Persuasion

Persuasion

Messages, Receivers, and Contexts

William Rogers

ROWMAN & LITTLEFIELD PUBLISHERS, INC.

Lanham • Boulder • New York • Toronto • Plymouth, UK

ROWMAN & LITTLEFIELD PUBLISHERS, INC.

Published in the United States of America
by Rowman & Littlefield Publishers, Inc.
A wholly owned subsidary of The Rowman & Littlefield Publishing Group, Inc.
4501 Forbes Boulevard, Suite 200, Lanham, Maryland 20706
www.rowmanlittlefield.com

Estover Road
Plymouth PL6 7PY
United Kingdom

British Library Cataloguing in Publication Information Available

Library of Congress Cataloging-in-Publication Data

Rogers, William, 1944 Feb. 13–
    Persuasion : messages, receivers, and contexts / William Rogers.
      p. cm.
    Includes bibliographical references and index.
    ISBN-13: 978-0-7425-3674-6 (pbk. : alk. paper)
    ISBN-10: 0-7425-3674-2 (pbk. : alk. paper)
    1. Persuasion (Psychology)—Social aspects. 2. Persuasion (Rhetoric) 3. Propaganda. I. Title.
HM1196.R64 2007
303.3'42—dc22
                                      2006017784

Printed in the United States of America

♾™ The paper used in this publication meets the minimum requirements of American National Standard for Information Sciences—Permanence of Paper for Printed Library Materials, ANSI/NISO Z39.48-1992.

Brief Contents

Detailed Contents

Figures, Tables, and Boxes

Figures

Tables

Boxes

Preface

PERSUASION IS especially useful for praising or blaming, for predicting the effects of present activities or future plans, and for explaining past causations of things. I could place before a group of people a seven-piece sterling-silver tea set by Tiffany and Company priced at about twenty thousand dollars and made in the style of the art-deco movement of the 1930s. Perhaps I will ask, Of all the possible things that could have come to exist in our world, what caused particular tea sets such as this one to come to exist? Aristotle might have offered several answers to my question, as might a modern philosopher such as Kenneth Burke. A postmodern thinker might offer yet other answers. Perhaps a first persuasive answer to my question would be that the very existence of silver ore on earth and the marvelous properties of silver both "demanded" that sterling-silver tea sets and other fine silver products should come to exist. A second possible answer to my question might be that the development of mining and smelting technologies made it possible, and therefore likely, that such metallic artifacts would come to be. Third, we could say that people actually valued and continue to value things like sterling-silver tea sets. A fourth answer might be that particular people intended that the above tea set and other ones like it would come into existence, either for profit or for personal desire. A fifth persuasive answer could be that the procedures commonly used by silversmiths had to actually be carried out so that each tea set in turn would come to exist.

It is my hope that readers will view these five persuasive explanations about the existence of sterling-silver tea sets as rational ones. However, I could have chosen less-rational approaches for explaining the existence of sterling-silver tea sets. I could have said that financial conspiracies were carried out long ago by Tiffany and Company to maximize profits from the use of silver. I could have told of undocumented visits prior to 4000 B.C. (the date of the first known use of silver) by space aliens, who left plans behind about how to mine and smelt ores. Or I could have argued that a tragic character flaw in the genes of the human race exists that leads people to accept false gods in the form of metal objects, especially silver ones.

Persuasion: Messages, Receivers, and Contexts is concerned with exploring human persuasive influence with three criteria in mind: rationality, proportionality, and communicative leadership.

The *rationality* of persuasion concerns things like the use of evidence, reasoning, and proof. Sometimes rational persuasion is more syllogistic (carefully proved, step-by-step) and sometimes more enthymemic (implied, to varying extents). Those who would influence us with less-rational approaches often try to gain our compliance by playing on our emotions; by creating the misleading appearance that something has been proved; by claiming undeserved sender, or persuader, credibility; or by using suggestion. *Rationality*, in this sense, means that the messages (or *symbolic maps*) we construct bear the maximum possible relation, or *calculus*, to objective reality (or *territory*), especially when we select people or policies to blame, praise, or count on in solving our problems. Propagandists and indoctrinators often resort to less-rational methods of influence out of their own fear, desperation, ambition, sanctimony, or sense of a "sacred" mission.

Proportionality in persuasion refers to a balance between the ends and the means. When tribalistic motives come to the surface, we sometimes say terrible things about others and their ideas (and occasionally do terrible things) to try and win the day. This tactic usually lacks proportionality. Hyper-emotionality, exaggerated statements, and extreme proposals may at times illustrate a lack of proportionality in the persuader's message. We should never take more liberty with the integrity of our messages and deeds than reasonable people might agree seems justified, at least at the time.

Finally, the *communicative leadership* of persuaders refers to the extent that messages seek clarity, reasonableness, and benefits for *senders*, *receivers*, and *third parties*—not just senders or their clients. Communicative leadership usually requires senders to exhibit the above two criteria of rationality and proportionality in guiding receivers through sets of ideas and their unifying themes.

A contemporary text on persuasion must almost, by definition, be comprehensive. But comprehensiveness is a tall order. When the ancient theorists studied persuasion, this persuasion was mostly spoken, although some examples may have been hand-written. Today, scholars must try to explain persuasion that can be verbal or visual, written or spoken, live or recorded, more cognitive in style or more emotional, created by single individuals or by whole organizations of people, and so forth. Further complicating matters is that visual persuasion can come in still forms (oil paintings, sculptures, photographs) or complex-motion forms (films, television advertisements, dance, theater, and other performance arts). Beyond these distinctions, the study of persuasion can be scientific or humanistic. It can try to *describe* how persuasion works or to *prescribe* what practitioners should do to succeed at it. It can be theoretical or intended for practical applications. Students of persuasion must also be familiar with scholarship that began in ancient times, then continued through the Dark Ages, the Middle Ages, and the Renaissance up to modern times (and now, for some, postmodern times). Moreover, persuasion topics can concern the ethical or the unethical, the spontaneous or the carefully prepared, the objective or the subjective, and the amoral, the immoral, or the moral. Lastly, persuasion scholars can seek culture-limited knowledge or universal truths.

Thus, any text on persuasion can easily become topically crowded. There is a wide variety of professionals with an interest in persuasion, including students of speech communication, advertising, media, the English language, sociology, history, and psychology. Reflecting the pluralistic nature of the field, materials selected for a text on persuasion might include receiver-oriented empirical studies and message-oriented critical studies. This book's approach is understandably eclectic because persuasion is so expansive a topic, and thus it makes use of many scholarly forms, whether they are a laboratory study that collects data to evaluate hypotheses, a philosophical treatise, a history of indoctrination efforts by various politicians, the contents of a teen magazine, websites of almost any type, or even a history of architecture used for political purposes.

Not only is the field of persuasion multifaceted, but the various paths to actual persuasion vary considerably. Consequently, a text discussing persuasion must find ways to synthesize what passes for persuasion in the minds of disparate groups of professionals, practitioners, researchers, and theorists. And while persuasion can be about building a logical case to support a proposition, it can also trade on the reality that people have psychological and physical needs that can be aroused by senders in powerful ways, such as by inviting their receivers to avoid fear or guilt, obtain or express love, practice greed or charity, or express anger. So if you as a sender can link your persuasive idea to my survival or prosperity, I may listen to you with great interest. One of the goals of this text is to try to draw a line between what counts as persuasion and what counts as propaganda.

Then there are the pedagogical goals all textbooks must come to terms with in one way or another. In particular, a text on persuasion must qualify to what extent it will be theory oriented or applications and skills oriented. Even the skills-oriented approach needs to qualify whether it is concerned with sender skills, receiver skills, or both. A text on persuasion needs to arm its readers with the best of the theories on communicative influence that have been created over the decades and even centuries. But the study of persuasive effects on receivers dominates the research literature. Thus, the author of a text on persuasion needs to estimate how much of this literature is needed to help readers reach justified conclusions about how persuasion works.

The creators of persuasive effects, or senders, have been studied in great detail. Researchers have asked, How important is sender credibility to persuasion? Will a sender's perceived attractiveness to audience members help? Will a sender's apparent similarity to audience members help? Similarly, theorists and researchers have looked closely at the structure of persuasive messages. They have tried to find out if it makes a difference whether you put your strongest argument first or last in your message. Should you concede points on both sides of an issue? Will discrepancies in your message hurt you? Which emotional appeals work better? The receivers of persuasive messages have been studied too. Here, to take another example, researchers have asked which sorts of people are more easily or less easily persuaded. A text like this one must find some optimal point for reporting on the above questions. Too little detail results in superficiality, and too much in drudgery.

Particular persuasive messages are often studied in isolation. But they can also be created in sets to support specific campaigns (e.g., to sell a product, solve a community problem, or elect a candidate) or to play a role in broader social movements. It is important for us in a free and open society to learn exactly how these campaigns and movements get started. How do they progress? What makes them succeed or fail? Who joins them and why? Thus, this text will also prescribe ways for citizens to persuade each other on matters of social policy, consumer purchasing, politics, and so on. And it will explore the persuasive and propagandistic methods used by cults, revolutionaries, and even terrorists.

I have organized the text into three sections. The first section deals with elements of persuasion, especially as they concern persuasive messages. The second section deals with receivers as audiences and as individuals about which theories are created and tested using empirical research. The last section deals with many of the most common communication contexts for persuasion and also offers materials to help readers improve their skill in creating persuasive messages and in critically evaluating the persuasive messages of other people. Each chapter begins with a list of goals for readers to keep in mind when reading the chapter. Quotes also appear at the beginning of each chapter to set a helpful tone. Each chapter concludes with a summary and conclusions section, review questions, a list of key terms, suggested projects and activities, and thought-provoking questions for discussion to enhance the reader's understanding of the ideas expressed in the chapter. Many chapters also include vignettes: examples of persuasion that are "unpacked" to illustrate the concepts of the chapter.

The six chapters in part I collectively provide detailed looks at various aspects of such messages as persuasion, propaganda, and argumentation (chapters 3, 4, and 5). The message emphasis in these chapters especially reflects the humanistic approach first taken by scholars in the ancient world. Chapter 1 sets the tone for the text and introduces readers to the basic elements of persuasion. Chapter 2 takes a microscopic look at the particular words and message details, including the persuasive use of visual images, found in persuasion. And chapter 6 reviews the ethical standards senders should employ during persuasion to protect receivers from being manipulated or treated unfairly by the messages they expose themselves to daily.

The four chapters in part II focus on the receiver and especially examine the scientific approach to persuasion research. Chapter 7 explores the nature of audiences exposed to persuasive messages, including the vulnerabilities of audiences, their subjective responses to messages, their objective responses to messages, and their tendency to take on personalities of their own. Chapter 8 looks at what motivates the people who become audiences for persuaders. Several rival theories of human motivation will give us here a good picture of what persuaders can do to link their messages to what goes on at deeper levels of human consciousness. These sequenced chapters on audiences and motivation try together to offer a balanced perspective—regarding potential manipulation of audiences—for readers to use when planning persuasive campaigns. Chapters 9 (theories) and 10 (research) go hand-in-hand to report on empirical, receiver-oriented theories and research findings that offer the foundations for building new theories or for changing existing ones.

The six chapters in the third and last section of the text are dedicated to examining persuasion in particular contexts and with particular applications. Chapter 11 offers practical materials for critics of persuasive messages. It reviews dramaturgic theories about persuasion as well as two recent and exciting theories on visual rhetoric and on *publics* (anonymous collections of people who, through their use of media and public communication, support, criticize, and revise collective attitudes about current political topics of the day). It also tries to summarize Aristotle's thoughts about persuasion. Chapter 12 looks at persuasion as used by political parties, governments, and interest groups. Chapter 13 examines the persuasion used by political activists, and the formation of such things as the environmental movement over the decades. Chapter 14 gives us a perspective on how the media helps make persuaders more powerful and on how the media itself exercises power through advertising, news, and entertainment formats. Chapters 15 and 16 then offer helpful materials on persuasive skills for senders and critical skills for receivers.

One other point to remember about this text is that my biases as an author have obviously affected the approach I've taken in it. One of these biases is my belief that a textbook should not just report on what is known about its subject, but should also offer a vision about that subject. As is true of many textbooks, this text will by necessity take a multitude of positions on topics, will select some things for inclusion and not others, will recommend some ideas and not others, and will openly make inferences on things that are not known for certain. Capturing a topic's essence also requires projecting the big picture while marshalling important details into a cohesive whole. The field of persuasion has become quite pluralistic with a wide variety of subfields now subsumed within it. Nonetheless, I hope readers will come away from this text with useful and detailed understandings of what it means in the contemporary world to persuade other people.

Readers can visit two websites for additional information about the text. The first of these is www.rowmanlittlefield.com, and the second is a personal **website** I maintain at **home.tiac.net/~wroger**, where readers will be able to download auxiliary materials and post questions or suggestions. My e-mail address is wroger@tiac.net.

Finally, I would like to thank the text's reviewers and the editors at Rowman & Littlefield—acquisitions editor Brenda Hadenfeldt, John Shanabrook, April Leo, and others—for their help.

PART I

Messages and Influence

CHAPTER 1

Introduction

◆ Chapter Objectives

After reading this chapter, you will be able to:

- ◆ Identify several historical highlights of persuasion study
- ◆ Define persuasion using communication terminology
- ◆ Identify four common objectives of persuaders
- ◆ Characterize the elements and processes of persuasion
- ◆ Understand differences in approaches used to study persuasion

To make converts is the natural ambition of everyone.

—JOHANN WOLFGANG VON GOETHE

How quick come the reasons for approving what we like!

—JANE AUSTEN

Homo narrans—a person who combines story-telling and analysis in a discourse that is rational, lively, imaginative, open to dialogue, entertaining and persuasive.

—STEVE DENNING

I RECENTLY KEYED IN the search phrase {persuasion storytelling} for a Google search and fetched a large number of relevant website leads. Examining the first twenty or so sites suggested, I thought that an old idea—using good stories to persuade people—apparently has once again become very popular, at least in corporate settings, the courtroom, classrooms, political campaigns, and the arts.[1] Later I searched the Library of Congress website, which lists books that have been published, and retrieved a list of about ten current books written about the use of storytelling for persuasion. Interestingly, this storytelling idea goes back to the classical scholars who understood the persuasive utility of a good story. And it certainly is tempting to envision people in prehistoric times trying to persuade each other while sitting around a campfire at the end of the day. Maybe the first person to conjure up persuasive words that could affect future actions convinced a friend or ally that the fishing would be better on the other side of a long-ago lake. The ubiquitous "fish stories" of human experience had to begin somewhere.

Such ancient scholars as Isocrates, Plato, Aristotle, Cicero, and Quintillian wrote and spoke about much more than just the usefulness of stories for rhetoric and persuasion. They were especially concerned with what we call "making a case" by assembling arguments supported by logic, facts, credibility-enhancing information about the speaker, and appeals to the emotions to encourage a sympathetic frame of mind in the audience. In fact by the classical period, the art of public persuasion had become a sophisticated activity that was informed by an organized knowledge about the basic principles of persuasion.[2] So impressive was the success of these classical figures of ancient Greece and Rome that lessons learned from them are still quite useful today and permeate much of modern thinking.

Today, both verbal and visual persuasive messages are seemingly everywhere, while a veritable army of theorists, researchers, and practitioners seeks ever more insight about how to persuade to win political debates, sell things with ads, preach about ways to find religious salvation, win cases in court, change opinions using newspaper editorials or television documentaries, and so on. Beyond its use in these obvious examples, persuasion is also exercised by narrowly defined interest groups (small and large) seeking to influence public policy in ways that suit or benefit group members. At last count, there were perhaps as many as twenty-five thousand such organized groups just in America.[3] Even teachers and students form national groups that try to get favorable treatment for things like pay and student-loan programs. Add to this the influence of the news media, and most recently that of bloggers, who with varying degrees of credibility broadcast from websites their own take on the news (the top fifty bloggers collectively had 29.3 million unique visitors during July 2005),[4] and you get a rich mix of persuasion and propaganda that invigorates the political, economic, and social processes of the world, for better or worse.

This chapter examines materials that will help flesh out the meaning of the word *persuasion*, beginning with a carefully worded definition that tries to capture the topic's essence. In addition, we will (1) look closely at four common objectives of persuaders: changing **beliefs, attitudes, values,** and **behavior;** (2) construct a visualization, or communication model, of the process of persuasion; and (3) explore the differing approaches that students of persuasion use to study this topic within the social sciences and humanities.

Understanding Persuasion

Over the past five or six decades there have been a healthy number of definitions of persuasion proposed in a variety of books. Let's sample a few of these various definitions. The easiest way to begin is with a simple one:

> Persuasion is the process of trying to "move" one or more people—by using credible information, evidence, reasoning and emotional appeals—to a new or changed belief, attitude, value, or behavior.

The word "move" in this definition means getting people to change in some way. One good way to prove to someone that a change might be justified is by producing evidence: facts, statistics, physical objects, recorded images, testimony, narratives, and specific examples of general points. This sort of proof often requires reasoning to show how the evidence supports your claim (e.g., "It's a *fact*. Your fingerprints are on the murder gun. How else would they *reasonably* get there if you weren't the shooter?"). On the other hand, emotional appeals encourage a sympathetic frame of mind in audiences, or receivers, and often involve connecting such emotions as fear, happiness, ecstasy, sadness, guilt, or anger to your claim. For example, you might link the adventure of rocketing to the moon and back to a persuasive proposal for funding a new space program that will enable anyone with the price of a ticket to get onboard. You might also provide information that enhances your credibility, saying for example, "I've spoken with numerous younger people about this. Of the one hundred college students I surveyed, 70 percent think this sort of space program ought to get started immediately."

The above definition was intended to be broad in order to help set the tone of this book and provide scope for explaining the many and varied aspects of persuasion. But students of persuasion sometimes create definitions that reflect the particular nature of the study taking place. Persuasion scholar Wallace Fortheringham, for example, defines persuasion as "that body of effects in receivers that has been caused by a persuader's message."[5] This emphasis on receiver effects might be very helpful in scientific studies of persuasion that seek to explain the relationship between what the sender does and how receivers typically respond. Another more specific definition is offered by another persuasion scholar, Charles Larson, who says, "Persuasion is the co-creation of a state of identification between a source and a receiver that results from the use of symbols."[6] This definition describes an important subtlety of persuasion that concerns receivers coming to see senders as "just like them," or as having viewpoints about a topic that are similar to their own. "Co-creation" suggests that both sender and receiver have roles to play in explaining how exactly the message is finally understood by receivers. Advertisers, for example, might demonstrate this particular definition when they create an ad that sells a product by portraying a lifestyle that viewers will find alluring, and then showing the viewers how the product fits into that lifestyle. But for this approach to work, the viewers have to already think that the lifestyle portrayed is desirable.

Moving beyond the above definitions that assert what persuasion is, we might now contrast persuasion with other forms of influence—that is, with what it is not. For example, if you needed money, you could *persuade* someone to give it to you by making an upbeat request such as "If you can see your way to the loan, I'll be more than happy to pay you back with interest." This approach is persuasive because you have tried to use evidence, reasoning, and a mild emotional appeal to move someone to a new behavior (lending you money). But there are other approaches to getting the money that would not be persuasive. For example, you could walk up to someone, knock that person to the ground, and grab their purse or wallet. This would be influence through *force*. Force is usually illegal and is not persuasion because it relies on physical power, not the use of evidence and reasoning. You could also use *coercive* threats or blackmail to get your money (e.g., "Give me the money or I will . . ."). This message may at first sound like persuasion. But it is not ideas in themselves that may gain compliance here; rather, it is the action that you, the sender, threaten to take that may gain the compliance. Similarly, through the use of *manipulation* you might embarrass a person into handing over money, perhaps by asking for the money in front of other people. Here too, your receiver may cooperate with the request, if only to avoid the negative consequences of your actions or to avoid the negative reactions of third parties.

We also need to distinguish persuasion from such things as (1) propaganda, (2) the making of a case for or against something by assembling a set of formal arguments, and (3) the unintended influence informative messages sometimes provoke. Put as simply as possible, propaganda differs from persuasion in the same way that tallness differs along a continuum from shortness. Some messages are good examples of persuasion, some messages are good examples of propaganda, and some messages exist in a middle region that is not clearly one or the other. As we will see in later chapters, propaganda messages are often broadcast in a more systematic way over time, are often less rational, are often more emotional, and are sometimes less ethical than are persuasive messages. As a propagandist, I could try to convince you to give me money by asking my supporters to mindlessly repeat at every opportunity a set of malicious lies about how you left your family in the lurch by not helping them financially when they needed help.

When messages are strictly *informative*, the principal difference between these messages and persuasion is that with the former there is no intent to persuade nor are any tactics used to bring about persuasion. The goal of an information giver is just that: to give information. Nonetheless, sometimes informative messages may have what seem like persuasive effects. For example, in a bit of conversational chit-chat I might mention that a newspaper just reported that the cost of living has gone up, and then you might offer to help me by giving me some money even though I do not want you to help and will certainly refuse the money outright. Your response seems like a result of persuasion, but it is really a spontaneous action on your part; it was not an intended persuasive effect of my informative message.

Lastly, students of persuasion distinguish between persuasion and **argumentation**. Some messages are examples of persuasion and argumentation. But the term *argumentation* is narrower in meaning than the term *persuasion*. For example, if by meticulously describing five benefits that will come from a public-works project I build the case that more money is needed for the project, I have argued my case. And I have also engaged in persuasion. But if I go about asking you to give me some money by first "buttering you up," I may end up being persuasive (mostly with emotion and maybe a bit of implied logic), but given the spirit of the message, we should not apply the word *argumentation* to the words in a message like "You're too far-sighted and intelligent not to let me have ten dollars for this project."

The above examples concern a target audience of just one. More often, however, persuaders concentrate on larger audiences that can range in size from several dozen to millions.

The End Product of Persuasion—Changing People

The basic aim of persuasion is to change individual listeners or entire audiences in some way desired by the sender.[7] This change commonly involves trying to alter four things: beliefs, attitudes, values, and behavior. Persuasion is probably most successful when attempted in small increments rather than giant leaps. One difficulty is that persuasion is often a competitive affair in which rival senders with competing ideas vie to persuade people. Persuadees themselves complicate matters when they accept some things said by persuaders and reject others, forming their own interpretation of the message and sometimes resisting the change altogether.[8] In some cases, people will be uninterested or ambivalent about what senders propose. A healthy personality should accept change when given good reasons but should not be too easily led.

The First Objective—Changing Beliefs

The beliefs held by people are usually about factual things, although we should distinguish here between "to believe in" and "to believe about." For example, what do I believe *about* water? I believe that fresh water will generally boil at 212° Fahrenheit at sea level. I also believe that water will freeze when its temperature drops below 32° Fahrenheit. I believe that if you boil water you will kill the bacteria in it that could make you sick if you drank the water without boiling it. Most people have an enormous range of "factual" beliefs about themselves, others, the physical world observed around them, and a metaphysical world they cannot see. Some of these beliefs can be more easily changed with persuasion than others. You could probably persuade me that the exact recipe used for making Coca-Cola varies in different parts of the world. On the other hand, some of our beliefs are more resistant to change. For example, you could not convince me under any circumstances that on earth the sun rises in the west and sets in the east. But in a whimsical moment you might have a chance to convince me that on the day I die, my name will be written in a cloud.

Let's suppose that you are a volunteer helping people in some remote part of the world and that your mission is to encourage them to boil water to kill the bacteria that can at times cause typhoid or other diseases. In some cases you might encounter people who believe that boiling water for drinking is only suitable for people who are already sick, people who want to remove the "cold" quality of water, or people who intentionally want to ruin the familiar taste of unboiled water. Thus, in order to encourage the water-boiling practice, you would first have to promote beliefs that more closely reflect the reality of bacteria's presence in uncooked foods and contaminated drinking water. What could you say to people who do not have a basic knowledge about the microbe world when you try to explain why boiling contaminated water is important? The problem is not insurmountable, but to succeed you first have to take into consideration any social norms and interpersonal networks that encourage change-resistant beliefs about boiling water.[9]

People can also believe *in* something. These beliefs usually involve matters of faith or the teachings of a particular religion. Or you may believe in the scientific method by which researchers try to answer questions by using methods designed to ferret out the truth about humanity and the universe in which we live. You may believe in the rightness of a political party, regardless of particular political issues. Gut feelings, loyalties, personal experiences, and so on probably make a person's belief in something harder for persuaders to change. But all beliefs can probably be changed if the time is right and the approach is right. Proselytizers have had great success over the centuries in converting people to the tenets of a particular religion. Political agitators are sometimes successful in getting citizens to commit treason. Potential lovers might try to persuade another person's spouse that infidelity is okay because the existing relationship "is not worth believing in anymore."

To study persuasion, researchers often measure beliefs. This can involve simply identifying the *direction* of a belief in someone's mind. By direction, researchers usually mean whether someone thinks a statement is true or false, as could be tested with a question like "Today the family dog dug up flowers in the backyard: True or False?" Believing the dog is guilty points in one direction, while believing the dog is innocent points in another. Researchers may also try to measure the *depth* of a belief. For example, consider the question "Which of the following best represents how sure you are that the dog is guilty: absolutely; probably; possibly; there's a slight chance; really don't know?" Depending on your answer, your belief will have lesser or greater depth. The *importance* of beliefs to particular individuals can also be measured and studied (e.g., if it is *your* garden, you may care if the dog dug up the flowers; but if it is your neighbor's garden, you may not care). Thus, analyzing receivers' beliefs about something in terms of direction, depth, and perceived importance can be useful to persuaders. And in the above example, influencing the direction, depth, or importance of family members' beliefs about the family dog's alleged digging up of flowers might be important if a family policy is being proposed to ban the dog from the garden. But the beliefs held by people are often components of another persuasive objective: attitude.

The Second Objective—Changing Attitudes

Attitudes concern the orientations we carry around with us about the social and physical settings we encounter day to day. One way to define an attitude is as a general evaluation of a person, situation, action, or institution that helps explain individual variation in social conduct. Attitudes can also be defined as predispositions to respond to things or situations in certain ways, or as a statement that summarizes our values as associated with the attitude's topic. For example, someone walks up to you on the street and says, "I need some money. Could you give me a dollar?" How would you respond? Would you say, "Sure friend, here's a dollar" or "No"? Would your response depend on the time of day or night, the person's manner or appearance, or the scene or location of the request? How you answer the above hypothetical questions will tell us something about your attitude about people who solicit money on the street. We have attitudes for a wide range of things such as saving money, honoring social responsibilities, buying on credit, cheating on tests, and acting patriotically, among many other possibilities. Attitudes often motivate our behavior when we are free to act as we wish. Thus, the argument goes, change someone's attitude about something and you may also change that person's behavior. Similarly, if you influence someone's behavior, then you may (in a reversed way) change the person's attitude toward that behavior.

Attitudes can also be understood by identifying the functions for which people use them. A number of category schemes have been suggested for analyzing **attitude functions**.[10] Some attitudes are the result of learning through experience and serve a *utilitarian*, adjustive, or instrumental function. For example, you might think it is important to mind your own business when in a strange neighborhood in order to avoid trouble (a practical, or utilitarian, idea). Trying harder after you have failed at something might also illustrate the utilitarian function of your attitude toward failure. A second function, *ego-defense*, might occur if you distrust the "people across town" because you secretly feel jealous of their financial success. This attitude serves as ego-defense for you when you think, "They're dishonest, so no wonder they succeed." With ego-defense, you protect yourself from unwelcome thoughts about yourself or the harsh realities of the world. In another example, you might try to reduce your guilt about a lie you told to a prospective employer by rationalizing that "Everyone lies during a job interview."

A third function of attitudes is that we sometimes enjoy publicly expressing our values through action. For example, you might pay considerably more money at a breakfast counter for a dish of scrambled egg-whites, in part to project your attitude about health consciousness. Similarly, keeping your fingernails always spotlessly clean and well-manicured could also project an attitude for others to see. This *value-expressive* function of publicly projected attitudes helps to express the self as a person with opinions and outlooks of quality.

The fourth and last function of attitudes is that they sometimes help us make the world seem more predictable, simpler, or more understandable. Thus for some, the smart voters may be the liberals, or the conservatives, or the independents. Other people may simplify things by believing that selling used possessions at auctions is for the rich, while poor people should sell theirs at yard sales or at secondhand stores. With this last function, we find meaning by developing ways to organize our perceptions and knowledge about the world and our place in it. Because of these attitudes, we do not have to spend as much time seeing shades of gray, but can rather see the world in terms of black and white. Beyond the above four functions, a number of similar functions that can be served by our favored attitudes have been suggested by authors.[11] As will become clearer later in the text, persuaders sometimes need to take the functions served by their receivers' attitudes into consideration when they plan a persuasive strategy, especially if the functions will make persuading those receivers especially difficult.

One further way to understand attitudes is to list all the salient beliefs that you or I attach to some particular attitude.[12] You might believe that saving money now will (1) offer protection against emergencies, (2) increase personal wealth, (3) serve as a sign of good character, and (4) provide fun in the future when spending it, but (5) provide fewer satisfying spending opportunities in old age than it would now. Four of the five beliefs seem to support a favorable attitude toward saving money. If a relationship could be established between the direction of your attitude toward saving money, in this particular case, and the underlying salient beliefs, a researcher might be able to predict that persuading you to alter those salient beliefs would encourage you to adopt the attitude toward spending money favored by a specific persuader. The premise here is that if you can change underlying beliefs, the generalized attitude may shift; and just as interesting, if you can find some way to change the attitude, the underlying beliefs may shift.

Attitudes are often measured by our answers to *scaled* survey items in which the answer may occur along a range:

> If asked to give blood today at work, I would donate.
> not likely 1 2 3 4 5 6 7 likely

Here the answer checked by a responder would range between 1 and 7. Which range the researcher selects will depend on the purposes of the research study. Historically, researchers have used scaled questions with possible answers that range between 5 and 9 in number. An odd number of answers allows for a middle, "unsure" position, while an even number forces the responder to select one side or the other. Sometimes each answer is given a characterization such as "always," "usually," or "sometimes."

The Third Objective—Changing Values

Values concern what we consider good or bad, important or unimportant, worthwhile or worthless. If you could only save three specific objects from your home during a fire, what would they be? Would your three choices include a particular piece of jewelry, cash, your birth certificate, a faded picture of grandma, a present you received when you were young, a set of antique dishes, or the sweater you made with your own hands? What you pick or do not pick says something about your values. There are also many abstract words to describe particular values, including *family, power, patriotism, wealth, fame, safety, health, immortality, youth, love, beauty,* and *salvation.*

Researchers describe two types of values: terminal and instrumental. **Terminal values** concern enduring things like desiring either a safe, predictable life or an exciting one. An **instrumental value** is one that may change as conditions change in one's life, such as having a convenient restaurant nearby to eat at when feeling too lazy to cook.[13] During one part of the year I may value the restaurant, but in another part of the year not value it. Said in another way, terminal values concern the "locations" of the happinesses people try to find. Instrumental values concern the momentary routes or means different people use to navigate toward those locations.

Values, especially terminal ones, are probably more resistant to change than are beliefs, attitudes, or behavior. Thus, it is not surprising that a television sitcom often reinforces the social values of the particular audience that makes the sitcom a success by watching it and buying the products advertised on it. Beyond television programs, it is also true historically that such groups as People for the Ethical Treatment of Animals (PETA), the NAACP, the Church, the AIDS Coalition to Unleash Power (ACT UP), or even the North American Man-Boy Love Association (NAMBLA) have sometimes sought to change our values.[14] Values have to come from somewhere, perhaps from childhood experiences or from living conditions that change drastically for adults.

What is a little more certain is that to help change beliefs, attitudes, or behavior, persuaders can offer messages that connect with the existing values of audience members. For instance, you might encourage people to give blood by linking giving blood to their valuing of "family safety." To get someone to join a particular organization, you might link the desired act to finding friendship or new respect among friends and neighbors. To get someone to buy your used car, you could link the purchase to saving money or to having a really "cool machine." Values too can be measured using scaled questions, checklists, or the sort of question that asks, "Is X more important or less important than Y?" or "Is X more valuable or less valuable than Y?"

The Ultimate Objective—Changing Behavior

Persuasion often concerns influencing our actions, deeds, or day-to-day habits as we work, carry out our social lives, and seek entertainment. Advertisers may try to get us to change the toothpaste we buy. Politicians may try to get us to vote for them. We may sometimes need to convince a noisy neighbor to quiet down at night so we can get more sleep. We may even try to persuade ourselves to be more efficient in our management of time. One reason that influencing behavior is so important during persuasion is that changed behavior almost always has consequences, big or small. Persuasion by others may affect whether we start or stop smoking. You may convince someone—for better or worse—not to marry a certain person. Someone may convince you to invest in a small business. When you are the persuader and your message affects other people, you must take some of the responsibility for the consequences of their actions, although they are probably more responsible because they accepted your ideas and proposals.

Measuring changes in behavior offers additional options compared to measuring changes in beliefs, values, or attitudes. These options include examining the outcome of persuasive messages such as changes in sales statistics after a new advertising campaign, the election outcome of a political campaign, or grade reports after particular curriculum materials have been taught by a teacher to a class. Sometimes researchers try to measure behavior directly, as we've seen. But at other times, they may again use scaled statements for measuring our *intended* behavior. An example:

I will visit the Grand Canyon this year.
not likely 1 2 3 4 5 6 7 likely

For practical reasons, the intended behavior of receivers is easier for researchers to measure than are the receivers' actual future behaviors, although one complication with measuring intended behavior is that we as receivers don't always carry out our intended behaviors.

Having tried to define persuasion with a technical nomenclature, I will now try to conceptualize it with a model.

A Communication Model of Persuasion

Communication models are constructed for several purposes: (1) they force the model maker to identify the important *components* of some communication process; (2) they require the model maker to show how these basic components *fit together*; (3) they then allow the model maker to *ask questions* about how, when, and why the process works; (4) they facilitate taking *measurements* and making *predictions* about the process of interest; and (5) they may even didactically *teach* the model's maker and reviewers something about the particular process, in this case, persuasion. The basic elements of persuasion can be identified using a persuasion steps model, which is the communication model arranged like a board game and shown in figure 1.1. Shown in the figure are five elements: Sender, Message, Receiver, Feedback, and Noise, which is any interference that may cause confusion or degrade the meanings understood by receivers.

Sender (or Source) Components

Defining the Purpose and Setting The model shows the persuasion process beginning in the lower left corner, where the sender defines a persuasive purpose within some communicative setting. For example, the sender might try to convince a jury to award financial damages to someone libeled by a newspaper.[15]

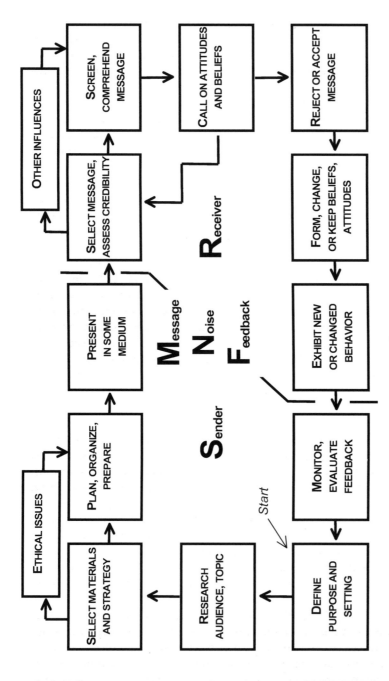

FIGURE 1.1 The persuasion steps model prescribes steps for persuaders to follow in creating persuasive messages and describes steps commonly followed by persuadees when exposed to persuasive messages.

Researching the Audience and Topic Moving up the left side of the model we see that senders, or persuaders, will to varying extents research and prepare what they need to know about their topics and their target audiences. Persuaders also need to learn about the rhetorical complications with which they will have to deal: Is the audience polarized or opinionated? Is the topic a hot-button one? What does the audience know about the topic? What are their existing beliefs, attitudes, values, and customary behaviors regarding the topic? Persuaders especially need to discover ideas or inducements that will help them accomplish their persuasive goals. In this example, at an emergency meeting the newspaper's managing editor may be able to convince the newspaper's stockholders that all is under control in the libel suit against the newspaper because the editor now knows that the individual bringing suit has a record of suing newspapers for bogus reasons.

Selecting Materials and Strategy The persuader selects materials in the form of reasons, factual support, emotional appeals, and credibility-enhancing personal information for use in persuading the audience. In our libel example, the lawyer for the libeled individual might select materials that suggest the individual suffered a damaged reputation and measurable financial losses because of the libelous comments made by the newspaper. The sender also creates a persuasive strategy by trying to answer such questions as "Which ideas or arguments will I encourage my audience to think about?" "What order should the ideas follow?" "Should I use an emotional appeal? If so, which one and how strongly worded?" One strategy might be to make the newspaper look like a crass, money-mongering organization that does not care about ruining reputations. On the other hand, this lawyer might decide to tread lightly on exactly how badly damaged the client's reputation is if this reputation was already low in the eyes of many in the community—that is, before the story ran in the newspaper. Other strategy issues concern such things as how intense to make whatever emotional appeals you include in your persuasive message, and how much factual detail to give.

Considering Ethical Issues Looking at the top of figure 1.1, we see that the sender must at some point consider whether the overall strategy selected is fair. This is about the ethics of the persuasion (i.e., Do unto others as you would have them do unto you). Propagandists worry less about this obligation. Let's say that the newspaper tries to defend itself in its libel suit by leaking a story about how the plaintiff's third-grader was recently disciplined by a teacher for taking another child's milk carton. This seems like hitting below the belt ethically. Or in a different situation, a defense lawyer might raise an alternative and exculpatory scenario of how a wrong was committed, in contrast to the scenario promoted by the prosecution.[16] But if the defense lawyer presents this alternative scenario while having no evidence for its occurrence whatsoever, the lawyer has not acted ethically.

Planning, Organizing, Preparing As we look across the top of the model, we see that the persuader must then plan, outline, organize, and generally prepare the message. Some messages will need a great deal of preparation and research, while others may come together at the last moment and with a minimum of effort. A public speech, for example, often requires (1) hours of library and online research, (2) a careful selection of main ideas and supporting detail, (3) the obtaining of feedback about the proposed speech ideas and their sequential organization from helpful critics, (4) the creation of visual aids such as charts or diagrams, and (5) several practice sessions where the speaker becomes comfortable and familiar with expressing the outlined ideas. A persuasive television documentary may go through hundreds of hours of preparation and planning by a team of individuals before the materials are photographed on film or videotape and then edited for broadcast. A book that seeks to change the outlook of millions of people about some topic may take several years or more to create.

Presenting the Message through a Medium The sender then presents the message in one or more *channels*, or media, on one or more occasions. Messages can be sent in such forms as a speech, a written or printed essay or story, a street demonstration, or in a variety of media-presentation formats including radio, television, stage, film, music, and the Internet. At this point the sender's job has momentarily halted, and our model now looks to what receivers do when exposed to persuasive messages.

Receiver Components

Because the persuasion steps model has a left side (the sender steps) and a right side (the receiver steps) a line appears between them in figure 1.1 to show this important divide.

Selecting a Message and Assessing Credibility As we see on the right side of the model, one or more receivers needs to attend to the message if it is to be successful. Receivers can be highly selective in exactly what parts or features of a message they take notice of. We call this **receiver selectivity**. Receivers also assess some degree of credibility for the sender. For instance, if in our libel case the plaintiff's lawyer chooses words very carefully and does not seem to exaggerate the extent of loss to reputation caused by the newspaper story, the jury may begin to form favorable impressions about the plaintiff's case. In contrast, if you receive an e-mail that asks you to accept a $10 million transfer to your bank account because the e-mailer is trying to find the owner of the money and needs to temporarily "park" the money somewhere, you will be correct in attributing low credibility to this sender, who probably has no money to give and is just trying to get you to open a foreign bank account with exorbitant fees. The loop at the upper right side of the persuasion steps model represents the receiver's assessment of **sender credibility**, which is an ongoing process that may change one or more times over the course of several seconds, minutes, hours, days, or months.

Taking in Other Influences Other receivers (or even competing senders) can influence individual receivers as they respond to a sender's message. Listening to a speech, you might be influenced by jeers against, or cheers for, the speaker. If someone proposes marriage to you, very likely your friends and family will react with supportive or nonsupportive comments, although some may remain neutral. Jury members in a court case will usually be admonished by the judge not to discuss the case with others until after the trial and not to discuss the case with fellow jury members until the beginning of deliberations. But jury members do not always follow these rules. Professional persuaders sometimes try to preempt rival persuasion from others by **pre-addressing** potential **counterpersuasion** (e.g., "I know this car is a bit expensive, but it offers the best ride on the road today").

Screening and Comprehending the Message As we move down the right side of figure 1.1, we see that for a message to be persuasive, receivers must comprehend what they are being asked to do or accept. They must also understand the inducements offered for whatever changes are suggested by the sender about their beliefs, attitudes, values, or behavior. The word SCREEN in the diagram means that receivers do not pay attention to, understand, or remember every part of a persuasive message. This is known as **screening**. Receivers sometimes try to understand and remember only what interests or motivates them in a message.

Calling on Attitudes and Beliefs At this point in the model, one of two things may happen. In some persuasive situations, receivers will intentionally call on their own relevant attitudes and beliefs in order to accept or reject the message's persuasion. In other persuasive situations, the sender's message may be dynamic enough to intentionally or unintentionally arouse particular attitudes and salient beliefs within the receivers. Some persuasion theorists think of this arousing activity as the creation of *presence* in the minds of receivers for particular message elements. The lawyer for the libel-case plaintiff might well arouse jurors' feelings by letting the jury know what it feels like when someone's friends, neighbors, coworkers, family, and children hear them called a thief by a local newspaper. Jury members may then feel sympathy or even anger as a consequence of the attorney's skill in arousing their attitudes and beliefs. But as addressed above, receivers sometimes have control over what attitudes or beliefs they call on when hearing a persuasive message. One juror may, for example, get angry at the idea of a lawsuit against the newspaper and may adopt the attitude that all the newspaper did was tell the truth about the plaintiff, and that the plaintiff is just trying to get money through a lawsuit.

Rejecting or Accepting the Message At some point, receivers start to take sides for or against the persuader. At the end of the libel trial, the jury members must come to terms with what they have heard and will begin leaning toward the case made by either the plaintiff or the defense. Will they find the arguments from one side more credible or believable? Will they accept the attitude or feelings suggested by one persuader or the other? Rejecting or accepting the persuasive message is closely intertwined with the next step where things either change in the receivers or fail to change; at times these two steps may seem to occur simultaneously, and at other times they may seem to occur one after the other.

Forming, Changing, or Keeping Beliefs and Attitudes If the persuasive message is rejected, any existing attitudes or beliefs in the receiver relevant to the persuader's topic will likely hold steady, unless none had existed. But if the persuasive message is accepted, new or changed attitudes or beliefs should form in the receiver. In a trial, jurors will probably move from an initial stage of not knowing how to respond, to a final stage of knowing how to respond. It is important here to note that the initial responses of receivers to persuasive messages can in some cases be later reversed. At other times, changes in belief or attitude may eventually disappear, or in the reverse, message failure may become message success.

Exhibiting Changed or New Behavior Not all persuasive situations will involve the possibility of changing receivers' behavior. For example, behavior may remain unaltered when two people debate which sports team is the better, or when a television audience watches a program that makes them like some historical figure better. Of course, there are many circumstances when changed beliefs or attitudes may indeed be accompanied by changed or new behavior or a one-time-only action. That is, persuasive messages sometimes do cause people to buy things, vote for candidates, or accept an offer of marriage.

Feedback—Coming Full Circle

Finally, at the bottom of the model, on the left, the sender again becomes the focus of attention for our analysis. Here senders monitor feedback from receivers to identify what about the message is working or not working. Monitoring feedback during face-to-face persuasion is usually easy, by noting audience vocalizations and nonverbal reactions. Either lawyer in the libel case can monitor the feedback of the judge or jury in order to assess whether a current approach seems to be working or needs to be altered. For example, one attorney might notice that the raising of constant objections to the proceedings is beginning to irritate the judge or the jury. If so, the attorney might try being more cooperative during the rest of the trial. Or a sales agent may discover that a favorite inducement is not working well with a potential customer and so may quickly switch to an alternate approach. However, there are times when senders and receivers are separated by time or space; here feedback may never appear, or may be delayed because it is indirect (e.g., letters to the editor about an editorial, product sales figures, taking a teacher's advice ten years after it was given). In either case, if feedback does show that the persuasion failed, the sender may start all over again at the beginning of the steps, altering their persuasive approach and message. Thus we can see that the persuasion process is both cyclical and co-constructional in nature (sender and receiver both affect the outcome of the persuasion). Figure 1.1 can also be used to illustrate how persuasion can occur all at once, or incrementally when used on repeated occasions by a particular sender. In other cases, multiple senders may communicate in tandem, or independently of each other, to cause a persuasive effect. This might happen, for example, when two different companies advertise over time to promote competing DVD recorders, but perhaps in the end cooperatively increase the sales for one or both companies.

Ways of Studying Persuasion

As noted earlier, the formal study of persuasion began with students of public address in ancient Greece and Rome. In our modern world, there are several different approaches to studying persuasion. In one approach, those with a historical bent search through documents and study historically important persuasive events in order to evaluate how such events influenced the times in which they occurred. A researcher could study Abraham Lincoln's Gettysburg Address, made during the Civil War, or Martin Luther King Jr.'s "I have a dream" speech, made in the 1960s, to try to evaluate how people at the time were affected by the speeches. When using the historical approach, the researcher must carefully extract details of these persuasive events and their aftermaths from newspaper stories, books, documents preserved in libraries, and current interviews with people present at the time if they are still alive and can be found, or previous interviews if they were documented. As time passes, it becomes harder and harder to form definite conclusions about the persuasive effectiveness of such events.

In a second approach, the researcher examines a persuasive event perhaps closer to the present and tries to critically evaluate the event by applying to it standards that have been proposed by scholars on rhetoric. Often these rhetorical critics glean lessons to be learned about persuasion from numerous case studies. Aristotle created one of the best-known sets of standards, which is still used today. Contemporary times have brought other systems of critical analysis. When critically analyzing a speech about teenage weight problems, you might for example examine the speech's use of evidence and whether audiences will find that evidence credible or not. Or you might examine how well the speech resonated with deeply felt beliefs about personal responsibility versus government responsibility with regard to such personal problems. Sometimes the two approaches for studying persuasion described above are linked together as two variations of one *historical-critical* approach.

Perhaps the most often-used approach for studying persuasion today uses the *scientific method*. For persuasion studies, the scientific method relies on investigating the effect of a carefully controlled exposure of persuasive messages to a sufficient number of people (subjects) in order to make generalizations about what things cause persuasive change. When the scientific method is used properly, the subjects are recruited through a random process, while the persuasive effects are identified and isolated with clever methods to remove the possibility that some extraneous factor beyond the message feature in question is causing whatever is being observed. In a study about the relative effectiveness of different types of evidence used in a persuasive message, three slightly different experimental messages may be exposed to three randomly composed groups of subjects. One group may get a persuasive message that offers proof with convincing statistics. A second group may get a persuasive message that offers proof with dramatic examples. Still a third group may get a message that offers no proof at all. If test scores taken after the exposure of the messages to the three groups of subjects show more persuasive movement on the topic when either the statistics or the examples are used, the researchers may argue that the observed test scores have proven that the particular type of evidence used in a message can affect its potential to persuade.

Chapter in Retrospect

Although persuasive communication has probably existed since prehistoric times, it is today seemingly everywhere, especially in our media. Particular persuasive messages are created by people to try and change other people. Since the need for all of us to cooperate is always high, the potential usefulness of persuasive messages is obvious, though the effects of given persuasive messages are not always good. As the theorists of the ancient world first observed, persuasive messages typically work by appealing to both the reason and the emotions of receivers regarding topic and sender. But persuasion needs to be distinguished from other behavior forms such as propaganda, force, manipulation, blackmail, formal argumentation, and the inadvertent influence that sometimes results from purely informative messages. The purpose or goal of persuasion is the influencing of receivers' existing beliefs, attitudes, values, or behavior salient to some particular topic.

To understand how persuasion works, we have identified a number of the general steps involved, which we can organize into a communication model of persuasion (see figure 1.1). Some of these steps prescribe what the persuader must do to be successful (such as identifying a persuasive purpose, researching the message, planning the message, and trying to be ethical in presenting the message). Other steps describe how audiences of persuasion typically respond to persuasive messages (such as when they attend to and understand an incoming message, assess the credibility of the sender, and call on existing internal attitudes and beliefs to evaluate the incoming message). The persuasion process is both cyclical (it may take repeated and altered efforts to get results) and co-constructional (both the sender and the receiver can have an affect on the final outcome).

Students of persuasion have taken several different approaches to the study of how it works. One of these approaches is the historical-critical approach, where persuasion critics use and develop theories that help them analyze case studies of actual instances of persuasion found in current or historical communication events. A second approach to the study of persuasion involves the use of the scientific method to uncover knowledge about persuasion through carefully controlled experimentation.

KEY TERMS

argumentation	communication models	screening
attitude functions	counterpersuasion	sender credibility
attitudes	instrumental values	terminal values
behaviors	pre-addressing	values
beliefs	receiver selectivity	

REVIEW QUESTIONS

1. What are the various meanings of the verb *to move* when defining persuasion?
2. Using your job, school, or social life as reference points, what is a good example of an actual persuasive message that tries to change a belief? Tries to change an attitude? Tries to change a value? Tries to change a behavior?
3. How is an instrumental value different from a terminal value?
4. How is it possible that the change the sender seeks to make in the receiver does not always occur as expected, as shown in the persuasion steps model in figure 1.1?
5. What does it mean to say that "Persuasion is the co-creation of a state of identification between a source and a receiver"?
6. What are some key differences between the historical-critical approach to studying persuasion and the scientific approach to studying persuasion?

SUGGESTED PROJECTS AND ACTIVITIES

1. Thumb through a popular magazine and find examples of persuasion in ads, articles, or other features. Analyze how the creators of a particular example have tried to persuade the magazine's readers. Are the techniques used emotional or cognitive? Are they simple or complex? Have the creators tried to enhance their credibility? If so, how?

2. Take something inexpensive out of your wallet, purse, or drawer at home. Plan a persuasive message to sell that item to someone you know. Remind yourself of how a person's beliefs and attitudes toward things can affect their behavior. Try to plan an appeal that will work for the particular person you have selected. Consider an appeal that is emotional or cognitive, or that concerns your credibility as a sender. Outline what you will say and do during your sales pitch. If you've never sold anything before, carefully work out your opening statement (e.g., "I have something here I think you'd like that I *might* be willing to part with"). Now try it out on your subject. (You can first practice your timing, choice of words, and vocal tones on the family pet if you have one.) Analyze the sales pitch's success or failure. If your first try is rejected before you get to give your pitch, work harder on composing your opening statement or selecting your inducements.

3. Identify several of your attitudes toward various activities (e.g., buying on credit; lending money to friends, relatives, or coworkers, or borrowing money from them; taking a leadership position among strangers in public; volunteering in class or at work; choosing a marriage partner; joining clubs). Think about each attitude in terms of (1) the functions it serves for you, and (2) the underlying beliefs that help support this attitude. Pick one of these attitudes and write a paragraph that starts with the words "My attitude toward _____ probably exists as it does because . . ."

4. Think about persuading a family member, coworker, dorm-mate, or friend. Maybe you'll try to convince this person to (1) do something differently or something new, (2) believe something new or disbelieve something old, or (3) feel differently about something. Using some of the ideas in this chapter, identify the biggest problem you will have in persuading this person on the topic you have selected.

5. If you are resourceful and just a little creative, build a physical model of what takes place during persuasion by using common objects found around your house, workplace, or school. Pick objects whose shape, color, texture, function, size, or other attributes bear some significance to the model element each is chosen to represent. For example, the clippings of a magazine ad might stand for the message, and an empty cardboard tube might stand for the communication channel. The five criteria listed at the beginning of the section "A Communication Model of Persuasion" may help you evaluate your model.

QUESTIONS FOR DISCUSSION

1. How easy or hard is it to persuade you on political topics? On domestic topics? On financial topics? On entertainment topics? For each of them, why?

2. Would you rather be easier or harder to persuade than you are? Why?

3. Why do you think it is possible to persuade people at all?

Notes

1. Cf. Paul N. Luvera, "The Art of Storytelling," Washington State Bar Association, March 2004, www.wsba.org/media/publications/barnews/2004/mar-04-luvera.htm (8 November 2005). According to this website, the basic steps of persuasive storytelling in the legal profession are:

First, set the stage. The story should have a clear and engaging opening. This includes introducing the characters as well as the background needed to understand the story. Next, state the problem—the catalyst that sets everything in motion. Then, tell the story. The sequence of events should be told in a way that is easy for the listener to follow. Every good story has a hero and an adversary—sketch it out for the listener. You will need to answer the question, what happened? Tell your story through a combination of words, sounds, and images. Words should be descriptive. Use body language where appropriate. Always end with a powerful and dramatic conclusion that stays with the listener.

2. Cf. The Internet Classics Archive (http://classics.mit.edu), where speeches by the following classical rhetoricians may be found: Lysias, who helped develop the study of persuasive speaking (classics.mit.edu/Browse/browse-Lysias.html); Isocrates, more than twenty of whose speeches can be read today in translation (classics.mit.edu/Browse/browse-Isocrates.html); Demosthenes, who may have been the greatest of the Greek orators (classics.mit.edu/Plutarch/demosthe.html); Aristotle (see his *Rhetoric*); Plato (see *Gorgias*, which is a criticism of the way rhetoric was practiced at the time, and *Phaedrus*, which offers Plato's conception of ideal persuasion); Aeschines (classics.mit.edu/Browse/browse-Aeschines.html); and Hyperides (classics.mit.edu/Browse/browse-Hyperides.html). Also see Cicero's *Rhetorica ad Herennium* [*Rhetoric to Herennius*] and *De Oratore* [*Concerning Oratory*] (humanities .byu.edu/rhetoric/Primary percent20Texts/Cicero-DeOratore.htm), and Quintillian's *Institutio Oratorio* [*Training of an Orator*] (msu.edu/user/lewisbr4/980/Intro.htm).

3. Jonathan Rauch, *End of Government* (New York: Public Affairs, 1999), 42–43, 86–87. It is a challenge knowing just how many people work in the "influence business" because this grand total includes full-time workers, volunteers, part-time workers, and those people who sometimes do this kind of work, such as lawyers, consultants, and experts.

4. Thomas Johnson and Barbara Kaye, "Wag the Blog: How Reliance on Traditional Media and the Internet Influence Credibility Perceptions of Weblogs among Blog Users," *Journal of Mass Communication Quarterly* 81, no. 3 (Autumn 2004): 622–42. Also see "Weblog-visitor ratings: August 2005 Nielsen// Net-Ratings Top-50 Web Sites," www.nielsen-netratings.com/pr/pr_050815 (8 November 2005).

5. Wallace Fotheringham, *Perspectives on Persuasion* (Boston: Allyn and Bacon, 1966), 6–7.

6. Charles Larson, *Persuasion: Reception and Responsibility* (Belmont, CA: Wadsworth, 1998), 8–12.

7. Although some scholars argue that a persuader merely stimulates receivers to create changes within themselves.

8. See for example Charles Berger, "Slippery Slopes to Apprehension: Rationality and Graphical Depictions of Increasingly Threatening Trends," *Communication Research* 32, no. 1 (February 2005): 3–28.

9. Everett Rogers, *Diffusion of Innovations* (New York: The Free Press, 1995), 1–5.

10. Cf. Daniel Katz, "The Functional Approach to the Study of Attitudes," *Public Opinion Quarterly* 24 (1960): 170–76.

11. See summary by Daniel O'Keefe, *Persuasion Theory and Research*, 2d ed. (Thousand Oaks, CA: Sage, 2002), 31–33.

12. Martin Fishbein and Icek Ajzen, *Belief, Attitude, Intention, and Behavior* (Reading, MA: Addison-Wesley, 1975), 1–18, 335–79.

13. Sandra Ball-Rokeach, Milton Rokeach, and Joel Grube, *The Great American Values Test* (New York: The Free Press, 1984).

14. ACT UP is said to be a diverse, nonpartisan group of individuals united in anger and committed to direct action to end the AIDS crisis; NAMBLA pursues a goal to end the "oppression" of men and boys who have mutually consensual sexual relationships.

15. The source of a persuasive message may comprise one or more persons who persuade in informal ways or who are parts of an organized message-creation campaign in the public or private sector.

16. Exculpatory evidence is used to clear a defendant of alleged fault or guilt.

CHAPTER 2

Language and Communication

◆ Chapter Objectives

After reading this chapter, you will be able to:

- ◆ Compare and contrast signs and symbols used for persuasion
- ◆ See the persuasive ways in which single words convey meanings
- ◆ Understand the effects of grammar and syntax on persuasive messages
- ◆ Illustrate the persuasive powers of common figures of speech
- ◆ Recognize language traps as they can affect both persuaders and receivers
- ◆ Identify several elements that help in persuading nonverbal communication

But words are things, and a small drop of ink, Falling, like dew, upon a thought produces that which makes thousands, perhaps millions think.

—LORD GEORGE GORDON BYRON

Once I knew only darkness and stillness. . . . My life was without past or future. . . . But a little word from the fingers of another fell into my hand that clutched at emptiness, and my heart leaped to the rapture of living.

—HELEN KELLER

IN THE POWER *of Words*, by an anonymous author, a group of frogs are traveling through the woods, and two of them fall into a deep pit. All the other frogs gather around the pit. When they see how deep the pit is, they tell the two frogs that they are as good as dead. The two frogs in the pit ignore the comments and try to jump up out of the pit with all of their might. The other frogs keep telling them to stop, that they are as good as dead. Finally, one of the frogs takes heed of what the other frogs are saying and gives up. He falls down and dies. The other frog continues to jump as hard as he can. Once again, the crowd of frogs yells at him to stop suffering and just die. He jumps even harder and finally makes it out. When he gets out, the other frogs ask, "Did you not hear us?" Eventually the frog understands them and explains to them that he is deaf. He thought they were encouraging him the entire time. The most important words in this frog story are "good as dead." The respective effect these words had on the two frogs in the pit can serve as an illustration for almost all the topics that follow in the first section of this chapter.[1]

Persuasion most directly rests on the power of the word. Sometimes a single word or two can be quite persuasive, as when a speaker says, "What goes around comes around" in order to get listeners to see themselves as part of some problem. Professional persuaders do in fact pay very close attention to each message element (e.g., word, grammar, gesture, tone of voice, action, visual image, and impression created). This chapter will look at persuasion from a microscopic perspective, including both the semantic elements that make up a message and those items of gestural or scenic context that help color persuasive messages. As many scholars have noted, words sometimes have an almost magical power to influence people when used in conversation, writing, or the mass media. Perhaps one of the most important jobs of formal education is to help free us of the magical influence of words so that we can then use verbal communication, persuasive or otherwise, more rationally.

What Words Do for Us

Words let us semantically divide up, categorize, and single out things of importance to us in the world, which then lets us conceptualize and "manipulate" these things in our heads. Words allow us to communicate about the here and now, the not-here and the not-now, the imaginary, and the minimally detailed world of abstractions. The classic game Twenty Questions makes use of the categories idea: Is what you are thinking animal, vegetable, or mineral? Is it smaller than a breadbox? Is it your engagement ring? Is it your car? Is it the breadbox? Words are **symbols** or abstractions of things we know about. For example, the word *chair* represents any piece of furniture (so it is not your lap) having a back (it is not a stool) that is designed for one person to sit on (it is not a sofa). An upholstered chair, a kitchen chair, and a rickety folding chair are all chairs. There are probably billions of objects in the world that can take the symbol *chair* as their name. I can imagine a chair, tell you I am thinking of a chair, and you can then imagine a chair—but perhaps in your mind it is not the same chair I imagine—unless I try to designate a particular chair with a clever series of words. In contrast, when a dog growls it can let you know that it is angry, but a dog cannot growl that it was angry with you two months ago; and a dog cannot growl that there is too much anger in the world today, or that anger is learned early in life. Dogs live in a here-and-now world of perception, relationship bonding, survival motivation, learned habits, and likes and dislikes. Dogs cannot use words to semantically divide up things of interest.

The exact words you use to describe something may alter how your receivers think or feel, as might happen if you coined the phrase "vanity divorce" to critically define what happens when a person wants out of a marriage for self-centered reasons, perhaps thereby creating intense separation anxiety for their younger children.[2] According to author Timothy Borchers, the act of naming something may with subsequent use of that name provide us with an attitude toward that something. To take a simple example, a reporter's use of the word *gaffe* (a social or political blunder) to describe a politician's remark can make us feel negative about that remark. In this case, the negative meaning comes both from the bits of meaning chosen to make up the entire meaning of the word *gaffe* and from the typical circumstances in which *gaffe* is usually uttered or written.[3] Borchers gives the example of the use of the compound noun *front-runner* in political elections. When a given candidate is called "the front-runner," that candidate may enjoy an edge, perhaps in getting campaign contributions. A word like *dinosaur*, when used to characterize someone who may have outdated social viewpoints, can create an entire scenario (true or false) about that person's alleged poor adjustment to the contemporary world.[4]

Words may even become "self-fulfilling prophecies." I might predict in a lecture that a particular student will become a success in the future. Will my predictive label come true? It may. Or perhaps a faith healer says, "Heal!" and the believer becomes well. Or a physician's prescription and prognosis ("Take this and it should clear up in a few days") may help you get better. Or we may talk pessimistically about something, and our project then starts to turn out wrong. Each of these examples illustrates the self-fulfilling power of words to "engineer" a social outcome.

Signs and Symbols

According to philosopher Suzanne Langer, a **sign** is merely an indication of something.[5] When a dog growls, this may be a sign that the dog is angry or about to bite you. Dark, menacing clouds are often a sign of a coming rain storm. A modern submarine may give away its undersea presence by an ever so slight curvature of the surface water just above it. Signs often signify to an animal or a person something in the here and now, as when you hear a nearby car start up and you expect the car to move, or you begin to doze and realize that you have worked a long day. Sometimes signs can signify something far away, as when early light at dawn signifies that the sun may soon appear, even though the sun is 93 million miles away. And archaeologists may uncover signs of ancient civilizations when they find artifacts buried in the ground.

An interesting question concerns how particular signs come to have the meanings they do. The linguist Ferdinand de Saussure and the philosopher Charles Sanders Peirce helped provide answers to this question many decades ago. Recently, semiotician Daniel Chandler summarized the work of Saussure and Peirce by describing three categories of **signifiers**, the first two of which are what we have called signs, and the third of which is what are called symbols. Chandler defines these categories as follows:

Index/indexical: a mode in which the signifier is not arbitrary but is directly connected in some way (physically or causally) to the signified—this link can be observed or inferred: e.g. "natural signs" (smoke, thunder, footprints, echoes, non-synthetic odours and flavours), medical symptoms (pain, a rash, pulse-rate), measuring instruments (weathercock, thermometer, clock, spirit-level), "signals" (a knock on a door, a phone ringing), pointers (a pointing "index" finger, a directional signpost), recordings (a photograph, a film, video or television shot, an audio-recorded voice), personal "trademarks" (handwriting, catchphrase) and indexical words ("that", "this", "here", "there");

Icon/iconic: a mode in which the signifier is perceived as resembling or imitating the signified (recognizably looking, sounding, feeling, tasting or smelling like it)—being similar in possessing some of its qualities: e.g. a portrait, a cartoon, a scale-model, onomatopoeia, metaphors, "realistic" sounds in "programmed music", sound effects in radio drama, a dubbed film soundtrack, imitative gestures;

Symbol/symbolic: a mode in which the signifier does not resemble the signified but which is fundamentally arbitrary or purely conventional—so that the relationship must be learnt: e.g. language in general (plus specific languages, alphabetical letters, punctuation marks, words, phrases and sentences), numbers, Morse code, traffic lights, national flags.[6]

As is evident in the description above, *symbolic* signs would include words that we use when we speak or write but would also include things like the American flag (a symbol of freedom), the two interlaced *R*s that serve as a company logo for Rolls Royce automotive and aerospace products, and the tree that is used to indicate the international environmental movement. If two spies are passing on the street, one may give a sign to the other by tugging twice on his jacket sleeve, which may mean that passing the contraband will be safe at that moment. This sign also is symbolic because it is arbitrary and has to be learned, as perhaps cardboard boxes would be a sign if I see them as an implication of homelessness. The gesture that uses a circling finger at the side of the side of the head may indicate in certain places or cultures that someone is mentally disturbed. This gesture would be *iconic* to an extent because it indicates that the brain materials have gotten jumbled up. And if your weathervane points eastward, you have an *indexical* sign of the wind's direction. Further, the nervous glances of a squirrel may indicate fear of nearby threats, and since these movements are probably connected to an apprehension inside the squirrel, we might call these indexical signs.

One of the things that distinguishes human language from the calls and gestures of animals concerns this distinction between signs and symbols. Both signs and symbols can be persuasive, but symbols can dramatically change the world while signs in and of themselves probably cannot. As units of thought, symbols can denote what is true, what is not true, what might be someday, what should have been, what could have been, and so on. Though symbols and the realities they try to represent are completely separate entities, a new symbol (or a new arrangement of symbols) can sometimes help some new, human-influenced dimension of reality come about through invention or accidental discovery. The concept of an airplane preceded the actual invention of airplanes (because people early on dreamed of flying like the birds). Because of symbols, the human race will probably someday escape the confines of earth to explore and populate the far reaches of the solar system and beyond. Because of symbols, the average life span of a person will probably extend beyond one hundred years in the not-too-distant future. Sign-using animals or humans deprived of language, left to their own resources, would never escape the confines of earth or learn to extend their life spans through intervention in the aging process.

Finally, we should also distinguish between signs that are a part of the human perception of the things within perceptual range (e.g., smoke as a sign of fire) and signs that are part of human communication, whether interpersonal, public, or even connected with the mass media. Signs are used during communication because people are good at imagining how other people perceive things (this is sometimes called *perspective-taking*). So we use signs during communication to augment our use of symbols. For example, if I visit your home you might offer me a snack, causing me to smile as an indication of appreciation. I may have smiled spontaneously (which would provide perceptual material for you), or I may have done so intentionally as part of our interpersonal communication, or it may have been a little of both, the smile being first spontaneous then extended on purpose. The **signification** (or understood meaning) of this signifier is something like "What a nice thing to do." Other examples of signs used during communication include sweeping your eyes across the several people listening to your story to include each in the storytelling event, wearing an outfit that says to your audience, "Yes, I *am* in style today," or pointing your finger to indicate an object of mutual attention for you and your listeners. Now let's look more closely at the connotative and denotative meanings of symbol-type signifiers.

Connotation and Denotation

Denotative meanings of words are found in dictionaries. The dictionary meaning of the word *girl* might be "a young, human female." In contrast, **connotative** meaning concerns the emotional, subjective, and personal meanings of words. We acquire connotative meanings from our ongoing experiences with the world around us and from our communication with others about things in the world. Sometimes connotative meaning concerns the word associations we might give for a specific word (e.g., the word *cat* might elicit from me the associations "cute," "cuddly," and "warm," or even "snobby," "scratchy," and "secretive"). When we say that a word connotes something, we usually mean that it has one or more similar associations. In some parts of the English-speaking world, the term *gin mill* denotes a tavern, pub, or bar. But the term also connotes a sense of seediness. Connotative meaning can also be analyzed using three rating scales.[7] In their simplest forms, these scales include notions of (1) strong versus weak, (2) active versus still, and (3) positive versus negative. That is, we could measure someone's connotative understanding of a word like *poison* as perhaps "very strong," "very active," and "very negative." In contrast, the word *cotton-candy* might be rated by someone as "very weak," "very still," and "very positive." The word *desk* might rate as "moderately strong," "very still," and "slightly positive." With these three rating scales, we could measure the difference in connotative meaning felt for a word by two different listeners, or by a speaker and a listener, and then use this difference to predict in detail communication failure or success.

God terms and *devil terms* describe connotative meanings in a special way. God terms are words that sound connotatively positive and good to a majority of people in a particular social strata. Examples of god terms might be *slim, rich, free, democratic, fair, successful, low-fat,* and *no-MSG.* Devil terms are words that sound negative to a majority of people in a social strata. Examples of devil terms might be *poor, skinny, racist, autocratic, high-calorie,* and *gas-guzzling*. What may be a god term to some may be a devil term to others and vice versa. The term *democratic elections* may have very different god-devil polar meanings for groups in different parts of the world. For different people, the words *socialism, capitalism, free-market, progressivism*, and so on will evoke different attitudes. Persuaders and others who would influence us usually take advantage of the attitude-encouraging properties of particular god or devil terms, depending on their persuasive goals. So if you wanted to convince me to take my life savings out of the bank and put it into the stock market, which one of the three sentence endings below would you choose for the following claim?

> You should take your life savings out of the bank, because now is the perfect time to pursue _____ .
> A. calculated financial risks
> B. stock-market gambles on future profits
> C. sound, equity-growth opportunities

If you picked answer C, you have selected several attitude-encouraging words: *sound*, as in "rock solid"; *growth*, as in "amassing more money"; and *opportunities*, as in "taking advantage of something good." Even the word *equity* here probably has a more positive ring for people who understand its meaning than would its more familiar synonym *stock*, which could have been used instead. Answer B has one or two positive words, but contains a devil word in this context: *gambles*. Similarly, answer A contains the term *financial risks*, which makes some people worry. Now we move from the subtleties of word selection to the subtleties of word order in sentences.

Persuasion through Syntax

When we speak or write sentences, we may compose simple sentences, compound sentences, or complex sentences. A *simple* sentence has one complete thought (e.g., "We will march on Washington tomorrow"). A *compound* sentence has two or more complete thoughts ("We will march on Washington tomorrow, and we'll tell the whole world what we think" or "We'll tell the whole world what we think; and then we'll go home"). A *complex* sentence has one or more complete thoughts and one or more incomplete thoughts. For example, the sentence "Since you've taken both sides of the issue, I will not vote for you tomorrow" is complex. This is because the first idea ("Since you've taken . . .") is an incomplete, dependent thought, and the second thought ("I will not . . .") is a complete, independent thought (the main thought). "Since you've taken both sides of the issue" by itself cannot stand alone; it needs completion in some way. "I will not vote for you tomorrow" is the main thought and can stand alone. Incomplete, dependent thoughts can come anywhere in a sentence, as can the main thought (e.g., "When I'm here, you seem okay" or "You seem okay, when I'm here").

Simple sentences can be used by persuaders to give *emphasis* to a singular thought: "Charlie Brown, go home." Compound sentences give less attention to a single idea because they focus on combining two or more ideas: "Charlie Brown, you are irritating; Charlie Brown, you are frustrating; Charlie Brown, go home." Notice that the third idea in the above compound sentence gets less attention than it did when it stood alone as a simple sentence. We can also balance the importance of two ideas by using a compound sentence: "The pro-choice groups have their points, and the pro-life groups have their points." Depending on whom I am addressing, I can switch the order of the above two ideas.

The main and subordinate (or independent and dependent) clauses in complex sentences, theoretically at least, should offer different emphases for the ideas placed in them. Consider the four variations that follow:

1. While we did not find any inaccuracies in your report, we did find it a bit brief.
2. We found your report a bit brief, although we did not find any inaccuracies in it.
3. We did not find any inaccuracies in your report, although we found it a bit brief.
4. Although we found your report a bit brief, we did not find any inaccuracies in it.

Perhaps the best way to assess the above four sentences is to try and select the one that makes the reader of the report feel the least put-off. I am leaning toward version 4.

Beyond sentence structure, there also are idea-order considerations. Consider the two sentences below. Though both would probably be unwelcome news to the children involved, which would be the better choice for the teacher?

1. The following students will not be allowed to go on the class trip today because they didn't bring in their parental permission slips.
2. Because they didn't bring in their parental permission slips, the following students will not be allowed to go on the class trip today.

Notice that the above two sentences both describe a cause-and-effect idea, but in different order. In the second sentence the cause comes first, and in the first sentence the effect comes first. Perhaps the cause–effect wording of the second sentence will be received better by those children who know they *did* bring in their notes on time—and therefore have nothing to worry about. Similarly with the cause–effect wording, those children who *did not* bring in slips on time are asked to focus more on the reason for the unhappy news than on the unhappy news. In contrast, the effect–cause pattern of the first sentence will momentarily worry the whole class. And those children who cannot go on the trip must first focus on the bad news before they are reminded of the good reason for the bad news. While there is no guarantee that the second wording will be more effective in this case, the odds are favorable that it will be. In another situation an effect–cause pattern might be more effective: "We will have a class party today, because I left my reading glasses home by mistake." Other thematic possibilities for composing persuasive sentences include problem–solution, solution–problem, and chronological steps for giving advice or partisan analysis of a process.

Later chapters will take note of other examples of persuasion shrewdly enhanced by selection of words and word order. Now we will turn to persuasive uses of figures of speech. Figures of speech also concern language choices, but for power rather than for tone or emphasis.

The Power of Figures of Speech

Recorded history tells us that figures of speech have long been used, first by clever persuaders in antiquity, then in sacred texts written over the centuries, and on down to the present.

Figures of speech often work by comparing one thing to another—even though the comparison is not perfect. It is both the aptness of these comparisons and the imperfections in these comparisons that give rhetorical power to figures of speech. The most common figures of speech include:

metaphor	two apparently unlike things compared
metonymy	using the name of one thing for that of another it is associated with or part of
personification	giving human characteristics to inanimate objects
rhetorical question	a question used to make a statement
simile	two things compared by using *like* or *as*
alliteration	repeating the same initial sound in two or more words
antithesis	presenting contrary ideas in parallel form
climax	presenting ideas in ascending order of power
hyperbole	extreme exaggeration
irony	using literal meanings that are opposite to their apparent intention

The *metaphor* is probably the most important figure of speech for the persuader and can be used in powerful ways. The phrase "Come in out of the dark and bask in the light" is a metaphor if the speaker means that someone should adopt a new idea. Here "dark" is used figuratively to signify not accepting a glorious new idea. For most people, the notions of dark and light probably have powerful and ancient associations. In another example, a parent might say, "You're tearing my heart out by taking that job" to a grown-up child. While "taking that job" is an intellectual notion, "tearing my heart out" is a visceral, bloody, and very emotional image. Recently the railroad station near my home had the cement floor of its waiting area repaved. Although it seemed a rather small job, it took the workers nearly three months to complete. Toward the end of the work I went into the station's coffee shop and said wryly to the owner, "How's the Great Wall of China coming?" which produced an instant, knowing smile. My comment relied on a metaphor (the idea of the repaving project metaphorically changed to the building of the Great Wall of China).

Metaphors can be categorized in numerous ways: archetypal, which means having to do with powerful, primordial entities such as fire, the earth, the sun, and the sea ("He was *on fire* with enthusiasm"); sporting ("Let's see if we can *hold the line* here"); cinematic or theatric ("He made quite a *scene*"); culinary ("These are the *salad days* of our lives"); architectural ("I'll take advantage of my *window* of opportunity"); militaristic ("Get out the *big guns*"); naturalistic ("That sailor has *eagle eyes*"); and so on.

Metonymy identifies something by using the name of something else closely akin to it or with which it is commonly associated. This allows the persuader to recharacterize or reduce the whole to the terms of the part. For example, middle- or upper-management executives in companies often wear suits. You will therefore sometimes hear management referred to as "the suits." The phrase "Will the suits agree to this?" emphasizes the power and formality of management. Of course, the suits in question here are much more than just symbols of power and formality. Similarly, the metonymy in "The *front desk* can help you with that" relies on an association between the people who give information in the front lobby of a hotel or building and the desks at which they sit.

When using *personification*, the persuader gives human characteristics to inanimate objects: plants and ideas, for example. The power here may simply be because we care more about humans. So when we imagine an object as a person, we care more. I once sold a car to a used-car dealer and felt sad all the way home—as if I had abandoned a friend or member of the family.

Asking *rhetorical questions* allows persuaders to make statements in the form of questions, the answer being implied by the question. Persuasive statements often need proof or backing, but questions, on the other hand, need answers not proof. So a rhetorical question can allow us to make a claim without having to offer proof. When I say, "Are we going to let these people continue to annoy us with their unsolicited phone calls?" I mean, "No, we aren't." Notice here that I haven't said, "I don't think we should continue to let these people annoy us with their unsolicited phone calls . . . and here's why." If someone says of your rhetorical question, "I don't agree," you can always say that you were just asking a question.

Similes work like metaphors except that you must use either *as* or *like* in the comparison: "like a ton of bricks" or "smart as a whip."

Alliteration is useful for bringing attention to an idea. The rhythmic punctuation of initial word sounds in alliteration is often poetic. One website I used to visit had a folder called Novice Nook, which explained how to use the site. One day I received a notice from the website manager that the Novice Nook folder would be renamed the Beginners Folder. I along with several other frequent guests of the site complained about the name change, and the manager then decided to keep the name Novice Nook, an alliteration. Alliterations can also be used to conveniently change the subject ("We have no freebies, but we do have Frisbees").

Using *antithesis* can get your audience to think about ideas: "Sometimes your best friends can be your worst enemies." "It was the best of times, it was the worst of times" is a famous antithesis from Charles Dickens's novel *A Tale of Two Cities*. As you think of these antitheses, you may try to come to terms with their opposing meanings. In the second example, Dickens uses the antithesis to help suggest that his story about the French Revolution will be interesting and tragic.

A *climax* is very useful for the persuader because it creates a sequence of ideas that can lead to persuasion. For example, in a debate on whether mercy killing should become the law of the land, a persuader who is against this proposition could use a three-phase statement: "What is permitted today . . . may be encouraged tomorrow . . . and then someday required." This sequence of ideas builds on the idea that unintended or unanticipated consequences can often ruin new policies. How could such a policy of mercy killing become encouraged or even required someday? Longer life spans and the increased cost of keeping older people alive in hospitals or nursing homes might make the policy seem economically advantageous.

Hyperbole sometimes separates what persuaders do from what propagandists do. Used properly, hyperbole allows a persuader to help us appreciate the significance of some idea through exaggeration—as long as we know it is an exaggeration used to make a point—as in "They'd give you the shirts off their backs." Of course, they probably would not. Propagandists may use exaggeration in ways where it is not clear whether they are speaking figuratively or literally: "Mayor X is a fascist."

Irony can help a persuader criticize something, say a diet program, by using a kind of semantic opposition: "This diet is supposed to help you lose weight, but when we checked, it actually caused people to overeat and gain weight" or "Can you believe it? They were actually robbed by the security guard who was there to protect them."

Language Traps

Though language is the most important tool we have, language nonetheless can be a source of trouble. We can fall into **language traps** when we think we know something about a topic that we really do not know. Perhaps the simplest example of how language can provide a false sense of security can be found in your medicine cabinet. You may have a bottle of medicine there that you have used several times in the past. Maybe you need to take the medicine one more time but fail to notice that the expiration date has come and gone. Are the contents of the bottle the same as they were the last time you took the medicine? Maybe, maybe not. There is probably a warning on the bottle not to use the medicine after the expiration date. Why? Over time, chemicals can change. What was once a good medicine may now be something that will harm you. And the fact that the name on the bottle is the same does not necessarily mean that the original substance still fills the bottle. Could someone have replaced the contents without telling you? Could you have done this and forgotten? Often we can be fooled by the very language we depend on to live intelligently.

The field of general semantics documents the ways in which we can be fooled by the words and sentences we use.[8] Those senders who would influence others may at times try to fool their audiences; but more importantly, senders who want to be ethical may also fool themselves with their language use and may then innocently pass on these language traps to their audiences. You may already be familiar with some of these traps, but they are important enough to review from time to time, as we can easily be tricked even when we are aware of a particular trap. One rule of general semantics is to keep factual statements distinct in your mind from inferential statements, and the failure to do so is the first specific language trap we'll examine.

Fact-Inference Confusion. A factual statement occurs when someone observes something and then describes the event or subject without adding any feature or detail that was not directly observed. For example, I could observe a traffic accident and then try to explain to investigators what I saw. If I say, "The larger car was coming from the east and the smaller car was coming from the west," I have offered a reasonably *factual* statement. But if I say, "The driver of the larger car didn't notice that the smaller car was in the way," I have offered not a factual statement, but an *inferential* statement. The reason the second statement is inferential is that I can only guess at what the driver of the larger car noticed or did not notice. Similarly if I say, "The light had just turned red for the smaller car," I am delivering a factual statement. But if I say, "The driver of the smaller car thought there was enough time to get through," I am offering an inferential statement. Inferential statements go beyond what is observed by the reporter, adding guesses, inferences, assumptions, and the like.

There is nothing wrong with making inferential statements; this is one of the most valuable ways we have to think and reason. The problem comes when we (1) create an inferential statement and then forget the inferences we have made in it, falsely thinking we have made a factual statement; and (2) reflexively make inferences that we are unaware of in our statement.[9] In either case, a false fact may then be passed on to listeners or retained by the speaker in making a second statement based on this possibly false fact. Now if I say the driver of the smaller car seemed to be trying to get though the light before it changed, that is fine because I am alerting myself and my listeners, with the words *seemed to*, that my statement is conjectural. But if I say that he was trying to run the light, I have made an important error. Yes, the driver of the small car may have tried to run the light. But it is also possible that he did not notice that the light was changing, or his brakes failed, or he missed the brake pedal, or he had a heart attack at that very moment, and so on.

It is a good idea to adopt the communication habit of tagging your statements with *certainty-level* phrases when you are not simply stating a fact about something as it was observed by you. Possible tags are *it seemed, if my memory serves me correctly, perhaps, it appeared to be*, and *I'm guessing that*. If you want to be a very careful communicator, you might limit your conversation and writing to just two things: factual statements and labeled inferential statements. This may be easier than at first it seems. For example, with the words *I seem to remember* or *it appeared to me*, you are using factual statements about what you have seen, heard, felt, thought, or imagined. Other labeled inference statements could be "I'm guessing we went off course" or "I bet the lost earrings are under the couch." With practice, these reminders can become a habit. Sometimes we do not take the above advice when making self-serving inferences that we then pawn off as facts.

The map is not the territory. We must always remember two things: descriptions of things are made by people, but the objective world exists before any descriptions are made about it. If I see a tree and point at it, saying, "Tree," we must remember that the tree is not in the slightest way affected by my calling it a tree (or a bush, light pole, or pogo stick). If I then go on to call it a "sick tree," it may be true that the tree is rotting; but it may also be true that I am wrong in my diagnosis. If I put a sign on the tree that says "Sick and Dying," I still have not altered the tree at all. But if you then come along and chop down this tree because it is "sick and dying," you may have fallen into the-map-is-not-the-territory language trap, in which there is a faulty correspondence between the map (words) and the territory (the thing described). In fact, a concerned neighbor may try to get you to not chop down the tree. But if you are, say, a worker for the highway department, you may trust the official-looking sign on the tree more than you do an opinion from a passerby, or even your own opinion. Listeners to persuasive messages especially have to remind themselves not to get carried away by a map with an ambiguous or incorrect relationship to a territory.[10]

Dating. Things change over time. For example, as a graduate you might say, "The high school that I attended would never allow someone in who was not a good student." General semanticists would urge you to date the important things you describe. Thus you should say, "The high school that I attended *ten years ago* would never allow someone in who was not a good student." Now even if it happens that the policy of this high school has changed over the years, you still have a chance of being reasonably accurate—assuming your memory and judgment of that past time are correct. Similarly, you should not say, "X, my old high-school friend, is self-centered." Instead you might say, "The X I knew in high school always seemed self-centered to me, although I am biased since he once stole a girlfriend of mine." There is an old saying, "You can't step into the same river twice." Why? Because the next time you step in, the river will have already changed—even if only slightly (e.g., in its currents, riverbed contours, the things floating on it, the positions of boats navigating in it).

Indexing. You should also index the important things you describe.[11] That is, a given oak tree may share many things with other oak trees, but there will always be differences between it and other oak trees (in size, configuration of branches and leaves, age, location, history, general shape, imperfections, number of squirrels and birds living within, resident insect populations, and so on). So to not confuse ourselves, we should index what we talk about. Subscripts might be one way of doing this: oak tree$_1$ and oak tree$_2$. Actually, it would sound more natural to index with words rather than subscripts: the only oak tree at the southwest corner of Main and Sixth Street, Mudville, for example. Anyone who has ever bought a new car that turned out to be a lemon knows only too well the importance of indexing objects of the same class. Even this subclass of lemons should then be indexed, however, as in lemon$_1$, lemon$_2$, and so on. So when a persuader says, "You can visit our franchises in the city where you live for great service," you might think, "Yes, but do *all* your individual franchise operations have the same great service?" Propagandists and occasionally persuaders may play a shell game with words that should really be dated or indexed to avoid misleading their audiences.[12]

Hypostatization. This is another idea of general semantics, although the word *hypostatization* predates the field, entering the English language in the early 1800s. Hypostatization refers to the problem of believing that because a word exists for something, then that something must necessarily exist or at least will come to exist at some future time. This may be the case of having a labeled category with no actual content. A simple example of hypostatization is the word *unicorn*. A unicorn is a mythical animal with the body and head of a horse, the hind legs of an adult male red deer, the tail of a lion, and a single horn in the middle of its forehead. Of course, no such animal really exists, but it is tempting to imagine such an animal, and the existence of the word can make it seem that unicorns really do exist. Other examples of hypostatization may not be so easy to keep in perspective. The existence of terms like *time travel* and *time machine* may tempt us to think that time travel will someday become a reality. But it may be that time travel does not make any sense. Just where would all these places that we would travel to in time exist? Where I am today, along with the entire universe, would have to exist in some particular space, as well as the universes of yesterday, a thousand years ago, and a thousand and one years ago, as well as the universes of tomorrow and two million years from now. And what about all the time points in between or beyond these?[13]

So when a persuader mentions "a peace process" that is currently in place at, say, the United Nations, we had better make sure that the phrase "a peace process" refers to actual things that are also labeled accurately. We should do the same when we confidently talk of investing next year's surplus money—because by next year there may be no money to invest. Real-estate "get rich" offers promoted in "informationals" on television may say that they will show you how to get rich buying all the "undervalued houses" in your neighborhood with no money down. Perhaps there are such properties. But maybe there are none. Or maybe there are in fact only one or two, and these will be competed for by numerous other people, some of whom may have an advantage because of their occupation or experience with the real-estate business. We are probably especially prone to hypostatization errors when words seem to magically solve our problems for us. However, words are not the only parts or types of messages that need to be considered by those who are bent on analyzing, understanding, and augmenting persuasion.

Influence through Nonverbal Communication

Though this book emphasizes verbal communication, sometimes the old adage "It's not what you say, but how you say it" is important. During conversation (in person, or as depicted on television or in films), we use a variety of nonverbal channels to augment our spoken words. And even written words have the nonverbal dimensions of the fonts used for their printing, the layout and arrangement of text, headlines, and so on. As we like to say, "A picture is worth a thousand words." It would take several books to tell the entire story of nonverbal communication, so here I will just highlight those nonverbal elements that help in persuading.

Semiotics (or Artifactics)

Semiotics concerns the symbolic meanings we associate with various objects. In old Hollywood Westerns, the heroes wore white hats and the villains wore black hats. And if I am giving a talk on investing your savings in stocks, I might well carry a copy of the *Wall Street Journal* or *Money* with me. If I am a preacher, I might speak with a Bible in my hand. If I am going on a job interview, I might try to create the impression of a competent worker by wearing a suit. The Goodyear blimp may announce to the world that some important sports event is taking place at this moment somewhere under the blimp. Politicians often pose for certain messages to their constituents either in front of a flag or in front of the building they legislate from. Even classical paintings may contain images that carry special meanings: a small dog portrayed in a family portrait that was painted during a particular period may symbolize something to knowledgeable viewers. In America, the presence of Air Force One at an airport conveys a powerful image of the presidency. Can these semiotic messages help persuade us? Very likely so.[14]

Communication theorist Roland Barthes has analyzed fashion in clothes, creating an extensive vocabulary for describing clothing using such terms as *size, weight, fit, plunging* or *hanging movement,* and *relief.* Clothing can also be analyzed by using the theory of signs discussed earlier in this chapter. Barthes mentions that raw silk used in a garment is a sign of summer. And so are things like short sleeves, light colors, and open shoes. Communication through clothing probably operates at three levels that are analogous to speech. When we speak, we utter sounds that are used to create words and effects that are in turn used to accomplish something. With clothing, these three levels (sounds, words, and effects) might be represented by fabric and design, the "message" of each garment worn, and the overall effect of these garments on the people who wear them or on the people who observe others wearing them.

How do *fabric* and *design* contribute to the message of a garment? Specific fabrics such as denim, silk, leather or suede, cotton, wool, hemp, jute, ramie, and the numerous synthetics lend themselves to communication quite well. Each of these carries its own connotations. Design concerns how the body will be redefined by the outfit. An outfit can suggest exactly where body parts or contours are, how small or large body parts seem, where the boundaries of body parts seem to be, and which body parts should get more attention or less attention. Some outfits desexualize, some sexualize, some create images of strength or weakness, and some are "loud" and some are "quiet." Some seem to imply thoughtfulness and some, mindlessness.[15]

Sometimes advertisers of particular garments try to create auras or associations through which a garment seems to say something about its wearer. This is the garment's *message*. Tight-fitting jeans are one example of this, whether worn to encourage simple attraction or actual seduction. Uniforms say to observers that the wearer works in some particular occupation. Barthes uses figures of speech, among other things, to describe how meaning is created by a garment. For example, a particular garment could be hyperbolic (by exaggerating, or its reverse, minimizing). Clothing experts advise us to wear dark clothes to minimize weight and shoulder padding to exaggerate body heft; wearing a hat may make us seem taller. Similarly, heavy boots that rise to the calf may serve as metaphors of power (as in "jack-booted soldiers"). If when people have seen you they can remember *only* your outfit, your clothes may have served the function of metonymy. And antithesis can occur when an outfit seems to say incongruent things, such as a red, white, and blue t-shirt in America that displays a criticism of the government.

The *overall effect* of outfits worn can concern things like (1) the psychological assurance extended to others whereby our clothing says, "I mean no threat to you, I am just a regular person," (2) the image management of the social and physical perceptions that others will form about us by noticing what we wear, (3) seduction or sexual attraction, (4) identification with a job role through either a formal uniform or an informal one, (5) lifestyle, and (6) neighborhood or ethnic affiliation. At this level, clothing is transformational. We see someone's clothing (e.g., a police officer's uniform) and are momentarily changed inside in small or large ways.

Kinesics

The **kinesics** class of nonverbal communication concerns gestures, facial expressions, and posture. Facial expressions are good for communicating such emotions as joy, fear, anger, surprise, sadness, and contempt.[16] Those who can communicate these emotions spontaneously in appropriate situations will probably enjoy more credibility with audiences. The posture of the body is good for communicating a speaker's mood and attitude toward the speaking situation and the audience. Since persuaders don't always monitor their postures, they need to learn to be careful of what their postures may be inadvertently saying. Hand and head gestures are commonly used by speakers (signifying "I do not know," "you," "me," "okay," "they are crazy," "go ahead," "good going," and so on). Persuaders need to be careful of such gestures because they may not always be decoded in the way the persuader intended. For example, the victory or peace sign using two fingers held up can in America be flashed with palm forward or backward (forward is more usual) and still mean what the speaker intends. But in England, if you flash the two fingers palm backward, you are making an obscene gesture, not the sign for victory or peace, which is made with palm forward.

Proxemics

Proxemics includes eye contact, how close you move to other people, and even how loud or soft your voice is (the volume of your voice can also serve another nonverbal function, as explained below).[17] The meanings of these proxemic messages usually concern things like (1) power, (2) level of involvement with others, and (3) positive or negative sentiments. A speaker who moves physically closer to the audience at a crucial moment of persuasion may be intensifying a powerful bond between the speaker and the audience. Politicians may persuade by moving closer and draping one arm around the shoulder of the target of persuasion. Some persuaders may even poke the listener in the stomach to emphasize a point (both of which, draping the arm and poking the stomach, add the separate element of a touch message to the proxemic message; see discussion of *haptics* below). Eye contact is a type of proxemics in that you "move in or out" on the other person with the amount of eye contact made. More-persuasive people may in fact use more eye contact than less-persuasive people. Authoritarian persuaders may use louder voices to get attention and encourage compliance from others.

Proxemics can also be applied to television, film, and still images because the camera "transports" viewers to apparent proxemic locations vis-à-vis the main subject of the visual image. This is especially important when the subject is a person. At one moment when watching a film, the viewer may seem to stand close to and facing two people who are conversing on a city sidewalk. But then the viewer is moved closer by the camera for a close-up reaction shot of one of the two. Then maybe the viewer is looking down from a second-story apartment window at the two on street level as they begin walking down the sidewalk toward the corner. Rapid cutting from shot to shot may at times provide viewers with perspectives impossible to duplicate during face-to-face communication. In another example of media proxemics, the camera angles in a television documentary may allow viewers to "tag along," acting almost like an assistant to an on-camera interviewer conversing with passersby on the street. In other cases, news broadcasts may warn viewers that "the following graphic images may be disturbing to some" before the camera allows viewers to peer directly down at several dead bodies found in a vacant lot. Media theorists such as Joshua Meyerowitz have argued that the modern media collectively disrupt the normal proxemic perspectives that people have used from time immemorial for orienting themselves within their social worlds and that were based on experiences that were mostly face-to-face.[18]

Vocalics

There are several terms I can use to identify communication through the dynamics of voice, terms such as *paralinguistics* and *paralanguage*. But I will stay with the term **vocalics** to explain how vocal pitch, loudness, word duration, and pause duration can be used to convey emotions or to affect how words are actually decoded. For example, the sentence "They decorated the girl with the flowers" has at least two possible meanings, depending on how you say it. In one, the flowers are used *for* the decoration, and in the other, the flowers are used to identify *which* girl was decorated. But perhaps a more important role of voice concerns the information that voice conveys about the speaker and about the speaker's emotions. Your speaking voice (but interestingly, not always your singing voice) may tell people such things as where in the world you are from, how much money your parents had when you were growing up, how much education you have, what your personality is like, and how much confidence you have. For talented speakers, the voice can convey a host of different emotions that can sway the audience one way or the other. In fact, demagogues like Nikita Khrushchev of the Soviet Union or Adolph Hitler of Nazi Germany relied on the power of their voices to augment the incredible political power each had in his time and place. Other notable political speakers with motivating voices were Franklin Roosevelt, Winston Churchill, and Ronald Reagan. Hollywood actresses who had engaging voices include Greta Garbo and Marilyn Monroe.[19]

Environmentalics

Environmentalics is a term I use to refer to the setting (a room, an outdoor scene) in which communication takes place. Colors, textures, arrangement of interior space, fixtures, furnishings, height of ceilings, area of floor space, sound levels, aromas, and so on are used to convey messages. These features of communication environments can encourage users to feel certain ways and act in certain ways. For example, does your living room or your parents' living room say to guests, "Sit down, make yourself comfortable, we're easy-going people," or does it say, "Be careful of what you do here; this is a museum"? Expensive hotel lobbies may say to guests, "You are important." Fleabag hotel lobbies more often say, "We're watching you, so don't loiter." Outdoor or indoor political rallies may be persuasive due to the orchestration of lights, loud music, flags, signs, and the order in which things happen. The longer you wait for the principal speaker, the more dramatic the eventual performance may be, assuming that every detail has been coordinated by a skillful event-planner. Abraham Lincoln's most famous speech, the Gettysburg Address, was made on a blood-soaked Civil War battlefield in Pennsylvania that was being turned four months after the battle into a cemetery. So when Lincoln said, "But, in a larger sense, we cannot dedicate . . . we cannot consecrate . . . we cannot hallow this ground. The brave men, living and dead, who struggled here have consecrated it, far above our poor power to add or detract," the audience probably felt a powerful appreciation for Lincoln's words as they looked around at what might have been the "still smoldering" aftermath of the battle.[20]

Chronemics

A clever persuader can use timing, or **chronemics**, as an ally. During a speech, you can use timing to create emphasis if you momentarily hesitate just before your key idea. And how early or late you arrive for a speech may communicate something, depending on who you are. Even the date and time of day can help or hinder the effectiveness of a message. A politician who complains about the national economy in a letter to his or her constituents will sound smarter or dumber, depending on how bad or how good the economy sounds in an economic report that surfaces at about the same time the letter is delivered in the mail. One word of caution, however, is in order. The codes we use to understand the meanings of timing may vary from culture to culture. What is considered late or early in a metropolitan area may not be considered the same in a small town or a remote part of the world. Precise timing serves important roles in the modern world. Greenwich, England, serves as the starting point for coordinating what time it is in various places on the globe. And an atomic clock in the southwestern United States now calculates the exact time in nanoseconds and then broadcasts a radio signal by which distant clocks can set their time. However in other places in the world, people sometimes avoid modern society's "rat-race" and get to things . . . when they get to them.

Haptics

Haptics is another name for communication through touch. Few public speakers spend much time touching people in their audiences, and media communication does not facilitate using touch, at least at present. A faith healer, however, might reach out and touch someone on the head to emphasize a bond with the audience. And some persuasive people may wrap an arm around your shoulders during persuasive encounters. But here too, the acceptability of touch during communication will vary from place to place, culture to culture, and rhetorical setting to rhetorical setting. There are many people who desperately want and need to be touched, yet in "non-touch" cultures like America, taboos prevent touch from being used in many social settings.[21]

Chapter in Retrospect

VIGNETTE Nonverbal Persuasion and the Statue of Liberty

The Statue of Liberty in New York Harbor is located on twelve-acre Liberty Island, formerly Bedloe's Island and Fort Wood (a fortress for the protection of New York Harbor in 1811). A gift from France, the statue was dedicated on October 28, 1886; designated a national monument on October 15, 1924; and recently restored for its spectacular centennial on July 4, 1986. The statue follows in the tradition of great monuments that includes the Bamiyan Buddha statues, Mother Russia, and the Colossus of Rhodes.[22]

The important symbolism of the Statue of Liberty includes (1) the seven *spikes* in the crown, which represent the seven continents or the seven seas across which ships risk life and limb on their treks to America; (2) the *tablet* held in Liberty's left hand to affirm the principles articulated in the Declaration of Independence—which has its date emblazoned on the tablet; (3) the twenty-five *windows* in the crown that represent the "natural minerals" of the earth; (4) the *toga*, which represents the ancient republic of Rome and the timelessness that links Liberty to past, present, and future; (5) Liberty's *crown*, which symbolizes majesty, along with her *gown*, which reveals her divine origin and eternal mission: to be a source of light and hope for humankind; (6) her *torch*, which represents enlightenment; and (7) the *chains* underfoot, which represent Liberty's crushing of tyranny. We should also note that Lady Liberty stands at the official entrance to America, not the entrance to New York City.

In terms of proxemic messages, the Statue of Liberty conveys meaning through its location in lower New York bay, centermost among such points as Manhattan Island, Staten Island, Long Island, Governors Island, and Ellis Island (where numerous immigrants once landed). The statue is the understandable pride of America as that statue looks nearly southward toward the approach from the sea, offering visual encouragement and navigational guidance to those about to enter the United States, and especially to ships in the night. The torch lights the way, and the first face that ship-born travelers see in America is that of Lady Liberty saying, "Welcome." The scene of those disembarking from these ships will be laden with social and political imperatives. Most of those arriving are welcome; but if a would-be entrant were to say, in passing Liberty Island, "I've come to try to end democracy and freedom in America," Lady Liberty would seem to reply, "You may *not* enter."

Liberty's face is serene, confident, and steady; her eyes gaze toward the sea. Her posture is very erect in her holding up the torch as high as possible. There is a Joan of Arc quality to her manner and appearance. The semiotic signs of the statue, which include the torch, crown, toga, and tablet, give her an almost biblical presence. And there is a timeless quality to the statue that addresses the ages. The poet Emma Lazarus, who campaigned in 1883 for financial contributions to build the base for the Statue of Liberty, describes Liberty with these words:

> Not like the brazen giant of Greek fame [the Colossus of Rhodes],
> With conquering limbs astride from land to land;
> Here at our sea-washed, sunset gates shall stand
> A mighty woman with a torch, whose flame
> Is the imprisoned lightning, and her name
> Mother of Exiles. From her beacon-hand
> Glows world-wide welcome; her mild eyes command
> The air-bridged harbor that twin cities frame.

And we can almost hear Lady Liberty speak as Emma Lazarus offers the now-famous words:

> Give me your tired, your poor,
> Your huddled masses yearning to breathe free,
> The wretched refuse of your teeming shore.
> Send these, the homeless, tempest-tost to me;
> I lift my lamp beside the golden door!

Though no one has ever heard these words actually spoken by Lady Liberty, it is not hard to imagine the vocal tones that would be needed to say these words with passion.

Summary and Conclusions

Like other forms of communication, persuasion relies on signs and symbols. With either of these, there is the signifier (the form or appearance) and the signification (the meaning understood). The exact relationship between given signifiers and their significations helps determine whether we have a sign or symbol. Simple signs concern things like smoke being an indication of fire (an index-type sign). But so-called iconic signs are used when people look for ways to communicate with signifiers that resemble what they signify (e.g., a posted sign in the forest warning not to build fires, the sign consisting of a simple drawing of a campfire and an X drawn through the campfire). The most sophisticated relationship between a signifier and its signification is the word and its arbitrary meaning (that is to say, we will find no clue to the meaning of the word *fire* in the letters of its spelling). Words are good examples of symbols. And nonverbal messages often function as signs but at times can function as symbols (e.g., a gesture of the fingers that means "peace"), depending on how they are used.

There are two types of word meanings: connotative and denotative. Denotative meanings of words can be found in dictionaries. These are the objective or official meanings of words. But a word's connotative meaning concerns the subjective and personal responses each person experiences when writing, reading, saying, or hearing the word. Clever use of words can help make a speaker persuasive, and so can cleverly composed sentences (syntactic or grammatical meaning). Words with special persuasive powers include such figures of speech as metaphors and rhetorical questions. Unfortunately, the power that language gives us can sometimes create traps that confuse us or cause problems. Some examples of language traps are when we think the inferences we make are actually facts, or when we fail to note that a term like *oak tree* does not always refer to the same object (every oak tree will be a different size, age, shape, and so on). Traps also occur when we falsely think that because a word or phrase exists, the thing or things to which it refers must necessarily also exist (such as all the "undervalued houses" in your neighborhood that you can easily make lots of money with by buying and then selling them quickly).

Sometimes persuasion rests not on what you say, but on how you say it. This influence through nonverbal communication can rely on a number of different types of communication that include (1) semiotics (or artifacts), by which a sender displays objects for persuasive effect; (2) kinesics, which includes facial expressions, gestures, and posture; (3) proxemics, which involves how we regulate for persuasive effect our physical distance from other communicators, our eye contact, and our vocal loudness; (4) vocalics, which refers to the tones of our voices; (5) environmentalics, which concern the messages conveyed by a room's colors, shapes, furnishings; (6) chronemics, which includes such communication tactics as arriving early or late to a meeting, speaking slowly or rapidly, or waiting before answering a question; and (7) haptics, which a speaker uses when touching the bodies of listeners to make a point or convey an emotion.

KEY TERMS

chronemics	hypostatization	sign
connotative	kinesics	signification
denotative	language traps	signifiers
environmentalics	proxemics	symbols
haptics	semiotics	vocalics

REVIEW QUESTIONS

1. How does the game Twenty Questions illustrate the nature of words and the things they represent?
2. Explain the notion of the self-fulfilling prophecy.
3. Give examples of three different type of signifiers and give sample significations for each.
4. What is the difference between the denotation and connotation of words? How does this distinction relate to the distinction between god and devil terms?
5. According to a theory in this chapter, the main and subordinate clauses in complex sentences can be used skillfully by persuaders. How?

6. Why are the aptness and imperfections in the comparisons apparent in many figures of speech important?

7. Why are indexing and dating important when using words?

8. Explain how symbols have already helped the human race explore space.

9. How do each of the types of nonverbal messages described in this chapter relate to the signifier-signification aspects of signs?

10. How many of the topics covered in this chapter were alluded to by the frog story given at the beginning of this chapter?

SUGGESTED PROJECTS AND ACTIVITIES

1. Make two sets of labels for common items found in your home (furnishings, appliances, rooms). One set should encourage people to use the items, and one set should discourage use. Hang the items on the things named and see how the labels encourage or discourage users (e.g., the kitchen could be named "chow dump" or "dining suite").

2. Write a persuasive paragraph in which the central motivation relies on one of the figures of speech discussed in this chapter.

3. Think of several examples in which people can be misled by a persuasive message that confuses something because of faulty indexing or dating.

4. Select a really appealing ad in a magazine and analyze how nonverbal messages in the visual part of the ad contribute to the ad's appeal for you.

QUESTIONS FOR DISCUSSION

1. Why do you think language is so powerful in the lives of people?

2. Do you believe that time travel is possible? Why? Why not? Explain in terms of hypostatization.

3. After reading the list of ingredients for a dog biscuit, could you then taste one? Explain your answer in terms of the power of word meanings and the realities represented by words.

4. When you suspect that someone may be lying to you, which channel do you rely on more, the verbal or the nonverbal? Why?

Notes

1. Stress Relief by a Simple Life, "The Power of Words," www.stresslesscountry.com/thepowerof (7 September 2005).

2. The Sapir-Whorf hypothesis posits that the lexicon of a language can affect the way we think and view the world (this is also known as *linguistic determinism*). The language we use probably weakly influences the way we think about things. Translating from one language to another may not always be easy, because certain ideas may be more easily coded in one language than in another, but it is usually possible to do so, even if the receiving language needs many words for an idea that takes only one or two words in the donor language. As such, the Sapir-Whorf hypothesis has been given less attention by linguists in recent decades; see for example Helen Cairns and Charles Cairns, *Psycholinguistics: A Cognitive View of Language* (New York: Holt, Rinehart, and Winston, 1976), 14–17.

3. These bits of meaning are sometimes referred to as *semantic features* by linguists and psycholinguists.

4. Timothy Borchers, *Persuasion in the Media Age* (Boston: McGraw-Hill, 2002), 173–75.

5. Suzanne Langer, *Philosophy in a New Key* (Cambridge, MA: Harvard University Press, 1976), 53–58.

6. Daniel Chandler, "Semiotics for Beginners," www.aber.ac.uk/media/Documents/S4B/sem02.html (1 September 2005).

7. Charles Osgood, George Suci, and Percy Tannenbaum, *The Measurement of Meaning* (Urbana: University of Illinois Press, 1957), 31–75.

8. See for example Martin Levinson, *The Drug Problem: A New View Using the General Semantics Approach* (Westport, CT: Praeger, 2002), 3, 117–18, 155–56.

9. One common way to make a fact-inference mistake is to treat a fallible sign of something as an infallible sign. An example of an infallible sign might be the first light that tells us that a new day is dawning. But a fallible sign might occur when we see someone on the street who seems to be talking on a cell phone. If we reflexively see the visual image of the cell-phone user as a sign that someone is talking at the other end of the call, we are treating a fallible sign as an infallible one. It may be that the cell-phone user is only pretending to talk to someone. To be safe, we should report that "the person appeared to be talking to someone over a cell phone." This way we remind ourselves and our receivers that we are making an inference that could be right or wrong.

10. A 100 percent correspondence between a map and a territory is probably impossible, but we can hope for a reasonably accurate correspondence in most successful instances. For example, if you speak precisely, you could probably advise someone to replace balding tires on his or her car (after you have measured the depth of the tire-treads using a tool designed for this), and thereby claim a fairly good correspondence between the map (your spoken diagnosis) and its territory (the tires with balding treads).

11. In some ways, indexing is the opposite of abstracting. By indexing, you remind everybody that one instance of something is always different in some way from other instances of that something. But with abstraction, you ignore the differences between all the instances of something and concentrate on what exactly these instances have in common with each other (e.g., two chairs may have their physical differences, but they are both the same kind of useful object: a piece of furniture having a back and designed for one person to sit on, and usually but not always having four legs).

12. Some critics of Abraham Lincoln like to question whether he was an abolitionist by playing a shell game in terms of dates. The Lincoln of 1850 may not have been the abolitionist he was to become, but the Lincoln of 1860 to 1865 (1) was responsible for waging the Civil War successfully (which ended slavery); (2) issued the Emancipation Proclamation after several states had committed sedition, thus activating his constitutional authority to free the slaves in those states; and (3) called for the Thirteenth Amendment to the Constitution, which was then initiated by Congress and later ratified by the states (ending slavery for all time, at least in America). In 1865 Lincoln even gave a speech that praised the outcome of the war. This speech was apparently attended by John Wilkes Booth.

13. Of course, exotic new theories can always be created to try to deal with these issues, such as a theory claiming that parallel, non-current versions of the universe could exist in compact form somewhere; but even this twist would be difficult to use for time travel because of the likely difficulty of "de-compacting" a specific past or future moment of the universe for multiple time travelers to use at will.

14. Mark Gottdiener, Karin Boklund-Lagopoulou, and Alexandros Lagopoulos, eds. *Semiotics* (London: Sage, 2003).

15. Roland Barthes, *The Fashion System*, trans. Matthew Ward and Richard Howard (New York: Hill and Wang, 1983).

16. Cf. Ray Birdwhistell, *Kinesics and Context: Essays on Body Motion Communication* (Philadelphia: University of Pennsylvania Press, 1970), 65–94.

17. Jinni A. Harrigan, Robert Rosenthal, and Klaus R. Scherer, eds., *New Handbook of Methods in Nonverbal Behavior Research* (New York: Oxford University Press, 2005).

18. Joshua Meyerowitz, *No Sense of Place: The Impact of Electronic Media on Social Behavior* (New York: Oxford University Press, 1985).

19. Cf. David Buller and Aune Kelly, "Effects of Vocalics and Nonverbal Sensitivity on Compliance: A Speech Accommodation Theory Explanation," *Human Communication Research* 14, no. 3 (Spring 1988), 301–32.

20. For a general description of environmentalics, see William Rogers, *Communication in Action* (New York: Holt, Rinehart, and Winston, 1984), 94–95.

21. As a "non-touch" culture, America has nonetheless become a nation of "huggers," at least during their greeting and departure rituals.

22. L. E. Bond, *Statue of Liberty: Beacon of Promise* (Santa Barbara, CA: Albion, 1999): 31–32.

Persuasive Messages

If you would persuade, you must appeal to interest rather than intellect.

—BENJAMIN FRANKLIN

You think that you are Ann's suitor; that you are the pursuer and she the pursued; that it is your part to woo, to persuade, to prevail, to overcome. Fool: it is you who are the pursued, the marked-down quarry, the destined prey.

—GEORGE BERNARD SHAW

At the heart of the First Amendment lies the principle that each person should decide for him or herself the ideas and beliefs deserving of expression, consideration, and adherence. Our political system and cultural life rest upon this ideal. Government action that stifles speech on account of its message, or that requires the utterance of a particular message favored by the Government, contravenes this essential right. Laws of this sort pose the inherent risk that the Government seeks not to advance a legitimate regulatory goal, but to suppress unpopular ideas or information or manipulate the public debate through coercion rather than persuasion.

—U.S. SUPREME COURT

COULD I CONVINCE you to sell all your belongings, quit school or your job, buy a sailboat, and set out for two years to see the world by boat? To persuade you to do this would require good arguments, a fitting **emotional appeal** or two, and an effort to build credibility about my persuasive motivations and knowledge of the topic. But in the end, I will have to come close to assuring you that my proposal is a good one, for you at least. I really do not want to trick or manipulate you into following my advice. Nor do I want to create false impressions about what a trip around the world would be like in a small sailboat. There is a good rule for persuaders to follow here: Be careful of what you try to persuade others to do or believe—you might get your wish. Then both you and the individuals who heeded your persuasion will have to live with the consequences of your persuasive success, for better or worse. Beyond sailboating promotions, persuasive messages are generally used to influence others on questions of what to do (policy), questions of what is good or bad (value), or questions of what is true or false (fact).

Over the years there have been two basic approaches to the study of persuasion. One approach focuses on the analysis of actual public messages designed to persuade, often in case studies of speeches or media messages by public figures or advertisers. A second approach focuses—often using the scientific method characterized in chapter 1—on what happens to receivers, in their minds and hearts, when they are exposed to a persuasive message. This and the following three chapters will usually take the **message-oriented approach** often favored by the humanist-oriented student of persuasion rather than the **receiver-oriented approach** often favored by the social sciences–oriented student of persuasion (see chapters 7–10).

A Message-Oriented Study of Persuasion

In the ancient worlds of Greece and Rome, persuasion was seen more in terms of messages than in terms of the psychological tendencies of receivers. For example, Aristotle envisioned the workings of logos, ethos, and pathos in persuasive messages (see figure 3.1). With **logos**, persuaders marshal facts, figures, and reason to make a good case for something. With **ethos**, persuaders emphasize in their messages that they are competent and honest, and have goodwill and a dynamic communication style. And with **pathos**, persuaders augment their messages with emotional appeals to encourage favorable attitudes in receivers toward a persuasive topic. Aristotle also described a very clever persuasive technique called the **enthymeme**. For now, we'll say that an enthymeme is a brief persuasive message that leaves one or more of its several ideas implied or unstated.

As an illustration of a persuasive message with respect to the concepts of logos, ethos, pathos, and enthymeme, let's consider the following case study. As a persuader, you start by observing that the Rocky Mountains are the tallest mountains in the United States, a fact you have learned from just-gathered information. If you then conclude from this information that mountain climbing will be more exciting in the Rocky Mountains than anywhere else in the United States, you have constructed an argument that a mountain climber might accept on where to best climb. With good preparation, your message about mountain climbing would then include elements of logos (reasons to go), pathos (descriptions of fun and adventure), and ethos (a reasonable idea from a reliable person). Enthymeme in this argument will refer to any basic premise you do not explicitly state but leave to your listeners to supply themselves. The benefit here is that receivers in some sense help persuade themselves when they supply an argument with a crucial element they already happen to believe.

For example, as part of your mountain-climbing message, you might say, "Take the trip because you will lose your breath the first time you stand high atop one of the Rocky Mountains." The enthymeme here concerns the unstated premise that if you lose your breath, you have certainly found a worthwhile place to climb mountains. In another example of an enthymeme, I could say to a weight-conscious audience, "You should drink lite beer because it has fewer calories." If you are in the audience, you may then supply the basic premise yourself, namely, that consuming products with fewer calories is better for weight control than consuming products with more calories. Of course, if you have not eaten for a few

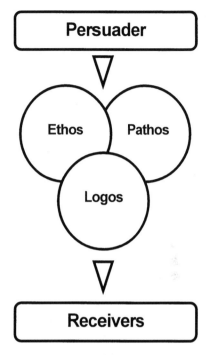

FIGURE 3.1 Message moving from persuader to receivers, helped by overlapping elements of pathos, ethos, and logos.

days, you may not supply this enthymemic premise. Moreover, if you end up drinking more lite beer, you probably have not benefited in any way and have spent a little more money. In fact, you might be better off drinking higher-calorie beer, but less of it, if you are concerned with the amount of money you spend on beer. Thus you might retort, "Drink regular beer; it has more 'carbs' per dollar."

Several centuries after Aristotle, the Roman orator and statesman Cicero prescribed five elements, or **canons**, to add to our understanding of persuasive messages, apparently with some earlier clarification by Aristotle and others. He advised that persuaders use the elements of invention, arrangement, style, memory and delivery.

With *invention*, you prepare to persuade by trying to identify convincing arguments for your case. These arguments do not have to be totally new arguments, they just have to be well selected, and cleverly adapted to the situation. For example, if I try to convince you to take up photography, I might assemble or invent several good reasons: you will have fun being creative; you may enjoy the photos long after you take them; you might make money if you can sell some of the photos; and you could eventually become a professional photographer and start your own business.

By using *arrangement*, you organize these arguments and other message materials in the most effective and efficient way for your topic and audience. Of the four inducements given above for becoming a photographer, which would be the most effective for a given audience? Should I put that best idea first to grab the audience's attention, or last to leave a memorable impression?

Style concerns the effective ways you find to word your persuasive ideas and includes how formal your text is, what figures of speech you'll select, and what tone the message will take. In a movie I once saw, a character said to a bird-spotter photographer, "These woods are lousy with birds." The line was supposed to make the speaker sound bad. If the line were persuasively rewritten to create a favorable impression of the character, it might have read, "The flora and fauna in this region offer spectacular opportunities for photographers who value naturalistic images."

As a persuader, you use *memory* to make sure that you have the most useful ideas and information at your fingertips when communicating your message. Being able to spout the names of several hundred species of birds, when needed, might help you persuade a would-be bird photographer.

Delivery means bringing your message to the audience in the most professional way possible, whether you are giving a speech, writing an essay, or creating a documentary, advertisement, or other media message.[1] Readers can revisit chapter 2 to review details about the finer points of delivering spoken messages.

The first organized studies of persuasive messages took place in ancient Greece, perhaps in a class taught outdoors near an olive tree. One of these first studies concerned answering a simple question: What can the speaker do to be more persuasive? One intriguing answer came with the stepwise description of a **syllogism**, which comprises three statements: a major premise, a minor premise, and a conclusion. And in the last 2,500 years, many others have offered different answers to this basic question. Syllogisms will be discussed in more detail in chapter 5. The twentieth century has spawned much thought on the question through scientific, historical, and critical studies of persuasion and rhetoric.

Answers to this question often involve models. In one such model, sometimes called the **Yale approach**, five steps, or milestones, are identified: attention, comprehension, acceptance, retention, and action.[2] In this model, receivers first attend to and understand the persuader's message. They then accept and remember the persuader's persuasive materials. Finally, they take action because they have not rejected the persuader's ideas. The action, in this model, concerns whether the receivers do something as a result of the persuasive message or at least are ready to act when the opportunity arrives.

When using the above model, the persuader has to discover effective ways to carry out each step. For example, someone may approach you in a shopping mall and say, "Did you know that the XY store is giving away free gift certificates to anyone who will appear in the background of a commercial they are shooting on site to help promote the mall?" This one statement may get you, the receiver, through the first step (attention). The person may go on to give you details about when and where to show up to appear in the ad. Assuming you understand what the deal involves and think it's a great opportunity to get the gift certificate, you have been helped through the comprehension and acceptance steps. If you are told to show up at ten o'clock Saturday morning and then you actually show up, the message has gotten you through the retention step and the action step. Obviously, the success of each subsequent step depends on the success of the previous steps.

A second model, called the **motivated sequence approach**, lists five steps: attention, need, satisfaction, visualization, and action.[3] These steps may seem similar to the steps in the Yale model, but they are somewhat different and can especially be applied to selling things. Here the persuader gets receivers' attention and then shows receivers that something is not right in their lives—they have an important need that is yet unmet. The sender then provides the solution and helps receivers see or feel what life would be like with this new solution. Next the sender asks for action. Thus, as a sales representative:

(1) You could stop me in a store by showing me a glass of water and a small water-faucet filter, saying, "You may think the water from your kitchen faucet is clean, but it's not" (attention). You sip the water and react with mock disgust.

(2) You then add an "impurities detection" chemical to the glass of water, and the water turns orange; this is to illustrate that my life is not perfect and that I have a problem to solve (need).

(3) Then you focus my attention on and describe the workings of the handy filter you are selling that is designed to solve my water problem (satisfaction).

(4) After you run another sample of water through the filter, it now seems to test clear (visualization). You now taste the water and smile and then invite me to taste it.

(5) You then ask how many filters I would like to buy and how I would like to pay for them (action). Here the main emphasis is on closing the sale.

Modern Forums for Persuasive Messages

Persuasive messages can assume a variety of forms. Sometimes a persuasive message takes the form of a well-chosen motivating *story*, sometimes a carefully developed *case* with several or more arguments, and sometimes just a simple *request*, such as "Can you give me a lift this morning? I'm very late for work." Persuasive messages can even take the form of a marriage *ritual*, a cleverly designed visual *image* such as an oil painting, or even a *token* or object such as a primitive totem pole. Then there are what researcher Kevin DeLuca calls *image events*. These events are often staged by groups to produce pictures that, when broadcast in print or electronic media, may influence the public. According to DeLuca, the first modern use of an image event to affect the political landscape occurred in 1861 when President Lincoln designated Yosemite as a national park after having viewed pictures of the land. But persuasion by visual image, like persuasion by the written word, can be honest, dishonest, or something in between the two.[4]

In modern societies, forums for persuasive efforts, whether visual or verbal, include speeches, debates, court trials, and the mass media.

Speeches

These are one of the oldest forms of persuasion and can be critically evaluated by researchers using tools created in the field of rhetorical criticism. Journals in this field publish studies of speeches in relation to theory.[5] Over the years a number of models have been worked out to accomplish this critical evaluation. The reader can investigate this field by reading such works as Aristotle's *Rhetoric* and Kenneth Burke's *A Grammar of Motives* (1945). As we've seen, Aristotle approaches a speech in terms of how effectively it uses ethos, pathos, and logos. A speech's pathos and logos can in turn be more closely examined in terms of how the speaker appeals to such virtues as justice, prudence, generosity, courage, and wisdom. We could also critique how well the persuader selects evidence that will be accepted by a particular audience. Burke's approach, by way of contrast, requires the speech critic to evaluate how effectively the speaker creates dramatic images in order to persuade. Does the speaker envision heroes pursuing heroic deeds? Does the speaker envision people caught up in situations beyond their control? For now, we will use a common-sense critique and simply ask if the main ideas selected for a persuasive speech would be likely to succeed were they used in an actual speech. You can decide this for yourself after reading the speech outline in box 3.1.

BOX 3.1

Sample Persuasive Speech Outline Showing Seven Inducements

A WALK OVER THE QUEENSBOROUGH BRIDGE IN NEW YORK CITY

I. Walk across living history, a grand bridge with a fairy-tale skyline
II. 1908 state-of-the-art bridge, nifty when first opened
    A. Trolley-cars and trolley-stations (on bridge)
    B. Bridge-level elevators to what was then called Blackwell's Isle
    C. Second Avenue el-train across bridge to Queens
    D. Unique riverscape views from bridge
    E. Romantic pedestrian-walks across bridge
    F. Stone staircase and turret-stairwells from street
III. Sadly, much is gone (traces still left to the keen of eye)
    A. Underground trolley station now a garage
    B. Ridges of stone staircase left in bridge wall
IV. Enjoy breathtaking vistas on pedestrian-walk high atop the bridge
    A. Manhattan Island, Queens, and East River below
    B. Eagle's-nest view of Roosevelt Island beneath (earlier island names: Welfare, Blackwell's, Hog)
V. Take a thirty-minute, zesty, 1 1/4-mile walk over bridge—great exercise
VI. For a memorable experience, prepare for the visit by doing research
    A. Website pictures of trolleys and bridge stations
    B. Movie *Mr. Buddwing* (1965 location shots on the bridge: walkways, stairways, old bridge signs that no longer exist)
VII. Visit other historical sites near the bridge to round out your trip
    A. 1833 Mount Vernon Hotel Museum (one block away)
    B. Tram ride to Roosevelt Island (ride high across the river)
    C. Roosevelt Island walk-around (lighthouse, old stone church, owner's house (ca. 1796), 25¢ around-island red bus)

Sources: Joseph Brennan, "Abandoned Stations," www.columbia.edu/~brennan/abandoned/willb.html; *Mr. Buddwing*, directed by Delbert Mann (1966); William H. Whyte, introduction, *The WPA Guide to New York City: The Federal Writers' Project Guide to 1930s New York*, American Guide Series (New York: New Press, 1995).

Debates

Debates are designed to test the goodness of a proposition by having two sides speak, one in support of and one in opposition to the proposition. Perhaps the two sides would debate whether public-school children should be required to wear uniforms. The affirmative side must explain why it supports the proposition. If the proposition is for a new policy, as it would be in this example, the affirmative must also offer a brief plan on how the policy would be implemented. The negative side then explains why it is opposed to the proposition. Each of the two sides must offer their reasons for supporting or opposing the proposition. Debate formats usually include time for rebuttal and sometimes cross-examination.

Box 3.2 compares the supporting reasons that might be used by affirmative and negative sides in a debate on another possible topic: legalizing drugs. In this illustration, each side presents a number of reasons that make its case seem the better. Each reason must also be cast in the form of an argument. For example item 1, "Would reduce crime because users would not have to steal to get money for drugs," would have to be supported by an argument such as "Users would not have to steal to get money for drugs because drugs would be cheaper to buy. And here are some facts to show this." Similarly, item 1 on the negative side of the debate, "Would increase drug usage because legal users would join illegal users," could be defended with this statement: "The people now using drugs illegally would continue to use them legally, while others would start using them because they have now become legal to use. For example, in Amsterdam . . ." The audience then decides who has won the debate, unless the debate is seen as a tie. And in a debate competition, there will be one or more judges who use rating scales to decide which side has won the debate. The judges will rate each side's analysis of the issues, definitions offered, evidence produced, adaptation of material to the

---

BOX 3.2

Sample Arguments for Affirmative and Negative Sides in a Debate

Drugs should be legalized
1. Would reduce crime because users would not have to steal to get money for drugs
2. Drugs could be taxed; revenue could be used for treatment programs
3. Government oversight would be safer for users
4. Would unclog courts and keep recreational users out of jail
5. Would be fairer to drug users: If alcohol can be legal, why not drugs?
6. Would deprive cartels and terrorists of income sources

Drugs should not be legalized
1. Would increase drug usage because legal users would join illegal users
2. Would have unintended negative effects (e.g., it would send the wrong message about national priorities)
3. Would not eliminate black market for underage or anonymous purchases
4. If taxed, would corrupt society and put us all in the drug business
5. Drugs like crack cocaine and heroin cannot be used without addiction
6. Would increase accidents and crimes because increased number of users

audience, refutation and rebuttal of the opposing side's materials, delivery skill, organization of ideas, courtesy shown to the other side, and effectiveness of cross-examinations.

The interesting thing about debates is that an assertion may at first seem convincing only to seem less convincing after the other side speaks. In a debate on banning private automobile traffic from the center streets in a city, the side arguing against the proposal might say, "Mass transportation will be overwhelmed by the greatly increased numbers of riders who leave their cars home." However, the other side might then say, "But you're assuming that we would not increase our mass-transportation capacity; we could add more buses and commuter trains and pay for these with increased fare-revenues from the added riders." Then the first side might answer, "But you're assuming an unlimited capacity to add more buses and trains; and at the height of rush hour, the buses and trains are already backed up one behind the other."

Court Trials

In some ways, courtroom trials are a type of debate. The affirmative side (the prosecution) has to create a series of messages that make its case on why the defendant should be convicted, say, of armed robbery. The negative side (the defense) need not actually make a case for acquittal—but usually does. This is because the burden of proof is on the prosecution, since it is arguing for a change in the status of the defendant (i.e., that the defendant be fined, put on probation, or imprisoned). There are significant differences between a debate and a trial. Trials are conducted under numerous rules of procedure. These rules concern such things as establishing whether there are grounds for a trial, introducing evidence during a trial, impaneling juries, giving instructions to juries (for jury trials), providing the defendant with the right of appeal, and protecting the defendant from double jeopardy.

Most important in the persuasive messages brought to a criminal trial is the concept of reasonable doubt.[6] The prosecutor must produce evidence and reasoning that proves guilt beyond a reasonable doubt. The defense must only show that there is a reasonable doubt. Judges and juries are persuaded by the very message variables that Aristotle mentioned: logos (the facts and logic of the case), pathos (the emotions aroused by the case), and ethos (how credible the various figures of the trial seem, including the defendant, the prosecutor, any witnesses, the defense attorney, and the judge).

In modern, high-profile trials, the two sides may even employ specialists who will advise each side on the most persuasive way to present its case to the jury. The social-science field of *impressions management* comes into play here, because there will always be some ambiguities in a trial, and the forming of impressions during a trial may help to resolve these ambiguities in the minds of receivers (the jury, judge, and spectators). For example, is the defendant a "monster," or only a "victim" of forces beyond his or her control? Wearing business attire and conservative-looking eyeglasses, writing with an expensive fountain pen on a yellow legal pad, and perhaps sliding notes across the defense table to counsel may go a long way in suggesting to the jury that the defendant is not the monster the prosecution makes him or her out to be. On the other hand, the prosecution may use language in court that implies the defendant is in fact such a monster, or it may bring witnesses inclined to describe the defendant as such. The judge has the obligation to see that the trial does not unfairly influence the jury along these lines—but this is often easier said than done.

While the proper mode of a trial is fact-oriented persuasion or argumentation, some high-profile trials make use of propaganda instead; these are sometimes referred to as "circus" or "celebrity" trials.[7] It seems, at least lately, that defense teams often try to create a "circus" environment to influence or pressure jurors. The goal at these trials is often to put the government, the police, larger society, or the prosecutor on trial and not the defendant. But at other times, it is the prosecution that may encourage a "circus" atmosphere. This may happen when a defendant is subjected to sensational but frivolous charges (for public relations purposes, to affect a future trial, or because the prosecutor is pursuing a personal agenda).

The Mass Media

Persuasion can be found in the print, broadcast, and electronic mass media, where sometimes the line between persuasion and propaganda (ideological or social) may be blurred. Common formats for persuasive messages in the media include editorials, ads, documentaries, news stories, talk-show discussions, and such media-covered public events as political demonstrations, "street theater," and planned political events. Even entertainment programming can sometimes be persuasive. In one recent study, sitcoms were shown to reflect (and for that matter, maybe project) norms for lying in family settings. The most common lie was told to protect someone's feelings. The family member most commonly depicted telling these lies was the husband or father figure.[8] Editorials in newspapers are other good examples of persuasive messages designed to influence public attitudes, beliefs, and behavior. And advertisements often contain mild propaganda (*white propaganda*) rather than persuasion. Numerous Internet sites contain persuasion or propaganda. Movies may also seek to both entertain and influence us.

Strategies and Tactics of Persuasive Messages

Strategies concern those plans made about the necessary broad steps in the path to persuasive success. One consideration here concerns whether a persuader should include just one side or both sides of an issue in a persuasive message. If you are trying to persuade your audience to sign a form that allows their organs to be donated after death, should you mention reasons why signing the form might be a bad idea? We could plot this strategically as (1) give good reasons, (2) give and respond to bad reasons, (3) make final plea. An alternative plot would be to give good reasons and make the final plea. Research has shown that the answer to this strategic question depends on at least two factors.[9] Of course, if the audience will later be exposed to counterpersuasion by someone who disagrees with you, then it may be best to give those downside arguments and answer them now, so that when your audience later hears these arguments from the third party, they will not be surprised and may even recite your rebuttal for you. This is called *inoculation*. If you are selling beachfront property, you may say, "This costs a lot—but these are the going prices." Later, if your customer hears from a friend, "Sounds a little steep to me," your customer may answer, "But that's what the prices are like these days."[10] Educated audiences are a second reason for mentioning both sides of an issue, because such audiences may expect decisions and solutions to problems to have both advantages and disadvantages.

Another strategic decision to make when planning persuasive messages involves the use of *climax* or *anticlimax organization*. Do you put the best elements of your message in the opening or closing sections of the message? If your audience will be opposed to some idea in your message, it may be better for you to place this idea toward the end of your message. This gives you a chance to build your credibility and create audience interest. If you were to place this problem idea at the beginning of the message, you would risk losing your audience before you had the chance to win them over. Unfortunately, the research on this issue is mixed, making generalization difficult, so persuaders must be guided by the details of their particular topic and what they know about their audience. Another strategic decision concerns *ego-involved* people, who may be difficult to persuade because of their strong feelings. Your strategic path here may be to avoid directly challenging their existing viewpoints, and instead to settle for partial success only. The prosecutor in a criminal trial may build a strategy around showing that a defendant had (1) motive, (2) opportunity, and (3) the means to commit the crime. But the defense attorney's strategy may consist entirely of showing that the defendant has an unshakable alibi and could not have committed the crime (or of showing that someone else had an even stronger motive). One other strategy might be to meticulously prove the same point in similar ways, one after the other.

Before moving on to discuss the **tactics** of persuasion, I should note that many issues can be important at both the strategic and tactical levels. The one-sided or two-sided strategic decision regarding inoculation may be reflected—tactically—when making a choice in phrasing a single sentence. In supporting one of my major points in a campaign speech, I could say, "A Gallup poll has Mayor X up by seven points," or I could say, "A Gallup poll has Mayor X up by seven points, although a *Time/Newsweek* poll has the mayor up by only three." When considering possible strategies or tactics, we can make good use of the concepts attributed to Aristotle: pathos, ethos, and logos, and those attributed to Cicero: invention, arrangement, style, memory, and delivery.

Persuasive tactics help us execute the various strategic steps in creating messages. If you were to try to convince a friend to become a vegetarian, you might consider using both logos and invention to create a general strategy built around four themes: (1) the environment (generating food from plants is better for conservation than generating food from livestock), (2) personal health (plants compare favorably with animals in terms of such dietary concerns as vitamins, cholesterol, drugs used for production, pathogenic microorganisms, worms and parasites, and fiber), (3) finances (vegetarians spend less on health care and food), and (4) ethics (animals used for food in large societies are not treated well in life or in death). But as you create your message to persuade your friend to become a vegetarian, what tactical decisions will you have to make?[11]

One set of tactical decisions in your message may concern how long or extensive each of the arguments based on your four themes will be. What types of evidence will you use? Will you use emotional appeals? As we will discover in chapters 5 and 10, evidence can take the tactical form of stories, pictures, statistics, examples, objects, quotations, demonstrations, factual reports, historical reports, social criticism, or even sound recordings. In a court trial, scientific evidence may take the form of fingerprints or the results of DNA tests. And in the sciences and arts, all sorts of sophisticated tests might be used as evidence to prove a theory or contention. The possibilities are almost endless. You could, for example, tactically provide vivid details about the health risks of eating meat. As I read the above list of problems with meat eating, the items about worms, parasites, drugs used for production, and pathogenic microorganisms make me feel squeamish. These arguments illustrate persuasion through the use of logos and also pathos. Another tactical decision concerning pathos might be whether to use pictures that show how livestock is raised, and what happens to cows, chickens, and pigs in slaughterhouses.

In another persuasive case, you might try to find a roommate by placing an ad in a newspaper or on a message board at school. Although you might create several strategic inducements in your ad, as you did for the vegetarian message, here you might also think about what tactical detail you will give about yourself (the sender) and your ideal roommate (the receiver). Your strategic arguments may mention cost, features of the accommodation (size, location), and terms of the rental. But a tactical issue would concern how you state the details of your preferences: if you sound too demanding, you may not get many responses; but if you sound very undemanding, you may get troublesome responses. Yet another tactical issue concerns exactly where you will place your ad. And what should you say, if anything, about your preference with respect to the ideal respondent's sex, age, or lifestyle?

You would have to make similar tactical decisions if you were to try to sell your used car, or if you wanted to get someone to volunteer at your organization, take up a hobby, switch majors, take a part-time job while at school, or decide to apply to graduate school. In any of these situations, you might use the tactic of enhancing your reputation as a persuader. This tactic might increase your effectiveness in the short run by making it more likely that receivers will at least listen to your message. Relying on your physical and personal attractiveness and likableness may also make you more effective. Presidential candidates often travel around the country trying to fit into local settings by eating the local food and maybe wearing a hat that local workers wear. These are all tactics. Let's now closely examine one specific form of persuasion, compliance gaining, and what is sometimes its result, compliance resisting.

Compliance Gaining

I have described persuasion in its broader sense. But there is a smaller body of knowledge concerning what is called **compliance gaining**.[12] This type of commonly used persuasive message concerns mundane, day-to-day, simple requests for favors. Such messages may not inspire much concern from people because they are simple in structure. For example, if you wanted a friend to return a book for you to the library, how would you word your request? Or how would you ask someone to watch your pet for the day, lend you a small amount of cash, have lunch with you, or stop doing something that annoys you?

Perhaps you would take the "honey" approach (flattering the person, making promises, predicting pleasant outcomes). Or maybe you would take the "vinegar" approach (threats, warnings, and temper tantrums). Using altruism, you might ask someone to do "the right thing" and help you. You might ask a family member to forego a weekend party and stay over at grandma's on Saturday night because she is not feeling well. You could also make a direct request, or simply explain why you need the favor. Some people are also good at hinting, which puts the request "between the lines," or they will use strong emotional appeals, which as might be expected, offer no cognitive support for the request.

One interesting analysis of compliance-gaining messages is offered by researcher Robert Cialdini, who has combined evidence from experimental work and the strategies he gathered while working as a salesperson, fund raiser, and advertiser for organizations that commonly use compliance tactics to get us to say yes. He organizes compliance tactics into seven categories based on psychological principles that direct human behavior: authority, consistency, contrast, liking, reciprocation, scarcity, and social proof.[13]

When you're using *authority*, you hope the person will simply do as you ask because of your authority, strength of personality, or superiority. If you are speaking to your employee in an office, you might say, "We'll need some help in getting these boxes opened. Will you start on these?"

With *consistency*, you emphasize how a request fits in with the status quo, and that the person should do such and such because it follows from what we all do in general and what the person has obviously also done. If you're a volunteer, you might say to another volunteer, "I guess we can sort the new recruit files the way we did all last week; maybe you can start with the list we got this morning."

Using *contrast*, you first ask for a greater commitment from the receiver and then settle for something less. Say you ask someone to drive you home (a fairly long distance). The person balks, pointing out how long the round-trip drive would be. Then you might say, "Well, can you at least drive me to the railroad station?" Now the person may say yes, partly out of feeling guilty about saying no to the larger request.

With *liking*, you seek the affection of the receiver, perhaps through gifts and compliments. The receiver is then encouraged to speak or respond positively (e.g., at a Tupperware party, the salesperson is also the hostess, and her friends who attend can be expected to have a good time and then feel obligated to buy Tupperware).

When using *reciprocation*, you encourage the receiver's sense of fair play by making the person feel an obligation to repay a past debt, perhaps by saying, "Look at all the nice things I have done for you."

If you're using *scarcity*, you try to sell something by suggesting that the buyer act before no more of the item is left. Or you might try to get someone to feel that their intended volunteerism must happen today or the opportunity to volunteer will be gone. Or you may ask someone to come to visit you before you go away for the summer.

In *social proof*, we have the lemming concept, which derives from certain rodents that are said to commit mass suicide by jumping off cliffs when their leaders jump. We also tend to do or not do things depending on what other people are doing or not doing. You may get up to open a window in a warm classroom when you are the only one in the room, but will not do so when others are present. Persuaders can even try to encourage compliance by arranging for role models to "start the ball rolling" (such as having a shill make the first purchase during a sales pitch to a group).

Still one other approach to categorizing compliance-gaining tactics is offered by researchers Kathy Kellermann and Tim Cole.[14] Here compliance gaining is analyzed using many of the items already discussed and some additional ones. The set includes (1) altercasting ("For you not to comply here would be bad"); (2) positive altercasting ("For you to comply here would be good"); (3) altruism ("Do this because it is the right thing to do"); (4) audience use ("Others will see that you do this or do not do this"); (5) negative self-feeling ("If you do not do this, your self-esteem will go down"); (6) self-esteem ("If you do this, your self-esteem will go up"); (7) suggestion, which uses a subtle approach to gently seek compliance through hinting or making an indirect request; (8) surveillance ("I'll see if you do this or do not do this"); (9) third party, which uses someone else to make the request, adding possible credibility and pressure; (10) status quo ("You should do this because that's the way things are"); (11) value appeal ("Do this because it follows from what you, I, and the rest of us think is right"); and (12) table-turning ("Prove to me why you shouldn't do this").

The above lists of compliance-gaining tactics have similarities and differences. But they all emphasize the pragmatic nature of this sort of persuasive message. Table 3.1 offers a composite of many of these compliance-gaining tactics. The specific tactical items are sorted into six strategic categories: trickery, power, soft sell, neutrality, pressure, and argument. Some of the specific items in rival lists overlap or are repeated. But as a pundit once said, "It's amazing what can be accomplished if you don't worry about who gets the credit." And we can

TABLE 3.1
Composite Categories of Compliance-Gaining Tactics

Trickery	**Turn the tables** (Prove to me why you shouldn't do this.)
	Hint (ask in a subtle way)
	Contrast (ask for more, settle for less)
	Suggest (take indirect approach)
	Altercasting (For you not to comply here would be bad.)
	Positive Altercasting (For you to comply here would be good.)
Power	**Use authority** (Do this because I say so.)
	Threaten (If you don't do this, I will . . .)
	Warn (If you don't do this, others will . . .)
	Apply aversive stimuli (There'll be hell to pay if you don't do this.)
Soft Sell	**Promote atmosphere** (Everyone's having a great time.)
	Make a promise (If you do this, then I will . . .)
	Use allurement (If you do this, then others will . . .)
	Play on self-esteem (You'll feel good.)
	Use ingratiation (You'll do this because you're smarter than most people.)
Neutrality	**Make a direct request** (Would you please do this?)
	Appeal to altruism (Do this because it's the right thing.)
Pressure	**Use audience** (Others will see that you do or do not do this.)
	Use guilt (How can you leave me in the lurch?)
	Use debt (After all the things I did for you . . .)
	Act hurt (Don't worry; I'll get by.)
	Threaten with surveillance (I'll see if you do this or do not do this.)
	Have third party ask (How can you say no to X?)
Argument	**Imply urgency, scarcity** (Do it while there's still time.)
	Suggest unique ability (Only you can do this.)
	Encourage consistency (You have done it before.)
	Produce social proof (Everyone's doing it now.)
	Note benefits (You will get this if you do it.)

leave verifying just how effective these items are to future field or laboratory researchers. It is important to remember that the fact that someone makes a compliance-gaining request does not mean that the request will be honored. People sometimes say no.

Compliance Resisting

The number of compliance-gaining messages we receive on any given day is probably extensive, whether we're working; conducting our social lives; meeting in public associations; shopping; being solicited to buy things by mail, phone, or e-mail; or dealing with requests from children. Sometimes compliance gaining occurs between peers (e.g., spouses, coworkers) and sometimes between nonpeers (parent and child, teacher and student, boss and employee). Nonpeer compliance gaining can occur, say, when a child asks his or her parent for a special favor, or a parent asks his or her child to do something not normally required.

A number of researchers have identified sets of tactics that are **compliance resisting**.[15] These can include such obvious things as direct refusal, offering an alternative, giving an excuse for not complying, or explaining noncompliance. But researchers Nancy Burroughs, Patricia Kearney, and Timothy Plax identify as many as nineteen compliance-resisting tactics used by students. These include "blaming the teacher for being boring or ill-prepared," "seeking revenge," "rallying other students to disobey," "being openly hostile," and "being disruptive." Many of these tactics involve *behavioral-avoidance*, such as pretending not to remember a request.[16] And in an interesting study of how people resist sales personnel in stores, researchers Amna Kirmani and Margaret Campbell report that *seekers* (customers who want help from sales personnel) and *sentries* (customers who want to buy with a minimum of help) each use different tactics when targeted by a sales worker.[17] Seekers use such control tactics as getting the clerk to work to find the desired purchase or giving verbal praise. Sentries on the other hand sometimes bring a friend to help control the situation, withdraw from conversation, act rude, resist help by going up the chain of command, or conceal their true intention to buy. A nicely balanced set of compliance-resisting categories has been used in a number of studies:

1. Negative identity management: Receiver attempts to make the persuader feel wrong or inappropriate in asking for compliance.
2. Non-negotiation: Receiver says no under all circumstances.
3. Negotiation: Receiver bargains or offers a substitute action or counterproposal.
4. Justification: Receiver explains why the request will not be honored.
5. Positive identity management: Receiver tries to reduce the compliance gainer's motivation.[18]

Making Sense of Compliance-Resisting Tactics

Let's organize the most common compliance-resisting tactics reported in the research summarized above in a new way, as shown in tables 3.2 and 3.3. Table 3.2 shows discursive tactics. These types of compliance resisting typically include conversational statements that address the request in a topic-appropriate manner. Table 3.3 shows the behavioral-avoidance tactics that simply try to circumvent or obstruct the request.

TABLE 3.2
Six Categories of Discursive Compliance–Resisting Tactics

Compliance Acceptance	*Justification*
full yes	explained no
reluctant yes	disqualification
partial yes	excuse
	objection
Positive Identity Management	*Non-negotiation*
begging for a pass	simple no
yes but no	nonverbal no
praise/build-up	assertive no
Negotiation	*Negative Identity Management*
conditional yes	rejection (censure)
redirected yes	blame
compromise	comparison

TABLE 3.3
Behavioral-Avoidance Categories of Compliance-Resisting Tactics

Avoidance	*Disconfirmation*
dodging	ignoring
yes then no	inappropriateness
diversion	turning the tables
Inducement Avoidance	*Aggression (Super-Assertion)*
favors	anger
scarcity	challenge
authority	power play
consistency	sabotage
contrast	ridicule

Discursive Tactics When we use discursive tactics for compliance resisting, we refuse by referring to something presently unacceptable about the request. These refusals often are couched in terms of (1) the setting in which the request is made, (2) some personal aspect of the asker or the complier, (3) the nature of the methods used in asking or the nature of the methods that will have to be used for complying, (4) the manner in which the request is made or the nature of the act requested, or (5) the purpose of the asker making the request, or those purposes involved or suggested for the complier in carrying out the requested act. The possibilities for wording these refusals are endless, although some of the above ideas will show up in the paragraphs that follow. We can, nonetheless, be much more specific about the general forms discursive refusals take. The first example below illustrates failed compliance resistance (see table 3.2).

Compliance acceptance means giving in to the asker's request. Sometimes we give a *full yes* (agreeing to everything the asker asks for), a *reluctant yes* (complying in a begrudging way), or a *partial yes* (perhaps agreeing to volunteer on Fridays only, not the entire week as requested).

Positive identity management takes place when we try to finesse the asker out of the request. Successful *begging for a pass* may get the asker to forget the request out of sympathy. *Yes but no* softens the rejection by accepting the request in principle but not this time ("I'd love to come over tonight, but . . ."). *Praise* seeks a free pass, as can mentioning the asker's existing assets in order to *build up* the asker so there will be no need to help ("I'm really impressed with how you seem able to do this stuff so easily by yourself lately").

Negotiation allows us to seek favorable changes in the request. With a *conditional yes* we request an added benefit: "I'll come over tonight if you clean up your apartment," "I'll try it if you're certain it'll work," "Include wine, and dinner's a yes," "Show me how the money is used before I contribute," or "Alter the deal to include . . ." The conditional yes may set conditions that can be met ("Add a 'sweetener,' and I'll say yes"), or conditions that are too steep to be met in the hope that the compliance gainer will not accede to the new conditions.

When using the *redirected yes*, we agree to a substitute action ("I can't lend you money, but I'll cosign a bank loan"). For dinner, we might seek a change of situation ("If we skip Burger Heaven and make it the Perdition Bar and Grill"), a change of the participants ("If we take Mom and Dad along"), a change in some detail ("If we walk instead of drive"), or a change in purpose ("If it's not a calorie binge but a light meal at Weight-Watchers Café"). It is also possible to redirect the request by asking the compliance gainer to think of a substitute. Or we may seek a *compromise*. For example, if the asker seeks donations in the form of old clothing, we may offer to sell our old clothing at less than its fair-market value.

Justification types of resistance take a "No, because . . ." pattern. The *explained no* states a simple reason for noncompliance, as in "I can't contribute in these trying financial times." Using *disqualification*, the resister may self-disqualify with an answer like "That's not my job, please talk to . . ." or other-disqualify with something like "No thanks, we want a gardener who knows a little more about the many varieties of orchids." An *excuse* allows the compliance resister to try to weasel out of a request in a sometimes transparent way that may be irritating to the compliance gainer, perhaps by saying, "Saturday is lawn-mowing day at our house, so I guess I can't go to the game with you." Finally, *objection* often employs one aspect of the request that seems to be very important to the resister: "No, I've already been on the rollercoaster twice" or "I don't want to go to bed; I'm not sleepy."

As a type of *non-negotiation tactic*, the *simple no* or *nonverbal no* need not be explained to the compliance gainer, or asker ("I have nothing more to say"). The main advantage of the simple no is that the compliance gainer is deprived of any "comeback" to the objection. Also included here is the *assertive no*, which is good for especially aggressive compliance gainers ("Forget it, not in a million years, not until pigs fly, not a chance, go away").

Negative identity management often tries to disarm the asker with strong criticism of some aspect of the request, as through *rejection* (or censure) of the compliance gainer with something like "I think going to a cock-fight is a despicable idea," "You know fireworks maim thousands," or "I don't mind smelling model airplane glue if we're building models, but to just get high is stupid." Sometimes we will *blame* the asker for our noncompliance by saying, "If you weren't so pig-headed I might try to help you out once in awhile" or "How can I do what you ask when you don't seem to know exactly what you want?" Negative identity management can also be accomplished by using *comparison*: "You're biased. You gave X an easy job, and now you ask me to . . ."

Behavioral-Avoidance Tactics Unlike discursive tactics, in which the compliance resister is at least willing to discuss the request in an appropriate manner, behavioral-avoidance tactics seek to circumvent the request by keeping the asker, or compliance gainer, from successfully communicating the request. This is done by seeming to discuss the request but in an insincere manner, by sabotaging the compliance gainer's confidence or legitimacy in asking, or by damaging the compliance gainer's likelihood of succeeding with other potential compliance resisters.

Avoidance offers the compliance resister clever tactics that do not always require actually saying no. One example is *dodging* local blood-bank workers seeking donors at a block party by keeping away from them or not staying nearby long enough to hear their requests. You could also dodge a request by procrastinating when asked. With *yes then no*, you initially agree to the request but later find a way to avoid fulfilling it, perhaps by claiming to be sick, by leaving town, or by claiming a forgotten appointment. A yes then no tactic might also be used to avoid correctly fulfilling the purpose of a request (e.g., you agree to supply valuable business information to a community group, then wait so long to send it that the information is useless). *Diversion* allows the compliance resister to focus the compliance gainer's attention on other situations, people, or motivations and to distract them from the original request ("Look at the cute doggie," a father might say when his child asks for a candy bar).

With *inducement-avoidance* tactics, we anticipate the five compliance-gaining tactics identified by Cialdini in which compliance gainers do favors for us, try to make us like them, point out our past behavior, speak with authority, or use implied scarcity by pointing out that our compliance is time- or opportunity-limited. By using inducement avoidance, we prepare ourselves for anticipated compliance-gaining tactics such as these. That is, inducement-avoidance thinking concerns a decision about intended avoidance, although the eventual tactic could be a behavioral-avoidance or discursive type.

Next come *disconfirmation* responses, which by implication deny the asker validity as a social actor or person. Here we might try not to comply by *ignoring* what is going on in some situation: its fundamental nature, the compliance gainers, the acts taking place within it, and so on. A good example of disconfirmation is when a small child says to its parent, "There's a lost cat out on the sidewalk that wants to come into the house," and the parent then says, "Wash your hands, it's almost time for dinner," thus disconfirming the child's status as a speaker requesting the parent to respond to the cat report. Or in some cities, men with squeegees may insist on washing the windshields of motorists stopped in traffic. A motorist may try, with varying degrees of success, to ignore these squeegee compliance gainers, or what they are doing, or what the implied offer is about. The tactic of *inappropriateness* is being employed when a panhandler asks a passerby for some spare change and the person says, "No thank you." The inappropriateness of the answer may catch the asker by surprise, giving the compliance resister time to easily move several paces out of earshot before a second request can occur.

In the tactic known as *turning the tables*, the compliance resister becomes the compliance gainer, and the compliance gainer becomes the compliance resister. If several neighbors ask you to contribute money for a block-beautification campaign, you might resist by asking them to fix up their own houses and saying that their houses are the principle eyesores on the block. The purpose and situation of the request have remained the same, but the neighbors have become the resisters now.

Finally come the responses that are considered *aggression* (or *super-assertion*) tactics, which entail acting out at the situation, the asker, or others. Resisters may engage in a variety of aggressive ploys, including (1) expressing *anger* (in words or deeds) toward the asker or the situation or the compliance-gaining message; (2) offering a *challenge*, such as when you call the police to complain about people canvassing the houses on your street, or when an employee sues an employer for harassment over work assignments; (3) orchestrating a *power play* (e.g., a student who tries to take control of a class by claiming the teacher is incompetent and has no right to make curriculum-oriented requests); (4) committing *sabotage* (perhaps by destroying a compliance gainer's printed requests after they've been placed in people's mailboxes, or by telling a lie about the compliance gainer that will turn off other people); and (5) indulging in heavy-handed *ridicule* ("As if we would really help such an idiot").

Balancing Compliance Resisting with Reasonable Cooperation

There is a difference between on the one hand protecting yourself from unwanted persuasion from askers and on the other living up to your responsibilities. For example, it seems reasonable to become skillful at turning down offers made by strangers in unsolicited phone calls. However, if your spouse wants to know where you have been for the past week, in most cases you owe some sort of explanation. The idea is to maintain your right not to be manipulated or pestered by other people while not tuning out all comers with a general attitude of "If I did not start this conversation with you, get lost." Discretion, common sense, and a positive attitude are the key words here.

Chapter in Retrospect

VIGNETTE 1 **Saying No at a Lawn Party**

At a gathering of suburban neighbors on someone's lawn, one neighbor in an attempt at compliance gaining may ask another for a lift to buy several six-packs of beer. We might analyze this compliance gaining as an example of social pressure, perhaps in the use of an audience, guilt, or debt, as defined in table 3.1. The resister then could say, "My car's not working." Here the compliance-gaining analysis could be:

1. Gathering of neighbors as the setting for the compliance gainer's request for a lift
2. Relying on the mutual obligations of neighbors as a means of social pressure
3. Getting beer as the purpose

In contrast, the compliance-resisting analysis could be:

1. Driving the neighbor to the store as the requested act
2. The car as the means
3. Performing neighborly assistance as the purpose

By saying, "My car's not working," the compliance resister objects with the use of justification, and more explicitly, the resister is using an excuse (see table 3.2).

But if the resistance comment is "I don't think this group should drink beer tonight," the resister's objection exploits a different means of negation by rejecting an aspect of the role of the asker who seeks to buy beer for the neighbors. This compliance resisting can be categorized as a negative identity–management tactic: rejection (censure). Similarly, if the response is "Ask someone else, I'm angry with you," the right of the compliance gainer to ask for a favor at this time is called into question, which is the negative identity–management tactic of blame. And last, if the response is "I'd be happy to, but I've just got to tell everyone what happened at work," the resister has chosen to engage in a more desired act that precludes doing the requested act—an example of a yes-but-no positive identity–management tactic (see table 3.2).

VIGNETTE 2 **Saying No at an Engagement Party**

In a brief conversation, the daughter of a wealthy family says to her fiancé, "Do whatever it takes, but get my sister to come downstairs to my engagement celebration." The fiancé answers, "I'll ask; but I'll do only what a gentleman can do under the circumstances." He has used the redirected-yes version of negotiation for compliance resisting (see table 3.2). The physical and social setting is a family party, an engagement announcement, and it includes all of the social motivations that such an occasion brings to the minds of the people involved. The daughter requests help on the basis of the obligations of a fiancé, her purpose being getting her sister to attend. But the fiancé's counteroffer seems to refer to an abstract setting we could call "polite society," where ladies and gentlemen flourish. The fiancé accepts the request to get the sister to attend, but only if he can do so without offending her. Although the asker, the fiancée, does not specify what inducements the fiancé is to use, the implication is that perhaps anything short of using a gun is okay. Thus, with the words "only what a gentleman can do," the fiancé has rejected using the asker's implied or recommended inducements and counteroffers with an allusion to the inducements he feels comfortable using.

Summary and Conclusions

This chapter examines the techniques typically used by persuaders to construct persuasive messages. Aristotle contributed to the study of persuasive messages by defining how persuaders often use logos (logic, factual evidence), pathos (appeals to the emotions), and ethos (attempts to seem credible to a given audience) to make a case. Cicero contributed the canons of persuasion, which say that persuaders should perfect the use of invention or discovery of convincing ideas, arrangement or the order of ideas in a message, style of language choices and sentence construction, memory of important information about the persuasive topic, and delivery skills such as voice and nonverbal communication. In more modern times, the Yale approach (attention, comprehension, acceptance, retention, action) and the motivated sequence approach (attention, need, satisfaction, visualization, action) have both added to our insight into the broad steps that persuaders, or compliance gainers, seem to go through to succeed with receivers, or compliance resisters.

Modern forums for persuasion include public speeches with their stated purpose and supporting materials (which are sometimes evaluated for effectiveness with the help of theories of rhetorical criticism); debates, in which two sides, one affirmative and one negative, make cases for or against something and then rebut what the other side says; court trials, which in a sense are specialized types of debates with unique rules because of the important consequences for the parties involved; and the mass media, including advertisements, editorials, documentaries, news stories, and even media entertainment, where particular social values can be reinforced or not.

Techniques of persuasion can be sorted into strategies and tactics. A persuasion strategy concerns the calculated experiential paths that receivers of messages go through over time on their way to the persuasive effect desired by the senders. Strategic decisions by persuaders can involve such issues as whether or not to address both sides of a topic, whether to put the most convincing materials first or last in a message, and how much persuasion to attempt with a given audience. Tactical decisions made by persuaders assist the various strategic steps in the overall plan, and concern such things as the amount and type of evidence to include in the message, whether to include emotional appeals, and, if such appeals are included, whether to use stronger or weaker emotional appeals of various types (e.g., anger, fear, joy).

Compliance gaining concerns the day-to-day conversational techniques we use to get others to provide favors, follow instructions, stop doing something that is irritating, buy something, and so on. A number of compliance-gaining tactics have been identified in the literature (e.g., using trickery, power, the soft sell, neutrality, pressure, and argument). Compliance resisting concerns the art of saying no to compliance-gaining requests. A number of compliance-resisting tactics have also been identified in the literature (e.g., justification, negotiation, and non-negotiation).

KEY TERMS

canons
compliance gaining
compliance resisting
emotional appeal
enthymeme
ethos

logos
message-oriented
   approach
motivated sequence
   approach
pathos

receiver-oriented
   approach
strategies
syllogism
tactics
Yale approach

REVIEW QUESTIONS

1. How do ethos, pathos, and logos differ in helping people persuade each other?
2. What are the canons of persuasion?
3. How could the motivated sequence approach be used by an encyclopedia sales representative?
4. What is one similarity and one difference between a debate and a court trial?
5. Give an example that explains the difference between a persuasion strategy and persuasion tactic.
6. What do the terms *compliance gaining* and *compliance resisting* mean?

SUGGESTED PROJECTS AND ACTIVITIES

1. Write a brief essay to defend one of the following assertions:

   Full employment is not necessarily a good idea in a free-market society.
   The rich should pay much higher/lower taxes than they do now.
   One should not start college until age twenty-five.
   One should not get married until age thirty.
   I urge you to become a vegetarian.
   Take up a musical instrument!
   Even if you've never painted before, start painting landscapes.
   Lend me $10,000 to start up a new small-business, where I will _____.
   Join the Democratic Party!
   Join the Republican Party!
   Do not vote unless you are prepared to vote intelligently.

2. Write a short list of suggestions to an imaginary persuader on how you can be best persuaded about one of the above assertions.
3. Select a newspaper editorial that you disagree with and write a response that is no longer than the editorial.
4. Write an e-mail to an advertiser in which you critique what was said or implied in the advertiser's ad.
5. Write a song or a poem that is persuasive, then analyze it for ethos, pathos, and logos.
6. Think of someone with sour interpersonal attitudes and imagine how you would convince the person that "You can catch more flies with honey than with vinegar."
7. If you are really brave, on a given day, test out in numerous and varied ways the truism "Ask and you shall receive." But be careful of what you ask for; you might get it.
8. Think up clever ways to respond to telemarketers who make unsolicited calls to your house. Perhaps you can start your list with the line "If you'd like to talk to me send $25 to my house and call back next week when I'll give you five minutes of my time" or "The person you want has moved to Finland; would you like the number?" Then when you get a call, try out one of the items on your list. But do not be rude, nasty, or verbally aggressive.

QUESTIONS FOR DISCUSSION

1. The notion that persuasion requires a state of identification between sender and receiver can be applied to one of the persuasion models explained in this chapter (attention, comprehension, acceptance, retention, action). How?

2. Can you imagine circumstances in which a disliked or disrespected sender may nonetheless be persuasive about certain things?

3. When conceptualizing persuasion, does it seem more useful to think of receivers as nouns or verbs? Objects or processes? As anchored in space or moving through time? Why?

4. Have you ever been persuaded by a work of art? If so, which one? And in what way?

5. What recent television commercial strikes you as particularly persuasive? Why?

Notes

1. James Murphy and Richard Katula, with Forbes Hill and Donovan Ochs, *Synoptic History of Classical Rhetoric* (Mahwah, NJ: Hermagoras, 2003), 131–33.

2. This five-step model was used for the "single-shot" analysis of attitude change developed by Carl Hovland, Irving Janis, and Harold Kelly, *Communication and Persuasion* (New Haven, CT: Yale University Press, 1953).

3. Kathleen German, Bruce Gronbeck, Douglas Ehninger, and Alan Monroe, *Principles of Public Speaking* (Boston: Pearson, 2004), 254–58.

4. Kevin DeLuca, *Image Politics* (New York: Guilford Press, 1999), 1–24.

5. www.ncapublicaddress.org/journals.htm offers a partial list of speech journals.

6. Standards for evidence vary depending on the type of event, whether it's a preliminary hearing, a criminal trial, a civil trial, and so on. In a civil trial, the standard for evidence is a "preponderance of the evidence." Standards can also vary in terms of how many jurors have to agree on the verdict.

7. Cf. Bill Lennon, "Circus Trials Can Teach Us How the Law Really Works," *Advance Titan*, student newspaper of the University of Wisconsin, Oshkosh, 16 February 2005. O. J. Simpson, Scott Peterson, Kobe Bryant, and Martha Stewart have all had well-publicized celebrity trials.

8. Michelle Mazur and Pamela Kalbfleish, "Lying and Deception Detection in Television Families," *Communication Research Reports* 20, no. 3 (2003): 200–207.

9. Actually, this is a complicated question that I will review in chapter 10 on research about message variables. For example, if your audience knows about both sides of a controversy, they may expect you to deal with both the "upside issues" and the "downside issues."

10. Apparently, the inoculation strategy was in play in the 2000 presidential debates because both Vice President Al Gore and Governor George Bush made sure that supporters and undecided voters were informed in advance of what the opposition would say about important issues and of what each candidate's response would be.

11. Cf. "49 Reasons Why I Am a Vegetarian," www.britishmeat.com/49.htm (18 June 2006).

12. Cf. Michael Cody, Mary Lou Woelfel, and William Jordan, "Dimensions of Compliance-Gaining Situations," *Human Communication Research* 9 (1983): 99–113; Lawrence Wheeless, Robert Barraclough, and Robert Stewart, "Compliance-Gaining and Power in Persuasion," *Communication Yearbook* 7 (1983): 105–45.

13. Robert Cialdini, *Influence: Science and Practice* (Boston: Allyn and Bacon, 2001), 17–272.

14. Kathy Kellermann and Tim Cole, "Classifying Compliance-Gaining Messages: Taxonomic Disorder and Strategic Confusion," *Communication Theory* 4 (1994): 3–60.

15. Examples of compliance-resisting tactics can be found in the following reports: Sandra Metts, William Cupach, and T. Imahori, "Perceptions of Sexual Compliance-Resisting Messages in Three Types of Cross-Sex Relationships," *Western Journal of Communication* 56 (1992): 1–17; Kevin Wright and Dan O'Hair, "Seeking and Resisting Compliance: Selection and Evaluation of Tactics in a Simulated College Student Drinking Context," *Communication Research Reports* 16 (1999): 266–77; Kathleen Reardon, Steve Sussman, and Brian Flay, "Are We Marketing the Right Message: Can Kids 'Just Say No' to Smoking?" *Communication Monographs* 56 (1989): 307–24; Jess Alberts, Michelle Miller-Rassulo, and Michael Hecht, "A Typology of Drug Resistance Strategies," *Journal of Applied Communication Research* 19 (1991): 129, 152.

16. Nancy Burroughs, Patricia Kearney, and Timothy Plax, "Compliance-Resistance in the College Classroom," *Communication Education* 38 (1989): 214–29.

17. Amna Kirmani and Margaret Campbell, "Goal Seeker and Persuasion Sentry: How Consumer Targets Respond to Interpersonal Marketing Persuasion," *Journal of Consumer Research* 31 (2004): 573–82.

18. Cf. Craig Hullett and Ron Tamborini, "When I'm within My Rights: An Expectancy Based Model of Actor Evaluative and Behavioral Responses to Compliance-Resistance Strategies," *Communication Studies* 52 (2001): 1–16; Christy Lee, R. Timothy Levine, and Ronald Cambra, "Resisting Compliance in the Multicultural Classroom," *Communication Education* 46 (1997): 29–44; Mary O'Hair, Michael Cody, and Dan O'Hair, "The Impact of Situational Dimensions on Compliance-Resisting Strategies: A Comparison of Methods," *Communication Quarterly* 39 (1991): 226–40; Margaret McLaughlin, Michael Cody, and Carl Robey, "Situational Influences on the Selection of Strategies to Resist Compliance-Gaining Attempts," *Human Communication Research* 7 (1980): 14–36.

Propaganda

The real persuaders are our appetites, our fears and above all our vanity. The skillful propagandist stirs and coaches these internal persuaders.

—ERIC HOFFER

The elegance of honesty needs no adornment.

—MERRY BROWN

If you tell a lie big enough and keep repeating it, people will eventually come to believe it.

—JOSEPH GOEBBELS

Ideas are more powerful than guns. We would not let our enemies have guns, why should we let them have ideas?

—JOSEPH STALIN

PROPAGANDA VERY likely got its start in prehistoric times as part of psychological warfare used for exaggerating tribal power in hopes of encouraging a tribe's warriors and discouraging the tribe's enemy warriors. Tribal chiefs may also have used crude propaganda to justify their privileged positions. The simplest forms of propaganda probably included drumbeats, drawings on walls, charms and totems, appeals to oracles, interpretation of omens, and war chants. The ancient region of Mesopotamia shows evidence of elongated stone monuments called *stelae* that were used to glorify kings and depict enemies being vanquished militarily, with the dying soldiers then being eaten by the king's private pride of lions. In ancient Greece, statues, public architecture, martial poetry, disinformation, and speeches were added to the options available for propaganda. Alexander the Great encouraged a cult dedicated to him, with great spectacles such as mass marriages between his soldiers and captured concubines; he also used artists to make portraits and statues to perfect his image as a god on earth. The Romans added triumphal processions after military victories as staged propaganda spectacles.[1]

In more modern times, perhaps the most significant propaganda campaign in American history was convincing the people of the thirteen original British colonies to commit mass treason. Political voices yelled, "Taxation without representation!" newspapers reported angrily on the Boston Massacre (five dead in a riot), Bostonians held a "tea party" to demonstrate against taxes designed to pay for national security provided by the British, and Minute Men rode everywhere to explain grievances. What started out as a political spat ended up as sedition. The cynical today can argue that the revolution was not about grievances but about political opportunism (i.e., a revolution would be successful because of the lack of consensus in England about the colonies and the great distance between England and the colonies; there would be economic and political advantages for the colonists if it worked; ergo, do it).[2] But others can say that, in the end, the right thing was done even if for the wrong reasons. Whose interests were best served at the time? We could debate this forever.

Although the word *propaganda* is used often in regard to political or historical events such as the ones above, it is a word that needs to be clearly defined if we are to use it consistently and intelligently. Unfortunately, defining propaganda will be a challenge. What is clear, however, is that the word *propaganda* derives from the Latin word *propagare*, meaning "to spread plants to new locations." In the 1600s a papal council formed the Sacra Congregatio de Propaganda Fide to spread Christianity around the known world. During the First and Second World Wars, propaganda acquired negative tones associated with the aggressive communication employed to help defeat an enemy. Total war meant doing everything and anything to prevail.

One way to begin clarifying the nature of propaganda is by listing some obvious forms or characteristics of it, including censorship, doctoring of information, and suggestion. By using **censorship**, politically sensitive information about public and private events can be selectively controlled, with information favorable to the sender's objectives being passed on to relevant audiences and unfavorable information withheld. The power of censorship is not about misinformation, but rather concerns the overall picture presented when some true things are passed on but others are not. There is today a cottage industry of conspiracy theorists who promote stories of government censorship and conspiracies about such events as the Kennedy assassination, alien UFOs in Roswell, New Mexico, and Elvis sightings.

Sometimes propaganda is created by **doctoring of information**. Persuasion scholar J. A. C. Brown relates the interesting story of how the Franco-Prussian War of 1870 was instigated by a newspaper-published telegram that had been doctored by Bismarck to instigate war.[3] The telegram's contents outlined the details of a disagreement between Kaiser Wilhelm and the French ambassador concerning succession to the Spanish throne. Bismarck subtly altered the telegram to give the impression that each side had insulted the other. With publication of the doctored telegram, the populations in both countries clamored for war, and 140,000 lives were subsequently lost. By today's standards, the doctored telegram was more subtle than outrageous; but to the diplomats and educated classes of the times it was, according to Brown, "a truculent challenge and a consequent snub." It was also a form of propaganda.

One other form of propaganda noted by Brown is the propaganda that seeks to circumvent the reasoning process, replacing it with some form of **suggestion** through words, visual imagery, or actions. Suggestion is a slippery technique that can create impressions or implied claims without the propagandist having to prove anything, as in "The people behind these attacks on me have political agendas." The suggestion leaves open the question as to whether "attacks" is the fairest word to use and what the actions described as "political agendas" actually involve. A more impartial person might in this case rephrase this statement as "The people who have criticized my actions have expressed their point of view."

Perhaps the first researcher to characterize propaganda in terms of suggestion was Leonard Doob, who emphasized that suggestion was not merely a common technique of propaganda, but the very essence of propaganda.[4] According to Doob, if suggestion is present in the message, we have propaganda—if it is not, we do not. Nonverbal cues, tricky wordings, and subtle innuendoes are all examples of how suggestion can work in a propaganda message. This is an elegant definition, but it may not account for some forms of propaganda, such as explicitly telling malicious lies about someone or using explicit but fabricated evidence.

More recently, Charles Larson has suggested that for a given message to be considered propaganda, it should (1) be *ideological* in nature, (2) use *mass media*, (3) *conceal* things from receivers, (4) seek *uniformity* among receivers about the topic, and (5) try to *circumvent* the reasoning process.[5] Items 3, 4, and 5 seem quite useful. But regarding item 1, we could argue that not all propaganda is ideological. For example, workers in a factory may seek a pay raise by airing messages that make the factory management feel guilty about paying lower wages. If the workers do not mention terms like *class struggle* or *worker exploitation* in their messages, have they not engaged in nonideological propaganda? A promotional ad for a soda is also nonideological. As for use of mass media being required in propaganda, an organized group of proselytizers could spread across the world preaching a common religion to potential converts—face-to-face. And the propaganda of the ancient world had to succeed without mass media. So perhaps item 2 should refer to organized communication, and not mass media.

Dictionaries typically give such definitions of propaganda as "the spreading of ideas, information, and rumor to help or injure an institution, cause, or person." Unfortunately, these sorts of very general definitions lack precision, especially when using such vague words as "spreading," "help," and "injure." For a better start in defining propaganda, we will first describe its possible *intensities*. Three degrees of intensity have been consistently recognized in the academic literature on the topic: **white propaganda**, **gray propaganda**, and **black**

propaganda. Early theorists used the terms *white* and *black* to indicate whether the source of the propaganda could be identified or not, since it was assumed that anonymous propaganda would take the greatest liberties with the truth.[6] However, here we will not be very concerned with the issue of anonymous or attributed messages and will use the term *black* for the most extreme form of propaganda where the propagandist pulls out all the stops to most seriously harm the other side. White propaganda will then here refer to messages that are self-serving and mild, with gray propaganda being more competitive in style but falling short of the aggressiveness of black propaganda. Other options for naming the three types might be *mild propaganda*, *moderate propaganda*, and *malignant propaganda*.

Describing the intensity of propaganda is helpful, but we still need a clear statement of what propaganda is. Propaganda scholars Garth Jowett and Victoria O'Donnell offer a good deal of help here; they define propaganda as a "deliberate, systematic attempt to *shape perceptions*, *manipulate cognitions*, and *direct behavior* to achieve a response that furthers the desired intent of the propagandist [italics mine]."[7] Now persuaders might also try to do these things by openly admitting their objectives and then providing evidence and reasoning to influence the audience. But when propagandists attempt the above three things, they often have an ends-justify-the-means mentality that treats receivers as things to be moved or as adversaries to be defeated.

Of particular interest here is the difference between how Jowett and O'Donnell describe the objectives of persuasion and propaganda. They say persuasion is intended to fulfill the needs of both the sender and receiver. For example, if I try to persuade you to save 20 percent of your weekly salary, presumably we would both benefit (you would accumulate money, and I would feel good about someone taking my wise advice). Or, you might persuade me to go into business with you; we would then both benefit if our joint business succeeded; and if it failed, we both would lose our investments—together.

On the other hand, the function of propaganda is to promote the objectives of the sender, but not necessarily the objectives of the receiver. A few years ago, some residents in my neighborhood banded together to try to stop the proposed construction of a ten-story apartment building on a street with just private homes, although there were apartment houses on adjacent streets. They collected signatures, put up posters, got a local newspaper to print sympathetic stories, hired legal counsel, and asked the county executive for help. They succeeded in portraying the developer as a greedy person unconcerned with increased congestion and the quality of life on their street. And they did finally succeed in blocking the construction. Although I felt proud of their success at the time, I have sometimes wondered if all those involved benefited. The apartment building would have provided homes for families in a neighborhood where it is difficult to find housing, and the construction project would have provided jobs. These particular home owners clearly benefited, but did all the passersby who signed the petitions benefit? Some in need of a better or newer apartment may not have. So here too, propaganda was intended for the best interests of the senders, but may not have been good for all the receivers. In addition, all members of society pay a price for increased propaganda use in the form of irritation from propaganda messages and the risk of becoming misinformed on the issues of the day.

Let's accept Jowett and O'Donnell's definition that propaganda messages "attempt to shape perceptions, manipulate cognitions, and direct behavior." I will then add to this definition by saying,

Propaganda is communication designed to influence receivers in a manner that compared with persuasion is more assertive and aggressive, more committed to gamesmanship, and less committed to rationality, proportionality, persuasive leadership, and ethics.

When I say that propaganda is "more assertive and aggressive," I mean that propaganda helps to organize receivers into groups of human assets or agencies that serve a mission. In comparison, persuasion at its best seeks to convince individuals. By saying that propaganda is "more committed to gamesmanship," I mean that propaganda sometimes seeks to gain advantage for senders or their clients at the expense of others. Being "less committed to **rationality**" means that ideas in propaganda do not always correspond objectively to receivers' best understanding of what is true about the physical and social worlds in which they live. Being "less committed to . . . **proportionality**" means that the ideas expressed in propaganda messages sometimes are more intense than seems justified (e.g., praising or blaming in the extreme, describing things in exaggerated or minimized ways, or proposing outrageous actions or policies). Being "less committed to . . . persuasive leadership" means that when using propaganda, the sender fails to guide receivers through a set of ideas and their unifying themes in helpful ways so that the receivers as individuals can make fair and reasonable judgments about the issues involved. Finally, by saying that propaganda is "less committed to . . . ethics," I mean that propaganda senders are not always honest and fair regarding receivers or regarding third parties described in their messages.

One last thought in defining propaganda is that communication may at times be what we have just called propaganda and sometimes merely propagandistic, because it possesses only some of the defining features of propaganda (e.g., a manipulative statement in a social conversation or letter).

To be fair propaganda appraisers, we should also note that there are times when those who opt to create propaganda will rightfully argue that their interests (or the interests of third parties) were in jeopardy and that they could not have afforded the idealism required by a commitment to persuasion, but rather needed to rely on the pragmatism of propaganda. But this last consideration should come down to what reasonable people will accept, after enough time has gone by to make sober assessments, about how right or wrong it was to use propaganda in that particular situation. Was the propaganda justified? Or was it merely an example of people motivated by economic, social, or political ambition or convenience?

Models of Propaganda

Let's try to understand propaganda with the use of two communication models that will help us visualize the propaganda process. Models such as these help us examine important factors simultaneously, rather than one at a time, as is the case with definitions or extended discussion. The first of these, the Rank model of influence, is a model proposed by author Hugh Rank. This model has been widely used by teachers for helping students evaluate propaganda and persuasion messages. The second model, paths to influence, is proposed here by me.

The Rank Model of Influence

Box 4.1 shows the method used by Hugh Rank to analyze propaganda messages.[8] This model nicely illustrates the "card stacking" nature of propaganda. It is important to note that Rank proposed his ideas as a how-not-to-be-fooled model for use by receivers. To create propaganda, you *intensify* the good points of what you support and the bad points of some alternative (remembering that even propaganda that is for something is often against something—explicitly or implicitly).[9] You also try to *downplay* the bad points of what you support and the good points of some alternative. If I want to convince the world to stop eating meat, for example, I need to make meat eating sound bad and make vegetarian diets sound good. I also need to downplay the problems with vegetarian diets and the joys of meat eating.

Intensifying Rank offers three terms to explain how **intensifying** works: repetition, association, and composition. *Repetition* means that you create favorable images about what you support and create unfavorable images about an alternative that you have identified for comparison by using slogans or recurring themes. For example, the theme of a website for a residential college might be a comparison of all the nice features of living on campus and all the negative things about attending a commuter college.

Another way to intensify is with *association*, in which you link your message with positive or negative values, or with such abstractions as health, wealth, patriotism, death, scandal, or failure. The U.S. Army recruits personnel in part by linking enlistment in the army with alluring values (being all you can be, seeing the world, protecting your country from harm). An ad for the military could also associate jobs in the private sector with boredom (a negative abstraction).

One mattress company I know of uses *composition* to intensify its good points; they get you to remember their phone number in a clever way: "Dial 1-800-Mattress, and leave off the last S for savings." You might also compose an ad for a weight reduction program by printing the word *thin* with thinly drawn letters, or by showing a rival weight-reduction company's exercise facilities in an unflattering photograph. The composed suggestion here is that your program will make its participants thin like the word *thin*, and that a shoddy building prob-

---

BOX 4.1

Rank Model of Influence: Intensifying and Downplaying Tactics

Intensify (own good points, others' bad points)
  Repetition (use slogans, recurring themes)
  Association (link to positive or negative values or abstractions)
  Composition (emphasize with graphics)
Downplay (own bad points, others' good points)
  Omission (omit evidence)
  Diversion (change the subject)
  Confusion (overwhelm the receiver; muddy the waters)

ably means shoddy service. Composition might also take the form of a picture showing a political candidate smiling at young children. Composition most often suggests something helpful to the propagandist through the use of visual images, but aromas (e.g., mailed ads with pleasing scents), sounds (music from ice-cream trucks), taste, and touch might also be used by resourceful senders.

Downplaying Rank also offers three terms to explain how **downplaying** works: omission, diversion, and confusion. When using *omission*, we will not mention the downside of what we are advocating (e.g., if I'm promoting the parking facilities at the college where I teach, I won't mention that it cannot handle all the people who want to park). Senders also often omit the benefits of some alternative. Army recruitment ads may or may not, for example, mention the higher pay, reduced marital stress, or greater personal safety available in the private sector.

Diversion downplays by changing the subject at difficult moments in the communication or by directing receivers away from unfavorable considerations. For example, a political candidate might not exactly answer the following question: "Just where are you going to get the money for your new highway construction project?" Instead, the candidate may divert our attention by explaining that jobs for highway construction are less likely to be outsourced to some other country. Diversion can also be used to take our attention from the benefits of an opposing point of view. In a political debate, I might divert your attention from an opposing plan's benefit, a benefit that my plan cannot match, to some benefit I can match. I might pull this rhetorical sleight-of-hand by saying something outrageous about the benefit I can match, hoping you will fall for the ruse and demand I explain my outrageous comment, forgetting the benefit I cannot match.

Confusion, finally, seeks to muddy the communication, with such tactics as (1) overwhelming receivers with details or statistics, (2) cleverly comparing "apples to oranges"[10] in a way that escapes attention, and (3) using jargon that is not really well understood by the audience. Employing this tactic is especially likely to produce propaganda. If we do not understand what is being said, the sender hopes that we will take the sender's word about what some or all of it means. Dictators sometimes avoid the embarrassing effects of their policies by using public-relations campaigns that flatly deny allegations and then publish disinformation and confusing data-analyses that help conceal the facts.[11]

Whether a message constructed with the help of the Rank model—or simply analyzed with it—should be seen as propaganda or persuasion depends on exactly how many self-serving liberties the message's originators or adopters take.

The Paths to Influence Model

Here I propose a model that summarizes the various paths open to senders via propaganda, persuasion, or argumentation. Let's say the news item of the day concerns a body discovered in a downtown alley. Imagine how different people with different motives might report the incident. A medical examiner might describe the cause of death in a purely factual way. A reporter might write a story that leaves lots of lurid questions partly unanswered. And a self-appointed community activist, with almost no evidence, might self-servingly explain the as-yet-unclear situation by blithely asserting that dark forces assassinated this local resident as part of a dire national conspiracy. Meanwhile, a local prosecutor and defense attorney might competitively fence over whether there is enough evidence to indict someone known to have hated the victim. Each of the above persons has chosen a different *path of influence*. Now we can translate the above scenario into model form. We see at the left of figure 4.1 that any sender (S_1, S_2)—a propagandist, persuader, or arguer—could opt for any one of five paths that each start on the left and move from the sender's selection of a *mission*, including a *sender preference* (motive) and *message type* (style), through *cues* created by the sender and finally on to the right where we see *receiver response* (bias factors) and final *acceptance*. Any path selected by a sender would be designed to influence some target audience via that path. Let's begin to describe the model by noting five motives that senders can adopt in creating messages.

Forensic assertion. Here the sender seeks to prove modest claims through meticulous treatment of evidence. This form of influence includes argumentation. The medical examiner might use this motive to influence a court proceeding as to the cause of death for the possible murder victim. Was it death by poison, or a heart attack? The evidence would be carefully marshaled and the conclusions reached with great care for the evidence. Similarly, scientists explaining how the universe was formed might use a similar and very careful line of reasoning that asks very little faith on the part of listeners. Influence through emotional appeal or by exploiting the positive qualities of the sender are left out of this motive for the most part. In other words, the message is left to sink or swim solely on the merits of its logical claims and supporting evidence.

Persuasive leadership. This motive concerns promoting rational beliefs, attitudes, or policies intended to serve the interests of both sender and receiver. As we've seen, one difference between persuasion and propaganda is whether the interests of the receiver are necessarily served (along with those of the sender) through the persuasive leadership of the sender. Senders engage in persuasive leadership when they sincerely try to help receivers come to the right conclusions about some topic. With persuasion, we expect the sender to use evidence and reasoning, but we may tolerate some enthusiasm and emotion, as well as comments about the sender's qualifications regarding the topic. In a debate, both sides may say opposite things about the same evidence. Did the murder suspect have motive, opportunity, and the means to commit the crime? The prosecutor will inevitably say yes to this question, while the defense attorney will usually say no to one or more parts of the question. We expect that persuaders will have some sense of the best interests of their receivers at heart—even if in the end a given persuader is wrong about what is good for everyone involved. Proof through pathos, logos, and ethos are all acceptable here. A possible test for a message's being categorized as persuasive leadership is whether a randomly selected set of reasonable people who are reasonably well informed about the topic and reasonably nonpartisan would accept the sender's position as a reasonably valid position on the topic.

Self-promotional gamesmanship. This is an option that includes white propaganda. Here the sender creates self-serving messages—but without damaging others. The defense lawyer for the accused murderer may release white propaganda "spin" messages in the newspapers by saying, "My client is loved by everybody in town." In a different circumstance, an ad for a cola might paint a picture of the good life available to those who drink the cola by using the slogan "Get on the bandwagon! Feel good! Be a beautiful person!" Note that no serious mention is made about competing soda brands. Pragmatic messages may also fit in this category.

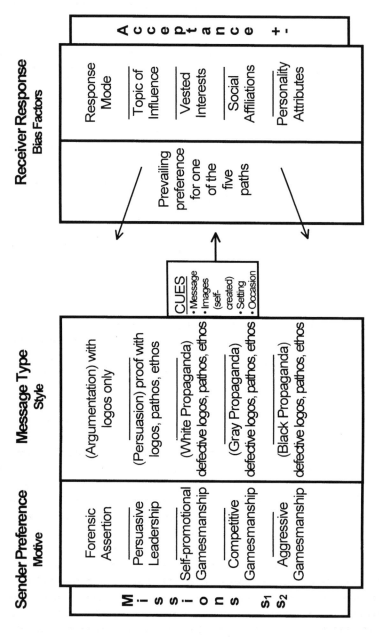

FIGURE 4.1 Senders must adjust messages to receivers' prevailing biases, or find an audience that will accept sender preference and message type.

Sometimes both the sender and receiver benefit from the message when the sender doubts the wisdom of the receivers to recognize a good idea when they see one.

Competitive gamesmanship. Here we could include gray propaganda, which often uses "card stacking" ("We're perfect on all issues, and the other side is just wrong") to outdo any competition. The tone of the messages here portrays the other side as an adversary, but not as an enemy. For instance, the above court battle could become quite competitive during news conferences, where perhaps the defense attorney will accuse the prosecutor of trying to get reelected by rushing an indictment through the grand jury before election day. Or in a different situation, a cable-TV company might mention in an ad that they offer hundreds of channels, hundreds of on-demand movies, no extra monthly charges for HDTV, exclusive local channels, less vulnerability to weather conditions, no annual contract or equipment to buy, service you can count on, and Internet access, whereas satellite, they will then say, just offers hundreds of channels.[12]

Aggressive gamesmanship. This can include black propaganda. Here the sender is willing to be destructive, make up malicious stories, tell lies, destroy reputations, plant false stories, and engage in name-calling. Stealing credibility and using false messages may also occur. Such a sender may falsely accuse the other side of destroying evidence or manufacturing phony evidence, or of tampering with witnesses or juries. The sender could even falsely accuse a judge of drinking vodka on the sly out of a plastic water-bottle in court. As is partly true with white and gray propaganda, black propaganda uses defective versions of ethos, pathos, and logos, due to such things as dishonesty, exaggeration, and irrational ideas.

Next in figure 4.1, moving from the left to the middle, we see the cues made available by senders for receivers. These cues are message, images, setting, and occasion.

The sender's *message* may be several speeches made by invited guests at a meeting, a TV ad, a flyer distributed in the street, a news conference held by a prosecutor to update reporters on the progress being made to solve a case, or any other means the sender uses for communicating with receivers.

Self-created *images* or impressions of the sender suggest how the sender wants to appear to receivers. We might ask several questions regarding these images. Do they imply the sender's competence? The sender's honesty? Do the images make the sender seem good-willed or dynamic? For example, a prosecutor may meet reporters while wearing shirt-sleeves rolled up to create the impression of doing hard, down-to-earth work.

The *setting* is where the communication takes place. A prosecutor could meet with reporters on the courthouse steps, or an executive could try to sell shares in a company to selected employees meeting in a top-floor executive boardroom (or in a small, dusty office next to the heating equipment in the basement). The scenic cues of the executive boardroom might include leather chairs; a long, highly polished, heavy wooden table; a sterling silver tea-service; large, staid pictures mounted in fancy frames with rich patinas; thick carpeting; and an extensive view of the city. Will these upscale cues get potential buyers to think "big?"

The *occasion* concerns why the communication is taking place. An occasion such as Thanksgiving, the Fourth of July, graduation day, a marriage ceremony, or a divorce can help to create an influence by setting a mood and encouraging certain expectations (e.g., relatives might decide to set up a nest-egg fund at a graduation-day ceremony for a grandchild). Or, as a good example of the chronemics described in chapter 2, demonstrators could hold a press conference counter to the one held by our prosecutor, and across the street from the courthouse steps, by which they would emphasize that the unsolved case has now gone on for one year without any progress.

The right side of figure 4.1 shows what happens to incoming messages. Receivers may have a *prevailing preference* for one of the five message paths, depending on the variables to the right of the preference box. Some people in town now may believe a cover-up has taken place to protect an important citizen from being prosecuted, and they may favor angry propaganda during their press conference. But supporters of the yet-to-be-prosecuted suspect will probably listen carefully to the defense attorney, who counsels that given the evidence, the prosecutor is nowhere near getting an indictment, and they may favor hearing persuasion or even argumentation that offers factual reassurance.

Thus, different audiences, or receivers, have different biases and preferences for types of influence. These biases are determined in part by receivers' current *response mode*, which may favor the upper paths of argumentation or persuasion if the receivers prefer proof. But in other instances, receivers may just want the reassurance provided by the white, gray, or black propaganda of the lower paths. In contrast, some receivers may respond better to the lower propaganda paths if their moods tend toward intense emotional reactions, partisan thoughts, or even the need to protect self-esteem. Similarly, the principal sender (S_1) may well succeed with receivers who have favorable beliefs or attitudes toward the *topic of influence*. Presumably, they will react well to almost any path of influence that supports what they already agree with. Receivers with neutral beliefs and attitudes can probably be influenced by either the principal sender (S_1) or a rival sender (S_2). Apathetic neutrals may not care enough to give much thought to the message and may be reached by lower paths; but disinterested neutrals may react better to upper paths because, as unbiased neutrals, they may be more discerning of S_1's message than receivers who already agree. And those who disagree with the principal sender (perhaps favoring an S_2 message) will be the most difficult to reach. Still, they may respond to S_1 message materials that take the higher two paths, do not attack, and make minimal claims based on sober evidence.

Real or material *vested interests* may also affect prevailing preferences for one of the five paths. For example, receivers may have a vested interest in the topic of downtown zoning restrictions because they own real estate in a downtown area and strongly favor loosening zoning restrictions on property development. These receivers may respond well to either pro-development propaganda or persuasion. But to convince receivers with no real-estate interests that some development is needed (or receivers who oppose tearing down historically significant buildings), you may need argumentation or persuasion, although propaganda might also be used to motivate them against development. Similarly, receivers' *social affiliations* with family, community, country, and culture may make them more or less responsive to propaganda on various topics. And *personality attributes* (or traits), such as authoritarianism or a tendency to group loyalty, may generally make receivers more or less responsive to various modes of influence. If a town council plans to install parking meters in a neighborhood, those receivers prone to loyal feelings for their community may respond to pro- or anti-meter propaganda that furthers the "neighborhood perspective," while individuals less prone to group loyalty may respond better to persuasion or argumentation that promotes an altruistic perspective. If all goes well for sender S_1, in any case, receivers will accept (+) what the sender asks and won't reject (-) it.

Finally, another sender (S_2) using propaganda may cause the principal sender (S_1) to switch midstream from using persuasion or argumentation to using propaganda. Or if S_1 is already using white propaganda, S_1 may feel provoked enough to switch to gray or black propaganda. These switches sometimes happen when one side in an election publicly states at the onset that they will not engage in any political mudslinging. But they may then reverse course when they see that the other side has begun a negative campaign, when they suspect that the other side is preparing to do so, or when they just get desperate. As with persuasion, if propaganda is to be successful, senders need to either find receivers who will respond to sender-chosen paths of influence, or select paths preferred by particular receivers.

Tactics of Propaganda

In 1937 the Institute for Propaganda Analysis set up shop, believing that

> It is essential in a democratic society that young people and adults learn how to think, learn how to make up their minds. They must learn how to think independently, and they must learn how to think together. They must come to conclusions, but at the same time they must recognize the right of other men to come to opposite conclusions. So far as individuals are concerned, the art of democracy is the art of thinking and discussing independently together.[13]

They identified seven propaganda tactics, including such things as name-calling, the glittering generality, the plain-folks approach, card stacking, and getting people on the bandwagon. This was a good start, but in the intervening years additional tactics have been identified.

As I've noted, tactics serve the interests of strategies.[14] Thus, a **propaganda tactic** is one that helps the propagandist win a point or evoke a feeling at some given point in time. A **propaganda strategy**, on the other hand, is concerned with success in the long term (e.g., get the public's attention this month, get them to believe something is true next month, and go for a policy change the following month). *Strategy* is a relative term here, as is *tactic*; so strategy could also be applied to the layout of one particular message. Thus, message-level strategy could be part of a campaign-level tactic; and in turn, a campaign-level tactic could be an element in a campaign-level strategy. Let's examine the many common tactics of propagandists.[15]

Table 4.1 summarizes common tactics used by propagandists.[16] These tactics have been loosely sorted into the three types: white, gray, and black. Black propaganda can use white and gray tactics (but with greater intensity) in addition to the tactics it uses exclusively. Similarly, gray propaganda can also employ the techniques of white propaganda. Also note that a given propaganda act may illustrate just one of the tactics that follow below or may illustrate two or more. For example, a propagandist might on the one hand make the *bold, sweeping assertion* that a political candidate is a child molester, though offering no evidence. This assertion would also *demonize* (use character assassination against) the political candidate because of the intense negativity of the accusation. Thus the same act could fall into two categories at once.

Table 4.1 Examples of White, Gray, and Black Propaganda Tactics

WHITE PROPAGANDA	bandwagon
	positive stereotypes
	mild appeal to emotions
	mild, unlabeled hyperbole
	mild substitution of names
	mild appeal to authority
	bold, sweeping assertions
GRAY PROPAGANDA	misdirection
	illogic
	card stacking / selective use of sources
	exploiting common misconceptions
	embedded propositions
	self-serving definitions of words
	fallacies in logic
	equivocation
	marginalizing the opposition
BLACK PROPAGANDA	demonizing (using character assassination)
	relentless attack
	unflattering images
	negative stereotypes
	unsubstantiated atrocity stories
	the big lie
	disinformation
	goading or baiting an action

Tactics of White Propaganda

White-propaganda tactics are generally self-promotional, do not attack anyone or anything, and are positive. White propaganda can also be pragmatic in form, when a sender with good intentions tells a few white lies in order to motivate lazy or apathetic receivers.

Bandwagon. This tactic is often used in advertising with such lines as "Join the Pepsi Generation!" or "Get with the program, Get ABC Toothpaste!" To varying extents, people are followers who feel insecure if they are not with the majority. Nonetheless, when the bandwagon tactic is used in a positive way, we have white propaganda.

Positive stereotypes. Stereotypes that make people feel good are common in white propaganda (negative stereotypes occur in black propaganda). A sales agent for a real-estate company might be portrayed in an ad as friendly, helpful, trustworthy, attractive, and professional.

Mild appeal to emotions. When using this tactic, we pick a positive emotion, such as joy or adventure, and invite receivers to follow us purely for emotional reasons (e.g., "Come to the Thrill-A-Minute Theme Park for Fun! Fun! Fun!").

Mild, unlabeled hyperbole. Hyperbole is a figure of speech meaning fanciful exaggeration. There are times when using hyperbole is a reasonable way to make a point: "Our picnic was invaded by zillions of ants" or "I know you haven't been late every day, but sometimes it seems as if you have." Properly used, hyperbole is not misleading. But there are ways to use hyperbole that are a "stretch." For example, if I write a computer program and then advertise that millions just love it, I am not being ethical if what I really mean is that 1,119 people have bought it so far.

Mild substitution of names. Most of us are good to some extent at winning points with self-serving word selections. Do we say "free-market system" or "capitalism"? Do we say we had a "spat," a "disagreement," or a "blood bath"? Do we say "doing drugs," "abusing drugs," or "enjoying recreational drugs"?

Mild appeal to authority. Advertisers may refer to what "doctors say," politicians may refer to what "the people want," preachers may refer to what the Bible says, and scientists may refer to what a highly regarded theorist has said. Mild appeal to authority allows the sender to say or suggest, "Don't rely on your own thinking, don't ask me for objective proof, but rather take it 'on authority,' and trust me." Not all appeals to authority are propaganda. But a sender should offer you convincing evidence that a particular authority has the best judgment at this time on the issue.

Bold, sweeping assertions occur when we make a claim and offer no evidence to back it up (some call this a "factoid"). Now it is true that a common-knowledge claim does not normally have to be supported with evidence (e.g., "Scotland is in the north of the United Kingdom" or "Water is a liquid"). But with a *bold, sweeping assertion*, we make a claim that *does* need support but we act as though our claim were common knowledge. An Internet ad might assert that "Each year tens of millions of dollars in college scholarships go unused; these funds could easily go to you if you respond to our offer!" Such unused scholarships may in fact go unused because of restrictive application requirements. Here are a few more examples of bold, sweeping assertions: "Space aliens landed in Roswell in 1949, but the visits were covered up by the army," "Teachers do not care about educating students anymore," and "Gas companies are conspiring to keep prices up." Although these assertions could be true, they would need lots of support to be taken seriously.

Tactics of Gray Propaganda

Gray propaganda uses a competitive approach to outdo the other side, but its techniques fall short of the aggressive techniques of black propaganda.

Misdirection. This is a way to change the subject when things get sticky. Or we can use misdirection to entice or manipulate receivers to pay attention to what will help our mission, not what will hurt it.

Illogic. One example of illogic would be arguing that it really is not all that bad if eight-year-old children have sex with adults because not all children exposed to adult sexuality grow up with personal problems. (The propagandist might then go on to argue that when problems do occur, other factors are responsible.) This confuses the concepts of necessity and sufficiency. The error is in saying that because such sexual experiences are not by themselves always sufficient to cause problems, they are not important. But quite likely such experiences are a necessary ingredient (in conjunction with other factors, such as a child's low self-esteem or strong belief that such behavior is wrong) for causing future problems to occur.

Card stacking and *selective use of sources.* Card stacking refers to airing all the things that support your case and none of the things that do not. Selective use of sources happens when the propagandist quotes particular experts but only when the individuals say (or can be made to seem to say) things that are supportive of the propaganda; the propagandist ignores whatever else the experts say that is not supportive.

Exploiting common misconceptions. At any given time, the general public probably misunderstands many things, such as when it thinks a community problem (1) is being taken care of when it is not, (2) is not being taken care of when it is, (3) exists when it really does not, and (4) does not exist when it really does. Propagandists can exploit these misconceptions, for instance, when they urge more, or less, government response to a public problem.

Embedded propositions say things obliquely rather than assert them. One example of an embedded proposition is the statement "Although we did not bother documenting their financial abuses, we found inaccuracies in their reports." The words "their financial abuses" will in some people's minds imply that there definitely were financial abuses. Another example is "Because of concerns about police brutality, biased judges, apathetic juries, and one-sided newspaper reports, many defendants are not cooperating when arrested these days." Here we have several embedded propositions: (1) police brutality is commonplace, (2) many judges are biased, (3) lots of juries are apathetic, and (4) many newspapers are anti-defendant. The problem here is the word "concerns." Were these concerns of the defendants justified ones that reasonable people would accept, or were they self-serving distortions? How common were these concerns among defendants? Were these just the invented concerns of the writer?

Self-serving definitions of words. When someone starts with what they say is the true meaning of a word, pay careful attention. Perhaps a government employee says, "I did not take a bribe when I received a discount for air travel from that lobbyist's cousin—a bribe must involve the exchange of money or valuable gifts." There have been ideologies in the past that argued that the true meaning of *peace* is not an absence of military conflict but an absence of class conflict.[17] One television advertiser, to give another example, apparently has a special definition for the term *hidden money* because he claims that anyone who buys his book will find at government agencies $350 million to be given away just for the asking. But according to the New York State Consumer Protection Board, this author "exaggerates the availability and purpose of dozens of grants and programs listed in his book. For example, a grant from the National Academy of Science [given to a physicist at Georgetown University] is advertised as money 'to travel the world.'" The board's report goes on to say, "There are some grants out there but the vast majority of these dollars are for low-income consumers or senior citizens."[18]

Fallacies in logic can occur in a number of ways that will be discussed in some detail in chapter 5. But for example, it is not logical to say, "There will be one more hour of daylight tomorrow because tonight we switch to standard time and set the clocks one hour behind." That may sound true to some, but it is not a logical conclusion.

Equivocation is a form of evasiveness. The word means using statements subject to two or more interpretations in order to mislead or avoid committing oneself to what one says. In an episode of the 1950s *Leave It to Beaver* television series, Beaver's parents give him money to get a haircut at the barbershop. At the shop, he realizes that he has lost the money and leaves without a haircut; he then talks his older brother into giving him the haircut at home. That night he wears a hat at dinner, hoping his parents will not notice his horribly botched haircut. When asked by his father, "Beaver, did you go to the barber for a haircut today?" he answers, "Dad, I went to the barber; and I got a haircut." The elements of his answer are technically true. The overall gist is misleading. He does not confirm or deny whether he got a haircut at the barbershop. Politicians sometimes use equivocation when caught in difficult situations.

Marginalizing the opposition. Here, instead of taking on the arguments of the other side, we slap a label on the side or its argument with words like "That's dinosaur thinking," "You're just a reactionary," or "I'm not going to respond to your propaganda." It would be better to offer these generalizations after we have made a good case for them, as might happen if someone urged that we return to the horse and buggy as our principal means of transportation and I carefully pointed out several huge problems with this idea. Or if you can show me that I disagreed with you several times but agreed with someone else about the same things, you might rightly accuse me of being a reactionary who has to say "up" when certain other people say "down."

Tactics of Black Propaganda

The tactics of black propaganda include malicious and dishonest messages that aggressively attack things in a rhetorical style congruent with foreign or domestic warfare.

With *demonizing* (*using character assassination*), the propagandist wants people to believe the adversary in essence is evil, or at least is a mean and nasty person who kicks dogs and snarls at hungry children. The purpose of this tactic is to render the adversary a low-credibility source who will not be believed or listened to by people. Character assassination can occur, for example, when we unfairly describe someone as a modern-day Stalin or Hitler, or when we use unproven innuendo to suggest that a person's ancestors were bigots or horse thieves.

Relentless attack against an enemy gives the propagandist a negative foil or target. Relentless attack is a characteristic of many propagandists; they are always "on message" and always "playing the game." They tend not to take time for other public activities.

Unflattering images or news items, another type of black propaganda, are sometimes used by newspapers against a politician they do not support.

Negative stereotypes seek to shape receivers' perceptions about members of *out-groups*, or people of some other religion, class, nationality, ethnicity, or political allegiance. Members of an out-group may be described as "animal-like" or "devil-like" or "criminal-like." Sometimes they are just described as stupid, greedy, ugly, manipulative, or conspiratorial. Practicers of black propaganda usually do not care if their characterizations are untrue.

Unsubstantiated atrocity stories. These occur when the propagandist fabricates a false story that claims the other side has purposely done terrible things to innocent people. You can very probably think of examples of this tactic yourself. Of course in the real world, atrocities do occur, and real events can also be exploited for their emotional power by propagandists. Sometimes enduring the pain of being a victim will pay off in the end, if you are a propagandist who seeks to score points against your adversary by using substantiated atrocity stories. And sometimes the atrocity story is merely about how the other side once used black propaganda against your side. This is a form of turning the tables on a propaganda adversary after the fact.

The big lie. This is a term that goes back to Nazi and Soviet propaganda: both governments used propaganda to lie about their respective massive killing of civilians. The term suggests that it may sometimes be easier to get away with bigger lies than with smaller ones. We are seldom surprised when other people speak or write with mild exaggeration, so we are usually more alert for mild lies. But we can be fooled by big lies because we do not expect the outrageous. Big lies work best when listeners are ill-informed, are too lazy to verify the facts, or like the lie so much that they do not want to question its veracity.

Disinformation is a fairly modern term that often (but not always) refers to trying to trick an adversary into making an unwise move; the adversary may then misstep because they have false information about something, information that was planted for them to "uncover." Army commanders, for example, may at times leak misleading information about where their troops will move next, hoping the enemy deploys in the wrong direction. In the same way, political campaigns and business rivals may at times leak misleading information about themselves to gain an advantage. A political contender may give the impression that he or she has personally taken unethical financial liberties when this did not in fact happen. When the other side falls for the bait and complains publicly for political advantage, the political contender then publicly denies the accusation and taunts the just-baited other side to prove their accusations, thereby trying to get them to admit that they are engaged in malicious mudslinging. Disinformation can be used to gain advantage in other ways, such as when we cover our tracks to avoid being held accountable for something, perhaps by planting misleading stories claiming that someone else has done what we in fact did.

Goading or baiting an action through interfering with people's daily activities, ridiculing others publicly, blocking public speeches, or issuing "fightin' words" is one of the most negative tactics of a propagandist. For instance, a politically hostile group might engage in disruptive actions that will bring the authorities to stop them. Then if the group does not cooperate with the police as the police interview or arrest them, the police may begin to treat the group roughly. If the group can get the police's rough handling of the group shown or discussed by news services, they can then denounce the police in hopes of winning the hearts and minds of the public. In some political settings, the roles of the goaders and baiters and their targets can be reversed, with the police doing the goading and baiting, and others being the targets.

Why Propaganda Works: Some Strategic Considerations

Earlier we looked at Doob's description of propaganda as suggestion, which might easily lead us to less than rational attitudes about things. But there are other routes to the less rational outcomes brought about by propaganda. Brown reminds us that children early in life learn to feel guilt and anxiety for not living up to the expectations of the adults around them.[19] So when a nineteenth-century country preacher (or a storefront revival preacher in a big city today) warns, "Hell has been waiting for six thousand years. It is filling up every day," the message is "You had better repent." Many people changed by propaganda messages do so out of a sense of conformity. Others, however, do so as individualists. It is with these individualists that propaganda, when successful, may be most enduring. Propaganda's influence on conformists may last only so long as the conformists are in a particular social setting; as soon as they move on, or back to a previous setting, the effects may end. Good examples of this may be found at residential colleges and in the army. In both cases, receivers will probably be changed somewhat by their new environment. But when they later return home, their attitudes may revert, unless they are individualists who changed without group pressure or changed because they simply matured. The propagandist has an edge when receivers are ignorant of important facts or have little experience defending one side of a given topic. If a propagandist's message is consistent with the social currents of the times, the propagandist may also have an edge. But propaganda can probably only retard or accelerate popular social trends, and will seldom reverse them without the use of widespread effort.

Message Flow and Propaganda

Propagandists can seek receivers and receivers can seek propagandists, especially when tribalistic mentalities prevail. In a tribalistic setting, strong emotions such as anger or fear can encourage group-loyal or **shibboleth thinking**. In modern times, the word *shibboleth* means "If you are one of us you will talk in a certain way about some controversial topic, especially in your use of vocabulary, and if you're one of them, you will talk in another way about the same topic."[20] Such thinking creates a justification for seeing the group we identify with, or belong to, as always good and always right—while seeing opposition groups as always wrong and always bad. Ergo, because what we say is true and good, it is not propaganda, but what the other side says, because it is not true and good, is propaganda. In addition, we in the modern world often seem at odds with each other over what should be considered the established virtues of the land. Which is more important, cultural diversity or cultural unity? Confrontation or accommodation toward adversaries and enemies? Religiosity or secularity? Cosmopolitanism or traditionalism? Nationalism, internationalism, or anarchy? Consumed or conserved societal resources? At times we sometimes even seem at odds over whether the soul of society should seem more masculine or feminine. Thus, to the extent that people are tribalistic, they will seek out propagandists skillful at reassurance.

Coming to terms with what constitutes propaganda has not been easy. But we can now begin to understand the word as referring either to types of messages (**forms**) or to processes (**functions**) that unfold as a result of an organized campaign that tries, as we noted earlier, to turn target groups into resources that facilitate a mission. Brown identifies propaganda strategy as unfolding in three stages: (1) The pre-propaganda stage of *attention and interest*: if people are not listening or watching, your chances of reaching them are not good; (2) *emotional hyper-stimulation*; and (3) *release*. It is in the last stage that the propagandist, having now gotten the receivers strongly concerned about something, must then offer a solution to the crisis that will release tension and promote whatever the propagandist seeks to change.[21] Communication scholars Anthony Pratkanis and Elliot Aronson describe steps of propaganda similar to Brown's, although they add a separate stage for building source credibility for the propagandist, and they emphasize shaping perceptions somewhat more.[22]

Jowett and O'Donnell remind us that a propagandist's message often reaches the receivers within some particular social network.[23] So the propagandist must try to anticipate how the message will be supported or opposed by opinion leaders within that network. Receivers may react to propaganda messages by voting, answering pollsters' questions, contributing money to the propagandist's organization, demonstrating for or against the propagandist's message, or joining groups of like-minded people—all of which may circle back to stimulate more propaganda. And completing the cycle, the receivers themselves may change their moods and concerns, which in turn may ripple back and influence the propagandist's goals and tactics. Making things more interesting, propaganda, like persuasion and other types of communication, must be understood in terms of the societal contexts in which it occurs.

Propaganda in Societal Contexts

To learn a little more about propaganda strategy, let's explore the contexts of (1) psychological warfare and propaganda, (2) agonism and propaganda, and (3) scientific mind-changing that may rely at times on both propaganda and persuasion. In certain political contexts, scientific mind-changing can involve **indoctrination**. With indoctrination, those with political power systematically inculcate some doctrine—about how people should live or how societies should be organized—into the minds of voluntary recruits, semi-voluntary recruits, or political prisoners. As we will see in chapter 16, indoctrination strategy involves the breaking down of the individual through induced trauma and anxiety, and then the building up of that individual by removing the trauma and anxiety in order to encourage acceptance of new beliefs, values, attitudes, and behavior. These changes often disappear when the person returns home, unless the person remains in the new setting permanently. Some of the changes may remain if the individual returns home but finds such changes especially appealing.

Psychological warfare refers to the careful coordination of propaganda with the ongoing tactics and strategies of actual warfare. Psychological warfare is probably as old as is human experience; even wild animals roar loudly, increase their apparent body size, or stare and howl with hostility at adversaries. However, the term *psychological warfare* is modern and especially became a familiar term in the cold war and world wars of the last century. According to Brown, the [strategic] goals of the propaganda used in psychological warfare are to:

1. Mobilize and direct hatred against the enemy and undermine the enemy's morale
2. Convince our side of the rightness of our cause and increase and maintain fighting spirit
3. Develop the friendship of neutrals and strengthen in their minds that we are right and will be victorious
4. Develop and strengthen the friendship of the allies fighting with us

The tactical goals of propaganda support larger strategic goals. And sometimes the tactical goals of psychological warfare occur in coordination with military actions. For example, prior to a military operation, propaganda might entail parading the impressive array of weapons to be used in the operation, or leaking a report about disarray on the other side. With coordination, tactical goals for fighting with arms or with words can help each other.

Agonism is an interesting word with a history that goes back to ancient times. It can refer to athletic competitions, animal threat-posturing (perhaps with snarls), or public policy infighting among those who can find a microphone, television camera, or authorial space in a newspaper, magazine, website, or book. The word *agonism* is enjoying somewhat of a revival today, not in terms of the contests mentioned above, but in terms of the so-called culture wars that are sometimes fought in the media. For example, social scholar Deborah Tannen sees agonism as a contemporary tendency to fight over public policy issues as if they were battles that must be won and not lost. She urges more cooperative public discussions. Do the heated arguments we often hear in the public arena actually help us see the strengths and weaknesses in the various arguments? Does everyone participate in this competition or just the most assertive or ambitious? Is agonism one of the root causes of a preference for propaganda use in modern society?[24]

Finally, *scientific mind-changing* is in some ways propagandistic and in some ways persuasive.[25] It can include psychoanalysis, general psychotherapy, hypnosis, and even what is sometimes inaccurately called "brainwashing." Brainwashing is probably better referred to either as *semi-voluntary indoctrination* or as a *coercive form of usually temporary mind-changing* that can occur when the victim is incarcerated in an incommunicado environment where information from and social contact with the outside are strictly censored by jailer "mind-changers."[26] Coercive mind-changing (and to a lesser extent, indoctrination) tries to strip the victim of all interpersonal and public support that would normally confirm the victim's feelings of self-goodness and rightness of idea and purpose. The idea is to attack the victim's core attitudes about self, family, and country. Then the mind-changer replaces these things with some rival, hostile, or sometimes unconventional worldview or doctrine—in part by treating kindly the victim who conforms while treating harshly the victim who does not conform. Historically, these mind-changing attempts have occurred in authoritarian dictatorships, ancient societies of obedience, or in domestic cult groups. Garden-variety psychiatric practices are quite tame compared to the above techniques. However, psychotherapy, boot-camp training practices, and even prep-school experiences can share some of the techniques of coercive mind-changing.

In a way, a psychotherapist is a specialized sort of scientific persuader with an audience of one person (or several people). Sometimes, for example, the patients of psychotherapists may seek help for problems when dealing with authority figures. These patients have difficulty with others who express authority that constricts the patient's behavior, and they become hostile and argumentative, or simply avoid situations where authority is asserted. Friends, relatives, or workplace personnel may try to convince such people that authority is sometimes a legitimate social force. But these arguments may fail because the problem or attitude is not based on a rational belief but on an underlying emotional function such as ego-defense, avoidance of irrational fear, or facilitation of unfocused anger. Either the helpful arguments will be rejected, distorted, or rationalized away, or they will be generally accepted but then ignored, as in "Okay, you're right about that part, but I'm still not going to let *them* tell me what to do."

The psychotherapist, in this case, may try to discover what psychological function the patient's antiauthority attitude serves, because the function that is served by the attitude probably disallows any acceptance of reasonable argument. When the therapist identifies the likely underlying cause, this knowledge can be passed on to the patient, or the therapist can try to arrange for the patient to discover the insight for themselves (depending on the methods used by the therapist). The therapist has thus directed the message to exactly where it may do some good. Our antiauthority patient, for example, may have a repressed memory about how as a six-year-old he was forced by his father and mother to kiss his dead grandmother lying in a coffin at a funeral. He may have cried, "No, no, mama I don't want to!" And his mother may have said, "But darlin' that's how grandma will know you still love her." Or perhaps a young girl, allowed to see her mother work as a prostitute at home, has come as an adult to hate men, whom she sees as selfish authority figures. Neither child was in a position to say no to the will of adults in order to avoid something traumatic. In both cases, persuasive, liberating insight into an underlying cause may help. Perhaps propagandistic mind-changing could be used here to undo the harmful effects of trauma-caused mind-changing. Or as Jowett and O'Donnell might say, the therapist tries to help the patient by "[re]shaping perceptions, manipulating cognitions, and sometimes directing behavior" to how things might have been had it not been for the original trauma.

Chapter in Retrospect

VIGNETTE 1 An Iron Cross at Ground Zero

A construction worker stumbled over an iron cross in the debris several days after the brutal murder by Islamic extremists of nearly 3,000 people in the twin towers of the World Trade Center in 2001. The cross had apparently been sheared in exactly the right proportions by the collapse of one of the two towers. It closely resembled a Christian cross and was later erected on a small stone base by construction workers. It still stands (as of this writing) on the empty site. There is an eerie feel to this icon, reminiscent of the monolith in the film *2001: A Space Odyssey*. The story of the iron cross appeared in a number of newspaper articles at the time, and spurred numerous websites to tell its story. The website American Atheists notes:

> With time, though, "ground zero" has taken on the aura of "sacred space," charged with religious, apocalyptic and prophetic significance. Everything from impromptu shrines to after-the-fact prognostication have become part of a new mythos surrounding this place and the dramatic events associated with it.
>
> On Thursday, news reports told of an iron "cross" found in the Trade Center rubble that has become an icon of faith for many of those laboring to recover the bodies of victims and clear debris following the September 11 attack. A laborer, Frank Silecchia, 47, reportedly found the 20-foot-tall cross standing "almost upright" on September 13. It consists of two metal beams that fell intact from one of the twin towers into a neighboring structure. (www.atheists.org/flash.line/islam10.htm [1 June 2006])

The website Bible Network News had this to say:

> Cross Becomes a Witness of Faith to World Leaders
>
> On Oct. 4th, the Feast of St. Francis, fire fighters, police and construction workers, some with their hard hats removed out of respect, all with their heads bowed, listened quietly while Father Jordan dedicated the massive iron cross. The Franciscan priest prayed for "redemption and healing for workers, victims and their families and for all America which was violated" by the terrorist attacks.
>
> Father Jordan told The Canadian Bible Society in a phone interview that for him, the cross symbolizes "the pain and suffering of Jesus on the cross and the redemption of all humanity." Almost every day Father Jordan tirelessly ministers at Ground Zero. What

would he want prayer for? "For the healing of the nation." (www.biblenetworknews.com/northamerica/102901_usa.html [1 June 2006])

The above two excerpts illustrate how icons can be employed by those who would influence us. In the case of the iron cross, the potential power of the icon is considerable. Given the cross's setting in the World Trade Center debris, it would not be hard for a propagandist to go beyond the moderate intensities of the above two website excerpts and to say perhaps that the wrath of the Christian God has been revealed by this icon to the Wahhabi fundamentalists who were apparently behind the attacks. The propagandist could go on and say that God has condemned this act of terror, that it has not gone unnoticed, and that they will be held accountable. In addition to its setting, the icon takes part of its power from its shape and size. And part of the power comes from the appealing story of the construction worker who found it and apparently cried for twenty minutes afterward. That the icon has stood in place for more than four years also gives it authority at the site, especially as local squabbling about how to rebuild the site continues. In fact, for four years this iron cross, sitting on its ad hoc stone base, has been the only noticeable object that remains untouched in the huge pit. All that remains for the propagandist here is to suggest what the icon's appearance can be said to foretell for the immediate future.

VIGNETTE 2 Communication outside the World Trade Center Site

In late summer 2005, a group of people stood outside the site of the World Trade Center on a sunny afternoon and spoke loudly to passersby. On the extra-wide sidewalk serving as the eastern perimeter of the site, about six individuals stood perhaps eight feet apart in two rows and took turns saying things in "headline" form, sometimes overlapping each other's statements. Two other individuals handed out sheets of paper emblazoned with fourteen "Whys." A center paragraph on each sheet said:

> America has waited long enough for answers:

> The government, the media, and the 9/11 commission [have] not honored the victims by providing the truth. [They obscure] the truth. You'll have to learn on your own. See the big picture, ask real questions. Discover the hidden agenda. See how the real conspiracy theory is the government's official story.

The sheet goes on to ask numerous questions that seem to say the 9/11 attacks were either the result of gross government-intelligence incompetence, or were known about before the event and nothing was done about it. The sheet then goes on to say what the reader can do about all this:

> Send people to the research Websites. Purchase videos like _____ and _____. Have 9/11 Investigation Parties to show them [the videos] and share information. Read _____. Download flyers like this and pass them out. The future is ours to save!

The term that probably best describes the above street event is the word *agitprop*. The term roughly means propaganda that is designed to influence people by means of highly emotional, aggressive language about social problems that may or may not exist in objective terms. Agitprop often identifies certain groups or individuals as bad, while identifying the creators of the agit-prop as good. The places you can find agitprop include the street, marches or events designed to draw large crowds, websites, films, documentaries, music videos, song lyrics, and pamphlets that are often distributed free. Agitprop might in some cases be employed by religious groups with fundamentalist orientations or by political groups with ideas that may not yet be popular with the majorities in various cultures. Historically, agitprop has been used along with other tactics by Nazis, Fascists, and Soviet and Chinese communists in the twentieth century to help destabilize weak governments prior to taking them over by force or political intrigue.

Summary and Conclusions

Propaganda was probably first used by people before recorded history. Definitions of prop-aganda vary somewhat from scholar to scholar, although the definition used here is based on one proposed by Jowett and O'Donnell, who argue that propaganda attempts to "shape perceptions, manipulate cognitions, and direct behavior" of audience members, or receivers. We have noted that propaganda when compared with persuasion is often more aggressive and more committed to gamesmanship (what one person wins, the other may lose), and less committed to the expression of ideas in a way that shows rationality, proportionality, per-suasive leadership, and ethics.

Some characteristics of propaganda involve the use of censorship, doctoring of infor-mation, and suggestion. The Rank model of propaganda relies on the concept of downplay-ing the unfavorable aspects and intensifying the favorable aspects of a propagandist's case. The paths to influence model relies on describing the paths to influence that a sender can choose from and that will be more likely or less likely to be accepted by receivers, depend-ing on the mood and motives of the receivers.

Propaganda can occur on a continuum that ranges from mild to severe. White propa-ganda refers to mild self-promotion in words and images. Gray propaganda refers to compet-itive but not malicious use of words or images between rivals. Black propaganda refers to malicious use of words, images, or acts between enemies or serious rivals. Numerous tactics of white, gray, and black propaganda have been identified.

Propaganda always plays a role in psychological warfare and in indoctrination into cults or in the coercive mind-changing of prisoners. A limited type of propaganda can sometimes play a role in psychotherapy.

KEY TERMS

black propaganda	gray propaganda	proportionality
censorship	indoctrination	rationality
doctoring of information	intensifying	shibboleth thinking
downplaying	propaganda strategy	suggestion
forms	propaganda tactic	white propaganda
functions		

1. Where and when did propaganda as a tool of influence probably begin?
2. How do Jowett and O'Donnell define propaganda?
3. How do Jowett and O'Donnell distinguish propaganda from persuasion?
4. What does the Rank model have to say about intensifying and downplaying?
5. Why can we say the paths to influence model is not just about propaganda?
6. How is competitive gamesmanship different from aggressive gamesmanship?
7. What alternative terms could be used to refer to white, gray, and black propaganda?
8. What are the strategic goals of psychological warfare?
9. What does the word *agonism* mean? What does the word *agitprop* mean?
10. Are there any circumstances where a psychiatrist's methods might be propagandistic?

1. Pick a politically polarized current-event issue (e.g., stem-cell research, global warming, a local election, freedom of speech on campus), then locate and analyze two propaganda messages (one from each side of the controversy). Look for messages in newspapers, pamphlets, the hand-outs people distribute in public, television news stories, magazines, advocacy news shows on cable TV, politicized points of view from professors, e-mail or website political opinions, and campus-organization speeches. Identify the leading participants involved, their motives and goals, their strategies and tactics. Have they used black, gray, or white propaganda? Have they also used other forms of influence such as persuasion or argumentation? Warning: You may have trouble seeing the side you might agree with as using propaganda. If you have this problem, think to yourself, "I hope this message is true; but it may nonetheless contain elements of propaganda. I had better know for sure in order to be prepared for future debates on the topic; I do not want to get blind-sided by something the other side brings up that I cannot refute." If a particular current events topic makes you feel so emotional that you have trouble remaining politically neutral and objective, pick a different one.

   Questions to answer in your analysis:
   A. What has each side actually said about the topic?
   B. What seems to be the goal of each side?
   C. What strategies and tactics can be identified on each side?
   D. Does one side seem to be winning the battle? Why or why not?

2. Find a short propaganda message in print form. Now translate this propaganda into a persuasive message. Are there any difficulties in doing this? Do you have to locate information not contained in the propaganda message in order to make a credible persuasive message? Do you have to change some of the vocabulary used in the propaganda message in order to make it persuasive? Have emotional appeals been used in an extreme way that has to be modified? Are there logical flaws that have to be corrected? Do you have to weaken any of the claims made in the propaganda message?

3. Find a short persuasive message and translate it into a propaganda message, just for fun. Use the techniques discussed in the last section of this chapter.

4. Visit an open trial at a courthouse. Do the attorneys or witnesses ever try to use propaganda? Note how the judge tries to protect the jury from hearing occasional propaganda (or other improper statements) introduced by the trial's participants. Keep in mind that in a criminal trial, it is accepted that each side can introduce evidence that favors either the defense or the prosecution without this evidence being considered propaganda. The same is true for the plaintiff or defendant in a civil trial. Occasionally, lawyers will find tricky or propagandistic ways to expose the jury to hearsay or popular prejudices about the trial—even if such statements are immediately stricken from the record by the judge.

5. Construct a set of criteria or rules that outline the boundaries teachers should respect when speaking in class on issues that may influence students' political attitudes (e.g., attitudes toward organized religion, political parties, ideologies, and government policies). You might consider this issue for all school levels: grade school, high school, college—or just the level that interests you most.

6. Construct a set of criteria or rules that outline the boundaries teachers should respect when speaking in class on issues that may influence students' social attitudes (e.g., attitudes toward family life, marriage, sex, money, technology, personal rights and civil responsibilities, and voting). You might consider this issue for all school levels: grade school, high school, college—or just the level that interests you most.

7. Listen to a popular song with "hard hitting" or aggressive lyrics. Analyze the lyrics as propaganda. Can you identify any of the tactics of white, gray, or black propaganda in the song?

8. Repeat the analysis in number 7 above, but this time for a Hollywood film.

9. The next time you have a political disagreement with a friend, teacher, or relative, try later to write down what you said. Then analyze your ideas or their ideas for propagandistic content; use the propaganda features suggested earlier in this chapter: assertiveness or aggressiveness, commitment to gamesmanship or a commitment to rationality, proportionality, persuasive leadership, and ethics. The more these features apply to what was said, the more likely it is that the ideas were propagandistic.

10. Some theorists (e.g., Jacques Ellul) believe that modern society is a type of walk-in propaganda environment (referring to a society's buildings, roads, architecture, technology, consumer products, education systems, media programming, and so on). Write an essay defending or attacking this idea. How broad must the definition of propaganda be to facilitate Ellul's arguments?

QUESTIONS FOR DISCUSSION

1. Do you think that contemporary societies are more prone to using propaganda than were the societies of the last two centuries? Are some contemporary societies more prone to using propaganda than others? Consider the tactics discussed in this chapter. What evidence can you bring to bear to back up your analysis?

2. Do nightly news programs contain elements of propaganda? Consider the tactics discussed in this chapter. What evidence can you bring to bear to back up your analysis?

3. Is the current generation in Western societies better able to deal with incoming propaganda than were people of previous generations. Consider the tactics discussed in this chapter. What evidence can you bring to bear to back up your analysis?

4. The next time you use communication to influence others, will you feel *more* or *less* comfortable using propaganda after having read this chapter on propaganda? Why?

5. In your personal opinion, should contemporary artists (painters, sculptors, media-graphic artists) be encouraged by society to more often seek the traditional artistic goals of portraying truth and beauty, or should they be encouraged to influence us socially or politically? Are the visual and acoustic arts the best place for political dialogue, or are they too prone to propaganda?

Notes

1. Philip Taylor, *Munitions of the Mind* (Manchester, UK: Manchester University Press, 1995), 19–48.

2. Taylor, *Munitions of the Mind*, 133–44.

3. J. A. C. Brown, *Techniques of Persuasion: From Propaganda to Brainwashing* (Baltimore: Penguin, 1963), 9–36.

4. Leonard Doob, *Propaganda: Its Psychology and Technique* (New York: Henry Holt, 1935), 88–90.

5. Charles Larson, *Persuasion: Reception and Responsibility* (Belmont, CA: Wadsworth, 1998), 339–40.

6. Taylor, *Munitions of the Mind*, 208–48; Garth Jowett and Victoria O'Donnell, *Propaganda and Persuasion* (Thousand Oaks, CA: Sage, 1999), 12–15.

7. Jowett and O'Donnell, *Propaganda and Persuasion*, 5–11.

8. Hugh Rank, *The Pep Talk: How to Analyze Political Language* (Park Forest, IL: Counter-Propaganda Press, 1984), 7–66.

9. Propagandists often "cherry pick" alternatives that help make their case look good (e.g., comparing an easy-to-use liquid stain-remover to the old-fashioned way of hand scrubbing a garment on a metal board).

10. People often get away with comparing "apples to oranges." For example, you might argue that a farm-subsidy bill fifty years ago saved families from bankruptcies and that the one you propose today will do the same. If the beneficiaries of fifty years ago were mostly at-risk small families but the beneficiaries of today are large farming industries, you may have a false comparison—the families of fifty years ago may have needed saving, but the farm industries may just want the subsidy for increased profits.

11. Robert Conquest, *Harvest of Sorrow* (New York: Oxford University Press, 1985), 106–7.

12. Competitive gamesmanship involving gray propaganda is different from the competition that occurs in persuasive debates or argumentation, to the extent that dishonest or misleading techniques are used in gray propaganda.

13. Cf. Robert Jackall, ed., *Propaganda* (New York: New York University Press, 1995).

14. Historically, these two terms have been especially used by the military to distinguish, for example, between tactical bombing (that helps win ground battles) and strategic bombing of factories and rail lines (that helps win wars).

15. As in the game of chess, some campaign strategists may favor a strong defense (win through endurance, and don't make any mistakes while probing and prodding the other side into making them), and other strategists may favor a strong offense (do the maximum to win early and decisively), while still others opportunistically switch back and forth between a strong defense and a strong offense, or steadily devote equal amounts of resources to offense and defense.

16. Nicholas J. Cull, David Culbert, and David Welch, *Propaganda and Mass Persuasion: A Historical Encyclopedia, 1500 to the Present* (Santa Barbara, CA: ABC-CLIO, 2003). In my sorting of tactics into white, gray, and black categories, I have tried not to be arbitrary, although some readers may see other ways of assigning particular items to particular categories.

17. For the Communist Party of the Soviet Union's definitions of war and peace, see Brown, *Techniques of Persuasion*, 121–22.

18. "Author of 'Free Money to Pay Your Bills' Admits There's No Free Money to Pay Your Bills," *New York State Consumer Protection Board*, www.consumer.state.ny.us/PressReleases/2004/december152004.htm (20 December 2004).

19. Brown, *Techniques of Persuasion*, 37–81.

20. Shibboleth thinking, pronounced in English "shib-uh-luth" or "shib-uh-leth," derives from a Bible story (Judges 12:5–6) in which people were screened by how they pronounced the word *shibboleth*. If they pronounced it one way (with a *shh* sound, not an *s* sound), they were known to be a Gileadite; if they pronounced it another way (with an *s* sound, not a *shh* sound), they were known to be an Ephraimite.

21. Brown, *Techniques of Persuasion*, 9–36.

22. Anthony Pratkanis and Elliot Aronson, *Age of Propaganda: The Everyday Use and Abuse of Persuasion* (New York: Henry Holt, 2001), 48–70.

23. Jowett and O'Donnell, *Propaganda and Persuasion*, 376–77.

24. Deborah Tannen, *The Argument Culture: Moving from Debate to Dialogue* (New York: Random House, 1998).

25. Brown, *Techniques of Persuasion*, 194–222.

26. Temporary mind-changing in cults may occur without the victim being incarcerated by force. But psychological incarceration may sometimes be just as effective as physical incarceration, if the victim is afraid to leave or perennially returns after leaving.

Argumentation

After reading this chapter, you will be able to:

- ◆ Distinguish between argumentation and persuasion
- ◆ Describe three types of argumentation
- ◆ Define the important parts of an argument
- ◆ Explain the importance of evidence and reasoning for arguments
- ◆ Contrast several models of argumentation
- ◆ Distinguish between syllogisms and enthymemes
- ◆ Describe common fallacies of reasoning

If thou continuest to take delight in idle argumentation thou mayest be qualified to combat with the sophists, but will never know how to live with men.

—SOCRATES

ARGUMENTATION, in its ideal form, should rely on logos to prove what the arguer believes to be true, wise, or good about something to a hypothetical audience that is reasonable, competent, and intelligent. In practice, most arguers seek to prove something to a particular audience of varying capacities. And while argumentation should not exploit ethos or pathos, it nonetheless has an obligation to be ethical, as shown in figure 5.1. But what exactly is argumentation? Consider the following class discussion:

STUDENT 1: I wore uniforms in school and I hated them; they deprive kids of the opportunity to express themselves without the school getting them to all look as if they're soldiers in some army.

STUDENT 2: Some kids who don't have money come to school and feel inferior to other kids wearing $150 pairs of sneakers; school shouldn't be a competition over clothes and jewelry.

STUDENT 3: It costs a lot of money to wear uniforms; kids grow out of them every term.

STUDENT 4: But you don't have to get up each morning and agonize over what you're going to wear that day.

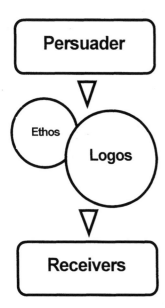

FIGURE 5.1 Argumentation through logos and ethos.

What we have in the above discussion are some of the elements of argumentation. The four individuals were in a sense testing an unstated idea that could have been formally worded in this way: "All children in public schools K–6 should be required to wear a uniform selected by the local school board." Each of the sides pro or con could marshal their ideas by researching for evidence and applying reasoning to support their respective arguments for or against the school-uniforms **proposition**. Both sides would then get several alternating time periods to make a case and to respond to each other's contentions, trying to convince an audience they are right. When the debate was over, a panel of judges (and the audience) would determine which side had made a better case on this one occasion. Communication scholar Annette Rottenberg defines argumentation in the following way:

> Argumentation is the art of influencing others, through the medium of reasoned discourse, to believe or act as we wish them to believe or act. . . . An argument is a statement or statements offering support for a claim. An argument contains three parts: the claim, the support and the warrant.[1]

She goes on to confirm our earlier contention that argumentation should give primary importance to logical appeals and that it is persuasion that can rightfully introduce the elements of ethical and emotional proofs, but she also notes that the difference between argumentation and persuasion is one of emphasis. In arguments about social policy, this difference is at times hard to measure; communication scholars Barbara Warnick and Edward Inch offer a slightly different definition:

> An argument is a set of statements in which a claim is made, support is offered for it, and there is an attempt to influence someone in a context of disagreement. . . . A claim is an expressed opinion or a conclusion that the arguer wants accepted.[2]

This second definition adds to argumentation the dimensions of competition and opinions.

The above definitions provide terms with which to analyze the debate above on whether children in elementary school should wear uniforms. One side might make a **claim** that "Wearing uniforms makes life easier in the morning." Well, does it? The **support** or evidence they might produce could be that without uniforms, you have to select different outfits each day while remembering what you wore previously. Well, so what? They might reason (here comes the **warrant**) that if you wear a uniform, you can get dressed with less time and less grief, both of which may be a valued benefit to students. The other side could then say that wearing uniforms deprives children of the opportunity to develop outfit-selection skills (claim). They observe that having to select a new outfit each day, while remembering what you wore previously, is a daily challenge (support). They reason, comparatively, that the skills learned in selecting outfits for school could be applied later in life when dressing for work (warrant). The first side might then say that children can develop outfit-selection skills when dressing on nonschool days. The second side may counter by saying that children would not feel a challenge dressing for play days. And on and on it goes.

There are three general approaches to argumentation. In one, arguers try to prove that they are right about something and that they have offered a sound argument; this is called **logical argumentation**. Here arguers try to demonstrate the truth about something. In a second approach, arguers try to help people better understand a topic. They delineate and evaluate the strengths and weaknesses of the topic's issues, and sketch the topic's applications; this is called **dialectical argumentation**. Offering reasonable opinions about a topic often occurs here. Moving from what is probable, acceptable, and reasonable to what is controversial also may occur here. A third possibility is called **rhetorical argumentation**. Here arguers try to influence a particular audience to accept positions taken on the topic. Matters of style, use of figures of speech, and message effectiveness are important considerations here. When using argumentation in actual communicative settings, as opposed to using it as an intellectual exercise, a good arguer may try to do all three of the above, but not necessarily to the same extent for each.[3]

Theorists Chaim Perelman and Lucie Olbrechts-Tyteca suggest that arguers also need to first identify what premises a given audience accepts. This identification can then be used as the starting point for making effective arguments. Forming your arguments to appeal to specific audiences is contrasted by Perelman and Olbrechts-Tyteca with analyzing what a universal audience might accept, if one could be found. This universal audience would theoretically consist of people who are intelligent, reasonable, and competent at evaluating reasonable arguments. Which should you do? Perelman and Olbrechts-Tyteca believe that the pragmatic approach is best, and recommend creating arguments for specific audiences if you are to succeed.[4] But an alternative approach might be to create the ideal case for the universal audience and then to fault specific audiences for failing to be convinced, rather than to fault the arguer for failing to accommodate those specific audiences.

Claims and Propositions

Claims are the workhorses of argumentation. In the course of a debate, the two sides will probably make many claims, some more general and some more specific. For example, in a debate about random drug-testing in the workplace, I might claim that employee drug abuse hurts company productivity. I might also claim that employee drug use can harm public safety. Someone else might claim, in opposition, that drug-testing people who have done nothing wrong is an invasion of privacy. The second side might also claim that the cost of conducting national drug-testing several times a year would be prohibitively high. Both sides would have to back up these various interlocking claims with supporting evidence and reasoning.

TABLE 5.1

Arguments and Subarguments for and against a Proposition

Affirmative Side	Negative Side
Claim 1: Productivity is hurt by worker drug-use.	Claim 1: Testing workers without cause is unfair.
Claim 2: Public safety is hurt by worker drug-use.	Claim 2: Testing workers nationwide is too costly.
Subclaim 2a: Drug-caused accidents can be deadly.	Subclaim 2a: Lawsuits alone would cost millions.

A *proposition* is broader than the many claims made during a debate. It is often used to give focus to an entire debate. In one sense, it is the most general claim in an argument or debate—a type of overriding or super-claim. It serves to define and limit, in an affirmatively stated sentence, the issues that make a debate or dispute. I can now structurally summarize the earlier mini-debate on drug-testing in the workplace. Notice in the drug-testing example, as shown in table 5.1, that in all but very simple argumentation, claims will probably be linked to each other (e.g., main claims and subclaims). The narrower subclaims serve to help develop broader main claims, while the main claims work together as equals.

Creating Claims (and Propositions)

The following applies both to the many claims made in a debate and to the overriding proposition that focuses that debate. It is important to word claims concisely. You also must define key words in the claim so that they are understood in the same way by all participants and listeners. You must then provide appropriate support for the claim. If I claim that traffic congestion downtown has increased significantly over the last ten years, I need to produce proof, perhaps in the form of traffic-flow analyses that show with comparable hard numbers what the traffic congestion was ten years ago and what it is today. I should also decide which of my claims are more important, then talk about these claims earlier in the debate and describe them with more detail. Similarly, the proposition for a debate should not be vague, ambiguous, or unnecessarily complicated. It should spark controversy, but it should not be worded in a leading way that expresses a bias (e.g., "We should do the smart thing and adopt plan A"). Debate propositions, and the lower-level claims that support propositions, answer implied questions that come in three common varieties.

Claims of Fact. A claim of fact asserts something that can turn out true or false. The claim can be about the past, present, or even the future. Claims of fact are usually inferences or conclusions because if they stated obvious facts (e.g., "The lights are on in the room we are in"), we wouldn't need to debate the issue. If I say that personal computers today outnumber typewriters, I have given a claim of fact and need to produce the numbers. If I say that I and not Christopher Columbus discovered America, I have also given a claim of fact—although an obviously untrue one. A few other examples of claims of fact:

- There are dozens of "occupations" for dogs.
- Dogs have been trained to comfort people awaiting operations in hospitals.
- Dogs can find people lost under snow or building debris.
- Dogs can find hidden bombs before they explode.

Factual claims need proof or else should be rejected.

Claims of fact that concern common knowledge need not be proven. These would include claims like "The sun rises in the east and sets in the west," "The Atlantic Ocean separates America from Europe," and "World War II ended in the 1940s." But other claims of fact may be contentious and will have to be defended with very convincing proof, claims such as "The loss of the rain forests of South America is harming the world," "Space aliens landed in Roswell, New Mexico, in 1949," and "America will still be a superpower in a hundred years." Some of the most contentious claims of fact occur when we publicly assert that something causes something else. For example, we could claim that children wearing "vanity" clothing in elementary schools causes discipline problems. Historical claims can also spark controversy, such as if I were to claim that the pilot Amelia Earhart, lost July 2, 1937, on route from Lae, New Guinea, to Howland Island, probably crashed on a small, unpopulated, Pacific Ocean island while carrying out reconnaissance for America just prior to World War II.

Claims of Policy. If I observe that dogs have so many "occupations" to fill these days, and then claim that those dogs that do work all their lives should be eligible for social security benefits, my claim would not be a claim of fact. Rather, it would be a claim of policy. While claims of fact are about what is true or false, claims of policy are about what should or should not be done. If I claim that traffic should be banned downtown, this is a claim of policy. If I claim that drug-testing should be done in the workplace, this too is about policy. When the students at the beginning of this chapter claim that the children in public schools K–6 should or should not be required to wear uniforms, this is also about a claim of policy. Claims of fact can be about the past, present, or future, but claims of policy are about the present or future.

Claims of value. These claims are about what is good or bad, worthwhile or worthless, important or unimportant. For example, we could argue over which new clothing fashions are the best. We could argue whether being a senator or being a Supreme Court justice is more prestigious. We could debate whether it is good or bad to be jealous of successful people. The previous three sentences could also be slightly reworded to formally become propositions of value. Here are examples of properly worded propositions of value: "It is wrong to allow children under sixteen to watch sexually explicit movies," "Capital punishment serves no useful purpose," and "It is unfair to the public to parole violent prisoners who may then commit additional violent crimes."

It is sometimes possible to confuse claims of policy with claims of value—if we presume that we should always do what is good (or avoid doing what is bad). The proposition "Uniforms are good for school children" is worded as a value, but in some people's minds, the proposition might imply a policy preference. However, there are many times when we might agree something would be best, but we will still not want to do it. I might agree that saving the bonus I just got from work is a wise idea (value), but nonetheless, I am using it for a trip to Cancun (policy). Sometimes we will have expedient reasons for not doing what seems best or for doing what seems worst—thus we need to make the distinction between claims of policy and claims of value.

In actual debates, a variety of claims will be made. Often a claim of policy will be defended with many claims of fact. Or one of several rival claims of fact may be argued for with a claim of value such as "More recent facts have to be given more weight." And chains of claims are often made, for example: "It will be hot today at the picnic; the perishable meats run the risk of turning bad from the heat, but an ice chest can keep things cold, and we can buy ice at the convenience store. Let's buy the ice." And changing a word or two in a claim can change its type. "Raising taxes would be fair" is a claim of value, but "Taxes should be raised" is a claim of policy.

Defining Terms

If I make the proposition that "Traffic should be banned in the government district of Washington, D.C.," I should be clear about how I define "traffic." Will it include automobiles? Trucks? Bicycles? Taxis? Limousines? Buses? Motorcycles? Emergency vehicles? Horses? Banning private cars might make sense, but banning delivery trucks or emergency vehicles would be a problem. Also, I need to define "banned." All the time? Just during rush hours? Weekends? I even need to define "government district" in terms of which streets would or would not be included. For more difficult terms, such as the term *black hole* as used by physicists, we might need an extended definition that uses a variety of techniques and takes up a paragraph or an entire essay. But the most common way to define a word is simply to describe it in a sentence:

> A brick is a unit of building or paving material, typically rectangular and about $2\frac{1}{2} \times 3\frac{3}{4} \times 8$ inches and of moist clay hardened by heat.

Sentence definitions of words often use short, better-known words to describe something by saying what it looks like, what it does, and how it is made. The definition may also give examples of it, say where it comes from, identify its synonyms, and describe how it may be categorized. However, for hard-to-understand concepts or contentious situations, we may also need to use more specialized ways of defining words.

An **etymology** gives the history of a word. For example, one dictionary says the word *persuasion* is from the Latin *persuadere*, meaning "to thoroughly advise," and *suavis*, meaning "sweet." Thus the word *persuasion* comes in part from the word *sweet*, as in "You can catch more flies with honey than with vinegar."

Negation tells us what a word does not mean. For example, the word *persuasion* does not mean using propaganda or manipulation. Or, if you mean to *save* money, you cannot spend it. And *going up* means not going down, staying in the same place, or moving sideways.

An *operational definition* defines by describing what something does, or by indicating what you can observe in order to understand something. An operational definition might define a *toaster* as "Something that warms and browns bread." This is what a toaster does. Or *improved typing* might be defined in this way: "You will type with at least 20 percent fewer typos." This is something that can be observed. This second type of operational definition is subject to differences among definers. One definer might use percentage of typos to operationally define *improved typing*, while another definer might use faster typing speed. As long as we are specific and consistent when we create operational definitions, confusion can be avoided.

Stipulation means that we will temporarily agree to define something in a particular way, as in "We will here stipulate that *driving while intoxicated* will be defined according to the laws of the State of Hawaii," or "Let us stipulate here that *freedom* shall refer to any behavior that does not harm other people or their property." Stipulation is intended for finding useful agreement about a term's meaning within a particular discussion or dispute.

Synonyms are words or terms with roughly equivalent meanings, such as *skillet* and *frying pan*, or *sundial* and *solar-shadow clock*. A synonym is the opposite of an *antonym*, which is a word or term with an opposite meaning. *Fat*, for example, is an antonym of *thin*. Antonyms are one way of using negation.

And when we say that "A tulip is a type of flower," or that "A typing course is a unit of a curriculum," we are using an *example*. Because they tend to supply detail, examples are especially useful definitions.

Supporting Your Claims with Evidence

The simplest definition for the word *evidence* is "Something that furnishes proof." According to Warnick and Inch, evidence comes in three types: (1) facts or conditions that are observable, such as whether a sewing machine is broken or not; (2) beliefs or statements accepted as true by the recipients, such as whether people think rap-music lyrics often celebrate violence; and (3) conclusions previously established, such as when I prove to you that eating-in can save bundles of money, and then go on to urge you to take a cooking class.[5] Without evidence, an arguer can only say, "I'm right, trust me." Without evidence, we live in a world of whimsy, communicative bullying, or irrationality. Let's here review the common types of evidence, ways to evaluate evidence, and the likely places to find the evidence that an audience will accept as proof of an arguer's claims.

Types of Evidence *Facts.* The most common type of evidence is the individual fact or factual report. To support a claim that watching violent television programs can cause children to become violent, you might find a psychological study done to see how such programming affected a sampling of children recruited for the experiment. Perhaps the study showed that boys were more likely to throw toys around after viewing a film that glamorized violent fighting. On a different topic, maybe facts about a new rocket engine will support a proposition on the likelihood of interplanetary travel. Or a government report on two-parent households and children's emotional health may prove helpful in a debate on divorce laws.

Testimony. Experts who know about something can give expert opinions, witnesses who have experienced something can state exactly what they observed, and anyone can give a personal opinion. In testifying for a lawsuit, a nurse might give expert testimony by telling about what injuries were treated; those who saw the accident that caused the injuries might give eyewitness testimony; and those interested in the case might post personal opinions on a website.

Statistics. There are times, such as with testimony, when words are the best evidence; but there are other times when numbers are best.[6] If I want to prove that car owners are using steering-wheel locks in greater numbers than ever before, I will perhaps use statistics that range over the last ten years. But if I walk down a street and count thirty out of sixty cars with a steering-wheel lock, I cannot say that 50 percent of car owners today use such locks. Why? Because the street I use for my study will seldom be representative of larger geographical areas.[7] I would need to randomly observe samples of cars on many streets and in many cities and towns. Nonetheless, statistics can be of great value when we are trying to show that one thing works better than others, that things have changed over time, that one thing is more numerous than others, and so on. If I want to show that one of my classes did better than the others on a midterm exam, I need to compute the average scores for all the classes that took the exam. But a statistician would then advise me to submit my data to an appropriate statistical test to judge whether any differences found are worth talking about or are just meaningless, chance fluctuations. Statistics generally should be collected by experts so that people are not misled.

Demonstrations. To prove that one computer printer is faster than others, I might perform a test in front of my audience. I might print the same document on three different printers while I time how long each takes to turn out the finished product. Lawyers sometimes try to convince a jury of something by staging a reenactment. And you might try to prove that security is lax in your workplace by walking into a restricted area without being challenged by security personnel. The power of demonstrations concerns the old adage that "Seeing is believing."

Physical evidence (artifacts). An archaeologist might try to prove that a long-dead civilization lived in a particular region of the world by showing pottery recently dug up at a site in the region associated with that society. A police investigator might show photographs of damaged door locks to prove a building was broken into recently. And a farming expert might bring in samples of extra-large vegetables to promote an exotic planting method.

Scientific evidence. Doctors often offer support for a medical diagnosis with the use of specialized blood tests, tests of heart functions, and so on. Scientists too may bolster their assertions about theories with the use of specialized tests. Even art experts may commission scientific tests to support a contention that an oil painting is the real thing or a fake.

Appeals to needs and values. Rottenberg reminds us that in addition to their use of objective evidence, arguers can also support their claims with appeals to personal needs and values. We all need interpersonal affection, job security, a sense of well-being, and the respect of others. We may also value such things as love, patriotism, fairness, peace, and wealth. Can these things be used to support a claim? Yes. For example, you might support your claim that someone should lose weight by first convincing them that their employer or possible dating partners will respond better to them after they lose the unwanted weight. Or I might claim that you should open your own business after I say, "You'll never get rich working for someone else."

Evaluating Evidence Supporting evidence needs to pass muster in a variety of ways. For example, evidence needs to be *reliable*. When you take advice on investment from a stockbroker, you probably want to know how much money the broker has on average made for clients in the past. *Expertise* is also important. Does the source of your information have credible knowledge and information relevant to the topic? I probably want my stockbroker to have a relevant advanced degree, job experience, and a current job at an established brokerage firm. Test results gathered with broken or poorly constructed test devices might also produce unreliable evidence.

Objectivity is important too in evaluating evidence. Your parents would probably be biased for or against you if they wrote you a reference letter for an employer. And asking supporters of the home football team whether their team or the visiting team is the better may not get you objective testimony. When juries are selected for a trial, the lawyers and sometimes the judge will interview the prospective jurors to see if they can objectively understand and evaluate the evidence. The *recency* of evidence can at times be important. This means you should not quote a twenty-year-old study on seatbelt compliance in your state, except to compare it with present statistics. Some topics, such as what styles of clothing people are buying now, require recent evidence. But proving that there are burial chambers in the Egyptian pyramids does not require especially recent evidence.

As we all know, in court you should tell the truth, the whole truth, and nothing but the truth. Similarly, evidence for argumentation needs to be *sufficient* to be useful. You need a balance of evidence that may cut both ways. And the best evidence suggests an appropriate completeness. If you are going to prove that certain methods of interviewing help when doing social work, how many case studies should you review? Two would not be enough, nor would it work to include only cases that support your contention. You can sometimes give too much evidence, such as may happen when you become super-enthusiastic about something. Evidence should also be *relevant* to your claims. Giving facts on what doctors believe to be true about a certain disease might not be relevant when you're describing what the general public believes about that disease. Even so, you might lose sight of the main topic and end up talking about what doctors believe as if that were what the public believes.

Finally, statistical evidence needs to be *timely*, *accurate*, and *correctly interpreted*. Statistics can be misleading if I am careless or dishonest in reporting them. How much money did Congress spend last year? If certain pet-project expense items are not included in the total, be skeptical of the final number given. I could also write a news report saying that "Four out of five students at my college had no date last weekend." Do I mean 80 percent of the college went dateless? Or do I mean that four out of the five students I interviewed in the college library at 7 p.m. Saturday night had no date? If you are the editor of the college newspaper, you had better ask some pretty skeptical questions about how I gathered my data, unless you want to create a lot of laughter among your paper's readers. And be especially careful when interpreting polls during election campaigns. Partisan pollsters sometimes report information in a biased way, perhaps by collecting more data from one side or the other in a political controversy, because such a tactic makes one side look stronger—assuming both parties have equal numbers of likely voters.

How Argumentation Works—The Big Picture

Arguers sometimes leave parts of their argument unstated; when this happens you have to put into words the unstated parts yourself. At other times the structures of arguments are convoluted and need to be parsed for analysis. Historically, there have been at least three ways to diagram the process of argumentation: (1) the general model, (2) the Toulmin model, and (3) the formal logic approach.

The General Model for Explaining Argumentation

Here is a simple argument:

> Voters have a broad, analytical set of accurate facts about the issues.
> They will make the right decision in the election.

This argument has two elements. Read it over several times and try to see which of the two is the claim and which of the two is the basic premise (or evidence). The claim is usually the more controversial of the two because it is what the arguer is asking you to accept. The claim is also often an opinion or a conclusion. In contrast, the premise (what we may just accept as true) or the evidence (what we can observe) is usually less in dispute and represents what we can perhaps take at face value, or what is the more certain of the two. Critics can also question the premise or evidence the arguer provides, saying it is not true. The claim in the above argument is that voters will make the right decision. The part that says "Voters have a broad, analytical set of accurate facts about the issues" is the evidence. Let's add the word *if* in front of "Voters have . . ." With the word *if*, our argument becomes conditional, but is still fairly similar in meaning. We can now evaluate the above argument in either its conditional form or its declarative form; perhaps we will agree with the argument, perhaps we will not. To evaluate the argument, we might ask if the evidence is relevant to the claim, if it is true, or if it seems reasonably objective.[8] In this case, the evidence does seem relative, objective, and true. But we might notice that the argument is very brief. Perhaps it is not a sufficiently developed argument?

Let us agree that our argument is not sufficiently developed and rephrase the argument as "If voters have a broad, analytical set of accurate facts about the issues, and if voters are not emotionally biased, they will usually make the right decision in the election." Here we have the original argument, but now with two premises, or pieces of evidence, and the original claim. In the version of the argument below, the bracketed words show the declarative form of the argument, and the complete statements show the conditional form of the argument:

> PREMISE/EVIDENCE 1: If [voters have a broad, analytical set of accurate facts about the issues],
>
> PREMISE/EVIDENCE 2: [and] if [voters are not emotionally biased],
>
> CLAIM: [they will] usually [make the right decision in the election].

It is also possible to make an argument where there is more than one claim, rather than more than one premise, as in "Because it's a warm sunny day on the boulevard, storekeepers will make money today, and strollers will have a good time." Parsing the ideas we get:

> PREMISE/EVIDENCE: It's a warm sunny day on the boulevard.
>
> CLAIM 1: Storekeepers will make money today.
>
> CLAIM 2: Strollers will have a good time.

It is also possible to create an argument with numerous claims and premises. Lastly, when you have more than one premise supporting your claim, the premises can work independently of each other or can work in a dependent way. For example you could say, "Work can be fun and work can bring in money; so get a job." Here the independent premises imply two separate arguments and do not need each other. Or you could say, "The cat is sleeping on an empty bookshelf, and the dog is barking at nothing in particular; maybe they'll get into a spat." Here you have dependent bits of evidence for one argument, both of which are needed for the claim to make sense.

The Toulmin Model for Explaining Argumentation

In writing his classic text *The Uses of Argument*, communication theorist Stephen Toulmin was concerned with a question that had not received much attention in the study of logic before he thought to address it: What is the relation of formal logic to the everyday practice of making good arguments? To answer this question requires defining the nature of logic. Toulmin reviewed the standard approaches to characterizing the nature of logic and came to reject many of them. He rejected seeing logic as a type of mathematics; he rejected seeing logic, from a psychological point of view, as the study of rational versus pathological thinking in the individual; and he also rejected seeing logic from a sociological point of view where logic is the study of the habits of groups of people and can be rational or pathological. Rather, logic for Toulmin was more concerned with the soundness of the claims we make—the solidity of the grounds we use to support them—and with the sort of case we present in defense of our claims. Logic is generalized jurisprudence (the rightful and correct application of the law in court), according to Toulmin. Toulmin also notes that there is one special virtue in the parallel between logic and jurisprudence:

> It helps to keep in the centre of the picture the critical function of the reason. The rules of logic may not be tips or generalisations: they none the less apply to men and their arguments—not in the way that laws of psychology or maxims of method apply, but rather as the standards of achievement which a man, in arguing, can come up to or fall short of, and by which his arguments can be judged.

In pursuing this line of thought, Toulmin selects six terms with which to analyze an argument, as shown in figure 5.2. This set includes more terms than we used in reviewing the general model above. At least two things have happened. One is that things that were left as unlabeled parts of the argument in the general model have now become labeled parts in the Toulmin model. Also, what were simply premises or evidence in the general model can now be divided into more specific things, giving us more precision. Let's take a closer look at Toulmin's terms.[9]

Basic Terms of the Toulmin Model *Data.* For Toulmin, data is a broad concept that refers to the grounds for an argument, whether that data takes the form of (1) observable evidence, (2) a general premise or belief accepted by an audience, or (3) a related argument that was proved previously in the message. If I say, "We only sold twelve burial plots this year," we now have the data part of an argument (observable evidence, in this instance). An assertion like "The magazine *Seventeen* appeals to young women" would also be an example of data, because it offers a premise that many people would accept. Or I could give a data statement by saying, "We know the butler didn't do it." This would be data if I had already proved to my

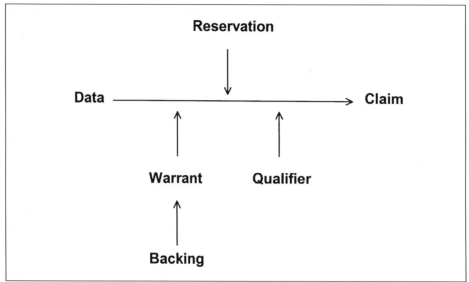

FIGURE 5.2 Six terms coined by Stephen Toulmin for analyzing arguments.

audience earlier in my summation that the butler had an unshakable alibi. Any one of the three above statements could serve as the data for a claim: "Let's declare bankruptcy—we've sold only twelve plots"; "Since *Seventeen* appeals to young women—let's advertise youth-market body scents there"; "We know the butler didn't do it—therefore you did it."

Warrant. Warrants provide the reasoning or linkage between the data and the eventual claim. Warrants tell us how or why the data supports the claim. Let's start with the data part of an argument: "We know the butler didn't do it." Now let's add the claim: "Therefore you did it." And last we will add the warrant: "No one else but you could have done it [eaten the soup] because there were just two possible suspects at the time in the dining room." Sometimes arguers leave out the warrant, as we did with our examples of the general model above, because arguers believe audiences can supply a warrant on their own. Warrants can take different approaches to linking the data to the claim. I could claim that my company's current Hollywood film "looks like a flop," and in offering data could say that "This weekend's gross receipts for the film were at the bottom of the current releases list." I could then give this warrant: "We want to make money not lose it; a low gross doesn't even cover our costs." Here I would have used a warrant based on a human value—profit in this case. If I leave out the last statement, I am assuming that you will know what I mean without stating it. This would be an implied warrant. In another example, I could say, "You seem unhappy [claim]; your eyelids are sagging [data]." My implied warrant is that your eyes are a good sign of how you feel.

Claim. Toulmin's model uses this term in the same way that we have been using it. In the example above, I asserted that the weekend's gross receipts for my company's recent film looked discouraging. But perhaps you will disagree with my claim and remind me that the film in question is a very recent release, so it has had less time to attract an audience. Here you accept my data but assert your own claim, rejecting my conclusion that the low numbers signal a flop at this point in time.

Reservation. The reservation in an argument is the argument's "escape clause." Someone might claim, "It looks like rain; see those dark, ominous clouds rolling in," which is data, leaving unstated or implied the warrant that dark clouds can be a sign or even a cause of rain. To express a reservation here, our arguer might add the words "unless the wind changes direction and the clouds roll out to sea." An argument's reservation is a way of saying, "Maybe I will be wrong under certain conditions or if certain things happen." Often the word *unless* is used to express the reservation: "I have enough credits to graduate after this semester, unless I fail biology."

Qualifier. A qualifier allows the arguer to express how strong the argument is. The most common examples of qualifiers are words like *scarcely, unlikely, possibly, probably, absolutely, without doubt,* and *written in stone.* I can express the relative strength of my reasonable claim by saying, "It will probably rain this afternoon."

Backing. Backing gives additional credibility to the warrant. Say I claim the new store on Main Street will do well today, opening day, because I already see several people waiting to get in and the doors have not yet been opened for business. So far I have the claim and the data. With this argument, my warrant could be "Having people just waiting to get in is a sign of healthy interest in the store." But if I felt that my warrant was not sufficient to convince a doubtful listener, I could back up my warrant by also adding, "Over the years, whenever a new store opens in town, people flock in during the first few days to buy and try out offerings." The warrant's backing uses additional facts or reasoning that my listener may accept based on experience or on principles supplied by experts.

Sometimes it can be challenging to apply the general model or the Toulmin model to a particular argument you encounter. You may on some occasions incorrectly identify the parts of an argument. But you can improve your ability to parse arguments if you are persistent and do not expect all arguments to yield to easy analysis. You can also go to the sources I have used to get a much more complete explanation of how argumentation works. Let's move next to what Rottenberg says about types of warrants, as these may help us see the logic underlying many arguments.

Types of Warrants Annette Rottenberg identifies seven types of warrants, and it will be helpful to discuss each one in turn.

Authority. These warrants usually explain that someone or something is assumed to be accurate as a result of their reputation, job, or function. Typically an argument that uses an authority warrant goes something like this: "I claim Rub-A-Dub will win the fifth race today. I know for a fact that several jockeys have said Rub-A-Dub is the best horse in the race." No warrant is given here, but obviously the arguer assumes listeners will provide an authority warrant something like this: "Jockeys are knowledgeable sources about race horses." Another example of an argument that uses an authority warrant would be "The American Medical Association recommends that you exercise frequently." Here not only is the authority warrant implied—that the American Medical Association should know what they are talking about—but the claim is also unstated. If this is a campaign to get you to start jogging, the implied claim may be "You should take their advice."

Generalization. This is sometimes called *inductive reasoning.* Say you're collecting signatures door-to-door to promote a change in a local law. You begin trying to predict who will sign and who will refuse. Perhaps you notice that people with toys on their porches are more likely to sign. You conclude that parents of young children find your proposal more desirable than people who are apparently not parents. The unstated generalization warrant here is that when something like this happens frequently, we may have found a general principle of human nature.[10] This form of reasoning assumes that we have picked a large enough sample of things from which to generalize and that we did not ignore exceptions.

Sign. This reasoning rests on a belief that one thing is a reliable indicator of something else. In *Hamlet*, a character says, "The lady doth protest too much, methinks."[11] If you use an altered version of this line to criticize someone, you make a subtle accusation that the person described feels differently than claimed. The sign warrant here is that when people contest something with greater emotion than seems reasonable, they may be misrepresenting their true motivations. Another sign warrant is implied in the statement "You have been sneezing a lot since you woke up this morning; you may be coming down with a cold."

Cause and effect. These warrants assert that something has the power to determine something else. They are commonly used in legal, scientific, or political arguments. Some examples are "You slipped on the ice for a good reason; the wet pavement was getting colder. When water drops below 32° Fahrenheit, water will freeze"; "You got caught because of an oversight: you didn't wipe the gun clean. Picking up the gun left fingerprints on the handle"; and "We have a higher unemployment rate because of higher interest rates. Higher interest rates suppress new business start-ups, and fewer new businesses means fewer new jobs." These types of warrants can flow from cause to effect or from effect to cause. Here is a labeled example of an argument with a cause–effect warrant:

CLAIM: Subsidizing people who lead counterproductive lifestyles may make their rehabilitation less likely.

DATA: Financial subsidy reinforces and conditions existing behavior.

WARRANT: People are shaped [effect] by psychological reinforcement and social conditioning [cause].

BACKING: Many textbooks on psychology say so.

RESERVATION: Unless the person feels guilty about taking help.

QUALIFIER: The word *may* in the claim

But as Rottenberg notes, cause–effect and effect–cause arguments are often more complicated than a simple outline like the one above suggests. Effects often have multiple causes, and causes may have multiple effects. Sometimes causes and effects are chained in a series.

Comparison. When using a comparison, you compare details about two things that are members of the same category, such as two countries, two vegetables, two leaders, two laws. You claim that what is true of the first must be also true of the second.

CLAIM: America should possibly adopt socialized medicine.

DATA: Many countries of Europe have adopted socialized medicine.

WARRANT: What works for Europeans will work for Americans [comparison].

BACKING: People in the West are much the same these days.

RESERVATION: Unless socialized medicine proves unpopular with voters.

QUALIFIER: The word *possibly* in the claim

Analogy. Unlike comparison, analogy assumes only a resemblance between two things on some issues; the two things may be of different categories, such as a country and a city, police and social workers, a vegetable and a new business, a person and a computer.

> DATA: Like artists, teachers don't want a boss telling them what to create and how and when.

> WARRANT: For creative human activities such as artist communities and schools, a heavy chain of command is stifling.

Obviously the strength of this argument rests on the strength of the analogy between a school administration and a community of artists. Critics of the above analogy may complain, however, that the arguer is comparing "apples to oranges."

Values. These warrants come from what people want and like. An example of a value warrant is in the argument "Take Professor X for Statistics 101; it's an easy A." The assumption here is that students will supply the value warrant that getting a high grade for little effort is superior to working hard for a possibly lower grade but learning something useful. A similar claim might be "Don't stay home by yourself tonight—like some hermit." The implied warrant here uses a common human need to suggest that the listener should be around other people to avoid loneliness. The implied data here is that the listener is planning to stay home.

The Formal Logic Approach for Explaining Argumentation

Argumentation goes back to antiquity when *syllogisms* and **enthymemes** were first identified. Using the formal logic approach, we reduce arguments to their essences and then organize them into three elements: a major premise, a minor premise, and a conclusion.[12] A syllogism expresses all three of these elements, while an enthymeme expresses just one or two.

Syllogisms A syllogism makes an argument starting with its major premise. It then adds its minor premise—which addresses one part of the major premise—and then reaches a conclusion, which addresses the other part of the major premise. Perhaps the most famous syllogism is "All men are mortal [destined to die]; Socrates is a man; therefore Socrates is mortal." The major premise, "All men are mortal," seems indisputable. That "Socrates is a man" also seems a reasonable assertion—and is the minor premise. Therefore, "Socrates is mortal" is the conclusion. This syllogism is called a **categorical syllogism** because it establishes that Socrates is in the category of men and that men are in the category of mortals. If the phrase "all men" were changed to "some men," the syllogism would fail. But "Some women are rich; Jane is a woman; therefore Jane may be rich" is a valid syllogism because of its use of the qualifiers *some* and *may be.*

Another example of a categorical syllogism might be "All the houses on Sixth Street were built in 1980; my house is on Sixth Street; therefore my house was built in 1980." This syllogism works if both the major premise and the minor premise are true. But note in figure 5.3 that some logical arguments may only seem to be valid. Take the argument "Over the years, all horses that have won the Bayview Race have eaten Winner's Circle oats [note that the

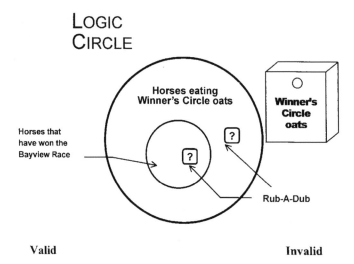

FIGURE 5.3 Valid and invalid arguments about Rub-A-Dub illustrated with circles.

smaller circle in the figure is entirely inside the larger circle];[13] Rub-A-Dub has eaten Winner's Circle oats; therefore Rub-A-Dub has won the Bayview Race." The problem here is that though we know all past winners have eaten Winner's Circle oats, Rub-A-Dub could be a winning horse or a losing horse that also happened to eat Winner's Circle oats. Rub-A-Dub is represented in figure 5.3 with two question marks. If Rub-A-Dub has won the race, Rub-A-Dub's arrow will point into the smaller circle, and if Rub-A-Dub has never won the race, Rub-A-Dub's arrow will point into the larger circle.[14] If Rub-A-Dub had never eaten Winner's Circle oats, the arrow would point outside the two circles.

Another type of syllogism is called the **disjunctive syllogism**. In this form, you as the arguer mention two possibilities in the major premise and then say in your minor premise that one of those possibilities is false. Your conclusion then declares that the remaining possibility is the true one. For example you might say, "In chess, one may play either the white pieces or the black pieces; my opponent has the white pieces; therefore I must be playing the black pieces." In another example I might say, "Since you are a player, you must be on either our team or the visiting team; I know you are not on our team; therefore you must be on the visiting team." But be careful with arguments that seem like disjunctive syllogisms, arguments like "Either you're with us or you're against us. Since you have not supported our candidate for office, you must be against us." In this case, there is the possibility that the listener supports neither candidate. In fact, there are very few pure disjunctive syllogisms in the world.[15] Yes, you can have only male or only female genes, and you can only be pregnant or not pregnant, and you can only be alive or dead, but other examples of disjunctives often require game rules like chess and football. So be wary of illusionary disjunctive syllogisms that seem to say something with a certainty they cannot claim.

A third category of syllogism is the *conditional* or *if-then* type.[16] In the example below, we assert an if-then condition in our major premise.

> MAJOR PREMISE: If public schools don't teach your children well [this is called the antecedent], then you should send them to private school [the *consequent*].

We then use a minor premise to affirm that the "if" part of the major premise is true.

> MINOR PREMISE: Public School no. 9 is failing miserably.

Now we argue in our conclusion that the "then" part of the major premise should be accepted.

> CONCLUSION: You should send your kids to Hillside Private School.

But if the listener decides to deny the "if" part (the antecedent) of our argument, this does not mean they have validly disproved the "then" part (the consequent). Maybe you say to a friend, "If you can't control your spending, you should consult a budgeting expert." Then after an inquiry into your friend's spending habits, you might say, "Apparently I was wrong, you can control your spending, therefore you don't need to consult a budgeting expert." Here you have created invalid reasoning. Even if your friend can control his or her spending habits, maybe he or she still should consult with a budgeting expert—perhaps to learn about handling money so that it grows through investment. In other words, there may be more than one antecedent that can justify accepting a consequent, which in this case was the consulting with a budget expert. Effects (or consequents) often have more than one cause (or antecedent), and causes can often have more than one effect.

If your premises can hold up to scrutiny and if your logic is without fault, you have concluded an argument that has both *truth* and *validity*. Validity relies on general rules of reasoning, and truth relies on whether claims can be objectively substantiated. So if your claims are faulty, even though you've reasoned correctly, your argument has no truth—though you have at least preserved its validity, for whatever consolation you can find in that. And perhaps in an odd way you might reason incorrectly but luckily arrive at a likely conclusion, perhaps because your claims were at least correct. So when analyzing or creating an argument, you must evaluate (1) the truth of its premises, (2) the validity of its reasoning, and (3) the likeliness of its conclusion.

Enthymemes Enthymemes are special types of syllogisms, and they are very commonly used in reasoned discourse and persuasion because they are effective. An enthymeme is a syllogism that leaves one or both of its premises unstated so that the audience can supply the unstated premises for themselves. One way to create an enthymeme is to assert something and then use a subordinate conjunction such as *because* or *as* or *since* to add something to support your claim.[17] For example, a beer ad might say, "Drink Miller Lite because it has fewer calories." The ad lets the audience, or the receivers, supply the reason why fewer calories are a good thing. For many people in the modern world, keeping their weight down is considered a good thing. So they will understand the argument as "It is sometimes good to consume food and beverages that are low in calories; Miller Lite is one of those nice products that are lower in calories; therefore buy and drink Miller Lite." This is a *categorical enthymeme* because it encapsulates related things in a nested way: the world of good things includes things low in calories, which in turn include Miller Lite.

Sometimes enthymemes (liberally defined) may leave two premises unstated, as with the following conclusion: "You should ideally get an Internet cable connection." For this conclusion, the unstated major premise might be "The speed of your Internet connection is the most important consideration." The unstated minor premise might be "Cable connections are faster than dial-up ones." For this disjunctive-like enthymeme to work, listeners must be familiar with Internet connections and how they're made. Interestingly, the enthymeme "You should get a dial-up connection" might also work well if the listener values low cost rather than speed, and if its major premise is "The cost of a your Internet connection is the most important consideration."

Identifying Faulty Arguments

Warnick and Inch sort faulty arguments into the following types: (1) **fallacies** of faulty reasoning, (2) fallacies of grounding, (3) fallacies of misdirection, and (4) fallacies of language use.[18] Let's take a closer look at each of these.

Fallacies of Faulty Reasoning

Fallacies of faulty reasoning occur when we make poor inferences in our arguments. For example, we could make a *false analogy* or comparison if we compare government-program funding cuts with cuts in scheduled funding increases. The false analogy might sound something like this: "In this time of economic recovery, all our programs are getting increased budgets; so why are we cutting program X?" If program X's cuts are actual ones, that is, if this year less will be spent on program X, allowing for inflation, than was spent last year, then we have a good comparison. But if program X's budget will increase—but just not as much as previously thought—we have a misleading analogy (between program X and programs with actual cuts). Another example might be this: "France has lower electricity rates than does the United States. Why can't people in the United States have similar low costs for energy?" Since France gets nearly 60 percent of its electrical power from nuclear energy (America's percentage is much lower), we have a false comparison with respect to the energy infrastructures of the two countries.

Hasty generalization occurs when we use too small a sample in making generalizations. If I say, "Two people in Mudville were rude to me—what a rude town," I am guilty of a hasty generalization. I can easily find two rude people anywhere in the world.

False cause is another type of bad reasoning. If you spill a glass of soda at a casino and then play a slot machine and win fifty dollars, you will be making a mistake if you keep spilling soda in hopes of winning again. This is a post hoc error that assumes that because something precedes something else, it was the cause of the second event. A false-cause error can also occur when an event has multiple causes, and we pick just one as the true cause.

A *slippery slope* argument assumes without evidence that a certain event will inevitably be the first step toward something else not wanted. I may be worried that as a teacher I will be asked to work more days in the year. So if my college asks its faculty to extend the semester by one week for this semester, I may worry that what happens this semester will soon happen every semester. Sometimes an interest group will oppose something not because they are really against it, but because they fear the slippery slope effect. To answer a slippery slope argument, you can say, "Yes, every new trend must have a first time, but there also are many one-time-only events. What's the evidence in this case as to whether the slippery slope effect will occur or not?"

Fallacies of Grounding

These fallacies provide faulty support for claims. *Begging the question* occurs when a definition masquerades as an argument, or when "the premises include the claim that the conclusion is true or, directly or indirectly, assume that the conclusion is true."[19] The statement "My salary has fallen because I'm not making as much money as I used to" begs the question of exactly why my salary is falling. "We believe they made false statements because what they said were lies" also begs the question.

A *non sequitur* occurs when what we say does not make sense, as in "There will be one hour more daylight tomorrow because tonight we switch to standard time and set the clocks one hour behind." This may sound true to some, but it does not follow. Likewise if I were to say, "To build a dam made of concrete and steel requires the permission of all within its planned domain: the hills and the valleys, the flowers and the trees, the squirrels and the bees." This may support a whimsical argument as part of a poem, but if used in wording an environmental law, it is a non sequitur.

Fallacies of Misdirection

These fallacies ask an audience to look in the wrong places to understand an argument. Say that arguers want to legalize nude bathing at beaches and the opposing side says, "Don't listen to what they say, they've just been indicted for insurance fraud." This is an *ad hominem* argument. With this fallacy you do not deal with your adversary's contentions, but rather with your adversary's character. In other words, you throw irrelevant "mud" at your adversary. With an *ad populum* argument, you might argue that someone should buy a cell phone because millions of people have done so already. But even if millions of people have bought cell phones, it might not make sense for this particular person to buy one. Similarly you could argue that I should do something because I have always done it; this is called an *appeal to tradition*.

One of the most popular ways to "spin" a political dispute is to use the *straw-man* fallacy. With the straw-man fallacy, you misrepresent what the other side says—that is, you weaken their arguments when describing these arguments to an audience. A politician might say of an opponent, "He wants to build a twelve-foot-high fence around the country for us to hide behind. It will cost zillions of dollars and won't work." If what the opponent actually said was "We need to set up checkpoints to see that criminal activities do not occur in selected border areas," we have a straw-man fallacy.

Fallacies of Language Use

When we *equivocate*, we exploit ambiguities in word usage. As a politician, I might say, "I would be the last person to vote this bill down." Do I mean I will never ever vote against this bill? Or do I mean I will vote yes, but only up to a point, and for instance, if it looks like the bill will not survive and I see no political expediency in being the only yes voter, I will change sides? If you ask someone, "Did you take money from that contractor?" and the person answers, "I've done nothing illegal here," is the person saying the money was taken or not? Or, say that you ask a group of acquaintances whether you can count on their support, and they answer, "Do we seem like people who would leave you in the lurch?" Here your acquaintances leave you to infer a one-word answer to their perhaps rhetorical question; but is that implied answer yes or no? *Amphibole* is similar to equivocation, but relies more on ambiguity in the grammatical structure of a statement: "When we compare the unpopularity of raising taxes with the inconvenience of canceling after-school programs, well we'll just have to do it." Do which?

Chaim Perelman has also described what he calls "quasi-logical arguments," which can at times be tricky because a casual reading may make them seem to be logical arguments when they are not. One form of a quasi-logical argument is the "transitivity" argument, which may seem like a syllogism, but is more like an enthymeme. Here's an example of this type of argument: "As a hotel on the boardwalk in Casino City, the Golden Goose certainly offers gambling." We could compare this transitivity, quasi-logical argument to a full-fledged syllogism:

MAJOR PREMISE: All hotels on the boardwalk in Casino City offer gambling.

MINOR PREMISE: The Golden Goose Hotel is on the boardwalk in Casino City.

CONCLUSION: The Golden Goose Hotel certainly offers gambling.

But in quasi-logical form, the argument "As a hotel on the boardwalk in Casino City, the Golden Goose certainly offers gambling" leaves unstated the assertion that all hotels on the boardwalk in Casino City offer gambling. If not all of the hotels do, then the Golden Goose might, or might not, offer gambling.[20]

Chapter in Retrospect

VIGNETTE 1 **The Big Lie**

Chapter 4 features a quote attributed to Joseph Goebbels: "If you tell a lie big enough and keep repeating it, people will eventually come to believe it."

MAJOR PREMISE (and unstated warrant): People do not normally expect their leaders to tell outrageous lies.

MINOR PREMISE: If you tell a lie big enough and keep repeating it . . .

CONCLUSION: People will eventually come to believe it.

There may be some truth to this argument. Besides the unstated warrant (People do not normally expect their leaders to tell outrageous lies), there is also an unstated backing (that such behavior is ever justified) underlying the unstated warrant.

The nature of the above quote also has something to do with what political news analysts refer to as "horse-race" analysis versus "issues" analysis. With horse-race analysis, the news report tells us about tactics. Is a specific line of political attack working, or is it being ignored by the public? Have the political effects of a scandal been neutralized, or are they still in play? Does admitting to be both for and against something help or hinder in the polls? With issues analysis, however, the news report can ask whether a stated policy preference is good or bad. Will decriminalizing a certain activity help or harm society? Is a proposed policy flawed or not? Goebbels's quote implicitly uses a horse-race approach to justify the telling of big lies. It avoids the issue that telling big lies is a bad way to govern or to attempt to gain control of government. The tactic of telling big lies helped the Nazis justify and commit heinous war crimes.

VIGNETTE 2 Thoughts of Osama's Deputy

The following quote has been attributed to Osama bin Laden's top deputy Ayman al-Zawahiri:

> Bush, reinforce your security measures. The Islamic nation which sent you the New York and Washington brigades has taken the firm decision to send you successive brigades to sow death and aspire to paradise.[21]

On the surface, this quote seems to offer advice, albeit unfriendly. Its unstated warrant is something like "What we have already done we can and will do again." But why give advice to your enemy on preparing for an attack that you obviously wish will be successful? Perhaps because the form of the statement (advice) is different from the function of the statement (taunting threat). The statement also contains several rhetorical sleights of hand.

For example, it links the notion of "to sow death" with "aspire to paradise." Who can fault anyone for aspiring to paradise? Who then can fault these people for making the firm decision to sow death in order to get to paradise? God must then want the people that Zawahiri speaks for to kill Americans, if by doing so they will get to paradise. The quote also contrasts the powers of bin Laden's "brigades" with America's power as vaguely defined in "security measures." The brigades will bring about destruction, and the American response will be to "reinforce . . . security measures." But how can the mere reinforcing of security measures stop the "successive brigades" that have been successful once and will supposedly be so again?

In addition, the quote is an act of psychological warfare. It seeks to justify terrorism and seeks to create the impression of invincibility. It expresses irreversible resolve. It taunts and it hates. It also portrays a political movement, Wahhabism, as a nation. Most importantly, it treats two different things as if they were the same: (1) the duplicitous and intentionally indiscriminate mass-murder of civilians, and (2) armed conflicts between professionally led, uniformed, armed, trained, and psychologically prepared combatants. Some in the West may dismiss the above quote as fanciful rhetoric. But to others not of the West, such a quote may be a compelling call to violent action.

Summary and Conclusions

Argumentation is the most rational and gentle of the various means to communicative influence, and the term *argumentation* overlaps in meaning with the term *persuasion*. Unlike persuasion, however, argumentation does not usually try to persuade with emotional arguments or with persuasive information about the sender's general credentials or characteristics. Most argumentation seeks to prove things with the use of evidence and reasoning. Argumentation seeks to persuade in a valid manner, or to identify what is true about something, or to educate people with clever questions and answers. Argumentation often tries to do all three of these, but perhaps with more emphasis on one than the others. At the root of argumentation is the argument, which makes a claim, including evidence and reasoning to show how the evidence supports the claim. Claims can assert a fact, or what policy should be enacted, or what is a good or bad value. Claims in turn are supported by evidence (facts, premises listeners already believe, or things proven by the arguer earlier in the argument). Reasoning, sometimes in the form of a warrant, serves to show exactly how evidence supports claims. A proposition is broader than a claim, and often serves to define or limit the issues in an argument. To analyze or create arguments, one can use the general model, which requires the identification of a premise and a conclusion. One can also create or analyze an argument by using the six parts of the Toulmin model: claim, data, warrant, backing for the warrant, qualifier, and reservation. Or one can use the formal logic approach. For many centuries, logicians have analyzed and created arguments, often using logic circles, or syllogisms and enthymemes. Good argumentation requires good preparation in the form of locating and using believable evidence. Nonetheless, argumentation may fail to truly prove something if common fallacies turn a good argument into a faulty one. And in addition to logical arguments, there are quasi-logical arguments, which can at times be tricky because a casual reading may make them seem to be logical arguments when they are not.

KEY TERMS

backing	enthymeme	reservation
categorical syllogism	etymology	rhetorical argumentation
claim	fallacies	stipulation
data	logical argumentation	support
dialectical argumentation	proposition	warrant
disjunctive syllogism	qualifier	

REVIEW QUESTIONS

1. Why are ethos and pathos less well suited to argumentation than logos?
2. How is support for a claim different from a warrant?
3. What are the differences between logical, dialectical, and rhetorical approaches to argumentation?
4. What is the difference between a proposition and a claim?
5. What are some criteria for evaluating evidence?
6. How is the Toulmin model of argumentation different from the general model?
7. Are enthymemes and syllogisms similar? How? Are they different? How?
8. How are fallacies of grounding different from fallacies of misdirection?

SUGGESTED PROJECTS AND ACTIVITIES

1. Create an argument about why you should be awarded $10,000 from your local community; use Toulmin terminology for your case.
2. Select a newspaper editorial and outline its claims, evidence, and stated or implied warrants.
3. Intentionally create several arguments that use the fallacies of faulty reasoning, grounding, misdirection, or language use.

QUESTIONS FOR DISCUSSION

1. Is there a market for actual argumentation and debate on television? Why? Why not?
2. Can you imagine a game-show format for television built around argumentation?

Notes

1. Annette Rottenberg, *Elements of Argument: A Text and Reader*, 7th ed. (Boston: Bedford/St. Martin's, 2003), 9–12.

2. Barbara Warnick and Edward Inch, *Critical Thinking and Communication: The Use of Reason in Argument*, 4th ed. (Boston: Allyn and Bacon, 2002), 6–10.

3. Joseph Wenzel, "Three Perspectives on Argument: Rhetoric, Dialectic and Logic," in *Perspectives on Argumentation: Essays in Honor of Wayne Brockriede*, ed. Robert Trapp and Janice Schuetz (Prospect Heights, IL: Waveland, 1990), 9–26; also see Chaim Perelman, *The Realm of Rhetoric*, trans. William Kluback (Notre Dame, IN: University of Notre Dame Press, 1982), 1–9; Warnick and Inch, *Critical Thinking and Communication*, 12–15. This distinction between dialectical, rhetorical, and logical approaches to argumentation should not be confused with the notion of dialectical argumentation discussed by Finocchiaro, who stresses the "dialogue" nature of dialectical arguments; see Maurice Finocchiaro, "Dialectics, Evaluation, and Argument," *Informal Logic* 23, no. 1 (Winter 2003): 19–49.

4. Chaim Perelman and Lucie Olbrechts-Tyteca, *The New Rhetoric: Treatise on Argumentation*, trans. John Wilkinson and Purcell Weaver (Notre Dame, IN: University of Notre Dame Press, 1969).

5. Warnick and Inch, *Critical Thinking and Communication*, 74–103.

6. Experts sometimes distinguish between *descriptive* statistics and *inferential* statistics. If you were to poll people before an election to try to establish who would win, you would be using inferential statistics because your sampling of probable voters would allow you to infer how people would actually

vote the next day. But if after the election you were to summarize how the various groups in your community actually voted, this summary would illustrate descriptive statistics because you would now be able to describe exactly how voters did vote.

7. In fact, I tried this experiment on my street but had to discard the data when I was reminded that the county district attorney's office is also situated on the same street—thus, law enforcement officers frequently park there. These individuals may not be representative of the county's general population with respect to concern for auto theft.

8. For example, the observation that "Voters have eaten lots of ice cream lately" would not be relevant, while the observation that "Mississippi voters always know best" would not be objective.

9. Stephen Toulmin, *The Uses of Argument* (Cambridge: Cambridge University Press, 2003), 1–10, 11–40, 87–100.

10. In other cases, a generalization might be that we have found a principle about the physical nature of things.

11. William Shakespeare, *Hamlet*, act 3, scene 2.

12. It may not always be easy or possible to translate all arguments into syllogistic form.

13. If some winners of the Bayview Race eat Winner's Circle oats and some do not eat this brand of oats, then the circle showing the winning horses would be shown partly inside the larger circle and partly outside of it.

14. Stating the Rub-A-Dub arguments in the negative can alter the arguments' validity. For example, the invalid version of the argument shown in figure 5.3 becomes valid if we state the argument in the negative: ". . . Rub-A-Dub does not eat Winner's Circle oats; therefore Rub-A-Dub has not won the Bayview Race." In other words, if all winners eat the oats, then a non-eater is a non-winner. And notice that the valid version of the argument shown in figure 5.3 becomes invalid when we state this in the negative: ". . . Rub-A-Dub has not won the Bayview Race; therefore Rub-A-Dub does not eat Winner's Circle oats." This is invalid because there are horses that eat Winner's Circle oats but do not win the race.

15. While you can claim neutrality on issues of, say, future foreign policy, a persuader might make the case that when your country needs you after a war has begun, being neutral is not good citizenship, although it is not as bad as rooting for or helping the enemy—which of course would be treasonous behavior.

16. Related to the conditional syllogism is the quasi-logical argument called *reciprocity*. The difference is that reciprocity arguments must state a reciprocal relationship between two things in the first premise (e.g., "Begging and charity are two halves of the same thing"). Then the claim asserts that the symmetry between the two things requires that we not, in this example, consider begging a crime but consider charity a virtue ("If it's okay to give to charity, it should be okay to beg"). The weakness of this argument may concern the asserted reciprocity or symmetry. That is, one can give to charity without waiting for another to beg, and begging can be an infringement that the potential charity-giver does not want; see Warnick and Inch, *Critical Thinking and Communication*, 114–15.

17. L. Kip Wheeler, web.cn.edu/kwheeler/enthymeme_checklist.html (3 February 2005; permission to quote is granted for nonprofit, educational, and student reproduction). Wheeler offers five criteria for stating an enthymeme: (1) Can you state it in a single sentence? (2) Does that single sentence contain (a) a clause that presents your argument—a thesis; (b) a clause that presents a reason to support your argument; and is it (c) connected together by a word like *because*, *since*, *so*, or some other subordinate conjunction? (3) Does the clause that presents a reason use a shared assumption—a statement with which even a hostile audience might agree and one that overlaps logically with the first statement? (4) Is the clause that presents your argument one that answers a question at issue? In other words, is there anyone who disagrees and takes the opposite stance? (5) Is it precise? Does it avoid vague terms that sound good and mean nothing?

18. Warnick and Inch, *Critical Thinking and Communication*, 135–60.

19. Michael Labossiere, "Fallacy: Begging the Question," The Nizkor Project, www.nizkor.org/features/fallacies/begging-the-question.html (9 February 2005). As an example, consider the following exchange:

> INTERVIEWER: Your résumé looks impressive, but I need another reference.
> BILL: Jill can give me a good reference.
> INTERVIEWER: Good. But do I know that Jill is trustworthy?
> BILL: Certainly. I can vouch for her.

20. Cf. Perelman, *The Realm of Rhetoric*, 53–80.

21. Muslim American Society, "Al-Qaeda Taunts Bush, Attacks France," citing a report by Agence France-Presse, 24 February 2004, www.masnet.org/news.asp?id=989 (22 April 2006); see also a transcript reported in the *New York Times*, 10 September 2004, A1, although with an incorrect date given for the Zawahiri statement. Date was corrected in the 11 September 2004 edition in an editor's note.

Ethics and Deception

Action indeed is the sole medium of expression for ethics.

—JANE ADDAMS

Relativity applies to physics, not ethics.

—ALBERT EINSTEIN

A man without ethics is a wild beast loosed upon this world.

—ALBERT CAMUS

E RELY ON the forces of socialization, parental supervision, and well-run schools to get children to behave well. But to get adults to behave well, we rely on the additional powers of enacted laws and social pressure in the form of moral standards and a sense of ethics. The word *ethics* derives from Aristotle's notion of ethos. Ethics refers to whether the sender has acted honestly, with goodwill, and without taking unfair advantage in a situation. There are times when laws work better to encourage good behavior, and times when social pressure works better. For example, most people would agree that protecting citizens from bodily harm at the hands of other citizens requires laws that are enforced. But should a person have to be good when, say, giving advice? What if you advise a friend to buy a certain kind of car without telling him that you own stock in the car company? Should this be against the law, as in, "Sir, you gave a friend selfish advice; this person bought a car not realizing you were only interested in boosting your stock portfolio; I will fine you $500"? No, this sort of wrong is better handled with a set of ethics that are enforced by social pressure—the car buyer can let his friends and neighbors know about your unethical behavior as a car tout.

Ethics are often used to judge fairness of behavior. If, in interviewing job applicants, you give your friends preferential consideration over candidates you do not know, your actions are unfair and unethical. But ethics can also be used to judge the fairness of communication, such as in the claims made by television ads, campaign promises, the personal information we might disseminate about other people, and any advice we might give. Admittedly, there are limits to our ethical responsibilities during communication with others. Say you have researched facts about a company to prepare for a job interview. Another candidate for the same job, who has not done any research, asks for your researched information just prior to the interview. Should you feel obligated to give this person the requested information? I do not believe so. You also have an obligation to be fair to yourself; you took the trouble to prepare, the other person did not bother. In other words, behaving ethically toward others does not require altruism in the extreme. There have been societies that have enforced a sort of altruistic extremeness on their citizens, as in "You are obliged to live for the benefit of others, especially others in the form of the State." Moderate amounts of altruism toward others is, however, consistent with the need to generally promote the public good and avoid unnecessary harm to others.

Perspectives for Judging Ethical Communication

Ethics are especially important during persuasive communication because successful persuaders do exercise a certain amount of power that, used recklessly, can hurt people. How do we decide what is ethical communication and what is not? Fortunately, there are a number of different ways to make ethical judgments. As summarized by philosopher Richard Johannesen, these include (1) examining the values inherent in particular political systems, (2) recognizing the essence of human nature, (3) evaluating the extent to which messages pursue a "dialogue," (4) looking to the situation or context, (5) consulting religious tenets, (6) evaluating the utility of communication, and (7) defining ethical concerns in legal terms.[1]

The Political Values Perspective

A political system's values can offer clues for evaluating what is ethical communication and what is not. In representative democracies, an individual's opinions should be important. In a democracy, each person has a right to speak (ideally, in an open, honest, balanced, equal, and clear way) to those who want to listen. The price of having listeners, however, includes the ethical obligation to create messages that do not demean, intimidate, manipulate, dominate, or trick. Democratic decision making requires multiple points of view and the freedom to evaluate ideas and policies in fair ways. The policies chosen should enjoy the consent of the governed and should have the public support that will make such policies legitimate ones. If a college newspaper that prints unpopular stories has its editions stolen or burned, we have unethical (and illegal) behavior on the part of those who sabotage the free and open airing of opinions. The same is true if college administrators refuse to let a newspaper publish because it has criticized administrative policies. But freedom of the press comes with responsibilities and does not, for example, include the right to advocate violence or to libel or endanger people.

Not all political systems support the above ideals. The Nazis in World War II Germany relied on propaganda messages that appealed to power, communicated hate in direct ways and through innuendo, played the blame-game by using minorities as excuses for government failures, created preposterous oversimplifications of complex social issues, and often left logic and factual truth "blowing in the wind." Communist regimes in the last century have been no better, preaching hatred toward the West, suppressing freedom of speech, requiring supreme love of country and party, and promoting communism with any communication technique that worked regardless of truthfulness or consistency.

American and other Western leaders have historically also had their seedier moments. Depending on your political point of view, you might easily connect various scandals or other political intrigues with presidents just upon the mention of their names: Roosevelt, Truman, Eisenhower, Kennedy, Johnson, Nixon, Ford, Carter, Reagan, G. H. W. Bush, Clinton, G. W. Bush. Some of these name-elicited recollections of scandal or intrigue may be more objective in nature and some more the result of passions emanating from party loyalty. And smaller countries also experience problematic ethics. As part of an anthropological study, Ethel Albert reported on the permissible public ethics of one third-world country in particular. She described a culture in which flattery was used as a means to get what one wanted and slander was the chief weapon in dealing with enemies day-to-day. As one of Albert's informants said when interviewed, "The man who tells no lies cannot feed his children." Albert noted that the truth seemed to be viewed by her informants as important for private judgments, but not for practical success.[2]

Thus, we shouldn't assume our democratic notions of openness and honesty and respect for individuals are universals for the world. There are places in the world that are quite hostile to such notions, as you might unhappily find out if you unwisely asserted your freedom of speech in the wrong place on the planet; you could end up in prison without charges being filed, or worse.

The Humanistic Perspective

Using a **humanistic perspective** is another way to evaluate communication ethics. The essence of the humanistic perspective is that human beings are distinct because of their ability to use symbolic thought in rational ways to come to conclusions on the issues of the day. The word *epistemology* refers to how we know what we know. Some human knowledge is based on mysticism or myth. Some is based on observation and logic. To be ethical within the humanistic perspective, you have to persuade others by using rational thought, accurate information, and appeals to human intelligence. So what would be unethical here? Trying to scare your listeners into heeding your words, intimidating them, or encouraging irrational, emotions-driven, mindless reactions to what you say. Within this perspective, we rejoice in human beings collectively trying to live better lives with shared ideas of merit in the hope that we can all benefit from each other's good ideas. The humanistic perspective seems to offer the highest ideal for human communication.

The Dialogical Perspective

The **dialogical perspective** is supportive of the humanistic perspective. It takes its name from the word *dialogue* (when two or more people communicate back and forth), as opposed to the word *monologue* (when one person or one side does all the talking and the others just take it all in). Propagandists often want to get their messages out to the public in efficient, standardized ways, with little competition from rival communicators. And propaganda is often a monologue when it treats its receivers as objects to be moved but not necessarily listened to. Dialogue, at its best, offers the possibility that the sender may persuade the receiver, or that the receiver may occasionally persuade the sender. Or perhaps sender and receiver will each admit that the other makes good points. On some occasions, they may so disagree that they part by saying, "Let's agree that we disagree," and leave it at that. What is special about the dialogical perspective is that it encourages the more personal "I-thou" relationship rather than the more impersonal "I-it" relationship.[3] Now you cannot always treat other people as a "thou" who should be understood in all their nuances (e.g., when you buy a ticket at a railroad station booth after standing in a long line, you may be short-tempered with the ticket seller), but at important moments, you should try. As an ethical communicator, evaluated by the dialogical perspective, you need to remind yourself that you are communicating with another person who has unique thoughts and perspectives just as you do. So do not try to bowl people over with your razzle-dazzle, wisdom, and skill—rather try to get them to see the possible rightness of your ideas, and do so with some degree of humility. Researchers Sonja Foss and Karen Foss have offered a recent twist on the dialogical perspective with what they call "invitational rhetoric," which is based on five core assumptions: (1) the purpose of communicating is to gain understanding, (2) the speaker and the audience are equal, (3) different perspectives constitute valuable resources, (4) change happens when people choose to change themselves, and (5) all participants are willing to be changed by the interaction.[4]

The Situational Perspective

The **situational perspective** accepts few if any universal ideas about ethics. In this method for judging ethics, only the circumstances of the communicative act are used. Is lying okay during communication? Some pundits today, using the situational perspective, would argue that in a political campaign for office it is okay to make up malicious lies about your adversary. The justifications for such a position may include that everyone does it these days, or that the stakes are too important to rely on the truth. There is an ends-justifies-the-means feel to the situational perspective. Situational perspectives may be a dangerous road to walk down, ethically speaking. If you can use lies and extreme exaggerations today to win an election, what will be acceptable tomorrow when someone decides to "push the envelope?" How about planting incriminating evidence? If anything can be justified, anything can happen. Now, situational details should occasionally be taken into consideration when judging the ethics of communicative acts. I certainly would lie to a known thief about how much money I had stuffed in a sock under my bed. But how often do I have to tell such lies? One other problem with easy-going ethical standards is that they encourage cynicism and defensive behavior. If you expect everyone you meet to take any shortcut with the truth that suits their current objectives, how can you use communication in any reliable way?

The Religious Perspective

The **religious perspective** has been around for a long time and can also be used to evaluate ethics. Johannesen notes:

> The Old Testament clearly admonishes Jews and Christians against use of lies and slander. . . . The Confucian religion generally has tended to shun emotional appeals and stress fact and logic, although some variations on Confucianism accept appeals to such emotions as joy, anger, sorrow, and so on. . . . Taoist religion stresses empathy and insight rather than reason and logic. . . . In Buddhism a number of sacred truths that seekers of morality must follow center on ethical communication: avoid anger, gossip and boasting; avoid quarreling; avoid lies and false speech; employ words that give peace and speak with a pure mind.[5]

In stark contrast, one could argue today that the Wahhabi sect of Islam includes ethics that allow for encouragement and coordination of terrorism and hyper-hatred of the West.[6] What may be ethical according to one religion may not be ethical according to another.

The Utilitarian Perspective

The **utilitarian perspective** (sometimes called *consequentialism*) looks to the outcome of communication to evaluate ethics. In one form or another, the question here concerns whether messages have good effects and benefit people or not. In some ways the utilitarian approach may overlap with the situational approach (which considers both means and ends). At its best, the utilitarian approach may justify lying to someone who is about to commit suicide in order to prevent his or her death. At its worst, the utilitarian approach may lead one to say, "I know what's good for people better than they do; so whatever I have to say to win the day is okay, as long as I can say everything worked out in the end." This too is a tricky path to walk down and can lead to authoritarianism.

The Legalistic Perspective

The **legalistic perspective** takes the position that if something is legal, it is by definition ethical. But you may remember that at the beginning of this chapter we saw that laws are sometimes better for getting people to be good, while social pressure in the form of morals and ethical codes is better at other times. It is difficult at best to legislate ethical behavior. But if we equate ethical behavior with legal behavior, we either abandon any notion of ethical behavior or we begin to legislate ethical behavior. Both of these options are problematic. The trouble with abandoning ethics is obvious enough, but what about legislating ethical behavior? Let's say that you ask a group of preschoolers to give you their lollipops voluntarily, with the intention of eating all the lollipops yourself. Now, you may not actually get the lollipops from many children, although some might give them over in a spirit of friendliness. Assuming you get the lollipops, have you done something unethical? Most reasonable people would say you have. Have you done anything illegal? Probably not. Therein lies the problem of equating ethics with legality. Would we then need to pass and strictly enforce laws that say it is illegal to talk preschoolers out of their lollipops?

Codes of Ethics and Challenges for Communicators

We began this chapter by focusing on the ethics of persuasive communication, including the ethical responsibilities and limits that individual communicators should adhere to. This section looks at codes of ethics and takes up the more difficult ethical challenges facing individual communicators in particular fields. Its purpose is to add to the ongoing dialogue on ethics by pointing to areas of needed improvement in various common arenas in which persuasion and propaganda take place.

One very interesting thought about ethics concerns whether one universal code of ethics could apply to the whole human race, or whether ethics should be defined universally in terms of single cultures. The extreme opposite to this *universalism* would be *moral relativism*, which argues that whatever ethical guidelines seem to work for some cultural group are okay for that group. With universal principles, the same ethical standards are identified for everybody. Universalists prescribe uniform obligations, rights, and virtues (this is sort of a philosophical application of the saying "What's good for the goose is good for the gander"). A weaker version of this ethical universalism is simply claiming that in applying ethical standards, exceptions should not be made only for some. Immanuel Kant probably stated the strongest version of universalism by saying, "Act only on that maxim through which you can at the same time will that it [your act] should become a universal law." In other words, if I sell my house without telling the buyer that groundwater seeps into the basement at times, I imply by my concealment that the whole world is rightfully entitled to act in a way similar to the way that I have acted. Kant might say to me at the closing of the sale of my house, "Are you sure you want to do this, given its worldwide implications?"

In some ways, moral relativism is similar to the situational perspective. The main difference is that the situational perspective can easily be applied to people in the same culture on different occasions or in different circumstances. Moral relativism, on the other hand, is more concerned with cross-cultural issues. Today moral relativism contains three branches of ethical standards. When using *descriptive relativism*, for example, the critic notes how differences among people in different societies affect how they see morality. *Meta-ethical relativism* then asserts that there is no one good way to judge the affairs of human beings because we are all much too egocentric or ethnocentric. And *normative relativism* advises people in a culture to "mind their own business" with respect to the ethical standards of people in other cultures. One problem with the moral relativism perspective is that it may take us down a road leading to nihilism or tyranny because we decline to identify meaningful standards for human behavior, based perhaps on some sense of self-evident truth.

Some of the standards we are considering here are **field dependent** (they vary from field to field) and some are **field independent** (or *field invariant*; they are common to many fields). In a courtroom, one field-dependent standard concerns physical evidence introduced by the prosecutor where there must be a credible "chain of possession" established (e.g., a detective gathers physical evidence associated with a crime, such as a gun, and delivers it to the police station where it is sent to the crime lab and then back to a property clerk who secures the evidence and later releases it for transport to the trial location, where it can be introduced as evidence). At the same time, the prosecutor would have to make logical arguments about any physical evidence introduced. This logic requirement would be a field-independent standard common to many persuasive arenas. Most of the discussion in this chapter has concerned field-independent ethics, so now we'll examine field-dependent ethics, especially concerning the more troublesome areas alluded to above.

A number of professional and academic societies have published ethical codes in the form of enumerated rules for their practitioners to follow. A common complaint made of professional codes is that they contain high-sounding but vague terms that can be interpreted in any way one likes. Critics also complain that creating and publicizing codes can sometimes function as a substitute for actually being ethical. Or they complain that devising a code can create the sense that all that needs to be done has now been done, or that codes can never be stronger than the membership of a sponsoring group will tolerate. Despite these complaints, there may still be some use for codes, if they are continually developed and written with the intention of actually improving public communication. So what makes a good code? Among other possible requirements, a code should (1) identify whether it is prescribing ideals or minimum standards, (2) be realistic in not requiring its followers to do what is "above and beyond the call of duty," (3) use specific terminology, (4) address the most troublesome areas for a particular communication field, (5) specify what actions should be taken by whom when code violations occur, (6) be enforceable and enforced, and (7) explain its moral basis.[7]

The Ethics of Political Discourse

Winning has become the supreme end in politics. And the goal of winning puts a strain on ethical considerations. A political candidate might call a rival a "fascist" or "communist" without any grounds for doing so, simply to create an extremely negative impression of the rival. Such a tactic might come from a strategy that assumes the only reliable way to get voters motivated is to get them angry or afraid, and to do so by whatever means it takes. There is nothing new about mudslinging in politics, but what is new is mudslinging in the twenty-four-hours-a-day news cycle. One hundred years ago, a farmer may have read in a newspaper a scathing attack against some political leader maybe once a week at most. Today we can witness the harsh words everyday—especially on political discussion cable TV, in the opinion columns of newspapers, and in commentary on the Internet. The election cycles seem to go on much longer today—in some ways, they never end. It would be nice if political discourse more often used the humanistic or dialogical perspective as a guideline for communicating ethically. Too often, however, a legalistic or situational perspective is used.

Ethics in Science and Education

Another challenge for ethics is the politicizing of science. "Junk science" has come to mean scientific findings publicized or created to prove a point helpful for a political or corporate agenda. Such communication is often intended to convince people that a problem is much more serious (or less serious) than can actually be proved. Junk science can even be used to create a problem that does not really exist. For example, if I dislike the fact that many people wear wrist watches, I might create a campaign to prove that battery-operated wrist watches have been associated with increased risk of insomnia for those who wear watches to bed. I could misquote medical articles on the subject. I might even recruit a rogue researcher to carry out bogus research designed to prove my point. With some public support, I might raise funds to widen public exposure to my claims. And if I really succeed, I might get a politician to introduce legislation on behalf of my mission.

Not all ethical issues in science and education are due to politicization. Perhaps an unethical scientist uses a faulty argument in order to secure more research funding. Cronyism among colleagues also raises obvious ethical issues, if a group of professionals "look out for each other" in securing grants or publications placement or even job opportunities. And allowing religious motivations to influence science-oriented policy decisions can raise serious ethical questions. As the old saying goes, "Mixing science and politics produces bad science and bad politics." The same can be said about religion, science, and politics taken together. In this sense, ethics can help us keep matters straight so that we can go on from there with less confusion.

Educators are not immune to the lure of politicizing educational curriculum. But teachers have an obligation to help their students learn to live more intelligently, get good jobs, become good citizens, and appreciate the finer things in the human experience. Perhaps a good rule for educators is to imagine that the parents of all their children are monitoring everything said in the classroom, as are all the clergy and all the lawyers in the neighborhood.

The Ethics of Art

Perhaps the most difficult area for which to discuss ethics is art (and in some cases, performance art). So, what are the ethics of art? Should artists be encouraged to feel a sense of ethics, especially when their art takes on political implications and perhaps has effects on public policy? If I paint a picture of a person held in high esteem by some particular group and publicly display the picture in a way that humiliates the subject of the art work, have I violated any sense of artistic ethics? Perhaps through its metaphorical images, my picture can be analyzed politically or socially as implying the following message in the form of an artistic enthymeme:

CLAIM: The subject of my painting is a person to be reviled [implied].

EVIDENCE: The subject publicly criticized things I value strongly [public knowledge].

WARRANT: Such criticism deserves public humiliation [implied].

Given this analysis, has the artist been unethical?

Art has long been used for political and social messages. The Romantic period (the late 1700s through the early 1800s) offers spectacular examples of art used for political and social influence. The Romantic period was a rebellious one. The old political and cultural order was despised by the Romanticists, who saw kings as evil, conformity and manners as unnecessary, and the older generation as worthy only of distrust. On the other hand, incest was okay, bandits and outlaws were admirable, and youthful nonconformism was the preferred lifestyle. Napoleon, who conquered half of Europe with his powerful armies, was adored by Romanticists as a symbol of rebellion. Social convention was a dirty phrase because it stifled the happiness and freedom of mankind. Within this context of thought (or feeling), the Romantic painters sometimes used their works to make political statements.[8]

For example, British artist John Henry Fuseli painted *The Nightmare* in the late 1700s.[9] It shows a woman in a white gown sleeping with her head half off the bed and her arms dangling to the floor. Sitting above her is a grinning image of the devil looking something like a raccoon. Behind her, pushing through closed curtains, is a luminescent horse with demonic eyes, glancing at the devil figure, which is glancing down at the woman, perhaps with a sexual motivation. What is the message of this painting? That depends somewhat on the individual who views it. But given the tamer artistic standards that preceded the Romantic period, there may be an assertion here that says, "Anything goes now, the beautiful, the ugly, the true, the false, the real, the unreal, the taboo." Socially or politically, you might argue that in the context of Romanticism there at times is a flirtation with nihilism, as in "Go where your feelings take you; go where you want. Worry not about conventions or consequences. The imagination and 'inner eye' are as valid or more valid than rational objectivity." So what is the message of *The Nightmare*?

> CLAIM: I reject the established rules of art, the existing political order, and the social mores that stifle the imagination, restrict personal freedom, and enslave the spirit.
>
> EVIDENCE: The existing social orders are rigged to benefit the established powers and justified by a suspect and self-serving rationalism devoid of the "subjective realities," nonrational perspectives, and power of raw nature.
>
> WARRANT: That which is corrupt should be mocked and replaced.

Assuming that the above analysis is reasonable, is the artistic enthymeme of *The Nightmare* ethical? Does it seek to influence in a fair and open way?

Ethics in art has become even more complicated today, as for example with the Danish cartoons of Muhammad that were reproduced recently in some newspapers and not in others. Of the seven criteria mentioned above about evaluating ethical codes, the ethics question arising from the cartoons controversy concerns our responsibility with respect to the fifth criterion to specify what actions should be taken by whom when code violations occur (e.g., what should newspapers, or their readers, do about the matter?). Complicating the ethics issue of publishing these images is the importance of freedom of the press in a free society. And further complicating the Danish photos issue was a similar one concerning images of Jesus and the Virgin Mary to which many Christians took offense. Some newspapers published one set of images but not the other. A consistent code of ethics should be followed by newspapers and other media outlets that publish such images. However, at present I doubt whether there is much consensus on the matter in the West, although there seems to be an almost absolute consensus on the matter in the Muslim world. But democracies definitely should not ask artists to follow a code of ethics in creating images, except perhaps if it can be proven beyond a reasonable doubt that such images could physically harm people even when only displayed in private areas (e.g., images that show how to construct illegal weapons).

The Ethics of the Media

One especially challenging area for ethical communication concerns our ever-developing technology. It is now possible for the media to create almost any image desired. You can easily today morph your rival into a video image of some well-known public villain to suggest perhaps that your rival is a sociopathic mass-murderer. Freedom of the press and freedom of speech regarding political figures make these types of attacks easy to justify legally. So it is only an informed public that can urge the ethics that will curb such abuses. Rapid-fire video montage can sometimes overwhelm receivers with images too numerous to be processed intellectually (but which further the objectives of their senders). Let's look at a few specific ethical challenges for the media such as in advertising, documentaries, news, and entertainment.

The Ethics of Advertising As shown in box 6.1, the American Association of Advertising Agencies (AAAA) adopted in 1924 and most recently revised in 1990 a state-

---

BOX 6.1
American Association of Advertising Agencies Creative Code

We, the members of the American Association of Advertising Agencies, in addition to supporting and obeying the laws and legal regulations pertaining to advertising, undertake to extend and broaden the application of high ethical standards. Specifically, we will not knowingly create advertising that contains:

a. False or misleading statements or exaggerations, visual or verbal
b. Testimonials that do not reflect the real choice of the individual(s) involved
c. Price claims that are misleading
d. Claims insufficiently supported or that distort the true meaning or practicable application of statements made by professional or scientific authority
e. Statements, suggestions, or pictures offensive to public decency or minority segments of the population. . . .

Clear and willful violations of these Standards of Practice may be referred to the Board of Directors of the American Association of Advertising Agencies for appropriate action, including possible annulment of membership as provided by Article IV, Section 5, of the Constitution and By-Laws.

Source: www.aaaa.org/eweb/DynamicPage.aspx?Site=4A_new&WebKey=d94ac5ca-e68d-4587-be89-5a8e7ea82e39, "Standards of Practice."

ment that can now be found on their website (actually a PDF file that you download) that requires that its members avoid intentionally producing ads that contain "false or misleading statements or exaggerations, visual or verbal," although it is not entirely clear if this concerns ideals or minimum standards.[10] And how the words "false or misleading" are defined is important here. Ads from larger organizations probably do not mislead on details like whether aspirin can cure a disease, although late-night "informationals" made by smaller entrepreneurs sometimes do say extraordinary things. Pain-relief products have in the past been promoted through such tricky phrases as "You can't buy a stronger pain reliever." But you often can't buy a weaker one either. Most aspirin products use the maximum strength allowed by law. And in the same sense, do commercials for jeans and other items of clothing sometimes give the impression that buyers of these products can become sexy by just wearing them?

The second item of the AAAA code says that testimonials should "reflect the real choice of the individual(s) involved." Here again, we have a definition problem. If I am a famous person and have been offered a large sum of money to speak well about a product, I may say that I like and use this product. But for how long? Have I also used competing products? And most importantly, has that large sum of money influenced my opinion of the product? The fourth item states that claims need to be supported. But much of consumer advertising deals not in claims but in vague suggestions. Will viewers get the attractive person in the car commercial if they buy the car shown in the ad? Not likely.

In sum, we can say that the AAAA's code (1) does not distinguish whether it describes ideal or minimum standards, (2) is quite realistic in what it proposes, (3) uses specific terminology sometimes but not at other times, (4) does not address the most troublesome areas such as competition between agencies and their advertising tactics, (5) does provide a statement on enforcement whereby those agencies that violate the code may have their membership annulled, (6) does create enforceable sanctions, and (7) suggests (on the website) that advertisers have a moral responsibility to be constructive, but within the context of competition among agencies. That is, advertisers have an obligation to compete on merit, not by simply trying to discredit rivals.

We can compare some of the above observations with the code posted by the Better Business Bureau (BBB) as a guide for advertisers. For example, on the issue of testimonials, the BBB advises,

> In general, advertising which uses testimonials or endorsements is likely to mislead or confuse if . . . while literally true, it creates deceptive implications . . . [or if] an endorser has a pecuniary [financial] interest in the company whose product or service is endorsed and this is not made known in the advertisement. (www.bbb.org/membership/codeofad.asp)

The BBB also has concerns about the use of the word *sale*. It advises that references to sales in ads should only be made when there is a significant reduction from the advertiser's usual or customary price, and that the sale should be time limited (several days, several weeks, but no longer). And predictions made by advertisers about future increases in prices should only be made when the prices will go up for a substantial amount of time. The details offered by the bureau concern a number of things that the AAAA code does not mention.

When examining the complete code (which came to eight pages when I printed it out), we find much detail on what constitutes fairness with regard to the pricing of merchandise and merchandise descriptions in ads. Of course, it will be easier for an organization like the BBB to arrive at its code than an association of advertisers. In sum, the BBB's published code (1) does not say whether it describes ideal or minimum standards, (2) is quite realistic in what it proposes, (3) uses specific terminology for those things it does choose to discuss, (4) does address one of the most troublesome areas—trickery used in some ads, (5) does not discuss enforcement, (6) does not create enforceable sanctions, and (7) implies that advertisers should be dedicated to truth.

The Ethics of the Documentary Author Bill Nichols points out that "every film is a documentary," and that there are two kinds of films: (1) documentaries of wish-fulfillment or fiction stories, and (2) documentaries of social representation or nonfiction stories.[11] Fiction films *can* show truths about the culture and times in which they were made. For example, the Audrey Hepburn film *Breakfast at Tiffany's* shows what the clothing styles, taxicabs, buses, office and apartment buildings, and streets of New York City looked like in the early 1960s. Nonfiction documentaries also tell stories from a certain perspective, just like their fiction-oriented cousins. The difference is that documentaries claim to represent, objectively or subjectively, some reality about the society in which the documentary was filmed. Nichols admonishes documentary makers that they have an obligation to ethically represent the narrow slices of society they choose to photograph. They have a similar obligation to the people represented in the film. As a paradigm ethical example, Nichols asks, Should we tell someone we film that they risk making a fool of themselves or that there will be many who will judge their conduct negatively?

To illustrate this question, he reviews several documentaries where informed consent was apparently not secured beforehand, and then he asks regarding one of these documentaries, Should the women in this documentary have been told in advance that viewers might see them as "coquettish, heterosexually obsessed, Southern belles?" Or should the people for a documentary made in Flint, Michigan, have been informed that they would end up looking foolish in order to make General Motors look even worse? Should the Hausa tribesman in another documentary have been informed that their filmed rituals would make them look bizarre if not barbaric? Should any of us be informed of the possibility that our participation in a documentary could end up being used against us in a future criminal trial? Nichols suggests a remedy built around an "informed consent" litmus test. Just as a medical researcher would be wrong to test a new drug on subjects without first advising them of the possible dangerous effects, documentary makers should get the informed consent of the people represented in the film before those people participate, actively or passively. We might add to this that the documentary maker should make clear to viewers what they need to know about production techniques (e.g., staged actions, morphing of images, multiple layers of images) to appraise the documentary's potential to misinform.

Communication researcher Teresa Bergman offers some interesting observations on the "production ethics" of film documentaries commonly shown on television and elsewhere.[12] In an analysis of one particular documentary about Alzheimer's disease, she concludes that its maker created an illusion of *naturalism* in several ways: (1) the author rehearsed the questions and answers of interviews shown in the documentary and then had someone ask the rehearsed questions in ways that would momentarily disrupt answers and make them seem more spontaneous; (2) the author narrates the film and at one point speaks directly to the camera to engage the audience—which encourages viewers to assume that thoughts, feelings, and observations that have never been revealed before are now being put before the audience; (3) the documentary consciously attempts to portray the author and her mother as real persons, and not as helpful participants in the documentary.

In addition, this documentary places the audience in the role of eyewitness spectators. This perspective allows the audience to "see" the truth rather than being asked to believe what the documentary maker asserts. And when the narrator speaks directly to the audience, the audience feels that the narrator is aware of its presence. This last point concerns the sense of dialogism. The mother in this documentary also speaks directly to the audience when she admits that she no longer can recognize her daughter. All the above tend to render the documentary producer as a believable and trustworthy narrator.

Another documentary, completed in 2004 and describing the making of the classic 1940s film *The Third Man*, offers some very interesting details about behind-the-scenes intrigues concerning one of the film's principal stars, Orson Welles.[13] We learn that Welles at one time said that he had codirected his own scenes (with the film's director, Carol Reed). The documentary then shows a clip of Welles clarifying that he did not in fact codirect his own scenes but did write much of the dialogue for the character he played in the film. At this point, the narrator dramatically says, "Fact or fiction. Orson Welles, alias Harry Lime. His first statement is fact [that he did not codirect]; his second statement is fiction [that he wrote the dialogue for his own character]. The real author of the *Third Man* is Graham Green." There are several problems with these statements. One is that Welles said he wrote much of the dialogue for his own character. But while the narrator emphasizes that Graham Green wrote the film, the narrator does not directly say that Welles did not write his own dialogue. At a later point in the documentary, the narrator mentions that the actress who played a landlady in the film did in fact write her own lines (spoken in German). The three statements are, at minimum, incongruous. Yet the vocal tone of the narrator's "fact" and "fiction" come across authoritatively.

In addition to the naturalism and spectator ideas discussed above, the use of the camera in a documentary can help to lend credibility to the assertions contained in the documentary. Through carefully selected camera placement, camera shots, and subsequent editing, the final product can sometimes facilitate the opinions and biases of the producers; we nonetheless allow ourselves as audience members to apply the adage that "Seeing is believing." We as an audience may also associate certain camera techniques with a documentary (e.g., the illusion of one camera almost constantly moving, and with a simple observational perspective).

Documentaries often portray their subjects in ways that are (1) **expository**, by which the producer takes a specific stance as would, say, an essay writer; (2) **observational**, and focused on life as it is lived, sometimes in real time; (3) **participatory**, such as when a documentary maker speaks with the film's subjects and answers their questions; (4) **reflexive**, because the production often includes reminders to the viewer that the particular documentary they are watching is a constructed reality; (5) **performative**, in that a documentary often involves an intentional mix of the objective and subjective; and (6) **poetic**, when the documentary "emphasizes visual associations, tonal or rhythmic qualities, descriptive passages, and formal organization."[14] Expository documentaries can be opinionated, but purely observational ones should not be. And we would not want an expository documentary masquerading as an observational one. In the final analysis, perhaps we can say that just as advertisements need to be identified so we can recognize that they are promoting something for personal gain, documentaries need to be identified so that we can recognize what they are trying to accomplish. If the goal is expositional or observational, we have a right as the documentary's consumers to know this. Should audiences for documentaries perhaps reflexively assume that every documentary is an opinionated essay in audiovisual form? If so, schools should teach this attitude to students just as they teach them about the commercial agendas of advertising.

We can take some of these ideas and informally create a code of ethics for documentaries. According to our code, a documentary maker should:

1. Accept responsibility for ensuring that any explicit or implicit claims made in representing the people, issues, or locations of the documentary not be misleading.
2. Accept an obligation to ethically represent the society that their documentary depicts.
3. Make clear to people portrayed in the documentary how they will be portrayed, and for what purpose.
4. Make clear to viewers to what extent production techniques used in making the documentary have the potential to misinform.
5. Make very clear to viewers the essential style of the documentary, that is, whether it is expository, observational, participatory, reflexive, performative, poetic, or some combination of these.

Since the above code is tentative, it does not try to define the ethics of documentaries in terms of ideal or minimum standards, nor does it address the most troublesome areas or propose enforcement or enforceable sanctions. The five items of the code do try to use specific terminology and to imply a moral responsibility in a realistic way.

The Ethics of the News A search of the Web using the search phrase {journalism ethics} will uncover numerous "hits," or results. In one such result, we learn that according to the Society of Professional Journalists, people in the news should seek:

- To promote this flow of information.
- To maintain constant vigilance in protection of the First Amendment guarantees of freedom of speech and of the press.
- To stimulate high standards and ethical behavior in the practice of journalism.
- To foster excellence among journalists.
- To inspire successive generations of talented individuals to become dedicated journalists.
- To encourage diversity in journalism.
- To encourage a climate in which journalism can be practiced freely.[15]

The Gannett Newspaper Division also offers a wide set of standards that they are committed to.[16] For example, according to Gannett, a news service should try to (1) seek and report the truth in a truthful way, (2) serve the public interest, (3) exercise fair play, (4) maintain independence, and (5) act with integrity. Gannett also offers a wide set of statements on matters of using unnamed sources, handling the wires (what happens when local sources of information conflict with information from wire services), remaining skeptical when editing, ensuring accuracy, and correcting errors.

We might evaluate the ethical code at Gannett in the same way that we evaluated the AAAA and BBB ethical codes above. The Gannet code (1) describes what seem to be ideal standards—minimums are not described; (2) is realistic in what it proposes—but there may be times when reporters and editors will not live up to the standards, such as during an election or ongoing political controversy in which each story may help or harm one political party or the other; (3) uses very specific terminology; (4) does not specifically address troublesome areas, but does not ignore them; (5) does not discuss enforcement; (6) does not create enforceable sanctions; and (7) is couched in terms of a sacred mission for journalism. Overall, Gannett seems very serious about creating a meaningful code.

Beyond what we've already said about ethics in journalism, additional tests that can help us decide whether news has been reported ethically include determining (1) whether the accuracy of information from sources has been tested (crucially important here is for the news staff to check the accuracy of sources with equal skepticism, whether the news story supports the staff's biases or does not); (2) whether sources' motives were questioned before they were promised anonymity (also important here is to be sure that anonymity is not being used to generate a story that cannot stand on its own when full disclosure of sources is given); (3) whether the news staff has made certain that headlines, news teases, promotional material, photos, video, audio, graphics, sound bites, and quotations do not misrepresent, oversimplify, or highlight incidents out of context (this can create a conflict of interest between those who produce the news and those who must keep the outlet competitive with other outlets); and (4) whether the news staff has kept a fair distinction between advocacy and news reporting (analysis and commentary should be clearly labeled).

One very interesting criterion for judging ethics in news reporting is the news organization's obligation to minimize harm—similar to the obligation that physicians have to do no harm. Thus, if publishing a particular news story will cause violence, the news outlet must balance the public's right to know with the need to minimize harm. Sometimes this may require satisfying the public's need to know by using carefully drafted words, and then minimizing harm by not using visuals or words that might incite violence. Ethical reporting should also respect as much as is possible the privacy of the people involved in news stories; the so-called paparazzi seldom respect this right when chasing down stories and pictures of well-known people. Other criteria include being careful not to name criminal suspects before formal charges have been filed, and balancing the criminal suspect's right to a fair trial with the public's right to know. News reporters especially need to avoid conflicts of interest that might influence their news reporting, whether the conflict involves the reporter or the source. Lastly, the power of individuals, groups, organizations, and governments can sometimes have a corrupting influence on society. The reporter is a countervailing force in holding these sources of power accountable—but pursuing this important mission fairly, consistently, and with a sense of proportionality can sometimes be easier or harder, depending on the biases of the news outlet.

The Ethics of Entertainment If you don't like what's on TV, just turn it off. The problem with this simple remedy to television programming is that television does not just affect the individual; it also affects the individual's family, community, and society. Violence in the media, for example, has been a subject of discussion for decades. Equally troubling to many people are the effects of television programs on children and teens with respect to a variety of problem behaviors concerning sex and drugs. One problem here is that many of the programs that possibly have undesirable effects are also popular with their selected audiences. In this respect, perhaps the biggest challenge for society in the coming decades will be reaching some consensus on the ethical standards to which entertainment programs should aspire. Other controversial entertainment products are music videos and video games, which are often accused of promoting an immature brand of nihilism and glamorized violence, while portraying various groups in stereotypically negative and degrading ways.

In the last decade, reality television shows have become especially popular, although their roots can be traced back to the 1950s program *Candid Camera*, which tricked unsuspecting people in public into possibly embarrassing themselves. By today's standards, *Candid Camera* was relatively tame. The ethical issue here concerns how far reality television programs should go in encouraging and portraying the suffering and humiliation of their participants. Given the explosion of cable channels in need of twenty-four-hours-a-day programming, given the casual way many of us accept what occurs on television, and given habituation—meaning that the intensity of reality TV programs needs to ever increase to keep an audience from becoming blasé and bored—where will all this go? Will programs in the next decade include a morning-television game show where contestants compete at bringing someone to sexual satisfaction, explicitly and on camera, in the shortest time or with the most unusual techniques? Will the studio audience be encouraged to cheer on the participants with applause, shouts, and suggestions?

Product placement is one other issue for ethical consideration in media entertainment. Here, sellers of household products, automobiles, sodas, and so on pay to have their product worked into the story line of a movie or television program. The potential of product placement to generate sales for the sellers of the products and fat fees for the producers of the entertainment program is considerable. But is this ethical? Some might say product placement is just another form of advertising. But critics could counter this by noting that magazine, television, and radio advertisements are usually identified for what they are. Product placements are not. Still, some might argue that everyone knows about product placement, so whether its use is formally identified is moot. But *does* everyone know about it? And can the people who generally do know about it reliably avoid being unfairly influenced? Do children and teens necessarily know enough about product placement? Do adults? Does acknowledging product-placement fees in a program's credits deal with the issue sufficiently?

Codes for ethical entertainment historically have been built around the notion of obscenity. However, because people have widely varying notions of what is obscene, these codes have largely been framed in terms of a small set of words that are sometimes kept off the airwaves and are sometimes not. Nudity and explicit sex acts have also been either kept off the airwaves or, as is done today, placed on cable channels with warnings to viewers. Creating a code that goes beyond these simple criteria is beyond the scope of this text.

Perhaps society will come to grips with the need for ethical or legal codes regarding entertainment in the future, and perhaps not.

Deception and Ethics

One of the best ways to encourage ethical communication from persuaders is to encourage receivers to be skeptical; this can help keep persuaders honest. Skepticism is an attitude that acknowledges the frailties of human nature. That is, it is the awareness that people sometimes lie, people sometimes are just wrong about what they say, and as Murphy's Law warns, if something can possibly go wrong, it will do just that. But skepticism needs to be distinguished from cynicism. Cynics are often skeptics who hope their worst fears about others' behavior will come true. Then the cynic can feel superior as the only "good" person in the world—and can also feel "right" about the predictions made. In contrast, skeptics, at their best, should hope that their fears will *not* come true. But as the old Russian saying goes, "Trust, but verify," which may encourage senders to be ethical—if only not to get caught at being unethical. In the interests of healthy skepticism, we will now examine deception.

Defining Terms for Deception

First, there is a technical difference between lying and deception. *Lying* is by definition verbal, although a single head nod could be considered a lie if given as a dishonest response to a pointed question. *Deception*, on the other hand, is a more general term and can be either verbal or nonverbal. Deception means creating a generally false impression about something through words, deeds, or nonverbal messages. Lying is a form of deception.

Similarly, *equivocating* can be a form of deception when you seem to answer someone's question, but really do not. If I ask a political candidate, "Will you be running again for mayor?" and the answer is "I'd have to be crazy to want to do that," did the candidate say yes or no?

A fourth term, which differs somewhat from lying, deception, and equivocating, is the word **masking**, which concerns socially approved white lies. For example, if a very sensitive friend asks what you think of an expensive new coat he or she has just bought, you might say something like "I love that color," while you carefully avoid mentioning (or mask) your dislike of the coat in general.

Under the rubric of lying, we can also distinguish between *lies of the mind* and *lies of the heart*. When you say that you have done something that you actually have not done, or when you misrepresent details about something, it is a lie of the mind. But when you express an emotion about someone that is not your real emotion, it is a lie of the heart.

Sometimes lies are *prepared* and sometimes they are *spontaneous*. When tempted to lie, some people prefer to have time to prepare their stories, and time to anticipate what they will say to challenges or requests for more information by listeners. Lying spontaneously, however, may sound more believable.

Still one other distinction concerns whether lies occur in *low-risk* or *high-risk* situations. If you tell a lie on a long-distance bus to a stranger you will probably never see again, you are lying in what seems like a low-risk situation. However, if you are smuggling contraband

and you lie when asked by a customs officer if you have anything to declare, you most certainly are telling that lie in a high-risk situation. Some people lie more effectively when the risks are low (and they are relaxed), while others succeed when the risks are high (and their adrenaline is flowing).

Finally, we come to the very important distinction between *lies of commission* and *lies of omission*. A lie of commission must be stated verbally, written, or in some other way made clear. Let us assume you know for certain that it's not raining outside, but you tell others inside, who are relying on your report, that it is in fact raining; this would clearly be a lie of commission. A lie of omission, on the other hand, requires that even though you tell some part of the truth, you leave out details in a misleading way. For example, you might assure a prospective client that your company returns fees should a client later decide that the service is not right for them and opt out of the service contract; then you say, "Last year, three clients opted out and we returned their fees." But you leave out the information that the three clients only got their fees back after they had successfully sued. There is wisdom in the oath required when a witness gives testimony in a court: Do you swear to tell the truth, the whole truth, and nothing but the truth?

Types of Deception

Having created a vocabulary for deception, we can now list some common ways in which people deceive one another.[17]

False information concerns lies of commission. These are usually lies of the mind, although they can occasionally be lies of the heart. Persuaders more often use false information in small ways, and propagandists use false information in both small and more significant ways.

A *mixed message* concerns half-truths. Here some elements in the message are true, and some elements are false. This is an especially difficult type of deception to deal with because the true parts of the message tend to give an undeserved credibility to the false parts. A sales representative's verbal guarantee, "We will return your purchase price if the product is defective or if you're unhappy with our product," would be a mixed message if you can return a defective product, but being unhappy with the product is only a legitimate reason for a return if the product is defective.

Concealment occurs when a sender does not want a receiver to know certain information. For example, a scam-artist may not want you to know the official-looking badge he's just shown you can be bought by anyone for $5. Or a mass marketer might not want you to know that the report they offer to sell you for $30 is distributed free by the government. And a teenager talking with their parent may want to keep secret what happened at a party last night.

Misdirection happens when a sender encourages a receiver to concentrate more on a safer part of a message than on parts that may cause the receiver to become skeptical of the sender's claims. Often companies that offer services with monthly fees mention in bold print what the temporary fee will be ("Zero percent interest on all purchases through April 30!"), while the usually much higher permanent fee is briefly mentioned in some obscure part of the promotional message. As we all know, the masters of misdirection are magicians when they get you to look at their right hand while the trick is being carried out by their left hand.

Less-than-ethical communicators may get you to think about the wrong things in their persuasive messages.

Using *minimization* or *exaggeration* simply means misrepresenting the extent or seriousness of something. Children quite commonly exaggerate or minimize things to their advantage or just to indulge their fantasies. Get-rich schemes in magazine classified ads or on late-night "informationals" may exaggerate how much money you will make if you pay for their guidance in getting rich. Bettors sometimes minimize how much money they lose. The saying "If it sounds too good to be true, it probably is" has a great deal of wisdom to it.

Research on Detecting Deception

There is a body of research that seeks to identify falsity in public statements (and even private ones). These investigations often look at either verbal or nonverbal indicators of the presence of deception in messages. Do liars take an instant longer to begin an answer than do truth tellers? You could test this hypothesis by asking sixty people to participate in a laboratory experiment where thirty are asked to lie to questions asked of them, and thirty are asked to tell the truth. A sample question might be "Where did you attend high school?" The experimenters would tape the questions and answers so that they could measure *response latency* (the time that elapses between a stimulus and a subject's response to the stimulus). But using response latency to judge the truthfulness of statements might not be all that easy in real situations, unless there also are other indications.

So what are these indicators? A number of works summarize past research on deception to identify possible cues, and table 6.1 shows items identified by these authors.[18] Some of the items are self-explanatory, but others may need brief definition. For example, in the voice category, *restricted pitch variety* and *pitch breaks* refer to the fact that the vocal pitch (melody) of the voice may at times seem unnatural, strained, or nervous. In the face category, *fleeting facial expressions* refers to changes in expression that take place in a fraction of a second and may briefly hint at a contradictory emotion, such as a fleeting smile during a frown. *Eyebrow flashes* are the upward movement of the eyebrows such as when someone says, "Really?" In the body category, *adaptors* are hand gestures that involve playing with keys or a pen or scratching or rubbing body parts. *Palsy* means temporary, poor control of body parts. And *illustrators* are hand gestures that emphasize spoken ideas (such as rotating your index finger when saying "spiral staircase"). In the language category, *circumlocutions* occur when you stall before giving an important part of your answer in order to give yourself time to think (e.g., "Well, okay, if you really want to know what happened, I'll tell you. The situation started several weeks ago").

It is important to keep in mind that a speaker acting in any one of the ways shown in table 6.1 is not necessarily lying (but you can now follow up a suspicion). But what makes a good liar? For one thing, liars apparently read feedback well and can often tell when receivers are suspicious of aspects of a story. The liar then makes adjustments to the story. Liars also tend to rate higher on such personality constructs as *Machiavellianism* (the desire to manipulate others) and *self-monitoring* (being very aware and controlling of the nonverbal cues they enact as speakers). People of at least high-school age are better at lying than younger people. General social skills help also, such as having good emotional control and an ability to role-play or act.

Table 6.1 Possible Cues to Deception during Communication

Voice	Language
1. Restricted pitch variety	1. Lower word variety
2. Pitch breaks	2. Verbal slips
3. Less variety in tone of voice	3. Repeated questions
4. More speech errors	4. Shorter answers
5. More pausing	5. Restricted topic development
6. Speaking frequency	6. Changing the subject
7. Response latency	7. Circumlocutions

Face	Body
1. Fleeting facial expressions	1. Adaptors
2. Pupil dilation	2. Hair grooming
3. Increased eye blink rate	3. Foot shuffling
4. Masked smiles	4. Posture shifts
5. Eyebrow flashes	5. Leg crossing
6. Lip biting	6. Palsy
7. Averted gaze	7. Fewer illustrators
8. Excessive frowning	8. Less nodding
9. Excessive or inappropriate laughing	9. Less-immediate seating choice
10. Muscle tension	10. Perspiration

Source: For headings, Jo Ruth Liska and Gary Cronkhite, *An Ecological Perspective on Human Communication Theory* (Fort Worth, TX: Harcourt Brace College, 1995).

The ability to plan out a story also may help liars be better at it. Especially successful liars may also be good at embellishing their stories with believable details that are hard to check.

Communication researchers Judee Burgoon, David Buller, and W. Gill Woodall also say receivers are poorer at detecting the underlying emotions of the speaker than they are at detecting the factual information asserted by the sender. Being familiar with a sender's usual style in communicating truthful information may help receivers detect deception. Just as age may help people be better deceivers, it also helps them detect deception a little more accurately. According to Burgoon, Buller, and Woodall, men may be slightly better at detecting deception than women, although this may be due to women's being on average more polite than men when visually monitoring nonverbal cues to deception during conversations (or to their not thinking the worst of speakers). Receivers who pay more attention to "leakier" channels of communication may do better at detecting deception. Monitoring a sender's tone of voice or movements of the lower body may be better than monitoring their face—which many people carefully control during conversations. Those who pay attention to certain aspects of what is said by speakers may do better at detecting deception than those who only listen to understand what is said. Things to especially notice when detecting possible lies include (1) greater use of word modifiers; (2) vagueness or lack of specificity in detail; (3) increased presence of humorous, negative, or irrelevant statements; and (4) increased presence of implausible, self-serving, and ingratiating responses.

Chapter in Retrospect

VIGNETTE **Developing a Personal Code of Ethics**

The personal websites of people unknown to me offer an interesting starting point for a personal code of ethics.[19] One of these individuals mentions a number of standards they use for personal guidance in dealing with others, including a desire to (1) practice the golden rule when asking others to do things you yourself might or might not want to do, (2) own up to mistakes, (3) be honest, (4) stay open to new ideas, (5) stick up for what you believe in, (6) not be argumentative, and (7) find ways to protect other people's feelings without being patronizing. This particular individual also notes that when they are living up to the above standards, things tend to go well, but when they are not living up to them, things tend not to go well.

Another individual mentions a commitment not to be violent toward others or take from them what is rightfully theirs. This individual also promises not to take advantage of other people's weaknesses and to help whenever possible to see that people are treated fairly. This individual apparently believes strongly in rational thinking and wishes to encourage this in their dealings with others so as to maximize the personal freedoms of other people.

Still a third person wishes to deal with others in ways that nurture them and are at all times lawful. This person is committed to self-improvement as an obligation to society. And this person tries to keep to a code of behavior that is objective, open-minded, fair, constructive, moral, and flexible.

With this admittedly small sample of personal codes in mind, I encourage you to make a simple list of statements of personal ethics, then sign the list, and put it where it can be reread from time to time. Items on the list might concern such things as (1) how you will treat others, especially those not as skillful or as capable as you; (2) whether you will seek to maximize gain for yourself or rather to set specific limitations; (3) what obligations to society, if any, you will set for yourself; (4) the sort of thinking you will encourage for yourself; (5) your concern for other people's feelings; (6) your respect for the laws of the land; (7) your respect for such classical virtues as courage, generosity, justice, magnanimity (being noble and gracious about things), magnificence (carrying yourself regally), prudence, temperance (controlling what you consume), and the pursuit of wisdom; (8) your sense of humility and appreciation of your limitations; (9) your respect for yourself, and commitment to yourself regarding your strengths, unique qualities, and potential to personally succeed and contribute to your community and society; and (10) your reverence for things spiritual. There is no need for the list to be long, but it should include things about which you feel strongly. It should be ambitious but realistic. It is intended for your use, so be careful of what you promise yourself and others.

Summary and Conclusions

Ethics involve standards of honesty, goodwill, and responsibility for actions. Persuaders need to evaluate the means and ends of their efforts as a matter of ethics. Seven ethical standards or perspectives are reviewed here: (1) examining the values inherent in particular political systems, (2) recognizing the essence of human nature, (3) evaluating the extent to which messages pursue a "dialogue," (4) looking to the situation or context, (5) consulting religious tenets, (6) evaluating the utility of communication, and (7) defining ethical concerns in legal terms.

Ethical challenges for senders commonly exist in politics, science, education, art, and the media (advertising, documentaries, news, and entertainment). One way for organizations to encourage ethical standards among their members is by promoting a published code of ethics. The quality of published codes can also be evaluated with standards. To evaluate a code, you should note the extent to which it prescribes ideals or minimum standards; requires code followers to act in reasonable ways and not in ways that might be considered "above and beyond the call of duty"; uses specific terminology; addresses the most troublesome areas for a particular communication field; specifies what actions should be taken by whom when code violations occur; offers enforceable guidelines (and is actually enforced); and explains the moral basis for guidelines. One of the most common ways persuaders can be unethical is by using deception to influence their audiences. Some common examples of deception include false information, mixed messages, concealment, misdirection, minimization, and exaggeration. Detection of deception is generally not very good among receivers, although cues that deception is taking place have been identified.

KEY TERMS

documentary types
(expository, observa-
tional, participatory,
performative, poetic,
reflexive)
field dependent

field independent
Machiavellianism
masking
misdirection
mixed message

perspective (dialogical,
humanistic, legalistic,
religious, situational,
utilitarian)
product placement

REVIEW QUESTIONS

1. Why is ethics especially important during persuasion?
2. Which of the ethical perspectives might be easier to follow? Which might be more difficult?
3. What is the difference between field-dependent and field-independent issues?
4. How can works of art be seen as rhetorical statements?
5. What criticisms have been made about attempts to publish ethical codes?
6. How are fictional films and documentaries similar?
7. What types of deception are identified in this chapter?
8. What are some of the cues to deception identified in this chapter? How reliable are such indicators?

SUGGESTED PROJECTS AND ACTIVITIES

1. Select a persuasive message from a print source and evaluate its ethics using several of the standards identified in the chapter.
2. Find an Internet site that contains very strong opinions and harsh language. Critique the site using the ethical standards defined in this chapter. Send your critique to the site managers, if possible.

3. Create a set of ethical standards for use in popular music genres.

4. Conduct a "liars clinic" with one or more friends, fellow students, or family members. To play, gather a fairly large number of magazine pictures (or other pictures), each of which has a reasonable amount of detail that could be described truthfully or falsely. Each person takes a turn describing one of the pictures (the others don't know what is in the picture, none of which they have seen before). There should be a uniform time limit for these descriptions. Using a secret, random procedure (perhaps shuffled index cards that each say either "lie" or "truth"), the person who is describing either lies or tells the truth about what is contained in the picture. Afterward, the others have to decide if the describer has lied or told the truth. Listeners should also mention how they decided that the describer was lying or telling the truth. Repeat this round-robin game as long as desired; keep score. In another variation of the game, the other players get to ask a limited number of questions about the pictures being described.

QUESTIONS FOR DISCUSSION

1. How important should ethics be in the classroom, at work, at home, on television, in politics, in your love life?

2. Is the legalistic perspective on ethics really a perspective on ethics? Explain.

3. Should artists feel obliged to be ethical in what they create?

4. Is it realistic to expect politicians to be ethical during campaigns?

5. Can companies advertise products ethically and still make money?

6. Is it possible to be too concerned with ethics? Why or why not?

Notes

1. Richard Johannesen, *Ethics in Human Communication*, 5th ed. (Prospect Heights, IL: Waveland, 2002), 1–19.

2. Ethel Albert, "Rhetoric, Logic, and Poetics in Burundi," *American Anthropologist* 66, prt. 2 (Decmber 1964): 35–54.

3. Martin Buber, see Johannesen, *Ethics in Human Communication*, 56–65, 210–12.

4. Cf. Sonja Foss and Karen Foss, *Inviting Transformation: Presentational Speaking for a Changing World* (Prospect Heights, IL: Waveland, 2003).

5. Johannesen, *Ethics in Human Communication*, 87–98.

6. This is specifically the Wahhabi (or Wahabi) version of Islam, as opposed to Islam in general.

7. Several of these have been suggested by Richard DeGeorge, *Business Ethics* (New York: Macmillan, 1986), 341–42; John Kultgen, "Evaluating Professional Codes of Ethics," in *Profits and Professions: Essays on Business and Professional Ethics*, ed. Wade Robison et al. (Clifton, NJ: Humana, 1983), 225–64.

8. Public Broadcasting System, "Romanticism," episode 44 of *Western Tradition*.

9. H. W. Janson, *History of Art* (Englewood Cliffs, NJ: Prentice Hall, 1967), 466–67.

10. American Association of Advertising Agencies, "Standards of Practice," www.aaaa.org/eweb/DynamicPage.aspx?Site=4A_newandWebKey=d94ac5ca-e68d-4587-be89-5a8e7ea82e39 (23 April 2006).

11. Bill Nichols, *Introduction to the Documentary* (Bloomington: Indiana University Press, 2001), 1–19.

12. Teresa Bergman, "Personal Narrative, Dialogism, and the Performance of Truth in 'Complaints of a Dutiful Daughter,'" *Test and Performance Quarterly* 24 (January 2004): 20–37.

13. Frederick Baker, *Shadowing the Third Man*, a television documentary by Media Europa, 2004.

14. Nichols, *Introduction to the Documentary*, 26–34.

15. Society of Professional Journalists, "SPJ Missions," www.spj.org/spj_missions.asp (24 April 2006).

16. Gannett Newspaper Division, "Principles of Ethical Conduct for Newsrooms (US)," www.aceproject.org/main/english/ei/eix_o060.htm (24 April 2006).

17. Judee Burgoon, David Buller, and W. Gill Woodall, *Nonverbal Communication* (New York: McGraw-Hill, 1996), 429–53.

18. Burgoon, Buller, and Woodall, *Nonverbal Communication*, 442–51; Jo Ruth Liska and Gary Cronkhite, *An Ecological Perspective on Human Communication Theory* (Fort Worth, TX: Harcourt Brace College, 1995), 265–99; Dale Leathers, *Successful Nonverbal Communication* (New York: Macmillan, 1992), 266–86; William Rogers, *Communication in Action: Building Speech Competencies* (New York: Holt, Rinehart, and Winston, 1984), 51–54; Mark Knapp, *Nonverbal Communication in Human Interaction* (New York: Holt, Rinehart, and Winston, 1978), 229–32.

19. Because the people who posted personal information on these sites may not have wanted their names and thoughts discussed in a college textbook, the ideas included do not contain information that could be used to identify these individuals. Additionally, I have paraphrased the ideas that were posted on these sites, so a keyword search cannot be used to breach the privacy of these thoughtful individuals.

PART II

Receivers
and Research

Understanding Audiences and Cultures

When an audience does not complain, it is a compliment, and when they do it is a compliment, too, if unaccompanied by violence.

—MARK TWAIN

MILLIONS OF people all over the United States and even in some parts of the rest of the world are watching the same program on their television sets. All the networks have crews working to cover the event. Newspaper reporters saturate the hallways of Congress. Members of the Senate and House of Representatives are present. Members of the military leadership are present, as are members of the Supreme

Court. The president's family members are present. The Secret Service is present in large numbers. Then we hear a loud announcement: "The president of the United States." Into the chamber walks the president, and even members of the opposition party position themselves to be seen on camera shaking hands with the president. The main business is, of course, a speech—in this case, a presidential State of the Union speech. Invariably this speech has gone through countless drafts and has been carefully crafted by speech writers, political consultants, and the president. One of their chief concerns is how the various audiences for this important speech will react to what is said in it. By tomorrow morning, every word will have been scrutinized in media reports and by many members of the public. As best as possible, the speech-writing team has made predictions about how the multiple audiences seeing and hearing this speech will react to it.

Persuaders and others who seek to influence do not communicate in a vacuum; they must connect with people in audiences—who in turn usually serve as constraining forces on the senders' communication. Audiences abound in modern societies, whether to hear public speeches, attend religious services, watch films or television programs, read newspapers or magazines or books, listen to music, visit websites, or even serve as a jury. Those senders who try to influence audiences must first study audience members: their characteristics, likely attitudes, beliefs and customary habits, and the prevailing circumstances that will be in place at the time of communication. For the propagandist, this means identifying the communicative techniques that will work best. For the arguer, the audience may or may not be studied depending on the arguer's purpose. For the persuader, the audience is studied to learn how to best provide communicative leadership. This chapter will sketch the steps persuaders often take to better prepare for persuading particular audiences.

We can simply define the word *audience* as "a group of spectators." Texts on communication often use similar definitions, as does communication theorist Denis McQuail, who describes an audience as the readers of, viewers of, or listeners to some channel of communication.[1] The word *audience* comes from the Latin word *audentia*. Each member of an audience is an **auditor** who audits the sender's message. Some auditors are better than others at auditing persuasive or propagandistic messages, in the same way that some accountants might be better than others at auditing the "cooked" books of a rogue organization.

But an audience is more than a collection of auditors: individuals in a face-to-face audience bond together psychologically to varying extents. This *audience bonding* is more complicated with mass-media audiences, but does partially occur for example among conversationalists who watch the same programs or who read about programs or films in magazines and newspapers or hear them discussed on talk shows and the like. It is taking into account this interactive nature of audiences that is the most complicated part of preparing to influence them. As a debater you may have discovered that more individuals in your audience initially support your proposals than do not. But if the more influential members of your audience do not support you, they may in antagonistic situations get the majority in your audience to switch positions against you by making derisive comments, asking questions that are difficult to answer, or acting in hostile ways.

Audiences can at times be quite vulnerable to the influence of communicators. In a courtroom, for example, elaborate legal procedures are used to try to protect juries from unfair influence: the judge rules on what evidence can be heard by jurors; juries are often asked to leave the courtroom while procedural issues are disputed by lawyers; jurors are admonished not to discuss the case with anyone until they deliberate at the close of the trial; the judge instructs the jury on applicable law; the lawyers marshal the evidence; and only at prescribed times (opening and closing remarks) are juries subjected to persuasive claims by both sides in the case. During jury selection, lawyers try to create a favorable audience to hear the case. And after jurors are selected, lawyers try to analyze the jurors' biases. The many other persuaders and propagandists who address either face-to-face or media audiences must also analyze their audiences' biases.

Audience Analysis

The term *audience analysis* usually refers to a systematic, often professional set of activities used to discover the most effective way to prepare a public message. One simple way to analyze an audience is with intuition. With intuition, a sender speculates on what will be the best approach to influence an audience. Say I am preparing a presentation to a group of local farmers. I might assume that they will support higher prices for the crops they grow. But my intuition could be wrong here if the farmers are afraid that in the present market, higher prices will discourage people from buying as much of their crops as they usually do. Intuition therefore may not always be a good way to proceed for audience analysis (depending on how well you know the individuals in your audience). It has sometimes been said that rather than sit around endlessly speculating on the number of teeth horses have, it is usually wiser to find several horses and simply count the number of teeth for yourself. What is good for studying horses may be good for studying audiences also.

Fortunately, there are several approaches to analyzing audiences that are more promising than intuition or speculation. One approach is to research what the audience actually thinks or feels about you and your ideas—sometimes called the **psychographic** approach. So if you find that your farmers are cool to the price-increase idea, you may discover another proposal that they will like. Similarly, if you find that a particular audience initially seems bored by the subject of stamp collecting, your promotional film on stamp collecting could dramatically illustrate how much money exotic rare stamps can sell for. Another audience research approach is to profile your audience using such categories as age, financial status, occupation, political affiliation, and place lived in. This is called the **demographic** approach. If you are to speak about the biblical story of Creation, the various religious affiliations of the people in your audience will be of obvious interest to you as you prepare. And third, you could perform a detailed analysis of the circumstances that might prevail when the audience sees or hears your message. We could call this the **topographic** approach, a phrase suggested by communication scholar Forbes Hill.[2]

The above analyses are done to learn how to achieve desired effects within audiences. According to researcher Theodore Clevenger, there are several different types of audience effects. Some effects are **idiosyncratic** and only concern individual receivers, as when someone purchases a room air-cleaner after reading a magazine story on air pollution that says nothing about buying anything. Other effects are **anticipated** because they are intended ones, such as when audience members vote for a political candidate after reading campaign literature delivered to their homes. And some are **surprise** (or unintended) **effects**, such as when a whole community abandons long-held social conventions after seeing a series of feature-length films—produced in another society and designed only to entertain, not influence.

Clevenger observes that when surprise effects are also idiosyncratic ones, the sender may not have much to worry about because each idiosyncratic effect involves small numbers of receivers; but when surprise effects are popular enough to rival intended, or anticipated, effects, something has gone wrong. For example, you might try to convince your neighbors to install home water filters; instead they start moving away from the neighborhood in droves because of the fears you have unleashed about contamination in the water supply.[3]

Audiences, or receivers, come to a message with preexisting attitudes, beliefs, feelings, and habitual ways of acting. One other thing they bring are images. Clevenger reminds us that receivers will invariably produce personalized mental images in reaction to messages. These images can easily affect how the receivers respond. If a sender uses the expression "sales job," some individuals may imagine sales people knocking on homeowners' doors to sell roof repair services. Other receivers may imagine a dozen or so sales agents sitting in a call center and making cold calls to sell banking services. Still others may imagine a plush, corporate setting where sales representatives sell network television airtime to national advertisers. Professional persuaders, and propagandists for that matter, try to anticipate the images their audiences will supply to key elements in their messages. You might say during a workplace meeting, "I know some of you think of shorter breaks when you hear me mention improved productivity, but in this case you'll be surprised at how it actually works." What you have done with this mid-message warning is to try to influence the images produced by your audience in a favorable way.

Now that we have looked at audience analysis in general terms, let's explore in more detail how audiences can differ. Senders need to prepare somewhat differently for each audience addressed, and audience analysis is a part of that preparation.

The modern, formal audience may have had its beginnings in the theaters of ancient Greece and Rome.[4] These were face-to-face audiences that developed the customs and roles we recognize today, including such things as vocal and gestural reactions, common focus of attention, and suspension of disbelief when appropriate. The roles played in any theater include the roles of the spectators, performers, directors, writers, and producers, and of those who provided the funds for the spectacle. Here we can see the dual nature of any audience: on the one hand, senders seek an audience for their messages in the way a job hunter seeks a job; and on the other hand, receivers "employ" senders to create and exhibit messages that provide the cognitive and emotional gratification desired by the audience. Audiences vary in terms of temperament, social makeup, and setting.

Audience Temperament—A Psychographic Analysis

Audiences can vary in their psychographic categories, such as in *temperament*. One factor here concerns how *willing* an audience is to listen to, view, or read the message.[5] A related factor is how *favorable* the audience is to the position expressed by the sender. Audiences may also be relatively more *active* or *passive*; the former will think critically and ask questions, at least in their minds, while the latter are not very assertive. Audiences can vary in *knowledge* about the sender's topic. Audiences can also be more *homogeneous* (similar in social or psychological makeup) or *heterogeneous* (varied in those things). Each of the above five factors (willingness, favorability, activity-passivity, knowledge, and homogeneity-heterogeneity) will obviously affect how a given message will be received and maybe acted on by members of an audience. Clevenger reminds us that audiences can also vary in how biased or polarized they are on an issue and on how orderly they may or may not be if assembled face-to-face.[6]

The favorability factor can be evaluated with help from the **social judgment** model developed by communication theorists Muzafer Sherif and Carolyn Sherif. This model will allow us to peer closely into the process of persuasion, almost as though looking through a microscope. But to do this, we need to define five basic terms: anchor, latitude of acceptance, assimilation, contrast effect, and ego involvement.[7]

The model insists that to analyze audience members, we first need to know their current position on some topic, assuming that they have a position. So we must learn what they think and feel about the topic. Let's illustrate the model by asking people whether private automobile traffic should be banned from the center of their city. One respondent disagrees with the proposition and circles the 6 on our questionnaire:

We should ban private traffic on the center streets of the city.
(circle the number that comes closest to your attitude about the above proposal)
strongly agree 1 2 3 4 5 ⑥ 7 strongly disagree

This person mostly disagrees with banning automobile traffic in the center city. So we've now identified the **anchor** for this person. We then need to know the **latitude of acceptance** our person has on this topic. Perhaps our subject is somewhat flexible and would agree that positions 5, 6, and 7 are somewhat similar. However, our subject would probably reject positions 1, 2, and 3, and might be uncommitted about position 4.

However, a more polarized individual might hate cars and drivers and select position 1 as the only acceptable position. Positions 2 to 7 would therefore be unacceptable, and because this person is so polarized, there might be no room for an uncommitted position. Obviously, our two subjects are different. It would probably be a little easier to persuade the first subject to take a different position, because of his or her broader latitude of acceptance, and it would probably be hard to persuade the second subject to take a different position. When receivers have a wide latitude of acceptance, they minimize objective differences between their current anchor on a topic and the position taken by the persuader. When a receiver has a narrow latitude of acceptance, that receiver maximizes objective differences between their anchor and the persuader's position. When we minimize objective differences, we are said to engage in **assimilation**, and when we maximize, we are said to illustrate the **contrast effect** (or to use a term unrelated to the social judgment model—a **boomerang effect** where the reverse of what the persuader is trying for happens). By charting an individual's latitudes of acceptance, rejection, and noncommitment, we can gauge just how much persuasion we should attempt. With large numbers of people in our audience, we have to learn what the average anchor is for the group and what the average latitude of acceptance is for the group. This can be done with surveys and interviews, by observing and listening to audience members speak on the topic, or if none of the above are possible, by using intuition and common sense.

More recently, communication scholars Ronald Adler and Jeanne Elmhorst have given the social judgment model, or theory, some further clarification. They point out that the theory works best when applied to issues involving high **ego-involvement** (that is, when receivers identify with something, often with strong feelings). They also report that messages from highly credible speakers will stretch the latitude of acceptance of receivers, and that the use of ambiguity may help place statements within receivers' latitude of acceptance. Dogmatic people have chronically wide latitudes of rejection. Most interestingly, Adler and Elmhorst remind us that (1) application of the theory creates ethical problems, (2) the theory assumes mental structures that are beyond observation, (3) much of the research has had problems confirming the contrast effect, and (4) even so, the theory is an elegant, intuitively appealing approach to persuasion.[8]

To move beyond the social judgment model, I should note that analyzing the psychographics of an audience means more than just cataloging the prevalent beliefs and attitudes held by a majority of the audience members about the sender and the sender's topic. As we saw in chapter 1 and will note in greater detail in chapter 9, listeners' attitudes sometimes serve functions that must be understood. Attitude functions can be *utilitarian*, *ego-defensive*, *value-expressive*, or *knowledge-enhancing*. For example, getting the fans of a local football team to admit that their side cheated during a game they won may run the risk of threatening their individual egos (their attitude function is ego-defensive). Or asking home owners to agree to fair increases in property taxes may run counter to their financial interests (their attitude function is utilitarian). If you run into an audience with strongly felt values that underlie a political attitude, your rational arguments can at times fall on deaf ears (their attitude function is value-expressive). This is partly why it is sometimes hard to get people who have pursued a vendetta against each other for many years to come to a compromise agreement: the bad feelings have been festering for so long that the entrenched attitudes of the antagonists may serve as ego-defense or another of the four functions. Senders who fail to learn what their audiences know or feel about a topic invite communicative disaster.

Audience Social Makeup—A Demographic Analysis

Each audience is composed of people who can be socially profiled. These profiles then allow the sender to adapt the message to the audience in commonsense ways, depending on age, gender, religious affiliation, and so on. For example, one audience for a political message might comprise mostly members of one political party or ideology, while another audience might comprise listeners of a wide variety of political persuasions. It may sometimes be easier to manage homogeneous audiences, because there is less variation among them, but heterogeneous audiences may provide a greater number of people actually open to change—because some may not have yet taken sides. Table 7.1 lists some common demographic categories used for making these profiles. Most of these categories are self-explanatory. Consumer membership could refer to the readers of a particular magazine, the regular viewers of a soap opera, or the loyal purchasers of a consumer product or service. Advertisers might discover a commonality within a particular consumer membership that could then be appealed to in an ad. Family membership refers to whether a person is an active member, communicatively or just psychologically, of a family, or else is what we would call an *isolate*.

Knowing the demographics of audience members may help the sender fine-tune the message. An audience for a specific advertisement might be made up of mostly suburban, middle-income high-school girls who all read *Seventeen*, which boasts to its readers that "Every month, you'll read about the hottest fashions trends for teens, beauty and style tips, relationship advice, and the latest news on today's biggest heart throbs. Staying cool has never

TABLE 7.1
Sample Demographic Categories for Audience Analysis

Self-Chosen	Born To
consumer membership	age/generation
education level	family membership
geographical affiliation	gender
hobby interests	nationality
marital status	racial/ethnic membership
occupation	
organization membership	
political affiliation	
religious affiliation	
socioeconomic status	

been this easy!" An ad designed to sell this audience a particular cell phone model might require different tactics than an ad selling that same cell phone to a group of males in their thirties from large cities who frequent basketball games and read *Penthouse*, a magazine that boasts to its readers that it has "sexually explicit content, dedicated to the sophisticated adult male, and offers photo essays of women, advice columns, contemporary commentary and titillating articles." By using a demographic profile of the audience, a sender can make logical inferences about what will work or not work. A newsletter for the supporters of a local school team could probably count on some interest among its readers in purchasing school-related paraphernalia. And an opinionated message on malpractice lawsuits may be received differently by an audience of doctors than it is by an audience of tort lawyers. Here the sender would be wise to create approaches that consider the sensitivities of the two groups on this issue. Audience research is therefore required before committing to a strategy for persuading some known group.

We now turn to one last method of audience analysis typically used by persuaders, propagandists, and to a very limited extent, arguers as they seek tactics and strategies in preparing messages.

The Communicative Setting—A Topographic Analysis

Senders must take many circumstances into consideration as they prepare their messages. These include (1) the *location, size,* and expected *life span* of the audience; (2) whether audience members will *interact* with each other in response to messages received; (3) whether the sender will actually make *social contact* with receivers, a contact that may range from a live speech to an anonymous street sign that warns, "Keep off the grass!" and (4) whether the audience *assembles* in one location or is *dispersed* in time and space via communication technology.[9] A live television broadcast has a mass audience dispersed in space but not in time (leaving aside those who record the broadcast for later viewing). A book has an audience dispersed in both space and time, since people can read the book in any geographic location at any time after the book is published. Much of today's media have audiences dispersed in both space and time (through the use of videotaping, CDs, and so on).

We also have newer forms of audiences that do not fit easily into this framework, such as the Internet audience, whose activities include online swapping of individually controlled or produced audio- or video-recordings, and automated telephone calling to large numbers of people. With the Internet, the message flow from a unified sender to a dispersed set of receivers does not always apply, as for example occurs with mutual Web links scattered among small website hosts.

In addition, audiences sometimes have a *collective history* that makes communicating with them on particular occasions unique. Viewers who watch the Academy Awards may have memories of previous shows and assorted expectations and feelings about awards for Best Picture and so on. The promoters and producers of these programs obviously need to understand their audience in order to maximize the positive effects of the programs. Another audience with unique characteristics might be that faced by attorneys who argue a constitutional issue before sitting justices (a small audience). Such arguers or persuaders have to know the prevailing procedures of the court, the conventions and courtesies expected of them, and the temperaments of the individual justices. Speaking to a graduating class at a particular school is another example of an occasion that requires the speaker to understand a particular audience, by perhaps considering the prevailing views of this particular generation and the school's history.

One last point about the communicative setting concerns whether the sender can treat media audiences as groups of isolated and easily manipulated individuals, as early theorists imagined. Should the producers of a television program on developing American woodland imagine that they are speaking to several million separate individuals? Most of us live in communities and social networks that share common attitudes, beliefs, and customs. These networks and communities can predispose us to react in ways that vary from place to place and region to region. If you live in the eastern section of the United States, you may be more biased toward preserving the woodlands in the western states. But if you live in the western states, you may feel that "Yes, it's okay for Easterners to think that way, but they had the chance to develop their wooded regions in the last century—we didn't." Not all media audiences comprise sets of neighbors; some audiences are sets of people with narrowly defined media-gratification interests, such as historians attending a seminar on nineteenth-century Portugal, science-fiction enthusiasts watching a television program on Star Trek trivia, at-home wine makers reading a how-to book, couples shopping for honeymoon locations, and political activists searching for voting records online.

Communication researchers Sorin Matei and Sandra Ball-Rokeach report that many Los Angeles neighborhoods now have an "Internet connectedness" that is associated with civic participation and indirectly contributes a sense of "belonging to a residential community."[10] This Internet-contributed social infrastructure can be a good resource for senders and audiences alike: the former can become more familiar with these "connected communities" and can use them to better understand how to approach geographically defined audiences, and the latter can use the local infrastructure to confirm or disconfirm their reactions to the messages created by public and professional senders. The authors say that not all people (especially in ethnic enclaves) have yet come to value learning to use the Internet as a means of incidentally enriching the communicative infrastructure of their local communities.

Methods of Researching Audiences—
An Audience Analysis

The methods described in the following paragraphs can be variously used to carry out much of the demographic, psychographic, and topographic audience analysis activities described above. These data-collection methods help to answer general questions about an audience and specific questions about how that audience will probably respond to given messages. I will briefly describe the use of focus-groups; interviews, surveys, and observations; and research libraries and the Internet in performing research into particular, intended audiences.

Focus Groups

Focus groups seem to have been first used in World War II by the U.S. Army for evaluating training and propaganda films.[11] As often happens, innovations are found by necessity. Focus groups involve perhaps seven or more individuals who are invited (or are sometimes given a small payment) to assemble in a room along with a moderator. The session usually starts with the presentation of a film, videotape, audio recording, an object of some type, or even a live performance. The purpose of the group meeting is to gather information on the group members' attitudes, emotions, beliefs, or likely behavior regarding the stimulus just shown in order to better understand similar audiences of interest. Typically, the moderator opens the discussion with a broad question, such as "Now that we've seen the film, I'm wondering what thoughts or feelings come to mind about it?" The discussion is usually taped or videotaped, and the group members' comments may be transcribed by typists. The moderator's main job once the discussion is under way is to keep the group on topic, while not influencing exactly what is said.

The moderators of focus groups use open questions to promote debate, challenge participants, and gauge the range of participants' perspectives about the topic. Moderators must keep things focused by encouraging discussion among all participants, and ensuring that the discussion is not dominated by some or avoided by others. We should remember that researchers have already analyzed the topic objectively, formulated research hypotheses about likely participant reactions, and developed a set of focused questions for obtaining subjective information from the participants. The discussions may be organized into phases that take up different issues over the one to two hours of the discussion, and may later probe what was uncovered earlier in the discussion. Moderators must keep their own opinions and biases out of the discussion so as not to influence what is said by participants. Thus, focus groups at their best are (1) interactive, because group members get to influence each other; (2) subjective, because group members are asked to consider their own personal perceptions and feelings; (3) nondirective, to varying extents, because the moderator tries to avoid influencing exactly what is said; and (4) re-creatively introspective, because moderators ask participants to think back to parts of the experience and tell how they were reacting to the stimulus at that moment.

Though moderators sometimes make comments, their most important job is to skillfully ask questions that stimulate discussion in hoped-for directions. The most general questions, often asked in the earlier stages, are unstructured: "What impressed you most in this film?" Semi-structured questions provide greater focus: "What did you learn from this pamphlet that you hadn't known before?" "How did you feel about the part where Karen and her friends were asked to leave the club?" Structured questions deal with issues that are of specific interest to the researchers, but are used only occasionally and toward the end: "Judging from this ad, do you think brand A cell phones offer more features than the cell phone you are currently using?" Transitional questions are used either when the group has gotten off-topic or someone has brought up a new issue that is on-topic. Mutational questions with varying levels of structure can be abruptly inserted at the end of a session if a specific topic has not come up spontaneously: "One last thing I'd be interested in hearing about is . . ." Follow-up questions can be more or less structured, to get greater depth on an issue: "What did you see in the film that makes you think that?" "How did you feel about that when it first came up in the program?" Some of the ways moderators subtly influence the discourse of focus groups involve ignoring certain comments or verbally redirecting the group's attention with a question; and though focus groups are designed to be interactive, moderators sometimes openly seek individual reactions and not group-created ones.[12]

The data obtained during focus-group sessions are then analyzed after the discussions are over. Usually, numerous focus groups, representative of a larger intended audience, are studied before any conclusions are drawn about the topic at hand. The larger audience could be an entire country, a region of the country, a locality, or some slice of the nation defined by one or more demographic categories such as teenagers, older patients in hospitals, or trainees for an organization. Say the stimulus for the focus groups is a tape of several speeches given by a candidate for governor of a state. The groups could be composed of registered voters in the state. Or for a more detailed analysis, the groups could be composed of registered voters from different regions of the state, or of registered voters segregated by age and gender, for example. Now if many negative comments about the speaking voice of the candidate turn up, the researchers might conclude that the candidate's speaking style will be a problem in the coming campaign. The data could be analyzed qualitatively by perhaps noting if comments were negative, positive, or neutral. The data could also be analyzed quantitatively by noting how many negative comments were made, and how many respondents said negative things. Some combination of both approaches could be used. Marketers also use focus groups to, among other things, discover interesting facets of consumer opinion. One marketer might find that many people apparently feel guilty about not cleaning their oven as often as they remember their parents doing; so a product that claims you do not have to clean your oven as often when using it might sell well because of this widespread guilt. Focus-group researchers often provide a summary of the themes they have discovered, with sample quotes to those who commissioned the research.[13]

Focus groups are an alternative to surveys, interviews, observations, and Internet and library research for analyzing audiences. All these methods can be used to study public attitudes, perceptions, and beliefs about things of interest to researchers: consumer products, political candidates, government policies, and social or organizational practices, for example. One important advantage of a focus group is that the collector of the data has a minimal amount of influence on the data, although some groups are run more pragmatically than others. Cues as to what the researchers are interested in are kept from the discussants as much as possible. One downside feature of focus-group research is that its data are less precise than the data collected in a survey or in multiple standardized interviews. And participants in focus groups may not always publicly mention things they think privately. Thus, focus groups may sometimes need to be used in conjunction with other methods of analysis.

Surveys, Interviews, and Observations

With either surveys or standardized interviews, the researcher defines topic areas and poses questions. The questions can be closed, "How old are you?" or open ended, "What, if anything, do you think about raising property taxes?" The chief advantage of asking standardized questions of a representative sample of an intended audience is that you can secure responses in an exhaustive way. You might learn, for example, that 43 percent of respondents support a proposed increase in property tax, 43 percent oppose it, and 14 percent are unsure or uninterested. Another advantage of the interview or survey is that you can directly seek the information you are looking for without having to wait for respondents to spontaneously speak up on your topic, as you would in a focus group. And just about anyone can be employed to ask scripted questions written to help uncover needed information.

It can be expensive to poll or survey large audiences. However, if the researcher's topic is of current interest, there may be survey data available online. The Cornell Institute for Social and Economic Research maintains a website where visitors can access surveyed information: www.ciser.cornell.edu/info/polls.shtml. Other organizations that provide a similar service include Gallup, the Roper Center for Public Opinion Research, and the National Opinion Research Center. You can do your own Web search for such sites using the search phrase {polls surveys}. All polling and survey information, whether you collect it yourself or get it from the pollster, must be taken with some skepticism, because some of the respondents may not have had much information on the topic or may not have given the topic much thought before they answered the questions. And clever commercial pollsters can at times patronize their prime clients by asking questions in ways that produce answers these clients are hoping to hear. As with other forms of research, it is best when you can confirm your information by using multiple sources independent of each other.

Propaganda dissemination is possible through surveys or interviews using a method called *push-polling*. Here the propagandists might claim to be conducting a survey, but they are really planting partisan-inspired ideas in the minds of the respondents, as when a telemarketer calls voters at home and asks, "Some people are now accusing Mayor X of suppressing a corruption investigation against Council Member Y, who supported the mayor's run for office. How do you feel about this?" People who are called and asked about Mayor X may begin to distrust the mayor—even if no proof of the accusation exists.

When the audience in question is located in the same geographical region, it is often possible to simply use observation to note their public behavior and then make inferences regarding a topic. People may say one thing in surveys, interviews, and focus groups and yet act differently in their day-to-day lives. If you discover that most people say they do not give money to beggars in the street, you might want to observe what happens when a sampling of these people are actually approached by panhandlers.

Research Libraries and the Internet

Learning about specific audiences and markets can also be done with the help of the thousands of reference books available in a good research library. There is a wealth of data about national groups around the world (e.g., *Information Please*), as there is about people belonging to larger domestic groups. Some resources include the *Encyclopedia of Private Organizations*; the *Encyclopedia of International Organizations*; the *Encyclopedia of Organizations*; the *Cyberlaw Encyclopedia of Organizations*; the *Encyclopedia of Associations, Fraternal Organizations, Environmental Organizations and Conferences*; and the *Encyclopedia of Medical Organizations and Agencies*. Specific groups of people often have their own websites where you can learn about what the groups do and even read a mission statement for some. The above list was compiled with an Internet search using the search phrase {encyclopedia organizations}.

Audiences' Attribution of Credibility for Given Senders

Inevitably, any audience will come to view the source of a message as credible or not, based on a set of rational or irrational factors. Whether the communication is face-to-face or through a mediated message (electronic or print), we can sort **sender credibility** into three general categories: (1) pre-message credibility, (2) during-message credibility, and (3) post-message credibility. Credibility can also be understood in terms of three perceived attributes of the sender: competence, character, and dynamism. Figure 7.1 shows how credibility can be tracked for the three perceived attributes.[14] As time passes, each attribute can independently rise, fall, or remain constant as a result of salient events before, during, and after a communicative act. We also see how the sender's message creates effects within the audience.

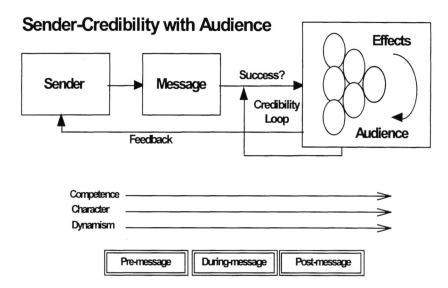

FIGURE 7.1 Factors affecting audience perceptions of credibility for sender.

The audience then provides feedback to the sender, who may adjust the approach the message takes in light of the feedback. And early credibility effects from messages reaching the audience may influence later credibility effects, for better or worse (this is known as a *credibility loop*).

Pre-message Credibility

Pre-message credibility concerns the existing images audience members have for a given sender, if any. *Reputation* is one good example of a pre-message image factor. If the sender of a message has a good reputation with the audience, the audience's expectations will be positive. Further, the extent to which a sender's image is well-defined for an audience will result in more helpful or more harmful effects. When the sender is unknown to the audience or a message is anonymous, as might occur with a political message posted on a public wall by an unknown source, there will be no reputation. Then the image will be formed by the message itself, possibly with some *heuristic*. Heuristics are simple signs we sometimes use to evaluate something. With sender-credibility, an example of a heuristic might be the speaker's manner of speaking or some general category in which the sender can be placed: drug-offender, clergy member, accountant, or homemaker, for example. In the case of public speakers, the moments just before the speech are also part of the pre-message period. The speaker's general appearance and manner, any audiovisual aids present (equipment, music, pictures, flags), and any introduction by another speaker may all affect an audience's sense of credibility for the persuader. With media messages, the reputations of the producers, distributors, or outlets carrying the messages may affect pre-message credibility. Any pre-message publicity for the message may also affect credibility. And the opening moments (e.g., the credits) of the message itself may affect credibility.[15]

During-message Credibility

During-message credibility especially concerns impressions of the sender formed by the audience as the message is experienced and processed. *Competence* concerns whether the creator or deliverer of the message has, among other things, seemingly worked hard, gotten the story straight, proved accurate and effective at reaching the obvious goals of the message, and been generally skillful as a communicator. *Character* concerns matters of honesty, believability, and integrity. Problems can occur here when the message appears to contain lies, exaggerations, or minimizations. And audience members' perceptions of these sender attributes may be inaccurate. For example, the speaker of a live message or media message may have an appearance and manner that seems honest or dishonest when the truth is just the opposite. A third during-message credibility component concerns *dynamism*, that is, whether the communicator exudes energy, enthusiasm, charisma, or a host of other attributes that may capture an audience's imagination and spirit.[16]

In one recent study, reaction shots of television-studio audience members were used to affect the credibility of selected guests as they gave their opinions. Reaction shots caught by the television cameras of either the moderator or the audience members were used right after a guest would say something. The director of the program selected camera shots in

ways that either helped or hurt the credibility of the guests. If a guest made a statement for
or against something, the reaction shots selected could show head nods of agreement or the
smiles of audience members; but at other times, the reaction shots chosen by the director
could show heads shaking in disagreement or negative facial expressions. The study found
that perceptions of trustworthiness were especially influenced by the selective use of supportive or nonsupportive nonverbal reactions.[17]

Post-message Credibility

Post-message credibility involves at least four things. The first concerns what the sender
might do or not do to *follow up* after a message. A public speaker, for example, might make
promises. But if the speaker's audience members then expect to receive materials in the mail
from the speaker, and those materials never come, the speaker's credibility may go down,
depending on the audience's standards and expectations about promises being kept. And if
the producers of a television-promoted product bill their customers for more than the advertised price, credibility can go down also. A second factor influencing post-message credibility concerns *public events* that occur after the message, events that are beyond the control of
the sender. If I urge the members of my community to form a block-watch organization to
patrol the neighborhood, my credibility may go up if the next day a violent mugging occurs
on the very streets the block-watch group is planning to patrol. Or a news anchor's credibility may go down if an ongoing news event turns out differently than the anchor predicts. A
third factor concerns the fact that members of an audience can *communicate* with each other
during a public event, or after a television program or a face-to-face sales pitch, and so on.
This communication can obviously affect the audience's perceptions of credibility for the
sender. And last, third parties may *intrude* on the communication event with their opinions
about the sender and the sender's message. These third parties might include opinion writers, politicians, or audience friends, neighbors, or family members.

Managing Specific Audiences

The most basic things audience members bring to the communicative event are their motives
for partaking in the communication and their individual personalities. For example, dogmatic or closed-minded personalities may be hard to influence unless the sender can invoke
authoritarian images that the dogmatic personalities can identify with. Open-minded people are just the opposite. According to Larson, much of the study on personality variables centers on the psychological factors of self-esteem, confidence, anxiety, and ego-defensiveness.[18]
Higher or lower self-esteem may make people easier or harder to persuade. Anxiety might
also make us more vulnerable to influence, and messages that reduce this anxiety may be
better received than messages that increase the anxiety.

People who are ego-involved also tend to develop strong feelings about a topic, tend to
learn the various arguments that support their positions, and tend to feel confident about
what they believe in. A very interesting point here is that ego-involved people may at times
be easier to influence than, say, apathetic people. This can occur when the sender's materials
support the ego-involved person's point of view. The new material is processed very efficiently and maybe without a lot of scrutiny. The ego-involved receiver's position may then

move from "I think we probably should" to "Boy, do I think we should!" In other words, because the sender's view is supportive of the ego-involved receiver's existing view, the receiver might be moved to a more extreme position on the topic.

So far we have discussed issues, one at a time, about influencing audiences. But what about an overall strategy that persuaders can use to manage particular audiences? One strategy for **audience management** is to *adapt* your message to the specific audience. You might try to adapt it to each member individually, but except with the smallest of audiences, say a family meeting, this is seldom possible. A more practical approach is to adapt the message to various segments of an audience. One way to do this is to appeal to those who are either supporters of the message, fence sitters, opposers, or some combination of these. Politicians sometimes try to energize the party faithful by saying just those things that the party faithful want to hear; this is sometimes described as throwing them "red meat." At other times, politicians appeal to the fence sitters. The rationale for this second approach is that the faithful are already on your side, and the opposition will likely never switch sides, but the fence sitters may eventually pick one side or the other, so why not yours? Although politicians do not often spend valuable resources on trying to convert the opposition, other communicators do, as sometimes happens when proselytizers of one religion try to convert nonbelievers or to get members of another religion to "switch sides."

Another audience-management strategy is to *appeal to the middle ground*, the *middle ground* being defined as either the modal, most popular position, or as the average position in a particular audience. This requires psychographically profiling your audience to find out where its "center of gravity" is on issues relevant to your purpose. If the most popular position is moderately for something, then your goal is to move the audience to be a little more strongly for that position, or a little less strongly for that position, depending on your purpose.

One other approach is to envision your audience as a "virtual person,"[19] or **virtual audience**. This approach assumes that an audience can take on a life of its own, or that the whole is greater than the sum of the parts. This approach also assumes that you can move a whole audience in ways that you could move few if any of the individuals within it.

In fact, demagogues probably move mass audiences in just this way, by swaying group feelings to create a momentum that individuals in the audience find irresistible. Demagogues, like other propagandists, also often resolve in self-serving ways the ambiguity that is found in most social and political situations. In many situations, questions about who did what, when, where, why, with what motives, and with what effect are often never totally clear and are usually open to discussion and disagreement. Historically, people like Hitler, Stalin, Mao Tse-tung, Napoleon, and Alexander the Great were able to sway audiences with demagoguery.[20] The virtual audience develops feelings, values, beliefs, and customs that can perhaps be addressed in a singular way. Other highly charismatic people may be able to accomplish this feat without necessarily becoming a demagogue or war criminal.

Culture and Persuasion (Sociographics)

To understand their audiences, senders need to consider the underlying cultural orientations of those audiences. If you wanted to convince people to teach their children a foreign language at an early age (perhaps at age three), what obstacles would you encounter as you addressed people in one country or another? Would your project be more successful in one part of the world than another? Would you have to use different appeals in this culture or that one? Social scientists Craig Thompson and Zeynep Arsel have studied the success of Starbucks coffee shops and have concluded that while this chain has had a "globalizing" effect on how coffee shops now operate around the world, local customers "nonetheless appropriate the meanings of global brands to their own ends, creatively adding new cultural associations, dropping incompatible ones, and transforming others to fit into local cultures and lifestyle patterns."[21] In other words, local customers still use their coffee shops in locally preferred ways, even when consuming a new product line with a globalizing influence. This interactive process in which both seller and buyer influence the scenes of the transaction has been called "glocalization." By altering its product lines, Starbucks has tried hard to deal with the criticisms offered by anti-Starbucks websites. While the company may not have placated its adversaries, it seems to have succeeded with local markets by partly accepting what works locally.

When drafting persuasive messages within a particular culture or subculture, we should keep in mind the notion of a **cultural premise**. A cultural premise is a core belief or basic assumption that people in a given scene or local culture have. It is not hard to get Americans to accept something that seems new and improved. This bias for innovation and change may sometimes result in a community losing, say, a historic building or social practice due to a campaign for something new. Let's review what is known about cultural premises in America and then briefly look at some interesting new approaches to studying cultural premises around the world.

Cultural Premises in America

Author John McElroy argues that Americans in particular have inherited core beliefs first formed in the colonial-frontier experience where survival was not certain and thus any means of ensuring it were deemed very important.[22] Because of this experience, Americans especially value work and the rightful benefits of work. As newcomers to a hostile continent with many natural resources and a good deal of land, Americans quite understandably came to believe that success was possible for those who dared to dream of it and then braved through tenaciously. Moving from the eastern cities and towns of the original American colonies to the undeveloped and sometimes dangerous West took courage, but many of the risk takers did succeed in building communities and success for themselves. Today, many a midwestern or far western town or city is a living testament to this belief. The frontier mentality also required a sense of individualism and self-reliance (at a cost to the native cultures that were pushed aside during this expansion). National confidence exudes even today in the unique notion that "What has to be done will teach you how to do it," and that individuals are responsible for their own well-being, although helping others helps yourself.

In addition, America was and is a very religious country; many Americans trust in God and trust that God gives them rights and responsibilities. Many Americans also believe in democracy and capitalism. And the eighteenth-century relationship between the royalty of Europe (especially in England) and America has had a profound influence on Americans, who are ever ready to suspect conspiracy and corruption from an established government; thus American presidents may serve no more than two terms, which is a way to wash out the old and bring in the new. According to McElroy, Americans believe that society is a collection of individuals, that people are sovereign, that the least amount of government possible is best as long as the majority decides, and that a written constitution is essential to government. Americans believe that people essentially want to do the right things, but that people will also abuse power when they have it. Given the American belief in progress that derives from the above cultural premises, it is easy to imagine how a persuader in America could, for example, persuasively link a specific idea with the idea of progress: "The time for thinking of a workplace as a physical address is coming to a close; the world of tomorrow will have most workers staying near home, but contributing their work electronically or by ground or air shipment."

Researchers Joshua Hammond and James Morrison identify cultural traits similar to the above when they describe Americans as insisting on choice, pursuing impossible dreams, wanting ever bigger things and more things, being impatient with time but accepting mistakes, having an urge to improvise, and being fixated with the new.[23] In fact, America is so caught up with change (which increases in speed with each decade) that in the not-too-distant future, it will have to worry about pursuing two seemingly incongruous things: diversity and unity. There already are neighborhoods in America that have become cultural "cocoons" where people might think they were in a foreign country. One other point about the American cultural premises reviewed so far is that they do not always describe all people in the nation. Not everybody shares these premises. So a persuader or sender cannot simply pick one of these premises and put it to use in a persuasive message. The premise must be chosen carefully, and the audience must then apply it to the message.

Larson summarizes a set of myths that describe America and offer persuaders underlying premises to use implicitly or explicitly during persuasion. Americans, according to Larson, sometimes believe that country or rural people are clever and resourceful. Presidential candidates in America often like to cite their rural origins if they have them. And Americans like Horatio Alger stories, in which someone young sets out to make their mark in the world and does so. Larson also speculates that Americans tend to believe in secular messiahs when things go wrong. For companies in trouble, this may mean the ax for a current CEO and the installment of a replacement. In politics, we Americans often look to a newly elected president for secular salvation. We love conspiracy theories. And we believe in challenge as that which makes people better, stronger, and more competent—whether for college students, interns in hospitals, or recruits in army boot-camp.[24] Author Robert Reich offers what he calls "parables." He portrays the American "psyche" as a belief in America as the last bastion of what is good and moral in the world. The "mob at the gates of civilization" includes drug traffickers, terrorists, nations willing to give in to political extortion, and weapons proliferators. Reich adds to this the conflicting images of the "benevolent community," which describes a community ever ready to lend a helping hand, and the "rot at the top," which envisions the corruption of a good society by the powerful and the greedy.[25]

How do the above cultural premises come into play within persuasive messages? Persuasive messages usually include a set of ideas that lead to a conclusion. Often these step-wise arguments have several components. Take the argument "You should eat an orange every day because oranges contain vitamin C, which strengthens your resistance to colds." Underlying this argument is the cultural premise that through rationality, problems can be solved, or that health and happiness are possible through knowledge and know-how. To take another example, I might argue that UFOs did land in Roswell, New Mexico, in 1949, but their landings were covered up by the U.S. government. Underlying this argument is the cultural premise that the government routinely covers up things in conspiracies that benefit the insiders at the expense of the outsiders. Here the cover-up hides the fact that the U.S. government is unable to protect us from UFO landings. Or I might try to sell you a big, plasma-screen, high-definition TV, and I don't have to say that bigger is better, and more powerful is better because that may be assumed as a cultural premise. But bigger is not always better, nor is more powerful always better. The next time you have a power blackout, you may come to appreciate an old-fashioned mechanical can-opener. Finally, persuasive stories that fit cultural premises or reinforce myths in a locale may be especially effective.

Cultural Premises around the World

It is beyond the scope of this text to try to fully characterize the various sets of cultural premises held by societies around the world, though this is now an unfolding project for some researchers. England and the United States probably share many cultural premises that can be used by persuaders and propagandists. But perhaps one important difference between these two nations concerns the self-reliant, colonial-frontier experience of America. England has a much longer history, which has been characterized by conflicts with such rivals as Ireland, Scotland, France, Germany, the Netherlands, and the Norwegians. England has also had its share of internal conflicts emanating from the history of its royal families, the Protestant Reformation, and the birth of the Industrial Revolution. But tenacity at overcoming trouble seems buried deeply in the collective British psyche, and it especially came to the surface during World War II. France probably also has a set of cultural premises that are different from America's. France seemed willing to accept defeat during World War II at the hands of the Third Reich rather than to have its beautiful cities destroyed or its soldiers killed in numbers that might have rivaled the heavy losses of World War I.

In Saudi Arabia, a Christian attempting to convert a Muslim to Christianity could in certain circumstances be subject to beheading. The value of free speech is not a basic cultural premise in Saudi Arabia. By comparison, the northern countries of Europe may have the most egalitarian cultural premises on the planet. In the Netherlands, prostitution is legal, drugs are somewhat legal, and social-welfare benefits are easily obtained. Self-indulgence, it might seem, is more a virtue than a vice in the Netherlands. The liberalism of the northern countries may have gotten started during the Protestant Reformation in conjunction with the Renaissance and national resentment over interference in local affairs by the Pope in Rome. What about the southern countries of Europe? In the film *It Started in Naples*, actress Sophia Loren begins to yell and gesture in Italian at her character's ten-year-old son, who yells back in a dispute that means very little if anything to them. Then they both stop and laugh at themselves, seeming to appreciate how yelling and gesturing are meant to be a pleasurable bonding and not a hostile rejection—as if to say, humans are warm-blooded beings, not ice cubes. This cinematic anecdote may provide us with a first clue to some of the cultural premises of Italy.

A good start for making a global comparison of nations and their underlying cultural premises may be found in the World Values Survey, www.isr.umich.edu, which surveyed one thousand individuals in sixty-six countries to report on how the peoples of these respective nations feel about such things as work, family, religion, and even who should do the housework. Similarly, the International Social Survey Program (ISSP), www.issp.org, has surveyed thirty-eight nations on the following broad topics: environment, family and changing gender roles, national identity, religion, role of government, social inequality, social networks, and work orientations. According to authors Dan O'Hair, Rob Stewart, and Hannah Rubinstein, researchers at the International Social Survey Program posed the same series of questions to a representative sample of subjects in each of the thirty-eight participant nations. For example, they asked subjects if they believed that the Bible is the word of God. The ISSP site is interactive, so you can go and research your topic by inserting a phrase such as {"belief in God"}. This work is just getting started, and there is a long way to go before these nations' "souls" will be understood intimately.[26]

Perfection is not possible in predicting how audiences will respond to a given message. And in a free society, perfecting the ability to predict the effects of propaganda or persuasive messages is not desirable. Such perfection would put a great deal of power into the hands of those who would influence us. And in the words of British historian Lord Acton, "Power tends to corrupt and absolute power corrupts absolutely."

Chapter in Retrospect

VIGNETTE 1 **Audience Analysis: A Local Election Campaign**

Say a sixth-grade teacher riles parents during Careers Week by inviting a self-described car thief as one of five people to speak to the class. The car thief proceeds to show the class how to break into a car and brags about how much money he can make stealing cars. Later events involve the mayor in a political fight over Careers Week during the campaign for the coming mayoral election. We might conduct an audience analysis to find out what voters believe about (1) the purpose of Careers Week, (2) the teacher's aims in inviting the car thief, (3) what the teacher did in class as the car thief spoke, (4) what went wrong, if anything, and (5) who bears the greatest responsibility. Our analysis would also need to find out where the sentiments of the voters will lie—with the teacher, the thief, the mayor, or the other parents who objected to what happened.

Our audience analysis might put voters into four groups. The first group attributes to the teacher a "morally corrupt" attitude for inviting the thief. The second group believes that the teacher was "asleep at the switch" and did not do enough to monitor the unfolding situation. A third group thinks that the teacher had an understandable lapse due to pressures brought by the principal (who organized Careers Week), the students (who found the incident very entertaining), and the parents (who often clamor for lots of classroom activities like Careers Week). And the fourth group attributes total innocence to the teacher, who is seen as a victim of circumstances, and as having been misled by the car thief.

In the coming campaign, the mayor will be running against a challenger who makes an issue of the Careers Week incident. The mayor might "test the winds" of public sentiment and adopt the most popular of the four positions regarding the classroom event. (A true leader, however, would champion the fairest, most constructive position.) The mayor's challenger might adopt one of the two positions saying that the teacher did something wrong, and then point out that the scandal occurred on the current mayor's watch. This may work if a sufficient number of voters already feel this way, and especially so if these people are also very ego-involved.

VIGNETTE 2 **Audience Analysis: A Social Justice Campaign**

Perhaps you believe that someone must speak up about animals used for research because these creatures cannot speak up for themselves and are at times the victims of intense loneliness, great pain, and early death. You look around campus and realize that the plight of animals used for research is not much of a concern for people. You even learn that animals are used on your school's campus for research and then killed after their usefulness is over. You and one or two others decide to try and make a difference—at least on your campus. Your first goal is to assess what the campus community knows and feels about the issue. Your questions are (1) What does the campus community know, if anything, about the current practices for using animals for research on campus? (2) Do people think it acceptable to expose animals to stress or early death, even if some good comes from the research? (3) How strongly does the campus community feel that using animals for research on campus is wrong? (4) Do students, faculty, and others think that the proven benefits of using animals for research outweigh the costs to the animals? (5) How motivated are students, faculty, and others to do something about this practice on campus? (6) Do students, faculty, and others think something can or should be done about whatever is current policy? and (7) Is this a topic that people in general do not want to think about?

After collecting data on what people on campus know and feel about the issue, you formulate a campaign to achieve your goals. What you do will depend a great deal on the data you have collected. Perhaps you find out that most people do not know very much about animal research on campus. Or perhaps people do know a fair amount about the issue but do not seem to care very much. Maybe people know about the issue and do care, but feel there is not much they can do about the status quo. With your findings, you would construct a strategy to educate, motivate, encourage, or do some combination of the three.

Summary and Conclusions

Audiences for persuasion are a dynamic part of the process that senders must consider because audiences bring to communication a set of motives for participating, attitudes, beliefs, and behavioral tendencies. Senders therefore study their audiences by using audience analysis. Audience analysis involves several activities: (1) psychographic analysis, which involves studying collective, topic-relevant factors that are true about an audience, such as how much information audience members have, and what their common attitudes toward the topic are; (2) demographic analysis of an audience, which involves considering such categories as sex, age, or educational level in order to predict likely audience responses to a persuasive message; and (3) topographic analysis, which involves examining the "lay of the land" upon which persuasion will be attempted. The analyst might ask, "What's going on in the news that might affect things?" "Under what circumstances will the message be delivered?" or "Will the audience interact with each other or not?"

Our methods of researching audiences include the use of focus groups; surveys, interviews, and observation; and research libraries and the Internet. Persuaders must monitor the levels of pre-, during-, and post-message credibility that an audience attributes toward them. Managing a particular audience requires a strategy. Some strategies include appealing to the party faithful, or perhaps to fence sitters. Finally, the cultural premises that an audience subscribes to often affect how persuasive messages are processed. These premises differ from place to place, people to people, and culture to culture.

KEY TERMS

audience analysis (demo-
    graphic, psycho-
    graphic, topographic)
audience effects (antici-
    pated, boomerang,
    idiosyncratic, surprise)
audience management

auditor
cultural premise
focus groups
sender credibility
    (during-message,
    post-message,
    pre-message)

social judgment
    (anchor, assimilation,
    contrast effect, ego
    involvement, latitude
    of acceptance)
virtual audience

REVIEW QUESTIONS

1. What does the term *audience bonding* mean? How is it important to persuaders?
2. How are topographic, demographic, and psychographic analyses different?
3. How can the social judgment model help you decide how strongly to word your claims?
4. Why are focus groups sometimes used instead of surveys or interviews?
5. What does the term *push-polling* mean?
6. Why distinguish among pre-, during-, and post-message analyses of credibility formation?
7. What cultural premises seem prevalent among Americans?
8. How are cultural premises within countries around the world now being studied?

SUGGESTED PROJECTS AND ACTIVITIES

1. Pick one of the following persuasive topics: abortion, income tax simplification, the environment, national defense, local schools, violence in the media, sex, or various groups' rights and obligations. Now state a persuasive proposition about the topic you've just selected. Next, consider how you would have to take one of the following demographic categories into consideration as you prepare to persuade a particular audience (you name it): age, sex, financial status, race, ethnic membership, occupation, religion, religious conviction, political party membership, ideological position (Left, Center, Right), marital status, or number of children, if any.
2. Make a study of a small group of people who could serve as an audience for some future persuasive message (perhaps a class you're attending, the people you work with, a group of friends, or your family). First pick a topic. Then conduct a psychographic analysis to collect data on (1) what and how much factual information your audience has about your topic, (2) what relevant attitudes your audience has about your topic, and (3) what relevant behavior your audience engages in that concerns your topic (if any). Now develop a strategy for persuading this audience. Try it out.
3. Select a well-known group of people (e.g., the National Rifle Association, the National Education Association, the AARP, the Teamsters Union, the American Taxpayers'

Association, Greenpeace, the American Medical Association, the American Bar Association, the Association of Oil Drillers, and so on). Now select a persuasive topic you predict will receive an unwelcome response from your selected group. Analyze demographically and psychographically why you think you will get such a response. Now construct a message that tries to deal with the objections you expect to get.

4. Do the same as the above, but pick a topic that you believe will be well received by the group you select.

QUESTIONS FOR DISCUSSION

1. What people are most easily swayed by an audience in which they are members?

2. Where do you draw the line on how much audience analysis is ethical?

3. Defend in an essay the proposition that people as audience members can be moved more easily than any of them could be as individuals.

4. Compare a street mob being led by someone intent on taking action with a panel of appeals-court jurists intent on reviewing an appeal to a lower-court verdict. Specify as many essential differences as you can between these two audiences.

5. Should we think of an audience as more like a noun or more like a verb?

Notes

1. Denis McQuail, *Audience Analysis* (Thousand Oaks, CA: Sage, 1997), 1–3.

2. Forbes Hill, personal communication.

3. Theodore Clevenger, *Audience Analysis* (Indianapolis, IN: Bobbs-Merrill, 1973), 38–42.

4. Perhaps the first audiences go back even further to prehistoric times, when people gathered around a campfire at night to hear their leaders speak.

5. See for example Joseph DeVito, *The Elements of Public Speaking* (Boston: Addison, Wesley, Longman, 2003), 230–43.

6. Clevenger, *Audience Analysis*, 109–18.

7. The model also includes other terms, such as *latitude of rejection* and *latitude of noncommitment*.

8. Ronald Adler and Jeanne Elmhorst, *Communicating at Work: Principles and Practices for Business and the Professions* (New York: McGraw-Hill, 1996).

9. McQuail, *Audience Analysis*, 43–64.

10. Sorin Matei and Sandra Ball-Rokeach, "The Internet in the Communication Infrastructure of Urban Residential Communities: Macro- or Mesolinkage," *Journal of Communication* 53, no. 4 (Autumn 2003): 642–57.

11. Robert Merton and Patricia Kendall, "The Focused Interview," *American Journal of Sociology* 51 (1946): 541–57.

12. Claudia Puchta and Jonathan Potter, "Manufacturing Individual Opinions: Market Research Focus Groups and the Discursive Psychology of Evaluation," *British Journal of Psychology* 41, no. 3 (September 2002): 345–63.

13. Puchta and Potter, "Manufacturing Individual Opinions."

14. Regarding James McCroskey's findings, see for example Dan O'Hair, Rob Stewart, and Hannah Rubinstein, *A Speaker's Guidebook* (Boston: Bedford/St. Martin's, 2004), 357–58. For evidence on the first two of these, see Daniel O'Keefe, *Persuasion: Theory and Research* (Thousand Oaks, CA: Sage, 2002), 181–215.

15. For some people, a Disney film may signal a general credibility that a movie created by a company called, say, "Expedient Films" may not.

16. Some theorists suggest that goodwill or a variety of other possibilities including power, idealism, and similarity to audience are the third component; others see insufficient evidence for any third component. I opt for dynamism as credibility's third component. As George Grice and Robert Skinner say, "Dynamism is more closely associated with delivery rather than content. We enjoy listening to speakers who are energetic, inspiring, spirited and stimulating." The two authors also advise that a flippant or detached style may hurt credibility (this is their case for including goodwill as part of the third component). See George Grice and Robert Skinner, *Mastering Public Speaking*, 5th ed. (Boston: Pearson, 2004), 349–50.

17. Robin Nabi and Alexandra Hendriks, "The Persuasive Effect of Host and Audience Reaction Shots in Television Talk Shows," *Journal of Communication* 53, no. 3 (September 2003): 527–43.

18. Charles Larson, *Persuasion: Reception and Responsibility* (Belmont, CA: Wadsworth, 1998), 73. Personality variables center on the psychological factors of self-esteem, confidence, anxiety, and ego-defensiveness.

19. I am not here concerned with whether audiences actually are virtual persons or, according to the more extreme concept, "collective minds." The virtual-person metaphor is merely a model that may help persuaders more effectively prepare persuasive materials.

20. Alexander was apparently tutored by Aristotle, presumably on the means of persuasion. But this may have been a case where the teacher's lessons about persuasion were altered to create self-serving propaganda, as when Alexander got his supporters to agree to consider him a god on earth.

21. Craig J. Thompson and Zeynep Arsel, "The Starbucks Brandscape and Consumers' (Anticorporate) Experiences of Glocalization," *Journal of Consumer Research* 31 (2004): 631–42.

22. John McElroy, *American Beliefs: What Keeps a Big Country and a Diverse People United* (Chicago: Ivan R. Dee, 2000).

23. Joshua Hammond and James Morrison, *The Stuff Americans Are Made Of: The Seven Cultural Forces That Define Americans—A New Framework for Quality, Productivity and Profitability* (New York: Macmillan, 1996).

24. Larson, *Persuasion: Reception and Responsibility*, 210–32.

25. Robert Reich, *Tales of a New America* (New York: Times Books, 1987), 53–100, 201–32.

26. O'Hair, Stewart, and Rubinstein, *A Speaker's Guidebook*, 90–95.

CHAPTER 8

Needs, Emotions, Motivations, and Vulnerabilities

◆ **Chapter Objectives**

After reading this chapter, you will be able to:

- ◆ Distinguish feelings from emotions
- ◆ Describe how consideration of human needs can be a part of a persuasive strategy
- ◆ Compare the persuasive uses of virtues and vices
- ◆ Explain how persuasive messages can make use of emotions
- ◆ Evaluate the potential of subliminal ads to actually work
- ◆ Identify pathos in advertising, fashion, architecture, and music
- ◆ Compare the pathos in traditional art and postmodern art

While a picture may be worth a thousand words, a word may be worth a thousand pictures, too.

—DAVID BLAKESLEY

Seeing is believing.

—ANONYMOUS

A **CHILD OF THE** streets sits on a curb and stares at you while you are dining at a sidewalk café and are about to begin eating an expensive gourmet sandwich richly stuffed with delicacies and accompanied with a blend of freshly squeezed, exotic fruit juices served in a chilled, tall glass. If you momentarily make eye contact with the child, will you feel guilt, annoyance, sympathy, empathy? This story image could be used to link the emotion you might feel to a persuasive argument: Give food to needy children because the cost of just one gourmet-restaurant sandwich could send ten hungry children to bed with at least some nourishment in their stomachs. The image itself would not try to convince you with good arguments and well-researched evidence; rather, it would try to evoke in you, the receiver, compelling emotions with the help of images created in your mind. These emotions and images then could later evoke a verbal argument if you translated them in your mind: Some children need help, and I can certainly help—well, maybe I should do something.

This chapter considers the emotional methods of persuasion, or what Aristotle called proof through **pathos**, remembering that pathos can in subtle ways support the logos of persuasive messages, whether it is to put receivers in the right mood or to serve as additional information translated by receivers into thought. The chapter also examines how needs, emotions, appeals to virtues and vices, and what have sometimes been called **subliminal messages** can serve to influence receivers. It also examines the pathos often found in the arts, which often are used by persuaders.

Beyond this, I will explain why the emotional elements of persuasive messages continue to interest contemporary researchers, many of whom believe that persuasion may not work at all without receivers feeling something about persuasive messages,[1] whether the emotions are envisioned on a continuum that ranges from positive to negative, or simply as distinct states (e.g., fear, anger, joy). Beyond simple emotions, there also are the deep-seated values, or virtues. In the ancient world, good qualities or virtues were identified, and these can be linked to a persuader's objective. But so can vices, which are sometimes used in persuasive or propagandistic messages to corrupt people. Finally, we will examine selected artistic genres: advertising, clothing and adornment, music, architecture, such traditional art as oil paintings, and a new electronic art form possibly on the horizon. Briefly describing these genres will help us describe the sensitivities or even vulnerabilities of the individual receiver. We will further discuss some of the ideas introduced in this chapter about visual arts in chapter 11 by describing a relatively new field of communication study, *visual rhetoric*. Visual images can especially be used to evoke strong emotional reactions in receivers. But let's begin by comparing several analyses of the human needs that are often pressed into service by persuaders who seek to influence us.

Human Needs

When some people wake up in the morning, one of the first things they do is have breakfast. Others (probably fewer) wake up but do not "break the fast." What makes the difference? Habits, motivations, and especially needs (biological needs, in the case of breakfast) do. Persuaders sometimes analyze the needs and motivations of audiences before planning a persuasive strategy. Thinking back to chapter 6, we might ask, "Is it ethical to dig into the subterranean layers of human motivation to influence an audience?" The answer may depend on exactly what sorts of psychological things the persuader digs into about the makeup of persuasive targets. For example, if you discover your audience members need reassurance about the value of some expensive new purchase, reassure them—if you can rationally justify such reassurance. But say you discover that your audience feels reflexively guilty about something. If you play on their guilt to get the audience members to become $30-a-month sponsors for children in another country, we may have unethical persuasion. So what are appropriate ways that senders may analyze the needs and motivations of receivers in preparing their persuasive messages?

Perhaps the best-known analysis of human needs was offered by American psychologist Abraham Maslow, who describes five such personal needs: **physiological** (for food, drink, sleep, sex), **safety** (from accidents, wild animals, temperature extremes, criminals), **social** (for love, affection, belongingness), **esteem** (from others, for self), and **self-actualization** (becoming the best you can be).[2] A persuader might on one occasion believe that a particular audience of subsistence farmers is very concerned about feeding their families (a physiological need). This might lead to a persuasive claim about the desirability of crop rotation to avoid bad crop yields. A representative of a local police department when giving advice to seniors on ways to protect themselves from being robbed might base the appeal on the need for safety from criminals. The social need for belongingness could be used to motivate lonely people to serve as community volunteers. And you could perhaps convince people that their need for esteem could be raised by their achieving a worthy personal goal. Finally, the need for self-actualization could be used to motivate college seniors to spend a year after graduation backpacking around the world.

Psychologist William Schutz offers a narrower analysis (of interpersonal needs) with just three terms: affection, control, and inclusion. Notice the overlap and the differences between this analysis and Maslow's.[3] The need for *affection* can serve as a persuasive motivation in, say, convincing people to improve their interpersonal skills so they can get to know people they will enjoy being around. The need for interpersonal *control* can be satisfied through the give and take of a relationship with another person: perhaps you and your date will bicker over what movie to see together (and maybe this time, you will win out). And *inclusion* concerns being a part of the lives of other people. Most of us want to be wanted by other people. So we may listen intently if a persuader can show us how to be accepted for membership in some highly desired organization or club. But the motivational power of inclusion may be best appreciated if you imagine how it would feel if were you suddenly to be excluded from the lives of those who mean something to you (e.g., you are disowned by your family, fired from a job, disbarred from a secret organization, expelled from college, dumped by the person you are dating, divorced by a spouse, kidnapped, stripped of your citizenship, thrown out of the band or off the team). Ads for personal-grooming products often link usage of these products with maintaining our inclusion in relationships with others.

Composite Model

Let's use the above two analyses of human needs to create a composite, topoi-like model, as shown in figure 8.1 (see chapter 11 for discussion of term *topoi*, sing. *topos*). This model builds on the personal needs identified by Maslow and on the interpersonal needs identified by Schutz. To these needs I will add *social needs*, meaning the needs we feel as members of a nation or community. The arrows shown in the composite model simply indicate portals from which the lists can be conceptually linked to one another. Since we have already

Human Needs and Virtues

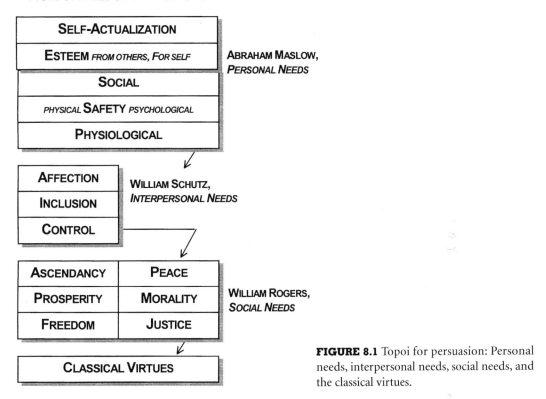

FIGURE 8.1 Topoi for persuasion: Personal needs, interpersonal needs, social needs, and the classical virtues.

discussed the needs as identified by Maslow and Schutz, we will now turn to the six social needs shown near the bottom of the model.

The need for *freedom* is something most people feel intensely. The anthropological-historical progression of humankind from tribes to larger autocratic and then democratic societies illustrates well this basic social need. But even a tiger pacing the perimeter of a cage demonstrates the origins of this human need for freedom. *Prosperity* concerns the need for the material success of individuals, families, communities, and entire societies. *Ascendancy* in this model concerns two things: (1) the need for individuals in a particular society to pursue and achieve ambitions vis-à-vis one another, and (2) the need for factions of or entire societies to pursue and achieve collective ambitions vis-à-vis other factions or societies. Here is the arena in which people compete for ascendancy on the national or world stage. Here is the place where groups shout out, "We're contenders!" Even the tribal mentality includes a sense of ascendancy in which one primitive tribe may feel that it is superior ("We are human") to surrounding tribes ("They are subhuman"). This all may sound like societal chest-beating, but recorded history tells us that political ascendancy is a recurring and powerful theme in the affairs of people, from the ancient societies of Egypt, India, China, Persia, Greece, and Rome down to the imperial powers and then superpowers of the sixteenth through twenty-first centuries.

Peace is a collective state of mind that anyone who has had to live for an extended time in a war zone, or even in a neighborhood that feels like a war zone because of its high levels of crime, can understand.[4] The need for *morality* can come in two forms. The first is a religious morality that can result in salvation for believers. The second is a secular morality that occurs when people just feel a need for goodness. At a minimum, morality can be valued by people as a way to feel that they have won the moral high ground in ongoing disputes. Last is the need for *justice* in the affairs of communities.

Persuaders can choose from items on all three lists to find links for motivating their audiences in desired directions. Certainly lawyers in a trial will often link their respective persuasive objectives to a jury's sense of justice. There was a popular song some time ago with the lyrics "Take this job and shove it!" These words very probably play on a sense of freedom from the excess controls of an employer. And the terms *peace* and *prosperity* are said by political consultants to have almost magical properties for an incumbent president, prime minister, or premier seeking reelection. Not all of the needs categories shown in figure 8.1 can be used in every persuasive message, but often more than one can be used on particular occasions. Finally, although the **classical virtues** are not examples of human needs in the sense in which Maslow or Schutz describes human needs, nonetheless we can list them in the composite model because they too can be linked to persuasive objectives. A virtue is an ideal that has universal appeal to people, although various cultures may differ over the importance of particular virtues. Virtues are emotional in nature and include courage, generosity, justice, magnanimity, magnificence, prudence, temperance, and wisdom.

Packard's Eight Needs Used by Advertisers

Vance Packard, in a very entertaining book *The Hidden Persuaders*, identifies a number of needs to which advertisers especially appeal.[5] As the old saying goes, "Sex sells." Many things are therefore sold by our associating them with *sex* (the first of the needs Packard identifies) or romance. Cosmetics, jeans, beer, cars, and toothpaste are just some examples of products that suggest that by buying them you can improve your social (and sex) life. The second of Packard's needs is the need for *power*. Power can be associated with cars, detergents, insecticides, and a host of other things. One recent car ad showed the vehicle practically driving straight up the side of a mountain. How many times would you need a car to perform this way? Nonetheless, some people feel good just knowing the "power is under the hood, should they ever need it." *Emotional security* is Packard's third need, and advertisers would have us believe that security is something we can purchase when we buy such things as home burglar-alarms, insurance, or a credit card such as American Express—the ads for which emphasize the security the card brings when we travel abroad. These products may sometimes provide physical security, but they can give us a sense of emotional security too.

Some products sell a sense of *roots*, Packard's fourth need. Sometimes a longing for roots infects people born and bred in a country other than the one they live in. Food and beverage products especially take advantage of this longing for roots when they can. But at other times, your sense of longing for roots may concern the place you call home now. In America, for example, Pepperidge Farm, a maker of bread products, has built its business partly with ad images reminiscent of a nineteenth-century, apple-pie, white-picket-fence America.

Packard's fifth need, *youthfulness*, is worshipped today in the media and in pop culture. Many products are now sold through their association with youthfulness and with on-screen personalities who are youthful; even dog-food ads sometimes show puppies. Going on to our sixth need, if an ad for a product tells you that it costs more but that you are worth it, the technique concerns what Packard calls the need for *self-gratification*. Upscale jewelry and clothing products may sell through an association with *glamour*, the seventh need. And with tongue in cheek, advertisers have marketed Grey Poupon mustard by associating it with *elitism* (the feeling that we are a little better, smarter, or nobler than other people), Packard's eighth need.

Persuasive Appeals through Common Emotions

An **emotion** is different from a **feeling**, although the two words are sometimes confused. An emotion is a mental state, and a feeling is a physical state. I might feel pain in my hand after an accident while I experience fear (an emotion) when I look at my wound. While I was born with the capacity to feel pain, I had to learn to fear the consequences of accidents. I might have learned this fear from my parents, teachers, or from my previous experiences with accidents. Emotions are sometimes analyzed as physiological arousal combined with a mental reaction to the arousal. Notice in the example that in order to experience the emotion of fear, I must first recognize that I may be in danger, perhaps of bleeding to death or losing the use of my hand. In other cases, I may learn to associate physical sensations (e.g., the "rush" of seeing someone to whom I am attracted) with an emotional state (happiness).

Connecting Emotions with Thoughts and Behavior

Why does eliciting emotions in their listeners help persuaders? The easy answer is that we often feel emotions when we take action—especially important actions. But our thoughts too can elicit emotions through associations, as when you think back fondly to some long-ago vacation with your family or remember some bitter, past incident when someone was nasty to you. When you enter an office to be interviewed by a prospective employer, you may feel a variety of emotions, including fear, confidence, or determination. Now if I want to sell you a pamphlet on how to be more successful as a job applicant, I may motivate the purchase by reminding you of the fear that you had in the past when on a job interview. I may suggest that you buy the pamphlet to remove that message-elicited fear. Perhaps then you buy it and feel more comfortable as you leaf through the reassuring pages.

The connection between emotions and cognitions can also be illustrated using conversations that contain abbreviated attempts at persuasion. Box 8.1 shows a snippet of dialogue from a Hollywood film. The story line involves a brother asking his sister for money to pay a gambling debt. When she refuses, he tries to make her feel guilty by bringing up the expectation of their now-dead mother that the sister take care of her "little brother." Notice how the persuasion of the brother includes just two statements. But these statements imply a mixture of emotional appeal (resentment, mock shame) and enthymemic argument. One of the statements signals the main argument and one a supporting argument. The sister's persuasion contains just one line. We can infer here that she will not give her brother the money (a claim of intended behavior) because of his implied past history of losing money to bookies

---

BOX 8.1

Pathos Used in Conversational Dispute

Both	*Drama dialogue of orphaned brother and sister*
Brother:	Give me the money to pay my bookie.
Sister:	Forget it; you've gotten the last from me.
Brother:	Mother expected you to take care of your little brother.
Brother	*Argument with emotion of personal resentment*
Claim	Give me the money to pay my bookie. [stated]
Evidence	Mother expected you to take care of your little brother. [stated]
Warrant	Paying my bookie will protect me from harm. [implied]
Backing	If I don't pay, they'll send the enforcers. [implied]
Sister	*Argument with emotional appeal of indignation*
Claim	Forget it; you've gotten the last from me! [stated]
Evidence	You've lost money time after time. [implied]
Warrant	Enough is enough. [implied]
Backing	The more I give you, the more you'll lose. [implied]
Brother	*Subargument to support evidence in his above argument*
Claim	Mother expected you to take care of your little brother. [stated]
Evidence	She was worried about me. [implied]
Warrant	Dying entitles sacred promises from children. [implied]

(factual data); the implied (authority) warrant is "Enough is enough." But the strongest element is an emotion: indignation. Conversations are often filled like this one with abbreviated bits of persuasion. The important thing to remember is that when condensed, such arguments may seem credible. But when you parse the implied elements of such persuasion, sometimes the persuasion will remain credible (as it did for the sister) and sometimes it will not (as it did not for the brother).

Connecting Emotion to Persuasive Objectives

Aristotle identified common emotions in pairs: anger and gentleness, friendship and hatred, fear and confidence, shame and shamelessness, graciousness and ungraciousness, and pity and envy or indignation.[6] Each of these can serve as a means to persuade with pathos. Envy, for example, can serve as a powerful motivation for persuasion and propaganda. Wars have been fought because persuaders and propagandists convinced people that they were entitled to what neighboring countries enjoyed. Similarly pity (more probably expressed as *sympathy*, *empathy*, or *compassion* in today's vocabulary) is often used by charity workers, religious leaders, and parents to encourage their listeners to help others. There are other words we can use to describe emotions, such as the ones reviewed in chapter 2: *joy*, *fear*, *anger*, *surprise*, *sadness*, and *contempt*.[7] And there are emotions that might be used by persuaders in very particular circumstances, including, interest, determination, resentment, delight, amusement, indignation, solemnity, melancholy, wrath, and rage.[8] We have already seen some examples of how fear and anger can be used for persuasion. Let's look at an additional aspect of the use of fear.

Fear Appeals One of the most researched uses of emotion in persuasion is the *fear appeal*, which can be defined in two different and sometimes confusing ways.[9] First, high and low fear appeal can be measured in a message, perhaps through the extent of the scary details depicted. But fear appeals can also be measured in receivers, by noting whether the receivers are actually made to feel more or less fearful. Researchers are divided over how freely persuaders and propagandists can successfully use fear appeals.[10] Fear appeals are often inserted in a problem-solution-action format, which provides a cognitive element to the emotion. The unanswered question about fear appeals concerns to what extent raw fear is responsible for any persuasive change, and to what extent the cognitive (problem-solution-action) format is responsible. If you tell me that my shoelace is untied, I may respond with (1) a very mild fear of tripping, and (2) a solution: I will tie my shoe. But the fear appeal for me may not be what it might be for an unmedicated hemophiliac, who could be in serious danger from the slightest cut. In my case, the action is probably more motivated by the needed solution to the problem; in the unmedicated hemophiliac's case, the fear appeal may be more important.

Psychologist Paul Mongeau says of fear appeals that (1) they describe a threat and indicate how severe the threat likely is (e.g., "Gum disease not only lowers the gum line, more importantly, it reduces the mass of bone material that anchors your teeth"); (2) they link the threat with some stated degree of probability of occurrence in a particular audience ("Many middle-aged individuals show some sign of the beginning stages of gum disease"); and (3) they link an action to removing the fear ("Thorough multisurface flossing one or more times a day can suppress gum disease").[11] This third, action stage also has to convince listeners that the solution is likely to work and that listeners have a likelihood of carrying out the solution. To complicate things, high-anxiety listeners to the gum-disease message may experience so much anxiety from the message that they either tune out the message or forget it as soon as they can. They probably do this in order to suppress the anxiety—when they should be suppressing the gum disease through flossing and regular dental care. Low-anxiety listeners may pay more attention to the message. Ironically, the ones who may need the message most may benefit the least from it, and the ones who need it the least, may benefit the most.

Just as fear appeals have both emotional and cognitive components, so do appeals to the other emotions. For instance, joy and delight can be both emotional and cognitive. Perhaps an unexpected pay raise makes you feel good and causes you to think about how to use the raise. Or someone who runs a curio shop may sell gift items that first catch shoppers' intellectual interest and then delight them enough to purchase. For whimsical buyers, these curios sell by cognitive and emotional appeal. In another example, resentment sometimes occurs between various nationalities around the world, often over a past grievance. The justification for the resentment is cognitive, and the negative reaction is emotional. Often such resentment is used by propagandists to incite political conflicts, sometimes resulting in simmering bad feelings and sometimes in violence or even terrorism.

Authority Figures and Persuasion Submission to authority and social conformity are also emotions-oriented inclinations that may be used to motivate listeners to accept claims without critical analysis. Cialdini describes a number of examples of how people can be influenced by authority figures, both legitimate and bogus.[12] Typical examples include a doctor asking a nurse over the phone to administer a prescribed medication when the prescription should be submitted in writing. There have been numerous studies of authority and social conformity over the decades, even one involving subjects giving what they think are electric shocks to the secretly cooperating confederates of the researchers, the confederates having been instructed to howl in apparent pain when the subjects turn up the intensity of the would-be electric shocks at the request of the white-jacket-wearing researchers.[13] Similar research procedures may involve someone confidently asking you to give up your place in line at the office copy machine—even though the person offers no legitimate reason for your doing so, but acts as though there is a perfectly justified reason for it. One reasonable explanation for the docility often observed of subjects in these situations is that many people want to be cooperative and helpful and will concede if they believe that the other person knows better or has the authority to intercede. The potential targets of influence vary in how compliant they are willing to be—ranging from the very cooperative to the completely uncooperative—depending on personality and knowledge about the social and physical setting where the attempted influence occurs. If I know an office intruder is actually a sidewalk-loitering social dropout, I will not be fooled by any illegitimate requests the intruder makes.

But are these authority-based examples of influence persuasion? And if so, are they examples of ethical persuasion? To answer these two questions, we must return to an earlier point made that ethical persuasion can be likened to leadership carried out for the benefit of both the sender and the receiver. If I believe someone is exercising a legitimate form of authority leadership, I may decide to comply. For example, my physician may ask me to hold my breath for five seconds while a test is made; I do not really know why I have to hold my breath, but I trust that there is a good reason. Now, of course, if my investment counselor advises me to buy a stock, the stock goes bust after I buy, and my counselor heads for Brazil after having rigged an investment scam, I have acted in good faith, but my counselor has been both unethical and criminal. So why do we sometimes give in so easily? Particularly dominating or officious people may remind us of parent-child interactions that occurred at an early age.[14] If the receiver can be induced to regress to a child's mentality, verbal requests may seem legitimate whether they are or are not. Saving face may also explain this pattern.

Appeals to Virtues and Vices

Virtues are commendable qualities to which given societies (or particular factions of societies) subscribe. As we said earlier, virtues are also emotional in nature and include courage, generosity, justice, magnanimity, magnificence, prudence, temperance, and wisdom. To the extent that a given group values particular virtues, persuaders can build a case atop those selected virtues. On June 18, 1940, at the onset of World War II, Winston Churchill gave his famous "This was their finest hour" speech. It was written to bolster the confidence of the British people at a low point just after the French had surrendered, opening a giant hole in the defense of Europe for the Axis powers to exploit. The final paragraph in this speech sums up Churchill's message:

What General Weygand called the Battle of France is over. I expect that the Battle of Britain is about to begin. . . . The whole fury and might of the enemy must very soon be turned on us. Hitler knows that he will have to break us in this island or lose the war. If we can stand up to him, all Europe may be free and the life of the world may move forward into broad, sunlit uplands. But if we fail, then the whole world, including the United States, including all that we have known and cared for, will sink into the abyss of a new Dark Age. . . . Let us therefore brace ourselves to our duties, and so bear ourselves that, if the British Empire and its Commonwealth last for a thousand years, men will still say, "This was their finest hour."

As you read the above final paragraph of his speech, notice that it is the virtue of *courage* with which Churchill is attempting to stir the British people and their friends around the world. He first describes what the British people are up against: "The whole fury and might of the enemy must very soon be turned on us. Hitler knows that he will have to break us in this island or lose the war." Churchill then asks his listeners to brace themselves to their duties in hopes of having the world say after victory that "This was their finest hour." To a lesser extent, he may also be appealing to the virtue of *magnificence* in asking his listeners to rise to the occasion as a great society should. He likens failure to sinking "into the abyss of a new Dark Age," and he likens success with moving "forward into broad, sunlit uplands."[15]

Selecting Particular Virtues for Persuasion

As almost every high-school student in America knows, President John F. Kennedy once said to Americans, "Ask not what your country can do for you; ask what you can do for your country." These words urged Americans to show *generosity*, or *magnanimity*, toward their country, rather than expecting their country to be a parental figure that doles out goodies. Listeners who heeded his words might then be less contentious about whether they were getting "theirs" out of the government and more likely to volunteer to do something good for everyone. Similarly, Martin Luther King Jr. asked that people be judged by their merits and not by the color of their skin—a request for the virtue of *fairness*, or *justice*. And Abraham Lincoln, speaking in his second inaugural address as the American Civil War was ending, volunteered *generosity* and *magnanimity* toward the Confederacy with the words "With malice toward none, with charity for all . . . Let us strive on to finish the work we are in, to bind up the nation's wounds, to care for him who shall have borne the battle and for his widow and his orphan."

But can the above virtues be used for more commonplace persuasive objectives? Yes. Courage, for example, could be used by a parent to motivate a child to stand up to classmates who say belligerent things. Generosity could be used by a preacher to ask parishioners to give used belongings to the elderly living entirely on retirement payments. Justice could be used by neighbors to convince authorities that a planned apartment complex will harm the quality of life in their tiny neighborhood. Magnanimity could be used to convince a teenager to forgive and forget having not been invited to a party. A high-school principal might use magnificence to encourage students to carry themselves in dignified ways that help them stand out among their contemporaries. Emphasizing the virtue of prudence, persuaders could encourage people to do something that is reasonable and not rash, irrational, or destructive. Endorsing temperance might help a drug counselor convince a substance abuser to become a person with iron-clad self-control. Wisdom can be used to ask people to guide their actions with knowledge, insight, and good judgment.

Appealing to Vices

Human vices concern moral corruptions, faults, or failings that ill-serve the individual who succumbs to them and ill-serve the society in which they flourish. And just as virtues can be linked to persuasive objectives, so too can vices. Examples of vices include gambling, substance abuse, **gluttony**, sexual promiscuity, violence, and perhaps even some forms of **nihilism**. While virtues appeal to our better natures, vices appeal to our weaker natures. And we should not underestimate the power of vices to influence; they can sometimes make the blood run very hot.

Gambling can get our pulse up when we enter a casino and see all the glitter and money and games of chance. Perhaps it is greed or the dream of a "free lunch" or the wish to live recklessly that invigorates people who are about to gamble. Advertisements for casinos can make use of the greed motivation or simply make reference to the high-style glitter. But in a sense, a casino is a walk-in advertisement for itself. One reason to consider casino gambling a vice is the possibility that the most vulnerable among us may destroy a good part of their lives in this way. They may lose their houses, the love of their children, their spouses, their self-respect, and a lot of money. On rare occasions, people sometimes even commit suicide when they have lost everything. But it is not just casinos that employ greed to lure people to gamble. Many local and state governments run lottery games with payoffs in the millions of dollars. One state has advertised its multimillion-dollar lottery with the very powerful idea "You've got to be in it to win it!" And if gambling is a vice, then we are all in the vice business, since our government budgets depend on the revenue from this state-sponsored gambling. Even charities may promote the vice of gambling when they run bazaars with dice and wheel games, and the amusement aspect of such bazaars may entice younger people to first gamble. My first experience with gambling occurred when I was delivering newspapers at age thirteen. Gambling went on at six in the morning in the newspaper storage hut where we delivery boys waited for the Sunday papers to be trucked in. For several weeks I could not resist the lure of the quickly dealt poker hands and the shiny coins gambled into the pot—which would hopefully be mine with the showing of the hands.

Substance abuse concerns addictive drugs, gateway drugs, alcohol, and cigarettes. Many businesses, legal and illegal, make their money with messages that lure people with vulnerable personalities to become substance abusers. Even family, friends, media role models, and acquaintances may help lure us into becoming substance abusers. Often the people in a community (especially older generations in our "kid culture") provide a leadership-by-example influence for younger substance abusers. Substance abuse is a powerful force because it makes us feel good for a time and helps us forget our troubles. But as most people know, the good times are short-lived, and the bad times last a lot longer. The substance-abuse vice has entrenched itself in society by targeting and attracting those who have the greatest difficulty saying no. In some ways, drug cartels engage in a kind of chemical warfare that extracts huge amounts of money, takes many—especially young—lives, and corrupts the politics and culture of the land.

Gluttony often leads to being overweight. Restaurants, food stores, and food manufacturers play on the common tendency we have to eat more than is needed to get through the day healthily. Gluttony, like drug abuse, can be a problem of self-control. We often give in to overeating when we habitually let the "child" part of our personalities make menu selections for us. Do we eat to live or live to eat? Sometimes food, like drugs, is a form of self-medication for clinical depression. Advertisements for food can tempt us with self-indulgence or tempt us with the allure of eating in a weight-conscious way that nonetheless leads to overeating. Some overeaters create delusions of weight consciousness when they finish a calorie-laden meal and then ask for Sweet'N Low with their coffee. Gluttony for food and drink perhaps is also similar to other "gluttonous" obsessions for cars, houses, clothing, jewelry, artwork, and so on. Imelda Marcos, former first lady and a public figure in the Philippines, apparently hoarded several thousand pairs of shoes.

Sexual promiscuity is a vice when the lure comes from sellers playing on an easily excitable lust. Newspaper advertisements for escort services that charge a great deal of money use engaging visual images and headlines to reel in their customers, as do pornography products, now on cable TV for the price of a Hollywood film. Certain bars where sex, liquor, and food have very high price tags use their attractive and sexually available personnel to extract incredible amounts of money—one story recently in the newspapers claimed that someone spent more than $200,000 in one evening at a topless bar in New York City on "tips," food, and alcohol. Prostitutes appeal to this vice by using their availability, sexualized clothing, seductive mannerisms, and explicit language about sex acts. From a secular point of view, it is not sex that makes promiscuity a problem; rather, it is the loss of personal control over sex that makes it a problem. The substitution of commercially provided sex in place of interpersonal relationships that may include sex also makes this vice a problem. To those with strong religious convictions, this vice is an invitation to sin and immorality.

Violence is a vice when one gets pleasure from inflicting physical or mental pain on others. Sometimes the violence is considered sadism if there are sexual overtones to the violence. Street gangs may in part lure new members in by stressing the glory of becoming a "banger." Lurid stories of how the gang has gone on a rampage against another gang or against outsiders from other neighborhoods or even against storekeepers in the neighborhood can glamorize gang activity for prospective members. Initiations for new members may require acts of random violence—even murder. Wall graffiti for particular gangs may in part be used to declare one gang's primacy within a neighborhood. Beyond gangs, the lure of violence can be marketed by manufacturers of electronic games with violent content and violent names or Hollywood films that portray violence in approving ways. And more recently, violence has been especially glamorized and politicized in **blood-lust** subcultures around the world that approve of terrorism and seduce teenagers into murdering innocent people by sneaking into populated areas of a city and blowing themselves up for religious glory.

Nihilism can be a vice in certain circumstances. Nihilism refers to an attitude that existence is meaningless and useless and that traditional beliefs and values are unfounded. It can also assert that conditions in the organized world are so bad that destruction of society is a good idea. In one early twentieth-century setting, nihilism referred to a policy of assassination and terrorism to change the world. As a political theory, nihilism is not a vice; it is just an idea. But as a call to people to give up and become self-destructive or destructive to others, it is an invitation to regress to the irresponsible urges of an infant. When I was about to graduate from high school, one of my friends said that he did not want to get a job; he just wanted to go "lay in the gutter" in a section of the city where social dropouts lived in shelters and drank cheap wine while lying on the sidewalks. He did go on to become a productive member of society. But he also illustrates how giving up and abandoning all sense of responsibility can be a lure and a vice.

Within the political realm, nihilism can be an aggressive force that undoes a society from within. Those who would corrupt a nation have only to convince enough of its citizens to cease caring about things like education, work, finances, family, community, obeying laws, and protecting the nation. When the constructive habits of enough people are neutralized by the forces of nihilism, a country can become balkanized, ungovernable, and undefendable.[16] When balkanization occurs, what is left of the society is probably "governed" by those individuals and organizations willing and able to be the most violent: roving guerrillas, organized crime, drug cartels, teen gangs, modern-day pirates, rogue motorcycle gangs, sociopathic personalities, and so on.[17] Perhaps a dictator will rise to put a stop to all the disarray, but a society can pay a steep price for turning to the services of a dictator.

Behavior Drivers

Beyond virtues and vices, one other emotions-oriented way to motivate receivers is with what are sometimes called **behavior drivers**. These can be divided into two groups: positive drivers and negative drivers. The *positive drivers* used for gaining compliance often include stimulation, creation, accomplishment, acknowledgment, fame, and fortune. Perhaps you're selling a cookbook. You say in your advertisement for the book, "There is nothing better in the world than just-baked bread. And there is nothing in the world more rewarding than making that bread with your own hands. My XYZ Cookbook will show you how to become *creative* in the ultimate sense of the word." *Negative drivers* include fear, guilt, boredom, fatigue, pain, and loneliness. Your persuasion might try to motivate receivers to avoid one or more of these several negative drivers. Perhaps you are selling a miniature DVD player. Your advertisement might say, "The next time you're on a long train trip or just sitting by yourself with nothing to do in a waiting room, take out your player, put on your ear phones, and watch one of your favorite movies."

Subliminal Sensitivities

The study of subliminal messages is currently mired in a confusion caused by a number of things: (1) the empirical research done on subliminal effects has not convinced skeptics that the subject is worth all the attention given to the topic by the media;[18] (2) popular books on the subject have created unrealistic expectations about the influence of subliminal effects; (3) the term *subliminal* is confusing because at least two techniques linked to subliminal messages have been defined, and they are different one from the other, so that what you say for or against one technique may not apply to the other; (4) some critics of subliminal research seem to have overreacted by describing subliminal techniques as an illegitimate branch of media or psychological study; (5) those who have defended subliminal research may have used criteria that were too easy for evaluating the findings of empirical studies; (6) advertisers have a built-in motive to want to deny that such techniques are sometimes used; and (7) some advertisers mock the criticism of the technique by using the technique in silly, obvious ways.[19]

There are two general techniques associated with subliminal messages. In the first, the pure form, a **subthreshold message** is hidden within a filmed, videotaped, or audiotaped advertisement, self-help product, or public-service message. Because the subthreshold message occurs so rapidly (when it is visual) or unobtrusively (when it is acoustic), it should not be overtly detected by the receiver. For example, several frames of movie film that last just a small fraction of a second could contain a persuasive message like "Don't shoplift!" A second type of subliminal message is the so-called **embedded message**, which is not subthreshold and can be seen or heard—some call this "semi-subliminal."[20] Such messages must be vague or ambiguous to have any chance of working. For example, an ad could contain a hint of the word "healthy" by depicting the letters in a way that barely suggests the word: the *h* might be missing part of its lower curve, the *e* might look more like a *c*, and the *t* might be missing one of its parts. And perhaps the word is camouflaged by the background coloring.

Subthreshold Messages

Subthreshold messages first came to public attention in the mid-1950s when popcorn and Coca-Cola sales were said to have increased in a movie house in New Jersey because the words "Drink Coca-Cola and eat popcorn" were interspersed for fractions of a second within the frames of the movies shown at the theater. Then in a study reportedly done on a college campus, a picture of a male model was shown to two groups of college students. One group just saw the picture. The second group was shown the picture, but with the word "man" flashed over the picture by a camera-like mechanism called a tachistoscope set at a 1/3,000 of a second exposure, every five seconds. The two groups then rated the picture on a scale of one to five for how masculine or feminine the model seemed to them. The groups were said to have seen the figure as more masculine when the subliminally flashed word was used.

Embedded Messages

Embedded messages are used quite commonly by magazine and television ads—especially as a type of visual double-entendre. An embedded message is usually identifiable once it has been pointed out to you. A good example of an embedded message appeared in the June 5, 1971, issue of *Time* magazine.[21] The ad shows a bottle of Gilbey's Gin and a glass filled with ice cubes. The cubes have been touched up by an artist. If you look very closely at the shadows on the cubes, you may recognize a faint image of the word "SEX." In addition, an erotic picture seems to appear in the bottle's reflection in the table on which it stands. According to author Wilson Key, subjects rated the ad as sexier when the touch-ups were present than when they were not. In another ad, this one for Camel cigarettes, two pictures are used. One picture shows a carton of ice cream and a pickle. The other picture shows a package of Camel cigarettes with several cigarettes protruding from the package. The caption over the ad reads, "Today a *man* needs a good reason to walk a mile."

No assertions have been made about whether the above magazine ads helped sell the products depicted. In fact, given the numerous variables involved in studying the effects of ads, it will always be a challenge to say just why one ad sells well and another does not, or to say what element in an ad helped it work. About the only thing that seems certain regarding embedded or double-entendre subliminal ads is that the advertising industry still seems to have faith in them.

Perhaps we should consider subliminal effects as an interesting theory and no more, because the research has one additional problem that we have not yet mentioned. When research is carried out by advertising agencies, its outcomes are sometimes considered proprietary knowledge and are not readily shared with rivals or with the public. Lastly, several bills were introduced in the U.S. Congress in the 1950s to outlaw the use of subliminal advertisements. Although none of these bills passed, today's broadcasters probably do not attempt to use subliminals as they were used in the early tests because such messages would be too easily detected on videotape machines with a freeze-frame feature. As for self-help tapes, reviewers of this branch of the research seem in agreement that such tapes have failed to perform as advertised. So in summary, while the research to date on subliminal messages offers more questions than answers, it would be foolish to dismiss the topic of subliminal advertising. The world will just have to wait and see what a new generation of researchers can discover about a topic that has continued to hold our attention for several decades. In the meantime, magazines still serve as the best place to monitor the use of embedded images.

Pathos and Audiovisual Art Forms

Persuaders from time immemorial have probably relied on what we today might call the "audiovisual arts" to accomplish their goals. A big advantage for persuaders who use these arts is that a common language is not always necessary to link sender and receiver. Perhaps there is a primitive or primordial dynamic operating in these nonverbal forms of persuasion. The following sections will briefly examine the persuasive use of pathos in advertising, clothing and adornment, music, architecture, traditional art, and what might be called postmodern art.

Pathos in Advertising

Today's advertising media are probably freer to overtly suggest sexual appeals than they were in the past. Nonetheless, advertisers may not always wish to make the appeals they use obvious to the consumer—so they can at least maintain a thin veil of plausible deniability. But walk past any fully stocked rack of popular magazines, and the emotionally oriented images will seem to jump off the rack at you with such names as *Raw, Self, Hot Rods, Glamour, GQ, Allure,* and *Jane.*

A recent issue of *Cosmopolitan* seemed almost exclusively dedicated to sex from the woman's point of view. For those who do not read this magazine, the issue reviewed was surprisingly explicit and seemed dedicated to images of alluring women. It offered graphic advice on performing various sex acts, it told racy stories about people engaging in sex in public only to be approached by police officers, and in its center pages it showed ideal males wearing small amounts of clothing. But surprisingly, there were more photos of super-attractive women in the magazine than of men. The tone for the issue was set on the cover with the teasers "Sex He'll Go Wild For," "Caught with Their Pants Off," "Feel Hot Naked,"

"The Sex Article You Must Read with Your Boyfriend," and "Rape Danger Zones Most Women Don't Know About." The ads seemed to occasionally have embedded subliminals or at least double-entendre visual features. One ad showed an erotic brunette eating an apple. The headline said, "Be Delicious!" Another ad showed an attractive model wearing skimpy underwear with her mouth open in a suggestive way. It was captioned with the phrase "Naughty or Nice." Still another ad showed a scantily clad blonde hanging onto a bottle of perfume larger than she was and hugging the squarish cap with her arms and head—while the headline said, "Chance, Chanel, Take It!" A milk ad showed a model dressed in a black evening gown and drinking milk out of an hour-glass-shaped drinking glass, while smirking with milk smeared on her upper lip. And finally, an ad for Cointreau orange liqueur showed a model, naked except for a giant orange peel that covered her some-what like a bikini, holding a large Cointreau bottle behind her and suggestively pointing it toward the small of her back.

A recent issue of *Penthouse*, being mostly for male readers, was sexually more explicit than was the issue of *Cosmopolitan*. There were plenty of pictures of naked women. It also had one or two pictures accompanying phone-sex ads that came close to explicit pornography. But aside from the obvious sexuality of the ads for phone-sex and the like, the ads for cars and high-tech equipment were mostly without sexuality, at least in this issue. Perhaps there is no need for sexualized advertisements in a magazine that offers entertainment that is sexually so explicit.

Taken as a pair, the above magazines seem like "his and her" companion editions, with complementary perspectives toward youth-oriented sex. Perhaps the apparent subliminals in magazines such as *Cosmopolitan* depend on or resonate with the racy entertainment features included in these magazines; that is, if you're thinking about sex, you'll sense it with varying levels of consciousness in ads that appeal to racy moods. One other magazine that appeals to some women is *Bitch*, which offers a feminist response to pop culture in a print magazine devoted to incisive commentary on our media-driven world. The magazine features critiques of TV, movies, magazines, advertising, and more, plus interviews with and profiles of "cool," smart women in all areas of pop culture. It also carries the occasional racy ad, such as "Lipstick . . . or Lip*trick*? Guaranteed to give you color! Lipstick vibrator, only $19.95! Sexual self-discovery tools for women."

Pathos in Clothing and Adornment

Youth-oriented clothing styles today offer a kaleidoscope of emotional images for those who want to go beyond "standard clothing" to communicate a personal style that can be either bought "off the rack" or self-assembled. A variety of Internet sites instruct the uninitiated in such styles as *gothic*, with lots of black, and generating almost medieval feelings; *60s*, which goes with long hair; *punk*, which evokes images of spiked hair; *industrial* and *fetish-bondage*, suggesting images of submission and dominance, along with a healthy dose of leather and slave collars that might be at home with riding crops and handcuffs; *cyber wear*; *alternative wear*; *subcultural*; and many more that sometimes combine more than one style, such as *punk bondage*, *vinyl*, and *cyber punk*. As a sign of the times, the following disclaimer appears on a website that advertises youth-oriented clothing:

Omenclothing.com, designers and manufactures of gothic, tribal, bondage, cyber and PVC clothing.

Warning: This Website contains information of an adult nature. You are not allowed to access this website if you are under 18 years of age. You should not access this website if easily offended.

YOU HAVE BEEN WARNED!

If you wish to proceed please click on the button below. (www.omen-clothing.co.uk/)

Pathos in Music

The earliest commercial use of music to create moods in public places was apparently Muzak, with its trademark name that was created in 1922 by Major General George O. Squier, who believed that workers could be more productive when music played in the background. The Muzak service, which "piped in" easy-listening music, became very popular with commercial customers. Perhaps the best-known use of Muzak was for what was called "elevator music." Today, Muzak offers dozens of background moods created by its automated music for stores, offices, and telephone services. Its product is still so popular today that in 2005, the company took in $60.9 million in revenues. Muzak also offers a range of music styles, including classical, country, jazz, Latin, and oldies.

Businesses often use various genres of popular music to create emotional images. For example, a storefront business could pick background music from the list shown in box 8.2 to create just the right mood or emotions to add to the store's particular ambiance. And as we've seen, persuasion may work better when its receivers are in a receptive mood. Even the conventions held by political parties set a tone these days with background music of various styles selected to appeal to a party's voter base or to undecided voters in an election. Might grocery-store owners even play sad love ballads (say from the 1970s) in order to make people feel depressed, in the hope that they'll compensate by buying junk food or more food in general? Perhaps. In any case, you surely can "color" your living room to induce moods with background music selected from box 8.2, just as you could select a lighting scheme that varies in color tones, brightness levels, shadow, and focus. A party could just as easily set a tone with music of one style or another. Of course, most people just listen to music rather than use it to create ambiance. But what is remarkable today is how the number of recorded-music genres has expanded over the last fifty years, although particular recordings will sometimes fit into more than one category. One of the more interesting genres is Sound Scapes, which, depending on the particular recording, may transport you to exotic, faraway places or just to imaginative places of the mind or heart.

Pathos in Architecture

Today, Second Empire or Victorian architecture can at times make us think of haunted houses, such as the house of the Addams family in the TV program, the house in the Scooby Doo cartoon introduction, and the haunted houses at Disney theme parks—at least when the house is shown at night with no one alive around (see figure 8.2). Like music and clothing, architecture can be used to communicate pathos, pathos mixed with ethos, or pathos

FIGURE 8.2 Wheelock House, photographed by Bernice Abbott, 1937. Courtesy of the Photography Collection, Miriam and Ira D. Wallach Division of Art, Prints and Photographs, The New York Public Library, Astor, Lenox and Tilden Foundations.

mixed with logos of a sort. The architecture of the American colonies borrowed heavily at first from Europe. Even the designs of early colonial "wigwams" and log cabins were very likely carried to the New World from rural, northern England.[22] But in the late 1700s, a new pathos developed, along with the belief that America should have its own architecture as a kind of "architectural declaration of independence" from its European roots, and thus the Federal style of architecture was born. To the casual observer, the Federal style looks a lot like the late-Colonial (sometimes called Georgian) style that directly preceded it, with white pillars, window shutters, roof-level railings, and windows made up of small, square panes of glass. The Federal period of architecture announced—or maybe just whispered—that the modern world had indeed arrived and that America was a nation unto itself.

The nation's capital, Washington, D.C., is laid out in a way that symbolizes the division of powers among the branches of government: executive, legislative, and judicial. Within walking distance of one another in a rectangle of streets are grand government buildings with important functions and symbolism: the White House (in a neoclassical style) and the Washington Monument (a neo-Egyptian obelisk and a reminder of the most important soldier of the great American experiment) sit on one end of Pennsylvania Avenue, and at the other end sit the Capitol, the Library of Congress, and the Supreme Court (all in neoclassical style), and Union Station (in the Beaux-Arts style, and a symbol of government accessibility). Secured between these buildings are the national museums and memorials that "guard" the approach from the sea (well, the Potomac River leading to the sea). These include the Jefferson and Lincoln memorials and the National Gallery of Art. The neoclassical architecture used for the White House, the Capitol, and the Supreme Court made a statement of revitalized interest at the time of the buildings' construction in forms of government first explored in ancient Greece and the Roman Republic.

Throughout America today we can see numerous examples of architecture designed to incite one emotion or another. For example, banks in America once used various classical styles that included pillars, cathedral ceilings, heavy stone exteriors, and steel doors to create a sense of security: "Your money is safe with us." More modern banks have lowered ceilings, casual streetfronts, and warm interiors that seem to say, "Relax, you don't need to get dressed up to visit us." The modern, big-city apartment building is sometimes built with glass and steel in an almost abstract way that gives its upper-floor tenants an atmospheric or "heavenly" address in three dimensions, not two. But perhaps the buildings that are most curious today are the commercial structures built to standardized formulas and in styles that are largely unchanged across the entire country or even the world, the structures that house fast-food restaurants, real-estate agents, rent-a-car companies, and so on. In a sense, these architectural structures are a type of mass media.

Perhaps only one city in the world has been designed almost from its inception to motivate visitors by using pathos, whether that pathos be for gambling, emotional escape, or other nighttime attractions: Las Vegas. Even the names chosen for the city's numerous hotels serve as convenient semantic advertisements for the dreamland appeal of the city: Stratosphere, Palace Station, Sahara, Riviera, Circus-Circus, Stardust, Fashion Show, Treasure Island, the Venetian, Harrah's, Casino Royale, the Mirage, Imperial Palace, Caesar's Palace, the Flamingo Hilton, Barbary Coast, Rio, Gold Coast, Bourbon Street, Bally's, Palms, Terrible's, Paris, Boardwalk, Monte Carlo, Aladdin, MGM Grand, Orleans, New York–New York, Tropicana, San Remo, Mandalay Bay, the Four Seasons. If you have never been to Las

Vegas, pick just one of these names and let your imagination take over. As I've suggested, casinos and high-style hotels are walk-in advertisements for themselves.

Other examples of architectural forms designed to influence our emotions, attitudes, and even beliefs are amusement or theme parks. Sports centers where we can shoot each other with airguns equipped to fire small pellets of liquid paint (paintball) can even make us feel like we are soldiers fighting in a war. Perhaps in the near future, we will truly have real-time, virtual-reality entertainment where almost *anything* we will want to experience will seem to come true when we are wearing the specialized sensory equipment for our eyes, ears, nose, skin, and mouth supplied by entertainment businesses. Perhaps we will be able to have conversations with famous people from the past; spend private time in bed with a movie star; explore rock-climber style the inside of, say, a tomato; travel to Mars; drop without a parachute out of a high-flying plane and return to reality at the last possible second; hit a home run in the World Series; take a nap in a cloud; or visit our hometowns as they were one hundred years ago.

Pathos in Traditional Art

Oil paintings, sculptures, and dance are especially created to make us feel things about beauty, truth, ugliness, evil, and so on. The periods through which the arts have evolved witnessed world events, changing philosophies, and technological development, and historically, the arts have always been used to persuade and propagandize. The painting *Guernica*, for example, was painted by the Spanish artist Pablo Picasso to visually suggest the harsh realities of modern warfare, and it was stimulated by the Spanish Civil War of the 1930s.[23] The body parts shown in the work have been dismembered in an abstract way. They might imply that humanity has learned to do incredible damage to the human form and that it is too late, that doom is around the corner. But most importantly, they seem to want us to revile the events. The painting *The Scream* by the Norwegian artist Edvard Munch communicates similar emotions and thoughts by portraying a hysterical individual—possibly caught in a nightmare—fleeing across a small wooden bridge, with two ambiguous human figures behind.[24] The swirling, striated brushstrokes used to depict the painting's background of sky, earth, and water resonate with the fear shown in the face of the screamer. Artists with political or philosophical motivations know that visual or acoustic images are quite powerful—maybe because these images can appeal to us in primordial ways, instead of in discursive or intellectual ways.

Pathos in Postmodern Art

The term *postmodern* is difficult to define. But postmodern art is sometimes said to be inner-directed, intentionally ambiguous, and perhaps oriented toward examining the underlying ideas in art that receivers find comforting, reassuring, and clarifying. Some critics would argue that postmodern art uses its methods to go beyond existing artistic boundaries. I will really only address one aspect of art in these postmodern times: a new approach to art that plays with the possibilities of the electronic media as a platform for high art.

Cartoons have long featured motion, visual transformation of images, and multiple-image interactivity, as have televised or cinematic dramas and comedies. But cartoons are hardly instances of high art, and televised drama and comedy are hardly new. What about computer screensavers and video-game images used as entertainment or for aesthetic pleasure on computers? None of these are usually high art either—at least not yet. But the latest high-definition plasma television screens look just like ornamental pictures when mounted on the walls of homes or in trendy bars that may arrange five or six such screens spaced out as if they were just pictures on a wall. Like other types of television screens and sets, these are used mostly for entertainment or for carrying art programs as content. Even so, home-furnishing stores already sell videotapes that quietly "loop," or repeat (with appropriate sounds), through action images of such visual events as rainbowed waterfalls, endless waves washing onto sun-drenched beaches, fields of flowers, crackling firesides, and sequenced scenes of Greece. Screensavers for computers also seem to get better and better each year. But could these flat screens and their images become a new form of art? Video art, according to columnist Bruce Bahlmann, has been around for about fifteen years, and there are already collectors of it.

> One notable collector of video art is none other than Peter Norton (the founder of Norton Anti-Virus [*sic*] as well as the Norton Family Foundation). Norton lives on the 40th floor of the Trump Tower in New York City (among other residences) and has amassed quite a collection of video art on flat screen television monitors scattered through his living space. Norton actually employs his own art curator and his homes proudly display many different forms of video art, some even in his bathroom.[25]

One could call flat-screen TVs "animated wall pictures." Perhaps artists are really at a new juncture where works of high art might be created to exploit television in three dimensions (height, width, and time) and as silent art, not noisy entertainment. Is it possible that high-definition plasma television screens along with dynamic computer-image memory devices, by separating artistic method and content, could allow artists to create works of electronic art to hang on a wall? Such art might exploit image motion, transformation, and occasional, augmenting sound.

Like other forms of high art, flat-screen wall pictures might embody visual metaphors that allow the artist to express the affective, inner lives of people by subjectively describing what can be seen in the outside world. Imagine an image like the *Mona Lisa* subtly changing moods over periods of days or weeks. Imagine an aesthetically pleasing image of a beautiful structure such as the Taj Mahal (designed entirely in white marble by the architect Ustad Isa) slowly coming to form as if being erected over a period of several days, weeks, months, or years. Or perhaps a portrait of someone would show that person's many characters, with gradual changes in posture, orientation of the eyes, facial expressions, clothing, or body shape.

Examples of artistic, electronic images might include (1) bipolar, complementary artistic images that morph from one to the other over a period of hours or days; (2) light-sensitive images that morph from one thing to another as daylight turns to night and vice versa; (3) season-sensitive images that morph from one set of things to others as the seasons change through the calendar year; (4) images that pursue a theme by slowly transforming from a more abstract version of an image into a more concrete one; (5) interacting pairs of images, such as two persons sitting in portrait style; (6) life-cycle images such as of a rosebud forming, blooming, and then withering; (7) construction images such as of San Francisco's Golden Gate Bridge, Chicago's Sears Tower, Taiwan's Taipei 101 (currently the world's tallest building), or Paris's Eiffel Tower; (8) dismantling images such as of a mechanical clock that gradually comes apart into its components; (9) slowly morphing, related perspectives of an image such as that of a rainbow-lit waterfall shown from successive viewing positions to the right, to the left, above, below, or even from behind the waterfall; (10) occasional sounds that in artistic ways might complement these slowly morphing visual images (an occasional "tic-tock" delicately sounded as part of the slow and whimsical morphing of a grandfather clock as seen at various times and from various perspectives, thus encouraging the viewer to experience nostalgia or melancholy).

Where will the artists come from who have the vision and manual skills of an oil painter or sculptor but who can also master computer-generated image manipulation suitable for the plasma screen? Will they use cameras, or just create and manipulate their images using computers and programming skills? Will the pathos contained in silent (or nearly so), moving, transforming images of video high art take art lovers and connoisseurs to aesthetic raptures heretofore never experienced by humanity? Could such artistic endeavors actually command the prices of oil paintings that sell for thousands or millions of dollars? Would they turn off automatically when sensing that no one was in the room where they hang? To facilitate the artistic uses suggested here, will video technology have to be further developed (e.g., offering nonstandard picture-scanning formats, higher-density screen resolutions, and other increased potentials for rendering contrast of images)? Some innovations have already arrived, which you can find if you search the Web using the search phrase {hdtv "video art"}.

Chapter in Retrospect

VIGNETTE **Appealing to Positive Emotions**

With each decade, people in the modern world seem to spend more and more money, time, and attention on their pets. Many people just love their pets. Some hotels now provide special meals for pets accompanied by people. Many parks have dog runs that people cannot enter without a dog. There are pet medicines and health insurance policies for pets. Apparently, some hotels on the Mediterranean Riviera provide special beach cabanas for dogs. Doggie daycare centers are common in upscale neighborhoods, providing daylong programs with special meals, exercise programs for weight loss and fitness, fun and entertainment, physical therapy, and grooming services. There are also websites such as www.sassytreats.com.au that offer a variety of special-treat food products for pets, including bone-shaped birthday cakes, holiday cakes, valentine cakes, special lunches and main courses, meals for pets with special diet needs, and goodies that fit in with the styles of local cuisines. These stores specialize in products for dogs, cats, and horses.

Could you market pet goodies and treats as a small business where you live? How would you appeal to your potential customers' fond feelings for their pets? Your audience analysis would need to find out how many pets people have, what kinds of pets they have, and how many people could be convinced to get new pets. Your analysis should tell you where and how your audience buys whatever treats they currently buy, if any, and what they buy. You would also want to assess how favorably your audience currently feels about spending varying amounts of money for special-treat foods. Here you may need to know to what extent your audience members perceive their pets as members of the family with human-like needs about such things as birthdays and other holidays.

With the facts in hand, you will then need to appeal to your audience in terms of the love and happiness associated with the pet members in their families. Most importantly, you will need to create messages to sell your products by reminding your audience of how much joy they can get by purchasing your very special products ("It's birthday time for Spot!"), and how good they will feel when they see their pets begin to enjoy their very own birthday cake. Probably your biggest asset in succeeding at this business venture will be your ability to inspire your potential customers with the joy you yourself experience as you "practice what you preach."

Summary and Conclusions

Persuaders often look for some emotional link to put their receivers, or audience, in the right mood for responding to the cognitive parts of a message. Maslow, Schutz, and this book offer unique lists of such links. In addition, Packard suggests eight emotional needs often addressed by advertisers. Emotions (which are more mental) are different from feelings (which are more physical), and the most researched technique for appealing to emotion through persuasive messages is the fear appeal. Fear appeals work best when they are believable and when the message shows the receiver how to reduce fear by following the advice in the message. Virtues (first identified by classical philosophers) and vices can also be linked to messages to make them more persuasive. The research on so-called subliminal messages shows mixed results at best, although advertisers seem to use them from time to time. Pathos can be found in a variety of message forms, including advertising, clothing styles, music, architecture, and art (traditional, modern, and postmodern).

KEY TERMS

behavior drivers	gluttony	nihilism
blood-lust	human needs (esteem,	pathos
classical virtues	physiological, safety,	subliminal messages
embedded messages	self-actualization,	subthreshold messages
emotions versus feelings	social)	

REVIEW QUESTIONS

1. What types of human needs can especially be used by persuaders?
2. How are personal, interpersonal, and social needs different?
3. Do we have unlimited potential to use increasingly stronger and stronger fear appeals? Or do receivers tune out when a fear appeal gets too strong and they can escape further exposure to the message?
4. How are virtues and vices used differently by persuaders?
5. Which emotions have proved especially useful to persuaders?
6. Identify the ways in which pathos is used in advertising.
7. What does the phrase "architectural declaration of independence" mean?

8. How can music be used persuasively by merchants?

9. How have the masters of oil painting used pathos in the past?

10. What exactly is a television "wall picture?"

SUGGESTED PROJECTS AND ACTIVITIES

1. Convince several people to volunteer for something (giving time to the elderly, for example). Use any one of the motivational lists discussed in this chapter to motivate your audience favorably.

2. Write a short essay that makes use of emotions to argue why people should agree in advance to donate their body organs when they die.

3. Analyze a song you like for its persuasive use of emotional content.

4. Visit a building—if you live, vacation, study, or work near one—that was constructed with artistic intent. Analyze its construction features, ornamentation, and internal detail to discover what the architect was attempting to make people experience emotionally or intellectually when they entered the building.

5. Thumb through a magazine with racy feature stories to see if any of the ads use visual or semantic double-entendres.

QUESTIONS FOR DISCUSSION

1. When exactly in your opinion does the use of emotional content in persuasive messages become unethical?

2. In what type of messages do you think emotional appeals work best? Work worst?

3. How exactly can club-style music playing in stores that sell clothing that might be worn in a club help sell the clothing?

4. Do appeals to virtues or appeals to vices seem more persuasively powerful to you?

Notes

1. James Dillard and Eugenia Peck, "Persuasion and the Structure of Affect Dual Systems and Discrete Emotions as Complementary Models," *Human Communication Research* 27, no. 1 (January 2001): 38–68; Michael Pfau, Erin Szabo, Jason Anderson, Joshua Morrill, Jessica Zubric, and Hua-Hsin Wan, "The Role and Impact of Affect in the Process of Resistance to Persuasion," *Human Communication Research* 27, no. 2 (April 2001): 216–52.

2. Abraham Maslow, *Motivation and Personality* (New York: Harper and Row, 1970), 35–46.

3. William Schutz, *The Interpersonal Underworld* (Palo Alto, CA: Science and Behavior Books, 1966), 17–25.

4. Peace is a more abstract need than is the physiological need identified by Maslow for momentary safety; you might feel a need for peace even during a safe, year-long lull in a war. Or you might fear war even if assured of your own personal safety.

5. Vance Packard, *The Hidden Persuaders* (New York: Pocket Books, 1969), 73–78.

6. See James Murphy and Richard Katula, with Forbes Hill and Donovan Ochs, *Synoptic History of Classical Rhetoric* (Mahwah, NJ: Hermagoras, 2003), 98–99.

7. Paul Ekman and Wallace Friesman, "The Repertoire of Nonverbal Behavior: Categories, Origins, Usage and Coding," *Semiotica* (1969): 49–98.

8. Summarized in William Rogers, *Communication in Action* (New York: Holt, Rinehart, and Winston, 1984), 80–81.

9. Daniel O'Keefe, *Persuasion: Theory and Research* (Thousand Oaks, CA: Sage, 2002), 224–28.

10. O'Keefe, *Persuasion: Theory and Research*, 222–23.

11. Paul Mongeau, "Another Look at Fear-Arousing Persuasive Appeals," in *Persuasion: Advances through Meta-Analysis*, ed. Mike Allen and Raymond Preiss (Cresskill, NH: Hampton Press, 1998), 53–68.

12. Robert Cialdini, *Influence: Science and Practice* (New York: Harper-Collins, 1993), 212–13.

13. Stanley Milgram, "Behavioral Study of Obedience," *Journal of Abnormal and Social Psychology* 67, no. 4 (October 1963): 371–78.

14. Persuaders communicating to adult receivers have an obligation to appeal to the adult part of their receivers' personalities. This notion is very similar to the parent, child, and adult "ego states" referred to in transactional analysis theory, as described by Eric Berne in his book *Games People Play: The Psychology of Human Relationships* (New York: Ballantine, 2004).

15. "Sink into the abyss of a new Dark Age" and "move forward into broad, sunlit uplands" are good examples of the archetypal metaphors that we discussed in chapter 2. There may also be a subtle reference here to the fact that Germanic tribes (the barbarians) had already brought about the first Dark Age by bringing down the Roman Empire.

16. *Balkanization* is a geopolitical term that gets its meaning from the seemingly unending wars over the last centuries among several small societies on the Balkan peninsula. The term means "to break up into smaller, often hostile, units."

17. The ongoing, brutally violent separatist struggle in Chechnya is a prime example. See www.cbc.ca/news/background/chechnya/; www.pbs.org/newshour/bb/europe/chechnya/; www.globalissues.org/Geopolitics/Chechnya.asp.

18. Anthony Pratkanis and Elliot Aronson, for example, have criticized studies that do not use double-blind research methods (in which neither the subjects nor those collecting the data know the purpose of the study). See Anthony Pratkanis and Elliot Aronson, *Age of Propaganda: The Everyday Use and Abuse of Persuasion* (New York: Henry Holt, 2001).

19. For an explanation of some of the complexities plaguing this topic, see James Hargart, "Semi-subliminal World," www.subliminalworld.org/fulls.htm (29 January 2005).

20. Hargart, "Semi-subliminal World."

21. Wilson Key, *Subliminal Seduction* (New York: New American Library, 1980), 78–80.

22. Fiske Kimball, *Domestic Architecture of the American Colonies and of the Early Republic* (New York: Dover, 1950), 3–10.

23. H. W. Janson, *History of Art* (Englewood Cliffs, NJ: Prentice Hall, 1967), 523–25.

24. Janson, *History of Art*, 509.

25. Bruce Bahlmann, "Broadband, HDTV, and Video Art: An Artistic Window with a View towards Next Generation Broadband Services," Broadband Properties, 8 April 2005, www.birdseye.net/article_archive/broadband_hdtv_video_art.htm (27 November 2005). Also see Michael Rush, *Video Art* (New York: Thames and Hudson, 2003); and Catherine Elwes, *Video Art: A Guided Tour* (London: I.B. Tauris, 2005).

CHAPTER 9

Empirical Theories of Persuasion

◆ **Chapter Objectives**

After reading this chapter, you will be able to:

- ◆ Explain several versions of learning theory
- ◆ Compare and contrast operant and classical conditioning
- ◆ Show how social learning theories are related to persuasion
- ◆ Show how consistency theory can explain changed behavior
- ◆ Explain two related theories of behavioral intention
- ◆ Describe the routes to persuasion predicted by the elaboration likelihood theory
- ◆ Explain a composite theory of the various persuasion theories

An inner voice tells me that it is not yet the real thing. The theory [of quantum mechanics] yields a lot, but it hardly brings us any closer to the secret of the Old One. In any case I am convinced that He doesn't play dice.

—ALBERT EINSTEIN

A **THEORY** tries to explain what may be true about something not yet completely understood. In some ways, a theory is a tentative extension of what is believed to be true about something—subject to further clarification by future research. Theories, like the models analyzed in previous chapters, provide a variety of services. Most importantly, they try to explain the underlying form and functions of something by specifying basic elements then showing how those elements work together. Good theories also serve as important guides for doing research on a subject; the resulting research findings can then be used to make the theories even more accurate, useful, and interesting. The particular theories selected for this chapter should serve as a guide for future researchers in persuasion, for practitioners who create or critique messages, and for those who simply want to learn about the subject. I will sort the theories of interest into several sections. The first section discusses the learning theories that follow a behaviorist tradition. These theories try to explain how people are influenced not so much by conscious logic but by underlying psychological forces. Next will come consistency theories built around the notion that people like to feel that they are consistent, and feel uncomfortable when they see signs of their own inconsistency (persuaders often try to remind receivers of this second possibility). The later sections will include several newer theoretical explanations, including two related behavioral intention theories and the elaboration likelihood theory.

The Behaviorist Tradition

The guiding voice in the behaviorist tradition was psychologist John Watson, who in the early part of the twentieth century rejected the introspective methods then sometimes used by researchers who studied what they called "consciousness." These introspective methods had focused on people's descriptions of inner thoughts and first-hand experiences. Instead, Watson advised researchers and theorists to study observable behavior using more scientific methods. As a consequence, researchers such as Ivan Pavlov and B. F. Skinner began to study how people and animals learned things one behavior at a time. Let's briefly examine three of these behaviorist efforts: the classical-conditioning type of learning theory pursued by Pavlov, the operant conditioning type of learning theory pursued by Skinner, and the less-orthodox, more recent social learning theory pursued by Albert Bandura.

Learning Theory: Pavlov and Skinner

Learning theory is more a theory of behavior modification than a theory of persuasion. Pavlov described one form of learning through **classical conditioning**, or how simultaneous events can become associated in the minds of people or animals, as when you are given food and you hear a bell ring at the same time, and this is repeated many times. Through this repetition, you come to associate the two events—that is, you hear the bell and then expect to be fed.[1]

B. F. Skinner described another form of learning through **operant conditioning**, which is how people learn through reinforcement of behavior.[2] If you perform behavior X and then receive a positive reward of some type, you will be more inclined to perform behavior X again. Thus, operant conditioning concerns the rewarding of desired behavior through reinforcement when the desired behavior occurs. Here the *change agent* uses **reinforcement schedules** to install the desired change. For example, animals can be trained to do things, such as jumping through hoops during a circus performance, by giving them food treats or compliments after they perform the desired act. This works with people also, but in more sophisticated ways. The schedule of reinforcement can be constant—you get the reward each time you perform as required—or intermittent. When the reinforcement schedule is intermittent, the rewards may come in predictable ways, perhaps every eighth time you perform accurately, or only if the correct performance occurs after a minimum time period elapses, maybe every thirty minutes. Intermittent schedules may also occur on a random basis. A first reward might come after a correct performance, but only if at least three performances have already occurred. Random payoffs may also be given for correct performances that occur after a minimum period of time—first after ten seconds, then after forty-three seconds, and so on. Apparently, the less-predictable schedules are the more effective ones, as when a gambler keeps putting in money and pulling the arm or pushing the button of a slot machine, while thinking, "I'll win this next time."

Although learning theory does not directly explain persuasion, it is relevant in an indirect way. A speaker may reward an audience every time the audience applauds a point made by the speaker, for example. The reward may take the form of complimenting the audience on their good sense in knowing a good idea when they hear it. With each reward, the speaker may be winning over the audience, at least emotionally. Behavior modification and persuasion can also be combined, as when an advertiser, in the first step, persuades people to buy some product—but only to give to friends as a present. In the second step, the purchasers of the product then engage in the self-reinforcing behavior of giving the product as a present (self-reinforcing because of the warm appreciation the friends will show when receiving the present). When both steps are successful, the seller will probably get repeat purchases from these customers.

The Social Learning Theory of Albert Bandura

Social psychologist Albert Bandura takes a less-orthodox view of learning theory than does Skinner to explain how people's behavior can be influenced.[3] Bandura does include Skinner-like conditioning of behavior through positive and negative rewards. But he also adds several other behavioral forces. One is *role-playing*. That is, if you act in a certain way, even in play, you are then more inclined to act this way in future, more realistic settings. And if a researcher should ask you to articulate a rhetorical position (on a political topic, let's say) opposite to what you really believe, the experience could cause you to actually change position in favor of the counter-attitudinal statements you've made. A teacher asking students to role-play a lifestyle that is not part of the students' social background may have a similar effect. Another force included in the theory is *role-modeling*. If we admire someone, we may begin to emulate their **attitudes**, beliefs, and actions. Interestingly, Bandura even adds to the theory the possibility that we may condition our own behavior with thoughts like "Yes, this is the sort of thing a person like me should do."

In considering behavioral theories in the abstract, we might speculate that some of the things we must learn are too important to be left to persuasion or individual decision making and are best shaped by the behavior-modifying forces in our surroundings. Examples might be learning to look both ways when crossing a street, avoiding dogs that growl at us, not saying things that irritate people, and wearing clothing appropriate to a social or public setting. Some of these behavior-modification forces are environmental and some are social.

Consistency Theories

Consistency theories reflect the premise that we like to see ourselves as consistent and rational in our thoughts and deeds. When we discover that we have been inconsistent, we then feel psychological discomfort. These theories also say that the resulting discomfort may cause us to change our attitudes, beliefs, and behavior to reduce the discomfort. So, senders bent on influencing receivers can create messages that point out the inconsistencies of the receivers. A sender could say to someone, "You seem to feel it is important to be honest. So why do you fudge on your income taxes?" If the receiver sees these two assertions as proof of his or her inconsistency, the motivation to change might occur. The receiver might then think, "I'll forget about trying to be honest" or "I'll stop fudging on my income taxes."

Consistency theories are only partly theories of persuasion because the influence involved relies as much on discomfort as on proof. Because consistency theories describe how people may be manipulated by messages that cause discomfort, they are of especial interest to propagandists. Though there have been a number of consistency theories, let us focus on two of them: balance theory and the theory of cognitive dissonance.

Balance Theory

Perhaps the earliest of the consistency theories, balance theory is built on the premise that we like to agree with people we like and disagree with people we dislike.[4] Balance theory supports the notion that sender credibility can help a persuader be more effective, and it is in part as much a communication theory as it is a psychological one. The theory can be visually illustrated by triangle 1 in figure 9.1. Imagine a sender talking positively about strawberry ice cream—indicated in the triangle by the plus sign between Sender and Topic. Triangle 1 also shows that the receiver likes this particular sender—as indicated by the plus sign between Receiver and Sender—but dislikes the suggestion that strawberry ice cream is a good thing—indicated by the minus sign between Receiver and Topic. The balance theory predicts that this receiver may now feel imbalance or discomfort because the receiver disagrees with the sender, and people like to agree with people they like and disagree with people they dislike. One of two things should now happen: the receiver either will come to like strawberry ice cream or will come to dislike the sender. Although the theory may not work well when the persuasive preference is for something whimsical, such as strawberry ice cream, it may indeed work well with such ego-involving controversies as capital punishment, political party rivalries, gun ownership, environmental issues, and immigration.

Each of the triangles in figure 9.1 is either balanced or imbalanced. One shortcut to identifying whether a given triangle is balanced or not is to multiply its three signs (remembering the rules for multiplying signs: a plus times a plus equals a plus; a minus times a minus equals a plus; and a plus times a minus equals a minus). If you end up with a plus, the triangle is balanced; if you end up with a minus, the triangle is not balanced. This arithmetic trick will not help you understand the theory, but it will let you check if your identification of balanced or imbalanced triangles is correct or not. As you examine each of the eight triangles, you will see that some predict change because they are not balanced, while some predict no change because they are balanced. For example, triangle 2 is balanced because sender and receiver are both positively disposed to the topic and the receiver likes the sender (a plus times

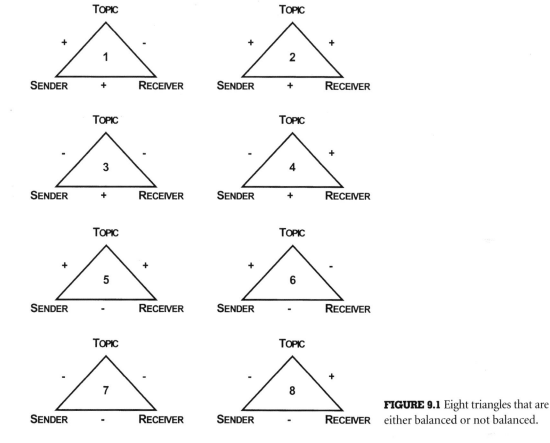

FIGURE 9.1 Eight triangles that are either balanced or not balanced.

a plus times a plus equals a plus). Triangle 6 is balanced because the receiver dislikes the sender and feels differently about the topic (a minus times a minus times a plus). Triangle 7, with three minus signs, is not balanced and predicts change (a minus times a minus times a minus equals a minus). Here the receiver dislikes the sender, but they are in agreement about the topic (they both dislike it); perhaps the sender can convert their agreement about the topic into a persuasive change in sender likeability. Balance theory is a good start, but it lacks flexibility because it does not show shades of gray when depicting attitudes.[5]

Cognitive Dissonance Theory

The cognitive dissonance theory of psychologist Leon Festinger has prospered with the times.[6] It too theorizes that we have a strong need to feel that we have been consistent in our words, deeds, and thoughts. When we do not feel consistent, we experience discomfort. This discomfort is called **dissonance**. Cognitive dissonance theory builds on the consistency theories that preceded it by adding features that make it quite flexible and useful to researchers and practitioners. One way in which it creates flexibility is with the notion of a **cognition**.

A cognition is a thought or focus of attention. Cognitions can be about almost anything: a belief, an attitude, an intended behavior, a memory of a past behavior, a self-perception of a current habit, a commitment, a perception of self in a social situation, a remembered promise. Any two cognitions can serve as possible *variables of interest* in the theory. For example, you may be about to buy a new car that is offered by a dealership at an attractive price. But someone may then say to you, "The manufacturer is recalling that model for a defect in the brakes." The knowledge that you are about to buy a new car and that it may have defective brakes can create two dissonant cognitions, which are variables of interest because in buying a car you would want it to have good brakes, but this car may have the opposite. Cognitive dissonance theory also has the advantage of being both qualitative and quantitative, in that it does not just ask if there is a discrepancy between two cognitive elements of someone's outlook, but it also asks how much discrepancy there is.

Greater discrepancies between cognitions should create more discomfort, or dissonance, and a greater possibility for change than should lesser discrepancies. In our example as depicted in figure 9.2, cognition A concerns how strongly or not you want to buy the car. If cognition A is placed more to the left (a lower number), you are less in favor of buying the car; if cognition A is placed more to the right (a higher number), you are more in favor of buying; if cognition A is placed somewhere near the middle (say a 4 or 5), you are unsure.

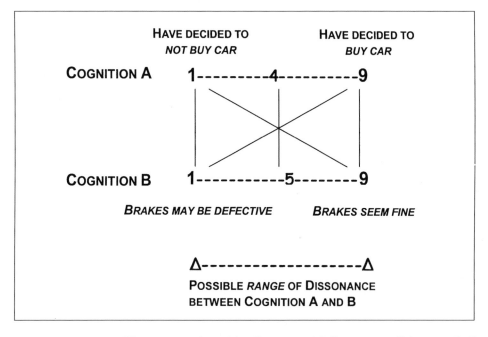

FIGURE 9.2 Four possible outcomes of cognitive dissonance: (1) dissonant condition prevails if car is bought and brakes are defective; (2) consonant condition prevails if car is bought and brakes are not defective; (3) consonant condition prevails if car is not bought and brakes are defective; and (4) dissonant condition prevails if car is not bought and brakes are not defective.

The same possibilities apply to cognition B, which concerns how strongly you believe or disbelieve that the car you intend to buy has defective brakes.

Depending on exactly where the two cognitions fall on the grid, there will be more or less discrepancy, possibly creating dissonance. The issue then concerns how much dissonance you will experience. If you have decided to buy the car but now strongly believe these cars have brake problems, the two numbers representing the cognitions will be far apart (say, 9 and 1), signaling likely dissonance. Similarly, if you have decided to pass on the car but begin to believe that the brakes are not defective after all, you might also experience dissonance (1 and 9). Maybe, you think, you should have decided to buy. The remaining two possibilities—you decide not to buy the car and yes, the brakes seem very likely to be defective; or you decide to buy the car and the brakes seem likely to be fine—create **consonance** (say, 1 and 2, and 9 and 8, respectively). If cognitions A and B both end up near the middle (perhaps 4 and 5) there will not be much consonance or dissonance because you are not sure about the purchase or the brakes. Now we must describe what happens when either dissonance or consonance occurs.

Dissonance, Consonance, and Irrelevance To review, dissonant cognitions cause psychological discomfort, depending on how much dissonance is present and on how important the topic is to you. Consonant cognitions do just the opposite. They make you feel comfortable, as when you call the car manufacturer about the possible brake problem and you are told that the particular model you want to buy does not have the problem—lucky you! Now you may feel good. The revised news is consonant in the case that you were intending to buy the car. Admittedly, sometimes two selected cognitions can be irrelevant to each other. If you now turn on the radio and hear that someone you know has just been arrested for multiple counts of bigamy, this news has no bearing on the proposed car purchase (although it might bear on your friendship with the alleged bigamist), so the theory is unconcerned with this last pair of cognitions (the new car not having bad brakes and the bigamy news), with respect to buying the car.

To apply the theory, a persuader could identify two possible receiver cognitions and select one as a persuasive objective. As a persuader, you might select (1) the attitude that "gambling to excess is bad," and (2) the fact that some of your friends do in fact gamble to excess at the horse races.[7] Now you might construct a message that reminds these friends who bet at the races that gambling to excess is bad, assuming that deep down they subscribe to this general attitude. Your message will be designed to first promote dissonance in them and then to promote a possible reduction of dissonance by their accepting your advice to reduce or eliminate their betting on horse races. The cognitive dissonance theory predicts three possible outcomes in this case: (1) your friends eliminate or reduce their betting, (2) they come to believe that gambling to excess is not all that bad, or (3) they find some other way to reduce their dissonance without changing their betting behavior or their attitude toward gambling in excess.[8] You, of course, are hoping for outcome number 1.

Clusters of Cognitions Often more than two cognitions can be simultaneously relevant. In table 9.1, we see a list of possible cognitions about betting on horse races. On the left are cognitions that may cause feelings of consonance for a person who bets. On the right are cognitions that may cause dissonance. The number shown before each cognition represents how important that cognition is for this sample receiver. There are several ways to measure consonance and dissonance in the table. First, the *direction* of the cognition will place it either on the dissonant or on the consonant side (e.g., the boss could approve or disapprove of gambling). Second, the *importance* felt about cognitions in the two lists can generate more or less dissonance or consonance. The fact that the spouse gets angry about the receiver's going to the races was given a 6 by our receiver; this should cause more dissonance than the belief that uncontrolled gambling is a character weakness, which is given just a 2. Third, we can *count* the number of cognitions on each side. If a certain receiver has six consonant cognitions and only three dissonant cognitions, that receiver may feel more consonance because of the prevalence of cognitions on the consonant side. In table 9.1, the number of consonant and dissonant cognitions happens, by chance, to be the same: five each.[9] Lastly, we can *calculate* total scores for consonance and dissonance. The consonance and dissonance lists shown in table 9.1 add up respectively to 16 and 13—thus the receiver in this illustration has belief clusters slightly more consonant than dissonant about betting on the races.

Now the story gets more interesting. As a persuader who wants the receiver to give up betting on horses (possibly you're the receiver's spouse or financial counselor), you can do a number of things:

1. You can urge the receiver to focus on a new cognition: "Please remember [add this dissonant cognition to your list] that your children see you as a negative role model."
2. You can urge the receiver to delete a cognition: "Picking horses doesn't challenge your abilities; nobody, including the horses, knows which horse is going to win a particular race." Adding, recategorizing, or deleting cognitions can change the relative sizes of the consonant and dissonant sets.
3. You can also encourage a change in how important one of the cognitions seems. For example, this receiver seems mildly concerned that the boss disapproves of gambling (giving it a low score of 2 out of a possible 7). But is it possible that the receiver was in

TABLE 9.1

**Clusters of Consonant and Dissonant
Cognitions for a Sample Receiver**

Consonant Cognitions	Dissonant Cognitions
3 I won $500 last week on a horse named Rub-A-Dub.	2 My boss does not approve of my gambling behavior.
1 The racing takes place in the comfortable outside.	2 I usually lose money over the long run.
4 I meet my buddies at the track for talk and laughs.	6 My going to the races makes my spouse angry.
5 Picking horses challenges my abilities.	2 Uncontrolled gambling is a character weakness.
3 Going to the races expresses my freedom to do as I like.	1 Going to the races twice a week is excessive.

Note: Cognitions are rated on a scale from 1 to 7.

fact passed over for a promotion recently—but kept unaware of this by the boss? If you have found out about the promotion denial, persuasion using this information could strengthen the importance attributed to the "boss does not approve" cognition, changing it from a 2 to perhaps a 5.

Other persuaders may attempt to influence the receiver. A fellow bettor at the track may get wind of the problems developing at home with the spouse and might try to persuade our receiver to continue coming to the track. The fellow bettor could take a different tack, saying, "Don't be fooled; your boss really approves of betting at the races and often comes here when you are busy at work." This assertion would be an attempt to move our receiver's belief about the boss's views on betting from the dissonant side to the consonant side of table 9.1. Cognitive dissonance theory can even illustrate self-persuasion, if our receiver does some soul searching on a long walk and experiences a change in attitude.

Reducing Dissonance One Way or Another From the persuader's perspective, the hope is that dissonance-reduction efforts will cause a persuasive change in the receiver. But as we've seen, receivers do not always reduce dissonance by accepting persuasive change. One common technique receivers use for avoiding change is *selectivity*. Selectivity can concern four things: (1) *selective exposure*: Will I read something, watch a television program, attend a speech or not? (2) *selective attention*: What details of the message do I notice or not notice? (3) *selective perception*: Exactly how do I evaluate or understand ideas in the message, as positive or negative, important or unimportant? and (4) *selective recall*: What parts of the message will I remember? Thus, if I have just bought an expensive home-entertainment center, I may worry whether I made the right decision. Now if I seek out promotional literature on the equipment I've just bought, I am selectively exposing myself to information that may help me reduce buyer's remorse (one type of dissonance) about my purchase decision. On the other hand, you may try to convince me that I should have bought a different system, but in this case I will only selectively attend to the details of your message because they too could create unwanted dissonance. Or maybe you look at my system and say that it takes up too much space in my living room, whereas I selectively perceive and see the equipment as a "jewel in the crown" of my living room. Or, as soon as you are out the door, I selectively recall not what you just said but what the sales clerk said instead.

In addition to these selectivity techniques, other dissonance-reducing tactics can include (1) *rationalizing* the dissonant situation away, as when I make an unwise purchase and then say I would only have spent the money on something even less worthwhile had I passed up the purchase; (2) *disbelieving* the information that causes the dissonance, as when I claim a scientific report on substance abuse exaggerates the bad effects claimed to be caused by prolonged use of the substance in question, when I am in fact a user of that substance; (3) *compartmentalization* of thinking, as when I dismiss my cheating on income taxes as not really being about honesty because it is a game that everyone plays; and (4) *denial* or *suppression* of dismaying information, as when I refuse to think about a horrible problem I have caused for other people, and that could have been easily avoided. The dissonance in the above situations could also be removed by actually changing one of my beliefs, attitudes, values (instrumental ones, as defined in chapter 1), behaviors, or habits.

Research and Applications of Cognitive Dissonance Theory Cognitive dissonance theory has some interesting applications. Boot-camp sergeants in the army may well understand that the best way to change recruits' attitudes and beliefs is by enforcing a change of the behavior of those recruits by giving them short haircuts, getting them up at five in the morning, getting them into physical condition, demanding that they use respectful language when speaking with officers, requiring that they do things that challenge their fears, and so on. In other words, if the recruits are *acting* like good soldiers, they may start *thinking* like good soldiers, because not to bring their attitudes and beliefs into accord with their behavior might cause dissonance. The reverse can also occur when changes in beliefs bring about changes in attitudes or behavior. If I keep my life savings in a bank account, you might convince me that over the course of a lifetime, my money would grow faster in a mutual fund. You might point out that with certain mutual funds, the fund's resulting portfolio will generally perform similar to the stock market—which historically has gone up with great regularity. If I come to believe in the superiority of this type of mutual fund, I might purchase shares in one of them to avoid the dissonance resulting from a sense of lost opportunity in leaving my money in a bank. Or I might discard your advice about mutual funds with the cynical rationalization that "only insiders make money in the stock market."

Interestingly, cognitive dissonance created by conflicts in public discussions may cause the members of a group to eventually seek consensus. This would be a persuasive effect of sorts. The dissonance felt by the members of such a group would reflect the undesirability or unpleasantness of being among adversaries on an ongoing basis. To reduce the dissonance, the members might then come to agree more with each other, which might make the situation more desirable and pleasant.[10]

Finally, the research on cognitive dissonance also focuses on (1) *decision-making patterns*, where a person first experiences conflict over what to do about something, then makes a decision, then experiences some amount of dissonance, and then tries to reduce that dissonance in some way; (2) *selective-exposure patterns*, where receivers only choose information that supports other cognitions, unless the new information is seen as having some degree of utility; (3) *induced compliance*, where the subject is given the opportunity to engage in counter-attitudinal advocacy—although the inducements or rewards for saying things the subject does not believe must be chosen by the persuader in optimal amounts to secure attitude change; and (4) *hypocrisy induction*, where a given belief or attitude is inconsistent with past actions by receivers, and the more salient the attitude or belief to the past behavior the stronger the effect (the receiver can always change the belief or attitude instead of the hoped-for future behavior, even though the persuader seeks the behavior change).

Theories of Behavioral Intention

We will now consider two theories of behavioral intention: the theory of reasoned action (Martin Fishbein and Icek Ajzen) and the theory of planned behavior (Icek Ajzen).[11] Theories of behavioral intention are true persuasion theories because they try to explain how a person's beliefs, attitudes, and so on influence the person's behavior. The reasoned action and planned behavior theories go hand-in-hand because the second one builds on the first.

With behavior intention theories, we can directly try to predict a particular behavioral intention by measuring an existing relevant attitude, such as whether the receiver considers it desirable to visit the Grand Canyon. But as we will see, it is more useful to identify and measure the beliefs that underlie an attitude than to simply measure that attitude. For example, we could identify a number of salient beliefs about a Grand Canyon visit and see where receivers stand on them (e.g., the belief whether a trip to the Grand Canyon will be a relaxing trip or not). By directly measuring these beliefs, we can indirectly measure the overriding attitude. A similar scoring method can be used for estimating the influence of *relevant others* on whether receivers decide on a certain action: Does the receiver think X would approve of the trip? With both the attitude score and social-influence score assessed and combined, the behavioral intentions of receivers can be predicted. The actual behaviors can then be predicted using these behavioral-intentions predictions.

The Theory of Reasoned Action

The theory of reasoned action, developed in the late 1960s, describes how people's actions can be predicted by two things: (1) their likely *attitudes* toward such actions, and (2) *subjective norms*, which are their beliefs about what the relevant others will think about the behavior. The attitude part is determined by **behavioral beliefs** (which are beliefs about the likely consequences of the behavior). In a similar way, subjective norms are determined by **normative beliefs** (which are beliefs about the normative expectations of the relevant others, that is, Will they approve on not?). An extended example will help explain this.

Determinants of the Attitude Component A person's attitude in part stands on underlying behavioral beliefs. We might ask, what are the likely behavioral beliefs someone might have about a trip to the Grand Canyon? Perhaps such beliefs will include (1) It will be relaxing; (2) It will be affordable; (3) It will be a memorable thrill of a lifetime; (4) I will need to plan extensively for the trip if it is to succeed; (5) It could be a dangerous trial of my abilities; (6) My friends will be envious of the trip; (7) I may embarrass myself if I come back home seriously injured.[12] Depending on your personality, values, and experiences, you in particular might believe one way or the other about the above seven assertions regarding the possible trip. We could use a seven-point scale to measure the strength of each of these beliefs for our respondents:[13]

A trip to the Grand Canyon will be relaxing.
[check the box below that most closely identifies your belief]
yes __ __ __ __ _✓_ __ __ no
      +3 +2 +1 0 -1 -2 -3

The theory also requires measuring how respondents will feel if the item in the belief comes to be or not (e.g., how desirable the relaxation factor is as a possible outcome):

As an issue, that the trip to the Grand Canyon be relaxing is
good _✓_ __ __ __ __ __ __ bad.
      +3 +2 +1 0 -1 -2 -3

[B₁] MEASURING BELIEFS COMPONENT [E₁]

THE GRAND CANYON TRIP WILL BE RELAXING.

YES __ __ __ __ __√__ __ __ NO   -3
   +3 +2 +1 0 -1 -2 -3

THAT IT BE RELAXING IS

GOOD _√__ __ __ __ __ __ __ BAD
   +3 +2 +1 0 -1 -2 -3

IT WILL BE AFFORDABLE.

YES __ _√__ __ __ __ __ __ NO   +4
   +3 +2 +1 0 -1 -2 -3

THAT IT BE AFFORDABLE IS

GOOD __ _√__ __ __ __ __ __ BAD
   +3 +2 +1 0 -1 -2 -3

THE GRAND CANYON WILL BE MEMORABLE.

YES _√__ __ __ __ __ __ __ NO   +9
   +3 +2 +1 0 -1 -2 -3

THAT IT BE MEMORABLE IS

GOOD _√__ __ __ __ __ __ __ BAD
   +3 +2 +1 0 -1 -2 -3

$A_0 = \sum b_i e_i = 10$ scales range from +3 to -3

FIGURE 9.3a Calculating behavioral-intention/prediction score: Beliefs component.

Figure 9.3a illustrates how to create a score using several of these pairs of scaled items to predict attitude by measuring the beliefs component.[14] If I think the trip will not be relaxing, I might indicate a -1 on the yes–no scale. And if I rate the relaxing issue as really good, I might indicate a +3 on this scale also. The theory asks that we multiply the two numbers (getting -3 in this case). I might also indicate that the trip will be affordable (perhaps a +2), and that I think it is good if the trip is affordable (a +2). This second pair of ratings will yield +4 when multiplied. After answering all the included pairs of belief scales (one belief scale and one evaluation-of-importance scale for each pair) and then multiplying pair members, we add up all the scores. Figure 9.3a shows a +10 at the bottom left, indicating that my attitude, on the behavioral beliefs component, is moderately positive (the maximum score for any three pairs multiplied is a high score of 27 or a low score of -27).

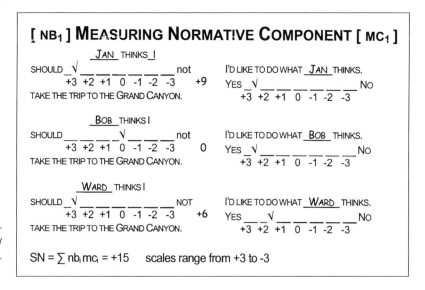

[NB₁] MEASURING NORMATIVE COMPONENT [MC₁]

JAN THINKS I

SHOULD _√__ __ __ __ __ __ __ not
   +3 +2 +1 0 -1 -2 -3   +9
TAKE THE TRIP TO THE GRAND CANYON.

I'D LIKE TO DO WHAT _JAN_ THINKS.

YES _√__ __ __ __ __ __ __ No
   +3 +2 +1 0 -1 -2 -3

BOB THINKS I

SHOULD __ __ _√__ __ __ __ __ not
   +3 +2 +1 0 -1 -2 -3   0
TAKE THE TRIP TO THE GRAND CANYON.

I'D LIKE TO DO WHAT _BOB_ THINKS.

YES _√__ __ __ __ __ __ __ No
   +3 +2 +1 0 -1 -2 -3

WARD THINKS I

SHOULD _√__ __ __ __ __ __ __ NOT
   +3 +2 +1 0 -1 -2 -3   +6
TAKE THE TRIP TO THE GRAND CANYON.

I'D LIKE TO DO WHAT _WARD_ THINKS.

YES __ _√__ __ __ __ __ __ No
   +3 +2 +1 0 -1 -2 -3

$SN = \sum nb_i mc_i = +15$ scales range from +3 to -3

FIGURE 9.3b Calculating behavioral-intention/prediction score: Normative component.

Determinants of the Subjective-Norms Component In addition to the above behavioral beliefs, we must now consider the normative beliefs. What are the likely normative beliefs that someone might have about a trip to the Grand Canyon? These concern how my decision to go to the Grand Canyon might be affected by people whose opinions about such things I respect. Here I will need to identify a set of relevant others and imagine how they will react to the news that I am thinking about a trip to the Grand Canyon; in other words, what are my subjective norms? I do not have to ask them (although I could if I chose to); I just need to imagine how they might feel. Perhaps I would list three people, one of whom might be my friend Jan, and then fill out the following two scales:

Jan thinks I should __✓__ __ __ __ __ __ should not go to the Grand Canyon.
+3 +2 +1 0 -1 -2 -3
I would like to do what Jan thinks.
yes __✓__ __ __ __ __ __ no

As shown in figure 9.3b, we can collect data on my relevant others (Jan, Bob, and Ward) and do the multiplications and additions to arrive at a score for the subjective norms (+15), shown at the bottom left of the figure.[15]

Adding both the *attitude* score and the *subjective-norms* score together will give us a prediction for my current behavioral intention about the trip (unweighted total = 25, calculated by simply adding the two totals listed respectively in the bottom-left parts of figures 9.3a and 9.3b.

Shown below is an equation that explains in a general way how the above two scores can be used for calculating behavioral intention:

$$BI = AB\,(w1) + SN\,(w2)$$

BI stands for behavioral intention, AB stands for attitude toward some behavior, w1 stands for the particular weight we need to give for the attitude portion of the score, SN stands for subjective norm, and w2 stands for the weight we will give to the subjective-norms portion of the score. For this example, there will be no weights assigned. But in an actual study, weights would have to be assigned because attitudes and subjective norms will not likely have the same power in determining future intended behavior. Such weights must be determined with independent research efforts.

Now, a fair question to ask of the theory is why bother to identify and evaluate these behavioral beliefs and subjective-norms beliefs? Why not just ask people to fill out a simple scale about their attitude toward some possible future action (e.g., good idea __ __ __ __ __ __ __ bad idea)? We do this because by identifying and measuring these two kinds of salient beliefs, a persuader or experimenter then can understand the underlying causes of receivers' attitudes on a topic. You as persuader could say to me that the cost of a trip to the Grand Canyon is not as high as I might now believe. Here you would be hoping to get me to change my attitude-salient belief about cost, assuming I actually thought it was salient. Or you might say, "Yes it is expensive, but this is a once-in-a-lifetime opportunity." Here you would be trying to get me to reevaluate the importance of the unfavorable attitude-salient belief I hold about the cost of the trip. Similarly, you could try to alter how I feel about a relevant other (e.g., "X really would approve" or "Why should you care about what X thinks?"). The respective weights given to the measurements of attitude and subjective norm can be established with pre-studies that calculate correlations between these two factors and direct measurements of behavioral intentions. That is, for a decision like this one, how important is attitude and how important is it what the relevant others think? Keep in mind too that researchers are not usually just interested in what one person thinks about a topic. Usually entire groups of people make up the persuader's target group—thus data has to be collected and then analyzed with respect to groups of people. Likert-like (graduated) scales are often used for this data collection.

The Theory of Planned Behavior

The second theory of behavioral intention, the theory of planned behavior, developed in the late 1980s, requires that one additional component be added to the equation given in the previous section: **perceived behavioral control**, which concerns how receivers imagine obstacles and resources that might impede or facilitate completing an intended action. Perceived obstacles and resources can include many things, such as information, objects, or tools; aspects of the terrain where the behavior will occur; the personal abilities of the actor; and other people who will help or hinder. For example, shopkeepers sometimes keep the front door to their store open (an aspect of terrain). Perhaps they think that a closed door is more of a psychological obstacle than an open one for potential patrons who might or might not decide to come inside. Noticing a security guard at a store may be an obstacle for a would-be shoplifter. Knowing exactly where a store is located might be an informational resource for a shopper.

So how will this new factor, perceived behavioral control, play out in the Grand Canyon trip, as illustrated in figure 9.3c? What things will affect my perceptions of perceived behavioral control? I might perceive the Grand Canyon as a remote location and wonder if I could actually find it. Or I may worry whether I can actually plan the trip and bring it off. I may even believe that having a traveling companion will be necessary. Or I may see my job as a facilitating resource for the trip if there is some job-relevant aspect to the trip.

Determinants of Perceived Behavioral Control Just as attitudes and subjective norms are based on underlying beliefs, perceived behavioral control is also based on beliefs. These *control beliefs* are about the presence of factors that may impede or facilitate performance of the behavior. We could formally illustrate this third feature with a newly added component to the equation given earlier, as shown below.

$$BI = AB\,(w1) + SN\,(w2) + PBC\,(w3)$$

The new part in the above equation is PBC (perceived behavioral control; illustrated with the scales in figure 9.3c). The determinants of perceived behavioral control also concern scaled pairs of evaluations, just as the measurements of attitude and subjective norms did earlier. With PBC, the pairs of evaluations first concern the strength of the individual's beliefs about the proposed behavior, as in:

The Grand Canyon is located in a remote area.

yes _✓__ __ __ __ __ __ no
    +3 +2 +1 0 -1 -2 -3

The second evaluation in each pair, shown below, concerns the facilitating or inhibiting power each control belief is imagined to have by the target:

Remoteness will make the trip

easy __ __ __ __ _✓ __ __ hard.
     +3 +2 +1 0 -1   -2 -3

Thus with the first item in the pair of scaled items above, we find out what I believe about the remoteness of the Grand Canyon. The second item in the pair (how important the remoteness issue seems to me) shows the facilitating or inhibiting power of the item for me. Another example of perceived behavioral control evaluation might concern requirements of elaborate planning for the trip and how much this requirement may be expected to help or hinder the trip. A third example might concern how useful a companion might be or not be. Perhaps I think it will take planning, but the planning will be simple. Other potential visitors to the Grand Canyon might have opposite evaluations for the location, planning, and companion issues.

Now having illustrated all three components of these two theories of behavioral intention with the planned trip to the Grand Canyon, we can predict whether I will go or not

---

[P_1] MEASURING PERCEIVED-BEHAVIORAL CONTROL COMPONENT [C_1]

THE GRAND CANYON IS REMOTE.

YES _√__ __ __ __ __ __ NO   -3
    +3 +2 +1 0 -1 -2 -3

REMOTENESS WILL MAKE THE TRIP

EASY __ __ __ __ √ __ __ HARD
     +3 +2 +1 0 -1 -2 -3

THE TRIP WILL REQUIRE ELABORATE PLANS.

YES __ √ __ __ __ __ __ NO -4
    +3 +2 +1 0 -1 -2 -3

ELABORATE PLANS WILL MAKE THE TRIP

EASY __ __ __ __ __ √ __ HARD
     +3 +2 +1 0 -1 -2 -3

I EXPECT TO GO WITH A COMPANION.

YES __ √ __ __ __ __ __ NO +2
    +3 +2 +1 0 -1 -2 -3

A COMPANION WILL MAKE THE TRIP

EASY __ __ √ __ __ __ __ HARD
     +3 +2 +1 0 -1 -2 -3

PBC = $\sum p_i c_i$ = -5   scales range from +3 to -3

Total Behavioral-Intention Grand Canyon Trip Score = (+10 +15 -5) = +20
Note: The first two scores (+10 and +15) were calculated in figures 9.3a and 9.3b respectively.

FIGURE 9.3c Calculating behavioral-intention/prediction score: Perceived-ability component and final score.

based on my answers shown in figures 9.3a, 9.3b, and 9.3c, and then summarized at the bottom of figure 9.3c. The third and last factor, my behavioral-control score, turns out to be -5. Adding this to the +10 and +15 of the previous two scores, we get a total score of +20—a somewhat positive score. A perfect score would be +81 (multiplying nine pairs times the highest possible value for each pair, which is 9). However, a positive score of 20 may not be all that bad. What we would have to do next is gather total scores for a reasonably large sampling of other people and see what the average score would be using the nine pairs of questions shown in our example. But most importantly, it would be very helpful to find out the scores for people who actually then take the Grand Canyon trip. We would then compare my score to the average score in general and to the average score of actual trip-goers.

Research and Applications for Theories of Behavioral Intention

To use these two theories for research, you would need to identify salient beliefs, individualized sets of relevant others for respondents, and perceived obstacles or resources. The methods for doing these things are more intricate than are the simple examples given in this text. For instance, to establish beliefs you would need to do preliminary research to see what beliefs a target population in fact associates with a given attitude about an intended behavior. One target group may be wary of the sugar content in breakfast cereal, fearing it will make children hyperactive (a behavioral belief). For a different target group, this possible connection between sugar and hyperactivity may be completely unknown and thus hardly salient. So to measure attitudes regarding sugared cereals, you must systematically identify which beliefs are considered salient by your target group. Perhaps you will identify these salient beliefs by using interviews and surveys, or through previously published research on the topic.

One other research topic concerns documenting the relationship between receivers' behavioral intentions and their actual behavior. Research studies have found that intended behaviors are actually carried out about half the time. The power of behavioral intention theory to predict subsequent behavior depends on such things as the degree of specificity with which behavioral intention and subsequent behavior are measured.[16] Similarly, the personalities of the receivers are also important. For example, some people may change their preferences with the weather, while others have preferences that remain constant. The relationship between intention and action will be stronger for the latter group. Whether people have engaged in specific planning of the intended behavior or not, have engaged in the behavior in question in the past, or have established routines for the behavior in question can all make the predictive power of behavioral intention theory stronger in the expected directions.[17]

These two theories of behavioral intention have been immensely popular with researchers, who continue to add to the body of facts and continue to fine-tune the theory. For example, in a recent study, researchers David Trafimow and Krystina Finlay asked a provocative question about how a double negative could become a positive in the theories of behavioral intention.[18] Here, you as a respondent in the study might believe that working as an elementary-school teacher will not likely result in high pay, so you respond to the high-pay assertion in the study with a doubtful -3. But perhaps you don't care about high pay, therefore assigning the high-pay assertion a -2 (i.e., low pay will not be an obstacle). The resulting belief score on the high-pay assertion would nonetheless be +6, giving us some encouragement in predicting that you will become a teacher. But should this double negative be considered as legitimate a predictive factor as, say, a response pairing where you believe teaching will result in high job satisfaction (+3) and feel that job satisfaction will make the job easy (+2), which would also equal +6? That is, when predicting what things may cause you to do something, is not caring about a negative feature of the behavior equivalent to caring about a positive feature of the behavior? As is often the case with quandaries of this sort, the likely answer may be "It depends." Trafimow and Finlay report data analyses that suggest that predictions based on double-negative scorings need more investigation.

In another recent study, researchers Julie Christian and Cristopher Armitage used the theory of planned behavior as a framework to investigate the likelihood that homeless people would participate in outreach programs in South Wales, UK. They found that attitude was the dominant predictor of behavioral *intention* (as opposed to subjective norms or perceived behavioral control). But they also found that behavioral intention and perceived behavioral control were predictive of actual behavior, and that contrary to expectations, subjective norms also exerted a direct effect on actual behavior. The authors speculate that subjective norms, usually the weakest of the predictors, found resonance with the stigmatized population they studied.[19]

Elaboration Likelihood Theory

Elaboration likelihood theory developed from the work of psychologists Richard Petty, John Cacioppo, and their associates over the last twenty-five years or so. Generally speaking, the theory speaks to important variations in how receivers of persuasive messages think about incoming messages. Elaboration likelihood theory offers a somewhat different perspective on persuasion than have the theories already discussed. The keyword in this theory is *elaboration*, which refers to the concentrated thinking receivers engage in about a message.

Elaboration likelihood theory assumes that people are motivated to hold correct attitudes. They want to feel rational and right about things that matter to them, and may define the word *correct* as what is "good for them." A second assumption is that although people want to hold correct attitudes, the amount and nature of issue-relevant elaboration in which they are willing or able to engage to evaluate a message varies according to individual and situational factors. Here we also see that different people respond to persuasive messages in one of two ways: centrally or peripherally (see figure 9.4).

Two Routes to Persuasion: Central and Peripheral

The central path is used when the receiver is (1) motivated to think about the message, and (2) has the ability to think about the message. When on this path, receivers may think favorably about the persuasive message as a kind of elaboration and may even add their own ideas. Critical thinking may occur during **central processing**.[20] Logic characterizes the central route when receivers consider the merits of an idea or proposal: Do I agree with this idea? Why do I like it? Are the facts in it true? But while central processing concerns detail, peripheral processing instead concerns the packaging of the message, or the context in which it is received.

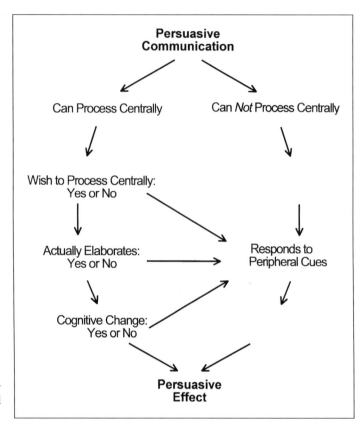

FIGURE 9.4 Two routes of the elaboration likelihood theory: Central and peripheral.

The peripheral path is used when the receiver is either not motivated or is unable to critically examine the message. Using **peripheral processing**, the receiver might accept or reject a persuasive message in terms of how trendy it seems or whether the sender is attractive or not. In other instances, a receiver might choose to buy something out of whimsy or for some superficial reason.

Peripheral processing often involves simple judgments about such things as (1) the perceived credibility of the sender—this helps receivers decide whether to agree or not with the persuasive message; (2) the likeability of the sender—this also helps receivers decide whether to agree or not with the message; (3) the consensus of peers or role models about the message—this causes receivers to accept the message bandwagon style; (4) the message's length in time or words—this may be seen as a sign that something right has been articulated; and (5) the number of persuasive arguments used—this can affect the message's apparent persuasiveness. Other variables probably also exist but have yet to be identified through empirical research. For example, the age or gender of a seller could affect whether I buy lemonade from that seller on some tree-lined street in the summer. These peripheral cues are sometimes called *heuristics*, which are helpful procedures for making decisions.

Elaboration likelihood theory is built around the notion that, unlike central processing, peripheral processing when favorable for a certain sender may lead only to weak changes that do not last long.

Elaboration Likelihood Variables in Play

Two sets of elaboration likelihood variables concern receivers' *abilities* and *motivations* to scrutinize the message. If these are favorable in a given situation, the receiver will more likely centrally process the message; if these are not favorable, then peripheral processing may occur. Other variables may help determine whether central processing, with its elaboration or scrutiny, will be more objective or more biased. For example, we might not want to see a flaw in a message we like, even if we are following the message fairly closely. At other times we may indeed try to see the truth as we process a message.

Another way to predict how receivers will respond concerns individual receivers' needs for cognition. Some people have personalities that make thinking enjoyable for them so they like to listen to arguments and parse each for truth and validity. Other people think rigorously when they have to, but not as a hobby. If you are fatigued, working hard at some task unrelated to the persuasion, or in a noisy environment, you may be less likely to take the central processing route and may opt for the less-taxing peripheral route. And if central processing causes dissonance, you may opt for peripheral processing. Prior knowledge of the topic may give you an enhanced ability to think centrally about the arguments you hear, making things easier. If you know a great deal about history, and I make the statement that President X was the first modern ecologist in his seeking public lands to be used as national parks, you may respond quite thoughtfully in agreement or disagreement.

One other assumption about variables of the elaboration likelihood theory is that as motivation and ability to process the arguments in a message go down, the importance of peripheral cues goes up. If you just cannot follow the arguments a scientist is making about what causes a specific disease, you may have to resort to noting that the scientist is from a very reputable university (thus you say to yourself the arguments are "probably true"). In contrast, as your ability to process the arguments goes up, the importance of peripheral cues goes down. Because you can follow the logic, you agree with or disagree with the explanation given about the disease, not caring who is saying what, but caring about what seems true or not. The elaboration likelihood theory also predicts that attitude changes that result from receivers' central processing of a message's arguments will show greater *longevity* in the minds of the receivers, greater *impact* on their actual behavior, and greater *immunity* to counterpersuasion than will attitude changes resulting from peripheral processing.

The Elaboration Likelihood Theory in Perspective

How should a persuader decide whether to assume that receivers will rely on peripheral processing (mental-shortcuts thinking) or central processing (issues-relevant thinking)? One criterion here is topic relevance. If the county you live in says that you will have to move to another house and neighborhood within six months for reasons of eminent domain, you will probably think long and hard about the reasons they give. But if I try to persuade you that the guitarist Les Paul and the singer Mary Ford pioneered multitrack sound recording in 1950 in a backyard garage in Queens, New York, you may not care all that much about evaluating the message and may then take a shortcut by saying, "He seems so enthusiastic, maybe he knows for sure." But if you are a recording-technology buff, you might scrutinize my statement, agree or disagree, and maybe take me to task on the particulars. Petty, Cacioppo, and Goldman illuminated this issue with an experiment that varied topic relevance to receivers in order to study the effects of argument strength and sender expertise.[21] One group of receivers were assigned a topic not all that relevant to them. The individuals in this group who were persuaded were apparently persuaded by the sender's expertise (a peripheral shortcut). But individuals who were assigned a relevant topic were apparently persuaded more by the strength of the arguments than by the expertise of the persuader (central-processing elaboration). This study illustrates the two general routes to persuasion.

Elaboration likelihood theory also has its complexities. The fact that receivers may use both routes within the same persuasive event means that more often we will have to expect trade-offs because as receivers make greater use of argument scrutiny, they may make lesser use of peripheral cues, and vice versa. But the most difficult complexity is that a given variable may play multiple roles during persuasion. For example, persuasion scholar Daniel O'Keefe summarizes several studies by Petty, Cacioppo, and Goldman on the complexities of message length.[22] Message length can serve as a peripheral cue of message quality. But in some cases, message length can serve as a cue telling us whether close examination is required of the message. Perhaps I will not completely read the last section of a chapter if it is a single paragraph. Another complexity concerns documenting statements with citations or believable personal experiences. This practice can serve three roles: (1) it can cause receivers to pay close attention in order to centrally process; (2) it can serve as a heuristic that says, if the message has lots of citations or personal testimony, it may be right; (3) it might encourage the creation of additional positive thoughts for central processing about the advocated view.

Finally, some critics of elaboration likelihood theory have tried to describe a shortcoming in it. That is, central processing and peripheral processing may not be two separate entities but merely end points on a continuum. For example, could one receiver scrutinize with great energy the arguments in a persuasive message while another scrutinizes the argument, but with just some effort, and while yet another just uses peripheral cues? You could also note that even peripheral processing requires some thought. However, peripheral processing often concerns "meta-things" (*meta*, in this sense, means "about," as in the term *metacommunication*, which signifies cues that help us disambiguate a message with two or more possible meanings). Peripheral cues often concern things like how long a message is, what color package a product comes in, whether the sender is attractive or ugly or young or old, and whether the sender has just a few arguments or many. Perhaps we could make a case that peripheral cues are indeed a different sort of entity than the arguments of a message. Beyond "meta-things," other terms that come to mind when thinking about the nature of peripheral cues are "summary things" and "parametric things" (referring to something not with a description of exactly what it is, but with coordinates that identify where it exists on a grid).

A Composite Theory

Now that we have reviewed several theories of persuasion, perhaps I can create a composite theory to show us the bigger picture, with some linkage among the theories. The composite theory model shown in figure 9.5 is in large measure an extension of the theories of behavioral intention and a theory described in chapter 1, attitude function theory. To these materials, the composite theory adds several external features: obstacles and resources (actual ones, not perceived or imagined ones) and others' behaviors in the actual setting where the intended behavior will occur or not (which are different from the subjective-norms ideas imagined about what relevant others might think about some intended behavior).

Incoming Persuasive Messages and Experiential Data

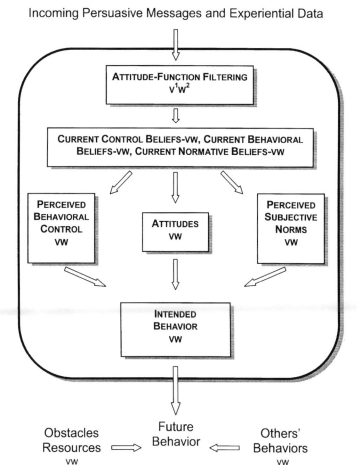

[1]determinant value
[2]relative weight of determinant

FIGURE 9.5 Future behavior is predicted from ratios of intended behavior, others' behaviors, and obstacles and resources; intended behavior is predicted from ratios of perceived behavioral control, attitudes, and social norms, which in turn are predicted from the ratio of current beliefs and attitude functions; future beliefs are predicted from ratios of attitude functions, current beliefs, and incoming data.

As you can see at the top of the model, persuasion enters the mind of a receiver in conjunction with experiential data from communicative settings. As you follow the arrows downward, you see attitude-function filtering, borrowed from attitude function theory. Below this are the current beliefs (control, behavioral, and normative). These are the underpinnings of the attitudes, perceived behavioral control, and perceived subjective norms that are parts of the two behavioral intentions theories discussed above. Then come perceived behavioral control, attitudes, and perceived subjective norms, followed by intended behavior. To these things the model then adds obstacles and resources, and others' behaviors. As noted above, these two elements are different from the perceived behavioral control and perceived subjective norms. The two outer additions refer to actual objects and people who may affect future behavior as it begins to play out. The internal elements exist in the person's imagination (e.g., I can imagine if a friend will approve of my climbing a tree in the park, but that imagined friend is different from the police officer who might see me start to climb the tree). Several brief illustrations of the composite model may help.

Perhaps we are eating lunch in a cafeteria, and you ask me to pass the salt. I had not intended to pass the salt. But my attitude toward things like that is positive. I believe that such courtesies do not cost much, and this attitude helps me feel like a good person. I also think that other people will approve, and I do not foresee any difficulty with completing the action—so all systems are go, and I pass the salt. In this case, the v's in figure 9.5, or the values of each determinant, say yes. The w's in the figure refer to the relative weights I assign to the various determinants in making my decision. The weights do not mean much in this first example because the v's are all for my saying, "Yes, I'll do it." But on another occasion, one of my salient beliefs about passing the salt could turn negative: perhaps I believe you are just being lazy this time. Still, my wanting to be seen as nice (an attitude function) may have a greater weight, and I will pass the salt; but on another occasion, maybe my attitude function will not have a greater weight, and I may say, "Get it yourself; it's closer to you."

Things may become more interesting and complicated if you are asking me to sign a petition to get our boss fired. Now many things become salient. I may believe the boss does deserve a pink slip. And I may believe that if we do not "kill the king," we may be in big trouble. But I may also wonder what my mother would think of my signing the petition (a subjective norm). I may be uncertain whether my signing the petition violates my employment contract (a perceived behavioral control, or imagined obstacle). Perhaps when I add up all the values and weights, I am inclined to sign (an intended behavior). But as the petition comes around, I am concerned about the other people present, whose behaviors may interfere with mine because they do not support the action. So I decide to go to lunch early (an actual behavior), while worrying that the security cameras could record my signing the petition (an actual obstacle). But you see me leaving and come running to convince me not to be a coward, and you want a yes or no decision from me. You remind me of all the things the boss has done in the past several months. You tell me that others in the workplace look to me for leadership. You even propose to put up a screen to let people sign in privacy (an actual resource). Now how will I respond? Will my beliefs carry the day? Will my attitude functions for personal survival carry the day? Will other people in the environment discourage or encourage me?

With a little effort, we can also see the theory of cognitive dissonance at work in figure 9.5. The principal cognition here is actually signing the petition, and the cluster of relevant consonant or dissonant cognitions include salient beliefs, attitudes, and attitude functions. We might even see the balance theory here when the person who puts the pressure on me to sign becomes the sender whom I want to agree with—because I want to agree with people I like. Elaboration likelihood is the most difficult theory to apply here. But if the listener responds with peripheral processing, the determinant values (the v's) will tend to be superficial, with perhaps just one determinant value carrying the day because it gets slightly more weight than the others (e.g., "X is usually right about these things, so I'll sign"). With central processing, the full array of determinant values and weights would all come into play in complicated ways.

One last thing we might note about the composite model in figure 9.5 is how it shows that at various points, given variables are dependent on what happens in the several variables shown nearby. This feature was borrowed from the theories of behavioral intention. Future behavior is predicted by intended behavior, the actions of others at the scene of the action, and real obstacles or resources. For example, I might intend to climb a tree in the park but stop short when I see others looking at me disapprovingly and a park sign that says, "Do not climb on the trees—$50 fine." Later that night, a drunk party-goer climbs the same tree because fellow revelers tear down the sign and offer loud encouragement. As we have seen, intended behavior is predicted from attitude, perceived behavioral control, and perceived subjective norms.

In one last example, a receiver may have a positive attitude toward bringing home stray dogs. Perhaps the receiver's beliefs about this include the idea that stray dogs taken home give back more than they get. The receiver may also have beliefs about perceived behavioral control and perceived subjective norms. But that receiver might think twice in this situation if his or her spouse would object (a subjective norm based on beliefs about the spouse), or because of thoughts about the next cold morning when the dog has to go out for a walk (a time-energy aspect of perceived behavioral control).

What about attitude function? In the above example, perhaps the receiver feels warm inside when bringing home a new dog that seems so happy and grateful to have a new home. Thus, even if the receiver's spouse is believed to disapprove of yet another dog, the receiver rationalizes that there is always room for just one more. The "warm-fuzzy" attitude-function filter trumps any beliefs about possible objections from the spouse, in this case. Attitude-function filters can be very powerful, especially when they concern a receiver's ego-defense, a value expression of something very important, a pragmatic benefit, or some way to simplify the receiver's understanding of the world.[23]

We might also note here that the one criticism that has been leveled at the theories of behavioral intention is that receivers sometimes intend to do things and then are unable to actually carry out these actions. The composite model answers this criticism by including the possibility that other people at the scene of the intended behavior can affect the receiver's actual behavior. This influence could also come from physical obstacles and resources at the scene. Consequently, the external variables at the bottom of the composite model have been assigned values (v's) and weights (w's) similar to the other elements of the model.

In addition to the major theories described in this chapter, there are numerous minor theories that describe some aspect or detail of the persuasion process, as shown in box 9.1.[24] The number of minor theories with something to say about persuasion are numerous, as can be seen in the table. But they are so numerous that summarizing what each has to add to the ideas already discussed in this chapter would take up more space than we can afford at the end of an already long chapter on persuasion theories. Nonetheless, those interested can use box 9.1 and a library or Internet search to find materials and to read further on one or more of the theories.

Chapter in Retrospect

VIGNETTE **A Message from Above**

Y ou are walking down the sidewalk and someone standing at the corner offers you a small, two-page pamphlet with the headline "Hey! You Gotta Problem?" Inside the pamphlet you read, "Is your problem about drinking and drugs? Is it about the lack of money? Sickness? Loneliness? Guilt?" The pamphlet then offers a solution to these problems. It directs you to the "expert problem solver," God. The pamphlet next reminds you that in the Christian Bible, God says, "Come to me all you who are weary and burdened and I will give you rest" (Matthew 11:28). According to the pamphlet, God also says, "Whoever comes to Me I will never turn away" (John 6:37). The rest of the pamphlet explains that God is concerned about you, and thus it is quite reasonable for you to consult God because he is the best problem solver available. At the end, the pamphlet asks you to say a prayer and invites you to visit a particular location for religious services.

How persuasive is the approach taken in the pamphlet? The answer to this question probably depends on a given receiver's religious orientation. Perhaps some receivers will ignore the pamphlet offer, and some will take it but throw it away after a quick, heuristic-applying look. Still others may carry it away, presumably to read closely at a later time. Although the theme of the pamphlet's message is religious, the message functions in a familiar rhetorical manner. There is a claim, evidence, and reasoning. If the receiver accepts the

---

BOX 9.1

Minor Theories about Features of Persuasion

Accommodation	Expectation States	Post-Decision Dissonance
Acquired Needs Theory	False Consensus Effect	Propinquity Effect
Attribution Theory	False Memory	Reactance Theory
Availability Heuristic	Framing	Regret Theory
Cognitive Evaluation	Groupthink	Risky Shift
Conversion	Halo Effect	Sapir-Whorf Hypothesis
Correspondent Inference	Impressions Management	Scapegoat Theory
Counter-Advocacy	Information Processing	Self-Fulfilling Prophecy
Deindividuation	Inoculation	Sleeper Effect
Empathy-Altruism	Language Expectancy	Speech Act Theory
Equity Theory	Outcome Dependency	Strategic Contingencies
Expectancy Theory	Personal Construct	Uncertainty Reduction
Expectancy Violations	Politeness Theory	

evidence (what Matthew and John have said) and the reasoning (i.e., If you have a problem, seek out the ultimate problem solver), perhaps the receiver takes the advice and attends religious services at the address given at the bottom of the pamphlet.

How does balance theory, for example, help us in analyzing the above religious message? The senders of importance regarding the pamphlet could be (1) the person who is handing it out, (2) the religious organization sponsoring the pamphlet distribution, (3) Matthew and John, or (4) God. But remember that with balance theory, we like to agree with people we like and we like to disagree with people we dislike. Hence, if we like whom we see as the sender of the pamphlet, we may take the pamphlet's advice and show up at the address given. But if we do not, we probably will not.

Cognitive dissonance theory may also add something to the analysis. To the extent that receivers believe they do have the sorts of problems described in the pamphlet, and to the extent they believe that things religious can help with their problems, they will either feel consonance or dissonance. Whether they feel consonance or dissonance will depend on their decision to either take the advice in the pamphlet or not. If you agree that you have one of these problems and agree that religion is the answer, you may feel dissonance if you fail to make the obvious decision to attend services. But the opposite can also be true. If you do not agree you have one of these problems, or if you do not believe that religion is the answer, you may then feel dissonance if you decide to attend services. And in the end you may choose to do something beyond what the pamphlet recommends: you may attend services somewhere else, pray, or read the Bible privately.

The theories of behavioral intention are perhaps the most interesting here since your decision to attend or not attend services seems to be the ultimate persuasive objective of the pamphlet. Thus, which factors will best predict whether you intend to show up at next week's services or not? First there is your attitude about attending or not attending. Second is whether you imagine how other people you know will feel about your current intention to go or not. The third concerns how easy or hard you imagine the trip to the church will be.

Another interesting dimension of the two behavioral intention theories concerns here your underlying beliefs about attending services and solving personal problems. What might some of these beliefs be? Perhaps two of them are "God cares about me as an individual" and "God exists." Further, the religious organization sponsoring the pamphlet is a legitimate one. "Is it possible," you might wonder, "for this organization to solve the sorts of personal problems I have?" Exactly how you answer each of these sample questions may have a significant effect on your general attitude toward attending services at a religious organization that promotes attendance with pamphlets passed out on the sidewalk. How positive or negative your resulting attitude is will significantly affect whether you now plan to attend services next week. Finally, whether or not you at least intend to go will affect whether you in the end do or do not go.

Elaboration likelihood theory concerns your general approach to evaluating persuasive messages. With one approach, you use superficial peripheral cues called heuristics to decide. Taking the above example, you might notice whether the pamphlet was created at significant financial cost or not, whether it has many arguments or few, and whether it seems to flow logically or not. Your response may hinge here on some small detail. Perhaps you will think to yourself, "This pamphlet looks very amateurish to me, so I will not give it much thought." Or you might think, "It quotes Matthew and John with reference numbers, so it must be legitimate." In both these examples, you have taken the peripheral approach of the elaboration likelihood theory. But instead, you could think long and hard about what you read in the pamphlet. You might engage in central processing in order to decide whether you will attend services or not, depending on how reasonable the message seems. You may even add to the mix religious thoughts, agnostic thoughts, or even atheistic thoughts you remember from previous discussions and experiences. But with central processing, your decision will rest on how carefully you have scrutinized the religious message, and on how knowledgeable you are about the topic, how logical you are, and how strong your religious faith is. Peripheral processing seems to be what the pamphlet writer was expecting you to do when examining the pamphlet you were handed on the street. The message was simple, brief, and pragmatic; perhaps people on the street are not likely to give things they are handed great amounts of thought—at least at first.

Summary and Conclusions

Learning theory describes the ways in which behavior can be modified without much rhetorical input, ways that include operant and classical conditioning and social learning theory. Consistency theories are built around the idea that people want to feel that they are rational and consistent. When we discover a discrepancy in ourselves, we are more prone to being persuaded. The two theories of behavioral intention tell us that intended behavior can be predicted by our attitudes. They also describe perceived behavioral control and perceived subjective norms as having an impact on intended behavior. Most important here is that beliefs about the desirability of performing actions will influence our attitude toward those actions. Elaboration likelihood theory posits that there are two routes to persuasion. One route is peripheral and relies on heuristics or minor decision techniques that we use to evaluate a message. The other is central, and here we give our full attention to the ideas in the message. A composite theory—built in part on the above theories and a theory about attitude function mentioned in chapter 1—may account for behavior by identifying internal and external variables.

KEY TERMS

attitudes	consonance	perceived behavioral
behavioral beliefs	dissonance	control
central processing	normative beliefs	peripheral processing
classical conditioning	operant conditioning	reinforcement schedules
cognition		

REVIEW QUESTIONS

1. Why are learning theories probably not really about persuasion?
2. What easy-to-remember saying can help you to understand balance theory? It begins, "We like to . . ."

3. What is the difference between operant and classical conditioning?
4. How is social learning theory different from learning theory?
5. How are balance theory and the theory of cognitive dissonance related?
6. What happens when we experience dissonance?
7. How is the word *cluster* used in explaining cognitive dissonance theory?
8. What is the main difference between the theories of reasoned action and planned behavior?
9. How are the two routes of elaboration likelihood theory similar? How are they different?
10. How many different theories are included in the composite theory?

SUGGESTED PROJECTS AND ACTIVITIES

1. Draw up a list of things around your home, school, or workplace that illustrate classical conditioning (e.g., I hear footsteps in the hall and instantly know who is about to enter the room).
2. Test out the ideas in balance theory. Think of someone in your neighborhood, at school, at work, or even among your relatives whom you do not like or get along with. Then think of a topic that the two of you probably disagree about. If the topic is lighthearted, maybe it matters very little to you. But if it is a very serious one, maybe the balance theory will illustrate the bad feelings.
3. Use the theory of planned behavior to try to predict whether someone you know can be persuaded to do something in particular (e.g., volunteer, take a vacation, ask someone out on a date).
4. When you are shopping in a supermarket, take note of when you use peripheral or central processing to decide what things to buy.
5. Suppose you are a volunteer trying to convince people you know to donate blood to a community blood bank. How could the theories of behavioral intention help you persuade? The elaboration likelihood theory? Cognitive dissonance theory? Learning theory?
6. Spend some time watching people assembled, say, on a playground or in a cafeteria. Can features of the composite theory and figure 9.5 be illustrated by what you see? What things can be understood about you (and anyone you might be with) by variables illustrated in the theory?

QUESTIONS FOR DISCUSSION

1. Balance theory seems to work for some subjects but not for others. Can you build an explanation about why it sometimes works and why it sometimes doesn't?
2. What are the many ways learning theories can be used to analyze what happens at casinos?
3. Which theory or theories in this chapter do you think offer the best insights into the type of persuasion that goes on in your life? Why?
4. What kinds of common habits of people can be explained by principles of operant or classical conditioning? Give examples.

5. Is it really possible that attitude functions as described in the composite theory can make it very difficult to influence someone's attitude when you offer factual information designed to help change their relevant beliefs on some matter?

6. What types of specific topics (e.g., relevant to sports, science, politics, business, family, sex) do you typically deal with by using peripheral processing? Central processing?

Notes

1. See the summary in Arthur Staats, Carolyn Staats, and Hugh Crawford, "First Order Conditioning of Meaning and the Parallel Conditioning of a GSR," *Journal of General Psychology* 67 (July 1962): 159–67.

2. B. F. Skinner, *The Behavior of Organisms: An Experimental Analysis* (New York: Appleton-Century-Crofts, 1966), 61–115.

3. Albert Bandura, *Social Learning Theory* (Englewood Cliffs, NJ: Prentice Hall, 1977), 7–14, 17–29.

4. Fritz Heider, "Attitudes and Cognitive Organization," *Journal of Psychology* 21 (1946): 107–12.

5. A researcher could add a quantitative dimension to balance theory by measuring degrees of like or dislike, for example, using Likert-like graduated scales: like 1 2 3 4 5 6 7 dislike.

6. Leon Festinger, *A Theory of Cognitive Dissonance* (Stanford, CA: Stanford University Press, 1957), 1–31. One other early consistency theory was congruency theory, which was somewhat more flexible than balance theory but not as useful as cognitive dissonance theory.

7. For actual research these pairs of scales might be turned into single bipolar scales, such as "My boss does not approve of my gambling behavior." Yes __ __ __ __ __ __ __ No

8. The psychological costs of reducing dissonance without persuasive change may add up over time, however, making future dissonance more likely to be reduced by persuasive change. Simply noting the number of items on both sides is a safe approach to measuring cumulative dissonance or consonance since it does not assume too much about the type of data involved (i.e., whether it is nominal, ordinal, interval, or ratio).

9. Here too, simply noting the number of items on both sides is a safe approach to measuring cumulative dissonance or consonance since it does not assume too much about the type of data involved.

10. Robert Huckfeldt, Paul Johnson, and John Sprague, *Political Disagreement: The Survival of Diverse Opinions within Communication Networks* (New York: Cambridge University Press, 2004), 1–26; David Matz and Wendy Wood, "Cognitive Dissonance in Groups: The Consequences of Disagreement," *Journal of Personality and Social Psychology* 88, no. 1 (January 2005): 22–37; and Daniel O'Keefe, *Persuasion: Theory and Practice* (Thousand Oaks, CA: Sage, 2002), 78–100.

11. For more detail on the theory of reasoned action, see Martin Fishbein and Icek Ajzen, "Attitudes and Voting Behavior: An Application of the Theory of Reasoned Action," in *Progress in Applied Social Psychology*, ed. Geoffrey Stephanson and James Davis (New York: John Wiley, 1981), 1:253–313. For more detail on the theory of planned behavior, see Icek Ajzen, "The Theory of Planned Behavior," *Organizational Behavior and Human Decision Processes* 50 (1991): 179–211. In addition, Bagozzi and Warshaw have extended the theory of reasoned action with the theory of trying, developed in 1990. This theory emphasizes consumer uncertainty when achievement of a consumption objective is not entirely within the consumer's volitional control; see Richard Bagozzi and Paul Warshaw, "Trying to Consume," *Journal of Consumer Research* 17, no. 2 (September 1990): 127–40.

12. In actual research studies using the theory of reasoned action, we must systematically collect possible salient beliefs through preliminary empirical research.

13. A Likert scale poses statements and then asks respondents whether they strongly agree, slightly agree, agree, are undecided, slightly disagree, disagree, or strongly disagree. Researchers sometimes

replace the words above with numbers: agree 1 2 3 4 5 6 7 disagree. Statisticians usually advise that we not calculate averages from data collected using these scales (unless we are certain that we are not violating any assumptions about our data), but rather to calculate medians, which makes fewer assumptions about the type of data we have collected. So if five people answer a question giving respectively the answers 3, 7, 1, 2, 5, we could calculate the average response (3.6 in this case), or the median or middle-score response (3). The safer report might in this case then be 3, not 3.6. When in doubt about how to proceed with summary calculations, check with a professional statistician.

14. If we were studying groups of people who held somewhat different relevant beliefs, we might want to average their relevant belief scores rather than just add them, so that the averages could be compared among group members.

15. Here again, we would average normative data for individual group members for comparison or for statistical tests done for entire group scores.

16. See for example Min-Sun Kim and John Hunter, "Relationships among Attitudes, Behavioral Intentions, and Behavior," *Communication Research* 20, no. 1 (February 1993): 331–64.

17. O'Keefe, *Persuasion: Theory and Practice*, 130–34.

18. David Trafimow and Krystina Finlay, "The Prediction of Attitudes from Beliefs and Evaluations: The Logic of the Double Negative," *British Journal of Social Psychology* 41 (March 2002): 77–86.

19. Julie Christian and Cristopher Armitage, "Attitudes and Intentions of Homeless People towards Service Provision in South Wales," *British Journal of Social Psychology* 41, no. 2 (June 2002): 219–31.

20. Richard Petty and John Cacioppo, *Communication and Persuasion: Central and Peripheral Routes to Attitude Change* (New York: Springer-Verlag, 1986).

21. Richard Petty, John Cacioppo, and Rachel Goldman, "Personal Involvement as a Determinant of Argument-Based Persuasion," *Journal of Personality and Social Psychology* 41 (1981): 847–55.

22. O'Keefe, *Persuasion: Theory and Practice*, 150–52.

23. James Dillard and Eugenia Peck, "Persuasion and the Structure of Affect Dual Systems and Discrete Emotions as Complementary Models," *Human Communication Research* 27, no. 1 (January 2001).

24. ChangingMinds.org, "Theories," http://changingminds.org/explanations/theories/theories.htm (7 November 2005).

Empirical Persuasion Research

Nothing has such power to broaden the mind as the ability to investigate systematically and truly all that comes under your observation in life.

—MARCUS AURELIUS

"The scientific method," Thomas Henry Huxley once wrote, "is nothing but the normal working of the human mind." That is to say, when the mind is working; that is to say further, when it is engaged in correcting its mistakes.

—NEIL POSTMAN

IN THE PREVIOUS chapter, we reviewed a number of theories that over the last half century have guided the scientific research that we will now discuss. Then in chapter 11, we will review the critical methods developed and used to study persuasive messages over the last 2,500 years. Much of the experimental research has tried to identify and understand the effects that persuasive messages have on a receiver. Persuasive effects mostly originate from variables in the communication process, including those variables that concern the sender, the message created by senders, the receivers themselves, the channel used, and the context within which persuasive messages succeed or fail. This chapter will (1) very briefly review the most commonly used empirical methods in persuasion research, and (2) characterize what can be said with some confidence about how, when, and where persuasion works—as we have learned from scientific study in the past five or six decades.

Quantitative Methods of Research

Quantitative research uses the scientific method to discover truths that can then be generalized to relations among the variables associated with a topic of interest. For example, researchers can ask what is true about the relationship between the variables *use of evidence* and *persuasiveness of message*, or they can ask what is true about the relationship between *message consistency* and *sender believability*. Experimenters often study persuasive effects on small numbers of people (perhaps fifty or one hundred) but then generalize their findings to larger numbers of people or even to all of humanity. To be useful, experiments must eliminate threats to **research validity**. Validity concerns inferences that can correctly be made about what is uncovered in research studies. One of these threats to validity concerns whether researchers have sufficiently controlled procedures in the study in order to be able to say, if the study succeeds, that something has indeed caused something else.[1] A second threat concerns the degree to which findings can be generalized.

A Simple Experimental Design

In chapter 1, I proposed a simple study that would test whether an emotional appeal would help make a message more persuasive. Continuing the illustration in this chapter, let's say that four videotaped messages are now planned that will urge people not to drive after drinking two or more alcoholic beverages. One videotaped message will make the case logically, and the other three will each make the identical logical case as the first but will also add an emotional appeal with one of three possible strengths (weak, moderate, or severe). Perhaps the severe form of the emotional appeal will show the horribly injured victim of an automobile accident, the moderate form will show an ambulance racing to the scene of an accident, and the weak form will include a worried plea, recorded by a fellow motorist, that we drive safely. Will the inclusion of one of these emotional appeals make the anti–drunk-driving message more persuasive? Perhaps.

The researcher will next create questions printed on sheets for subjects to answer after viewing the persuasive messages about the dangers of drinking and driving. This proposed study will also need a minimum number of subjects (perhaps thirty or more for each of the four test groups). It will need valid procedures for recruiting the subjects, assigning each to receive one of the versions of the persuasive message, communicating with them, and collecting the data they generate. Afterward, the researcher will look at the data to see if what was expected to occur actually did. The actual procedures needed for such a study would be more complicated than this, as will become apparent. The following section of this chapter will briefly outline the research steps commonly taken by researchers. A discussion on evaluating research studies will later provide those readers unfamiliar with **research design** with a big-picture overview of the empirical process used by many of the studies cited in this chapter, and will offer help to those students who wish to go on and read for themselves the actual empirical studies I cite.

An Overview of Empirical Research Steps

Figure 10.1 offers an overview of the steps often taken by empirical researchers. The top half of the diagram shows the steps for a laboratory-style **experimental study**. The far left of the diagram shows the origins that researchers use to develop ideas for a study, whether the ideas flow from past research, theory, speculation, observation, folklore, or even just hunches. Often a researcher will become interested in a topic because of a noted anomaly, a contradictory set of facts, a curious exception to a rule, or a knowledge gap in the research literature. This budding interest gradually results in stating a research problem, characterized by a guiding or topic-defining research question such as "Do people who wear eyeglasses actually look more intelligent than people who do not?" Next the researcher will use this guiding question in an examination of the existing literature on the topic to draft a research hypothesis or hypotheses and specific research questions.

A hypothesis asserts that something is true about a topic. The hypothesis must come from the investigator's best judgment about relationships between topic variables. The above topic-defining question about eyeglasses might result in the following hypothesis, labeled in the study as H1: *People wearing eyeglasses will be perceived by others as more intelligent than will be people not wearing eyeglasses.* This hypothesis can justifiably be asked only if the researcher has at least some theoretical foundation or previous data-analyses for making the assertion. But maybe the researcher does not believe there is enough prior research evidence or existing theory to justify an actual hypothesis here. In this case, a research question (RQ) may have to do for now instead of a hypothesis. Thus we have RQ1: *Can eyeglasses affect how intelligent the wearer will seem to other people?*

Often new technologies or social innovations create knowledge gaps that invite empirical inquiry. Just as often, stating a hypothesis may be put off until additional knowledge is added to the available empirical evidence, leaving the research question as the best approach for the time being. A second example of a research question might be RQ1: *Has the increased popularity of using cell phones in public made people less likely to rely on fellow pedestrians for needed directions to destinations?* A researcher studying the "direction-asking inclinations" of pedestrians in various age groups could include the above question in the study. If RQ1 fails to find support in initial studies, it may never find form as a hypothesis in later studies. But if support is found, a subsequent study could then restate the question as hypothesis H1: *Younger cell-phone users* [under age 30] *are less likely than older cell-phone users to ask strangers for needed directions when out walking.* As is often the case, this hypothesis may involve a variety of interesting complications, such as the extent of cell-phone usage, gender, and personality of the subjects. Some studies may take a simpler approach than this and include a statement of the research problem, a guiding question, and one hypothesis or one

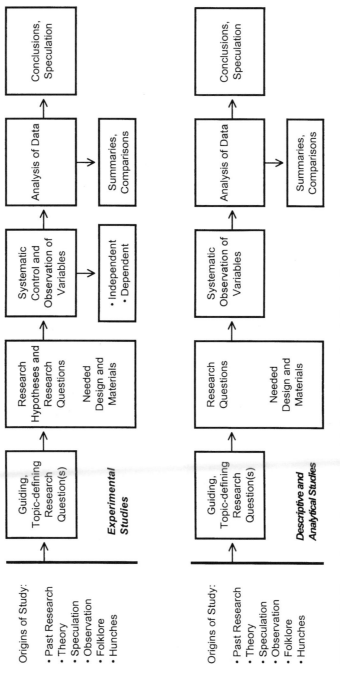

FIGURE 10.1 Research steps for experimental, descriptive, and analytical studies.

research question. Other studies may be broader or more ambitious in scope, opening their report with a sophisticated discussion of a research problem that leads to perhaps six research hypotheses, H1 to H6, and three research questions, RQ1 to RQ3.

Figure 10.1 shows the design and materials part of the study, just below the research hypotheses and research questions. The *design* of an experiment concerns such things as how many subjects will be used, what will happen to them, and how their reactions will be recorded. *Materials* include the physical or informational paraphernalia and the tools used (e.g., answer sheets, videotapes of persuasive messages, and questions to ask subjects). The study next identifies independent and dependent variables with which to organize the data collection, the analysis of findings, and the final conclusions.[2] These variables should be operationally defined (see chapter 5) to avoid confusion or ambiguity. The *independent* variables concern what the experimenter manipulates (e.g., whether the people observed by the subjects will be asked to wear eyeglasses or not, or whether persuasive messages will be spoken by people who slur their words or not). *Dependent* variables concern what is observed about the subjects' behavior in response to the independent variables manipulated by the experimenter. The data collected during the experiment concern the dependent variables. For example, a dependent variable could be the numerical estimates given by subjects of how intelligent each of ten speakers looks when wearing eyeglasses or not wearing eyeglasses. Another example of a dependent variable could be how many people buy inexpensive jewelry from a sidewalk seller who either wears eyeglasses or does not wear eyeglasses (an independent variable) when touting jewelry.

Details of the steps for a **descriptive study** or an **analytical study** are given in the lower half of figure 10.1. These studies too identify variables of interest to facilitate data collection, analysis, and final conclusions. But with descriptive studies, nothing is manipulated—whatever happens in these studies happens spontaneously and without interference from the researchers or the research assistants. Here the researchers may note which variables they observed did in fact vary, and with which others and in what ways. In analytical studies, a comparison group is used, although nothing is manipulated by the experimenter and random assignments are not used. An illustration of a descriptive study may help here.

A descriptive-study researcher plans to observe how volunteers on city streets will use a variety of appeals to persuade people to donate money for a particular cause. If all the study's observations are lumped together, the study will simply be a descriptive one. But if comparison groups are used in a meaningful way, the study will be analytical. In these types of studies, nothing will be influenced or controlled by the researcher. But as is true with the experimental studies, several variables have to be defined, one or more research questions have to be stated, and a procedure for collecting and analyzing data has to be put in place. Here the researcher might identify several streets in the city where the volunteers are scheduled to be, and might then plan to observe their behavior with a carefully designed, nonintrusive procedure. Some variables of interest might concern how much time the volunteers spend speaking, the type and number of appeals they use when speaking, their loudness of voice, and the type and number of hand gestures they use. Important variables will be how many people stop to give money and how much they give. The researcher will then have to sort out what types of appeals seemed to produce how many donors and how much money. Other moderating variables that could be observed in this study might be the age, sex, appearance, and manner of the volunteers and donors. Finally, the researcher will draw conclusions about research questions earlier identified.

Evaluating Experimental Studies

For the purposes of this book, we will not get into the intricacies of research design. But let's look at several criteria that will help us evaluate the validity of studies cited later in this chapter.

Some issues concern the *outcome* of a study. For example, we might ask, "What was the direction of the effect? Did the training of interviewers help or hinder their accuracy in assessing job seekers' skills during interviews? Is this newly reported finding on the effect consistent with what has been found in previous studies? Has only this one study to date demonstrated the present outcome? Have a few? Many? An impressive number?"

Researchers also may use statistical tests on data collected to help them decide whether any differences found among subjects' scores were due to the manipulation of the independent variables or were simply chance fluctuations. When these statistical tests are deemed positive, then the effects found in the study are accepted as *statistically significant*. The study's hypotheses are then reported as having "survived" an opportunity to be proved untrue or unfounded. This is called "rejecting the null hypothesis."

However, statistically significant findings are not always important ones. Thus, a good empirical report will often estimate the *size* or practical significance of an observed effect. Size can also be understood as the magnitude of a treatment effect compared to the effect in a control group, as when researchers want to know if the outcome of a study on psychotherapy interventions is clinically significant, not merely statistically significant. Perhaps the training of interviewers did significantly result in more-effective questioning of clients, statistically speaking. But to what extent? Was the observed improvement extraordinary, moderate, or ever so slight? Tests for estimating the size of an effect should be calculated along with the tests of statistical significance.

Other issues concern the *methods* used for the experimental study. When recruiting subjects, for example, care should be taken not to rely exclusively on subjects whose backgrounds will make interpreting the study's outcomes difficult. If you want to generalize your findings to people in an entire college, city, or occupation group, your subjects should be *representative* of the population you wish to study. In a study about the persuasiveness of advertisements for life insurance, recruiting high-school students as subjects would obviously create problems since life-insurance purchases are more often made by adults than by high-school students. Similarly, recruiting tourists visiting a country to participate as subjects in a study about attitudes toward the income taxes in that country would create problems when interpreting the data.

Experimental studies rely on **treatment groups** and **control groups**. Something unique will happen to the subjects in the treatment groups, but not to the subjects in the control groups. Using both types of groups helps to establish whether an independent variable was responsible for the study's outcome, or whether some confounding or extraneous factor was in fact responsible (e.g., subject fatigue, a radio news program inadvertently playing in the research area, or pretesting subjects to see what attitudes they came to the study with).

Using a control group also provides a benchmark for evaluating the independent variables in a study. Sometimes several treatment groups are used without a control group, but each treatment group in a sense then serves as a control group for the others.

So if several treatment groups of subjects are asked to evaluate the visual appeal of a candy bar to be sold in a green wrapper, a red wrapper, or a blue wrapper, the control group could be asked to evaluate the same candy bar but wrapped in a colorless, plain wrapper. Perhaps the red wrapper will get the best results. But maybe all three colored wrappers will do about the same, though the plain wrapper will do very poorly. Using a control group here helps us see that color is important, but not any specific color. Or in a study on interview skills, subjects in one group might get training about how to ask effective questions. Control-group subjects would get no training. Both groups then would be tested in their ability to obtain certain types of information from interviewees. Afterward, the training method could be evaluated by seeing how well the trained subjects did in comparison with the untrained ones.

Subjects should be recruited and assigned to the treatment and the control groups using *random* procedures. When random procedures are not used, the method by which the subjects were recruited and assigned to groups becomes a major obstacle to explaining the effects of the independent variables. For example, if the subjects who arrive early to a study site are all put in one group and those who arrive late are put in another, the subjects' attitudes toward arriving on time for appointments may explain how much work is done by the subjects in the two groups. And if subjects' attitudes about being prompt indeed played a role in the study, then an independent variable that varied the instructions given to the subjects on how to efficiently complete some research task has been jeopardized.

Experimental studies have the advantage of better explaining causality among variables, while descriptive and analytic studies have the advantage of studying the actual behavior of subjects in real circumstances. Thus, while experimental researchers often have more confidence when identifying which variables caused which effects, the experimental setting itself sometimes results in subjects not behaving the way they would in the world beyond the controlled experiment. On the other hand, while descriptive or analytic studies usually can say with more confidence that what was observed occurred spontaneously and was not affected by data-collecting procedures, they have a problem in trying to identify what caused what. Used in conjunction, at different times, and perhaps by different researchers, the experimental and descriptive or analytic approaches can often complement the other's efforts.

Empirical Research on Persuasion

To characterize the empirical research on persuasion and persuasive effects, we can organize these studies into five categories as suggested by such persuasion scholars as Daniel O'Keefe and Charles Larson: (1) sender variables and persuasive effects, (2) message variables and persuasive effects, (3) channel variables and persuasive effects, (4) receiver variables and persuasive effects, and (5) context variables and persuasive effects.[3] The number of empirical studies on persuasion is quite large.

Sender Variables and Persuasive Effects

Some people are generally more persuasive than others. Why this is true has probably interested analysts for all times. Some obvious factors to consider here concern matters of sender **credibility**, **likeability**, and physical or personal attractiveness, and the extent to which the sender is perceived to be similar to audience members. Some of these factors may be more reliable assets for persuaders than others.

Perceived Sender Credibility Credibility does not actually reside within the sender, even though we commonly refer to "source credibility"; but perceived sender credibility does exist in the minds of receivers. For example, a given public speaker may enjoy high credibility with some audiences but may have low credibility with others. Similarly, a given speaker may enjoy high credibility when speaking about one topic but may have low credibility when speaking about another. In fact, as we saw in chapter 7, the credibility attributed to a sender may even vary moment to moment during the message. Here we will look at dimensions of credibility now generally accepted in the field, factors that seem to underlie perceived credibility, and persuasive effects on audience members that can be attributed to perceived credibility.

Specifying exactly what factors lead to sender credibility is best done with something called *factor analysis*, which is a statistical technique. Generally speaking, in these analyses subjects are asked to answer scaled questions about something (credibility, in this case); their answers are then analyzed to identify common threads or themes relevant to the topic. However, a factor analysis is only as good as the particular items included in the analysis. As a result, different factor analyses have identified varying descriptions of the dimensions of sender credibility.[4] Nonetheless, two dimensions of sender credibility have stood the test of time: the *perceived expertise* (or competence) of the sender, and the *perceived trustworthiness* (or character) of the sender. Some factor analyses of credibility also report a third factor: *dynamic style* (or apparent goodwill).[5]

Factors of credibility concern what things audiences will note about a sender when attributing high, middle, or low credibility. A number of source characteristics have been examined, some of which seem more predictive than others. For example, the sender's *educational history*, *occupation*, and *experience* apparently are used by audiences to decide on credibility, although it is not yet clear exactly how these things add or detract. Also, the relevance of a credibility factor can be an important qualifier. So if I am speaking about modern firefighting in the wilderness, sometimes called "smoke jumping," my liberal arts degree may not be relevant to my credibility with the audience, but my having spent two months as a smoke jumper in the great forests of the American West might. In a different example, if I mention that I graduated from Harvard Business School and have worked for fifteen years as a broker for a leading brokerage firm on Wall Street, I may enjoy higher credibility when I advise a client about which stocks are more likely or less likely to show improved earnings in the coming year.

Speech nonfluencies of the sender are a source characteristic that can nudge audience perceptions of credibility downward. These nonfluencies include such things as the use of "um," word repetition, and slips of the tongue. However, speaking faster or slower apparently does not affect credibility, even though common sense might lead us to believe the opposite. Citing authors' names, and the titles and dates of published studies can boost credibility, but in minimum ways. If your audience likes you, you may benefit from higher credibility on the trustworthiness dimension but not on the expertise dimension. Using humor is unpredictable at best. But the position you take on a topic offers an interesting twist. If you take a position that seems to run counter to your self-interest, you may gain credibility with an audience. For example, a Democrat or a Republican might speak to members of the opposing party and say something in agreement with them. Although we might think this would sound patronizing, the logic is that there must be some profound reason why the speaker is willing to concede this usually partisan issue ("It might surprise some of you to learn that I'm not happy with my party's platform statement on issue X; in fact, I agree with the position taken by your party").

Communication researcher Eun-Ju Lee reports an interesting study about the self-proclaimed competence of the sender. Here the source characteristics of the influence agent's gender and "self-proclaimed competence (high or low)" were used as independent variables, as was the "qualitative or quantitative" means used to express this competence in statements heard by subjects. The dependent variable was the "persuasive conformity" exhibited by the audience. The procedure involved subjects playing a trivia game with an anonymous partner portrayed using computer-mediated communication (the subjects didn't actually see the partner but learned about the partner through give-and-take computer messages). Verbal self-descriptions of confidence concerned whether confidence was present or not in subjects; quantitative descriptors concerned indications of how much confidence was present.

> Of interest in this study is that when the computer-character portrayed confidence in quantitative ways its effect on conformity was more pronounced among men than women; but when confidence of the characters was expressed in verbal ways its effect on conformity was more pronounced among women than men.[6]

How effectively an audience can be influenced by a sender's perceived credibility can be measured in two ways: *credibility direction* (whether higher or lower credibility would result in either greater or lesser persuasive power), and *credibility magnitude* (how much of an effect there is).[7] Surprisingly, credibility is not always important. Elaboration likelihood theory would suggest that when a topic is especially relevant, receivers may be more inclined to centrally process the ideas in the message and be less influenced by sender credibility. But when the topic is less relevant, peripheral processing may make credibility a more important factor in whether the audience is persuaded or not. Also, credibility is more important when the audience gets information about the sender before getting the message. When this information is withheld until after the message, credibility differences are less important.

The effects of higher or lower credibility direction on receivers also have an interesting twist. High credibility usually helps and low credibility often hurts (the direction we would normally expect). But low-credibility senders may sometimes be more persuasive than high-credibility senders if they give a pro-attitudinal message, such as when agreeing with what the audience believes or feels. The explanation for this unexpected outcome may be that receivers expect high-credibility senders who agree with them to do a good job; but receivers' expectations of low-credibility sources who agree with them may be less optimistic. In their minds, receivers may then even root for or "help" the low-credibility sender make the pro-attitudinal case. In contrast, agreeing receivers may feel more competitive with high-credibility senders and therefore be more critical of what they hear. This is an area that could benefit from further research, as not enough studies have manipulated other important variables for this counterintuitive finding, such as topic relevance or whether information about the sender is given before or after the message.

Sender Likeability Whether a sender is liked or not by audience members seems like a good factor for explaining why some persuaders are more effective than others. But being a liked sender may not be as important as being a sender perceived as credible. Authors Arthur Lupia and Mathew McCubbins provide evidence for this weaker role by suggesting that when credibility is high but the sender is not liked, credibility seems to trump.[8] Similarly, topic relevance also qualifies the extent to which being liked helps with persuasion. As the topic becomes more relevant, being a liked sender becomes less important. And our discussion of cognitive dissonance theory in chapter 9 may help us explain why disliked senders can sometimes be more persuasive than liked ones. If a disliked person talks you into doing something you initially did not want to do, you will experience dissonance for obvious reasons. You will probably not feel so much dissonance if someone you like talks you into doing something you initially didn't want to do. Thus, because you did something for a disliked person, you may have to talk yourself into thinking that there was in fact very good reason to go along with that person's persuasion.

Likeability and persuasiveness can be a two-way street. Communication researchers Bryan Whaley and Lisa Smith were interested in how the use of *rebuttal analogy* would affect the likeability of persuaders. Rebuttal analogies often take a *that's like* form: "That's like trying to reinvent the wheel and then coming up on square one." The authors point out that rebuttal analogies tend not only to be criticisms of ideas, but also character attacks on the people who stated those ideas. So if you use the rebuttal analogy, will the people who hear you think you are rude, impolite, or unfair—and as a consequence, less likeable? In testing their hypothesis, Whaley and Smith used four topics: medical use of marijuana, whaling, logging, and safe sex. Their analysis of this study led to several conclusions: (1) rebuttal-analogy users were rated as less likeable, especially when the topic was whaling or logging, but less so when the topic was medical use of marijuana or safe sex; (2) receivers exposed to rebuttal analogies produced more negative thoughts in response to the rebuttal analogies than to the other persuasive forms tested; (3) receivers exposed to rebuttal analogies were more inclined to counterargue; (4) receivers generated more counterarguments to the rebuttal analogies, although they did not, contrary to expectations, generate negative thoughts about the analogy user; and (5) the use of rebuttal analogies was not all that successful in creating attitude change among receivers.[9]

The Sender's Similarity to Audience Members The problem with expecting that perceived similarity felt by audience members will help senders be more persuasive concerns the word *similarity*: it is vague and can mean many things to different people by involving associations that include age, sex, occupation, political-party membership, agreement about some topic, personality, group membership, race or ethnicity, geographical birthplace, body build, wealth or social class, hobby interests, neighborhood affiliations, religion, and citizenship. If I am hoping to appeal to an audience by promoting my similarity to them, how do I know which particular similarity factors will be salient for them? The word *similarity*'s broad references have probably led to the inconsistent findings in persuasion research.[10] However, it is possible that if an audience actually sees a sender as similar to them, this will translate into greater liking of the sender and then to some modest increase in persuasiveness. Good persuaders may in some cases find rhetorical ways to bond with an audience on an issue of similarity. And a dissimilar sender may occasionally enjoy greater persuasiveness if seen as someone with different but credible experiences relevant to the topic, as for example might an Australian speaking about kangaroos to an audience in Italy or an Italian speaking about the Isle of Capri to an audience in Australia.

Sender Attractiveness and Other Attributes There is a host of other source factors that might make good candidates for improving persuasiveness. However, they tend to have one thing in common: the evidence supporting them is inconclusive, possibly because these factors are helpful in some circumstances but not in others, and in some circumstances are even harmful.[11] For example, an attractive speaker might have trouble convincing an audience that physical attractiveness is the most important qualification for being hired for any job. This proposition would be a tough sell for any persuader, but a less-attractive person might succeed here where a more-attractive person might fail because the less-attractive person might be seen as making an argument that runs counter to personal interest, while the attractive person might seem to be just arguing for personal advantage.

Message Variables and Persuasive Effects

A number of message factors have received a good deal of attention from researchers over the years, including the structure of messages, their contents, and their temporal strategies. For example, persuasion theorists Ann Gordon and Jerry Miller studied the debates between Governor George Bush and Vice President Al Gore for the 2000 presidential election. They argue that undecided voters were very much affected by which one of two particular values, egalitarianism or individualism, was stressed by the candidates during the debates.[12] Obviously, what gets said in a message is important. But now let's focus not on the particular arguments used but on the common methods used by persuaders in hopes of making the best use of whatever materials they have chosen. The message factors we'll discuss here include the use of evidence in messages, message structure, message content (including fear appeals), foot-in-the-door and door-in-the-face tactics, and other tactics such as low-ball, bait and switch, and labeling

Use of Evidence Communication scholars Rodney Reynolds and Michael Burgoon reviewed much of the research on relationships with respect to belief processing, reasoning, and evidence.[13] They formulated a number of propositions about what the past literature might show upon inspection, and then reviewed a large number of these studies. Their summary indicates:

1. Using evidence to change attitudes is better than not using evidence or simply mentioning sources.
2. Using irrelevant evidence or poorly qualified sources, or omitting citations will lower sources' credibility and produce effects opposite to the ones desired.
3. Providing the qualifications of sources cited and clearly explaining the evidence provided by the sources will produce more persuasive success.

4. Citing highly credible sources increases an advocate's credibility, and placing citations of less-credible sources after a description of the evidence helps.

5. Poor delivery hurts the advocate.

6. Evidence is most effective when receivers have not heard it before; evidence helps, regardless of the credibility of the advocate.

7. The credibility of the advocate is positively related to receivers' evaluation of message attributes.

8. Receivers tend to evaluate a message's evidence in terms of whether it is consistent with their own attitudes, regardless of the quality of the evidence.

9. Evidence in messages that is inconsistent with the advocate's arguments is harder to detect than evidence that is irrelevant or is from unqualified sources.

Message Structure The first question to take up is whether it makes a difference if you put your best materials in the beginning of the message or the end. As I mentioned in chapter 3, this issue is commonly referred to as **climax** or **anticlimax** organization of a message arrangement. Finding convincing support for either side of this question has been elusive over the years.[14] Apparently, there isn't a good reason for placing your best arguments at the end or at the beginning of your persuasive message, although situational factors specific to particular messages may require the placement of one argument or another in the earlier or later parts of the message. However, the omission of a conclusion is a different story. This concerns whether you explicitly state the major point or position of your persuasion, or leave it implied. If you have given several good reasons for taking notes when reading a book, chapter by chapter, section by section, thought by thought, should you then go on to say, "You have much to gain by taking well-organized and specific notes from a text just as you would a lecture?" Or should you state the reasons for your conclusion but leave the general idea implied, hoping that listeners will be more persuaded by a conclusion that they reach themselves than by a "spoon-fed" conclusion? Stating the conclusion is generally better unless a unique situation argues for not doing so (e.g., an ego-involved, disagreeing listener).[15]

A related issue concerns *recommendation specificity*, which means giving or not giving details when urging an action of some sort. I might recommend that you visit Gettysburg, Pennsylvania, where the famous Civil War Battle of Gettysburg was fought. Should I include details about exactly where the park is, how to get there, and also include website information, telephone numbers, and suggestions for how long to plan on staying and exactly where to find accommodations? Here again, there is no ambiguity. Specificity works well, possibly because of what we said about the theories of behavioral intentions in chapter 9; that is, sometimes persuasion fails because receivers imagine obstacles in the way of compliance or fail to notice resources that would facilitate compliance. For example, behavioral theorists Richard Evans et al. found when studying compliance for dental-care suggestions that providing specific details for compliance helped.[16]

Message Content Here we will address four common questions about message strategy and content: (1) Should persuaders amplify both sides of an issue, or just the side they want to promote? (2) How much discrepancy should there be between what the persuader argues for and what members in the audience currently subscribe to? (3) Should persuaders seeking change use fear appeals, and to what extent? and (4) Are persuasive messages more effective when they contain statistical summaries or good examples?

The first question concerns the use of **one-sided messages** versus **two-sided messages**. This is a complicated question. The quick answer is that this is a good place for generalizations. But a better answer may turn on what O'Keefe refers to as "refutational" versus "non-refutational" two-sided messages.[17] A refutational message is one in which not only do you argue your side, but you also systematically refute what the opposing side says. There are two generalizations to be made here. First, two-sided messages that refute are dependably more persuasive than one-sided messages. Second, non-refutational, two-sided messages are less persuasive than one-sided messages. A non-refutational, two-sided message simply acknowledges the best points for the other side and then goes on to make a persuasive case for the side taken by the persuader. So if you don't intend to systematically refute what the other side says, use a one-sided approach. But if you intend to refute, use a two-sided message.

Marketing researcher Cornelia Pechmann reports an interesting effect regarding two- and one-sided advertisements. In one test ad, an ice-cream product was described as having the primary attribute of "rich taste" and the secondary attribute of being "high in calories." An alternate version of the ad also mentioned the rich taste attribute, but here admitted the shortcoming that the ice cream had a secondary attribute of high salt content. The difference between the two ads concerned whether these primary and secondary attributes were seen by the test subjects as negatively related (high calories bring rich taste, and low calories bring lesser taste) or unrelated (higher or lower salt content does not lead to better or poorer taste). In this experiment, the negatively related, two-sided ad was more effective than either the unrelated two-sided ad or the unrelated one-sided ad. It produced more positive ratings for the advertiser, the product, and the product's primary attribute—rich taste. Apparently the negative secondary attribute of higher calories also reinforced the positive primary attribute of rich taste within the audience of college students who served as subjects. However the high-salt attribute did not help reinforce the rich taste feature because salt content did not seem especially relevant to taste, at least for this audience.[18]

Our second question of message strategy and content concerns the *discrepancy within message* issue. How ambitious should messages be for maximum persuasiveness? For example, you could urge that I reduce my credit-card usage by 10 percent, 50 percent, or 100 percent (as in "Go get a pair of scissors and be done with them"). In chapter 7, I reviewed the social judgment model offered by Muzafer Sherif and Carolyn Sherif, which advises that senders not go beyond the latitude of what receivers will accept. Perhaps this advice will help explain things here.[19] According to the social judgment model, a persuader needs to know two things about persuadees: what their general attitudes are toward the topic, and how strongly they feel about it. If they have very strong feelings and are perhaps ego-involved, they may reject almost anything the persuader say that varies in the slightest way from their attitudes. But if they are easy-going on the subject, the sender may succeed with an ambitiously persuasive message.[20]

Turning to our third question regarding message strategy and content, in chapter 8 we considered the message element *fear appeals*, which have interested researchers for a long time, probably because of concerns that it might be easy for propagandists using this element to crank up the fear emotion and manipulate everyone in sight about anything and everything. Fortunately, things are not as simple as that, as recently noted by communication researcher Charles Berger, who found that some receivers reduce the effects of fear appeals because they "appear more likely to heed cues that serve to reduce the amount of apprehension they experience in response to graphically presented information [in news reporting] about increasingly threatening trends."[21] For example, you might view a news report about a threatening disturbance on the street then quickly notice someone laughing in the rear of the crowd. But fear appeals do sometimes work, stronger fear appeals can at times be more persuasive, and messages that actually arouse fear are more persuasive. Consider the following advice about cars: "Owning and driving a small car is more dangerous than owning and driving a larger one. Small cars are lethal for the family and friends who ride with you—thousands of motorists die on the road each year. So do the right thing and buy a larger car." For this fear appeal to work with people who are about to buy a new car, they have to (1) allow themselves to hear, understand, and remember the message; (2) agree that they are more likely to have an accident while driving a small car; (3) actually feel the fear generated by the persuasive message; and (4) give more weight to this safety issue than to other issues such as the car's price, useful features, style, and symbolism.

In one recent study of fear appeals, researchers David Roskos-Ewoldsen, Jessy Yu, and Nancy Rhodes sought to clarify how fear-arousing messages might help to get women to perform breast self-examinations. They posited five hypotheses and one research question about the relationships among four variables: threat, efficacy, accessibility, and behavioral intentions. For this study, efficacy concerned how likely an action would be to solve the problem brought to mind by the threat, and accessibility concerned how quickly an attitude about responding to a threat could be retrieved from memory. One finding was that low-to-moderate fear appeals worked well, but high-threat messages had a decreased usefulness:

> Specifically, people are more likely to orient their attention to an object [breast cancer] if they have an accessible attitude [self-examination] toward that object. . . . Fear appeals that emphasize the efficacy of the action function by increasing the accessibility of the attitude toward the behavior, strengthening intentions to perform the adaptive behavior.[22]

In other words, if the fear appeal not only makes us fearful of a problem but also motivates us to do something that will decrease the problem, the fear appeal will be especially helpful when it prompts us to retrieve an adaptive attitude regarding the problem. But if the fear appeal is overwhelming, we may just become defensive and tune out, or rationalize the problem away.

Our last question here concerning message strategy and content concerns the effectiveness of examples versus *statistical summaries*. Some studies have found that statistical summaries can work better than examples (cf. James Baesler and Judee Burgoon) or that vivid examples did not work as expected (cf. Shelley Taylor and Suzanne Thompson).[23] This too is probably a question that depends on the topic and on receiver bias. When I ask my classes which they prefer, examples or statistics, the majority often support examples over statistics. Nonetheless, there are times when statistics can be quite compelling (especially when they are true) and even if they are not accurate or relevant, as in "We're 30 percent of the population but we're getting 50 percent of the tickets out on the highway." Perhaps some of the cynicism expressed toward statistics is a result of our belief that persuaders sometimes abuse statistics to make points. Examples, on the other hand, are often compelling because of how clear they are and easy to understand. The best advice here seems to be that the persuader should make judicial use of both at various times.

Foot-in-the-Door and Door-in-the-Face Tactics Returning to our discussion of message tactics, let's look at the **foot-in-the-door** technique. Here a persuader first asks for a small commitment from the audience and then later asks for an increase in the commitment. Psychologists Jonathan Freedman and Scott Fraser asked selected home owners in California as part of "Drive Safely" and "Beautify California" campaigns to either sign a petition or display a small sign in their front windows.[24] Two weeks later, a different person dropped by to ask the same group of home owners to erect large, ugly, Drive Safely signs on their front lawns (this was the experimental treatment). A different selection of home owners served as a control group—they were only asked to display the large, ugly sign and were never asked initially to display the small sign or sign a petition. The difference here was that the experimental group was asked a small favor before being asked a big favor, and the control group was just asked a big favor. More than twice the number of experimental-group home owners agreed to do the big favor than did the control-group home owners. There is disagreement in the field as to what explains the above findings. But cognitive consistency theory may help here. We could argue that initial compliance with the favor-asker will result in dissonance if the initially complying home owner then later contemplates saying no to the second request for displaying the large sign. If this explanation is correct, it should warn people who agree to comply with small requests that they may be proceeding in a persuasive direction that will be hard to reverse.

A persuader using the **door-in-the-face** tactic first asks for more than seems reasonable. After the initial rejection by the receiver, the persuader then asks for a smaller commitment. For example, I could first ask you for a loan of $500 and than reduce the request to $20. Perhaps receivers feel guilt because of the first rejection, and they then try to reduce this guilt by giving in to a smaller request. It is also possible that they may just feel that the smaller commitment is justified and the larger one is not.

Psychologist Murray Millar tested the guilt hypothesis and found that higher levels of guilt in fact produced the effect. Subjects in a study on nutrition were first either asked to keep a detailed log for three months or were not asked to do so. If a subject in the first group refused the request, the experimenter would say, "Your refusal will cause considerable damage to the department's efforts to help others eat healthy diets." Subjects in both groups were then asked to keep a log for four days, which request got more volunteers among those to whom the more extreme request had been made.

In two other door-in-the-face studies conducted by researchers Michael Patch and Vicki Hoang, nearly three hundred people in either a large college or shopping mall were asked to volunteer two hours of their time for an interview or to hand out one hundred flyers; both requests were for "good causes." The two-hour request was reduced to twenty minutes for those who refused, and the one-hundred-flyers request was reduced to ten. But in an interesting twist on door-in-the-face–type studies, the researchers encouraged half of the subjects to *metacommunicate* about the appropriateness of the requests. By metacommunicate, they meant that subjects could talk about the fairness of the requested behavior with reference to the specific relationship involved between requester and subject (the requester and the subject were strangers). These researchers found that when subjects were given an opportunity to comment on the appropriateness of a request, subjects more often complied with the request. Support for the door-in-the-face tactic was also found. Both findings were made by comparing subject compliance rates in the experimental treatments with subject compliance rates in control groups, who were simply asked to comply with one of the two smaller requests.[25]

Communication researchers Danette Johnson, Maichael Roloff, and Melissa Riffee have studied response refusals and whether such refusals would potentially result in a threat to *face*. This study was not a door-in-the-face study, but instead concerned *politeness theory*, which posits that people have two faces they generally want to protect: a positive face, where they will feel good if others like, respect, and approve of them; and a negative face, where they may feel bad if others can constrain them in any way. Both of these faces may be threatened when we make a request of someone. And often when we seek to protect one type of face, the other may suffer. For example, if I ask for a favor in a super-polite way, my target may begin to think I am an "easy" social actor who can be trod upon. But if I act tough, others may see me negatively. The researchers found that a threat to a requester's face (positive or negative) is positively related to a desire in the requester to persist after the refusal with additional persuasive statements.[26]

Low-Ball, Bait and Switch, and Labeling Tactics With the **low-ball** technique, the persuader initially offers what sounds like a good deal in order to gain a commitment from the target. A telephone service might advertise a low monthly rate that brings in new customers, who later learn about the additional costs for things that they thought were part of the basic rate.[27] This tactic seems based in part on cognitive dissonance theory because the target is encouraged to walk part of the way down the road to a desired behavior so that they then feel a commitment or "investment" that makes backtracking harder to do. And we have all probably heard of the **bait-and-switch** technique, in which a store advertises something at a good price, but when customers arrive, the customers are told the product is out of stock, or that it has in fact "undesirable" features; the customers are then offered a more expensive item in the original item's place.

Labeling means using a form of flattery to get people to buy something or do something. Sometimes it's an attempt to create a self-fulfilling prophecy. Here the persuader uses a message to assign a "trait" to the target (e.g., "You seem smart to me" or "You seem like the sort of person who will vote this year"). Then anything that would seem consistent with the trait can be touted by the persuader. In one study, elementary-school children were told they seemed like the sort of boys and girls who knew how important good writing is. Apparently, the children flattered in this way were more likely to sign up for a voluntary project on good penmanship later in the term.[28] Lovers sometimes also seduce each other with affectionate terms of endearment.

Channel Variables and Persuasive Effects

Timothy Borchers reminds us that the **channels** used for messages are never simply a pipe through which information is sent. And communication researcher Herbert Simons points out that not only do persuasive effects vary in terms of the channels used to transmit them, but senders and receivers vary in terms of their attitudes toward the various channels used for a persuasive message.[29] You might respond favorably to a persuasive message made in person and asking for your help, but you might not respond well if the request is made on a scribbled note slipped under your front door. Prospective employers might prefer to send bad news (you didn't get the job) by mail or e-mail, while informing the happy new employee by a phone call or in a face-to-face meeting.

I have studied the effectiveness of television-monitor versions of face-to-face messages sent in one of either two channels, and accompanied by varying degrees of distraction (white noise later added to these videotaped messages with noise-generating equipment). The channels used for the laboratory experiment were audio, audiovisual without facial cues, and audiovisual with facial cues. In noisier conditions, the audiovisual messages that included facial cues seemed superior to either the audio messages or the audiovisual messages that did not include facial cues. Data was collected for twelve conditions that were created by independently varying how the message was sent (using the three presentation modes, or channels) and by using four degrees of noisiness (none, light, medium, heavy). The subjects gave answers to printed questions about the messages. The questions tested what the subjects remembered about claims made in the videotaped messages.[30]

Larson notes that the channels used for persuasive messages can be at times important: "Usually messages sent via the audiovisual medium result in greater attitude change than do those in the audio channel alone." On the subject of distractions or noise added to messages by experimenters, he summarizes an interesting observation in the literature on channels used for persuasive messages—that such distractions accompany more attitude change when the topics run counter to the original attitudes of the receivers, although these changes are usually short-term ones. One other point Larson makes is that for very complex persuasive messages, the written channel may be superior to other channels.[31]

In a study on the persuasive effects of messages that use computer graphics, persuasion theorist Wesley C. King Jr. reports that when the alumni of a business college were asked for donations, the channel used for the request was important. The independent variable in this study was created as follows: one group of receivers received the request on a plain white piece of paper (text only); a second group viewed the same printed text request used in the first condition, but projected onto a 60 x 60 inch computer screen (that also used still graphics to support the text message); and a third group viewed the same request used for the first two conditions, but with the above-described computer-screen text, augmented here with moving or dynamic computer-generated graphics (e.g., image "wipes," "explosions," and "scrolls"). The two dependent variables in this study were the subjects' inclination to make a financial contribution to the college and their agreement to make the contribution by a specific date. According to King,

> The data indicate that subjects exposed to the dynamic graphics treatment were more likely to pledge to donate than were those exposed to the text-only treatment; however, the analysis revealed no significant differences between the willingness to pledge for those subjects exposed to the dynamic graphics treatment versus those exposed to the static graphics treatment.[32]

Apparently, whether a persuader augments text with graphics or uses electronic screens for transmission may be important decisions.

Receiver Variables and Persuasive Effects

Sometimes the success of persuasion will depend on exactly who the receivers are and what their attitudes, beliefs, and behaviors are prior to persuasion. It would seem reasonable that some people will be more responsive to persuasion and others less. For example, psychologist Dolores Albarracin et al. examined studies on condom-use among at-risk populations.[33] The authors reviewed 42 studies that included 96 data sets carried out by various researchers collectively studying 22,594 individuals, and then performed statistical tests, finding strong evidence that the predictive models of the two theories of behavioral intention were indeed quite helpful for understanding which particular receivers of persuasive messages would or would not use condoms when engaging in risky sex. Some *receiver characteristics* were already present when persuasion was tried, but at other times the persuader had to induce receiver characteristics before attempting persuasion.

Receiver Characteristics Gender has been sometimes studied in relation to general persuadability, with a mild expectation among researchers that women would be more easily persuaded. Here the confounding problem concerns the systematically differing social values and social objectives of men and women. Self-esteem, however, may predict persuadability at the middle ranges. In other words, people with very low self-esteem (perhaps they are disoriented or unable even to take advice) and people with very high self-esteem (therefore perhaps overly confident of their own judgments) are less easily persuaded. And perhaps the very intelligent receiver is better at evaluating arguments for defects, and thus less persuadable. Other factors that are too uncertain to make any generalizations about include "sensation seeking" as a personality characteristic, age, and cultural background—all three of which might be proved in the future to make a receiver more or less persuadable.

Persuaders can analyze receivers in terms of the sources of information consumed. Communication scholar Patricia Moy et al. examined the effects of newspapers versus television on whether people actually participate in the political process, and found differences depending on how and where one gets information. One other study examined who is more likely to become politically mobilized (thus becoming persuasive senders themselves) and found that it is people who pay more attention to political discussions and take part in them when opportunities occur.[34]

Induced Receiver Factors Our first induced receiver factor is one you'll recognize from chapter 3: **inoculation** against **counterpersuasion**. Say I try to sell an expensive radio to a group of people, offering the radio for $400. I explain the radio's best-selling features and tell the group I can keep the offer open for three days only. At least some of my potential clients will talk to other people over the next three days and maybe read items about various other radios. What will happen here is that my persuasion will likely be met by counterpersuasion. Perhaps one member of the group will hear from a friend, "Sounds kind of pricey to me." This comment could ruin the sale. What I could have done to prevent this would have been to use inoculation when I made my initial sales pitch. I could have said, "You may think this radio is expensive—and it is—but it has features not available in cheaper radios. For example . . ." If I had inoculated my persuadees, perhaps one of them would now say to the friend volunteering the "pricey comment" as counterpersuasion, "Yes, but this radio has features not available in cheaper radios." With inoculation I have found an ally—my persuadee.[35]

Inoculation may also assist persuaders with social or political objectives. A *truism* is a belief given wide acceptance in a given culture. (Remember that we discussed in chapter 7 the underlying cultural premises that people carry around with them, depending on where they were born and currently live.) For instance, the citizens of Western countries often say, "This is a free country. I can do what I want as long as I don't hurt anyone." Such statements are seldom questioned. But truisms can be vulnerable to attack because their users often have no experience in defending them. A provocateur might come along and say, "You're not free; it's all an illusion—just try criticizing this or that and see what happens to you." Inoculation can work here if the persuaders have given their receivers refutational arguments to use against such anti-truism attacks. But although refutational inoculations seem to create an immunity to these attacks, supportive-argument inoculations that just reinforce the truism do not. In other words, do not just assure me of X; rather, tell me that when someone says something that is anti-X, I should then say Y.

Recently, communication researchers Hua-Hsin Wan and Michael Pfau reported that inoculation approaches may at times run into problems or may simply offer no additional advantages over the more traditional approach of just saying positive and reassuring things to an audience during a crisis. They created a hypothetical crisis for study subjects about an industrial gas-line explosion in which five people had died and twenty-three were injured. To prepare an inoculation message, they created imagined attacks from the media and the public. To refute the attacks, for example, the company whose gas line had exploded might say why each of the attacks was bogus, exaggerated, or out of **context** (e.g., "Every employee gets X hours of training in handing hazardous material" or "In the last year alone, we have spent X dollars in upgrading the following equipment"). Nonetheless, the authors were unable to report the superiority of the inoculation strategy in this case:

> The results of this study revealed that inoculation treatments, although effective in conferring resistance to negative influence, are no better than traditional supportive treatments. Further, in this particular case, inoculation may hurt the company's image if there is no crisis.

Perhaps in this case there was a trade-off where in order to prepare receivers for the media and public attacks, the company had to mention questionable things about itself before anything had occurred that would require self-defense.[36]

Context Variables and Persuasive Effects

Sometimes what makes persuasion work will not be found in the persuader or the receiver or even in the persuader's message. At these times, we must look to the bigger picture to see what else is going on in the background politically, socially, and historically. For example, persuasion theorist David Whiteman counsels that persuasion in documentary films (the message) needs to be understood in newer terms that examine how activist groups have used documentaries as tools for achieving political impact for their social movements (the context). He points to activists' roles in the distribution of these films as being even more important than their roles in the films' production. Thus, understanding the persuasion of a particular documentary may require analyzing the place that documentary takes within the wider political agenda of its makers.[37] Context also includes the factor of time. As persuasion plays out over time, effects may change in interesting ways. After several months go by, you may remember a criticism about a proposal but not who made the criticism or why. Let's examine two examples of this time-sensitive issue: **primacy-recency** and **persistence of persuasion**.

Primacy-Recency Primacy-recency should not be confused with the debate over climax-anticlimax organization already discussed. While climax-anticlimax organization concerns where in your message you place your best arguments, primacy-recency concerns who talks first or last in a debate or in any other sequence of persuasive messages that involves more than one persuader. But as was the case with climax and anticlimax, there is little to report here that might convince you as a rule to choose to speak first or second in a debate; however, pragmatic considerations that might vary from topic to topic and situation to situation might well cause you to consider this factor. If two politicians will give speeches on television on a Monday night, one at 10 p.m. and the other at 11 p.m., given the reality of people going to bed for work the next day, it is probably better to have the earlier time slot. And sometimes a particularly effective persuader who goes first may get the opportunity to define the issues in self-serving ways that are difficult for the second speaker to redefine. On the other hand, sometimes having the last word is important. In our example of the two late-night speakers, for instance, the second speaker can respond to what the first has said, but the first speaker can't respond to what the second speaker says. Sometimes in an informal debate, people will compete to get in the last word.

Persistence of Persuasion Psychologists Thomas Cook and Brian Flay have summarized how persuasive effects decay over time.[38] Some effects dissipate quickly, some slowly, and some may stay with receivers for a lifetime. Strategic-minded persuaders probably want to time their persuasion so that it will be in place at exactly the right instant for some decision or other action, such as in a campaign for elective office where the key moment will be election day. The elaboration likelihood theory may help here to explain why some persuasive effects may last longer, by suggesting that these are the effects that were centrally processed, not peripherally processed. Nonetheless, this is a murky area. For example, most of us can probably remember certain details of something that happened a long time ago but cannot remember other details. Cognitive dissonance theory may also help clarify one of the issues with this topic. You may persuade someone to do something that will eventually cause that person dissonance, even though it does not at the moment. It may not occur to your target of persuasion until later that his or her spouse, boss, or friend will be unhappy with the new behavior, thus creating potential dissonance. But for the moment this is not a salient consideration, and your persuasion has temporarily succeeded.

This decay can also be linked to the **sleeper effect**. Decay and the sleeper effect can occur if, say, a receiver hears two things: (1) an effective message on a persuasive topic—perhaps you advise a high-school student to consider a particular occupation for the future; and (2) a second, bogus message in which someone criticizes the first message—such as by saying that the recommendation you gave the student is bad because it was filled with ideas that might have been good advice twenty years ago, but are terrible now. What apparently happens is that the first message is suppressed, perhaps because the receiver does not quite know what to do with the two discrepant messages. But after a period of time, the first message eventually succeeds. Why? Because the "suggestion" message and the "discounting" message have different decay times. The suggestion message has outlasted the discounting message (a sleeper effect), presumably because of its superior quality.

Chapter in Retrospect

Quantitative research must be planned very carefully if it is to help us understand something about persuasion. A number of standard designs for research can be used to carry out empirical studies so that they can avoid threats to research validity. Reviewing the empirical research done to date shows that a good variety of things are known about the effects of persuasive messages on receivers. For example, the credibility assigned to a persuader by an audience apparently can make the persuader more successful, as can the persuader's citing research that has not been heard by the audience. Inoculation also seems to help persuaders avoid having their messages sabotaged by rival persuaders in the post-message environment. Some variables that would seem to help determine persuasiveness have been difficult to prove, such as a persuader's apparent similarity to an audience. We can categorize studies on persuasive effects under the following five headings: sender, message, channel, receiver, and context.

KEY TERMS

analytical study	descriptive study	persistence of persuasion
bait and switch	door-in-the-face	primacy-recency
channels	experimental study	research design
climax or anticlimax	foot-in-the-door	research validity
context	inoculation	sleeper effect
control groups	likeability	treatment groups
counterpersuasion	low-ball	two-sided messages
credibility	one-sided messages	

REVIEW QUESTIONS

1. What is a control group?
2. Why should groups of subjects used in a study be randomly recruited? Randomly assigned to treatment or control groups?
3. How is the significance of an observed effect different from the size of that effect?
4. What is the difference between a hypothesis and a research question?
5. What is the difference between an independent variable and a dependent variable?
6. What things seem to be reliable predictors of senders being seen as having higher sender credibility?
7. What is the difference between climax-anticlimax and primacy-recency?

8. Are two-sided messages always better than one-sided messages? Explain.
9. What are some things known about sender variables and persuasive effects?
10. What are some things known about message variables and persuasive effects?
11. What are some things known about channel variables and persuasive effects?
12. What are some things known about receiver variables and persuasive effects?
13. What are some things known about context variables and persuasive effects?

SUGGESTED PROJECTS AND ACTIVITIES

1. Read one of the research studies cited in this chapter and write a summary that outlines the study's hypotheses, methods, results, and significance (use the library or the Web when you search for the title of the study).
2. Do you think the experimental, descriptive, and analytical research approaches are likely to produce different insights into persuasion because of their differing approaches? If so why? Or if not, why?
3. Construct a step-by-step outline of what you would do to prepare and then carry out a simple experiment to test the following hypothesis: *People in public will donate more money for a good cause when approached by a volunteer who _____ than they will when approached by a volunteer who _____. [fill in the two preceding blanks with parallel words, phrases, or clauses that spark your interest]*

QUESTIONS FOR DISCUSSION

1. How can the results of an experiment on persuasion be cast in doubt due to threats to research validity?
2. How can descriptive research and experimental research complement each other?
3. What topics on the empirical study of persuasion do you find most interesting?
4. Can we learn *too* much about how persuasion works? Why? Why not?
5. Which of the findings mentioned in this chapter about the persuasion process seem the most practical to know about for the sort of persuasion with which you personally are likely to be involved in?

Notes

1. This is true unless the study uses correlations. Correlation means that two or more things serve as a sign of each other's presence in a situation, process, or thing. When one is present, there is a tendency for the other to be present. Correlation makes no statement about causation.

2. Experimental laboratory studies can be conducted indoors or outdoors, as can descriptive studies.

3. To help provide a bigger picture of the empirical research on persuasion, two previous works used similar categories or schemes for grouping empirical studies: Daniel O'Keefe, *Persuasion: Theory and Research* (Thousand Oaks, CA: Sage, 2002); Charles Larson, *Persuasion: Reception and Responsibility* (Belmont, CA: Wadsworth, 1998), 3. This text combines the schemes used in these two books and selects five categories—sender, message, channel, receiver, context—to help build an easier-to-understand profile of what is known to date empirically about persuasion.

4. David Berlo, James Schweitzer, and Robert Mertz, "Dimensions for Evaluating the Acceptability of Message Sources," *Public Opinion Quarterly* 33, no. 4 (Winter 1969): 563–76; and Ronald Applebaum and Karl Anatol, "Dimensions of Source Credibility," *Speech Monographs* 40 (August 1973): 231–77.

5. Cf. Dan O'Hair, Rob Stewart, and Hannah Rubenstein, *A Speaker's Guidebook* (Boston: Bedford/St. Martin's, 2004), 357–58.

6. Eun-Ju Lee, "Effects of the Influence Agent's Sex and Self-Confidence on Informational Social influence in Computer-Mediated Communication: Quantitative versus Verbal Presentation," *Communication Research* 32, no. 1 (February 2005): 29–58.

7. We expect that high credibility will always make senders more persuasive, but this may not always be the case. The same is true with low credibility—which at rare moments will lead to more, not less, persuasiveness.

8. Arthur Lupia and Mathew McCubbins, *The Democratic Dilemma* (Cambridge: Cambridge University Press, 1998), 184–201.

9. Bryan Whaley and Lisa Smith, "Rebuttal Analogy in Persuasive Messages: Communicator Likeability and Cognitive Responses," *Journal of Language and Social Psychology* 19, no. 1 (March 2000): 66–84.

10. See for example Jesse Delia, "A Constructive Analysis of the Concept of Credibility," *Quarterly Journal of Speech* 62 (1975): 361–75; Donald Atkinson et al., "Ethnicity, Locus of Control for Family Planning and Pregnancy Counselor Credibility," *Journal of Counseling Psychology* 32 (1985): 417–21; and Teresa Swartz, "Relationship between Source Expertise and Source Similarity in an Advertising Context," *Journal of Advertising* 13, no. 2 (1984): 49–55.

11. O'Keefe, *Persuasion: Theory and Research*, 196–211.

12. Ann Gordon and Jerry Miller, "Values and Persuasion during the First Bush-Gore Presidential Debate," *Political Communication* 21, no. 1 (January-March 2004): 71–92.

13. Rodney Reynolds and Michael Burgoon, "Belief Processing, Reasoning, and Evidence," *Communication Yearbook* 7 (1983): 83–104.

14. See for example Howard Gilkinson, Stanley Paulson, and Donald Sikkink, "The Effects of Order and Authority in an Argumentative Speech," *Quarterly Journal of Speech* 40 (April 1954): 183–192.

15. O'Keefe, *Persuasion: Theory and Research*, 216–18.

16. Richard Evans, Richard Rozelle, Thomas Lasater, Theodore Dembroski, and Bem Allen, "Fear Arousal, Persuasion, and Actual versus Implied Behavioural Change: New Perspective Utilizing a Real-Life Dental Hygiene Program," *Journal of Personality and Social Psychology* 16, no. 2 (October 1970): 220–27.

17. O'Keefe, *Persuasion: Theory and Research*, 219–21.

18. Cornelia Pechmann, "Predicting When Two-Sided Ads Will Be More Effective than One-Sided Ads: The Role of Correlational and Correspondent Inferences," *Journal of Marketing Research* 29, no. 4 (November 1992): 441–54.

19. Muzafer Sherif and Carolyn Sherif, *Attitude, Ego-involvement, and Change* (New York: Wiley, 1967), 1–17.

20. Little persuasiveness occurs with extremely small or extremely large attempts at persuasive change; but in the middle, some optimal point exists.

21. Charles Berger, "Slippery Slopes to Apprehension: Rationality and Graphical Depictions of Increasingly Threatening Trends," *Communication Research* 32, no. 1 (February 2005): 3–28.

22. David Roskos-Ewoldsen, Jessy Yu, and Nancy Rhodes, "Fear Appeal Messages Affect Accessibility of Attitudes toward the Threat and Adaptive Behaviors," *Communication Monographs* 71, no. 1 (March 2004): 49–69.

23. James Baesler and Judee Burgoon, "The Temporal Effects of Story and Statistical Evidence on Belief Change," *Communication Research* 21, no. 5 (October 1994): 582–602; and Shelley Taylor and

Suzanne Thompson, "Stalking the Elusive 'Vividness' Effect," *Psychological Review* 89, no. 2 (March 1982): 155–81.

24. Jonathan Freedman and Scott Fraser, "Compliance without Pressure: The Foot-in-the-Door Technique," *Journal of Personality and Social Psychology* 4, no. 2 (August 1966): 195–202.

25. Murray Millar, "Effects of a Guilt Induction and Guilt Reduction on Door in the Face," *Communication Research* 29, no. 6 (December 2002): 663–80; and Michael Patch and Vicki Hoang, "The Use of Metacommunication in Compliance: Door-in-the-Face and Single-Request Strategies," *Journal of Social Psychology* 137, no. 1 (February 1997): 88–94.

26. Danette Johnson, Maichael Roloff, and Melissa Riffee, "Responses to Refusals of Requests: Face Threat and Persistence, Persuasion and Forgiving Statements," *Communication Quarterly* 52, no. 4 (2004): 347–57.

27. Robert Cialdini et al., "Low-Ball Procedure for Producing Compliance: Commitment then Cost," *Journal of Personality and Social Psychology* 36 (1978): 463–76. This technique is also explained in Robert Cialdini, *Influence: How and Why People Agree to Do Things* (New York: William Morrow, 1984), 79–81.

28. Robert Cialdini, Nancy Eisenberg, Beth Green, Kelton Rhoads, and Renee Bator, "Undermining the Effect of Reward on Sustained Interest," *Journal of Applied Social Psychology* 28, no. 3 (February 1998): 253–67.

29. Timothy Borchers, *Persuasion in the Media Age* (Boston: McGraw-Hill, 2002), 88–89; and Herbert Simons, with Joanne Morreale and Bruce Gronbeck, *Persuasion in Society* (Thousand Oaks, CA: Sage, 2001), 87–88.

30. William Rogers, "The Contribution of Kinesic Illustrators to Speech Comprehension," *Human Communication Research* (Fall 1978): 54–62.

31. Larson, *Persuasion: Reception and Responsibility*, 71–72.

32. Wesley C. King Jr., "Computer-Mediated Communication," *Computers in Human Behavior* 7 (1991): 269–79.

33. Dolores Albarracin, Blair Johnson, Martin Fishbein, and Paige Muellerleile, "Theories of Reasoned Action and Planned Behavior as Models for Condom Use: A Meta-Analysis," *Psychological Bulletin* 127, no. 1 (2001): 142–61.

34. Patricia Moy, Marcos Torres, Keiko Tanaka, and Michael McCluskey, "Knowledge or Trust: Investigating Linkages between Media Reliance and Participation," *Communication Research* 32, no. 1 (February 2005): 59–86; and Nojin Kwak, Ann Williams, Xiaoru Wang, and Hoon Lee, "Talking Politics and Engaging in Politics: An Examination of the Interactive Relationships between Structural Features of Political Talk and Discussion Engagement," *Communication Research* 32, no. 1 (February 2005): 87–111.

35. With the possibility of counterpersuasion, at least four strategic paths to influencing the audience might occur, with some path elements under the control of the sender and some not:

1. Rejection-Outcome
   - good reasons for complying
   - final plea for action
   - later counterpersuasion from rival source
   - audience acceptance of counterpersuasion
   - audience rejection of primary message
2. Acceptance-Outcome
   - good reasons for complying
   - final plea for action
   - later counterpersuasion from rival source
   - audience rejection of counterpersuasion
   - audience acceptance of primary message

3. Acceptance-Outcome–II
   - good reasons for complying
   - refutation of downside issues
   - final plea for action
   - counterpersuasion from rival source
   - audience rejection of counterpersuasion
   - audience acceptance of primary message
4. Rejection-Outcome–II
   - good reasons for complying
   - refutation of downside issues
   - final plea for action
   - counterpersuasion from rival source
   - audience acceptance of counterpersuasion
   - audience rejection of primary message

36. Hua-Hsin Wan and Michael Pfau, "The Relative Effectiveness of Inoculation, Bolstering, and Combined Approaches in Crisis Communication," *Journal of Public Relations Research* 16, no. 3 (2004): 301–28.

37. David Whiteman, "Out of the Theatres and Into the Streets: A Coalition Model of the Political Impact of Documentary Film and Video," *Political Communication* 21, no. 1 (January–March 2004): 51–69.

38. Thomas Cook and Brian Flay, "The Persistence of Experimentally Induced Attitude Change," in *Experimental and Social Psychology*, ed. Leonard Berkowitz, vol. 11 (New York: Academic Press, 1978), 1–57.

PART III

Contexts and Skills

CHAPTER 11

Verbal and Visual Rhetorical Theories

◆ Chapter Objectives

After reading this chapter, you will be able to:

◆ Understand the humanistic perspective of persuasion

◆ Apply Burke's dramaturgic theory of persuasion

◆ Apply Aristotle's theory of persuasion

◆ Apply Goffman's model of impressions management

◆ Explain what visual rhetoric is

But since we have the ability to persuade one another and to make dear to ourselves what we want, not only do we avoid living like the animals, but we have come together, built cities, made laws, and invented arts.

—ISOCRATES, who predated Aristotle

He had a daughter named Hortensia, whom he greatly loved for the subtlety of her wit. He had her learn letters and study the science of rhetoric, which she mastered so thoroughly that she resembled her father Hortensius not only in wit and lively memory but also in her excellent delivery and order of speech.

—CHRISTINE DE PIZAN, perhaps the first feminist, ca. 1365–1430

Here the painter's aid gleams a picture of Rhetoric's power of colour and thus a picture adds colour to a picture.

—ALAIN DE LILLE, perhaps the first to comment on visual rhetoric

THIS CHAPTER is concerned with what might loosely be called the humanistic perspective of persuasion. We will be concerned here with theories very old and very new. For the old, we will review a classical theory of rhetoric, and for the new, we will review what has come to be called in recent years **visual rhetoric**. With the inclusion of visual rhetoric, I will attempt to examine the intermeshing operations and effects of verbal and visual rhetoric when they co-occur in the same communicative event. We will also examine two relatively recent dramaturgic theories. The theories reviewed here will add to and build on what has already been said in previous chapters, and they will prepare the way for the remaining chapters. Unlike the previous two chapters, which explored the relationships between empirical theories of persuasion and empirical research studies, this chapter explores the relationships between humanistic theories of persuasion and the case-study approach for carrying out research. Case studies that can be explored with humanistic theories not only include examination of the persuasive essay or speech, but also include analysis of political campaigns, social movements, political demonstrations and street theater, attempts to indoctrinate prisoners with new attitudes and beliefs, cult experiences, advertisements, and what chapter 13 will describe as a *counterpublic*.

Burke's Dramaturgic Theory

The philosopher Kenneth Burke is thought by some to be the most important and influential communication theorist of the twentieth century. To try to understand his outlook, we can look to his own summary:

> The basic function of rhetoric [persuasion] is the use of words by human Agents to form attitudes or to induce actions in other human Agents. Language is a symbolic means for inducing cooperation in beings that by nature respond to symbols. Therefore, we can deduce that language motivates people to behave and is the means by which we can identify with one another in an attempt to become consubstantial [similar in mental outlook].[1]

Burke assumes that persuasion occurs when receivers can identify with the sender—especially the persuasive story or drama the sender uses to describe some persuasive situation. He also seems to say that we all have an inborn responsiveness to symbolic expression that sometimes can bring us together in purpose and action when a persuasive message is skillfully created. Burke distinguishes between the simple "motion" of objects and the purposeful "action" of people. He employs five technical terms[2] (his *pentad*) to analyze how senders dramatize the actions of social actors:

Scene (the place or situation where the actions or events are said to occur)

Agent (the people said to participate in some way in the actions or events)

Agency (the alleged means or tools used by those participating in the actions or events)

Act (whatever motivated deeds are said to be done)

Purpose (an explanation of why those who take part in the actions or events do whatever they do)

Applications of the Theory

For example, a persuader could describe the *scene* of the final football game of the season as a "grudge match" between University X and University Y. Another persuader might feel that the true conflict is between the two coaches of the teams who are intense rivals (*agents* both). The respective teams could be seen as human *agencies* for the coaches' motivations, as might be the coaches' material *agencies*, the playbooks. The obvious *purpose* is to win bragging rights that will last for the coming year. And the coaches' respective demands for aggressive play on the field are their *acts*. Another persuader, perhaps a sociologist, might analyze the final game differently by suggesting that the general *scene* of organized football caused all the competition and aggressiveness, not the personalities of the two coaches. While Burke spends a good bit of time talking about the individual five parts of his pentad and using it to analyze persuasive messages (as we have just done), he also refers to pentad items in pairs, or **ratios** (as in, a *scene-act ratio*). Thus, he says:

> For instance, by a "scene-act ratio" one would refer to the effect that a scene has upon an act, and by an "act-scene ratio" one would refer to the effect that an act has upon the scene. The Supreme Court would be exemplifying a "scene-act ratio" in deciding that emergency measures [acts] are admissible because there is a state of emergency [scene]. And we should be exemplifying an "act-scene ratio" in fearing that an arms race [acts] may lead to war [scene]. At still other times, however, there is merely a state of conformity between scene and act, without any notion of cause and effect.[3]

Incidentally, we might note that these ratios are essentially analogies exploited by persuaders. That is, the term *scene-act ratio* means that the nature of the act is implicit, or analogously present, in the nature of the scene. Therefore, a persuader might encourage an audience to see forces in a scene as causing an act. Perhaps a child is described as a rowdy in the schoolyard but as an angel when visiting its grandparents, the scene in either case being possibly responsible for the child's acts. The left side of the ratio points to the grounding for what is on the right side. This is not always the formal grounding that is required for formal arguments, but often an informal, broadly defined grounding. The reason persuaders can build their messages around Burke's pentad ratios is that receivers in general can relate to ideas couched in these ways. Burke's terms seem fundamental to human thought.

For example, as a prosecutor at a trial you might summarize to the jury, "What we have here is a grizzly stabbing [act] with an illegal stiletto knife [agency] of an innocent neophyte by the defendant [agent], a lifelong gambler, over one roll of the dice [simple motion] in a back-alley craps game [scene] and all for twenty bucks [purpose]. But don't let the defense fool you here; this was no disagreement that got out of hand; this was callous greed and face-saving on the part of the defendant." You might also remind the jury that one does not carry and use a stiletto knife as a matter of style—the stiletto knife is a weapon of aggression. The more you talk about the defendant's aggressive impulses and decision to carry the knife, the more the jury will sense the agent-act ratio. On the other hand, the defense might say to the jury, "The gambling caught hold of all the players as they rooted for or against the dice shooter, emotions flared, and the defendant lost control when he was accused of cheating by the victim, whose friends began to act in menacing ways when they

TABLE 11.1

The Ten Ratios of Burke's Pentad

Ratio	Ratio	Ratio	Ratio
scene-act	agent-act	agent-agency	agency-purpose
scene-agent	agency-act	agent-purpose	
scene-agency	purpose-act		
scene-purpose			

Note: Each ratio can also be reversed for analysis. For example: scene-agent, where the agent can be seen as influenced by the scene; or agent-scene, where the scene can be seen as influenced by the agent.

asked to examine the dice." Here the defendant's motive is to be understood in terms of the scene-act ratio: one of self-defense in a situation out of control. In our analysis of any persuasive or propagandistic situation, one or more of the possible pairs may seem more powerful than the others for stressing a particular point of view. In an extended analysis, more than one ratio may be needed.

Burke's pentad can also be employed in an analysis of the stage play and subsequent movie *The Music Man*. In this story, a huckster makes a living barnstorming American midwestern towns selling band instruments and uniforms to townspeople for their teenagers. He uses a variety of rhetorical tricks to make these sales, expressed creatively in the song lyric "There's trouble, right here in River City." The song alludes to the likelihood of town teenagers getting into trouble in such places as pool halls. As the huckster tells his story to the townspeople, the townspeople might apply the scene-act ratio and tell themselves, "Maybe by hanging out in pool halls [scene] our young pool players will get involved with theft or aggressive behavior [acts], and they will certainly not study for school very hard." They could also look at the scene-agent ratio by asking, "What will be the long-term effects on the character of our kids [agents] who hang out in pool halls [scene]?" Our huckster has a solution for all this: he wants the town to buy marching-band instruments and uniforms (agencies both) and get the kids involved with playing marching music (acts). So one way to analyze this is by seeing our huckster as emphasizing a beneficial act-scene ratio to the parents (i.e., let the kids play band music for a better town or youth culture).

According to Burke, scene and agent are often at odds with each other in public disputes:

> One may deflect attention from scenic matters by situating the motives of an act in the agent (as were one to account for wars purely on the basis of a "warlike instinct" in people): or conversely, one may deflect attention from the criticism of personal motives by deriving an act or attitude not from traits of the agent but from the nature of the situation.[4]

Although Burke did not create his theory for persuaders to use for building their strategies, let's apply his ideas by creating a twenty-first-century media campaign to reinvigorate the U.S. space program, which some believe reached its apex with the Apollo 11 spaceflight in 1969. Our campaign could use an agent-act ratio as the basic strategy by saying, "People accomplish great things because of who they are and by how their shared internal traits guide their destiny." Our second theme could be the reverse of the first, using an act-agent ratio: "Accomplishing great deeds will make a people great." A third possibility would be to describe the human scene as it will be on earth in the near future and characterize the act of space flight as a logical outgrowth for which we must prepare. A simple outline for this campaign is shown in box 11.1. To actually create a persuasive message about spaceflight, additional details and descriptions could be developed around one or more of the ratios suggested above used as basic themes. Perhaps the message would resonate with Americans because it includes a primordial drama that will appeal to a basic part of the human psyche, as long as that appeal is open and honest.

Research Stimulated by Burke's Critical Approach

Burke's theory has sparked research using critical and sometimes historical methodologies. In some ways, the critical approach works in reverse to the empirical approach. Empirical researchers consult theory, create and control cleverly designed studies, and then observe and explain the effects of persuasive messages on receivers. Critical researchers first identify a message, perhaps an important message in the public arena; generally appraise its success or failure; and then study the message to identify the likely reasons for that success or failure, consulting theory and possibly amending the theory based on the analysis.

For example, persuasion theorist J. Clarke Rountree III summarizes what rhetorical critics need to do when analyzing the statements about human motives made by persuaders in their persuasive messages. According to Rountree, critics should (1) look in the persuasive message for ways that statements direct attention to particular pentadic items (scene, agent, act, agency, purpose), and (2) characterize those terms (that evoke images of pentad items).[5]

BOX 11.1

Sample Outline for a Persuasive Message on Space Exploration

We should explore the moon, Mars, and beyond.

I. People accomplish great things because of who they are
   A. America was founded as a nation of explorers
   B. It is America's destiny to explore the universe
   C. Only America has the needed unity and resources for space exploration
II. Accomplishing great deeds will make a people great
   A. By taking on this adventure, we will unite the world
   B. We will obtain replacements should earth's resources falter
   C. We may learn the secrets of the universe
III. Space flight is an inevitable part of our future
   A. Earth's population is ever expanding
   B. Technology marches on
   C. We are curious about what is beyond
   D. Famous scientist Stephen Hawking believes that humanity must begin preparing without delay to evacuate the earth to survive probable man-made or natural disaster

Rountree refers to a study of Senator Edward Kennedy's Chappaquiddick speech (given after the passenger in a car Kennedy was driving drowned as a result of a car accident). In the speech, Kennedy explains that what happened was beyond his control. This explanation of the accident is one that directs our attention to the scene. In another study, scholar Jane Blankenship uses Burke's pentad to analyze one of the past Republican presidential primaries in which Ronald Reagan transformed himself from an actor (no pun intended) contained by the scene to the container, that is, the scene itself.[6] And in one other study, the Reagans' "Just Say No" anti-drug campaign is also described as an example of transformational rhetoric. In using the word *no*, the campaign implied higher expectations or purpose for individuals and "shifted the responsibility for drug-abuse problems from the arenas of politics and medicine to that of morality."[7]

One last thought about Burke's theory concerns how persuasive messages are used to encourage favorable frames of mind in receivers for accepting the individual persuasive claims in those messages. As we have already noted, Aristotle sees **pathos** being used by persuaders to help create a favorable mood in receivers for evaluating persuasive ideas in the persuaders' messages. When we turn to Burke's theory, however, it may seem that Burke sees all message elements (what Aristotle calls pathos, ethos, and logos) functioning to encourage favorable frames of mind in receivers and to promote specific persuasive ideas. Some of these message elements are literal, and some metaphorical. Thus I might say, "This town casts an evil spell on everyone who lives here; no wonder we have these sorts of illegal things happening every day." Here, pathos helps create the right mood (e.g., using the emotional connotations carried by the term *evil*), as does the idea (logos) that an evil spell might have the required power to haunt a town and cause crimes to be committed.

Aristotle's Classical Theory

Those who study Aristotle say that he identified four good reasons for learning about rhetoric or persuasion: to uphold the truth, to teach, to analyze both sides of issues thoroughly, and to defend oneself. Upholding the truth concerns improving our ability to distinguish between truth and falsehood. In Aristotle's time, the challenge was in obtaining accurate knowledge and in learning to think clearly. For us today, the challenge more often concerns a glut of information that can obscure knowledge, and a glut of people who have learned to manipulate this information to their advantage. The second reason to learn about rhetoric is that it enables us to teach and learn. For example, studying persuasion may help us understand what reasoning would motivate people to try to blow up the world (if they do not get their way). Learning how this reasoning has come to be is crucial to the survival of the world. The third reason why Aristotle believed that studying rhetoric or persuasion was useful was the fact that they can help us see both sides of an issue. Debate coaches often apply this knowledge when they require debate team members to prepare to defend both sides of a proposition before knowing which side they will actually be asked to defend. And fourth, studying persuasion can help us better defend our ideas and beliefs against the arguments of others. This is especially true when we are defending the things we take for granted and thus seldom feel a need to justify to ourselves—that is, until someone raises questions that had previously gone unraised.

Roughly 2,300 years ago Aristotle, building on the work of such previous scholars as Isocrates, gave the critical study of persuasion additional formalization, which culminated in the writing of his book *Rhetoric*. Aristotle defined rhetoric as "the capacity [*dynamis*] to observe, in regard to any subject, the available means of persuasion."[8] He also saw it as closely related to the study of logic, on one side, and the study of ethics and politics, on the other. He probably developed the theoretical ideas he did by observing the successes and failures of the speakers of his time and borrowing some of the less well-known ideas of the rhetorical observers who preceded him. He then perfected a theory that has served as a standard for creating and evaluating persuasion over the centuries.

A team of modern scholars could try retracing Aristotle's theory-building steps today by perhaps listening to one hundred persuasive speeches in a variety of contexts, carefully noting what was effective or ineffective in each. The group could create generalizations of what they thought were the best approaches to giving persuasive speeches, coining concepts as they went along. They could then look at more speeches, but this time anticipating that they would compare them to the generalizations they had just created with the original one hundred speech analyses. If this succeeded for them, they could encourage the use of these generalizations by analysts outside the team, and encourage these other analysts to suggest improvements in or elaborations on the theory. But starting from scratch on such a project might in the end become an exercise in reinventing the wheel.

Aristotle's Proofs, Topoi, Style, Enthymemes, and Examples

Aristotle's understanding of persuasion or rhetoric centered around rhetorical proof, not intellectual sleight of hand, mental trickery, or emotional outbursts. Certain tricks of the trade had been favored by some of those rhetoricians who preceded Aristotle; thus to some extent, he set out to correct the field of rhetorical study. He believed that people would be persuaded when they thought something had been proven. Forbes Hill notes that with Aristotelian theory:

> Rhetorical proofs are either artistic (intrinsic) or inartistic (extrinsic); the former must be constructed by the speaker, the latter are preexisting data that one must discover. The artistic proofs are of three kinds: those that pledge the speaker's good character (ethos) to establish his credibility; those that bring the audience into a certain state of feeling (pathos) favorable of accepting the arguments made in the speech; and the arguments themselves (logoi) as they appear to prove or disprove the speaker's conclusions.[9]

Enthymemes (arguments with implied premises) and *examples* were briefly described earlier. Continuing with Hill, we could add to what has already been said by noting that the enthymeme is "an argument from premises that are probable principles or from signs." Saying that an enthymeme can rest on a premise (that is, a probable principle) simply means that the enthymeme will be justified by what seems true about the world we live in (e.g., "If I can hold my breath for one minute, I can surely hold it for ten seconds"). Further, saying that an enthymeme can rest on a sign-type premise simply means we get an argument that will be valid if the sign on which it rests is infallibly correct (e.g., "I have had a 103-degree temperature while lying in bed all evening; I must be sick"). This specific example is argument from one particular to another. Both examples work from the premise that what is true about one thing in a class will be true about another in that class (e.g.,

"What we have here is extortion; you might as well have put a gun to my head as what you have just done").[10]

The persuasive application of **topoi** (sing. *topos*) has not yet been discussed. Topoi are handy lists of basic assumptions commonly accepted by people about the world around them. Enthymemes proceed from these topoi. Topoi are blueprints of persuasive ideas in general form; persuaders then apply these topoi to particular situations. To be a good communicator, you must learn about, and learn how to use, these topoi to help create your arguments or to criticize arguments heard from other people. This is true whether your persuasion is designed to influence (1) the perceived advantages and disadvantages of the future **deliberative** choices of others regarding elections, court verdicts, or product purchases, for example; (2) the **forensic** judgments others should make about past events, such as who committed what crime, what caused what disease, or what has been just or unjust; or (3) the **epideictic** attitudes others should adopt toward current events, as for example, who or what deserves blame, or who or what deserves credit or praise.

Aristotle identified specific topoi to be used for specialized subjects like physics, politics, and law; he also identified topoi for creating arguments for all subjects and kinds of discourses. The topoi identified in Aristotle's *Rhetoric* are too numerous to be summarized here. But as an example, let's make a list of the issues a lawyer or prosecutor might employ during that segment of a court proceeding that assesses whether someone has been a victim of a crime or not. Assuming there is physical evidence and a set of facts that are not in dispute (**inartistic proofs**), where does the legal persuasion go from there? Perhaps the lawyer or prosecutor will begin the case by starting with one of the following topoi that help establish that complaints by victims are probable:

- Among the likely victims of crime are persons who have what the criminal needs and also helpless persons like the weak and lonely.
- People living far away and also those near at hand can be said to be equally likely victims: the former because revenge [justice] will be slow, and latter because the gain is immediate.
- Crimes are often committed against the meek, easy going, or unskillful, and against persons not on their guard; also against victims who are unpopular or hated by nearly everyone, and especially those who have committed crimes of the same kind now committed against them, for such a crime may appear to be almost an act of poetic justice.[11]

Many of the above typical victims (e.g., the elderly, or a drunk sleeping on a park bench) can be found in the news stories of the day. Examples of victims who are hated by nearly everyone include (1) the serial killer who preys on prostitutes, hoping that no one will notice or care when they disappear; (2) the spouse murdered after years of being abusive and now seen as deserving this "poetic justice"; (3) the hired assassin who finds no sympathizers when he is preemptively murdered by a scheduled victim. A prosecutor may emphasize to a jury that the defendant especially picked elderly or drunk victims because they were easy to rob. And the defense attorney of the abused spouse might suggest to the jury that years of abuse had resulted in understandable retribution. The above two topoi therefore offer ideas for legal strategies.

Aristotle also describes topoi for creating arguments common to all subjects. For example, he identifies an enthymeme based on the topos of *more or less*. A persuader could use this topos with the argument "If the smartest people in the world cannot figure out how to build a time-travel machine, then surely you or I cannot." The conclusion here is that you or I will not invent a time machine. The minor premise for this conclusion is that the smartest people have failed to do so. The missing major premise is "If something is or is not the case when it is more probable, it certainly is or is not the case when it is less probable." Another enthymemic pattern is based on the inconsistency between what someone will do now and what someone has done in the past. A son might tell his parents, "You sent my older brother and sister to college; you should now send me." Here the missing premise might be "To be fair, you must treat equal people equally." Still one other pattern is based on consequences. I could say, "Conserving your money is certainly a good idea because you will then have it for a rainy day." Thus, unintended consequences aside, if something results in something good that causal something must too be good. Aristotle also identified a number of fallacious enthymemes, some of which we identify in chapter 5 as fallacies.[12]

Another aspect of persuasive or rhetorical style concerns word choice, especially the use of metaphor, which we discuss in chapter 2. Aristotle categorized metaphors in four ways, which we will modernize somewhat as (1) using the general to refer to the specific (e.g., "I bought the dinner wines at the local *establishment* on the corner"), (2) using the specific to refer to the general (e.g., "We're counting our *pennies* to get back on a sound financial basis"), (3) using the equally specific to refer to the equally specific (e.g., "They dutifully *laundered* the family car for the happy occasion"), and (4) using analogy (e.g., "*Waves* of locusts descended onto the crops").

One Modern Example of Research Taking an Aristotelian Approach

In a study by Jane Blankenship, the metaphors used in contemporary politics were analyzed to tell us something about how communicators in the political arenas view the actors they discuss and the activities in which they're involved. Some common categories of metaphor identified in the study were (1) general-violence metaphors, such as "brass knuckles," "assaults," "nailing an opponent," and "blasting back"; (2) warfare metaphors, such as "scorched earth," "battleground states," "blitzes," "beachheads," and "ambushed by the press"; (3) sports-and-games metaphors, as in "horse race," "playing ball," "up in the major leagues," "lottery winner," and "out of their playbook"; (4) natural-phenomena metaphors, as in "bucking the tide," "storm clouds," "putting out fires," "flooding the neighborhoods," and "avalanche"; (5) animal and hunting metaphors, as in "flushed out," "swimming upstream," "an albatross around the neck," "like ostriches," and "stalking"; (6) vehicle metaphors, as in "showboating," "any port in a storm," "ships in the night," "rocketing up in the polls," and "rocking the boat"; (7) personal metaphors, as in "a modern-day Hitler in drag," "busted in Bonnie-and-Clyde style," "asking Saint Peter for admittance," "the Devil incarnate," "pancake flippers"; and (8) show-business metaphors, as in "a last hurrah," "their dog-and-pony show," "his swan song," "showdown," and "box-office success."[13]

Aristotle did give advice about using metaphors. For example he said, "If one means to disparage, he draws the metaphor from something worse in its class; to adorn, from something better."[14] So if a political pundit describes a vice-presidential candidate as "an albatross around the neck" of the presidential candidate, we have disparagement. One last point here is that new and fresh metaphors may be especially useful for analysis because older, heavily used metaphors can sometimes become dead metaphors, or vocabulary words that have lost their metaphorical power—as in "time is running out," probably an old ambulatory metaphor, or "deadline," which was formerly a death metaphor deriving from the line in a machinegun-guarded prison courtyard that prisoners could not cross if they wanted to go on living. The number of studies based on Aristotle's theory is very large.[15]

Goffman's Dramaturgic Theory— All the World's a Stage

William Shakespeare reminds us in *As You Like It* that human communication occurs on a stage of sorts and that we all act to a certain extent to control the **impressions** we make when in the presence of others—either face-to-face or in media formats. Shakespeare's actual words are:

> All the world's a stage,
> And all the men and women merely players.
> They have their exits and their entrances;
> And one man in his time plays many parts. (act 2, scene 7)

Psychologist Erving Goffman has offered a set of *impressions-management* concepts to formalize Shakespeare's dramaturgic insight.[16] In the next paragraphs, I will propose a model to visually illustrate much of what Goffman has to say about impressions management during communication (see figure 11.1). Persuaders and propagandists need to manage the impressions they make on audiences, because audiences will inherently form such impressions, for better or worse, and whether the sender wants them to or not. A communicated impression often results from the sender doing something or saying something. Doing something is a kind of *presentational* message. But when you say something about your topic—perhaps analyze or describe something or make an argument to support something—this is a *discursive* message. These two types of messages do indeed support each other during persuasion.[17]

The primary concern for impressions management is the creating of impressions for some target audience by employing the elements shown in the model during communication. Some of the impressions a persuader creates are general ones. *General impressions* (see figure 11.1) tend to be about the personal attributes of a persuader (e.g., the speaker is honest, concerned, experienced, unbiased, or a host of other possibilities that will depend on the situation). General impressions can also concern conditions in situations (e.g., things are quite normal here, this is a special place, there is danger here). *Specific impressions* concern things a persuader seeks to imply are true or false. For example, to seem surprised when you are not, you could raise your eyebrows and squeal, "I can't believe you threw a party for me!" Or if you are a waiter creating the impression that patrons' leftover food is not "recycled" in your restaurant, you could gather untouched bread slices off the table in a rough way while saying to the diners, "Let me clear off this stuff for you." Compare that impression to your impression of the waiter who carefully picks up untouched slices of bread, gently dusts them

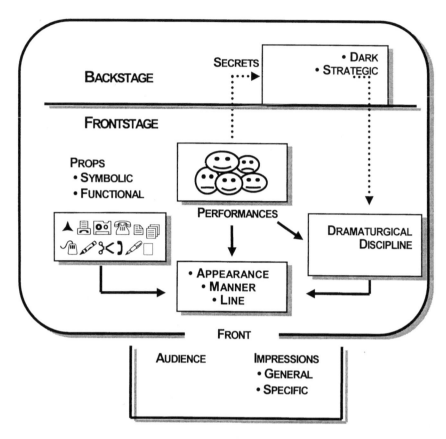

FIGURE 11.1 Model of impressions management showing terminology provided by Erving Goffman, which was inspired by act 2, scene 7, line 139 of William Shakespeare's *As You Like It*: "All the world's a stage."

off, and then stacks them with great care on a tray, saying cryptically, "Waste not, want not." Or, if you are a mischievous student sitting in the back of a class, you could touch, or "ping," the person sitting in front of you in the back of the head, and when your victim turns around to see what is happening, you will look very busy, writing in your notebook as if you have no clue as to what is going on.

Impressions are usually conveyed in the **frontstage** area where the audience can see things. **Backstage** is where the audience cannot see, and so here frontstage impressions management can be discontinued, unless you want to play to fellow players backstage. The frontstage of a restaurant is the dining area, the frontstage of your home (for guests) may be the living room, and the frontstage for a game of Three-Card Monte is the street where it takes place. Backstages are places like the kitchen in a restaurant, your closet and bedroom at home, or an alley around the corner from the Three-Card Monte game.

Secrets concern information that could harm the creation or ongoing maintenance of impressions. *Dark secrets* are about terrible things, such as a restaurant having rats in the basement, or a family that physically abuses the children in the hours before the guests arrive on Saturday night. *Strategic secrets* are less serious and may be thought of as the tricks of the trade practiced by impressions managers. If you are asked out somewhere, you might say, "Let me check my appointment book," even though you know you're free. Or when a customer calls your company with a complaint, you might create the impression for the customer that such problems are rare by pretending to conduct an investigation. You might claim to want to find out what has gone wrong, even though you know immediately what has happened. Perhaps you even say, "Can I call you right back? I need to check with the sales department on this." Persuaders can also use tricks to convince us that a product is scarcer than it actually is, that they like us more than they in fact do, that everybody's doing it, and so on. Or a food-service counter person might keep a certain amount of money in a "tips" dish in full view to encourage favorable tipping by customers.

Strategic secrets tend to be about managing several common impressions:

1. You want to seem uncertain about things of which you are certain.
2. You want to seem certain about things of which you are uncertain.
3. You want to seem as if you believe something that in fact you do not believe.
4. You want to seem as if you don't believe something that in fact you do believe.
5. You want people to think you like a thing or person you actually dislike.
6. You want people to think you dislike a thing or person you actually like.
7. You want people to think that other people have done something you prefer.
8. You want people to think that other people have not done something you dislike.

In addition, sometimes people may not have an accurate impression of you, and so you may turn to certain tricks of the management-impressions trade to get them to believe what *is* true, though this is what they think is not true. For example, you may like X, but for some reason people assume you do not. Perhaps then you will use specific tactics to convince people of the truth, that you like X.

Symbolic props are objects that help create impressions but do nothing else. The large key a wine steward may wear in an expensive restaurant may in some cases not be a key to anything, but may rather hang there just for show—to create the impression of an old, dusty wine cellar with tiers of priceless wine bottles and kegs. A bogus license hanging on the wall of a confidence artist might also be considered a symbolic prop. **Functional props** serve a dual purpose: they help convey impressions (as do purely symbolic props), but they also do something practical. An expensive watch may create the impression of wealth, but it also tells the time. Oversized menus in a restaurant are functional props because they create fancy impressions but also tell you what's being served. But a Bible in a court trial is a symbolic prop because it is not likely to be consulted for the trial. An upscale magazine placed on a coffee table is a functional prop because it can also be read.

Individuals create impressions—as you may be doing at this moment if you are reading this book around other people. **Teams** or groups often create impressions too. A restaurant crew is a team. The people who are paid to conduct trials (judges, court officers, and so on) are a team. The people who run a Three-Card Monte game also are a team. **Dramaturgical discipline** refers to a team's cooperation in creating impressions. A nurse in a doctor's office will usually refer to the physician as "Doctor," will act deferentially toward the doctor, and may even ask questions around patients when the answers are already known—this helps create impressions about the doctor's importance. A team can lose dramaturgical discipline when, for example, someone at home (and in a snit) says, while the guests are present, "Why don't you tell them that before we invited them, we first invited the Jones family, but they canceled at the last minute?" This would destroy the impression that the family was trying to create for its guests. Often social situations involve one team (the family, in this case) and an audience (the guests). But on occasion, rival teams may compete to create favorable impressions for the "home team" and unfavorable impressions for the "visiting team." One way teams do this is by revealing damaging information (strategic or dark secrets) about the other side.

In a restaurant, team *roles* include things like server, cashier, host, busboy, and manager. At home, the family team roles for entertaining guests might include main host, jokester, helper, conversationalist, and "evening-ender." In the Three-Card Monte game, the roles might include dealer, shill (the person who pretends to win to encourage actual players), and lookout. *Performance* refers to each time or occasion a specific role is played.

As an impressions manager, your **appearance** concerns your clothing, any props you may carry, and your body itself. Your **manner** concerns the way you walk, talk, sit, address others, and so on. And your **line** concerns what you would have people think you are up to at the moment—your particular motivation in this situation. If you are listening to the conversation of people you do not know, you might pretend to read a newspaper or gaze into the distance. Here, your line is that you are not paying attention to their conversation. If you are a host in a restaurant, you may ask newly arrived customers whether they have a reservation, even if you don't care whether they do. Your line here is that "This is a busy place and you can't just show up when you want." If you are a scam artist, you may show up at someone's front door carrying a baby and plead for some water with the line "My baby is choking." Your true motive may be, however, to case the house for a future robbery. Lines can be true or false. Finally, **front** refers to the general area where impressions management is carried out. The front can be a building, an organization's name, an outdoor location, or even a website.

When analyzing the persuasion or propaganda of a person or a group, you want to attend to more than the things they say in their formal message (the discursive part). It may pay for you to examine the general conditions (the presentational part) from which the formal message comes. I once listened in on an outdoor meeting with angry speakers who were opposed to a public policy important to them. The speakers eventually urged the crowd to go out onto a nearby highway and "close it down" as a protest. The idea for blocking the highway actually came from someone standing in the front of the audience. The suggestion was immediately accepted by the four or five speakers on the improvised platform. To this day, I am convinced the idea came from a shill planted in the audience to make the idea seem spontaneous. But whether the person was a shill is not the point. The point is that in order to more completely understand the influence you feel at public meetings or through public media messages, you might run through the vocabulary that Goffman has provided and try to understand how each concept may be contributing to the overall persuasive or propagandistic effect of those influences and messages.

Visual Rhetoric

For many reasons, scholars of communication since antiquity have paid much more attention to the spoken word than to the visual image. But recently, some theorists have argued that the field of rhetorical theory has been transformed, or is being transformed, and is taking a turn toward images. The reasons given for this new emphasis include the fact that the world is now saturated with visual images—many of which are used to encourage persuasive effects—and that visual symbols can provide access to a range of human experience not always available through verbal discourse. Nonetheless, communication scholar Nicholas Mirzoeff notes that there exists a wide gap between the wealth of visual experience in the modern world and our ability to analyze this wealth.[18] The communication field still needs additional critical methods with which to analyze visual images.

However visual rhetoric is eventually understood, we can nonetheless say at present that visual images can sometimes stand alone or be a part of a verbal message. Persuasive messages exist on a continuum between being more verbal and being more visual—and more visual is often more vivid (although particular persuaders can produce dull visuals or vivid words, depending on their personal skills). Theorist Charles Hill proposes categories for evaluating persuasive messages along just such a visual–verbal continuum, including actual experiences, moving images with sound, static photographs, realistic paintings, line drawings, narratives, descriptive accounts, abstract and impersonal accounts, and statistics.[19] Visuals give persuasive messages more presence, meaning that the messages can command more attention from receivers and perhaps cause more change in receivers because of this presence, although verbal elements such as vivid stories may also have presence. Visual images are organized in spatial terms and not in the linear terms of sentences that unfold one word at a time. They can be broadly processed with great speed. Even films that unfold over time consist of single images that too are organized spatially, not linearly. *When visuals and verbal text occur together, the verbal text tends to limit what the visual may mean to receivers, and the visual then tends to expand what the verbal text means*, although this may not always be the case. Further, visual images consist of signs that may help create symbolic meaning, especially with help from verbal elements.

Analyzing Visual Rhetoric

Rhetoric theorist Sonja Foss asks, How should visual images be analyzed? Should analysts use inductive and deductive reasoning in tandem to understand visual rhetoric? Or should they use *abductive* reasoning—a kind of intuition to search for patterns for forming hypotheses about particular images? Whichever critical methods develop, they will need to analyze visual images that are symbolic, that involve human intervention, and that are presented to the audience for the purpose of communicating.[20] These methods will need a vocabulary, basic laws, and analytical tools for sorting through the commonly used strategies and tactics of those who would influence us with visual images. Some of the most common places to find visual rhetoric are advertisements, business cards, political cartoons, websites, propaganda posters, news photos, illustrations in textbooks, murals, speeches that use presentation software, music videos, and posted signs on the street.

Communication scholar Jonah Rice reviews several recently developed rival analytical tools for analyzing visual images. One, a model proposed by Foss, offers an analytical tool by posing three steps for the analyst: (1) identify the message originator's persuasive intention in producing whatever text provides context for the image in question; (2) identify the details of the visual itself (e.g., color, line, and perspective) while at the same time picking apart any accompanying details of the textual materials; and (3) analyze the function of the persuasive message that contains both the visual and text. The second tool, also a model and proposed by another communication scholar Valerie Peterson, offers a revised set of steps that, among other things, reverses the first two steps in the Foss model.[21]

Roland Barthes, in several early analytical works, reminds us that a visual image, like a word, can have both *denotative* and *connotative* meanings.[22] Denotatively, an image refers to a visual idea; connotatively it inspires personal or emotional reactions. When combined with verbal text, visuals can add denotative and connotative meaning to (1) the words used in the verbal message, (2) the implied or stated particular ideas of the verbal message, and (3) the implied, summary ideas of the verbal message. A recent ad for the U.S. Coast Guard illustrates this combining of meanings. It shows several Coast Guard personnel on a small Coast Guard boat pursuing a hazily defined, suspicious-looking ship. The two Coast Guard personnel in the front of the boat are aiming a machine gun as the small boat bravely takes on the waves in pursuit of whatever trouble lies ahead. The headline uses the words "Command," "Compassion," and "Courage." The picture adds denotative and connotative meaning to the word "Courage" and to the implied summary message of the ad: "You too could be part of the Coast Guard." Thus, the visual speaks in the third person about the individuals portrayed in it, but the overall implied message speaks in the second person to the viewer.

According to Kevin DeLuca, **image events** can be quite effective rhetorically. In one of DeLuca's examples, we have a picture of three medium-sized boats at sea and a small power-boat big enough for two people. One of the riders in the powerboat is standing as if looking ahead at the three larger boats. The picture by itself seems devoid of action; it is somewhat bland and offers little that is connotative for the viewer. But when we read the extended caption under the picture, we learn that the two men are Greenpeace activists "confronting" a Soviet whaling fleet, prior to 1990. The text further explains the use of large, explosive harpoons by the whaling boats. After we have read the caption, the picture takes on new meaning for us. The difference in scale between the whaling boats and the small powerboat now seems to carry connotations of brave confrontation, a connotation that the textual materials by themselves cannot capture. Thus, the picture and the text work together rhetorically in ways that neither could accomplish independently. Of course, the picture is a "snapshot" taken from a particular perspective. It includes details and excludes details. The photo was obviously taken from a second Greenpeace boat positioned behind the first, but we do not see the second boat, leaving the first boat looking more alone then it actually was. We also do not see what may have happened before the photo was snapped, if anything, or what may have happened afterwards. DeLuca illustrates other similar image events created by activists, in one case on a road used by loggers, and in another at the site of a radioactive-waste dump in upstate New York.[23]

To understand visual rhetoric, it is not enough merely to demonstrate with empirical research that, say, a picture showing very graphic violence may affect an audience's reaction to the accompanying text—it is also desirable to describe the grammar of visual rhetoric. At present, this is still an elusive mission. But several models of visual rhetoric suggest the use of figures of speech to analyze the rhetorical dimension of visual images. Actually, we might call these aspects of a picture *visual figuratives*. To use visual figuratives, an image might exaggerate one of its visual elements, as a type of visual hyperbole. Or one visual element might be metaphorically substituted for another. Communication scholars Edward McQuarrie and David Mick do in fact propose an analytical tool that uses visual, analytical applications of figures of speech. They use such terms as *rhyme, alliteration, hyperbole, ellipsis, metaphor, irony,* and *paradox* to describe how elements in a picture might be persuasive. In one example, they analyze an ad for a Mercedes-Benz SL. In the ad, a small image of the vehicle is portrayed inside the opened shell of an oyster, as if the car were a pearl. This technique is an example of visual metaphor because the Mercedes is visually described as a pearl. The two authors go on to say that the ad "destabilizes" the viewer because the viewer has to make sense of its highly irregular visual image, and must do so by making the necessary perceptual corrections to understand what is happening in the picture. The viewer may then form a positive attitude about the Mercedes because of processing this novel visual metaphor. Perhaps some viewers will be changed by the ad and become more likely to purchase the Mercedes.[24]

In fact, as our earlier discussion of Aristotle alludes to, there are many more categories of figures of speech (or thought) that might be exploited in studies of visual rhetoric in the future, including **epanaphora** (consecutive verbal images in a persuasive message shown in a similar way), **antithesis** (opposite meanings), **juxtaposition** of verbal image contraries, climax, reduplication, repetition of a verbal image for emphasis, **asyndeton** (a verbal image presentation in separate parts), **synecdoche** (a figure in which a part is used to suggest the whole), **catachresis** (the inexact use of a verbal image in place of a more precise and proper one), and **allegory** (a set of verbal images related to a theme).[25]

Groupe Mu offers a model that distinguishes whether elements of an image are shown together or in separate areas of an ad. The model also distinguishes whether an image element in an ad has implied meaning or explicit meaning. A car ad for example might show the car (explicit) or might talk about it without showing it (implicit). Or the wheels of a bicycle might overlap the round shapes of eyeglass lenses in one ad but be shown in a separate area in another ad. In either case, the eyeglass lenses and bicycle images could be used to connect two disparate visual meanings in a way that helps sell the bicycle by reinforcing the purchase with the suggestion of admiring glances through eyeglasses.[26]

Theorizing about Visual Rhetoric

In describing the power of visuals to explain and convey information, theorist Edward Tufte reminds us that visual images are good at illustrating quantities, including number, amount, size, and scale.[27] The visual image can show these things all at once in spatial terms and as a kind of Gestalt. Images can force us to see comparisons shown in parallel form (such as two people standing together, one dressed in a suit and the other dressed in rags). Images can also be made powerful through repetition (e.g., an endless number of poor people marching to the "poorhouse" on some drab roadway). Images are good at graphically illustrating change (the "before" and "after" images used to sell diet products, for example). Tufte also uses the word "confection" to describe visual images as sometimes involving an assembly of many visual elements that have been juxtaposed to illustrate an argument, present and enforce visual comparisons, and combine the real and the imagined to tell a story.

Visuals do seem to work in part by telling a story. For example, in one recent political cartoon, a well-known newspaper reporter is depicted sitting in a trashcan about to be emptied by two sanitation workers with their truck. Several other trashcans also sit at the curb, labeled "cans," "paper," and "glass." The can the reporter is sitting in is labeled "reputations." The cartoon by its analogy criticizes the newspaper at which the reporter worked because this newspaper at first had supported the reporter in an ongoing conflict about protecting the identities of sources for stories, but had then attacked the reporter in print when this became expedient. All that is needed by the viewer to understand this picture-story is a little background knowledge of the news story about which the cartoon comments rhetorically. This cartoon appeared in a rival newspaper out to lampoon the newspaper that had politically abandoned its reporter. The story of the cartoon is told in the third person, but the rhetoric is directed at the viewer, the second person, by the storyteller, who is the first person. And although as a newspaper image the cartoon exists in two dimensions, it nonetheless implies a third dimension, depth, by allowing its viewers to observe the scene as if standing on the sidewalk across the street. And as these viewers imagine the action that is about to take place (the emptying of the "reputations" can), the image implies a fourth dimension: time.

In chapter 8 when we briefly discussed one new aspect of postmodern art, I laid the groundwork for the next part of this section. In a sense, visual images exist as figurative forms somewhere between what is real and what is not real. An oil painter begins with a blank canvas, adding details that may eventually come closer to depicting reality than did the very first brushstroke. For some projects, the painter may create a photograph-like image of a person. In other cases, the painter may create an image that represents something that does not actually exist as depicted or perhaps just indicates the artist's attitude toward the subject of the painting. A photographer, on the other hand, may begin with a straightforward picture of something that as yet offers no artistic metaphor other than a reduction of three dimensions to two, and the selectivity involved in defining a subject with a particular camera position, lens, and moment as captured when the picture was snapped. But with successive changes in exactly how the image is to be photographed and then processed in the darkroom or "computer darkroom," an artistic metaphor may be created that takes the image beyond mere realistic depiction of what had existed in front of the camera. Each of these two artists' creations, that of the painter and that of the photographer, may end up somewhere between what is an attempt to be objective and what is an attempt to be subjective. Through these visual figures, we may experience (1) what is beyond that which is easily perceivable with our senses, (2) what may not be visible to our eyes because it exists only in the realm of our emotions, (3) what may not be exactly true, (4) what is imaginary, or (5) what only exists in the abstract. With either a photograph or an oil painting, we may "see" the character, hopes, fears, and social perspectives of another person, as "seen" by the artist. And if no one in particular posed for the image, we may see what the artist thinks is inside the quintessential person. While visual art may more often be created for aesthetic purposes, it can also serve rhetorical ones.

An artist recently constructed a super-large dining-room set for public exhibit in an office-building lobby with a very high ceiling. This three-dimensional sculpture consisted of six oversized chairs and an oversized dining-room table that stood about ten feet high. Although the artist offered no explanation for the sculpture, a banner headline for it might have been "What If Your World Was Larger Than Life?" With or without a headline, the effect of the artwork seemed to encourage viewing a common setting from a very uncommon point of view, perhaps the point of view of a toddler. The details of this artwork were incredibly realistic, and the chairs and table looked exactly like dining-room furnishings you might find in countless homes. How might the oversized sculpture of the dining-room furniture rhetorically complement the headline above? Would the sculpture and headline imply, "Remember back to what it was like to be little?" Or maybe this hyperbolic pair would say, "In some ways you are not such a big deal after all." Alternatively, we might juxtapose the headline "What If Your World . . ." with a picture of earth from the perspective of a circumnavigating satellite; now the headline and satellite picture might make the viewer feel more god-like.[28]

Earlier I reviewed some of the theoretical work of Kenneth Burke. His pentad of scene, agent, act, agency, and purpose may also help us discover the grammar of the visual image. In a pentadic analysis, the political cartoon described above portrays scene in two ways: the sidewalk setting with trash cans, and the ongoing news controversy about the reporter. The agent can be seen as the newspaper being lampooned. The act is that of abandonment. The agencies will be the stories written that have criticized the reporter. And the purpose is the expediency of the abandoning newspaper, looking out for its own interests at the expense of its reporter.

Also of interest in analyzing visual images using the pentad is what Burke calls "manner" (the sometimes-included and sometimes-excluded sixth part of the pentad). Manner is especially useful in describing the graphic details of an artistically created image. Returning to the political cartoon, we might note that its image is quite grainy, which helps to create the sense of "seediness" that the cartoonist tries to give to the event. The image also flows from left to right by depicting the one-way street on which the garbage truck is proceeding in collecting the garbage. This graphic flow is especially useful in creating a sense of time unfolding toward an ending for the story—perhaps that the reporter will end up, in our imaginations, sitting inside the back portal of the garbage truck.

Finally, the symbolic power of any visual image has much to do with communication through implication, suggesting things about the not-here, the here, the not-now, the now, the might-have-been, the could-be, the may-be, the untrue, the never-was, the never-will-be, the seeable, the not-seeable, and so on. For example, when viewing a picture of a person walking down a country lane, the viewer may imagine where the person is coming from or where the person is going to. The viewer may imagine what the purpose of the walk is, what the larger geographical context is of which the country lane is part, or what the minute details of a bush at the side of the lane look like. Elements in the picture may also serve as concrete examples or tokens of more abstract types, such as countrysides, country lanes, rural neighborhoods in general, or the sort of society of which the country lane is part. In one sense, looking at a still visual can be likened to looking through a window or looking at a stage on which characters act.[29]

On a different plane of implications, a picture of a fashion model may imply a host of values, attitudes, or feelings about what is important or not important, what is attractive or not attractive, or even what is good or bad. On still a different plane, a picture of a vase of roses may imply something very abstract, such as the Romantic poet John Keats's assertion that "Truth is beauty." But a picture that contains representations of several pictures—including the picture of the vase of roses—may imply something about the philosophical staleness of rhetorical plat-itudes. In all of the above cases, the implications may also serve as visual enthymemes.

Researchers' recent concern with the importance of visual images is not entirely a new one. In the days of the early Christian church, the **iconoclasts** objected to the use of visual images as part of religious worship because such images might compete with the reverence due to God through verbal prayer. In the eighth century, Byzantine emperor Leo III ordered all images in churches to be covered or destroyed. Later, Empress Irene, also of the Byzantine Empire, permitted images as long as they were subdued. Still later, the Eastern Church found a compromise that accepted pictures but not whole statues. In the Roman Catholic Church, pictures and statues have regularly been used because the Roman popes did not join the iconoclast movement of the Eastern Church.

Chapter in Retrospect

VIGNETTE Dramaturgic Theory and Scams

Year in and year out, many people fall victim to scams (sometimes called "bunko crimes"). One of the nice things about the dramaturgic model discussed in this chap-ter is that it can add clarity to how scams work. News stories often explain why people fall for scams—often because of their own greed. Community policing campaigns warn people that "If it seems too good to be true, it probably is." In a common scam using lotteries, a stranger will walk up to the target asking for directions (the *line*). An accomplice soon joins the conversation (the *strategic secret* is that these two conspirators know each other but do not want the target to know this). The person last to arrive skillfully switches the conversa-tion from directions to a winning lottery ticket that "can't be cashed" because the third per-son is not a citizen (another *strategic secret* because in most locales, you do not have to be a citizen to claim lottery winnings). The *dark secret* is that the pair are engaged in a felony, not an ad-hoc business transaction. The general *impressions* of the proposed transaction seem friendly and legal, but these impressions are quite false.

An important *prop* here will most likely be a lottery ticket that is either a forgery or a losing ticket at which the target is not allowed to get a good look. Sometimes the prop is just discussed because it is "safely" being kept back home or at a hotel. The line of the scam now switches to an offer to share the lottery winnings with the target, who presumably can cash the winning lottery ticket without problem. The line is then further developed with what the third person will call a "good faith" deposit, where the target is asked to withdraw sev-eral thousand dollars or more from the bank in order to buy a share in the winning lottery ticket. Once the cash is handed over, the two conspirators disappear into the crowd, leaving the carefully selected target holding an empty promise. By carefully selected, I mean the tar-get is the sort of person who seems not likely to put up a fight or chase after the perpetra-tors down the street. The *front* in this case is the street where the conversation takes place. The *performances* of the two criminals have probably been practiced over and over again until they're right in terms of their nonverbal and verbal impact.

Manner and *appearance* are also very important in scams like these. Most importantly, the scam operators have to come across as believable and sincere. The target has to believe that the lottery ticket is legitimate and that the two operators are who and what they say they are. In order to maintain *dramaturgical discipline* the two operators must also get their stories straight and must support each other's lines without seeming to be trying to do so. In one recent case, a pair of scam operators used a sock as a prop to fool the target:

> The person returned to meet the couple and handed over the money. They then pretended to give it back in a stuffed sock and said they were going to retrieve the winning ticket from home, but never came back. The victim then opened the sock once the pair left—and found it stuffed with newspapers.[30]

In summary, the old saying that knowledge is power is quite true when protecting yourself from scams. Goffman's model goes a long way to giving you that power.

Summary and Conclusions

The humanistic study of persuasion predates the scientific study of persuasion by many centuries. This chapter focuses on the humanistic theories that function as analytic tools for understanding the workings of speeches and other communicative events. Burke's dramaturgic theory helps us analyze rhetorical events by defining the categories of scene, actor, act, agency, and purpose. Each of these categories can be used by the analyst to persuasively explain why a specific human event is said to have occurred the way it did, or why some new course of action should be undertaken. Aristotle's classical theory of rhetoric can be used to analyze persuasion by examining the rhetorical choices available to the persuader, including the artistic proofs of ethos, pathos, and logos; construction of enthymemes and syllogisms; and the application of topoi in creating arguments. In some ways, Goffman's theory of how people manage the impressions that others form of them emanates from Shakespeare's witty line that "All the world's a stage." Some conceptual connections can be made between Goffman's more specific theory and Burke's more general theory. Visual rhetoric concerns researchers' recent interest in accounting for how visual images can in isolation or in connection with verbal rhetoric lead to persuasive effects on attitudes, beliefs, values (especially instrumental ones), and probable actions.

KEY TERMS

act	enthymemes	logos
agency	epanaphora	manner
agent	epideictic	pathos
allegory	ethos	props (functional,
antithesis	forensic	symbolic)
appearance	frontstage	purpose
artistic proofs	iconoclasts	ratios
asyndeton	image events	scene
backstage	impressions	synecdoche
catachresis	inartistic proofs	teams
deliberative	juxtaposition	topoi
dramaturgical discipline	line	visual rhetoric

REVIEW QUESTIONS

1. How is a case study different from a scientific experiment?
2. What do scene, agent, agency, act, and purpose have in common?
3. How do scene, agent, agency, act, and purpose explain human events differently?
4. What is a pentadic ratio?
5. How are artistic and inartistic proofs different?
6. What are topoi?
7. How are impressions formed, according to Goffman?
8. What is the difference between a functional prop and a symbolic prop?
9. How may figures of speech apply to visual rhetoric?
10. Why is visual rhetoric more difficult to analyze than verbal rhetoric?

SUGGESTED PROJECTS AND ACTIVITIES

1. Choose either Burke's theory or Aristotle's theory and analyze the persuasion in a television commercial that tries to make a case for a specific purchase.
2. Explain what a visit to a fortune teller would be like, using the terminology suggested by Goffman's theory of impressions management.
3. Find a magazine-ad image that interests you. Analyze the visual rhetoric in it by asking, "What story does the image tell? Exactly how?"

QUESTIONS FOR DISCUSSION

1. How can Burke's theory and Aristotle's theory be compared and contrasted?
2. Do we ever get offstage, according to Goffman's theory? If so, where and when?
3. Is visual rhetoric more prone to ethics problems than verbal rhetoric? Explain.

Notes

1. Jo Liska and Gary Cronkhite, *An Ecological Perspective on Human Communication Theory* (Fort Worth, TX: Harcourt Brace College, 1995), 89.

2. When discussing these five terms, Burke sometimes adds a sixth term, *attitude,* to the pentad to describe the manner employed in performing an act as opposed to the means or agency used for performing the act. Kenneth Burke, *A Grammar of Motives* (Berkeley: University of California Press, 1969), 443.

3. Burke, *A Grammar of Motives,* 443–44.

4. Burke, *A Grammar of Motives,* 17.

5. J. Clarke Rountree III, "Coming to Terms with Kenneth Burke's Pentad," www.acjournal.org/holdings/vol1/iss3/burke/rountree.html (25 January 2005); David Ling, "A Pentadic Analysis of Senator Edward Kennedy's Address to the People of Massachusetts, July 25, 1969," *Central States Speech Journal* 21 (1970): 81–86.

6. Jane Blankenship, Marlene Fine, and Leslie Davis, "The 1980 Republican Primary Debates: The Transformation of Actor to Scene," *Quarterly Journal of Speech* 69, no. 1 (February 1983): 25–36.

7. Susan Mackey-Kallis and Dan Hahn, "Questions of Public Will and Private Action: The Power of the Negative in the Reagans' 'Just Say No' Morality Campaign," *Communication Quarterly* 39, no. 1 (Winter 1991): 1–17. We might note in passing here that attribution theory deals with similar prob-

lems of analysis when it asks if a given problem is attributable to external causes beyond the control of the individual or motivations within the individual.

8. James Murphy and Richard Katula, with Forbes Hill and Donovan Ochs, *Synoptic History of Classical Rhetoric* (Davis, CA: Hermagoras, 2003), 63.

9. Murphy and Katula, *Synoptic History of Classical Rhetoric*, 63.

10. Murphy and Katula, *Synoptic History of Classical Rhetoric*, 63, 101–15.

11. Murphy and Katula, *Synoptic History of Classical Rhetoric*, 79.

12. Murphy and Katula, *Synoptic History of Classical Rhetoric*, 105–15.

13. Jane Blankenship, "The Search for the 1972 Democratic Nomination: A Metaphorical Perspective," in *Rhetoric and Communication*, ed. Jane Blankenship and Hermann Stelzner (Urbana: University of Illinois Press, 1976), 236–60.

14. Murphy and Katula, *Synoptic History of Classical Rhetoric*, 115–16.

15. Cf. Lee Honeycutt, "Aristotle's Rhetoric," www.public.iastate.edu/~honeyl/Rhetoric/cite.html (23 November 2005).

16. Erving Goffman, *The Presentation of Self in Everyday Life* (Garden City, NY: Doubleday Anchor, 1959), 208–37.

17. This distinction is somewhat similar to the distinction made in chapter 3 between two types of compliance-resisting tactics: discursive and behavioral.

18. Nicholas Mirzoeff, *An Introduction to Visual Culture* (London: Routledge, 1999).

19. Charles Hill and Marguerite Helmers, eds. *Defining Visual Rhetorics* (Mahwah, NJ: Lawrence Erlbaum, 2003), 1–40.

20. Sonja Foss, "Framing the Study of Visual Rhetoric: Toward a Transformation of Rhetorical Theory," in *Defining Visual Rhetorics*, ed. Charles Hill and Marguerite Helmers (Mahwah, NJ: Lawrence Erlbaum, 2003), 303–14. For more on abduction, see Robert Almeder, *The Philosophy of Charles S. Peirce: A Critical Introduction* (Totowa, NJ: Rowman & Littlefield, 1980).

21. Jonah Rice, "A Critical Review of Visual Rhetoric in a Postmodern Age: Complementing, Extending, and Presenting New Ideas," *Review of Communication* 4, nos. 1/2 (January/April 2004): 63–74.

22. Roland Barthes, *The Fashion System*, trans. Matthew Ward and Richard Howard (New York: Hill and Wang, 1983).

23. Kevin DeLuca, *Image Politics: The New Environmental Activism* (New York: Guilford, 1999), 1–22.

24. Edward McQuarrie and David Mick, "Figures of Rhetoric in Advertising Language," *Journal of Consumer Research* 22, no. 4 (March 1996): 424–38; cf. Margot van Mulken, "Analyzing Rhetorical Devices in Print Advertisements," *Document Design* 4, no. 2 (June 2003): 114–28.

25. Murphy and Katula, *Synoptic History of Classical Rhetoric*, 139–49.

26. For a brief summary of the model discussed in *Traité du signe visuel: Pour une rhétorique de l'image* (Paris: Seuil, 1992), see van Mulken, "Analyzing Rhetorical Devices," 114–28.

27. Edward R. Tufte, *Visual Explanations: Images and Quantities, Evidence and Narrative* (Cheshire, CT: Graphics Press, 1997), 79–99, 105–15, 121–28.

28. My example here was inspired by a work of art by California artist Robert Therrien, who, in this untitled sculpture, created an oversized dining-room table and separate chairs to perhaps explore the forgotten perspectives of childhood. This resulted in an artwork that at once perceptually destabilized and transformed both the viewer's internal perspective and the viewer's external physical setting, which in this case was the lobby of an office building. The work was completely realistic, looking exactly like the real thing except larger (the table and chairs appeared to have been made of a hardwood of some type, but were actually made of lightweight metal).

29. Marguerite Helmers, "Framing the Fine Arts through Rhetoric," in Hill and Helmers, *Defining Visual Rhetorics*, 63–86.

30. Selim Algar, "Cruel Lotto Scam: Victim Loses 20G," *New York Post*, 2 August 2005, 29.

Persuasion and Politics

In politics, an organized minority is a political majority.

—JESSE JACKSON

The right to be heard does not automatically include the right to be taken seriously.

—HUBERT H. HUMPHREY

Whenever two good people argue over principles, they are both right.

—MARIE EBNER VON ESCHENBACH

He that goeth about to persuade a multitude, that they are not so well governed as they ought to be, shall never want attentive and favorable hearers.

—RICHARD HOOKER, ca. 1554–1600

MODERN GOVERNMENTS use a variety of message forms to influence the actions of other governments and their respective societies. These forms include diplomatic notes and memos, state visits, "hot line" telephone calls, communicating with ambassadors and other representatives, and speeches. As part of this external communication, governments sometimes involve their own people in the process by conducting investigative hearings and holding press conferences and publicized trials. Speeches in particular are a favored way for governments to engage their people in building political resolve during an external crisis. In addition, governments have always had the need to use persuasion or propaganda to manage the political affairs of their citizens through an orderly process—democratically or autocratically.

People and political factions also seek to influence the actions of their own governments. As communication theorist Dan Hahn notes, one unifying theme underlying most of this **internal political communication** concerns **freedom** versus **order**. On particular issues, blocks of people may desire maximum freedom to serve their own interests on matters of finance, religion, education, business, national security, welfare, and so on.[1] At the same time, other blocks of people may seek order on these very same issues. You may want order when it comes to conserving the nation's economic, political, or cultural resources; I may want the nation to have the freedom to use those resources for what I consider good reasons. Or I may want to express my political point of view in a style or with purposes that violate your perceived need for order. Political communication is also about the ever-ongoing question of who will do the accommodating on the various issues of the day and who will not. In the following pages, I will examine and analyze examples of the persuasive communication used by government, organized **interest groups** that seek to influence government, and political parties seeking to legally gain or maintain control of government. In the next chapter, I will then examine persuasive forces seeking political change through campaigns, movements, and publics.

Political communication often concerns matters that are difficult to see up close, such as the operation of the economy, foreign policy, taxation, social services, and education. Political leaders must as a consequence find rhetorical means to communicate the big picture for each of these policy matters. This communication often depends on figurative language, such as the archetypal metaphors of earth, wind, sky, sun and stars, sea, and fire. As we've noted, political persuasion also relies on the cultural premises and myths accepted by people in particular societies. Thus, when a politician argues, "We must continue to build a future that is safe, secure, and does not saddle our children with massive debt," that statement resonates well with a basic value of many people who see the success of their children as an extension of the success they themselves have achieved or in some cases have not achieved. The statement also resonates with the mental picture that many Americans have of building a nation where there had been only wilderness. When a U.S. secretary of defense uses a phrase like "shock and awe" in describing a future military action, the American public may become politically divided by the intense tone of the words and their implications about what constitutes acceptable policies for national security. The theme of order versus freedom can even be seen in political intrigues among nations, as happened in America at the time of the American Revolution, the Civil War (which also included meddling by foreign powers), the world wars, and the cold war.

Presidential Persuasion

In the next sections, we examine the order versus freedom issue as it provided a context for two presidential speeches: John F. Kennedy's Cuban Missile Crisis speech of 1962, and Abraham Lincoln's Gettysburg Address, given during the American Civil War. In both cases, one side wanted the freedom to do as it wished, and the other side wanted the security of an orderly status quo. In the first instance, the Soviets wanted maximum flexibility in pursuing what they claimed were their legitimate security interests, and the United States wanted the Soviets to play by the rules on the matter of installing offensive nuclear weapons in Cuba. In the second, the American South wanted, among other things, maximum flexibility in deciding whether to remain in the Union; and the North wanted, among other things, the South to live up to the commitment it had made in joining the Union. This section will also examine the persuasive potential of the modern presidential press conference as it is practiced in the twenty-four-hours-a-day news cycle of today's political arenas.

The Cuban Missile Crisis Speech

On September 28, 1962, U.S. Navy reconnaissance aircraft photographed ten crates on the decks of the Cuba-bound Soviet ship *Kasimov*. These photographs and others (of other Soviet ships en route to Cuba) were later interpreted as showing Soviet Ilyushin bombers that could carry nuclear warheads. A small number of tactical nuclear warheads were also believed to have been delivered. Two weeks later, a U.S. U2 reconnaissance plane got photographic evidence of ballistic missile sites on Cuba (at least three SS-5 IRBM [intermediate range ballistic missile] sites, which could fire missiles with ranges up to 2,200 miles). U.S. defense secretary Robert McNamara had previously outlined six scenarios for possible U.S. military action in Cuba: (1) another Soviet blockade of Berlin, (2) evidence of offensive weapons on Cuban soil, (3) an attack against the U.S. naval base at Guantánamo, (4) a substantial uprising in Cuba, (5) Cuban armed assistance to other parts of the Western Hemisphere, and (6) presidential national-security decisions. A debate now began on whether to blockade Cuba, attack and destroy the offensive weapons, or invade to topple the Castro regime. As the White House began talks, experts tried to estimate how long it would take before the weapons in Cuba would be operational. The estimates, initially of weeks, became days, and finally hours.[2]

On October 16, 1962, Soviet premier Nikita Khrushchev received U.S. ambassador Foy Kohler and stated that the USSR was helping the Cubans build a "fishing port" and had no military interest in Cuba. A Soviet spokesman, Andrei Gromyko, met with President Kennedy, assuring him that Soviet military actions in Cuba were purely defensive. Kennedy did not tell Gromyko that the United States had photographs suggesting the presence of missiles. Next, U.S. attorney general Robert Kennedy asked that a document be drawn up justifying the blockade option. When President Kennedy was told by military advisors that an air strike would at best be 90 percent effective, the decision was made for a blockade (called a "quarantine" to avoid a public perception of belligerence). According to author Raymond Garthoff, the decision caught Soviet leaders by surprise: "Ambassador Dobrynin called in by Secretary Rusk and given a copy of the speech an hour before it was delivered, arrived in a relaxed mood but left 'ashen-faced' and 'visibly shaken.'"[3]

Analysis of the Speech On October 22, President Kennedy turned to the most powerful rhetorical force he had, a speech on nighttime television to the American people and the world (see box 12.1).[4] Actually, Kennedy had prepared two speeches to keep his options open until the last minute, one announcing the "quarantine" and one an air strike. As it happened, he gave the quarantine speech, which took about seventeen minutes. Kennedy told startled Americans, some hearing the news for the first time, that he had "unmistakable evidence" that there were Soviet MRBM (medium range ballistic missile) and IRBM sites and nuclear-capable bombers on Cuba. He then explained what, as president, he would order to be done. First, there would be a strict quarantine on deliveries of all offensive military equipment. Kennedy chillingly then stated that any missile fired from Cuba would be regarded as an attack by the Soviet Union on the United States, requiring a full retaliatory response against the Soviet Union. (To make things even more harrowing, Khrushchev would subsequently (1) order Soviet ships, under surveillance by the U.S. Navy, to hold their courses for Cuba; (2) refer to the quarantine as piracy on the high seas; and (3) threaten unnamed responses to any U.S. interdiction of Soviet ships.[5]) The initial success of Kennedy's speech can be measured in a poll taken October 23, in which Gallup found that 84 percent of the U.S. public that knew about the Cuban situation favored the quarantine, with 4 percent opposing. This speech took a *problem-solution* pattern.

In characterizing the USSR's motives, President Kennedy speaks as one who has identified a problem: "The purposes of these [missile] bases can be none other than to provide a nuclear strike capability against the Western Hemisphere." Kennedy describes the USSR as transforming Cuba into a forward nuclear-attack base. He alludes to their trying to sneak a powerful weapon past U.S. intelligence services. (We could argue today that the actual purpose of these installations was probably not war, although Kennedy hedges on this, but rather to gain a power advantage, perhaps forcing America to withdraw U.S. missiles from Turkey or concede further political inroads by the USSR in Central or South America.) Thus, by saying what the Soviets are employing (secrecy) and what they are deploying (dangerous military

---

BOX 12.1

Excerpts from President John F. Kennedy's
Cuban Missile Crisis Speech

October 22, 1962

Good evening, my fellow citizens. This Government, as promised, has maintained the closest surveillance of the Soviet military build-up on the island of Cuba. Within the past week unmistakable evidence has established the fact that a series of offensive missile sites is now in preparation on that imprisoned island. The purposes of these bases can be none other than to provide a nuclear strike capability against the Western Hemisphere....

The characteristics of these new missile sites indicate two distinct types of installations. Several of them include medium-range ballistic missiles capable of carrying a nuclear warhead for a distance of more than 1,000 nautical miles. Each of these missiles, in short, is capable of striking Washington, D.C., the Panama Canal, Cape Canaveral, Mexico City, or any other city in the southeastern part of the United States, in Central America, or in the Caribbean area....

The size of this undertaking makes clear that it has been planned for some months. Yet only last month, after I had made clear the distinction between any introduction of ground-to-ground missiles and the existence of defensive antiaircraft missiles, the Soviet Government publicly stated on September 1 that, and I quote, "The armaments and military equipment sent to Cuba are designed exclusively for defensive purposes." . . . That statement was false.

Only last Thursday, as evidence of this rapid offensive build-up was already in my hand, Soviet Foreign Minister Gromyko told me in my office that he was instructed to make it clear once again, as he said his Government had already done, that Soviet assistance to Cuba, and I quote, "pursued solely the purpose of contributing to the defense capabilities of Cuba." . . . That statement also was false. . . .

For many years both the Soviet Union and the United States, recognizing this fact, have deployed strategic nuclear weapons with great care, never upsetting the precarious status quo which insured that these weapons would not be used in the absence of some vital challenge. . . . American citizens have become adjusted to living daily on the bull's eye of Soviet missiles located inside the U.S.S.R. or in submarines. . . .

Acting, therefore, in the defense of our own security and of the entire Western Hemisphere, and under the authority entrusted to me by the Constitution as endorsed by the resolution of the Congress, I have directed that the following initial steps be taken immediately:

First: To halt this offensive build-up, a strict quarantine on all offensive military equipment under shipment to Cuba is being initiated. . . .

Second: I have directed the continued and increased close surveillance of Cuba and its military build-up. . . .

Third: It shall be the policy of this nation to regard any nuclear missile launched from Cuba against any nation in the Western Hemisphere as an attack by the Soviet Union on the United States, requiring a full retaliatory response upon the Soviet Union.

Fourth: As a necessary military precaution I have reinforced our base at Guantánamo, evacuated today the dependents of our personnel there, and ordered additional military units to be on a standby alert basis.

Fifth: We are calling tonight for an immediate meeting of the Organ of Consultation, under the Organization of American States, to consider this threat to hemispheric security and to invoke articles six and eight of the Rio Treaty in support of all necessary action. . . .

Sixth: Under the Charter of the United Nations, we are asking tonight that an emergency meeting of the Security Council be convoked without delay to take action against this latest Soviet threat to world peace. . . .

Seventh and finally: I call upon Chairman Khrushchev to halt and eliminate this clandestine, reckless, and provocative threat to world peace and to stable relations between our two nations. . . .

Finally, I want to say a few words to the captive people of Cuba, to whom this speech is being directly carried by special radio facilities. I speak to you as a friend, as one who knows of your deep attachment to your fatherland, as one who shares your aspirations for liberty and justice for all. And I have watched and the American people have watched with deep sorrow how your nationalist revolution was betrayed and how your fatherland fell under foreign domination. Now your leaders are no longer Cuban leaders inspired by Cuban ideals. They are puppets and agents of an international conspiracy which has turned Cuba against your friends and neighbors in the Americas—and turned it into the first Latin American country to become a target for nuclear war, the first Latin American country to have these weapons on its soil.

hardware not needed for security back home, a point that even they conceded after first deny-ing placing missiles in Cuba), Kennedy shows us what he believes Soviet motives are. Now Kennedy can argue that Cuba has been altered in unacceptable ways by the USSR's actions.

What was most effective in this speech was the use of aerial photographs that were said to show installations for offensive nuclear missiles on Cuban soil. Perhaps none of the words spoken by President Kennedy would have been credible if the pictures, as *visual rhetoric*, were not available. While Kennedy in this address would next speak about what America would deploy as a response to the missile emplacements, the photographs were a pivotal force in themselves for the success of his speech.

President Kennedy's characterization of America's problem-solving role in the crisis portrays the American president as acting on behalf of Americans and people of the Western Hemisphere. The solutions listed by Kennedy include standing orders to blockade Soviet ships nearing Cuba and found to contain offensive weapons, "continued and increased close surveillance of Cuba and its military build-up," and the placing of "additional military units . . . on a standby alert basis" (to be used against the Soviet Union for any missiles launched against America from Cuban soil). Kennedy's purpose is defined as protecting peace, secu-rity, and the status quo in the Western Hemisphere—especially the basin in which Cuba sits and the geographic ranges that Soviet-installed missiles will now reach with ease.

In analyzing the success of President Kennedy's handling of the Cuban Missile Crisis, there now seem to be two schools of thought. The more traditional perspective is that Kennedy took a calculated risk and went eye-to-eye with the Soviets, and the Soviets "blinked." A more recent revisal of this perspective suggests that the crucial factors for resolv-ing the crisis were two concessions: one that the United States would dismantle its missile sites in Turkey (this idea did come up as a possible bargaining chip in the White House delib-erations), and second, that the United States would promise never to invade Cuba. So from a political perspective, which of the two leaders, Kennedy or Khrushchev, got the better of the other, if either one in fact did? Kennedy may have been the smarter of the two, but Khrushchev may have been the shrewder of the two. Notice that Kennedy and his advisors worried about the moral and legal aspects of their decisions; we can only wonder if Khrushchev and his Politburo worried in a similar way. Both men had powerful nuclear and conventional arsenals behind them. Some historians today even argue that what Kennedy did was roll the dice in an unjustified gamble that could have led to nuclear war.

Perhaps the crucial detail of the crisis came down to who would persuasively commu-nicate significant resolve first. Would Khrushchev install, arm, and present the missile instal-lations as a fait accompli, or would Kennedy have the resolve to act before the missiles were armed and could be used or "saber-rattled?" As a claim of first resolve, Kennedy made use of his ample persuasive skills in his televised speech. In the speech he accomplished several rhetorical goals that connected well with Americans and their allies at that time by describ-ing (1) the Soviet Union's provocative behavior, which would seriously threaten security in the Western Hemisphere; (2) Soviet and Cuban ambitions, deceitfulness, and aggressiveness; (3) his own plan to seek remediation for the situation; and (4) his confidence that the American spirit would bring the crisis to a peaceful resolution. Kennedy further reminded Americans of how their nation had failed to act soon enough prior to World War II, and because of their national timidity had allowed fascist dictators to almost conquer the world—thus Americans had a sacred duty to respond.

Lastly, Kennedy spoke directly to the Cuban people. He reminded them of their history of rising up to throw out tyrants, and how they had been recently betrayed by an international conspiracy that had turned Cuba against its friends and neighbors in the Americas. He also argued that nuclear weapons would not give them more security, but just the opposite. It may be possible that Kennedy was playing a wild card here, hoping to cause a popular uprising. Kennedy closed by reminding Americans that the cost of freedom is always high—but Americans had always paid it, since the beginning—and by saying that Americans would act and would never take the path to surrender or submission. Had the nuclear weapons and launching sites not been removed in 1962, we should remember, they might still be there today.

Persuasive Lessons Learned What can be learned from the Cuban Missile Crisis speech may be that persuaders sometimes do succeed when taking bold, calculated risks. The speech was apparently carefully researched, strategically organized, and very carefully worded. The likely reaction of its audiences, including the press, would have been considered. At the same time, the speech was not a diatribe, though neither was it apologetic, timid, or unsure. It seems to have spent its rhetorical capital shrewdly (although not all contemporary critics would agree with this assessment). Kennedy's risk taking in making this speech paralleled his risk taking in setting the policy that was announced in the speech. He could have apologized for taking the actions he announced—but did not. He could have been bellicose in manner—but was not. He could have been accommodating and compromise oriented—but would not. The speech's boldness seemed to catch everyone by surprise. Most importantly, the speech's timing had to be perfect. At a different point in time it might have backfired horribly, or just failed.

Governments also use internal political communication to promote unity of purpose and to provide for such things as the common defense and the general welfare of their citizens. In healthy societies this communication moves both ways—from government to citizens and from citizens to government—and at important moments in the history of some societies, a leader may come to the forefront to communicate in an exceptional way. The following case study of Abraham Lincoln's Gettysburg Address illustrates some of the personal qualities that are needed by leaders for these special historical moments. Actually there were two Gettysburg Addresses, one that lasted nearly two hours and was given by Edward Everett, the main speaker of the day, and Lincoln's, a formal, dedicatory statement in the funeral tradition of the ancient Greeks, and which lasted barely several minutes. It was Lincoln's brief speech, not Everett's, that stood the test of time.

Lincoln's Gettysburg Address

On the morning of November 19, 1863, Abraham Lincoln, having journeyed by train to Gettysburg, Pennsylvania, presided over the dedication of the Soldiers' National Cemetery at Gettysburg, now reserved for those who had fallen at the Battle of Gettysburg. He gave a brief speech consisting of about 270 words, or one double-spaced page of modern typing, but it was one of the most notable (and perhaps one of the most persuasive) speeches in history. The Battle of Gettysburg had occurred four months earlier in July, and Lincoln probably felt an obligation to say something about the great losses of the battle that had raged for several days. But he was also in the midst of a political nightmare and could not just go off to have a good time at a dedication ceremony. He needed to make the ceremony and his speech count for something. And the speech's brief length meant that it could be printed on the front pages of the nation's newspapers in the North and the West. Lincoln may have gotten as much exposure for his talk as would today a State of the Union address.

As the website for the Gettysburg National Cemetery notes, Gettysburg was probably the most decisive battle of the Civil War and the highwater mark for the Confederacy. Confederate casualties neared twenty thousand, with Union losses slightly higher, before the Southern soldiers began their retreat on the fourth of July. It was a bloody battle with rifle- and saber-wielding soldiers, cavalry, and cannons going at each other from extremely close distances. After this battle, the overall momentum of the war gradually shifted to the North. Perhaps the Gettysburg Address began a political momentum to match the military one.[6]

One line in the speech turned out to contain a wrong prediction; here Lincoln modestly says, "The world will little note nor long remember, what we say here, but it can never forget what they did here." Perhaps we can forgive this error in light of Lincoln's sense of personal modesty. Or perhaps it was merely a part of his technique to move his listeners in the profound way in which he needed them to be moved, given the dire circumstances of the war. The world has long remembered what Lincoln said there, and what he said reads almost like a poem. The speech contains five paragraphs. Each paragraph serves a very definite purpose in moving its readers (and original listeners) along a carefully prepared rhetorical path. In practical terms, Lincoln skillfully transforms a speech of dedication to one of persuasion—and does so in the space of a minute or so (see box 12.2).

Analysis of the Gettysburg Address The first paragraph of the speech begins with the familiar words "Four score and seven years ago," a reference to 1776, the date of the Declaration of Independence. In this first paragraph, Lincoln wants to remind his listeners and readers of the birth of a **Great Experiment** whereby a new nation would place the common people in a prominent position within the political power structure. Previous to the founding of America, most nations and empires of the world were ruled by tribal chiefs, kings, emperors, or dictators who jealously guarded power, perhaps sharing some of that power with family members or aristocratic supporters. For the American Founding Fathers and then later Lincoln, this Great Experiment envisioned God giving power to the people—who then temporarily lent it to elected sets of representatives for limited amounts of time. It is not unlikely that the great ruling powers of the world privately scoffed at such a novel way to create a country, perhaps predicting that such a nation could not last. One key concept for our understanding of this speech's opening paragraph is that of historical context. Lincoln wants his audience to remember that as they stand with him at Gettysburg, they are profoundly participating in the eighty-seventh year of this Great Experiment in democracy.

The next paragraph of the speech also has a historical context, but this time it refers to a time span of just several years, encompassing the then raging Civil War. Here Lincoln wants his listeners to remember that they are now witnessing a great threat to the Great Experiment. Perhaps they can almost imagine hearing distant cannon fire as he speaks. And we should remember that the powers of the world, upon learning of America's civil war, may have said to themselves, "We told you so—you cannot put power into the hands of common

BOX 12.2

President Abraham Lincoln's Gettysburg Address

November 1863

[1] Four score and seven years ago, our fathers brought forth upon this continent a new nation: conceived in liberty, and dedicated to the proposition that all men are created equal.

[2] Now we are engaged in a great civil war . . . testing whether that nation, or any nation so conceived and so dedicated . . . can long endure. We are met on a great battlefield of that war.

[3] We have come to dedicate a portion of that field as a final resting place for those who here gave their lives that this nation might live. It is altogether fitting and proper that we should do this.

[4] But, in a larger sense, we cannot dedicate . . . we cannot consecrate . . . we cannot hallow this ground. The brave men, living and dead, who struggled here have consecrated it, far above our poor power to add or detract. The world will little note, nor long remember, what we say here, but it can never forget what they did here.

[5] It is for us the living, rather, to be dedicated here to the unfinished work which they who fought here have thus far so nobly advanced. It is rather for us to be here dedicated to the great task remaining before us . . . that from these honored dead we take increased devotion to that cause for which they gave the last full measure of devotion . . . that we here highly resolve that these dead shall not have died in vain . . . that this nation, under God, shall have a new birth of freedom . . . and that government of the people . . . by the people . . . for the people . . . shall not perish from this earth.

people." That Lincoln saw the Civil War as an angry wind set upon the flickering candlelight of worldwide democracy shows through with his words "testing whether that nation, or any nation so conceived and so dedicated . . . can long endure." His listeners have now been reminded of where things stand politically and historically.

The third paragraph reminds Lincoln's listeners of the obvious occasion of the speech. But in a way this short paragraph sets up his audience to have the "rug pulled out from under their feet," rhetorically speaking. Thus, Lincoln says, "We have come to dedicate a portion of that field as a final resting place for those who here gave their lives that this nation might live. It is altogether fitting and proper that we should do this." At this point, listeners attending the speech might have heard a *but* coming, and indeed, a momentous *but* comes in the next paragraph.

The fourth paragraph is where this good speech became a great speech. Lincoln begins by telling his listeners that the assembled "cannot dedicate . . . cannot consecrate . . . cannot hallow" the ground on which they are standing. His humility again shows through here when he says his words have "poor power to add or detract" from what has occurred. His main point is that the lifeblood of the soldiers who fell three months earlier has soaked deeply into the ground underfoot; it is this bloodshed that hallows, consecrates, and dedicates the land to be now used as a cemetery. And with Lincoln having rhetorically admitted that the dedication ceremony has little real import, the unasked question meandering through the audience on that perhaps chilly November day may have been "So what *can* we do here if we cannot honor this ground?"

The fifth paragraph provides the answer to the unasked question of the fourth. Here Lincoln sets a standard: We the living must do much to accomplish the task before us. How much must we do? Let us use the standard followed by the fallen soldiers to judge what we must do in the coming days, weeks, and months of the war. Let us inspire ourselves as we take on these difficult tasks by remembering what the fallen youthful soldiers have contributed to our cause—their limbs, their eyesight, their lives, the impact their future lives might have had on their families and communities back home. Lincoln also suggests that failure in completing the task will mean that what the fallen have given will have been for nothing. The latter part of this paragraph sets forth a vision—that the Great Experiment will eventually become a great nation. At its birth, America set in place the principles of freedom, equality, and justice. But for political and economic reasons having to do with the plantation economy of the South, those principles were not yet in place for African Americans. But with the phrase "a new birth of freedom," Lincoln delicately forecasts that these great principles will eventually become great practices over the coming decades and into the next century.

One of the nicest things about the Gettysburg Address is its kindness to both sides. There is none of the insistence on the evil of the opposition forces that might have come from the lips of a lesser person. The only allusion to evil is perhaps in that the speech serves as a sort of second Declaration of Independence, this time not from Great Britain, but rather from the Old World evil of slavery that had been practiced for thousands of years in Europe, Asia, and Africa. And looking back today, we see that Lincoln's vision indeed became the practice of the land (and of much of the world for that matter).[7] As one of the last significant things he did with his life before being assassinated by John Wilkes Booth, Lincoln gave a boost to the cause of human freedom by promoting the Thirteenth Amendment to the American Constitution, which outlawed slavery. In the last line of the Gettysburg Address, Lincoln may have hit his highest point when he says so poetically, "that government of the people . . . by the people . . . for the people . . . shall not perish from this earth." So far it has not.

Persuasive Lessons Learned Visually, Lincoln spoke from the actual battlefield on which so many had died. Given what we said in chapter 2 on environmentalics, he could not have chosen a better place from which to make the persuasive arguments he spoke. Lincoln made persuasive use of three historical contexts: (1) the Great Experiment, which was then in its eighty-seventh year; (2) the greatest threat to the Great Experiment, then in its third year; and (3) the dedication ceremony for the fallen soldiers. Lincoln skillfully used these three contexts to help listeners and later readers envision themselves as people who would see the war to its successful completion with acts of patriotism and self-sacrifice. His audience would especially need courage and persistence to succeed.

One insight gained from this analysis of the Gettysburg Address might be that persuasive messages should never be longer than minimum standards of success require. I once sat on a jury and heard an attorney begin to summarize his case with the words "I have here written on my pad thirty-eight reasons why you should not convict my client of driving while intoxicated." I thought to myself, "I hope you are not going to talk about *all* of them." The attorney did.

A second insight concerns the sincere use of modesty. A more aggressive persuader than Lincoln might have bombarded his audience with overwhelming persuasive points that would seem to say, "I'm really right in what I say; you too can be right if you'll just take my words as the definitive explanation." If you think you have a definitive explanation, let others proclaim this. Actually, confidence does often work in a persuasive message, but the hyperbolic confidence sometimes expressed by partisan persuaders or propagandists may not win over as many converts as such people imagine. Then you end up preaching to the choir.

Also evident in this case study is the need for successful persuaders to build on what an audience already believes in or agrees with. The first three paragraphs of the speech state obvious facts about the situation, facts that few reasonable people would contest. Lincoln then tells the audience that there is one thing—that some of them may believe—that is probably not true (i.e., that it is possible for them to consecrate, dedicate, or hallow the ground). But even here he softens this analysis with the phrase "in a larger sense." This allows his audience members to retain a sense that their assumptions about what can be done are both true *and* false. Thus, Lincoln too may have spent his persuasive capital wisely in the speech, asking for no more indulgence from the audience than was rhetorically necessary for his purpose. Persuaders today can put this idea to work by analyzing any rhetorical situation with two lists: a list of those things that are not in dispute, and a list of those things that are in dispute. Do not waste your persuasive capital trying to convince people of what they already accept. Rather, remind them of these things, but only as you build an area of agreement. And then for those items that are in dispute, choose your goals for persuasion judiciously. Do not engage in every battle you encounter. Pick today's persuasive objectives selectively so that your credibility with an audience can survive for providing persuasive leadership tomorrow.

Many others over the past 140 years have analyzed the Gettysburg Address. Rhetorical theorist Edwin Black noted that Lincoln's speech at Gettysburg addressed the ages, had an oracular quality, followed a theme that ran from life to death to resurrection, skillfully transformed important ideas, made historical contexts relevant, distanced itself from ceremony, and played on the words and sense of dedicating a cemetery and dedicating an audience.[8] Anthony Pratkanis and Elliot Aronson observed that Lincoln needed to use the speech to justify the war, justify the **Emancipation Proclamation**, and heal the nation. And in Lincoln's referring to 1776 (the date of the Declaration of Independence) rather than 1789 (the date of state legislatures' ratification of the Constitution, which at its inception did not outlaw slavery), Pratkanis and Aronson portray Lincoln as using rhetorical sleight of hand.[9] Ronald Reid reported that the newspaper responses of the day were animated, if partisan.[10]

Major presidential speeches with such lasting effects are infrequent, but the **press conference** is used frequently today and apparently is also a very persuasive form.

Presidential Press Conferences

Q Getting back to Social Security for a moment, sir, would you consider it a success if Congress were to pass a piece of legislation that dealt with the long-term solvency problem, but did not include personal [Social Security] accounts?

THE PRESIDENT: I feel strongly that there needs to be voluntary personal savings accounts as a part of the Social Security system. I mean, it's got to be a part of a comprehensive package. The reason I feel strongly about that is that we've got a lot of debt out there, a lot of unfunded liabilities, and our workers need to be able to earn a better rate of return on our [sic] money to help deal with that debt.[11]

One of the most direct ways a president can communicate with the public is with a news or press conference. Though these events may seem at first to be more informative, political researchers Judith Trent and Robert Friedenberg remind us that in many ways, a presidential press conference can be persuasive. Trent and Friedenberg identify several purposes of press conferences: (1) they give the president the attention of a variety of media audiences because the conference in itself is somewhat novel, the president can focus the conference around a newsworthy event, and because reporters have come to rely on such conferences for reliable information; (2) they give the president the opportunity to focus the public's attention on one or a few issues of concern; and (3) they give the president the opportunity to establish rapport with reporters whose help the president may need in future times to get messages out to the people. Over the decades, some presidents have been more inclined to hold press conferences and some less inclined. During these conferences, as most of us know, reporters ask questions for the president to answer.[12]

Trent and Friedenberg believe that there are at least seven reasons why presidents really control these conferences and therefore have the opportunity in them to persuade the public who hear, watch, or later read about the conference. First, a president gets to pick the time of the conference, which may favor the salience of one or more issues of current public concern over others. Second, the president picks the place of the conference, which can offer a helpful or even symbolic background for the ensuing give-and-take. A third especially important feature is that the president will often read an opening statement, which can set the tone and agenda for the coming questions. Fourth, the president can restructure the questions asked in order to answer them on friendlier terms. A fifth reason is the $Q = A + 1$ tactic, in which the president answers a reporter's question, perhaps very briefly, and then adds a point that helps the president's case on an issue beyond or only loosely related to that one question. Sixth, presidents in more modern times have been known to have friendly reporters ask questions that the president wants badly to have the opportunity to answer. And seventh, the president may acknowledge particular reporters and so allow them to ask their questions, perhaps favoring certain reporters and not favoring others.

It should be noted, however, that during times of crisis or scandal, the reporters at press conferences may at times dog the president (or the president's press secretary) with questions the president would rather sidestep or answer briefly before moving on to other topics.

While presidents by definition try to influence citizens, at other times citizens try to influence presidents and government. At such times these citizens need to band together and speak with a unified voice, because in larger societies it is often difficult for one individual to be heard. If you have ever tried solving a problem you may have had with a large bureaucracy or corporation, you may appreciate the problem. Perhaps one of the oldest methods for communicating with government is the petition. But in modern societies, communicating with government has become a finely tuned art, if not a science. You might go out today and buy a book that will tell you how to amplify your voice by organizing an interest group that seeks to influence the policies and laws of the nation. Here too you will see the underlying theme proposed by Hahn of order versus freedom that we mentioned at the beginning of this chapter. Interest groups usually have very clear ideas about how either more order or more freedom will serve the interests of their members, issue by issue.

Influence by Interest Groups

As I've noted, there are perhaps as many as twenty-five thousand interest groups in America alone, many of which send representatives to Washington, D.C.[13] Social commentator Jonathan Rauch thinks it is better to call these organizations "interest groups" rather than "special interest groups" because the word "special" creates the false impression that interest groups solely seek the interests of the rich, famous, and powerful. Almost everyone is represented by interest groups by choice or just by happenstance. If you are a student, perhaps the nation's paper-products industries want to make sure that you can go to college so they can sell you notebooks and other paper goods. Even U.S. taxpayers are represented by the American Taxpayers' Association, whether they join or not. Rauch believes that the government's ability to solve problems is constrained by the collective influence of these groups; the groups limit the government to moving in directions where existing privileges beneficial to one group or another can be improved but seldom reduced and almost never taken away. How do these groups protect their turf? They use political action, which especially requires political communication.

To give you an idea of how much political communication goes on today, I might tell you that in 1955 there were only five thousand registered associations lobbying in Washington, D.C. The **AARP** (American Association of Retired People) had no members before 1960 but has more than 35 million today. Twenty-five thousand corporate executives have also banded together to pursue their interests. And municipal employees unions have more than 12 million members.[14] Today, many types of people and organizations form interest groups, including companies, trade employees, reformers, activists, the aggrieved, and a host of smaller, "me-too" types. They all play by the same rules regardless of their ultimate goals. And while we understandably think of corporations as having power and money, the National Wildlife Federation had 4 million members in 1997, $80 million in revenues, a plush headquarters, and a president who earned more than $300,000 a year in salary and benefits. The reason for all this added political organization is the increased size of the public sector. The more money collected through taxation, the more money there is with which the government can influence society through spending (to pay government staff and to buy goods and services for entitlements, programs, and policy enforcement); thus, better-organized groups can benefit more from the outflow of money and influence from government.

Tactics and Strategies of Interest Groups

One prime activity of interest groups is lobbying members of legislative bodies. Interest-group staffers mobilize their members or lobbyists to visit representatives' offices, arming them with "talking points" designed to persuade the representatives to vote one way or another on a specific bill identified by the interest group as important to its goals. The strategy is to suggest with this communication that if the representative votes the wrong way for the interest group's members, they will remember the next time the representative seeks reelection. These persuasive visits can be augmented by phone calls, e-mails, faxes, letters, and signed petitions. The messages more than likely take a "good citizen" tone, speaking about what's good for the entire nation, but the benefits of the positions promoted will often go disproportionately to the group's members.

It has also become much easier today to create organizations that will communicate with government on behalf of a newly defined set of members. Personal computers, database software, e-mail, websites, **weblogs**, and mailing software make it much easier to recruit and coordinate members, raise funds for them, and seek benefits on their behalf. In fact, there are organizations such as Advocacy Institute Training that will help newly formed organizations learn how to plan strategy, build coalitions, use the media for advocacy, and make use of the latest communication technology. The Whetherstone Project does similar things. And you can buy *The Lobbying Handbook* (John L. Zorack [collected by], Washington, D.C.: Professional Lobbying and Consulting Center, 1990), which contains important information on how to proceed. There also are a number of how-to books designed for specific groups (e.g., scientists, engineers, church pastors). Sometimes small organizations can get grants from larger organizations such as the Unitarian Church Environmental Charity. The National Association of Home Builders, to take another example, has a manual that explains how to organize and run telephone banks, house-to-house canvassing, and "victory caravans" to transport volunteers. Not only can you find help in getting started, but organizations sometimes will help each other out in mobilizing against an opposed government policy or legislative initiative.

Unfortunately, there is so much grassroots, politically organized, persuasive communication today that it is very difficult for government to engage in helpful solving of large problems. If a politician were to propose curbing for environmental reasons the use of disposable diapers (millions are used and thrown away every day), numerous interest groups could come together to defeat the proposed policy. Or if that politician proposed forming a "homeland-security draft" for patrolling airports, harbors, and so on, numerous interest groups might rise up to support or oppose the proposition. Changing the status quo is a most difficult thing to do—usually because those who benefit from the status quo will have more to lose than those who might benefit from a change. For example, I might be upset about a tax break given to manufacturers of widgets, but the manufacturers in turn would stand to lose substantial amounts of money each year if the tax break were eliminated. However, even if I or my interest group were successful in ending the tax break, my federal taxes would probably not go down even one cent. How hard will a group of tax reformers fight, in this case, compared to how hard the widget people will fight to protect their tax break?

The AARP: An Interest Group in Action

One of the biggest and most influential interest groups in America is the AARP, which represents more than 35 million Americans over fifty. The AARP has a national headquarters; offices in every state, as well as in the District of Columbia, the Virgin Islands, and Puerto Rico; and 3,500 local chapters.[15] The AARP's national headquarters coordinates the activities of the field operations and state offices, and it has approximately 1,800 paid staff, which provide members, volunteers, and the public with administrative support and issue and technical expertise. The staff work under the direction of the AARP's executive director and CEO, who in turn reports to the Executive Committee of the policy-making board of directors.

In addition, over 160,000 AARP members serve as volunteers to help fulfill the AARP's mission, including the twenty-one member, all-volunteer board of directors. The organization gets its funding from members' annual dues and from royalty fees paid by commercial companies that provide AARP-endorsed services.

With all of this organization and funding, how does the AARP influence the public policies of the day? Very effectively. AARP-lead volunteers often appear before the U.S. Congress to testify about a wide array of issues affecting people over fifty. According to the AARP, the organization keeps daily watch on proposed federal legislation and works hard to keep legislators informed of the AARP's views. The AARP also participates in coalitions with other national groups to support or oppose specific legislation. Recent issues have included seeking consumer protection against predatory lending practices, fighting discrimination that is based on age or disability, and lobbying for a prescription-drug benefit in Medicare. AARP attorneys identify cases whose outcome could have a significant impact on a broad segment of the older American population or could set important precedents. The AARP files amicus briefs and supports third-party lawsuits to promote the interests of its members.

The AARP explains that it is nonpartisan and does not use a political action committee (PAC). And although it does not endorse political candidates or contribute money to political parties or candidates' campaigns, it does engage in voter education. To educate its members and others, the AARP asks political candidates to explain their views on specific issues so that its members can make more informed choices in elections. Volunteers from the organization in various states hold workshops to educate voters on important issues, and organize candidate forums where voters can question candidates about their positions.

Final Analysis and Lessons Learned

In addition to the AARP and other large, well-known interest groups like the National Rifle Association (NRA), which supports gun ownership, and the National Education Association (NEA), which is often concerned with teachers' salaries, there is an interesting variety of smaller associations worldwide, including the World Bartenders Training Organization; the Canadian Honey Producers Association (an association for the beekeepers, not the bees); the American Bed and Breakfast Association; the Great Lakes Lighthouse Keepers Association; the Grand Canyon Hikers and Backpackers Association; the Surrey Association of Church Bell Ringers; the National Governors' Association; the American Kite-Fliers Association; the Association of Chinese Philosophers in North America; the World Association of Detectives; the National Association of Milk Bottle Collectors; the American Hat Pin Society; the Montana Draft Horse and Mule Association; and the Abduction and UFO Research Association—to name just a small few. These organizations provide services to members, often collect dues, and seek to further their members' narrowly defined political interests in government policy making.

What is interesting about all this activity is how complicated it can be. For example, it might happen in certain peculiar circumstances that the producers of, say, corn syrup, the chief ingredient in soda, might be in favor of government subsidies for sugar production—even though they do not produce sugar. The corn syrup companies' rationale would be that if the price of sugar could be kept artificially high, the soda companies would continue to use corn syrup and would not be tempted to switch to using sugar. With subsidized sugar, international sources of sugar could not compete well with domestic sugar producers, keeping the price of sugar high, and ensuring that soda continued to be made using corn syrup. Or a private commuter rail system might be in favor of strong safety rules for bus services. These safety rules would add to the cost of running bus lines, making it easier for the rail system to compete with the bus service. The means to promoting these beefed-up safety rules might involve a "citizens' committee" for safer mass transportation, or a letter-writing campaign, or any of a number of other means of persuasion.[16] As Rauch cleverly says, the interest groups all play by the same persuasive rules in an Interest-Groups-R-Us game. Who is to blame? Probably no one in particular. Many of us want favorable treatment when we can get it—without thinking of the hidden, cumulative costs created by everyone's favorable treatment. Unfortunately, we do not always respect our own money after it has been taxed and redistributed back to us. What had been the result of hard work may now seem like free money that can be used less discriminately.

As we have seen, if you feel a compelling reason to organize an interest group, you do not have to start from scratch. And there are twenty-five thousand blueprints already in place to help if you now want to practice the trade. Once you get going, your momentum may help you keep going. Interestingly, Rauch describes only one antidote for the calcifying effects of ever more interest groups plying their trade in modern societies: cataclysmic event.[17] Such an event seems to mean for Rauch things like major defeat in war, nationwide famine, a massive pestilence attack, or cosmic collisions with earth of the type that 60 million years ago probably ended the dynastic rule of the dinosaurs and left the world open for colonization by the mammals, especially humans. Hopefully someone can find a countervailing force something short of an incoming comet or meteor.

Influence by Political Parties

Here we will look at how political parties within societies try to influence the political process. As long as there are at least two viable parties involved in the political process, citizens have a chance of getting diversity of opinion and at least some degree of fairness. As history has shown us, especially in the twentieth century, when just one party gains a monopoly on the political process, we are well-advised to remember the truth of historian Lord Acton's words: "Power tends to corrupt and absolute power corrupts absolutely."[18] So even if the rancor of political-party hostilities in open societies becomes understandably annoying at times, this is still preferable to the artificial calm that can appear when a one-party system keeps a tight lid on the pressure-cooker of conflict perpetuated by enforced political accord.

The Functions of Political Communication for Political Parties

Political parties work at recruiting members, raising funds, fielding candidates for office, creating images of the party, defining where they stand in the political spectrum, and getting out the vote come election time. Office winners also give out political patronage or favors to loyal members of the party and generally try to exert their party's influence throughout government. Political researchers Brian Schaffner and Matthew Streb report that many voters are highly dependent on party identification when they state their voter preferences. As they explain, "Less educated survey respondents are substantially less likely to express a vote preference when party labels are not available to them." Schaffner and Streb attribute this, in America at least, to a weak appetite for politics that especially shows itself when voters must make decisions at the bottom of the ballot in elections for offices where information may be more difficult to come by. Thus, the major parties can serve a heuristic function for some voters (e.g., "If a candidate or policy initiative is sponsored by party X, okay, I'm probably on board; but if party Y is for this, then I'm probably not).[19] For some voters, party identification may involve a lesser-known party, of which there are quite a few in the United States, including the Green Party, which is a spin-off of the European Green environmental movement; the Libertarian Party, which straddles the middle of the political spectrum and stands for individual liberty and total economic freedom; and the Constitution Party. Box 12.3 lists some of the other lesser-known political parties in America.

Political Parties and Presidential Elections

Candidates for president communicate with the electorate in a variety of ways, one of which is to influence their respective party's **platform statement**. Platform statements must accomplish two things that sometimes are difficult to do together. They must make a positive political case for voters, and they must also minimize the opportunity they offer news agencies and rival parties to nitpick platform specifics. Nonetheless, platform statements may still provide material for analysis—if we consider the historical and political contexts in which these statements occur. Knowing how the issues of the day have played out in the months prior to the conventions that draw up these platforms can make platform statements indicative of differences between the parties. Below are the headline issues published in the Republican and Democratic **party platform statements** for the year 2004 (the bracketed materials are my clarifications). Perhaps even here we will notice a pattern with respect to the underlying issue of order versus freedom. Are the Democrats more inclined toward order on domestic issues? Are the Republicans more inclined toward order on foreign policy? This may be a more complicated question than it at first appears. But such themes drive the politics of the two parties at very subtle levels.

BOX 12.3

Minor Political Parties in America

America First Party	Marijuana Party
American Independent Party	Peace and Freedom Party
American Nazi Party	Personal Choice Party
Communist Party USA	Prohibition Party
Constitutional Action Party	Socialist Party
Family Values Party	U.S. Pacifist Party
Freedom Socialist Party	We the People Party
Grass Roots Party	Workers World Party
Labor Party	Working Families Party

Strong at Home, Respected in the World
The 2004 Democratic National Platform for America

[The Problem]

For the first time in generations, we have been attacked on our own shores. Our brave men and women in uniform are still in harm's way in Iraq, Afghanistan, and the war against terror. Our alliances are frayed, our credibility in doubt.

Our great middle class is hard-pressed. Millions of Americans have lost their jobs, and millions more are struggling under the mounting burden of life's everyday costs.

In Washington, the President and his allies stubbornly press on, without regard to the needs of our people or the challenges of our times.

[The Plan]

It is time for a new direction.

John Kerry, John Edwards and the Democratic Party bring a new vision for America—strong at home, respected abroad. An America that offers opportunity, rewards responsibility, and rejoices in diversity.

We have a plan to build a strong, respected America: protecting our people, rebuilding our alliances, and leading the way to a more peaceful and prosperous world.

We have a plan to build a strong, growing economy: creating good jobs, rewarding hard work, and restoring fiscal discipline.

We have a plan to help our people build strong, healthy families: securing quality health care, offering world-class education, and ensuring clean air and water.[20]

A Safer World and a More Hopeful America
2004 Republican Party Platform

[Goals]

Today, the Republican Party gathers to renominate a man who carries on the best traditions of our Party by carrying the banner of freedom.

. . .

Ushering in an Ownership Era . . . because a vibrant entrepreneurial spirit will keep our economy strong and provide more opportunities for workers and families.

Building an Innovative Economy to compete in the World . . . because America can compete with anyone, anywhere, thanks to our entrepreneurs and risk-takers who keep us on the cutting edge of technology and commerce.

Strengthening Our Communities . . . because our children deserve to grow up in an environment in which all their hopes and dreams can come true.

Protecting Our Families . . . because we respect the family's role as a touchstone of stability and strength in an ever-changing world.

[Decisions]

This platform makes clear that the American people will have a choice on November 2nd.

A choice between strength and uncertainty.

A choice between results and rhetoric.

A choice between optimism and pessimism.

A choice between opportunity and dependence.

A choice between freedom and fear.
And a choice between moving forward and turning back.
The 2004 Republican Party Platform makes clear:
We choose strength. We choose results.
We choose optimism. We choose opportunity.
We choose freedom.

And we choose moving forward with President Bush. A man of courage and compassion, of integrity and action.[21]

Analysis of the Two Platform Statements The Democratic National Committee (DNC) uses the title "Strong at Home, Respected in the World," while the Republican National Committee (RNC) uses "A Safer World and a More Hopeful America." These two titles say a great deal, by implication, about the contrasting foreign policy preferences of both parties regarding preemptive military action, for example, and using the United Nations (UN) Security Council as a legitimizing force for American foreign policy (especially for U.S. military actions). The phrase "strong at home" implies defending America against such adversaries as the Wahhabi terrorists. But the phrase "a safer world" implies that the nation needs a preemptive offense, and not defense. The phrase "respected in the world" is a reference to the options of unilateral action, informal multilateral action, or formal, UN-sponsored multilateral action. The DNC favors the last of these three, and the RNC favors the first two of these three.

On the economy, the DNC focuses on unemployment, the cost of living, and a yet-to-be-stated plan for improving these two things. The RNC focuses on the entrepreneurial spirit that will keep the economy strong and provide more opportunities for workers and families. The DNC also refers to "rejoicing in diversity." Perhaps this is an allusion to immigration policy. The RNC makes no mention of this, although President Bush had proposed a policy idea of amnesty for illegal immigrants that was very unpopular with his party, especially with those party members from states that border Mexico. Both platforms later address limiting weapons of mass destruction (WMD), and especially limiting the ability of terrorists to get their hands on such weapons.

The RNC argues that diplomacy should be used for enforcing agreements about WMD, for handling North Korea, for holding Iran to its atomic-energy treaty obligations, and for promoting UN Security Council Resolution 154, which requires states to enact legislation that criminalizes proliferation activities. The RNC will offer help to Russia in securing its nuclear materials, and asks Group of Eight (G8) nations to refrain for one year from initiating new transfers of uranium enrichment and reprocessing technology to additional states. On operational details, the RNC proposes creating "Biodefense for the twenty-first Century," and signing into law "Project BioShield, which provides new tools to improve medical countermeasures protecting Americans against a chemical, biological, radiological, or nuclear attack." The RNC also proposes deploying missile defenses; detecting, disrupting, and blocking the spread of weapons and technology; confronting emerging threats from any person or state before those threats have fully materialized; and improving the nation's ability to respond to WMD.

The DNC argues, regarding operational details, that the world should be on notice that America will take every opportunity to defend itself: "If such an attack appears imminent, we will do everything necessary to stop it." The DNC also advises that "If such a strike does occur, we will respond with overwhelming and devastating force." The DNC proposes to use diplomacy to win an international consensus for early preventive action to lock up and secure existing nuclear weapons and material; help Russia secure its nuclear weapons; lead an international coalition to put an end to the production of new nuclear materials; conduct a global initiative to remove nuclear stockpiles in dozens of countries within four years; lead international efforts to shut down nuclear efforts in North Korea, Iran, and elsewhere; work with every country to tighten export controls, stiffen penalties, and beef-up law enforcement and intelligence sharing; and take steps to reduce tension between India and Pakistan and guard against the possibility of their nuclear weapons falling into the wrong hands.

Applications of Insights   What we can learn from the above two platform statements is that wiser heads sometimes prevail in politics. There is a time for rhetorical fisticuffs and a time for diplomacy. The soft sell has its place. However, notice one difference between the strategies used in the two platform statements. The DNC refers briefly but directly to what they dislike about the administration's policies, while the reverse does not occur. This is because when asking for change, the party out of power has the burden of proof to show that things are not acceptable as they stand. The incumbent does not have to do this because there is no burden of proof required in defending the status quo. The incumbent projects images of well-handled, smooth sailing, and the challenger counterprojects images of poorly handled, rough seas. In specific campaign messages, the charges and countercharges can get hot because the stakes are high.

To vote intelligently, the voter has to assemble a combination of things that include (1) the past history of the candidates' words and actions, (2) the candidates' current statements on the issues, (3) an analysis of how strong the political forces will be both for and against the specific policy issues that the candidates promise to act on (e.g., If a candidate promises something that is in fact not likely to come to pass, what good is it?), and (4) the voter's intuition about what will probably happen if one or the other candidate is elected. It would be nice if candidates always said what they meant and always meant what they said, and always did what they promised to do and always promised to do what they eventually did do. But such candidness and brutal frankness might create more conflict than predictability. The two-party system has worked for countries like America, thus providing encouragement that the wisdom of the political marketplace (with all its hostilities, uncertainties, ambiguities, and vagueness) is still the best.

Chapter in Retrospect

VIGNETTE   **Political Ambition**

Sometimes it is easier to see what motivates political actors if we can step back and view something in which we have no current personal interest. Perhaps these political acts will be from far away, or from a time long gone by, or even from a work of fiction that was written to tell us something true about human motives. The following fictional anecdote has survived the passage of several centuries and still offers us insight into what can motivate political acts.

Shakespeare's *Macbeth* offers a good example of the trouble sometimes caused by political actors with unreasonable ambitions. Macbeth, a general in service to the Scottish king Duncan, at first serves the king well by helping to put down a rebellion. But later, when three witches in the woods together prophesy to Macbeth that he will become king, he and his wife begin plotting to murder King Duncan in order to make the prophecy come true.

We see illustrated in the play at least five characteristics of unreasonable or illegitimate ambition. First, the Macbeths are dissatisfied with the status quo. Although Macbeth is a lord, he and his wife are no longer satisfied with his being anything but king. Second, Macbeth lacks the resources needed to achieve a legitimate ambition. He would need the birthright to be king—which belongs to Duncan's son Malcolm. Third, Macbeth lacks any sense of inhibition or personal reproach in taking an illegitimate route to his goals. That is, he takes the law into his own hands and commits regicide to become king. Fourth, although Macbeth lacks the birthright to be king, he does have the resources needed to cheat his way to the crown: Macbeth is physically and emotionally capable of committing murder, if that is what it will take to succeed. Moreover, he has a wife who will taunt him whenever his resolve falters and who will be a willing coconspirator. (She in fact hatches the plot. She drugs the wine of the king's guards on the night of the murder; and she, not he, completes the conspiracy by entering the now-dead king's room, after Macbeth has lost his nerve to revisit the crime scene, to rig the evidence against the drugged guards, whom Macbeth later kills.) Fifth, Macbeth is not initially consumed with any debilitative fears, worries, or anxiety that will interfere with completing the murder (although guilt and fear come later). This first lethal act by the Macbeths leads inevitably to other outrageous acts and finally to personal tragedy.

Thus in Macbeth, we see the five common characteristics of a syndrome that underlies much of the trouble that has plagued the human race throughout its history. This syndrome has caused much tragedy, death, enslavement, theft, parasitism, unhappiness, suffering, and, at times, the self-destruction of the unreasonably ambitious themselves. Said another way, when we want to keep up with or surpass the Joneses and then fail, we can become frustrated and angry.

Yes, *Macbeth* is a work of fiction, even if Shakespeare partly based it on historical fact. Nonetheless, we can find numerous other examples of unreasonable ambition in the news stories of the day as well as, or perhaps especially, in history books.

Summary and Conclusions

Political communication internal or external often concerns matters that are difficult to see up close, such as the operation of a nation's economy, foreign policy, taxation, and education. Political leaders must as a consequence find rhetorical means to communicate the big picture for each of these policy matters. One theme underlying most of this political communication concerns freedom versus order. Often what is good for one group of people will not be good for other groups, so the political process has to find ways to compromise short of armed conflict. Speeches, press conferences, televised proceedings in Congress, advertisements, and private communications all have their place in this communication process. From time to time great speeches, such as the Gettysburg Address or the Cuban Missile Crisis speech, have illustrated the importance of persuasive political communication. Political parties, organized interest groups, and the general public also participate in this process.

However, there is so much public persuasion in the modern world of politics that some observers fear the ability of modern societies to address social problems is being hampered by political power expressed at cross-purposes. Nonetheless, political communication works best when it results in an accommodation between the order that serves the public interest, or some part of it, and the freedom that serves our personal or partisan interests.

KEY TERMS

AARP
Emancipation
   Proclamation
freedom versus order
Great Experiment

interest groups
internal versus
   external political
   communication

party platform statements
press conference
Q = A + 1
weblogs

REVIEW QUESTIONS

1. What is the difference between order and freedom as discussed in this chapter?
2. Exactly how did President Kennedy describe the main problem in his speech?
3. What was the most compelling visual evidence offered in Kennedy's speech?
4. What is the Great Experiment?
5. What exactly did Lincoln want his listeners to do after hearing the speech?
6. About how many interest groups are there in America today? Why?
7. Why are reporters sometimes at a disadvantage when covering a presidential press conference? Can the president ever be at a disadvantage during these conferences? Why or why not?
8. Does the AARP seem to be a successful or unsuccessful interest group? Why?
9. What was one difference between the Democratic and Republican party platform statements in the election year of 2004? What was one similarity?

SUGGESTED PROJECTS AND ACTIVITIES

1. Do Internet or library research on an organized interest group. List the group's apparent political objectives in order of importance. Identify its communicative strategies. Evaluate its effectiveness. Give your opinion about its good or bad effects on society in general.
2. Visit the official websites of the Democratic and Republican parties. Analyze the two sites by comparing their similarities and by contrasting their differences.
3. Do the same as in item 2, but for two opposing websites that promote extreme or radical points of view.
4. If you were running for president of the United States, what would your positions be on several of the most important policy issues today (e.g., national defense, the federal budget, education, immigration, the UN, terrorism, national parks, climate studies and policy, organized crime, energy problems, drug use, space exploration, civil rights of

people, obligations to animals)? Once in office, how would you try to implement these policy positions? Would there also be downsides to your initiatives? If so, what might these downsides be?

5. Review either Aristotle's or Burke's rhetorical theory as explained in chapter 11 and try to apply that theory to one of the speeches described in this chapter.

QUESTIONS FOR DISCUSSION

1. Do you think that you have the persuasive skills to become a politician? Why or why not?

2. Do you think it is good or bad that some of the larger interest groups can be so successful in influencing the political process to the extent that they can?

3. Think of one contemporary topic of national controversy. What do you think is the root cause of this controversy?

4. Which world or national leaders do you think have the strongest persuasive skills? Explain why, using reasons and examples.

Notes

1. Dan Hahn, *Political Communication: Rhetoric, Government, and Citizens* (State College, PA: Strata, 2003): 4–11.

2. National Security Archive, "The Cuban Missile Crisis, 1962: The 40th Anniversary," George Washington University, www2.gwu.edu/~nsarchiv/nsa/cuba_mis_cri/ (10 November 2004). After the crisis subsided, aerial photos of Soviet ships removing missiles, with holds wide open for inspection purposes, would provide further visual data for analysis.

3. Raymond Garthoff, *Reflections on the Cuban Missile Crisis* (Washington, D.C.: Brookings Institution, 1989), 137; Laurence Chang and Peter Kornbluh, eds., *The Cuban Missile Crisis: A National Security Archive Documents Reader* (Washington, D.C.: National Security Archive, 1998), 360.

4. For video, audio, or printed text of Kennedy's speech, see "Cuban Missile Crisis Address to the Nation," www.americanrhetoric.com/speeches/jfkcubanmissilecrisis.html (20 October 2005).

5. In a letter dated October 24, Chairman Khrushchev wrote to President Kennedy:

> Our instructions to Soviet mariners are to observe strictly the universally accepted norms of navigation in international waters and not to retreat one step from them. And if the American side violates these rules, it must realize what responsibility will rest upon it in that case. Naturally we will not simply be bystanders with regard to piratical acts by American ships on the high seas. We will then be forced on our part to take the measures we consider necessary and adequate in order to protect our rights. We have everything necessary to do so. (Chang and Kornbluh, *The Cuban Missile Crisis*, 173–74)

6. National Park Service, "Gettysburg National Military Park: Facts," www.nps.gov/gett/pphtml/facts.html (10 November 2004).

7. America may not have been the first nation to outlaw slavery, but it certainly was the only larger nation heavily dependent on slave labor to do so.

8. Edwin Black, "Gettysburg and Silence," *Quarterly Journal of Speech* 80 (February 1994): 21–36.

9. Anthony Pratkanis and Elliot Aronson, *Age of Propaganda: The Everyday Use and Abuse of Persuasion* (New York: Henry Holt, 2001), 53–56. Although the words "three score and fourteen years ago" do not have the same ring.

10. Ronald Reid, "Newspaper Response to the Gettysburg Addresses," *Quarterly Journal of Speech* 59 (1973): 50–61. Though the vast number of slaves were African, Europeans and Asians could also be legally held as slaves.

11. Press conference of President George W. Bush, 8:00 p.m., 28 April 2005, www.whitehouse.gov/news/releases/2005/04/20050428-9.html.

12. Judith Trent and Robert Friedenberg, *Political Campaign Communication: Principles and Practices*, 5th ed. (Boulder, CO: Rowman and Littlefield, 2004), 241–51.

13. Jonathan Rauch, *Government's End: Why Washington Stopped Working* (New York: Public Affairs, 1999), 42–43, 86–87.

14. Rauch, *Government's End*, 87–90.

15. AARP, "About AARP," www.aarp.org/about_aarp (11 November 2004).

16. Rauch, *Government's End*, 67–99.

17. Rauch, *Government's End*, 34–38, 123–63.

18. Lord Acton (1834–1902) issued epic warnings that political power is the most serious threat to liberty. Born in Naples, Acton was educated in England, Scotland, France, and Germany, developing an extraordinary knowledge of European political history.

19. Brian Schaffner and Matthew Streb, "The Partisan Heuristic in Low-Information Elections," *Public Opinion Quarterly* 66 (Winter 2002): 559–81.

20. Democratic National Committee, *Strong at Home, Respected in the World*, national party platform, 2004, http://64.233.161.104/search?q=cache:CWAErzmeKfAJ:a9.g.akamai.net/7/9/8082/v002/www.democrats.org/pdfs/2004platform.pdf+democratic+party+platform+2004andhl=enandgl=usandct=clnkandcd=1 (1 June 2006).

21. Republican National Committee, *A Safer World and a More Hopeful America*, national party platform, 2004, http://64.233.161.104/search?q=cache:ySPb1xloCA0J:www.gop.com/media/2004platform.pdf+republican+national+platformandhl=enandgl=usandct=clnkandcd=1 (1 June 2006).

CHAPTER 13

Campaigns, Counterpublics, Movements, and Cults

I felt everyone knew I was lying. But my parents said, "You're doing fine. Don't worry." And everyone was saying how proud they were of me.

—KYLE ZIRPOLO, apologizing for false
accusations of child molestation, twenty years later

An estimated 5,000 economic, political, and religious groups operate in the United States alone at any given time, with 2.5 million members.

—MARGARET SINGER

CAMPAIGNS AND movements seek, among other things, social goods, solutions to societal problems, and the goals of human ambition. When the motivation is for a social good or a solution to a problem, campaigns and movements might promote space exploration, better education for children, new jobs, research for disease cures, or fairer laws. But when the motivation concerns human ambition, some segment of society often strives for more of something, be it power, privilege, respect, material resources, or avoidance of responsibilities. Sometimes campaigns and movements begin seeking a social good but then simply try to fulfill ambitions, as when a group first asks for fairness but then seeks partisan advantage. In the following sections, we will examine a variety of campaigns and movements. Some of these will seem more noble and deserving of our admiration. But others may simply involve goals that lead to bad government policy, defective laws, organized or unorganized crime, civil war, international war, or even terrorism. In addition, all campaigns and movements risk unintended consequences that can sometimes undo whatever gain was intended.

What is the difference between a **campaign** and a **movement**? What is a **public** and what is a **counterpublic**? A campaign is an organized effort by a person or a group to accomplish a particular goal. Some campaigns seek to get their candidate elected to office, promote the success of a consumer product, or gain acceptance of an idea, social practice, or policy. Although on occasion campaigns can last for decades, they usually last for several weeks, months, or years. A movement is much broader than a campaign and may include a large number of individual campaigns that come and go over the years, as well as the occasional *movement organization* that turns out similar campaigns year in and year out. Movements are less focused than campaigns. For example, the environmental movement has been around for more than a century. But if you look for its leaders, you will find them associated with specific campaigns, such as Teddy Roosevelt's effort to preserve large tracts of land for the great national parks of the American West or Rachel Carson's campaign to outlaw DDT. By way of contrast, publics and counterpublics, as we will see in detail later in the chapter, refer to public communication involving politically oriented people, but within a process that is often ad hoc, informal, and without much centralization of effort—at least when compared to what goes on in campaigns or movements.

Historically speaking, the study of campaigns and movements has been an offshoot of the research on persuasive speeches.[1] Because of the broadness and complexity of campaigns and movements, it is more difficult to document their effects on society through the empirical methods outlined in chapter 10. Critical case studies of campaigns have often been the preferred method of research, by which scholars try to describe the drama of a campaign. Case-study methods also can describe or prescribe the steps that campaigns and movements go through from their inception to their culmination.

Campaigns

Campaign strategy concerns what things must get done, and in what order, to achieve success. According to political researchers Leonard Binder et al., campaigns pass through stages in which its executive members must (1) identify the purpose of their campaign for recruits, supporters, and society at large; (2) build sufficient surface credibility so that at least some people will listen, understand, and respond favorably to the messages; (3) succeed in getting people to buy something; volunteer for something; support a policy, position, or ideology; write letters; sign petitions; or vote in some way; (4) achieve a minimum level of success over time; and (5) in the end, offer benefits to target populations.[2] We can contrast these five steps with the seven steps proposed by Herbert Simons.[3] The five-step approach concentrates a little more on the end part of a campaign, while the seven-step approach concentrates a little more on the beginning part of a campaign. Nonetheless, both reinforce each other's descriptions.

Simons's analysis of campaigns involves seven steps: (1) setting campaign goals, (2) doing research and development, (3) strategizing, (4) mobilizing resources, (5) seeking legitimacy as a force of change, (6) promoting campaign goals, gaining credibility, and presenting a winning case, and (7) activating audiences. This last step may involve moving voters, consumers, and activists, with a detailed plan that is publicized, by which people are oriented on exactly what to do (e.g., where, when, and whom to vote for; or when and where to buy a product). Whatever plans have been made must be followed through, and if the campaign is successful, a degree of *penetration* will be reached: the product or organization will now be a contender in its category, or the candidate will have been elected or at least nominated by their party.

A Model for a Citizens' Campaign

While single individuals can carry out informal campaigns, organizations are a more effective tool for carrying out campaigns.[4] Figure 13.1 shows how citizens trying to conduct a campaign can organize. At the campaign organization's center is either an *executive*, who could be one person with a personal interest in and motives for running a campaign, or a team, committee, or director of a wider organization. The executive sees to it that the campaign's *mission* is

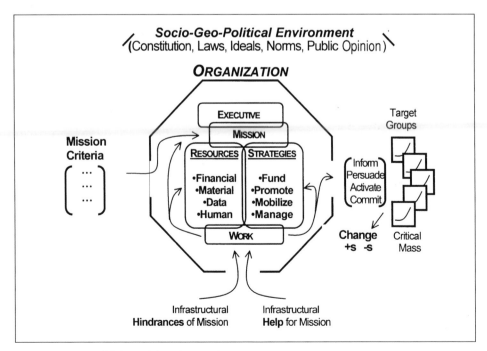

FIGURE 13.1 Model for a citizens' campaign.

defined, that *resources* are acquired or recruited, and that *strategies* are adopted and adapted. *Work* can be directed toward engaging **target groups** or toward refining the campaign mission, campaign resources, or campaign strategies. It is very important for a campaign to identify the target groups that will be necessary for carrying out the campaign's mission. A campaign's work can be evaluated by how well focused the campaign is on its mission, and how much it gets done in a timely, effective, and efficient manner.

Target groups fall into several categories, including (1) communities of people defined by where they live or work, their social affiliations, age, gender, race or ethnicity, and so on; (2) other organizations, private or public, including both the leadership and the membership of those organizations; (3) authorities, whether in the executive, legislative, or judicial branches of government, and whether local, regional, or federal; (4) the press, including editors, journalists, and writers; and (5) professionals or experts who can provide knowledge or services to the campaign. Thus, to mobilize help for gaining historic landmark status for several blocks of old houses in a neighborhood, a campaign might identify these target groups: affected homeowners, county residents, local business proprietors, community organizations interested in helping, local political leaders, local newspapers, and local radio and televisions stations. A lawyer, a real-estate professional, and a scholar of domestic architecture might each offer valuable services.

The term **Socio-geo-political environment** refers to the social, physical, and political settings for a campaign—all of which will help determine the possibilities for, and limitations placed on, campaign activities. That is, things that go on in wider society may be reflected, in adapted forms, within a campaign. For example, the constitution of a country may give its citizens freedom of speech, while the unwritten constitution of a campaign may give campaign staffers the right to call a meeting at any time. Laws, norms, ideals, and public opinion outside the campaign may also appear in a campaign in adapted forms, emanating in nonlinear ways from the wider circles of the socio-geo-political environment.

At the bottom of figure 13.1 we see the **infrastructural forces** that operate beyond the organization and its selected target groups. These outside forces are also part of the socio-geo-political environment. As independent forces, they exist either in opposition (as *hindrances*) to the mission, or in an unsolicited alliance with (as a *help* to) the mission of the campaign and its selected target groups. These outside infrastructural forces include (1) individuals with social or political agendas; (2) national, regional, or local media outlets with their own business or political agendas; (3) organizations with agendas; (4) the government with its agendas; and (5) the physical terrain within which the campaign must operate. *Physical terrain* here refers to the geographical settings where the campaign operates, whether mountainous areas, forests, plains, farmland, coastal areas, or locations out at sea. Physical terrain also includes the built-up resources within and by which the campaign operates: cities and towns, roads and transportation networks, communication utilities, goods and services, tools, local sites, and supplies.

On the far left of the model are the *mission criteria*, which describe the problems addressed by, and the intended solutions associated with, the campaign's mission. Examples of the criteria governing intended solutions include whether a proposed solution is specific, ambitious, popular, legal, possible, affordable, or reasonable. Examples of the criteria governing possible problems addressed include whether the problem is seen as important, simple, or visible. Perhaps a more specific solution will make that solution more appealing, or a more ambitious solution will make that solution more challenging. A problem that is difficult for people to see or appreciate (and which is therefore said to have "low visibility") may make it harder for the campaign to recruit workers or to generate cooperation from its target groups.

In the center of the model are two lists. *Resources* include money; material such as supplies and offices; information and knowledge; and people working inside the campaign. *Strategies* concern effective, efficient organization procedures for handling money, promoting the campaign's mission, mobilizing target groups, and managing the day-to-day work that gets done by workers.

It is important for an organization to monitor the effects of its campaign activities. This is shown on the right side of the model as *change* in terms of good outcomes (+s) and bad outcomes (-s). Often such outcomes concern how successfully target groups have been informed, persuaded, activated to do things, and committed to playing a role in the achievement of the mission. *Critical mass* is here a figurative term meaning that at a specific point in influencing a target group, a sufficient number of people may be convinced to help. Within each target-group icon on the far right of figure 13.1 is a line that can be thought of as moving upward in relation to the number of people who respond to campaign promotions and mobilizations. Critical mass occurs when the minimum number of people in a target group necessary for the campaign's success gets on board. Target groups can be defined very generally, such as "All the residents of town X," or very specifically, such as "The editors of newspaper Y" or "The shopkeepers on Main Street, Mudville."

Ultimately, this model can be used to (1) prescribe how to organize a monomorphic campaign for one mission, one time only, or a polymorphic campaign to be used for a variety of related missions in different places and times; (2) analyze an already existing campaign or predict the possible success of an intended campaign; or (3) plan research studies on campaigns. The likelihood of success for a campaign generally depends upon the preparation made in putting resources and strategies in place, the mission-relevant focus of the work completed, the quality and quantity of the work completed, and how difficult the mission is.

The model can also help generate questions about particular campaigns. Sometimes campaigns seek to conceal their true executive resource or to conceal whom their executive resource represents. A good idea when analyzing anonymous campaign propaganda is to ask, Who will probably benefit from this campaign? One political party may use an anonymous organization, or front, to create propaganda against an adversary so that it will not have to pay the political costs associated with disseminating harsh propaganda. At other times, campaigns may want to conceal that they are saying incompatible things to different target audiences. When speaking to immigrant groups, a campaign may say they are for "higher immigration quotas," but when speaking to workers in occupations that employ new immigrants, they may say that they are for "better control of immigration policies."

Funding, a resource, can also be used to analyze organized campaigns. If we want to learn what motivates people, there is a saying to keep in mind: Follow the money. Perhaps a campaign is funded through a complicated network of "paper organizations" that conceal who is donating money and with what motives. The human resources or membership of a particular campaign organization may have a telling history that defines what the campaign intends to accomplish. Members of the oil or Hollywood film industries, for example, might want to support a certain public policy while remaining individually anonymous. A campaign organization's promotional strategies may also be analyzed for motivation, especially when those strategies involve such things as the careful timing of message dissemination. In America, the term *October surprise* has come to refer to a presidential candidate's not releasing a bombshell, propaganda news item until the time (late in the campaign) when it can most hurt the opposing candidate.

Actual campaigns, of course, may not run quite as smoothly as the model suggests. For example, researchers Claes de Vreese and Holli Semetko report that in the referendum campaign in Denmark to adopt the euro, the electorate became quite cynical. They attribute this cynicism to "strategic news reporting" in the media. This style of reporting was described in chapter 5 as "horse-race" analysis: Who's winning? What are the ulterior motives of the parties or candidates? And we saw that the opposite reporting style was "issues" analysis: Is this a good idea? What will be its long-term effects? De Vreese and Semetko nonetheless believe that many voters can get through this "hot," news-coverage-caused cynicism and vote intelligently. They report that a campaign to get middle-school kids (a target group) to think negatively about marijuana had qualified success. This campaign involved a media program and a school-based curriculum (i.e., discussions to inform, persuade, activate, and commit the students). In de Vreese and Semetko's words, "Amount of exposure to the campaign directly impacted perceptions in kids that marijuana use was inconsistent with personal aspirations." Sometimes campaigns must settle for partially good results.[5]

Public Relations Campaigns

According to researchers James Grunig and Tod Hunt, there are four approaches to understanding **public relations** campaigns.[6] Figure 13.2 condenses these approaches and illustrates how public relations campaigns can be related to the study of persuasion. The figure shows four double-ended arrows, each depicting a continuum along which actual public relations campaigns can be characterized. Along the power kept–power shared continuum, one campaign might *keep power* to run things all to itself, while another might *share power* with the host community within which it is based. In the latter situation, a nonprofit organization's campaign style could, for example, allow its community to help determine what the organization's missions will be. A second continuum describes to what extent a campaign wishes to *promote* the interests of the organization or just to *inform* its host community. A third continuum concerns whether communication between organization and host community is *one-way* or *two-way*. And the fourth continuum illustrates whether the organization's public relations efforts will *be biased* in favor of the organization or will *be objective*. Organizations' efforts at public relations obviously will vary along all four continua. Some public relations efforts will be more propaganda oriented, some more persuasive, and some more informative.

Garden-variety public relations campaigns are almost always positive in tone and mostly intend to maintain a pleasantly positive or carefully defined public image for the organization or a well-known individual. But there are those occasional times when individuals, groups, or political administrations might pursue a negative public relations campaign organized by an in-house **political guru** (e.g., a valued idea creator, policy originator, or specialist) and not by a public relations team. This could happen when individuals or groups feel that they are politically vulnerable and need to be more aggressive, negative, or even

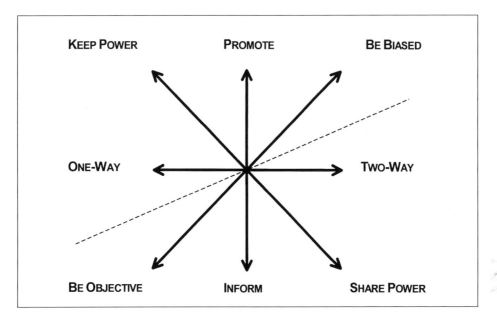

FIGURE 13.2 Four continua for categorizing public relations campaigns: (1) power shared or not with host communities; (2) point of view, whether objective or sender-biased; (3) type of objectives, to promote or inform; and (4) information flow, one-way or two-way. The dashed line separates two opposing styles for public relations, the upper more traditional, and the lower more future oriented.

malicious in order to keep their public image from being damaged. If you were the mayor of a middle-sized city, your political adversaries might try to hold you accountable for what they regard as your corrupt excesses. To deal with your adversaries, your political guru might hatch a strategy in which you (1) bait your adversaries into persistent criticism of your administration's record, (2) wait for the number of criticisms to amass because you "stonewall" in refusing to discuss the matter publicly, and (3) then begin to finally speak out, but only to characterize your adversaries as "obsessed" with the matter that you "stonewalled" in the first place. To protect your public image, you try to create a negative public image of the group that is out to damage (rightly or wrongly) your image.

Case Studies of Various Campaigns

Let's turn to actual case studies of successful campaigns that had clearly stated missions. The first case study is of a spontaneous citizens' campaign that successfully addressed a community problem that at first few seemed willing or able to face. Next we discuss a twenty-year-long effort to undo what campaign organizers felt was a terrible wrong, but in which their success turned out to be quite limited. Three summaries of case studies then follow: one for an unusual consumer product, and two for well-known individuals seeking elective office. All of these last three campaigns were quite successful.

The Brooklyn Heights Restoration Project Brooklyn Heights, New York, looks across the East River to the lower Manhattan skyline, out across the harbor to the Statue of Liberty and Staten Island, and still farther out to the shores of metropolitan New Jersey. The primary development of the Heights took place after 1814, when the Fulton Ferry began shuttling passengers from Manhattan across the East River to Brooklyn. For the next fifty years or more, grand townhouses were built, first in the Federal style, then in Greek Revival, next in Gothic Revival, and finally in several other styles including Renaissance Revival.[7] Nonetheless, this neighborhood fell into disrepair in the first half of the 1900s, with some of the grand structures becoming rooming houses, or worse. Ominously, developers began eyeing some of these historic houses for replacement with apartment and other commercial buildings, and even began considering an extension of the Brooklyn Queens Expressway. Although the neighborhood had been the first suburb of Manhattan, it was now in danger of becoming a lost American treasure.

Otis and Nancy Pearsall lived in the Heights in a basement apartment on Willow Street. One late summer evening in the early 1960s, Jack Blum, another resident, was visiting the Pearsalls. The three talked about the problems of the Heights and wondered whether some type of zoning could protect its charm and history from the Slum Clearance Committee that was preparing to swallow up the entire northeast section of the Heights. They began to meet over the next weeks and gradually attracted enough other concerned residents to create a historical-landmark campaign called the Community Conservation and Improvement Council (CCIC). The campaign eventually held open meetings in the undercroft of the First Unitarian Church at Pierrepont Street and Monroe Place, elected officers, and formed committees. One of the group's first campaign tactics was to print up a leaflet to define a proposed historic district geographically and announce its aims to limit any development that would ravage the neighborhood of its historical significance and nineteenth-century charm.

Next, the *Brooklyn Heights Press* joined the campaign with a news story that outlined plans by a well-known developer and regional planner to demolish some of the historic streets and houses in Brooklyn Heights. A local community association then joined forces with the CCIC. The campaign drew up a plan "for the preparation of an appropriate ordinance, the compilation of a survey of antebellum [pre–Civil War] structures on the Heights, supplying proof of worthiness of the cause, and the establishment of relations with allied parties." In this case, timing was important for the campaign. As it happened, the New York City Planning Commission was already studying citywide zoning rules to handle problems such as the one in Brooklyn Heights—so it seemed an opportune time to act by presenting such a plan. Sensing momentum, the *Brooklyn Heights Press* published a supportive editorial, "How to Make History," about the preservation aims of the campaign. A key player now joined the campaign, Clay Lancaster—a former teacher of fine arts at Columbia University and Cooper Union, a lecturer at the Metropolitan Museum of Art, and a specialist in American architecture; he agreed to survey the properties in need of historic landmark status. Lancaster also wrote six serialized articles for the *Brooklyn Heights Press* that tutored readers on the major styles of period architecture that existed in the Heights, and then delivered these articles in a speech with slides to an overflow community meeting.

Now the focus of the campaign switched to a golden jubilee celebration that was to include a special exhibition called the "Brooklyn Heights Story," followed by a photograph contest about the Heights as well as a restoration-theme exhibition of paintings, sculpture, graphics, and even three one-act plays. All of this activity culminated at the St. George Hotel of Brooklyn Heights, where a winner was declared for the contest and the exhibits were shown to audiences. Another milestone was reached here when Richard Howland, president of the National Trust for Historic Preservation in Washington, D.C., spoke in support of the proposal. Building on the momentum of the speech, Leonard Moore, a U.S. Court of Appeals judge and a Heights resident, added a substantive announcement about the proposed ordinance. More than seven hundred persons attended this meeting.

The culmination of the Heights campaign involved acting quickly to recruit block captains to explain the exact wording of the proposed ordinance to home owners in the Heights—whose support for the Heights's historic status would understandably be crucial. The final actions occurred when the mayor of New York City, the Landmarks Preservation Committee, and the City Planning Commission began considering the proposal. In the end, Brooklyn Heights got its protection and saved much of what deserved preserving, although some properties were lost before the ordinance was passed. What is fascinating about this campaign is that it all started in the basement of one house when three residents wondered if something could be done. And fortunately for the neighborhood, these three and their later allies not only conjured up a dream for the historically significant houses of Brooklyn Heights, they drafted a plan, and persistently pursued that plan. Over its several years of existence, the campaign chugged inevitably toward its conclusion. Having a good cause did not hurt.[8]

The five-step model and the seven-step model of campaigns might both now be used with good effect to explain the events of the Brooklyn Heights campaign. According to the five-step model, first came the identification of *purpose* and target populations. Next came a *credibility* effort, which was given a big boost by a survey of the properties (carried out by an architectural expert) in need of historic landmark protection. With each new supporter and politician signing on, and each additional supportive newspaper article, the campaign's credibility went up. In the third step, the campaign *succeeded* in getting interested parties, especially home owners living in the neighborhood, to formally register their support. And in the fourth step, landmark status was *achieved*, although only after some rough negotiations ("Would a second neighborhood be added to the proposal?" "No." "And would existing home owners be able to alter their properties if they could prove hardship?" "Yes, but they could not make their structures any taller"). Finally, the fifth step, *offering benefits*, has been going on ever since—as anyone who visits or lives in the neighborhood will surely confirm. Interested readers might now analyze the campaign by applying the seven-step model, just as I have applied the five-step model.

The organizational model reviewed in the discussion of figure 13.1 can also help us analyze the elements of this campaign. An *executive* (the campaign leadership) drafted the *mission*, identified the *target groups*, and began seeking helpful *resources* (mostly people and knowledge). *Strategies* were created to inform, persuade, activate, and gain commitment from the community and beyond. The campaign staffers worked continually for nearly two years to gain the change they sought. Their mission to save the neighborhood was specific, ambitious, apparently popular, legal, possible, affordable, and reasonable. The solution of a zoning ordinance seemed simple, visible, and important. The communication *work* relied on producing and disseminating informational, legal, and persuasive public messages, and on activating and committing an increasing number of concerned people and groups. The one example of infrastructural *hindrance* came in the form of the Slum Clearance Committee, which was outmaneuvered at almost every turn.

A Controversy in Court

> Interviewer 1: A long time ago some of the kids . . . said that there were some secrets from that school—some crummy things happened. And, um, we told 'em about our secret machine right here, and our puppets who are real smart guys like Mr. Snake Here's Pac-Man And, um, we told 'em how smart our puppets were and how they helped kids talk about some stuff sometimes and we've been playing detective . . . and maybe Pac-Man could talk for you, or Snake, so you wouldn't have to. . . . What do you think?

The above transcript was published in the *Los Angeles Times* on October 30, 2005, and illustrates one tactic used in the past to convict adults of child abuse by gathering testimony from school children. In the above instance, the *Times* article was written in part to allow one of the now grown-up students to apologize for having made false accusations against a teacher as a result of pressure by parents, prosecutors, and professional "interviewers," who used these accusations to create stories about abuse. The following case study is another example of an abuse prosecution that seems to have gone terribly wrong.

On the morning of April 30, 2004, Gerald Amirault walked out of the Bay State Correctional Facility in Massachusetts after serving eighteen years.[9] Nearly ten years earlier, his mother and sister Violet and Cheryl Amirault had also been released from prison. All three had been accused and convicted of multiple counts of child abuse and sentenced to long terms. (Gerald had been sentenced to thirty to forty years.) They had all been associated with Fells Acres private school. The case began in 1984, when an aide at the school informed Gerald that a child had wet his pants, which Gerald reported to the parent. The child apparently had a bed-wetting problem, which his mother had been brooding over. She had heard that bed wetting was sometimes a sign of child abuse, so she took the child to a psychologist. After several months of questioning by the mother and the psychologist, the child began to tell lurid stories of sexual abuse at the hands of Gerald Amirault. After several years of investigations and prosecutions, all three Amiraults were convicted of numerous counts of abuse involving several children and were sent to prison. But a small group of family and community supporters did not believe them to be guilty. Had they been victims of a modern-day witch hunt? By an ironic coincidence, the very court system in which they were tried had been in continuous operation since it was created to bring some sanity to the Salem Witch Trials of long ago.

The prosecution of these three was built around what seems today highly questionable methods. The children who eventually made the accusations were interviewed at length by people with reputations for handling these types of cases and who were hired by the prosecutor's office. The interview procedures apparently went on for weeks and involved asking the children leading questions over and over until the children gave the answers that the prosecutors sought. These interview methods secured allegations involving bad clowns, magic rooms, animal butchery, the consumption of urine and feces, anal abuse, and oral sex. The children whose testimony would eventually convict the Amiraults had initially offered no complaints. In fact, when they learned that the Amiraults were moving on to another place, many of them felt bad. But the state insisted that despite the initial reaction of the children to the interview questions, the Amiraults had continued this litany of crimes over a two-year period—though none of the children complained to other teachers or parents in all that time. However, as the case gained notoriety, other parents did come forward to join the prosecution's case.

The Amiraults' small group of supporters campaigned to have the convictions over-turned and the reputations of the Amiraults rescued. By the end of this saga, several appeals court judges, notably Justice Barton and Justice Borenstein, were convinced that fair trials had not been held. In addition, the *Massachusetts Lawyers Weekly*, which at that time had a twenty-seven-year-long policy of not criticizing court decisions said,

> The Supreme Judicial Court had rendered a decision that reflected shamefully on the Massachusetts judicial system of which [the editor] and his colleagues had always been proud. In six different decisions in the Amirault cases the SJC has seemed determined to defend the prosecutors and insist that these defendants belong behind bars, virtually scoffing at any possibility that an injustice may have been done; the justices have been unyielding in their refusal to let a new trial take place.[10]

Also convinced of the Amiraults' innocence was Dorothy Rabinowitz, who became interested in the child-abuse cases of the 1980s while working at a television station in New Jersey as a commentator. She remembers watching a bank of monitors showing another woman, in New Jersey, who had just been convicted on hundreds of counts of sexual abuse of the most grotesque kind. Dorothy wondered how all this could have happened undetected, and asked the station's news director if the station could report on questions now being raised about the convictions; apparently, this was not a popular proposal at the station.

The Amirault case actually involved two campaigns, each attempting to reach opposite goals. On one side was the pro-Amirault campaign, and on the other was a coalition of pros-ecutors, judges, and families, many of whom were convinced of the trio's guilt, although some may have believed that even if the Amiraults were innocent, society in sentencing them had done something good against child abuse by "drawing a line in the sand." The campaign to keep the Amiraults in jail may be partly explained by the theory of cognitive dissonance. In other words, how do you admit after a decade or two has passed that you may have been wrong in sending a family of educators to long prison terms and turning them into satanic public figures? Moreover, the Amiraults could have all gotten early releases and forgiveness if they had confessed and asked for rehabilitation. None of the three did, with Gerald refus-ing to take this route for eighteen years.

The pro-Amirault campaign strategy involved (1) publicizing the details of the prose-cution's methods, (2) persistent and repetitive appeals motions to overturn the convictions, and (3) requests for early parole. The two Amirault women had to be protected initially from the other prisoners, who banged things on the bars all during their first night at the prison, threatening violence against the two who could easily be seen in a centrally located cage with no walls; the older woman held the younger woman in her arms all night, both apparently still in a state of shock. These legal procedures had their ups and downs and false hopes for nearly a decade (for the women) and two decades (for Gerald). The final result offered con-solations for both campaigns. The prosecution could say the three had served lengthy sen-tences even if not the maximum. The defense could say that public opinion and sympathy for its side were increasing with each year that went by. One book and a number of editorial articles by Dorothy Rabinowitz have recently helped in publicizing this case—in favor of the Amiraults.[11]

Bose Headphones Perhaps one of the more unique products on the market today is a headset that masks unwanted noise and allows the wearer to experience either near-total silence in a noisy environment or full, rich, audio entertainment minus the background noise. The designer of this headset, Bose, is the same company that markets a small, $400 radio that is said to *almost* give the sound quality of larger sound systems. The company's advertisements say that in today's sometimes very noisy world, the Bose noise-cancellation headset can help you think in comfort and relax in quiet—for about $300. In a glossy sales pamphlet, Bose uses an imagined trip on a jet plane as a persuasive drama, saying, "The roar of the engines and whoosh of air is actively reduced by a Bose noise-cancellation innovation—TriPort headset technology . . . Enjoy the movie or music with full, rich sound. Step off the plane feeling less tired—then try this headset at home and in the office." The company offers a thirty-day, money-back "test flight" of the headset.

To add credibility to the claims, Bose quotes the magazine *Popular Science*, which praises the headset by saying it "reduced [the] background noise of 84 decibels of a Boeing aircraft—to a point at which the hushed dialogue . . . could easily be heard." Bose also quotes the president of American Airlines, who states that passengers prefer the Bose headsets by a wide margin; and the *Boston Globe* says, "The airplane roar became a whisper." Similarly, *Sound and Vision* magazine repeats the praises of the other reviewers and then adds that the headset is good for reducing the roar of a neighbor's leaf blower. To get you to act, the company gives you a 1-800 number with which to place your order and an interest-free payment plan of twelve installments of $24.92. For those potential customers who are still uncertain, Bose invites visits to its website, where the purchase can be explored in greater detail.

According to our five-step model, the campaign seems to work because it (1) has a clear and worthwhile purpose: to remove irritating noise from the customer's life (for the technically inclined, Bose provides a description of the process, which was pioneered for use by pilots: the technology uses a miniature microphone inside the headset to analyze background noise and then produce "an equal opposite sound" that cancels the noise [perhaps the way two sumo wrestlers with equal strength pushing at each other might stand frozen in place for a time]); (2) builds credibility from magazine critics who may have been recruited or may just have offered unsolicited reviews; (3) succeeds at getting its customers to buy the headsets, which keeps the product rolling off the assembly lines; (4) achieves success by promoting something that apparently works well and sells well; and (5) provides a benefit (peace and quiet) to the company's customers (the target group).

The seven-step Simons model may perform even better for analyzing the Bose campaign, by suggesting that Bose has (1) set product design, production, and marketing goals; (2) conducted product and consumer research; (3) created a marketing strategy; 4) mobilized in-house resources and consumer support; (5) sought legitimacy through published recommendations secured from experts; (6) promoted the product in ads; and (7) got people to buy. Regarding the last step, we can also say that Bose has achieved market penetration (at this moment, Bose may "own" the noise-cancellation headset market).

In a full-page newspaper ad published several months after the above promotional pamphlet circulated in the mail, Bose tells readers about "Quietly Setting a Whole New Standard." Bose updates the campaign by telling the newspaper's readers about airline passengers who have been avoiding the noise of jet engines by using the headset. But now, Bose sells its noise reduction technology to the newspaper's readers by stressing the satisfaction they'll have when listening to music or movie dialogue or when just seeking tranquility. And as in the pamphlet, Bose quotes a reviewer, this time in the *Philadelphia Daily News*: "Even in the noisiest environment, wearing these phones creates a calming, quiet zone for easy listening or just snoozing." In the ad, Bose again offers a thirty-day, money-back trial during which you can return the product for a full refund; it also offers to throw in a free Bose CD player ("a $50 value") to sweeten the deal. The CD player must be returned, however, if you want a full refund for the headset.[12]

Winning Elective Office Two recent campaigns for political office involved respectively Governor Arnold Schwarzenegger of California and Senator Hillary Clinton of New York. Both were running for the first time; both had plenty of previous media exposure to the voting public. What was amazing about Arnold Schwarzenegger's campaign was that political pundits had predicted that the recall of previous California governor Gray Davis had no chance of happening, and even if it did, that the election of Schwarzenegger would not happen either. Hillary Clinton had to deal with the issue of being an outsider in the State of New York, and had to overcome scandals that had dogged the Clinton administration for eight years. Both succeeded by making the best use of their resources. Mrs. Clinton campaigned using White House air transportation, and Arnold Schwarzenegger had the advantage of a very successful Hollywood career as, among other things, "the Terminator."

Not every campaigner has the good fortune to be well financed for advertising blitzes, especially newcomers to politics. However, a report by researcher Ruthann Weaver Lariscy et al. reminds us that old-fashioned, nonpaid campaign activities are alive and well, especially in U.S. state legislative races.[13] These nonpaid activities and communications can include endorsements from community leaders, supportive newspaper editorials, guest appearances on television and radio talk shows, door-to-door canvassing, ad hoc nighttime news appearances, news conferences, attention-getting stunts, and simply standing out in public shaking hands with people walking by. By succeeding early on with these less-expensive tactics, a politician may find future campaign contributions then rolling in for a more expensive media campaign.

Counterpublics

The term **public** often is used to mean "everyone," as in the term *public opinion*. To use the term *public opinion* usually means to ask, "What does the public as a whole think about this issue at this moment in time?" The term *a public*, however, refers to a slice of the public— not so much to particular members of the public but to particular sets of concerns, attitudes, and beliefs held by a fluid set of people about an issue or set of issues.[14] A public, then, is a sort of limited, meandering, collective consciousness about the ongoing text of a social or political issue, with numerous people contributing to the text on and off. Some of these contributors are identifiable public figures; others are anonymous. From this unfolding development of individual texts layered within society come accumulating communicative effects on that society. For example, the now popular use of the expression "date rape" is an effect of the ongoing textual dialogue of people who might loosely identify themselves as feminists. In addition to the above, we also have the term *counterpublic*, which refers to special publics involving *outsiders* who oppose the more mainstream publics, or the state. The term also concerns a relatively new set of theories that try to describe the political influence emanating from pockets of society that use nontraditional rhetorical strategies. These pockets of society seem to function not under a central locus of control but rather as almost spontaneous collaborations among strangers with overlapping interests.

One early team of writers on the subject, John Bowers, Donovan Ochs, and Richard Jensen, wrote about social change emanating from people who perceive themselves as outside the main political process and who then turn to agitative or demonstrative means of influence. More recently, persuasion scholar Robert Asen has urged other persuasion scholars to understand that counterpublics should never be confused with actual groups of people in physical locations; rather, counterpublics exist in the abstract and can only be understood in terms of the individual and societal texts mentioned above.[15]

Asen believes as well that counterpublics exist because some people in modern society feel excluded from the public channels of communication and power. They feel denied the power to induce or compel others to act in a desired way. A counterpublic, then, is an almost abstract rhetorical force in the form of a conversation that operates at the bequest of a vaguely defined set of strangers whose political interests overlap. This idea is also based on theorists' seeing nations like America as run more by the state than by elected officials. Political expression in the form of voting, contributing money to preferred candidates for office, running for office, writing letters to newspapers, attending community meetings, visiting local political officials at their offices, talking to neighbors, joining well-defined campaigns, writing essays, and so on are considered inadequate to bring political influence to those who describe themselves as being excluded. The Internet, the academic press, and other modern-day confluences of social identification may surface to support anonymous "conversations" within layered spheres dedicated to providing an alternative to the dominant public spheres. But counterpublics can also exist to disrupt the homogenizing and universalizing process of global mass communication that promotes uncritical consumerism. This second mission seems not so much designed to give power to the excluded as to give more power to those who already are included but who want more influence, an additional influence that they believe to be deserved.

In addition, counterpublic theory would portray the mainstream public as bourgeois. That is, counterpublics do not appeal to the bourgeois public sphere (those people concerned with middle-class values for personally owned, material things, for example). Rather, counterpublics exist to affirm differences in race, gender, sexuality, and ethnicity. The theory also seems to stress a redefining of the boundary between what is public and what is private. In other words, counterpublics have a better chance of succeeding if they refuse to let certain matters of social behavior be taken "off the table" in public policy debate as matters of private concern. Counterpublic theory stresses that modes of influence by counterpublics are not solely rhetorical, but are also poetic and demonstrative. Presumably then, those who feel themselves to be members of a counterpublic might try to exert influence by creating artistic messages, writing essays, giving speeches, or entering a public or semi-private meeting to shout slogans in order to disrupt the proceedings. Counterpublic theories often describe irregular methods used by some people to achieve variously defined collective ambitions.

Sociologist Daniel Brouwer, in describing the group ACT UP (AIDS Coalition to Unleash Power), refers to a kind of surfacing in which members gain skills for influence in the bases and training grounds of organizational meetings, committee meetings, caucus meetings, and affinity-group meetings. In these meetings, members choose enemies, suggest alliances, propose direct activities, debate means and ends, praise and condemn each other, articulate versions of justice, and engage in a multitude of other activities that foster the creation and refinement of oppositional discourses that are counter to the dominant and mainstream discourse about AIDS. They then seek to influence the AIDS discourse on talk shows, in community meetings, in medical symposia, and in the streets.[16]

In chapter 11 we reviewed the image events that play out in public spheres and discussed DeLuca's description of the especially visual rhetorical activities of activist groups, including Greenpeace. In explaining the form used for his text about image events, DeLuca captures some of the character of at least one of the counterpublics alluded to above when he says his text "is designed to question, interrupt, and disrupt a certain drive to clarity, transparency, and a transmission of authorial intentions in a translucent text."[17] On the use of image events by radicals engaging in confrontation, he says:

> I am exploring how radical environmental groups are using image events to deconstruct and articulate identities [for themselves], ideologies, consciousnesses, publics and cultures in our modern industrial civilization.

According to DeLuca, the individuals in these groups reject rhetorical notions about reasoned discourse and accuse traditional, rhetorical theorists and practitioners as serving the interests of those in positions of authority, thus allowing the established virtues of civility and decorum to hide the realities of protection and privilege. In some ways, it will be hard for the members of these groups to prove this denunciation if they reject the methods needed for proving things—that is, if they reject the notion of rational proof itself. If they reject the notion of rational proof, then they are left to making their case with the "Trust us, we know better than you do" argument. We should also keep in mind that reasoned discourse can be evaluated for truth and validity somewhat more viably than can an image event. Image events, because of their emotionality and their selectivity of visual details, seem more often to be propagandistic in nature (although not always). Some will point out that image events can just serve to bring our attention to a matter.

Finally, there is the diffusion of innovation theory formulated by theorist Everett Rogers to explain how various social innovations and practices come to be fully or partly adopted by a nation's population. The theory identifies a four-stage process that the public goes through in coming to adopt something new. These milestone-type stages include (1) acquiring new information and knowledge about an innovation, (2) becoming persuaded that adopting the innovation will be a good idea, (3) adopting the innovation on a trial basis, and (4) confirming through evaluation that the adoption will be relatively permanent.[18] Thus, an innovative attitude may at first surface in just one specific, anonymous public and then later become a widely accepted attitude by the public in general.

Rogers also identifies five categories for charting how an entire population may come to adopt something. A very small percentage of the population (less than 1 percent) are the **innovators**, or risk-taking people, who first discover or innovate something. Then come the **early adopters** (perhaps the next 10 percent). Next are the **early majority** (the next 40 percent to adopt), followed by the **late majority** (perhaps the next 40 percent), then followed by the **laggards** (the remaining 9 percent of the population). To combine the diffusion of innovation theory with the theories of publics and counterpublics would require charting the eventual acceptance over time of particular attitudes on matters of social concern.

Movements

Movements, as I have said, are broader in scope than campaigns. Some scholars today might argue that the study of publics should replace the study of movements. However, I will discuss movements in addition to publics. Studying movements is a murky area for communication scholars. Some have also argued that "movements are not inherently different from other forms of collective behavior in their rhetorical activities and . . . There is no need for a theory of the rhetoric of social movements."[19] Other scholars seek a communication theory for movements. Though I will offer no theories of movements, I will review several movements because they have had significant effects on society.

Often a movement will consist of a long succession of loosely related campaigns. Movements, as I note above, sometimes also contain movement organizations that run campaigns from time to time. These organizations should not be confused with the movement itself; rather, they are just individual elements in a movement. Theorists Charles Stewart, Craig Allen Smith, and Robert Denton Jr. explain the common stages movements go through:

Genesis. This is where a problem is defined by leaders, sometimes called "intellectuals" or "prophets." (These leaders may also be self-serving opportunists.) The leaders are good at articulating issues and pointing to those institutions that have not yet addressed the problem. This is a restless period in which nothing seems to be happening and there is not much practical organization, but there is an articulation of unhappiness with the state of something. Stewart, Smith, and Denton say here, "The most important contributions of the genesis stage are the apprehension of an exigence [a problem] and the cultivation of interest in the exigence within an audience."

Social unrest. Here the movement becomes larger and seeks public exposure and the moral high-ground vis-à-vis social authority. At this point, two sides may begin to emerge, one for the movement and one against. A manifesto, proclamation, or declaration is often produced. The ideology evoked by the movement at this stage is often built around myths and common beliefs (e.g., The rich get richer and the poor get poorer). Depending on the particular group involved, the chosen ideology will also employ a set of god and devil terms (e.g., liberal/conservative, social safety-net/free enterprise, communism/capitalism, Democrat/Republican).

Enthusiastic mobilization. At this stage, energetic supporters try to give life to the movement, often with a religious or secular-religious fervor. Now the movement begins in spurts to organize for action; it may become aggressive, perhaps burning things or violating laws. Polarization may also take place, forcing the public to choose between the movement ("us") and those outside the movement ("them"). The boiling point may be reached here, with resultant success or failure for the movement.

Relative quiet. The agitators of the movement have retired for the moment, and the politicians come to the forefront. This stage becomes an endurance challenge: Will the movement persist in limbo? Will it negotiate toward success? Will it return for a second mobilization stage, perhaps with new leadership? Will it die?

Termination. Either the movement has failed or succeeded at this step. One example of a failed movement is the temperance movement, which had a brief success in banning the consumption of liquor in the United States between 1920 and 1933. A more recent movement to protect animals from being used for research (cosmetic or medical), clothing, or food has mostly failed because the public seems divided or generally apathetic on this issue.[20]

The high-profile movements of recent decades have been about civil rights, as energized by the Reverend Martin Luther King Jr.; feminism, in its equity or identity-politics forms; treatment of animals; gun policy; the environment; alcohol consumption; and the ominous political diseases of Nazism and communism, or the religious expansionism sought through global terrorism. But as chapter 4 suggests, perhaps America's most significant movement was the American Revolution, in which the leadership for independence convinced the British subjects of the thirteen colonies to commit mass treason. This movement succeeded, but had it not, the British would have had the legal right to consider the movement's leaders traitors. As Benjamin Franklin said (perhaps not originally) at the signing of the Declaration of Independence, "We must indeed all hang together, or, most assuredly, we shall all hang separately." Leaving America aside, Europe's most significant movement over the last decades has created the euro and the European Union, for maximizing economic strength. Worldwide, there has been a movement to relocate many of the third-world peoples of Asia, Africa, South America, and more recently, Eastern Europe to new homes in Western Europe and the United States. This last movement may be an example of how the early stages of a movement are not always easy to identify as a movement.

In characterizing the tactics used by political actors who identify with various social movements, Stewart, Smith, and Denton describe what often amounts to gray and black propaganda.[21] For example, they describe the use (in movements) of ridicule, obscenity, slogans, polarization, an "us against them" mentality, song lyrics that often make accusations but seldom offer proof of the type a court of law or a scientific journal would accept, sowing of distrust, selling of conspiracy theories, the identifying of "devils," name calling, and bold assertion. The use of obscenity, I might note, implies that the audiences chosen by these political actors are not good enough or smart enough to respond to reasoned arguments, but can only be reached and motivated by four-letter words. This assumption does not treat people with respect and sanctimoniously regards others as inferior to the political actors.

You might, for example, while toiling in a political movement, say, "In California state colleges, the faculty are screwed regularly and vigorously by the governor and the legislature. For students, there is a kind of castration that goes on in schools."[22] Some of the people who hear this message might get angry and form attitudes that resonate with what you have boldly asserted. But, what do you mean—in fact? College teachers work about 60 percent of the year and come in three or four days a week for perhaps five hours a day. And how are these students, who are getting a subsidized education at institutions run by PhDs, being "castrated"? What kind of proof would you need and offer for such accusations? Often people making these sorts of statements do not clarify what they mean or add reasonable proof. Such speakers will sometimes say that this means of communication is the only one that works. But even this meta-statement needs reasonable support that provides proof. When hearing or reading messages such as this, we are well advised to evaluate what form of influence the people in the responsible movements have opted to use: argumentation, persuasion, propaganda (gray, white, black), indoctrination, coercion, or temporary mind-control.

The Temperance Movement

Substance abuse has probably been around since mankind first learned how to ferment fruit and vegetable juices to make alcohol. Efforts to curb drunkenness and encourage either temperance or total abstinence have been international. In America in the 1800s, there was a growing concern among citizens, especially among religious Christians, that drunkenness was a problem reeling out of control. Saloons had become commonplace on Main Street and in the big cities. Drinking to excess, especially among lower-class males living in the cities, caused rowdyism and crime.[23] At first, temperance seemed the solution. But it was just those urban males who needed temperance who were the most hostile to it. Temperance advocates gradually came to believe that total prohibition was the solution. This century-long effort culminated in the passing of the Volstead Act on October 28, 1919, for enforcement of the Eighteenth Amendment to the U.S. Constitution, which prohibited the manufacture, sale, or transportation of intoxicating liquors.

With hindsight, we now know that the Eighteenth Amendment was a terrible mistake. It was eventually rescinded in 1933, again by constitutional amendment. But by then, organized crime had gained a significant foothold in America through the black market that quickly developed to sell liquor illegally in "speakeasy" establishments that often operated with the full knowledge of bribed law-enforcement figures. The underlying problem was that many Americans insisted on drinking, whether legally or not. And with the mob-run speakeasy businesses, mobsters grew rich, enjoyed a bit of undeserved social legitimacy, and used their newfound money and power to engage in other illegal activities and generally corrupt the communities in which they plied their criminal trades. They fought wars with impunity over "turf" and intimidated citizens who got in the way. The temperance movement was a classic case of unintended consequences coming from a policy undertaken with good intentions. How did it all happen?

Perhaps the most flamboyant figure in the American temperance movement was Carry Nation, of Medicine Lodge, Kansas, whose husband drank himself to death in the early 1900s, leaving her with a small child. She came to hate the drunkenness in the liquor joints in Kansas and demanded that the state enforce the anti-saloon laws it had enacted in the late 1800s. But as the old song sort of goes, "Carry Nation couldn't shut them down," even though she is said to have attacked a number of saloons with a hatchet. The State of Kansas eventually sought tougher enforcement of its laws. But in doing this, it inadvertently stimulated rum-running, bootlegging, and moonshining. Other notable women also worked to end alcohol abuse in other states (such as reformer and educator Frances Willard). Some of these women went on to work in the women's suffrage movement. The temperance movement even attracted song writers, who sometimes wrote anti-drinking songs, including, "I never knew I had a wonderful wife until the town went dry."[24]

A Brief History of the Temperance Movement   The American Temperance Society was formed in 1826 and began a signature campaign, gathering numerous pledges of abstinence from signers. The State of Maine later enacted laws that allowed each county in the state to declare itself either "wet" (alcohol could be purchased) or "dry" (alcohol could not be purchased). The Washington Temperance Society was also formed and held revival-style meetings that encouraged moderation in or abstinence from alcohol consumption. In 1846, Maine became the first U.S. state to pass legislation curtailing the sale and consumption of alcoholic beverages.

By 1865, thirteen states had "wet-dry" laws. The Prohibition Party was founded in Chicago, and several of its candidates campaigned for president with prohibition of liquor as their major issue, but none of these candidates succeeded in getting elected. Although the candidates also favored women's suffrage and currency reform, they never did better than 2.5 percent of the vote, the total received by John Bidwell in 1892. The Women's Christian Temperance Union was created in 1874 to discourage excessive drinking, hopefully among those abusive husbands prone to violence or family desertion. Though some Americans, such as recent immigrants from Catholic European countries, enjoyed moderate drinking, the "bite" of the temperance issue concerned public and private drunkenness.[25] The Anti-Saloon League was formed in 1895, and probably had its greatest success in persuading Americans to begin taking problem-drinking seriously, especially when that drinking took place in public saloons.

The Anti-Saloon League held its sixteenth annual convention in Atlantic City, New Jersey, July 6–9, 1915.[26] With eventual U.S. involvement, World War I helped the temperance movement because of a temporary wartime need to conserve the grains that otherwise might have been used for making whiskey. Partly as a result of the war effort and partly as a result of the movement, by 1919, twenty-five states had enacted liquor-control laws of some type.

The Eighteenth Amendment to the U.S. Constitution, the so-called Noble Experiment, was passed in 1919. Enforcement, however, was spotty. It was not long before six masked men invaded a railway yard and took $100,000 worth of liquor from two boxcars: Chicago's gangsters had begun the undoing of the Noble Experiment, not so much driven by a disagreement on ideological grounds, but instead motivated by personal ambition and a willingness and ability to be violent.

After 1920, a "wets" campaign was initiated to reverse the Eighteenth Amendment. This also was the time of the Roaring Twenties when Americans, especially in the big cities, were in a partying mood. Apparently even women, many of whom had previously felt that saloons were undesirable places, began drinking at the speakeasies, which perhaps had an air of romance and mischief, even though they were serving liquor that was at times unhealthy or even dangerous to consume. America was now poised to switch gears on temperance and abstinence. In 1933, the Twenty-first Amendment to the U.S. Constitution was passed, undoing Prohibition and the Eighteenth Amendment. But with the best of intentions, the damage had been done: those too lazy to do an honest day's work were now ensconced in the organized-crime underworld. The residue of the temperance movement today is not a ban on alcohol consumption, but rather a meandering network of bureaucratic rules about who can drink what, where, and when.

Radical Political Movements

Radical political movements often recruit people who are very unhappy with their lives and who see themselves as society's losers.[27] They look to the movement as a type of secular salvation, somewhat in the way religious people look to religious salvation by practicing a particular religion. The leaders of radical political movements are often the rejected or the psychologically disturbed who have unrealistic ambitions for themselves and the society with which they most identify. Adolph Hitler (with his storm troopers and concentration-camp bullies) and Joseph Stalin (with his internal security apparatuses and Gulag bullies) quickly come to mind. But there have been many other less well-known examples. When these radical leaders can successfully attract enough followers, they may engage in revolution through military operations or political coups. Lower-placed members in these political movements may find a "family" and new social and economic privileges to replace their previously ungratifying life styles.

Cults

Cults especially rely on their leaders. So what is it that cult leaders do to attract the sorts of members who can be relied on to stay in the fold and do what they are told? According to Pratkanis and Aronson, a cult's originators promise something pleasing to cult members, such as happiness, power, purity, immortality, freedom from guilt, or a sense of being smarter than everyone else.[28] These promises may never come to pass, but they can seem ever around the corner for believers. Here too, the leaders create an "us against them" mentality between the "good" insiders and the "bad" (or potentially good) outsiders. The leaders encourage myths about themselves that emphasize their attractiveness, power, and sympathetic auras. Cult leaders work hard at creating cult-believed realities that may seem irrational or weird to outsiders, but can be made to seem rational or reasonable to insiders because everyone on the inside talks the party line. If you are around fifty people who all talk convincingly about the world ending two months from now, you may get caught up in the whirlpool of fantasy if you do not hear anyone else speaking in doubtful tones—especially if you have been selected, or have self-selected yourself, because you are already vulnerable to the cult's take on the world.

Cult leaders may also be pragmatists, at times thinking up ways to distract their followers, and especially their new recruits, from doubts. When you are hungry or tired or never left on your own, you may be less likely to think doubtful ideological thoughts—especially if you as a new recruit are immediately and continually being challenged by the emotionally stronger and conversationally disciplined insiders. Cults sometimes need money and replacements for deserters—so members may be sent out on the streets to panhandle and recruit new members. Last, cult leaders further create commitment through *rationalization traps*.

These traps are built on the theory of cognitive dissonance, which as we've seen suggests that if potential cult members are first asked for small commitments, such as to come to the cult center for dinner and discussion, they may later be profitably asked for greater commitments, such as to come to the center for three days of celebration, followed perhaps by a field trip and an invitation to move into the facilities. Further requests for total commitment come next: Sell your possessions! Donate your money to our cause! Abandon your family, friends, and spouse! Proceed confidently down the road to . . . !

Author Robert Lifton suggests eight criteria for evaluating the "mind controlling" techniques used by cult leaders ("techniques of indoctrination" is probably a better phrase).[29] *Milieu control*, the first criterion, means that cult leaders control the communication in environments where cult business takes place, and competitive, outside influences are usually banned unless being criticized. The second criterion, *mystical manipulation*, concerns a tactic whereby the leaders of a cult manage what takes place day-to-day, but also try to make these daily agendas seem spontaneous to give the agendas enhanced credibility for members and to leave little responsibility for the leaders if something goes wrong. In most cults, members are required to be "pure" in their commitment to the cause, and stark contrasts are maintained between orthodoxy among members and the "great unwashed" rabble that exists beyond the cult. Therefore the third criterion, absolute *purification*, is an ongoing obsession that will never be completed. Hand-in-hand with the purification process is *confession*, where members admit to their past or present impurities, sins, or other transgressions regarding the ideals of the cult.

Sacred science, the fifth criterion of a cult leader's controlling technique, means that a patina of science is carefully devised, perhaps by selectively quoting experts or charlatans, to show that the cult's ideas are scientifically supported. *Loading the language* requires that a vocabulary be chosen by cult leaders that supports the doctrine of the cult, a vocabulary that may be especially evident in slogans and clichés. *Doctrine over person*, the seventh criterion, should prevail when what the cult member feels or experiences seems in conflict with what the dogma or doctrine of the cult says he or she should feel or experience. When there is a conflict here, the member should guiltily feel that the self is wrong, not the doctrine. Finally, *dispensing of existence* means that those in the cult will have a totalistic vision of truth and the right to live, while those who have not accepted the cult's truth will not have a metaphorical right to exist, and will be secondary and of little importance. In extremist political cults, nonmembers or suspect members may be killed or enslaved with impunity because of their lack of social importance and because they are seen as impurities or as a threat to the movement.

Well-known examples of social cults in the past include the one created by Jim Jones that committed mass suicide in Guyana; the Heaven's Gate cult that committed mass suicide in California; David Koresh's Branch Davidian religious group—a number of whom were killed when, after they had refused to surrender and had killed several government agents, an order was given to storm their hideout. Other examples include the Hari Krishnas, who have been panhandling and proselytizing in the Western world since the 1960s, and the Reverend Moon's followers, who proselytized and panhandled in the 1960s and 1970s. Some of the above cults had Christian or Eastern-religion themes. Other cults have been political, as was the case with cult-leader Charles Manson, who led his cult to commit brutal murders in the 1960s in the belief that a war between blacks and whites in America was about to erupt and that Manson and his followers would be the leaders of the new world-order that would follow the war. Another example of this type of cult was the Symbionese Liberation Army, which kidnapped the newspaper heiress Patty Hearst in 1974, indoctrinated her with its class-warfare propaganda, committed bank robberies, killed people, and fought it out to the death with the police, thinking that they could start a civil war between the "moneyed classes" and the "underprivileged."[30] History is replete with revolutionary and terrorist groups that have done terrible things on a grand scale in the name of some doctrine.

But cults go back to ancient times. In the Hellenistic period, there were primitive mystery religions such as the cult of Dionysus, in which members learned the secrets to the mysteries of life and were thus promised salvation.[31] These cults were often built around themes associated with renewal of the earth, fertility, and worship of the moon, stars, or sun, as in the Persian cult of Mithras. Interestingly, some of these cults offered visions of escape from the discomforting aspects of life on earth. The mystery cults were also exclusive; benefits would only go to those who had been admitted. The knowledge that would get the cult members to whatever "promised land" the cult described would have been taught by prophets, priests, or teachers within the cult.

Today we have cults that seem more out of the mainstream than were the ancient cults. Today's cults seem more given to extreme and sometimes erratic behavior that involves mass suicide, murder, or just living at the edges of society.

The Heaven's Gate Cult

The Heaven's Gate cult was a mixture of UFO-fiction and of religious thinking of the type first found in the mystery religions of the ancient world. In March 1997 in Rancho Santa Fe, California, several dozen bodies were discovered in an expensive mansion (the cult "temple") by sheriff's deputies. All were victims of an apparent mass suicide. The members all had short hair and wore dark pants and sneakers. They also had maintained a website to chronicle their activities. The victims died in shifts over several days, by taking phenobarbital mixed with vodka and having plastic bags placed over their heads. Their leader, Marshall Applewhite, who had perfected an alien-like appearance with protruding eyes, had led the group to believe that it was leaving earth for a ride behind the Hale-Bopp comet, which was making an appearance in the sky at this time. The cult members seemed to believe that human bodies were "vehicles," or containers, that could be shed through death, allowing them to move to a "higher plane" anywhere in the universe. In religious terms, they seemed to believe that they could control their souls and live wherever they wanted to. There is some reason to believe that what actually triggered their departure was the suspicion that their leader was dying of cancer, though he had not been medically diagnosed as such.

One striking thing about the Heaven's Gate cult is the uniformity their leader achieved, persuading the members to dress alike and eat identical meals. But what is even more extraordinary was their apparent belief system: that they could hitch a ride in space by committing suicide. How they planned to actually make their way to the comet boggles the mind.

Some observers say that Applewhite may have been "sexually confused." Given his obsession with bodies as vehicles, perhaps he had tired of his own body and the mixed signals it sent him. In any case, one question in need of an answer is whether cults like Heaven's Gate exist more for the benefit of their leaders or their members.

Chic Occultism

One recent cult-like group involves a group of individuals who practice a modern version of medieval occult activities and mysticism, kabbalah, whose practitioners believe in creation through emanation and use a cipher method of interpreting Holy Scripture. This present-day group is said to have attracted well-known media favorites as part-time members, including Madonna, Ashton Kutcher, Demi Moore, Lucy Liu, Soleil Moon Frye, and Britney Spears.[32] The underlying idea of this "success" cult is that a person is an "empty bowl," and that 1 percent of reality concerns everyday comings and goings, while 99 percent concerns the spiritual realm to which these "kabbalists" are trying to get closer.[33] Members are supposed to transform themselves with spiritual light, to avoid selfishness, and to give away money with which they feel uncomfortable—a created social reality. "Negative energy" causes illness, and "positive energy" can bring health, the ability to cure others, and the ability to see into the future, which is said to be "a fixated vision on a phantom." Much of the practical knowledge needed by adherents to this chic cult can be found in a twenty-three-volume set of books written by a leader of the cult. One woman, in fact, believes that she saved her mother from kidney infection by running her fingers over the printed letters of the books. And one man claims that he undid his need for root-canal work by meditating. This mostly part-time cult claims to have 3 million members and fifty centers around the world; it also claims that the average member devotes twelve hours a week to study.

Chapter in Retrospect

Campaigns usually have a specific purpose that is pursued by an organized group of people for a modest amount of time. Campaigns can be organized to promote acceptance of a new policy or idea, a consumer product, a person running for office, a "celebrity cause," and so on. To organize a campaign, campaign leaders select a mission, gather resources (human, informational, material, financial), and cooperate in carrying out needed activities directed at completing the mission. The term *counterpublics* concerns a relatively new set of theories that try to describe political influence emanating from pockets of society that use nontraditional rhetorical strategies. Movements are broader in scope than campaigns and may include a variety of separate campaigns or movement organizations (that conduct various campaigns over time). The specific campaigns and other efforts that loosely make up a movement usually come and go over the course of a long time. One good example of a movement is the temperance movement, which existed in America from the 1830s to the 1930s and tried to convince Americans not to drink alcohol. The temperance movement is an example of a failed movement. Cults can sometimes function as movements, as can radical political organizations if they take on serious tones and become intense enough to start a civil war or revolution.

KEY TERMS

campaign	innovators	relative quiet
counterpublic	laggards	social unrest
early adopters	late majority	socio-geo-political
early majority	movement	environment
enthusiastic mobilization	political guru	target groups
genesis	public	termination
infrastructural forces	public relations	

REVIEW QUESTIONS

1. What general uses are made of campaigns?
2. In what different ways were the common steps of campaigns described in this chapter?
3. Why did the campaign described in this chapter to save a historical neighborhood succeed?
4. In the model of a citizens' campaign, how does the socio-geo-political environment affect what a campaign can do or not do?
5. What is a counterpublic?
6. What stages do movements pass through?
7. Why did the temperance movement fail?
8. Who typically joins cults, and why?
9. What were the mystery religions?

SUGGESTED PROJECTS AND ACTIVITIES

1. Volunteer to work on the campaign of a local politician during an election.
2. Do a Web search with the key word {movement} or the phrase {"political movement"}. Select a real movement and do a study of it, trying to discover the methods, goals, and motivations that drive the movement you have selected.
3. Try to find someone who has been a member of a cult but has since completely severed connections with the group. If you can, have several discussions with the person to find out what the experience was like. Or if you can't find someone who has been in a cult, research the experience through books.

QUESTIONS FOR DISCUSSION

1. What particular things do you think separate the citizens' campaigns that succeed from the ones that fail?
2. How does a counterpublic seem similar to or different from a social movement?
3. People join cults and other movements often for more than one reason. One obvious reason can involve ideological or intellectual matters. Another can involve social or emotional factors. Which do you think is the more motivating for people who join, the former or the latter? Why?

4. Do you think movements are driven more by noble and altruistic people or by people with personal agendas that happen to fit into the movement?

Notes

1. Campaigns and movements have generally been studied by communication researchers; however, movements are also studied by sociologists and other social-science researchers, who may bring their own methods, terminologies, and assumptions.

2. For a summary of these stages, see the final chapter in Leonard Binder, James Coleman, Joseph LaPolombara, Lucian Pye, Sidney Verber, and Myron Weiner, *Crisis and Sequence in Political Development* (Princeton, NJ: Princeton University Press, 1971), 283–316.

3. Herbert Simons, with Joanne Morreale and Bruce Gronbeck, *Persuasion in Society* (Thousand Oaks, CA: Sage, 2001), 212–23.

4. Ralph Nader's campaign against General Motors (GM) was initially something of a one-man effort to get GM to discontinue manufacturing one of their smaller car models; and Rachel Carson, as I noted earlier, campaigned to outlaw DDT.

5. Claes de Vreese and Holli Semetko, "Cynical and Engaged: Strategic Campaign Coverage, Public Opinion, and Mobilization in a Referendum," *Communication Research* 29, no. 6 (December 2002): 615–41; also, Michael Slater and Kathleen Kelly, "Testing Alternative Explanations for Exposure Effects in Media Campaigns," *Communication Research* 29, no. 4 (August 2002): 367–89.

6. James Grunig and Tod Hunt, *Managing Public Relations* (New York: Holt, Rinehart, and Winston, 1984); Denis McQuail and Sven Windahl, *Communication Models for the Study of Mass Communication* (London: Longman, 1993), 193–96.

7. Clay Lancaster, *Old Brooklyn Heights: New York's First Suburb* (New York: Dover, 1979), vii–xxxii.

8. Although interested in preservation, Otis and Nancy Pearsall probably also helped boost the cost of buying the Heights house they obtained later; Jack Blum was already a Heights home owner.

9. For a summary of this case, see Dorothy Rabinowitz, *No Crueler Tyrannies: Accusation, False Witness, and Other Terrors of Our Times* (New York: Wall Street Journal Books, 2003).

10. Rabinowitz, *No Crueler Tyrannies*, 169–71. The editorial was titled "Travesty of Justice."

11. See Dorothy Rabinowitz, "Homecoming: Gerald Amirault Enjoys His First Days of Freedom in 18 Years," *Wall Street Journal*, 28 May 2004, editorial section; Dorothy Rabinowitz, "The Sacrosanct Accusation," *Wall Street Journal*, 28 April 2003, editorial section; Dorothy Rabinowitz, "Epilogue to a Hysteria," *Wall Street Journal*, 27 March 2003, editorial section.

12. Bose Corporation, "Quietly Setting a Whole New Standard," *New York Post*, 21 December 2004, 24. This full-page advertisement appeared in the 2004 winter-holiday, retail-buying period. Product review is cited from the *Philadelphia Daily News*, 29 May 2003.

13. Ruthann Weaver Lariscy, Spencer F. Tinkham, Heidi Hatfield Edwards, and Karyn Ogata Jones, "The 'Ground War' of Political Campaigns: Nonpaid Activities in the U.S. State Legislative Races," *Journalism and Mass Communication Quarterly* 81, no. 3 (Autumn 2004): 477–99.

14. Michael Warner, "Publics and Counterpublics," *Quarterly Journal of Speech* 88, no. 4 (November 2002): 413–26.

15. John Bowers, Donovan Ochs, and Richard Jensen, *The Rhetoric of Agitation and Control* (Prospect Heights, IL: Waveland, 1993); Robert Asen, "Seeking the 'Counter' in Counterpublics," *Communication Theory* 10, no. 4 (November 2000): 424–46.

16. Daniel Brouwer, "ACT-ing UP in Congressional Hearings: Counterpublic Oppositional Discoursive Space," in *Counterpublics and the State*, ed. Robert Asen and Daniel Brouwer (Albany: State University of New York Press, 2001), 87–110.

17. Kevin DeLuca, *Image Politics: The New Rhetoric of Environmental Activism* (New York: Guilford, 1999), xiii.

18. Everett Rogers, *Diffusion of Innovations* (New York: The Free Press, 1995), 4–19.

19. Dan Hahn and Ruth Gonchar, "Social Movement Theory: A Dead End," *Communication Quarterly* 28 (Winter 1980): 60–64.

20. For a description of how these stages were suggested by various observers, see Charles Stewart, Craig Allen Smith, and Robert Denton Jr., *Persuasion and Social Movements* (Long Grove, IL: Waveland, 2001), 129–50.

21. Stewart, Smith, and Denton, *Persuasion and Social Movements*, 171–98.

22. Stewart, Smith, and Denton, *Persuasion and Social Movements*, 182–97.

23. *Encyclopedia Americana: International Edition*, 2001, s.v. "Prohibition."

24. Words by Lew Brown, music by Albert Von Tilzer, 1919.

25. *Encyclopedia Americana: International Edition*, 2001, s.v. "Temperance." Some contemporary analysts confuse the distinction between ethnic preferences for social drinking on the one hand and drunkenness and alcoholism on the other.

26. In 1915, Atlantic City, New Jersey, was a fashionable beach resort and was decades away from today's casinos.

27. J. A. C. Brown, *Techniques of Persuasion* (Baltimore: Penguin, 1973), 104–30.

28. Anthony Pratkanis and Elliot Aronson, *Age of Propaganda: The Everyday Use and Abuse of Persuasion* (New York: Henry Holt, 2001), 302–7.

29. Robert Lifton, *The Future of Immorality and Other Essays for a Nuclear Age* (New York: Basic Books, 1987).

30. Hearst was held incommunicado and told that no one would find her, after initially being kept in a closet where she was physically and sexually abused by various members of the gang. She feared for her life. The gang convinced her that they had been oppressed by society, and she eventually recorded messages critical of her family and participated in armed robberies.

31. Public Broadcasting System, "Hellenistic Kingdoms," episode 8 of *Western Tradition*, 1989.

32. Marianne Garvey, "Inside Madonna's Religion," *New York Post*, 24 October 2004, 22–23; 29 October 2004, 24–25; Yehuda Berg, "The Power of Kabbalah," www.powerofkabbalah.com (28 November 2004).

33. Kabbalistic groups interested in occult mysteries were first formed in medieval times and had informal associations with Judaism. The modern example mentioned here is a private organization.

CHAPTER 14

The Media Influence: Advertising, News, Entertainment

◆ Chapter Objectives

After reading this chapter, you will be able to:

- ◆ Identify general sources of power for the mass media
- ◆ Understand media theories such as uses and gratifications theory, dependency theory, and cultivation theory
- ◆ Better appreciate the workings of advertisements
- ◆ Evaluate effects of the media on such things as violence and education
- ◆ Define such terms as *subvertising* and *culture jamming*
- ◆ Recognize the power of entertainment and news dissemination

The media's the most powerful entity on earth. They have the power to make the innocent guilty and to make the guilty innocent, and that's power. Because they control the minds of the masses.

—MALCOLM X

The news media are, for the most part, the bringers of bad news . . . and it's not entirely the media's fault, bad news gets higher ratings and sells more papers than good news.

—PETER McWILLIAMS

Today we are beginning to notice that the new media are not just mechanical gimmicks for creating worlds of illusion, but new languages with new and unique powers of expression.

—MARSHALL MCLUHAN

The media's power is frail. Without the people's support, it can be shut off with the ease of turning a light switch.

—CORAZON AQUINO

THE INFLUENCE of modern media got its start around the year 1450 when Johannes Gutenberg, a goldsmith in the Rhine Valley, adapted a wine press to create the first movable, metallic-type printing press.[1] It was first used to print the Bible, and then helped spread the ideas of the Renaissance throughout Europe. The power brought by the printing press especially concerned the ease of reaching numerous people over wide spaces and long time periods with massive numbers of copies of a printed message; by the 1500s, 20 million books had already been printed. The focus of this chapter, however, is on the contemporary print and electronic media that splash into our lives day in and out. To appreciate the impact of the mass media on you personally, you would have to spend a month or two totally deprived of television, film, radio, books, magazines, newspapers, store signs, billboards, computers, audio recordings, videotape machines, CD and DVD players, and so on. Even your cell phone might need turning off, if you use it for anything other than a simple call.[2]

Modern media persuade us not just with advertisements and editorials, but also with news and entertainment. Role models on televised football, baseball, or soccer games may influence us, as may the actors on sitcoms or soap operas. Cartoons may influence how children play together. News broadcasts may sway the outcome of an election. Popular music may affect what teenagers think is "cool." A column in a financial magazine may determine the stocks we buy. Hollywood films since their inception have probably influenced the lifestyles of people around the world. The outcome of high-profile trials may at times be influenced by the day-to-day, sensationalized coverage these trials get in the press and on television programs. Automated telephone calls or e-mail can help sell products or raise funds for political candidates. And our Internet experiences can persuade us to buy and do things. Below we will examine the sources of media power, the effects of the media on our lives, and the techniques of influence used by the print and electronic media in advertising, news, and entertainment formats.

Sources of Media Power

Informational power. There is a saying that knowledge is power. The organizations that run media outlets benefit from this type of power with research staff, reporters, access to expensive databases, files kept over the years, and their ability to reach people with information that is in demand. When the lights go out in our community or when disaster hits, we especially rely on radios and televisions and newspapers, if they can get at them, for information and advice. Like giant beacons, the media are charged with surveilling the environment.

Gatekeeping power. Another power of the media is the power to set public-discussion agendas, promote agendas, and discourage agendas by selecting what materials to disseminate, with what tone to disseminate them, and how much detail to disseminate. Thus, media outlets that wish to reflect a social or political bias can do so very easily. Beyond this gatekeeping power is the power to evaluate and interpret what goes on. Sometimes this is a simple thing, as when the media tell us what the latest employment figures mean for new graduates; but sometimes media outlets need to recruit experts with technical expertise. Dictators especially prize controlling the media, and those conducting military invasions often seek to gain control of the local media outlets in order to gain some control of the local population. In a study by researchers Elizabeth Burch and Joseph Harry, California newspapers were content-analyzed to see if they operated with what the authors called "**hegemony**" (authoritative influence). The authors opined that on topics such as pesticide-use, newspapers are part of a "ruling hegemony," though they sometimes make room for selected other "voices" such as farm-worker organizations.[3]

Technical-expertise power. We also have come to rely on the expertise of the media for unraveling the confusing, the ambiguous, or the conflicted. A news story might mention that arsenic has been detected in a local lake, but we may then rely on the report to inform us that small amounts of arsenic are naturally found in such bodies of water. Now we want to know what is considered a safe level, whether the current level of arsenic in the lake is above or below the usual level, and whether it is above or below a safe level. We may also want to know whether the lake's arsenic content has changed significantly over the last several decades. Perhaps the news outlet will interview several chemists, physicians, or health officials. But in weaker moments, reporters may interview those with political agendas.

Legitimacy power. The most-popular media or the highest-regarded media benefit from the legitimacy that their consumers, readers, or viewers bestow on them by tuning in and then possibly regarding them as having high credibility. What newspaper would you turn to about a news item of the day you think important? If you could only watch one television program this week, which one would it be, if any? Which music groups do you appreciate the most? Without legitimacy power, it is difficult for those in the media to influence people. When the media are controlled by dictators, media outlets usually lack legitimacy. Any popularity of the media in closed societies can sometimes be explained by the scarcity of other more legitimate outlets.

Uses and gratifications power. That service we rely on for our cognitive and emotional gratifications has power over us because we value the service and would feel lost without it. This too is a type of power. Media uses and gratifications may include (1) personal identity, such as when we reinforce personal values by comparing ourselves to the characters or real people shown on television or by using them as positive or negative role models; (2) integration and social interaction, such as when we discuss programs with friends and coworkers, or just note how other people live; and (3) diversion, such as when we use the media for escapism, entertainment, or cultural or aesthetic enjoyment. In the special case of digital interactive television, the five categories of uses and gratifications found in one study included:

- entertainment and companionship
- the utilities of digital television, such as viewers' ability to change camera angles when viewing programs
- information, escape, and news

We consume those media materials that best serve our needs. Being the best at offering uses and gratifications for receivers may be media outlets' first step in achieving the legitimacy described above.[4]

Narcotizing power. The mass media can provide us with a substitute for taking action. For example, if a frustrating problem is aired in the mass media, we may feel that something has been done just because it has gotten attention. A news program may run a series of pieces on how tanker trucks that transport milk are not clean inside, having been used for carrying unsanitary substances prior to being used for carrying milk. If you see the story discussed two or three times on the local news, then you may assume that something will be done about it. But perhaps this is an intractable problem that is difficult to control for whatever reason, and nothing permanent ever gets done.[5]

Ethicizing power. This is the opposite of the above. Here the media can sometimes create a demand that something be done. By bringing the issue before a mass audience, the media can make everyone feel that something must be done, and quickly. If a number of people die in a fire at an unlicensed drinking establishment, the authorities, under pressure from a barrage of media accounts of the fire, may close down similar establishments. Since the attacks of September 11, a number of security practices have been implemented, although not all the things that people thought would change have in fact been changed.

Status-conferring power. The media can make people seem important by giving them increased media exposure in such venues as magazine stories, news spots on television, talk show invitations, and biographies. The status conferred can at times be so powerful that others are awestruck when they meet a media star face-to-face. This power is a special case of the gatekeeping power mentioned above. As a result of this power, people like Donald Trump (real-estate tycoon), Paris Hilton (entertainment figure, party girl, great-granddaughter of hotel magnate Conrad Hilton), and Kato Kaelin (O. J. Simpson houseguest) have become "famous for being famous," although the original famous-for-being famous icon was 1950s blonde Zsa Zsa Gabor.[6]

Perhaps the most electrifying example of media power in America occurred when actor Orson Welles sat at a radio microphone on a Sunday evening in October 1938 at CBS radio to present a program called *Mercury Theatre on the Air*. The dramatic program began, and the audience heard an announcer say, "Good evening, ladies and gentlemen. From the Mermaid Room in the Park Plaza in New York City we bring you the music of Ramon Raquello." After several minutes of music, the audience then heard, "Ladies and gentlemen, we interrupt this program to . . ." What followed was an incredible set of reports describing landings by invaders from Mars, battles between U.S. troops and the invaders, and descriptions of mass casualties inflicted by the invaders' "phaser" guns. There were announcements before, during, and after the program that the show was a dramatization. But many listeners who did not hear the announcements or forgot that they had heard them panicked, thinking they were hearing the real thing. Listeners prayed, cried, and tried to escape. Some telephoned loved ones to say good-bye, or called newspapers or the police for further information. More than 5 million people probably heard the broadcast, and perhaps a million of them thought that their world had come to an end.[7]

Although this type of incident could probably not happen today, it does illustrate the power of the mass media, especially the broadcast media. Consider that the Battle of New Orleans was fought a week after the War of 1812 had ended, because it took a week for the news of the truce to reach Louisiana. Before radio and television, we got our news after the event. Today we often hear and see news as it happens. In a sense, most of us are plugged into the informational heartbeat of the world. We sometimes see military fire-fights from the foxhole level. Several years ago I spent about two hours on a quiet afternoon monitoring the story of a stray dog stranded on a floating piece of ice in some distant river because one of the cable-news outlets kept returning for updates and live pictures of the dog—which it flashed around the world. If only the dog knew how many people were caught up in its ongoing rescue.

Media usage by people has also been described with dependency theory, and uses and gratifications theory.[8] Some scholars argue that media effects are **deterministic**, so we become dependent on the media in ways beyond our control, whether because we have less time or are increasingly bewildered by a complex world. These effects can operate at the microscopic level on the individual or at the macroscopic level on entire societies. Unlike dependency theory, uses and gratifications theory sees us as volunteering to use the media to attain individually selected gratifications or entertainment, information, social guidance, and an escape from monotony. As with most conceptual problems, the truth here probably lies somewhere in between. Yes, some of us become dependent on the media, but some of us control our media use rationally, while still others switch back and forth.

Advertising and Influence

Here in the West, our economies depend on advertising to grease the wheels of production and consumption. But as with many things, there are unintended consequences associated with the advertising arm of the free market. Do advertisements make children violence-prone or aggressive? Do we suffer lower self-esteem when we compare ourselves to the attractive people often shown in advertisements? Are children mentally capable of dealing with the influences of ads designed for them? Are parents manipulated by their children's advertising-stimulated desires for toys and games? Do advertisements for expensive personal products sow seeds of envy and unrealistic ambition among those with limited means of consumption? Healthier and stronger personalities may fare better than weaker ones.

As I noted in chapter 4, advertising is often a mild form of propaganda that in the West serves a function similar to that of the poster propaganda that was used in the Soviet Union to promote communism—for example, by showing good citizens working at their plows or proudly doing "wholesome" work in factories.[9] Even large billboard ads for products in the West have their analogues in the once-common larger-than-life billboard depictions of Soviet leaders. In the West, we see handsome people driving shiny new cars or doing high-tech household management at home. In both cultural settings, we have (or had) a symbolism that constructs an ideal world rather than reflecting the world as it is. But individual advertisers in the West are not really in the culture-creation business because no one is paying them to do this. They get paid to promote particular products and services. Culture creation is a by-product or secondary result of what advertisers do collectively. Because we consumers selectively respond well to one ad and perhaps not so well to another, we are all in the advertising-driven culture-creation business—just not to the same extent.

In fact, some of us consume advertisements for their own sake as a kind of window shopping or just as a way of watching the world go by. Sometimes we want advertisers to figure out how to grab our attention and help us decide what is worth buying or not. We want to be made to feel enthusiastic about the things we buy. We even rely on ads for a part of our education about what is going on in the world—or at least about the current vogue symbols parading through the media world. But not all of us want the above things done for us by advertisers. Rather, we are content to fast-forward through commercials in our recorded programs, to delete ads from our DVD recordings, or to watch noncommercial programming. We then use rational decision making for product purchases—or so we tell ourselves. The problem even here is that we may be influenced by friends, relatives, coworkers, and even strangers who *do* watch commercials.

Most advertisements are for consumer products, public-service messages, or political promotions. According to political observer Kathleen Jamieson, there are three types of political advertisements: the advocacy ad, the attack ad, and the contrast ad.[10] The **advocacy ad** concentrates on creating an image for a political contender. Such ads may tell us about the candidates' backgrounds, where they grew up, what positive things they did before entering politics, and the like. Though the word *advocacy* is used for this type of ad, little actual advocacy takes place. However, with the **attack ad**, one side may broadcast the perceived policy failings of the other side by saying things like "They've brought us the worst economy in the last one hundred years." "Going negative" is a common practice of both major political parties in the United States and in many other countries in the West, although such characterizations as "going negative" and "attack advertising" may at times be exaggerations. The **contrast ad** is a blend of both image and issues materials. Jamieson believes that advocacy ads are the most effective means of advertising, but attack ads can also be effective if the content is seen by receivers as fair.

Historical Trends in Advertising over the Past One Hundred Years

A century ago, ads mostly touted products in newspapers, as in the ad below for a pot-and-pan maker in the late 1800s.

> Agate Nickel-Steel Kitchen Utensils are Safe!
> No Poison has ever been found in the enamel of Agate Nickel Steel Wear.
> The Blue Label, Protected by Decision of US Court pasted on every piece, proves it.
> If substitutes are offered, write us:
> New York, Boston, Chicago—Lalance and Grosjean Mfg. Co.

The wording in this ad would probably not be effective today, although it may have been in its day. Advertising especially became popular when brand names started to appear. There was a time when you would go into a hardware store and buy a half pound of nails out of a large barrel. Today, we buy a small amount of nails packaged in a box with a name like Red Brand printed on it. When nails, crackers, and jellybeans were sold with a scoop, barrel, and scale, the seller decided what manufacturer or distributor to buy from. Today, the consumer decides what to buy from a menu of different brand names, each with a varying amount of marketing value added or invested in it to build name recognition, brand image, brand association, and brand loyalty. This value added to products from marketing efforts is **extrinsic**

value. Examples of products with extrinsic value are magazine- or store-advertised garments that are in style this season but might not be next season; car models that are "cool" to drive in public, perhaps because they have been showcased in a successful Hollywood film; an American Express credit card that emotionally reassures its users; and pricy alcoholic beverages that advertising has assured us will be the life of our party. In contrast, **intrinsic value** is designed into a product or service by its manufacturer, provider, or creator. Certain wines may be rare, which can affect their price, but rarity is an extrinsic feature of particular wines and cannot affect one of the intrinsic features of such wines: their taste.[11]

Advertising has come a long way, and now a single Super Bowl advertisement can have a tremendous impact on the sales of a product. But for less-privileged advertisements, the competition is fierce, with estimates of the number of ads that reach an individual now set at three thousand per day. And as we have seen, even entertainment programs sometimes carry ads through what is called product placement. This advertising clutter has developed because the number of media outlets has increased dramatically over the last one hundred years. The amount of time devoted to ads has also increased (especially on television), and sometimes similar types of ads are grouped together—which may increase the perception of clutter.

Author James Twitchell suggests six causes that contribute to the success of advertising in general. First, ads for things are **ubiquitous**; they are all over, on TV and radio, in newspapers and magazines, and out on the street on billboards, bus shelters, buses, and commuter trains; they are in your mailbox and your e-mail inbox, on website banners, and sometimes on your home telephone when it rings. In large cities, strip-clubs sometimes advertise by throwing their business cards (late at night from passing cars) onto sidewalks where men will sometimes pick up the cards the next day. Second, ads are *anonymous*; we do not know who the real sender is, and so perhaps we assume the sender is interesting, likeable, good-looking, and smart. Third, ads are **syncretic**—meaning they ride atop motivating cultural events to sell, say, Christmas presents or Mother's Day cards. Fourth, ads can be *profane*, in the sense that they are sometimes noisy, aggressive, annoying, repetitive, or outrageous. And I might add here that an ad's profanity may have a short decay time, helping gain our attention early on then disappearing from our memories before it might harm the chances for our purchasing the advertised product. Fifth, ads are **symbiotic** when they rely on icons and events in pop culture for sales, such as the famous people advertisers hire to help sell their products. Sixth and finally, ads sometimes rely on *magic* by encouraging us to believe that something can change our lives for the better. Can we become sexier by wearing an article of clothing or a cosmetic product, remove stains with an incredible cleaning agent, or become successful because of a razzle-dazzle photocopying machine?[12]

In some cases, advertising seems to be the price of gaining membership in a club. The club, of course, is for famous products (or services). Coca-Cola is a truly famous brand name. Microsoft is a truly famous brand name. So too is Bayer's Aspirin. In a sense, when we go shopping we can hobnob among the rich and famous. By buying one of these branded products, we can purchase a bit of that fame. Advertisers collectively help create images of stereotypical consumers, each of whom would be more likely to buy this product or that product but not some other product. Given this, I might at times feel awkward buying a product that is intended for demographic groups of which I am not a member. If I am going to buy a hair dye, it better be intended for men to use, or I may feel weird when I get to the checkout. All of this *purchase organization* provided by ad makers gives people in a modern society a common culture, a common set of values, and a common set of valued objects. With time, some of these ad-created cultural artifacts may become art of a sort.

A Simple Model of Advertising

When selling takes place at the point of purchase, the buyer is able to handle the merchandise, rub it, stretch it, knock on it, and try it out. The purchaser can also ask the seller questions about the object being sold. Today in the modern world, much of our purchasing is done in a two-step process: (1) we are exposed to ads everywhere, and (2) later when we go shopping, we are ever ready to notice things we have become familiar with through ads. However, during the first step, or the media portion of this process, we cannot reach out and touch the object in question, cannot squeeze it, cannot rub it, cannot try it out. It is not there. A logical response to this analysis might be to say, "The ads must then make up, verbally or with visual images, for the sensuous experience lost in our modern ways of doing things." Actually, ads are not that good yet—even the visual channel is usually reduced to two dimensions, and the acoustic channel is not real-time in that I might, for example, tap on a product and simultaneously hear my tapping sounds.

Consequently, ads must find a way to offer an alternative way for us to become interested in a purchase. So they create symbolic inducements as a substitute for the "sensuous ones" that occur on a shopping trip. As I suggest in chapter 11, the visual and acoustic senses have to be hyped, perhaps with **visual figuratives**. Examples of these are conversational *hyperbole* (people yelling, "Wow!" about a product); graphic *metaphors*, such as we might have with printed statistics that grow larger before our eyes; and animated *personifications* of inanimate objects, as with plants or animals that talk to us on screen. By the time we purchase the product, these figurative advertising tactics may be gone from our memories because they have short decay times. But if the ads have been successful, our general impressions of the products will survive, having longer decay times. Such media experiences do not have to always mirror reality, but rather can just encourage a subjective response to the product and a partial suspension of disbelief about what is said about the product. These subjective inducements then become part of the product's extrinsic value.

Advertisements, whether on television, radio, or in print, need to focus our attention on the product, make sure we remember the name of the product, and then motivate our purchase by using extrinsic value. As I've noted above, clothing created in a specific style for a specific fashion season may be seen to have a value beyond what the manufacturing process gives it. A shirt sold out of season often costs less. Why? Because ad campaigns have advised us on what is in or out or new. Sometimes extrinsic value derives from a simple association with a desirable notion.[13] In many cases, this appeal concerns the advertising-earned fame of a product— the "halo" or "spotlight" that appears over or illuminates it—at least for particular consumers. In chapter 3 we discuss the motivated sequence approach model of persuasion as built around identifying an unmet need in the consumer, promoting a product or service as the solution to the unmet need, helping the consumer visualize the benefits of using the product or service, and closing the deal.[14] The following five steps for creating ads have been inspired by that model and include some of the ideas mentioned in the above paragraphs:

1. Get attention
2. Make product or service name memorable
3. Motivate intention to purchase; or partly motivate intention to purchase that will be completed at the point of purchase, using
   A. Simple association (sex, youth, elitism, power, roots)
   B. Simple appeal (headline, slogan, song, pictures, visual icons)
   C. Problem or unmet need, provided solution, and visualization
   D. Suggested fame, notoriety, or secular "grace" of the product
   E. Presentation of product as an ideal and of consumer as the ideal consumer
4. Encourage timely purchase
5. Encourage loyalty for product or service

Getting Attention There are many ways for an ad to grab the attention of consumers. *Novelty* is a good attention-grabber (e.g., a cosmetics ad that shows "before" and "after" photos of a young woman, but the "before" picture is cut into strips and the headline says, "Oops . . . dropped it in the shredder"). *Humor* also works, such as when a dog owner brags about Purina's Beggin' Strips, saying something like "Dogs don't know it's not bacon" (the cartoon dog then yelps with glee at the strips, and Beggin' Strips now also has an added value). *Suspense* can grab our attention when we have to wait almost to the end of a commercial to find out what is being advertised. One recent television ad showed a series of filled water-glasses standing oddly alone in public places: on an outdoor escalator, on an empty seat in a bus, on a park swing, in a parked car, on a sidewalk. At the end, an announcer tells us that dry skin can cause us to lose a pint of water a day; therefore, we should "buy Vaseline Total Moisture." A long-ago lite-beer campaign was very successful in using *conflict* to attract attention by producing a series of ads that fretted over whether the product was "the best" because of its "great taste" or its "lower calories." *Activity* may grab our attention with fast cars, music, or rapid flashes of visual images. *Familiarity* relies on well-known images, say of dollar bills or a wallet full of pictures and credit cards. *Vitalness* grabs our attention with quick references to valued things (money, health) or feared things (sickness, debt, crime). And *beauty* is an old standby that works (and works and works) to add value to, say, a pair of jeans.

Making the Name Memorable Plays on words work well here, as in a Clinique cosmetics ad for December titled "Merry Clinique" and showing a female model running down the street with presents. Simple repetition of the name can work in print ads and television commercials. And the font size and location of a product's name in a magazine ad may direct our attention to motivational appeals, as in a lingerie ad where the product name, Vassarette, appears near the garment's location on the model's body. One ad for a Range Rover automobile prints the car's name in an unusual way, reading vertically along the right edge of the ad, from bottom to top (I couldn't resist reading it). The cover of *Penthouse* magazine often shows the name of the magazine partly set behind a picture of an attractive woman. Another clever technique involves a dialogue in which one person cannot seem to correctly hear the name of the product, and keeps saying, "What? What? What?" each time the other person repeats the name. The variations are endless.

Motivating the Purchase Associations are often used in clever ways to link a product or service with such motivating abstractions as love and sex, youth, power, rebelliousness, security, glamour, roots, self-gratification, health, and elitism. But often ads also try to identify an unmet need for consumers and then offer a product as the solution. For example, an ad for eye drops claims that the product can help produce "natural" tears for people with dry eyes. This unmet need (the need for more tears) is visualized in a television commercial for the product Restasis. An attractive woman talks about her problem, dry eyes, and a great solution, the eye drops. The solution is visualized when we see the woman lounging around her beautiful country house (a white exterior with window seats and plush pillows on the closed portion of the porch). Later we see her casually doing a number of things that emphasize comfortable eyesight, including playing in the yard with a white and brown dog, typing on a laptop while sitting on the porch, reading a book in her hammock in the yard on a pleasant summer afternoon, strolling slowly by herself through the woods behind the house using a video camera to record the beautiful flora, and then walking down a country lane with her bicycle at her side. It is a woman's bike with an old-fashioned wicker basket and a bell attached to the handle bars. This ad combines a problem–solution motivation with alluring associations.

In another ad, a young woman is walking in an open country field of two-foot-high, wheat-like yellow grass below a blue sky devoid of any signs of humidity. Almost everything looks beautiful but dry, including a dreary, dead tree in the background with no leaves (presumably, it has died for lack of water). Suddenly a six-foot-high fountain materializes in the middle of the grassy field, and the fountain is overflowing with cool, delicious water cascading in sheets over the side. Then raindrops the size of grapes start to fall from the sky. One of the drops lands in the woman's hand and morphs into an AquaDrop, which she casually munches. AquaDrops, it turns out, is a product designed to quench your thirst or your dry mouth. Numerous other ads use problem–solution techniques, including ads for fix-it products, time-savers, boredom-enders, kitchen helpers, beauty aids, and cheap solutions for expensive problems.

As I've suggested, a brand name that is famous may help motivate us to buy because it portrays the product as an ideal object and creates extrinsic value for the product. This value goes well beyond the intrinsic value the product may have as a result of manufacturing. Merchandise that never sells still has an intrinsic value, but apparently has no value that can be marketed. To take an extreme example, the pet rocks that were popular several decades ago had no intrinsic value to speak of, but for a brief time they did have extrinsic value, as did tulip bulbs that for a brief, frenzied time several centuries ago in Holland were worth hundreds of dollars (Tulip mania), and as did certain stocks in the stock-market bubble of the 1990s. Expensive cosmetics have a great deal of extrinsic value and perhaps only a modest intrinsic value (a product that sells for $50 on Fifth Avenue in New York City might sell for $20 in the factory district in Long Island City, New York, just a subway ride away). But we should not scoff at the illogic of the situation. If you had lots of money and your child needed life-saving medical treatment, might not you be disappointed if the prescribed medical procedure was inexpensive? Would you almost *want* to spend more money? In the final analysis, advertisers do not trick us into buying things we do not want. They do not trick us into paying more than we should. We want to buy things, and we want to feel we have bought things with value. Advertisers, perhaps opportunistically, give us what we want. If you are unhappy about all this, dedicate your life to trying to change human nature.

Encouraging Purchase and Loyalty Closing the deal quickly is important for most ads. Some ads provide 1-800 numbers to get you to call immediately. Department stores often run sales to get you in that week. Simple slogans for some businesses often say, "Stop by today." Very slick ads may say, "But wait! If you call in the next ten minutes, we'll throw in this beautiful pancake turner at no extra charge! A $20 value!" Product loyalty is especially important for products like Coca-Cola, whose producer invests huge amounts of money just keeping its already well-known name in people's minds and on their shopping lists. Repeat purchases are very important for these companies. When companies are especially fortunate, they may earn customers for lifetimes. An ad showing three generations of one family using a product might encourage this type of lifelong product loyalty.

The Language of Advertising

Weasel words are sometimes used in ads. These words or phrases include *up to*, *helps*, *like*, *little as*, *as much as*, *a fraction of*.[15] They are called weasel words because they let advertisers "weasel out" of responsibility for their claims. If I say I will sell you something at "a fraction of" its original cost, you may think you will get a real bargain, perhaps half off. But my idea of a fraction may be 99/100 (in fact, 3/2 of the original cost is still "a fraction"). If I claim you can make "up to" $20,000 a year in your spare time by opening the franchise I offer, I have not really said anything about what you will probably make. If just one person in the past has made this amount, my claim could be considered legitimate. "Like new" is an opinion, not a specification. And "helps" is so unspecific that if something provides just a minute service, it can still be said to have helped.

  Glittering generalities make us feel good, but they say little. Examples of glitter words are *fabulous*, *incredible*, *great*, *phenomenal*, *powerful*, *sparkling*, *wonderful*, and *fantabulous*. You might use words such as these to say in an ad, "Our incredible mousetrap will bring phenomenal results when used as directed." A more recent set of glittering generalities has environmental connotations: *all natural*, *environmentally friendly*, *safe for the environment*, *recycled*, *biodegradable*, *kind to animals*, and *organically grown*. The words may sound reassuring, but what exactly do they mean? Many of us probably consume these descriptives peripherally, and not with central processing.

  Slogans have helped many companies promote many products over the years: "You are in good hands with Allstate," "Just do it," "Reach out and touch someone," "Don't leave home without it," "The ultimate driving machine," "Absolutely, positively overnight," "The choice of a new generation," "We bring good things to life," "Fresh Mex," "It does a body good." Slogans provide a shorthand values summary that advertisers hope receivers will remember for a long time.

  Name substitutions give latitude to advertisers. But as one standup comic has noted, calling a snack "trail mix" does not make it any more nutritious. And as author Michael Geis points out, the phrase "more tomato for your money" is vague compared to "more tomatoes for your money."[16] The second statement could probably be proved true or false, but the first will depend on how the "tomato" quality of the product is defined. Similarly, adding a *y* to a word such as *meat* makes the word a vague reference, as in a dog food that is said to be "meaty." Similes may allow ads to make enhanced claims: "Cookie Crisp tastes like little chocolate-chip cookies." Geis also notes how advertisements for over-the-counter drug products can mislead if the claims made are too general or vague. For example, if a product claims it is good for an upset stomach, it is claiming a great deal. An upset stomach could be related to heartburn, acid indigestion, stomach gas, hiatal hernia, stomach ulcers, stomach cancer, food poisoning, or stomach virus. There is no product that can deal with all these problems. Further, sometimes grammar is important. Something with a "cheese flavor" doesn't necessarily have to contain cheese, but "orange juice" must contain the juice of an orange. The difference here is that *cheese* refers only to a property of the product, while *juice* refers to the product itself. Consider "lemon taste" versus "chocolate cake," and "almond flavor" versus "almond extract." In other words, you can buy an extract or a cake or juice, but you can't just buy a flavor or a taste.[17]

The Common Formats Used for Television Ads

Since television's inception in the late 1940s, television ads have used medium-friendly formats. The formats do not seem to have changed much, although the popularity of particular formats has risen or fallen from decade to decade, and new production techniques have come forth on a regular basis, such as computer graphics, morphing of images, and the electronic video-editing used today to create ads. The following formats should be recognizable to most television viewers.

With the use of a **barker**, or a **sales pitch**, someone stands facing the camera and delivers a promotional sales pitch (it can be low-key or high-key). This format probably originated in traveling tent shows and outdoor bazaars. Late night "informationals" sometimes feature a glib speaker who uses phrases like "an incredible bargain" and "at a fraction of the price you would pay in a store." In a specific ad for a diet product, a woman says, "Over thirty, over stressed, belly fat. It's not your fault. Diet failure is caused by a hormone called cortisol." The woman then goes on to make a pitch for a product named Relacore. Barkers usually exude confidence. Their job is to make you feel that you cannot let this opportunity get away from you.

Interviews (staged or spontaneous) have been a staple of television ads over the years. The interviewees usually like the product very much and plant ideas about the product in viewers' minds. This format is much more low-key than is the barker format. And because the interviewee is portrayed as giving unsolicited testimony, some of us may be tempted to give a higher credibility to what we hear in this format. Ad creators have total control, however, over staged interviews. And even with spontaneous interviews, ad creators can gather numerous interviews and then select just a few for broadcast. The people who show up to participate in these unscripted interviews may also try to anticipate what the sponsor wants to hear in order to "make the cut."

Given the never-ending popularity of talk shows, ads can always create a talk-show atmosphere where guests speak with a moderator about the product. As is the case with interviews, the talk-show format encourages receivers to assign more credibility to what they hear—because they think they are hearing unsolicited and spontaneous testimony. This format is also used more frequently in late-night "informationals."

Demonstration is another old standby. Here we get to see how something works in all its variations and uses. Five common subclasses of this format demonstrate (1) the product's basic use; (2) the product's versatility, by showing all the different things you can do with it;

(3) the product's durability, by showing the product being put through its paces under extreme conditions and suggesting that if it can pass this test, it surely can last a long time with more moderate usage;[18] (4) the product's benefits, which sells the product by showing its power to get something done (cosmetics and weight-loss programs often use this "before and after" technique, as do household cleaning products and closet organizers); and (5) the product's performance relative to the competition (this technique may be used when selling such things as napkins, vacuum cleaners, spot removers, batteries, and mattresses).

For want of a better term, I'll use *song and dance* to refer to any ad that features lots of music, and people moving around with lots of energy. The purpose of this format may be to put us into a partying mood, thereby hoping we'll be more likely to buy the product. Often the name of the product is liberally included in the goings-on. One good place to find examples of this format is on the MTV channel. In one ad for GAP clothing stores, the song "That's the way I like it" is used as background music for a montage of mostly younger girls prancing about showing things found at the GAP that they liked.

Dramatization formats tell a thirty- or sixty-second story with settings, characters, props, dialogue, and action. Dramatization often contains three ad segments: a problem, a solution, and a happy aftermath. A recent ad for AARP auto insurance showed an older man being pulled over by a female motorcycle cop. She says, "Drivers license, registration, insurance card." He says, "What's wrong officer?" She says, "Your insurance; you're paying too much. AARP has a program for people over fifty." The woman is tough until the last second of the ad, and then she cracks a slight smile. And in an ad for Hoover Floor-Mate floor cleaner, a six-foot-tall kangaroo invades a woman's kitchen, leaving muddy paw-prints all over the floor. The woman shrieks, and then a muscular man dressed as though from the Australian outback enters the kitchen and cleans up after the 'roo. He reassures her, in his Australian accent, that Hoover Floor-Mate is a "fast way to clean up down under." The still muddy-pawed kangaroo obligingly hops out of the kitchen into the backyard—but now leaving no paw-prints on the shiny, protected floor—and all is back to normal.

Video montage is a more recent technique. This format uses a rapid montage of sounds and flashing images, with the product cleverly centered within the sequence. The montage often switches rapidly from showing the product to showing people to showing print messages to showing situational contexts for using the product.

Surreal images occur in dream-like ads. The locations for these ads seem far away or seem part of a land of make-believe. In one ad for the Turner Classic Movie channel, we see a series of scenes that include representations of a 1940s theater ticket booth, a dance hall, a model in a second-floor window display for a fur company, a street-bus filled with people and idling under an overhead el-station, a barber shop with a sidewalk pole, and a "blue-plate special" diner with several lonely-looking people drinking coffee in the dead of night. The scenes all use minimal amounts of visual detail that nostalgically take us back to a long-ago time when the Turner Classic Movie channel's movies first ran in the movie houses of the day.

Story-telling narratives and testimony are very commonly used today, probably because they help to create a feeling of legitimacy: we believe that we are hearing the unsolicited testimony of someone who has discovered a great product or service. In an ad for Hallmark greeting cards, a woman tells a story with a tone of voice that suggests she is writing in her diary. Her now-deceased father (who by sad circumstances was both father and mother to her) apparently kept wrapped with a ribbon all the Mother's Day cards she sent him when she was younger—and she has just found the cards while going through his belongings in his room. In another ad, this one for Toll House Cookies, a mother seems to be writing poetry about her children, who are helping in the kitchen, and she says with a mixture of happiness and sadness,

> Little hands . . . how deeply I feel their sweet touch . . . tugging at my leg . . . so eager to help . . . tomorrow . . . too soon . . . their hands will reach beyond my grasp . . . but today . . . for a time . . . these little hands fit sweetly into mine.

The voice-over then says, "You're not just baking cookies, you're making memories."

Lastly, I will mention the political act of **subverting**, a merging of the words *subvert* and *advertising*. Subverting concerns the practice of creating spoofs and parodies of corporate and political ads. A related term is **culture jamming**, which is borrowed from the notion of jamming the radio frequencies of hostile media in times of war. Culture jamming tries to use the existing mass media to criticize the media, and especially to criticize the media's promotion of materialist culture. One place to sample the politics of subverting and culture jamming is by examining a copy of *Adbusters*, which is a Canadian political magazine founded by Kalle Lasn and Bill Schmalz and published in Vancouver, British Columbia. The magazine is anticonsumerism and anticapitalist in nature. It has spoofed Obsession perfume, Absolute Vodka, Prozak, MacDonalds, and Marlboro cigarettes, among other products. A similar organization is the Billboard Liberation Front, which believes, among other things, that each citizen has a right to a personal billboard. The front says that until each citizen has that billboard, it will continue to encourage everyone to take over such advertising media and alter specific displays to their own design (mentally, or even by climbing up the billboard to add graffiti or alter the text and images). Actually, this is not entirely a new idea. In the early 1950s, a film titled *It Should Happen to You* told the story of a young and lonely woman who rents and plasters her name on a centrally located, big-city billboard and becomes the talk of the town. One problem with the front's idea is that a nation of 300 million people would need 300 million new billboards.

News and Influence

When we rely on the media to deliver the news of the day, we put power into the hands of those who sort through the events of interest to pick what stories will appear and how they will be treated. *Story treatment* involves placement of the story within the larger format, the length of the story, which details are included or not included, and the overall point of view taken. Communication researchers Eric Freedman and Frederick Fico discuss an idea that I have briefly mentioned when they describe the inclusion of horse-race or issues experts in newspaper stories about ongoing elections. Horse-race experts talk about poll results, fundraising successes, political ads, endorsements, debate performances, and the candidates' personal scandals. Issues experts comment on the policies that the candidates promote in their speeches, position papers, ads, debates, and press conferences. Freedman and Fico analyzed stories in fifteen daily newspapers covering seven open races for governor between Labor Day and Election Day 2002. They report that 37 percent cited experts of some type, 27 percent cited horse-race experts, and 14 percent cited issues experts.[19] I should note that the focus on horse-race details concerns a candidate's potential to win, while the focus on issues details concerns the repercussions of policies. From a Burkean point of view, I might also say that the language of the horse-race report is more about competitions among agents and about the success of their agencies, while the language of the issues report is more about the political purposes of agents regarding the transformation of the social, economic, or political scene. Which of the two focuses is stressed more in a given story, assuming one is stressed, can significantly affect how readers or viewers are influenced by the story.

According to researchers Andrew Mendelson and Esther Thorson, newspaper gatekeepers also have to keep in mind the mental sets of readers for pictures and text:

> The advantage for verbalizers [text-oriented readers] in learning from newspapers was unmistakable. . . . When photos were absent, high verbalizers remembered the most. . . . Low verbalizers were helped [by the presence of pictures with a story].

The authors caution that their study may not have given the low verbalizers, the ones who presumably liked pictures, an opportunity to show better visual memory. Nonetheless, the study poses questions about newspaper strategies that rely on an extensive text versus an extensive visual layout.

Gatekeepers, working in both print and electronic news outlets, also have to contend with accusations of bias. There are two issues here. First, is the outlet *objectively* biased to the left or right? And second, do partisans on the left or right view the outlet *subjectively* as biased or not? Researchers Kathleen Schmitt, Albert Gunthert, and Janice Liebhart report, on the second issue, that a subjective accusation of bias may arise out of the three ways in which partisans process the news: (1) partisans sometimes use *selective recall*, meaning that they will only remember what will allow them to justify their accusation of bias; (2) partisans often use *selective categorization*, which means that opposing partisans will assign different valences to the same news content, and will see the information in it as favorable, unfavorable, or neutral regarding their respective points of view; and (3) partisans may use different standards for identifying bias, that is, opposing partisans may agree on what the news content is in a story, but may see any information in it that justifies the other side as either invalid or irrelevant. According to the study, if I think of newspaper X as biased, I will forget any instances in newspaper X of non-bias, will be super-sensitive to stories in newspaper X critical of my side, and will disvalue objective information in a newspaper X story that helps the other side or hurts my side. This study focused on selective categorization as a key issue.[20]

A number of other considerations affect the gatekeepers who decide whether and how a story is covered. To some extent, they set the agendas of the day regarding what people will talk about, praise, condemn, worry about, feel good about, and so on. The management of media outlets are concerned with profits. The advertisers are concerned with who actually consumes or does not consume the ads (and products) appearing with the news or in the general vicinity of the news. Programming decision makers are concerned with ratings and circulation figures. And consumers may be happy or unhappy with the news-reporting policies of the outlet. Bias is inevitable with all these dynamics in play, although journalists are supposed to overcome these dynamics and to report and analyze the news with nonpartisan objectivity. Sometimes they succeed, and sometimes they fail. News reporting is at its worst when news outlets all seem to focus on a single story for several days, weeks, or months, resulting in a symbiotic feeding frenzy between the news outlets and their audiences: the more the outlets report, the more their audiences are assumed to be interested, and the more the outlets then feel they must report to keep up with the competition.

Each of the individual media used for news dissemination also brings with it general biases. Television news is biased toward the visual image, people doing things, and such events as accidents, fires, demonstrations, and riots. Newspapers, on the other hand, can tell longer stories and with more detail. Many newspapers favor local stories, with such notable exceptions as the *Wall Street Journal*, the *New York Times*, and the *Times* (London). Radio news these days is often more headline oriented. Magazines are concerned more with news that is slightly less time sensitive: a magazine reporter may follow a candidate running for president along the campaign trail for a week or longer. Television-news viewers may at times bring short attention spans to their consumption of news, and so the news stories have to be accessible to the "lowest common denominator." Other factors that influence the news are how easy it is for reporters to actually get a story, what the financial cost will be in getting the story, how much time it will take on the air or in print space to tell the story, and what stories the competition is running or likely to run. Also, much of the news of the day originates from several epicenters—UPI, AP, BBC, Reuters, the *New York Times*, the *Wall Street Journal*—and is then copied almost verbatim by local outlets. Whatever bias exists, if any, in a story, can then be multiplied.

Even when individual news stories are objective in detail, the reporting styles of local news outlets can distort the perceptions that develop in the minds of those who view local news. Researchers Daniel Romer, Kathleen Hall Jamieson, and Sean Aday report that

> the results of a recent survey of over 2,300 Philadelphia residents . . . indicate that across a wide spectrum of the population, and independent of local crime rates, viewing local television news is related to increased fear and concern about crime. These results support "cultivation" theory's predicted effects of television on the public.

By referring to **cultivation theory**, the authors are addressing the tendency of prime-time television to portray a world more filled with menace than the one most of us inhabit, thus worrying us unnecessarily. A contrary theory is that individual viewers have differing appetites for worrisome media content and so eliminate dreary or threatening content with their remote controls. Making this issue more interesting is a study by Bernd Henning and Peter Vorderer, who report that those viewers in Germany who watch more television in general, not just the news, have a lower need for cognition and thinking; hence, as they escape into the world of television, they may be the most affected by whatever media biases they encounter there. The final word on this issue awaits future studies.[21]

Technically, there are three formats that news materials can use: news, news analysis, and opinion or editorial. *News* should be objective, nonpartisan, and fact-oriented. *Opinion* or *editorial* is allowed to be partisan and value based. The trickiest format is *news analysis*, where the news outlet tries to tell us what a news story, or a batch of news stories, means in general. This last format leaves "wiggle room" for the analyst to be political without seeming overtly so. A news analyst could write, "That party X has consistently relied on attack ads in the last decade may signal a new era in the politics of this country, dominated by the ugly, the negative, the hostile, and the aggressive." How the term "attack ads" is defined is very important here, as is the word "signal." It is possible that party X is using attack ads because an unmentioned party Y also uses them. It is also possible that the "attack ads" are about true things that the writer's news outlet has ignored because it backs party Y.

One final point here is that there was a time when news producers tended to be professionals, especially if they worked for big media outlets. Today, however, anyone with a video camera, a website, or a multitrack digital recorder can become a news producer of sorts. Steven Livingston and W. Lance Bennett report on event-driven, spontaneous news items that may begin with someone standing on a street corner with a videotape camera—as opposed to events that are created for news consumption, such as press conferences, interviews with officials, and interest-group demonstrations.[22] They note that cheap electronic equipment makes event-driven news more likely to be carried in broadcast news, such as when a bystander with a video camera records the crash of an airplane. However, they also note that "when an unpredicted, nonscripted, spontaneous event is covered in the news, the one predictable component of the coverage remains official sources [as in asking a public figure for information or an analysis of the event]." Lastly, being a news consumer is more challenging today than it was yesterday and will be still more challenging tomorrow. This is because of increases in the volume of media output, the increasingly more sophisticated techniques being used to produce media content, and the constant creation of new media uses. Perhaps educators and parents need to adopt a greater sense of urgency in promoting in children a greater communication literacy for the written and spoken word and the audiovisual media message.

Entertainment and Influence

Product placement is perhaps a trivial example of the influence contained in the media's entertainment formats, although lots of money can sometimes be at stake. But when we expose ourselves to professionally created drama, comedy, music, and sports, we allow the creators of these performances to influence our values, attitudes, beliefs, and intended actions, even if they don't intend this. How many of us would just love to own one of the cars driven by James Bond in the Bond movies, even without the gadgets? How many of us have seen attractive furnishings in a house used as a set for a film and then have gone out the next day to see if we could duplicate the visual appeal? How many of us just wish we could find a dating or marriage partner just like a character we have seen portrayed in a movie? How many people in other countries might see a movie about life in a free country in the democracies of the West and then be ready to tear down a barbed-wire fence to free themselves of a local tyranny? How many tyrannical governments control the content of media entertainment because they are afraid of the media's potential effect on their monopolies of power?

Perhaps the most powerful effects of entertainment in the media concern the formation of attitudes, beliefs, instrumental values, and habits of younger people. A summary of the effects of media violence on children is provided by a report by the Media Awareness Network, a nonprofit academic organization based in Canada, which says in part:

Whether or not exposure to media violence causes increased levels of aggression and violence in young people is the perennial question of media effects research. Some experts, like University of Michigan professor L. Rowell Huesmann, argue that fifty years of evidence show "that exposure to media violence causes children to behave more aggressively and affects them as adults years later." Others, like Jonathan Freedman of the University of Toronto, maintain that "the scientific evidence simply does not show that watching violence either produces violence in people, or desensitizes them to it."[23]

Researcher Andrea Martinez at the University of Ottawa has concluded that the above controversy stems from several problems with trying to research this issue.[24] One problem is that it is sometimes hard to define and measure variables about program violence and effects. She points out that some researchers, as did the late George Gerbner, define violence as the act or threat of injuring or killing someone even within the genre of cartoon violence. But others, such as University of Laval professors Guy Paquette and Jacques de Guise, do not study cartoon violence because of its fantasy content. She also points to a problem with correlation research when studying the effects of media violence. Does the content cause the behavior? Or are violence-prone people more attracted to media violence? Or does some third set of variables affect viewing preferences and aggressive behavior? In her final report to the Canadian Radio-television and Telecommunications Commission, Martinez concludes "that most studies support a positive, though weak, relation between exposure to television violence and aggressive behaviour." Although that relationship cannot be confirmed systematically, she agrees with Dutch researcher Tom Van der Voot, who argues that it would be illogical to conclude that "a phenomenon does not exist simply because it is found at times not to occur, or only to occur under certain circumstances."[25] I might also add here that whether violence is portrayed in an approving or disapproving way, or whether the viewer sees things from the victim's point of view or the aggressor's point of view may be important in understanding the effects of media violence.

Whatever its effects, violent programming has, according to media researcher Nancy Signorielli, "remained stable in prime-time network programs broadcast between the spring of 1993 and the fall of 2001 and similar to levels found in studies of the 1970s and 1980s."[26] Violence is in about 60 percent of TV programs and is somewhat sanitized. Notably, however, violent characters often avoid the consequences for their acts and seem to get a free pass on the morality of aggression. Interestingly, Signorielli reports that regardless of actual crime statistics, television-portrayed crime is proportionately committed more by men than women and is committed in equal proportions by whites and minorities. As the decades come and go, some people perennially complain about violence in the media, while other people cannot apparently get enough of it.

Beyond the use of violence, the use of stereotypes to portray various people is also criticized in media entertainment. Parents complain that excessive television consumption harms their children's intellectual development. And women worry about the effects of pornography on the social and criminal behavior of men. For a long time, critics have complained about the shallowness of entertainment. Now with the coming of **interactive media**, the issues will get even more complicated because consumers will use media content in more personalized ways. One thing we can be certain of is that there will be an ever-increasing need for media researchers to try and understand what is happening to people in their increasingly more media-saturated lives, a saturation now starting at younger and younger ages.

According to researchers Victoria Rideout and Elizabeth Vandewater, very young children are now a part of the world's mass-mediated societies:

> Recent years have seen an explosion in electronic media marketed directly at the very youngest children in our society: A booming market of videotapes and DVDs aimed at infants one to 18 months, the launching of the first TV show specifically targeting children as young as 12 months, and a multi-million dollar industry selling computer games and even special keyboard tappers for children as young as nine months old. . . . Despite this plethora of new media aimed at very young children, next to nothing is known about how these changes have played out in young people's lives.[27]

Rideout and Vandewater report (1) children six and under spend an average of two hours a day with TV and videos; (2) TV watching begins at very early ages, and well before the medical community recommends; (3) a high proportion of very young children use new digital media, including the 50 percent of four-to-six-year-olds who have played video games and the 70 percent who have used computers; (4) two out of three children up to the age of six live in homes where the TV is usually left on at least half the time, even if no one is watching, and one in three lives in a home where the TV is on most of the time, while children in the latter group appear to read less than other children and to be slower to learn to read; (5) many parents see media as an important educational tool and beneficial to their children's intellectual development, and parents' attitudes on this issue appear to be related to the amount of time their children spend using each medium; and (6) parents think that their children's watching television has a direct effect on their behavior and are more likely to see positive rather than negative behaviors being copied.

What is very interesting about this study are the attitudes of parents. If they are using the television as a baby sitter, we might speculate that their positive attitude toward increased television watching by their young children can be explained by cognitive dissonance theory: if I am doing something for my own convenience, I may want to see the effects of that practice as positive, especially when my young children are involved.

Historical Trends in News and Entertainment Media

Though newspaper readership today is high, it is down from what it was before television news became competitive in the 1960s. But perhaps the most dramatic format changes in the media have occurred with radio broadcasting over the years. In the beginning (the mid-1920s to the late 1940s), radio was the prime electronic medium; it offered music, news, comedy, and especially, dramatic entertainment. Housewives of the 1930s and 1940s would often use the radio as a companion while they ironed clothes, mended garments, pruned the bushes in the backyard with a window open, cleaned, prepared meals from scratch, paid the delivery tradesmen at the front door, and watched the younger children and pets. One of the most popular radio personalities of the 1940s and early 1950s was Arthur Godfrey, who put on a live variety-show in the mornings. In the evenings, people could listen to radio sitcoms, drama programs with a new story each week, and big-band music. Then television came along and relegated many of today's radio outlets to market-segmented music, "All news headlines all day," and talk radio.

Television has undergone its own changes since its inception in the late 1940s. As surprising as it might sound today, local television stations signed off late at night in the 1950s and 1960s, often playing a recording of the National Anthem as they switched to a test pattern and then stopped broadcasting any signal at all. A television viewer magically transported from 1950 to today would be shocked by tuning in a cable-station that shows explicit sex acts in living color. The amount of programming available today is mind-boggling when compared to what was available in the fifties; big cities then had three network affiliates and one or two local outlets, while rural locations had even fewer choices, with one local affiliate carrying perhaps just some of the programming from all three networks. There have also been astonishing changes in the ongoing competition between television and the cinema. In the 1950s, Hollywood films tried to compete with the new upstart television by turning to wide-screen movies, 3-D (which was a flop), and vivid color. Today, the latest television sets are as big and flat as smaller movie screens and offer features such as wide-screen and HDTV.

Chapter in Retrospect

VIGNETTE **An Idea for a Children's Cartoon Program**

We have discussed some of the unfortunate effects of television on children, but there are notable children's programs that have been very successful, while also having constructive effects on their audiences. Perhaps we could imagine another type of interactive television, and one in which viewers might make suggestions to television producers about the particular programs made available to their children. So in the spirit of trying to encourage things that are both constructive and popular, I'll make a suggestion here for a future television program for children. Perhaps the best way to create an idea for a children's television cartoon is to have fun coming up with the idea, hoping that what was fun for the creator will be fun for the consumer. Below is an idea built around a mythical group I have dubbed the Barrel People, who are barrel-shaped cartoon characters. I am creating this idea in hopes that a producer will like and develop it.

What would a typical day be like for a group of people who live in Barrel City and do barrel-like things all day? The general idea for the cartoon show might revolve around Bernie and Beth and their two children, Bianca and Brian, and pet dog Bobo (whose ears flap like airplane wings when excited). Episodes would find fun in dramatizing the hopes, fears, and antics of this barrel family along with their friends, neighbors, and the many other peculiar people of Barrel City. The following are idea-generators:

What are the Barrel People's biographies and histories?
How exactly do they get around?
What do the interiors of their homes look like?
What are their conversational styles and voices like (occasionally an echo)?

What is their sense of humor like?
Do they have fears and hopes? Likes and dislikes?
Schools? Jobs? Finances?
Entertainment? Sports?
Politics? Art? Philosophy?

Where on earth did these barrel people come from? What do they do for entertainment? Roll around all day? What kind of work do they do? If they play at sports, is it some kind of roller-derby? Someone once said that if history were written by cats, history would be mostly about cats. So what would barrel-people history read like? Perhaps there is a barrel philosophy built around rotten apples? Would it be fun to actually be a barrel person and roll around in Barrel City for one day? Would Barrel City be built with large, multitiered barrels and small cute barrels? If Barrel People must roll to get around, flatness would be a very important feature of Barrel City. Perhaps there is an ongoing battle among the people of Barrel City against "unflatness." Some Barrel People might be empty and some filled to the brim with things like crackers. In any case, a group of program developers might have fun playing with these possibilities and then come up with ideas that will entertain children in positive but fun ways, as long as the barrels do not crash into each other too often.

Summary and Conclusions

The mass media have been with us since the development of the metallic, movable-type printing press in the 1400s, and the world has not been the same since. The media by their very nature express their power to influence the affairs of people across both space and time. In the twentieth century, the power of the media increased dramatically with the invention of radio, film, television, sound recordings, computer programs, and the Internet. The actual content of the media provides such user gratifications as information, escape, social knowledge, and interaction. But this content may also foster dependency on the media. Advertising brings with it consumerism; the news media bring social and political influence; and entertainment influences us socially. Younger generations especially have had parts of their education provided by media experiences.

KEY TERMS

advocacy ad
attack ad
barker
contrast ad
cultivation theory
culture jamming
deterministic
ethicizing
extrinsic value
glittering generalities
interactive media

intrinsic value
media power (gatekeeping, hegemony, informational, legitimacy, narcotizing, status-conferring, technical-expertise, uses and gratifications)
name substitutions
sales pitch
slogans

story-telling narratives
subvertising
surreal images
symbiotic
syncretic
ubiquitous
video montage
visual figuratives
weasel words

REVIEW QUESTIONS

1. What are the common sources of power for the mass media?
2. How is uses and gratifications theory different from dependency theory?
3. What common steps can be followed to construct an ad?
4. In what ways can news stories become biased?
5. What does the term *product placement* mean?
6. What is the two-step process for purchasing consumer products? How does it help explain what ads seek to do?
7. What does the term *video montage* mean?
8. What are six things that contribute to the success of advertising in general?
9. How can news and entertainment programming have persuasive effects?

SUGGESTED PROJECTS AND ACTIVITIES

1. Use a program like Microsoft Word or work by hand to create a print ad for a public-service message you strongly favor. Include a banner headline, a visual of some type, and a brief message.
2. Have someone block out the headline of a newspaper news story so you cannot read it. Then read the story and write down what you think the headline should be. Now unmask the actual headline as it was written by the newspaper. Are the two different? In your opinion, did the original headline fairly frame the story? Which headline was better? Why?
3. Write a letter to your favorite television character (drama or sitcom) and explain why you enjoy watching the program week in and week out. List all the media uses and gratifications you obtain by watching the program. Send the letter or not, depending on how you feel about the letter when it is finished.
4. Write an idea for a new television program (sitcom, drama, or reality). Analyze what uses and gratifications your proposed program will provide for viewers. If you have time, develop more and more detail (e.g., add character names, possible themes for individual episodes, and locales).

QUESTIONS FOR DISCUSSION

1. Does it seem ethical for a reporter to leave out important details of a story because the source of the story might not be so cooperative the next time if the negative details are included this time?
2. Should television news tell viewers when someone interviewed is not just a person on the street but is a representative of an interest group?
3. Should advertisements directed at younger children be carefully censored to prevent advertisers from taking unfair advantage of children, or should parents be solely responsible for what their children watch? Are there idealist and realist perspectives here? How do they apply?
4. Are our interpersonal experiences in public suffering because of the portable media we carry around with us?

5. Is product placement in movies ethical?

6. If you had your own personal, large, outside billboard, what would you print on it?

Notes

1. Simpler versions of printing presses were developed in China centuries earlier, but these were not nearly as powerful as Gutenberg's.

2. If you have a nervous stomach, the jitters, or worry about world events you have no control over, you might give this a try.

3. Elizabeth Burch and Joseph Harry, "Counter-Hegemony and Environmental Justice in California Newspapers: Source Use Patterns in Stories about Pesticides and Farm Workers," *Journalism and Mass Communication Quarterly* 81, no. 3 (Autumn 2004): 559–77.

4. General categories provided by Denis McQuail, *Mass Communication Theory: An Introduction* (Thousand Oaks, CA: Sage, 1987). Examples for general categories and digital-television categories are from Julia Livaditi, Konstantina Vassilopoulou, Christos Lougos, and Konstantinos Chorianopoulos, "Needs and Gratifications for Interactive TV Applications: Implications for Designers," Athens University of Economics and Business, http://csdl.computer.org/comp/proceedings/hicss/2003/1874/04/187440100b.pdf (11 February 2005).

5. Paul Lazerfeld and Robert Merton, "Mass Communication, Popular Taste, and Organized Social Action," in *The Communication of Ideas*, ed. Lyman Bryson (New York: Cooper Square, 1964), 95–118.

6. Lazerfeld and Merton, "Mass Communication, Popular Taste, and Organized Social Action."

7. See for example William Rogers, *Communication in Action* (New York: Holt, Rinehart, and Winston, 1984), 281–82.

8. Karen Johnson-Cartee and Gary Copeland, *Strategic Political Communication: Rethinking Social Influence, Persuasion, and Propaganda* (Lanham, MD: Rowman and Littlefield, 2004), 127–34.

9. Michael Schudson, *Advertising: The Uneasy Persuasion* (New York: Basic Books, 1984), 210–17.

10. Kathleen Jamieson, *Everything You Think You Know about Politics: And Why You're Wrong* (New York: Basic Books, 2000), 97–106, 160. In the 1990s, the concept of a campaign "war room" was coined. The war room is intended to manage, as if in a crisis, incoming and outgoing attacks, whether in political ad form or news form.

11. As Kenneth Burke reminds us, intrinsic assessments of something or someone concern issues of "substance"; extrinsic assessments of something or someone concern issues of "standing." Intrinsically, you may be a skillful person; extrinsically, your peers may think of you as a skillful person. Thus, people can assess you both by noting your actual skills and by noting your reputation with regard to such skills among your peers. Such extrinsic factors as reputation do not always have to be true or accurate, as long as they are generally believed or commonly applied by others, but other extrinsic factors may require truth or accuracy, such as locating your office in an exclusive part of town in order to project a credible image for your business.

12. James Twitchell, *Adcult USA: The Triumph of Advertising in American Culture* (New York: Columbia University Press, 1996), 9–40.

13. Vance Packard, *Hidden Persuaders* (New York: D. McKay, 1957).

14. Raymie McKerrow, Alan Monroe, Douglas Ehninger, and Bruce Gronbeck, *Principles and Types of Speech Communication* (Boston: Allyn and Bacon, 2003), 153–70.

15. See for example Rogers, *Communication in Action*, 276.

16. Michael Geis, *The Language of Television Advertising* (New York: Academic Press, 1982), 109–30.

17. For additional description of these techniques, see Charles Stewart and William Cash, *Interviewing: Principles and Practices* (Dubuque, IA: William Brown, 1978), 224–26.

18. This tactic was popularized for television by Timex when in the 1950s it dramatized a watch's durability by placing one in a top-loading washing machine on live television (with a security guard

posted) at the beginning of a popular show. Just before the end of the program, the watch would be fetched from the machine and held up to a boom mike through which it could be heard to still tick. This is how Timex popularized the slogan it has used over the decades, "It takes a licking and keeps on ticking." Also see discussion in chapter 11 on Aristotle's *more or less* enthymeme: If something is not the case when it is more probable (the luggage is not damaged when it is abused), it certainly is not the case when it is less probable (the luggage will [therefore] not be damaged when it is properly used).

19. Eric Freedman and Frederick Fico, "Whither the Experts? Newspaper Use of Horse Race and Issue Experts in Coverage of Open Governors' Races in 2002," *Journalism and Mass Communication Quarterly* 81, no. 3 (Autumn 2004): 498–510.

20. Andrew Mendelson and Esther Thorson, "How Verbalizers and Visualizers Process the Newspaper Environment," *Journal of Communication* 54 (September 2004): 474–92; and Kathleen Schmitt, Albert Gunthert, and Janice Liebhart, "Why Partisans See Mass Media as Biased," *Communication Research* 31, no. 6 (December 2004): 623–41.

21. Daniel Romer, Kathleen Hall Jamieson, and Sean Aday, "Television News and the Cultivation of Fear of Crime," *Journal of Communication* 53, no. 1 (March 2003): 88–104; Bernd Henning and Peter Vorderer, "Psychological Escapism: Predicting the Amount of Television Viewing by Need for Cognition," *Journal of Communication* 51, no. 1 (2001): 100–120.

22. Steven Livingston and W. Lance Bennett, "Gatekeeping, Indexing, and Live-Event News: Is Technology Altering the Construction of News?" *Political Communication* 20, no. 4 (October–December 2003): 363–80.

23. Media Awareness Network, "Research on the Effects of Media Violence," 2005, www.media-awareness.ca/english/issues/violence/effects_media_violence.cfm (13 February 2005).

24. Media Awareness Network, "Research on the Effects of Media Violence," 2005, www.media-awareness.ca/english/issues/violence/effects_media_violence.cfm (16 June 2006).

25. Media Awareness Network, "Research on the Effects of Media Violence," 2005, www.media-awareness.ca/english/issues/violence/effects_media_violence.cfm (16 June 2006).

26. Nancy Signorielli, "Prime-Time Violence 1993–2001: Has the Picture Really Changed?" *Journal of Broadcasting and Electronic Media* 47, no. 1 (March 2003): 36–57.

27. Victoria Rideout and Elizabeth Vandewater, "Zero to Six: Electronic Media in the Lives of Infants, Toddlers, and Preschoolers," Henry Kaiser Foundation, 2003, www.kff.org/entmedia/7239.cfm (13 February 2005).

Skills for Senders

Have you ever said to yourself, "I wish I had spoken up"? Or, "If only I had introduced myself"? Or, "Did I say the wrong thing"? Conversational Confidence is the answer. Just by listening, you'll master the proven interpersonal skills you need to deal with every individual, every group, every occasion. The result? New doors will open to you. You won't hesitate to accept an invitation, to approach someone important, to seize an opportunity. You'll never again feel like an outsider. Success will naturally flow your way—and with less effort than you ever imagined possible.

—VERBALADVANTAGE (advertisement in the *New Republic*, 12 March 2001)

PERSUASION AND leadership are closely intertwined: leaders usually need to be persuasive, and persuaders always need to provide communicative leadership for their audiences. You might provide persuasive leadership for just one other person in a conversation. Or you might provide persuasive leadership to a small group, a larger audience, or even a large segment of society. For persuasion, you may need to use a mix of three styles of leadership. When you ask an audience to trust you about something or ask them to put faith in what you argue but cannot directly prove, you are relying on a type of **authoritarian** leadership, built in part on your credibility, or ethos. When you simply place the facts before an audience and summarize the possible conclusions to draw, but do not recommend any of them, you have chosen **laissez-faire,** or nondirective leadership, by giving them wide latitude in accepting your influence. When you involve the audience in your reasoning process and then recommend a course of action, belief, or attitude, you have opted for a **democratic** style. Here you encourage consensus and compromise, built on what the audience already accepts, to then negotiate alterations, additions, or even deletions in their beliefs, attitudes, or intended behavior.

Persuasion in Public

Two persuasive genres that require a good deal of preparation are giving or writing a speech, and taking your case to small-claims court. When you write or give a speech, you provide communicative leadership for your audience. You lead them through an orchestrated mix of thoughts, feelings, and attitudes. Your audience relies on you to help them get through this mix profitably. When you take a case to small-claims court, you also provide leadership for listeners (especially the judge) while you are speaking. This is true even though the judge is in charge of the proceedings. The judge, like everyone else present at court, will rely on you to lead them through a thought process while you speak persuasively about your claims.

Giving or Writing a Persuasive Speech

There are many texts devoted entirely to the mechanics of public speaking.[1] Nonetheless, we can highlight the basic steps here. In many cases, you should plan to give an *extemporaneous* speech, using an outline to prompt or remind you about what to say. However, *written* speeches are sometimes preferred when, for example, you are running for office, speaking to members of an organization, or addressing a graduation class.[2] *Memorized* speeches are best left to the dramatic arts, while *impromptu* speeches given without preparation are best used in emergencies when there is no time to prepare, but you already have the information your audience needs without delay. Box 15.1 summarizes the process of planning an extemporaneous persuasive speech.

First, write down your tentative **speech purpose**. The speech's purpose identifies in a single sentence the intended outcome of the speech. Often purpose statements for speeches will contain words or phrases like *convince, persuade, gain support for*, and *prove*. The sentence should also describe what change there will be—if you succeed. Sometimes your statement of purpose identifies your intended audience: "To get members of my class to feel more positively toward donating blood," and sometimes it doesn't: "To prove that crash-diets are often harmful."

Next, write down your tentative **thesis** just under your purpose statement, as best as you can word it at this point. The thesis statement tells in a single sentence what your speech is about. A thesis statement is your theme: it verbalizes the most general claim in your speech.

BOX 15.1
Preparing an Extemporaneous Persuasive Speech

Identify the speech's purpose: to convince my family to take a vacation together next summer at the Grand Canyon

Identify thesis: Vacationing at the Grand Canyon is an educational and enjoyable experience.

Identify your audience: immediate family members

Analyze your audience: demographics of members, psychographics of members, topographics of the occasion when proposal will be made

Research the topic: travel directions, accommodations, costs, attractions, history

Identify the main points you want to make: adventure, the Grand Canyon as national asset, the Grand Canyon's spectacular views, the making of family memories, good value for money and time spent

Identify the supporting details for each point: facts, descriptions, examples, definitions

Informally sequence and organize your main ideas: what and where, who, why, when, how

Create two different outlines: (1) a fully worded outline using sentences, and (2) a speaking outline that abbreviates the ideas with single words or brief phrases. Use conventions (e.g., roman numerals, capital letters).

Consider adding presentation aids: maps, photos (e.g., the Colorado River, Kaibab National Forest, Dragon Corridor, the majestic North Rim)

Practice your delivery: concentrate on timing, wording, familiarity with flow of ideas

Sometimes the thesis explains why your audience should do as your specific purpose suggests. A particular, specific purpose could be achieved with any number of different theses, each one serving as the single theme for a separate speech. Say I want to convince people to become wilderness firefighters, sometimes called "smoke jumpers" (my speech purpose). One thesis I could use to achieve my purpose might be "Spending a year as a volunteer smoke jumper will help you round out your résumé when you start looking for a career position." In this example, the speech purpose will describe what I want listeners to do (become smoke jumpers), and the thesis explains why they should do it. An alternative thesis that could be used to motivate listeners might be "There is a critical need for volunteer smoke jumpers in the far West." And still a third thesis might be "Forest fires kill defenseless animals—you could save them by becoming a smoke jumper." Each of these three potential theses would result in a somewhat different speech. I could even put them together for a longer speech: "There are three gratifying reasons for becoming a smoke jumper." All of these theses could end up accomplishing the same specific purpose, but by differing routes.

Sometimes speech purpose and thesis statements may sound just a little too similar (e.g., "To convince people that the roof leaks" and "The roof really is leaking"). If the statements sound too similar, you may need to think a little harder about what you really mean. Perhaps you could better write your thesis here as "This old house shows ominous signs of a roof leak."

With a speech purpose and thesis in hand, you next need to identify and analyze your audience. For this, you can review the tools described in chapter 7: a *demographic* analysis of the social categories auditors fall into; a *psychographic* analysis of auditors' current knowledge and attitudes about your topic and you; and a *topographic* analysis of "the lay of the land" rhetorically speaking—that is, where, when, and under what circumstances the speech will be given. In box 15.1, I have identified immediate family members as the audience to be analyzed. Here, one part of demographic analysis might concern the ages of the family members, and another might concern the family's finances. A third might concern the geographic region in which the family lives, vis-à-vis the destination of the trip. Psychographically, your analysis would want to take into consideration the personalities, attitudes, values, and beliefs of particular family members. And topographically, your analysis should concern the wisdom of or problems with picking a particular occasion that will set a helpful tone in which to discuss the proposed trip (perhaps the occasion will be dinner this weekend, or a local trip scheduled for next week, or when watching television together tonight).

Next, do your *research* at the library, online, with interviews or letters sent to experts or witnesses, with visits to particular places of interest, and the like. After you have completed this research, your speech purpose, thesis, and analysis of your audience may need adjustments in light of what you find out. For the proposed trip of our example, perhaps you will want to do your research through (1) the Grand Canyon's history, (2) factual information about how to get to the Grand Canyon and what to expect when you get there, and (3) descriptions from someone your family members know who has visited the Grand Canyon and had a good time.

With the results of your research in hand, identify the *main points* of the speech. You now ask yourself, "What broad, general reasons support the thesis?" In identifying main ideas that support the Grand Canyon trip, you might want, depending on your audience analysis, to focus on adventure, the Grand Canyon as a national asset, the Grand Canyon's spectacular views, the making of family memories, or the Grand Canyon's good value for money and time spent. Or to take a slightly different example, say you want to get your audience to think more fondly of the United Kingdom, and so you write this thesis: "Historically, socially, and politically, the mother country of the United States is the United Kingdom." You might then list four or five broad main ideas that support this thesis: (1) America began its life as a group of English colonies; (2) Americans speak the *English* language on Main Street, in corporate business settings, in public schools, in government, on network television, and in Hollywood films; (3) America's legal system has inherited features of English law, and America's Constitution and laws are written in English; (4) America has often been on the same side as England in times of war; and (5) many Americans can trace their ancestry back to England. It is important to put great care into assembling the list of main ideas for your speech. Ask yourself, "Do the main ideas develop the thesis adequately?[3] Do any of the main ideas stray off the main thesis? Are there too few or too many main ideas?"[4] In choosing your main ideas, ask or think about what the audience will find persuasive. If the audience for the United Kingdom speech is Americans with college educations, you could use ideas that require knowledge of American and European history. If you will be speaking to sixth graders, you might choose simpler main ideas.

Identify the *supporting details* of your speech. Now you can employ the full set of Grand Canyon facts, statistics, stories, personal statements of people, descriptions of events, details, demonstrations, examples, case histories, and anecdotes that you discovered during your research. These supporting items flesh out your main ideas or arguments. If one main point in the speech is that "We'll all become healthier from the walking we can do at the Grand Canyon," you might give examples of the benefits to be had from walking, such as improved cardiovascular strength, reduced psychological stress, and weight loss. For each of the examples you might also give specific details, such as your personal experiences with stress reduction from walking, or a scientific report about increased physical fitness from walking. In any speech, the supporting materials are like the leaves of a tree, while the main ideas or arguments are the branches, and the thesis statement is the trunk. To finish the analogy, the specific purpose of a persuasive speech is getting the audience to favorably view and then be influenced by the tree.

Now *outline* your ideas, using standard conventions. For example:

Speech's purpose: To convince my family to take a vacation together next summer at the Grand Canyon.

Thesis: Vacationing at the Grand Canyon is an educational and enjoyable experience.

I.   The trip will be an adventure.
    A.   It will be exciting, fun, and full of surprises.
    B.   We will be a team having fun together.
II. The Grand Canyon is one of the nation's grand geographical assets.
    A.   It is interesting geologically.
    B.   It is an important region in the Southwest.
III. The Grand Canyon is filled with spectacular views.
    A.   The size and depth of the canyon are extraordinary.
    B.   The textures and colors of the landscape are unique.
IV. We'll make family memories that we'll treasure over the years.
    A.   We'll have a treasure-trove of pictures.
    B.   We'll remember each other there together.

Experts on giving speeches advise that you make at least two outlines. The first one should use reasonably well-developed sentences and a **full-sentence outline**, so you can see how well your ideas fit together. But your **speaking outline** should be more abbreviated, using phrases rather than long sentences. The longer the sentences are in your speaking outline, the more time you will take looking down at your notes each time you look for the next idea to talk about.

As you order your main ideas (and minor ideas under each main idea) in outline form, you can proceed in several practical ways: (1) arrange by chronology or time periods, perhaps by listing steps to convince a doubter how simple it is to do something, or by claiming a country's foreign policy has followed a particular strategy over the decades; (2) arrange topically, such as by listing together all the practical or objective benefits of taking the family trip to the Grand Canyon, and then listing together all the subjective or emotional benefits; (3) arrange spatially, as a parent might do to show their children how best to keep their rooms looking neat, or as land developers might do when they outline a clever plan to acquire adjacent properties for building a future shopping center ("To the north we have . . . , to the south we have . . ."); (4) arrange by cause–effect, where you might move your message in several steps from a description of what happens when you stop changing the oil in a car's engine to a description of how oil deprivation will eventually ruin the engine; (5) arrange by effect–cause, where you might claim to have solved a mystery by reasoning backward from the crime to who did it, how, and why; and (6) arrange by problem–solution, as for example, you might instruct a novice baker in what to do when bread dough becomes too dry or too moist during preparation. Other more specialized arrangements may be found in a text on public speaking.

At this point in your preparation, you could *consider adding presentation aids*. Modern speakers use a variety of aids for gaining audience attention, orienting listeners, communicating information both effectively and efficiently, and projecting a professional image. As mentioned in chapter 3, the options at your disposal include physical props, diagrams, pictures, maps, posters, graphs, charts, tables, slides, sound recordings, videotape, overhead transparencies, and more recently, computer-generated graphics (e.g., Powerpoint). But with all these things available to you, be careful that your visual aids do not come to dominate your speech—a speech relies most heavily on the spoken word. In the extreme, visual aids can turn a speech into a media production, for better or worse. To take our Grand Canyon example, you might include pictures of the Colorado River carved through the landscape; beautiful Kaibab National Forest, as might be taken from an off-road safari jeep; Dragon Corridor, the widest and deepest portion of the Grand Canyon; and the majestic North Rim.

Finally, it is important to *practice your delivery*. Every speech you give should be rehearsed at least once before you talk to your group. Some experts, such as those at Toastmasters International (a public-speaking association), advise that you rehearse four or five times to get your speech right and to become familiar with wording your ideas and with following the flow of your outline. You also need to rehearse to find out how long your speech will last. And remember that presenting your speech occurs both with sound and sight. Revisit what we said about nonverbal communication in chapter 2, because the impressions audience members form about you and your topic can make or break even a well-researched speech.

Techniques of the Written Speech

Sometimes what you need to say in a speech is so important that you will decide to write out your ideas, sentence by sentence, and then read them to your audience, or have someone else read them—or even have someone else write them, if you have the resources to delegate this. To facilitate reading to the audience, the speech writer often uses relatively short paragraphs with double spaces between them. While the canon of invention is used similarly in either an extemporaneous or written speech, the canon of style may at times vary between the two, with written speeches made up of very carefully selected words, perfect grammar, and great economy of expression (you may want to review canons of persuasion in chapter 3). The following is an excerpt of an excellent written speech delivered in November 1998 by Tony Blair, who made history in becoming the first British prime minister ever to address the Irish Parliament. The opening lines of his speech illustrate his efforts to create a bond with his audience.

> Members of the Dail and Seanad, after all the long and torn history of our two peoples, standing here as the first British prime minister ever to address the joint Houses of the Oireachtas, I feel profoundly both the history in this event, and I feel profoundly the enormity of the honour that you are bestowing upon me. From the bottom of my heart, go raibh mile maith agaibh [a thousand thanks].

Ireland, as you may know, is in my blood. My mother was born in the flat above her grandmother's hardware shop on the main street of Ballyshannon in Donegal. She lived there as a child, started school there and only moved when her father died; her mother remarried and they crossed the water to Glasgow.

We spent virtually every childhood summer holiday up to when the troubles really took hold in Ireland, usually at Rossnowlagh, the Sands House Hotel, I think it was. And we would travel in the beautiful countryside of Donegal. It was there in the seas off the Irish coast that I learned to swim, there that my father took me to my first pub, a remote little house in the country, for a Guinness, a taste I've never forgotten and which it is always a pleasure to repeat.

Even now, in my constituency of Sedgefield, which at one time had 30 pits or more, all now gone, virtually every community remembers that its roots lie in Irish migration to the mines of Britain.

So like it or not, we, the British and the Irish, are irredeemably linked.

As illustrated above, the *introduction* may be the one place where a written speech must especially shine. You sometimes need to pay attention to protocol in exactly how you welcome various people in the audience (e.g., "President Goodperson, proud parents, esteemed faculty members, honored guests, happy graduates"). Next you do your best to grab the audience's attention, build rapport, motivate interest in what is to come, and orient the audience by stating the theme or thesis of the speech. The several sentences of the introduction must also function as a transition from the central theme to the beginning sentences of the body of the speech. Effective introductions often revolve around one of the following rhetorical devices, which should be chosen for their effectiveness and appropriateness to the main topic.[5]

Controversial or *startling statements*. "Sometimes your best friends can be your worst enemies. There are times when the people closest to us feel threatened by our ambitions or successes. Feeling threatened, some may even try to sabotage our efforts."

Quotations. "'O what a tangled web we weave, when first we practice to deceive'—so said novelist-poet Sir Walter Scott two centuries ago. Nearly twenty centuries ago, Quintillian, the Roman rhetorician, wryly noted that 'A liar should have a good memory.' Telling the truth is always much easier than lying, because you need not keep track of what you said last week or last year—just report the facts as best you understand and remember them."

Stories or *anecdotes*. "A bus had stopped to take on a passenger close to where I was standing the other morning, when I noticed a man about a quarter of a block away running toward the bus. I was about to call to the driver, 'Someone's coming for the bus,' but for some odd reason, said nothing. Then just as the man got to the still-open front door of the bus—he ran right past it. He was jogging, not trying to catch the bus. The lesson here is to be wary of treating inferences about our perceptions as though they were facts. Had I asked the driver to wait, I would have been embarrassed when the delay I caused turned out to be unnecessary."

One-liners or *jokes*. "Gorgeous, intelligent, kind, sweet, charming, witty, hilarious, friendly . . . well, enough about me. How are you?"[6]

Witty observation. "'Few sinners are saved after the first twenty minutes of a sermon,' according to Mark Twain."

Aphorism (a succinct statement of opinion or self-evident truth): "There is a saying, the more indebted the speaker to the audience, the shorter should be the speech. That creates a problem here, because in asking me to speak you have made me feel honored; but there is a subject that is crucial to us all . . ."

Current events. "As anyone must know who has been on planet Earth over the last several years, security procedures for getting on planes have moved in some very strange directions, with elderly people being asked to remove their shoes before they can board."

Personal experience. "Without mentioning it on the monthly statement, my ex-bank took a $10-a-month penalty fee out of a passbook savings account in which I kept less than the minimum balance required. After two years, my balance of $200 was down to zero even though I had made no withdrawals. What has happened to civilized banking ethics?"

Thought-provoking questions. "How many hidden problems loiter in our midst, threatening our organization's well-being as I speak here tonight? While hidden problems can be buried deeply in the infrastructure beneath our feet, they can also stand in full view, masquerading as harmless bits of the status quo."

Illustrations of the theme. In the Irish Parliament speech above, Tony Blair describes how Ireland is in his blood by citing several examples.

When you are speaking to a high-powered audience with which you want to establish your credibility, a skillful opening will suggest that you know exactly what you are doing as a speech maker. The first thirty seconds or so of your opening will go a long way to projecting the credibility and confidence you need to keep the audience on your side and anticipating a good speech. Perhaps beyond the protocol welcoming statement, your first one or two topic-salient sentences will be the most important part of your introduction. Introductions can also personalize the speech by saying something nice to the audience, referring to the occasion for the speech, or maybe sharing personal reactions or thoughts you had about the opportunity to give the speech.

The written *body* of your speech should say in sentences what you might have said spontaneously had you given an extemporaneous speech. But as I've already mentioned, a written speech should at all times use good grammar, the word choices should be the best possible, and the text should flow with an economy of words that is easy to follow. One other feature of a written speech is that you can insert written reminders in the speech, such as the word *PAUSE* to remind you to give the audience time to react or think, or words that remind you to refer to a visual that you have prepared (e.g., *POINT OUT WESTERN CANADA ON THE LARGER MAP*).

The *close* of your speech is an opportunity to (1) summarize the main points of your speech or remind the audience of your thesis and speech purpose, and (2) leave your audience in the right frame of mind. Here too you can make use of quotations, stories, challenges, and so on, as in the opening.

Taking Your Case to Small-Claims Court

Small-claims court is a venue in which you try to persuade a judge that your case has merit and that you should be compensated financially by the person you are suing (provided that you are the plaintiff). The other person will try to persuade the judge that your case does not have merit. Facts (logos) and credibility (ethos) both have important weights in court. The small-claims court is one place where you do not need a lawyer (or need to be a lawyer) to have your day in court.[7] According to the website MyLawyer.com, small-claims courts provide an easy procedure to assert your rights and settle disputes. One limitation concerns the dollar amount of the dispute, which can range from $2,000 to $15,000. You can check what limits apply where you live by going to www.mylawyer.com/disputes/limits.htm (U.S.) or www.compactlaw.co.uk/free_legal_information/small_claims/small_claims.html (U.K.) for basic information.

Your only cost for bringing a case in small-claims court is the filing fee. General suggestions provided on the U.S. website include the following:

1. If possible, attend a small-claims court for an hour or two to see how it works; also ask for information. If you can get any free legal advice, all the better (but remember that this advice may or may not be reliable, depending on whom you're asking).
2. Gather the documents for your case, including written contracts, correspondence, estimates for repair or replacement, warranties, canceled checks, photographs, or similar materials.
3. You can use a time line to organize your presentation or some other technique, depending on how you plan to explain your case to the judge.
4. If possible and appropriate, bring the item in dispute with you to court (a damaged coat, say).
5. Discuss your case with potential witnesses who have personal knowledge of the case and who may provide evidence that can help in court. Witnesses can provide written, signed statements, or they can appear in person. Appearing in person is better for your case.
6. Sometimes the person you need to provide information may not want to appear or even submit a written statement. You can ask the court clerk to subpoena this person to come to court to testify. Check to see how much lead time you must give the court to issue the subpoena.
7. You also may want to bring an expert witness, who in a damaged automobile case might be an auto mechanic. However, you may have to pay such witnesses for their time in court.
8. If you are unhappy with the outcome, see if you can appeal or ask for a new trial.

Filing Your Case After you have decided to bring a case to small-claims court, you will need several basic items of information to get started, including the name of the defendant, the current address of the defendant, the amount of your claim, and the basis of the claim. Remember that you will also need sufficient funds to pay the filing fee and any sheriff's fee for serving the warrant. In choosing whether to go to court, consider the following examples of small claims: car-accident repair bills, property-damage compensation, collection of money owed, breach of a written or oral contract, return of money used as a down payment, consumer complaints for defective merchandise or faulty workmanship, payment for work not performed, bad checks, recovery of back rent, return of a security deposit. A book by Ralph Warner, *Everybody's Guide to Small Claims Court*, offers some ideas about how to proceed.[8]

Persuasive Performance in Court When your case is called, walk to the front of the court with the intent to persuade ethically. You will talk to the judge, who will ask you and your witnesses to give your side of the case. Show the judge your physical or paper evidence as you tell your story, rather than giving the judge all the evidence at once after finishing your presentation. The plaintiff and plaintiff's witnesses go first, then the defendant and defendant's witnesses. Both plaintiff and defendant are given an opportunity to introduce evidence, ask questions of the witnesses, and explain why the judge should decide one way or the other. Do not argue with the judge or the other party. Remember, you must only convince the judge that you are right, not the other party. There is no jury. Be courteous to everyone. Have all your evidence (pictures, papers, estimates, witnesses) ready for the judge. The burden is on you to prove your side of the case.

Each case is tried in an informal manner. If your case is uncontested by the defendant, you can reduce your story to several persuasive statements. For example:

> Your Honor, I own the Racafrax Auto Repair Shop. On January 11, 2xxx, I repaired defendant's 2006 Ford Explorer. He paid me $500 and agreed to pay another $500 on March 1. He has not made the second payment. I have copies of the contract he signed and of several unpaid bills I sent him. I am asking for a judgment of $500 plus $55 for my court filing fee and the cost of having the papers served.[9]

But if the case is contested, then you will have to tell your story even more persuasively. Be as brief as you can while you explain and document your case; start with the end of the story, not the beginning (that is, what exactly is your loss and for how much). Do not read your story, but rather use a "show and tell" style. Do not interrupt anyone: a good judge will let all with an interest in the case have their say. For any parts of your story that are difficult to explain, use photos, actual objects, even short videos in some cases; use the blackboard if this will help.

You will have to document whatever the defendant is likely to contest: perhaps that the accident occurred where and when you say it did (use the police report or witnesses), that you were driving through a green light (use the police report or witnesses), that the defendant ran a red light (again, use the police report or witnesses), and that your damage as described amounts to what you say it did (use the mechanic's bill, paid in full). Now the defendant will get a chance to persuade the judge by presenting the other side of the case. But if you are the defendant, do not bother repeating uncontested background facts already mentioned by the plaintiff.

> Your Honor, it's true that the bumper of my truck hit the defendant's fender and pushed it in slightly. But, the key thing to understand is that this happened because the defendant's pickup entered the intersection before it was clear of cars, which were already there, including mine. Therefore the accident was his fault. Let me give you a little background. I was driving south on Cedar and entered the intersection just as the light first turned yellow. I slowed briefly near the center line behind a car that was turning left and then continued across, at which point defendant's car darted in front of me. Therefore when the defendant says the intersection was clear when he entered it—and that I ran a red light—he is not correct. Let me introduce you to Mr. Ed Jones who witnessed what happened and will back up everything I've told you.[10]

Now the judge will have to decide which side has made the most persuasive presentation of the facts, as each side remembers or can document them, and then apply existing traffic laws to reach a finding. The judge will decide if anyone is owed any money. This may be done immediately after the judge's hearing both sides, or the judge may wait to think about the case and then mail you the decision. Once the judge announces the decision, the judge cannot help you any further. Do not argue with the judge. If you have any questions afterward, direct them to the small-claims clerk who helped you file your claim. If you win, neither the judge nor the clerk will collect the money for you. You may be able to appeal a finding you do not like, but unlike the rules for small-claims cases themselves—which are fairly similar in most jurisdictions—the rules regarding appeals of a small-claims finding vary from jurisdiction to jurisdiction.

Pursuing Personal Campaigns

For my more ambitious readers, this section will outline how to contribute something bigger than what one person normally can to their community or even their society. Here I will consider two small **missions** and one larger mission as examples of what we can attempt when sufficiently motivated. In the first case, I will consider the prospects for changing something for the better on campus or in your community, or even in your workplace. Second, I will outline one way to open a small business (as an act of persuasive leadership for your potential clients or customers). Finally, I will briefly look at what it takes to run for high political office.

Pursuing a Community or Campus Campaign

Before you start, review the material in chapter 13 on the steps of a campaign and on the organizational elements of a campaign (see figure 13.1). Then read the following paragraphs and select a sympathetic or compelling topic from either option A (campus issues) or option B (community issues).

Option A. Curriculum offerings, campus housing, extracurricular activities, student services, dining-hall food, clubs, parking, tuition costs, scholarships, relations with surrounding neighborhood, campus visitors policies, speakers invited to campus, course requirements, cultural attractions, campus newspapers, radio and television stations, freedom of speech, faculty qualifications and workloads, use of part-time faculty, laboratory research done on campus, maintenance of buildings and grounds, on-campus use of alcohol or drugs or cigarettes, campus entertainment, majors requirements, library hours, athletic programs, physical-fitness resources, photocopy and computer services, noise, fundraising and recruitment policies from outside organizations, internship opportunities, post-graduation employment help, campus crime.

Option B. Local school policies, taxes, crime, parks and recreation, housing costs, regulation of local stores, roads problems, local elections, real-estate development, zoning regulations, policing policies and practices, noise abatement, mass transportation, public parking, social services, garbage collection, illegal activities (prostitution, drug sales, gambling, child pornography), public nudity, policies about dogs and pets, services for the elderly, religious displays in public, smoking bans, sexual activities in public, outdoor-advertisement restrictions, panhandling on the streets, proper relationship of Church and local government, proper relationship of God and local government, the environment and public and private community properties, nighttime street curfews for children, eating on the beaches and in public parks, public consumption of alcohol.

With topic in hand, follow these steps:

(1) Research your chosen topic for background and to identify a problem to solve. As the promoter of a campaign, you must be among the best informed on the subject, including your subject's relevant history, geography, economics, legalities, and cultural significance. You must also be more motivated than are other people, at least for now. For example, regarding the celebration of Christmas in the public square (religious displays in public), as an activist you should have already learned that in America, Christmas has not always been celebrated publicly. In Boston it was not publicly celebrated until the 1850s (the Puritans did not approve of the public holiday of Christmas). However, Clement Clarke Moore in 1822 gave the public holiday some of its magic for children with the poem "A Visit from St. Nicholas" ("'Twas the Night before Christmas"). In the seventeenth century, public celebration of Christmas was outlawed in England (as a pagan holiday) and did not return for more than a century. And publicly celebrating Christmas in some parts of the world today could get you assassinated.

(2) Identify your mission (a problem or unmet public need to change for the better, at least as you personally see it). This is the most important step, because what exactly you seek to accomplish may ultimately cause people to become happier or unhappier with you, end up done or undone, and turn out to be a good or bad investment of your time and energy. For example, seeking a community ban on cable television has little chance of succeeding. But setting up a rescue center for abandoned or battered pets has a chance of doing so if there is an unmet need for one in your neck of the woods. And as we've now learned in our discussion of persuasion, there will often be the risk of unintended consequences for any campaign. These consequences usually cannot be anticipated in detail, but may be lurking in the shadows.

(3) Gather supporters—because most things with important social ramifications will be difficult or impossible to do alone. You must find a way to motivate these supporters. Ask yourself, "What is in it for them?" And to convince those who will be affected by the outcome of your campaign, ask yourself again, "What is in it for them?" If you want your college or your local community to create more parking spaces for drivers, the people who need more parking space will probably be happy, but what about the people who do not? What can you do to keep them happy? New areas designated for parking might inconvenience people or deprive them of that space for doing other things. Some might simply dislike the idea in principle. If you don't find a way to placate these latter groups, you will have adversaries against your proposals. But perhaps you can win over these critics by pointing out how more parking will create new business opportunities and jobs (e.g., secondary benefits).[11]

(4) Communicate publicly. Sooner or later you will have to broadcast your ideas to wider and wider circles of people and collect the responses of affected people toward your ideas. You might start with a formal or informal survey of attitudes and knowledge within various affected populations. Or you might kick off your campaign with a letter to the editor of a local newspaper (on campus or in the neighborhood). If this is the first public communication in your campaign, put a lot of effort into this letter, because you might lose confidence if your letter goes largely unnoticed or unpublished. But determined people often

will not let early failures discourage them; they pursue things on and on. You might also give a speech at an appropriate community or campus meeting. Or you might place your campaign issue as the centerpiece of a run for local or campus office. With help from others (expertise, emotional support, volunteer efforts, money), you will need to later organize public meetings, events, maybe even fund-raising activities. Then you must soldier on and take the necessary actions for success.

In chapter 13 we also reviewed a campaign started by several people who wanted to save the historical character of their neighborhood. One of the first things they did was write down exactly what they wanted to accomplish. They did so by defining a proposed historic district geographically; announcing publicly their aim to limit development that would ravage this neighborhood of its historical significance and nineteenth-century charm; drafting an appropriate ordinance; arranging for the compilation of a survey of antebellum structures; supplying proof of worthiness of the cause; and seeking the establishment of relations with allied parties. Next, they began to hold weekly meetings, encouraging other residents of the neighborhood to attend. They got a tiny neighborhood newspaper to support them with regular articles and editorials. Eventually, they filed applications, sought political help, asked people with needed professional skills to volunteer services, completed detailed surveys of the properties, and put on events to garner public attention and support.

(5) Assess how much actual progress has been made toward your mission and identify and fine-tune the next things to be done. Persistence and efficiency pay off. And when looking for successful ideas and solutions to problems, remember one U.S. Marine motto that advises that to get things done, you *Adopt* [what has worked for others in similar situations], *Adapt* [what you adopt, to meet the needs of the current situation], and *Perfect* [what you have adapted so that it works effectively and can be employed efficiently]. Also remember the saying that "What needs to get done will show you how to do it."

(6) Strategize in an ongoing way. In planning a campaign, you can consult the citizens' campaign model introduced in chapter 13 that includes descriptions of resources, strategies, and countervailing forces (infrastructural hindrances).

Pursuing a Small-Business Enterprise

The ultimate dream for many is to find success running their own business. You might find a sense of self-sufficiency in making your living as a proprietor. And there is the old saying "You'll never get rich working for someone else." (Actually, a few people at Microsoft *have* gotten rich working for the boss.) A crucial part of starting a business is convincing people to become your customers or clients. With a good idea and lots of potential clients, you have already won a good part of the battle. Even start-up funds are not hard to attract from small investors when things look like they are going to succeed. You can use what you've learned about audiences and persuasion to work on the beginning steps.

(1) Find a mission worth pursuing. Somewhere there are people with unmet needs or wants whom you can satisfy. In a modern, ever-changing society, unmet needs always develop somewhere—so find one. The problem is to identify a want or a need that is currently not being met satisfactorily, at least for some people in some setting. Sometimes the problem is to identify a product or service that people do not yet know they will want or need. Your market may be on the Internet, in your neighborhood, in a big city, at school, or in the classified

section of a magazine or newspaper. Some entrepreneurs think of this problem as finding a *niche*. Others think about finding an ideal location from which to run a business, believing that if they are in the right place at the right time, they cannot help but do well with something needed or wanted.

(2) Get things going. Depending on what your mission becomes, you need to assemble resources (information, knowledge, tools, supplies, a work site, human help, credit, cash). You also need plans for managing whatever staff you may employ, the money, the technical operations of the business, and the ongoing promotion. Most importantly, you must marshal your own executive talents (good judgment, personal motivation, expertise, persistence, skill at motivating others, time management skills).

(3) Plan your promotional strategy. Sales to customers or clients will in large part depend at first on the customers' contact with you, their knowledge about your product or service, and their purchasing motivations. To appreciate what makes people buy things, think about things you have bought recently. What made you buy each of them? You may have just bought a television set. Why now? Why the particular model you bought? Why did you buy it where you did? You may have just had your nails manicured. Why today? Why the person who did them? You may have just bought a frozen dinner in the supermarket. Why a frozen one today? Why this particular dinner? Did you eat breakfast out this morning? Why? Where? Will you buy a pamphlet advertised in the back of a magazine? Why? As you do this analysis, keep tabs on the motivations you bring to your purchases and the knowledge you had about each of these purchases. How important was the location of the place where you bought the item or service? How important was the particular seller to you?

Now build a theory of what things will make potential clients buy your product or service. Talk to friends, relatives, and coworkers about your marketing theory. I personally wrote and sold a typing-tutor computer program on the Internet. It was not a big success, but my product sold to people looking for a cheap, effective way to improve their typing. The tutor sold best to people between the ages of about thirty and sixty and who had children or grandchildren. After paying the income tax on my profits, the net profit was modest—but it was really fun while it lasted.

There are numerous ways to communicate with the people in your potential markets, including word of mouth, the Internet, direct mail, newspaper ads, storefront displays— even a corkboard notice posted in a public space. You must experiment with and find messages that will educate, motivate, and help your future clients or customers get acquainted with you. Feedback will come from people's verbal responses to your pitches and whether they buy or not. Feedback can also come from surveys of customers or potential customers, and from consultations with experts or family and friends. Some marketing counselors may actually work for free on the Web or at a government agency. If you are really fortunate, there may be a newsgroup online that attracts people who have helpful ideas and information you can use. I once got great advice from a newsgroup devoted to song writing. I was not including a stamped, self-addressed envelope (SASE) with my queries, so song publishers were not answering them, but as soon as I started including an SASE, almost every contact responded politely, even if to just say no thanks. You can find the titles of books about small businesses and other useful resources by searching the Web with the search phrase {book "starting a business"}.

Pursuing Political Office

In chapter 13 we review common, inexpensive techniques candidates for office can use to get started. The candidate might try to get endorsements from community leaders, get the editorial support of local newspapers, or make guest appearances on television and radio talk shows. Or the candidate might engage in door-to-door canvassing, seek ad hoc nighttime news appearances, hold news conferences, perform attention-getting stunts, or simply stand out in public shaking hands with people. By succeeding early on with these less-expensive tactics, an office seeker may find campaign contributions then rolling in for a more expensive media campaign. As we also note in chapter 13, Herbert Simons offers practical ideas for starting and managing campaigns.[12] I will not repeat Simons's suggestions here, but will describe how he characterizes the general stages in running for president (and perhaps other elective offices). He first describes the stage of **surfacing**. Here, a candidate must seem credible and able to transcend politics to see to the nation's domestic and foreign policy interests, or possibly the world's interests, depending on the political ambition. The candidate needs to be taken seriously by a political party, by the news media, and by potential money contributors, small and large. In each election cycle, a number of contenders will appear who to varying extents fit the above criteria. The next stage is **winnowing**, where contenders play to their individual party's core constituents in trying to become the nominee. One candidate after another now drops out of contention in this endurance race.

Next comes the *convention period*, filled with hoopla, confidence-building, and the launching of the campaign ticket and its platform. Here is where the campaign team is consolidated and resources are built up after varying degrees of depletion in the run-up to the convention. Most importantly, of course, is the *general election*, where candidates must now delicately balance the desires of their core constituents with the sensitivities of the electorate as a whole (a tactic sometimes called "moving to the center"). Voters in states thought impossible to win may be written off. Voters in states thought to be shoo-ins may be left to their own resources. But the states in play are often given the lion's share of attention and resources, unless the opposition makes unexpected inroads with the shoo-ins, which then requires costly time and money to guard the "home front." In the end, however, the voting public will use a mixture of rational decision making, emotional attraction, and a hard to define "collective intuition" to select a winner. Running for office can be a rigorous and stressful process, but successful persuasion skills go a long way toward making a political campaign successful. Political researcher Donald Abelson adds an additional insight on what it takes to run for president by noting when and why presidential candidates turn to think tanks (small organizations that recruit professional policy experts) for help in formulating campaign issues. Sometimes they do this to get ideas, and sometimes to help establish public perceptions of their credentials on national or domestic issues.[13]

Interpersonal Persuasion

As we saw in chapter 3, sometimes we seek only to influence others in small (perhaps trivial) ways, as when we ask for a favor from a friend. But for many, one of the biggest challenges in interpersonal persuasion is asking someone out on a date.

Asking Someone Out

When you have identified someone you think will be a good match, your problem is not entirely dissimilar from that of a job applicant (the person you have identified, in this case, being the employer). Obviously, date-making is not as formal an endeavor as job-seeking. But in some ways, you can prepare similarly. For example, you might analyze yourself by assessing your strengths and weaknesses as a dating partner. Table 15.1 offers suggestions about your possible selling points. (You might need to make changes in yourself after the analysis.) Once you have picked the things you think will most interest the other person, the question then becomes how to motivate interest without seeming too obvious. Picking the place, time, occasion, others present, and so on for the "interview" is an important decision to make, as are your opening remarks. Some of the items suggested in table 15.1 are best said; others can be implied by your personal style, demeanor, appearance, and actions; and others will be left unsaid, but are still potentially knowable to those interested in looking beneath the surface.

I compiled table 15.1 from an informal survey completed in several of my lecture classes (about ninety students) to see what students claimed they valued when considering possible dating partners. Their responses suggested that for young, urban women at a public commuter college, the single most-important category is "can be trusted." Several other

TABLE 15.1

Four Types of Interpersonal Characteristics for Persuading a Potential Dating Partner

1. **My Attributes**

financially well-off	confident	good dresser
good job/business	approachable	creative mind
good-looking/cute	friendly	artistic talents
very smart	considerate	conversationalist
classy	funny/fun-loving	good in bed
well-traveled	conventional	well-read
important contacts	unconventional	good listener
sexy/hot	liberal/conservative	spontaneous
interesting friends	generally happy	business mind
respected family	interesting hobbies	other
cool car	virtuous	

2. **My Thoughts about You**	3. **Desirable Partnership Qualities**	4. **Potential Signs of a Good Match**
I like your looks.	not afraid of commitment	similar interests
I'm interested.	can be trusted	similar background
I think you're cool.	helpful	similar life goals
I like your style.	attentive	friends in common
other	affectionate	other
	open	
	other	

popular choices were good listener, funny/fun loving, good-looking/cute, sexy/hot, attentive, friendly, generally happy, likes your looks/style, helpful, and similar interests/life goals. When asked to write informal comments at the bottom of the survey, female respondents said things like "A friendly smile when saying 'Hi!' is a good way to start up a conversation with someone," "A compliment about your smile or something you're wearing is a good opener," and "An admission that you have been wanting to speak up and finally built up the courage." Nice compliments like "I like your smile" are good, but crude or rude compliments like "Hey, hottie," or "I like your [this or that part of the anatomy]" are not welcome for most. For young, urban men at this public commuter college, the responses were not as different from the women's as I had expected, but several items did come up a little more often, including sexy/hot, good at sex, funny/fun loving, confident, classy, and likes your looks/style. The women more often added things to my list of attributes in the box called "other." But this was a very informal survey, the respondents knew I was collecting answers for a textbook, and the sample size and makeup would need to be broadened for an actual study.

Icebreakers are important for making contact. If the other person is shy, you may have to be persistent and follow up your first icebreaker with another icebreaker or two. You have to decide, however, whether the other person simply does not know what to say, or would rather not pursue a conversation with you at this time. If the icebreakers do not work, then find a way to exit without adding unnecessary discomfort. Sometimes you have to take reasonable risks because you can probably never be absolutely sure if the other person's reaction will be positive or negative. Many people need to build up a "thicker skin" and be prepared for the occasional rejection. (Yes, there are cannot-take-no-for-an-answer type people who might be better off with a thinner skin.) Rejection can be a good learning experience, especially if the risk you have chosen concerns a person who was worth taking a chance for.

It may be that people who have trouble meeting other people have never given the persuasive situations they are confronted with much thought. The icebreakers you pick should not be clever lines. Rather, they should reflect one or more of the above characteristics about yourself that you think will make you more appealing to a particular person. The following are some suggestions for breaking the ice:

1. Flashing a sincere smile and saying, "Hi."
2. Walking over, smiling, and saying, "Hi. My name is _____; I noticed that you were _____. Would you mind if _____?"
3. Offering a friendly comment about something the person is wearing or carrying.
4. Asking a question, if you think the person knows the answer to your question and will want to answer.
5. Saying something about yourself.
6. Offering self-deprecating humor or a positive, good-natured attitude about bad luck.
7. Reciting a well-selected joke.
8. Getting a third party to introduce you to the person (usually a very good choice).
9. Asking if the person minds if you sit down (if the seat next to them is empty).
10. Asking for help with a minor, momentary problem you are having.

If you are a very confident person, you may even say something glib like "You know, fate has brought us together here" or "I predict a bright future for the two of us." But be prepared for a sharp comeback if you take glib chances with icebreakers, since such statements may at times be intrusive, or may seem shopworn or "off the rack." Lastly, Burke's pentad can once again be put to use, this time as a checklist for finding things to talk about. Conversational topics can be found having to do with the scene, agents, acts, agencies, and purposes found in our social encounters with others.

Face-to-Face Selling

Author Rolph Anderson offers us a strategy for selling things to people. In the first stage, you need to prospect for and qualify leads to find out exactly who may need or want your product or service.[14] This requires finding adults who have the necessary disposable income for making the purchase. It also requires a demographic analysis to discover what client categories are of interest to you (e.g., if you want to sell used Land Rovers, you need to identify by age, gender, income, occupation, educational level, lifestyle, and so on the people who tend to own Land Rovers). And it will require a psychographic analysis of the sorts of beliefs, attitudes, and customary habits your likely customers will have. Next, a topographic analysis will concern external matters of time, place, activities, and surrounding events that can affect sales. If you sell imported bamboo to antique dealers for use in making display racks, are there times in their selling year, such as certain holidays, that will make them more responsive to this or that selling point? Is there an alternative display-rack material just on the market with which you now need to compete? Has it gotten around that your last shipment from Asia had a higher-than-usual number of defective bamboo rods?

Planning a sales call requires that you do five things: (1) identify the specific objectives of today's call—a sale? Market development? Goodwill? Market protection and defense against competitors? (2) choose a persuasive strategy; (3) plan exactly how the meeting will transpire to avoid wasted time and effort; (4) anticipate the client's likely objections to any suggestion and your overcoming response for each (e.g., "It costs too much" might be followed by "But if you work it out, in the long run it's less"); (5) learn to seem confident and professional.[15]

Next, give thought to the impressions you make (and review impressions management in chapter 11). What does your outfit say? Your handshake? Your smile? Your speaking voice? Your vocabulary? Your eyes? Here you will also lead with the best feature of what you are selling, and with a quick demonstration if appropriate. If the cosmetic you are selling was used in a recent Hollywood film to make an actress look stunningly beautiful, you might mention this.

Negotiating resistance requires that you distinguish between valid and invalid objections. Invalid objections are often a way for the client to put off making a decision or avoid having to say no. Valid objections are legitimate concerns the client has about your product or service. Sometimes you may save a sale that is faltering by:

- describing or showing an alternative product or service that you sell
- explaining that similar clients have voiced the same objection but came to like the product or service once they started using it

- comparing your product with a competitor's product to show that your competitor's product has greater disadvantages
- confirming the client's objection, but then showing how the disadvantage is an advantage in disguise
- denying the client's objection by showing how a belief about the product is false or is an invalid myth or rumor
- offering proof that the product will work well, perhaps with a trial period for using the product without financial commitment[16]

Closing the deal can be done with the **yes, yes, yes technique**, where you ask a series of leading questions that have tested well with particular clients in the past: "Wouldn't you like the benefits of this product? Wouldn't you like to use it for many years worry-free? Would you like to make the purchase today?" Closing can also be done with a forced-choice set of questions: "So, would you like model A? Model B? Model C?" "Will you be paying with cash, check, credit card, or debit card?" or "Will you be taking this with you or can we deliver it?" Or you could start writing up the receipt while asking any of the above questions. With all the above techniques, you need to be ethical and to proceed in a nonoffensive way. I sometimes walk out of a store when I think the clerk is being too pushy in using the above tactics, but when it is done in moderation and without trying to rush me, I usually will not object.[17]

Creating Your Own Public-Service Print Advertisements

Chapter 14 introduces us to some of the influences and effects of advertising. Ads are one way to communicate with the communities and wider social circles in which we live. Let's construct two simple public-service ads that might run in a local newspaper or magazine. They will each need a persuasive purpose. In the first ad, I want to encourage more people to walk across a bridge, and in the second ad, I want to encourage more people to take trains instead of driving cars.

The intricacies of ad design are varied and many, and there are numerous books, professional programs, and other resources devoted to this. For these examples, however, let's stick with a few basics. If you examine ads in magazines or newspapers, you may notice that many of them have three common elements: a **banner headline**, a visual element, and text (called **copy**). The two ads shown in boxes 15.2 and 15.3 illustrate this approach to ad making. They began with pictures I had taken a while back as an amateur photographer. But any type of visual could be used: a drawing, a cartoon, a diagram. The headlines of advertisements are often attention-getting questions or pithy assertions. When composing your own headlines and copy, remember to keep them concise. Edit, reedit, and reedit until you get the ad to say what you want. Ask others' opinions, but stay true to your project's purpose. After you have selected a basic theme and layout strategy, you might look through magazines to get ideas for formatting, such as font style and size and the visual proportions of the elements in your ad.

One other feature to work toward in designing your ad is *unity*. Try to make the banner headline reflect one or more features in the graphic, and vice versa; also try to

Barney's keeping an eye on this bridge!

As a beaver, he appreciates things that are well constructed.
Walk over the Brooklyn Bridge; *you'll* appreciate the view!

make the copy relate to the graphic and the banner headline, and vice versa. In box 15.2, the banner headline resonates with three things in the picture: the beaver named Barney, the telescope, and the bridge. Prominent in the picture is the beaver's large eye, which is reflected by the phrase "keeping an eye on." The copy in turn tries to resonate with the three ideas in the banner headline and with several things in the picture. The copy in this ad tries to put the viewer into the setting by saying "Walk over the Brooklyn Bridge; *you'll* appreciate the view!" The ad shown in box 15.3 also tries to create unity between the headline, the visual, and the copy. The train seems to be visually disappearing into the night, and the ad cautions us against letting the train service as well disappear into "the night." The nice thing about creating public-service ads is that they are not just pedantic or pretended exercises; they can serve to communicate something you really *do* feel strongly about, and you do not need to have an actual product or service to sell.

BOX 15.3

**Mock-up of Commuter Train Public-Service Ad
with Headline, Copy, and Visual**

Don't let this train disappear into the night!

Trains are a Community Resource: they're energy-efficient, fast,
and convenient. Leave the car home—*TAKE THE TRAIN!*

Chapter in Retrospect

This chapter discusses skills for persuading in either interpersonal, public, or media settings. The skills outlined here include those required for (1) giving or writing speeches (including the steps needed for making effective speeches), (2) arguing a case in small-claims court when you think you have been financially harmed by others' actions, (3) carrying out a campaign to help your community or to run for office, (4) convincing people to be customers for your small business, (5) asking someone out on a date, (6) face-to-face selling, and (7) creating your own public-service ads. Except for the simplest of these activities, each requires a stepwise preparation that is carried out with a specifically stated objective. As the adage says, "What needs to get done will show you how to do it." You can also find help for persuading from library materials, on the Web, and from other people who can serve as role models because they have succeeded at what you intend to try doing. As you apply the persuasive techniques you've learned, you will need to try several or more times, learning from any mistakes you make as you go along. Corrective feedback can help make an initially unsuccessful project a successful one.

KEY TERMS

banner headline	leadership (authoritarian,	speech purpose
copy	democratic, laissez-	surfacing
full-sentence	faire)	thesis
outline	missions	winnowing
icebreakers	speaking outline	yes, yes, yes technique

REVIEW QUESTIONS

1. What similarities and differences do written speeches have with those given extemporaneously?
2. What did Prime Minister Tony Blair of the United Kingdom attempt to do with his speech to the Irish Parliament in 1999?
3. What is the difference between a speech purpose and a speech thesis?
4. Why are small-claims courts of special interest to students of persuasion rather than lawyers?
5. Who must you especially convince in a small-claims suit?
6. How would you go about starting a campus campaign to improve the food at the cafeteria? Or to get the library to stay open later in the evening?
7. Why are secondary benefits important in a community-based campaign?
8. Why is the notion of a niche important in opening a small business?
9. Why is the concept of unity important when creating public-service ads?

SUGGESTED PROJECTS AND ACTIVITIES

1. Use a video camera to make a documentary. Begin by selecting a documentary type (expository, observational, or interactive) and by selecting a topic. Perhaps your topic will be the morning rush hour at the local train station, or the public buildings in town, or kids playing in a park, or a coming election, or a festive occasion on campus. If appropriate and possible, spend some preliminary time loitering in the locations where you will make your documentary in order to develop a purpose and theme for your project (and to make test shots). Then plan what the final product will be like, including whether it will use shots of background scenes; actions of people or animals; on-camera interviews; narration by you the producer (unseen on camera); introductory or closing comments by you the producer (unseen on camera); auxiliary images such as pictures, diagrams, maps, or objects; scripted dialogue; or editorialized statements. Next, create a plan or shooting script, shoot the documentary, and edit it to the extent that you can, given your equipment and editing skills. Finally, be fair to anyone depicted in the documentary and be fair to your audience, who may put trust in what you portray (see chapter 6 for the ethics of documentaries).

2. Do a detailed analysis of someone you regard as an exceptional persuader. List the person's persuasive assets and skills on a sheet of paper. Include verbal and nonverbal examples of the person's persuasive skills. Consider the person's handling of the ethos, pathos, and logos aspects of persuasion.

3. Do a detailed analysis of your own persuasive skills and list them on a sheet of paper, including verbal and nonverbal examples. How well do you use ethos, pathos, and logos? Identify weaknesses that you can try to improve. Can you think of one communication activity at which you may be best suited to persuade others (e.g., making sales, getting minor favors, giving advice, winning social arguments, making friends, debating, teaching, impressing authority figures, preaching, leading groups, seducing dating partners, creating visual art or music, reassuring stray animals, soothing the sick, calming the upset)? If one or several similar activities are your strong suit, explain why it is that (or those) and not others.

QUESTIONS FOR DISCUSSION

1. What are the benefits of becoming more persuasive?

2. Are good persuaders born, made, or the beneficiaries of opportune circumstances?

3. To lead a happy life, in what specific ways do you think you might need to persuade others, if at all?

Notes

1. Some examples would be Dan O'Hair, Rob Stewart, and Hannah Rubenstein, *A Speaker's Guidebook* (Boston: Bedford/St. Martin's, 2004), 19–32; Joseph DeVito, *The Elements of Public Speaking* (Boston: Addison, Wesley, Longman, 2003), 230–43; Albert Vasile, *Speak with Confidence* (Boston: Pearson, 2004), 96–216; Kathleen German, Bruce Gronbeck, Douglas Ehninger, and Alan Monroe, *Principles of Public Speaking* (Boston: Pearson, 2004), 155–218; and George Grice and John Skinner, *Mastering Public Speaking* (Boston: Pearson, 2004), 269–90.

2. Politicians' speeches may be given intense scrutiny by the press, so politicians often *read* carefully written speeches to avoid becoming victims of the "gotcha games" played by rivals or the press.

3. Ideally, your main points should efficiently exhaust the possibilities implied by your thesis, and should do so in a mutually exclusive way so that the individual main ideas do not overlap.

4. Remember that in many speeches, three to five main ideas often are best.

5. For additional ideas on and resources for writing an effective speech introduction, consult books on public speaking or use the search phrases {"written speech introductions"}, {"speech introductions"}, or {"speech writing"} for a Web search.

6. Humorsphere.com, "One liners," 101 SMS Jokes, www.humorsphere.com/sms/one_liners.htm (3 May 2006).

7. Ralph Warner, *Everybody's Guide to Small Claims Court*, 8th ed. (Berkeley, CA: Nolo, 2004), 13/1–13/11; also see summary of text at www.mylawyer.com/disputes/trial1.htm (6 November 2005).

8. Warner, *Everybody's Guide*, 15/1–15/10.

9. Warner, *Everybody's Guide*, 15/5–15/10.

10. Warner, *Everybody's Guide*, 15/2–15/3.

11. Secondary benefits can sometimes be quite persuasive, as shown by one of my former students in a speech in support of accommodating wheelchair users by "ramping" sidewalks at intersection corners;

the speaker pointed out that this sidewalk feature is also very welcome to those pulling shopping carts, riding tricycles, and pushing baby carriages.

12. Herbert Simons, with Joanne Morreale and Bruce Gronbeck, *Persuasion in Society* (Thousand Oaks, CA: Sage, 2001), 212–23.

13. Donald Abelson, "Policy Experts in Presidential Campaigns: A Model of Think Tank Recruitment," *Presidential Studies Quarterly* 27, no. 4 (September 1997): 679–98.

14. Rolph Anderson, *Essentials of Personal Selling: The New Professionalism* (Englewood Cliffs, NJ: Prentice Hall, 1996), 190–217.

15. Anderson, *Essentials of Personal Selling*, 218–49.

16. Anderson, *Essentials of Personal Selling*, 280–311.

17. Anderson, *Essentials of Personal Selling*, 312–41.

CHAPTER 16

Skills for Receivers

After reading this chapter, you will be able to:

◆ Employ skills for critical listening and reading

◆ Analyze advertisements more critically

◆ Ask specific questions to help assess and respond to propaganda

◆ Identify strategies of indoctrination and possible techniques for resistance

There are petty-minded people who cannot endure to be reminded of their ignorance because, since they are usually quite blind to all things, quite fool- ish, and quite ignorant, they never question anything, and are persuaded that they see clearly what in fact they never see at all, save through the darkness of their own dispositions.

—MAGDELEINE SABLE, ca. 1599–1678

THE FIRST SECTION of this chapter, will characterize skills for responding to *rational* messages mostly of a persuasive nature. The second section will characterize the skills for responding to less-rational, *motivation-driven* messages, including sales campaigns, compliance-gaining tactics, and persuasion or propaganda with lower standards of ethics. And the third section will characterize the skills for responding to **coercive influence** brought about by manipulative and, in the extreme, criminal "persuaders." These latter skills concern withdrawing from situations where **indoctrination** is used by promoters of a doctrine, or where receivers are involuntarily exposed to demands for confessions or exposed to coercive, temporary mind-changing methods used for political or military purposes.

One good method for responding to persuasive messages is to render the implicit, tentatively explicit. Some of the power of communicative influence occurs when messages are compressed or abbreviated—which sometimes masks important weaknesses or conceals realities. This power may also rest on questionable assumptions (spoken or written) that remain hidden. When persuaders take a rational approach, you want to identify and evaluate their interlocking claims. When persuaders take a motivational approach, you want to identify the underlying intent that may drive their tactics (e.g., if someone "butters you up" to get a concession from you, ask the person in a friendly way, "What will this 'buttering up' cost me?"). When exposed to a coercive approach to influence, you want to make the underlying intent of incoming messages explicit, at least to yourself (e.g., they are pressuring me to admit this or that is true or false, good or bad, intended by me or not).

Receiver Skills for Rational Messages

Persuasive listening, reading, and visual perception require similar types of evaluation and critical skills. Listening is harder because you cannot go back to re-listen to the message, unless it is recorded. Reading materials can be repeatedly scanned, but at times are more abstract than spoken messages. Skills for visual perception are somewhat different from either reading or listening skills, although what I have said about distinguishing factual and inferential assertions (see chapter 2) applies to all three activities. Receivers do not always pay attention to how visually persuasive materials affect them. They can be at a disadvantage because professional persuaders—whether they be advertisers, media producers, preachers, lawyers, politicians, teachers, cult leaders, police interrogators, or political dictators—often have considerable resources at their disposal.

Persuasive Listening Skills

In face-to-face situations, good listeners are nonverbally involved with speakers. They provide obvious feedback conveying understanding and agreement, and they encourage speakers to do their best. In most situations, good listeners also try hard to remember the key points in what they are hearing. To be a good listener, you need not memorize ideas, but rather summarize them in your own words. Good listeners also evaluate what they hear (Do I agree or disagree? Like or dislike? Believe or disbelieve?). Evaluation also means distinguishing between what seems certain and what seems speculative or opinionated. As we've seen, language intended to influence can at times be tricky and hard to evaluate for truth and validity. And in some listening situations, you will have to decide to say yes or no to some request. If you decide to say no, you may need to use one of the refusal or compliance-resisting tactics described in chapter 3.

Listening Barriers and General Listening Techniques Listening can sometimes be difficult because of several common **listening barriers**. *Daydreaming*, of course, makes listening more difficult. *Laziness* as a listener means you will listen well when the speaker is interesting and you are familiar with the topic, but as soon as listening becomes challenging, you will tune out. *Being tired* makes extended listening difficult because listening is an intensely energy-consuming activity. Your *emotions* can be distracting. *Trying to understand everything* said does not work because speakers can speak much faster than we can take notes or commit things to memory. And *expecting to be bored*, because you judge a speaker or a topic to be boring, also hurts. I could make the argument here that no topic is boring, and that what often makes topics seem boring is our not knowing enough about them or having immature notions about what is important. For example, once someone realizes how much money rare stamps can sell for, that person may associate stamp collecting (sometimes seen as a boring topic) with hunting sunken treasure at sea or seeking lost gold mines on land. Rare stamps may also be considered works of art and icons of history and geography.

Techniques for improving general listening skills include (1) sitting in a good location front and center, (2) getting yourself oriented to what is to come, (3) being ready to listen at the very start of communication, (4) visually imaging what you hear, (5) anticipating what will come next, (6) concentrating, (7) reducing ideas to brief notes in your own words, (8) mentally rehearsing the several key ideas in what you have heard or taking summary notes, (9) asking questions when permissible, (10) looking near the speaker's face to note nonverbal details of the message, (11) having faith that you will remember lots of material if you employ some of the first ten tactics, (12) comparing notes and thoughts with others who also listened, and even doing your own subsequent research.

Critical Listening   Tactics for improving critical listening include (1) putting the thesis of the message into words if the speaker has not already done so, (2) identifying the main ideas that support the thesis, (3) noting the supporting material provided for each main idea so you can evaluate the truth and validity of the speaker's claims. Chapters 2 and 5 say a great deal more than I will repeat here on becoming a critical listener. Critical listeners pay consistent attention even when they are tired; they make sure to remember much of what they hear at important moments; and they bring a **skeptical**, not **cynical**, attitude to assessing how much stock to put into what people say. Professional listeners also ask probing questions, when possible, to help them verify what is being asserted by senders. They monitor their own emotional reactions to a message—in hopes of not getting carried away by the message. And they are very good at saying no, when necessary. When possible, avoid making immediate decisions on senders' requests—give yourself a chance to cool off.

Persuasive Reading Skills

Professional critiques of rhetorical messages are carried out with theory-based, established procedures, such as those mentioned in chapter 11. But to generally critique a written persuasive message, see box 16.1, where the ideas of reading experts Mortimer Adler and Charles Van Doren have been summarized.[1] Remember that when reading, it is often desirable to reread the material several times. Good readers will first scan the message to get the gist of the material. Then they will read the material closely. Finally, they will go back and forth to analyze the message and reduce it to its essential elements (this is called by Adler, "owning" the book or article).

Let's use the ideas listed in box 16.1 to apply a general critique to a letter to the editor from a newspaper's opinion pages:

BOX 16.1
Box 16.1 How to Read and Criticize Written Persuasion

Phase 1 Evaluate message (light reading, scanning)
  Classify the message: topic, type, likely goal
  Write the thesis or theme in one or two sentences
  Enumerate major parts of the message in outline form
  Define the problem the author has tried to solve
Phase 2 Interpret contents (close, multiple readings)
  Interpret key words (especially technical terms)
  List the leading propositions that support the thesis
  Determine which of the problems the author has solved
Phase 3 Criticize contents (fair and informed appraisal)
  Suspend judgment until the end; avoid illogical, biased, or partisan contentiousness
  Show where author is possibly uninformed, misinformed, illogical, biased, or partisan
  Show how author's account is possibly incomplete
  Summarize what the message has successfully defended

We should allow professional athletes to use steroids, whether the sport be baseball, football, hockey, or basketball. Many adults consume coffee, alcohol, cigarettes, vitamins, antidepressants, tranquilizers. Athletes should have the same rights. Professional sports are a form of entertainment—they are children's games played by overpaid adults. And if keeping sports records honest over the decades really matters, what about the effects on statistical records of the designated hitter in the American baseball league or the use of metal bats in minor leagues? Modern players also can have advanced surgery that the old-time players couldn't. If steroids help the performances in athletics, so be it; let the entertainment and games begin. We want to see more and better action.

—John and Joan Fan, Mudville

Using the items in box 16.1, we can say the above letter to the editor promotes the thesis that steroid use among professional athletes is an overblown issue; if the letter succeeds with readers, they will agree that the issue is not worth fretting about, or they may root for even more steroid use by players. Though this is a brief message, it has three parts: it identifies an issue, it offers several arguments, and it reaches a conclusion.

Steroids, as many of us know, are chemicals that can increase the size and strength of the body in somewhat the same way that the body's own hormones can. Three very important words used in this letter are "games," "entertainment," and "athletics" because many people feel differently about what these activities should be like. If baseball, for example, is nothing more than a business that provides an entertaining game, how important is the issue of steroids? But if professional baseball is an athletic field of honor for the nation, then the issue is important. The letter's main arguments, explicit or implied, assert:

1. All adults use stimulants or chemicals—it is hypocritical to complain about steroids use by professional athletes.

2. Professional athletes as adults can make their own decisions.
3. Professional sports are entertainment provided by businesses—that is all.
4. Worrying about steroids is a waste of time for our society.
5. Sports purists have already lost the battle because of many other innovations that make the performance statistics in sports historically incompatible.

Which problem have the letter writers solved? The writers have tried to identify what they consider a bogus problem that amounts to unnecessary meddling in sports, while they see no need to address specific problems associated with steroid use.

One principal problem that the writers mention but with which they only partly deal, at least for sports purists, concerns the integrity of records. Yes, as they point out, there are several other modern developments besides steroids that make it difficult to compare a current career home-run leader in baseball with an earlier record holder. But they overlook a complication here. Not every player wants to use steroids, and if steroids are allowed, then nonusers will be at a disadvantage. Now either they must risk harming their bodies with steroids, or they must compete at that disadvantage. Another issue omitted by the writers is that athletes, whether they like it or not, serve as role models for children. Will children trying to get on the little-league team start using steroids? Will some of their parents actually encourage this? And what is the next step? Already players are bigger than they have ever been before, due to a number of other factors including, diet, weight training, recruitment biases, and the passing on of genes in multigeneration player families. What substances or technologies lie around the corner to create an even more nonrepresentative class of human giants reminiscent of the gladiator classes in ancient Rome—only much bigger? That the modern "gladiator" classes are recruited disproportionately from minority groups also makes the topic a hot button one.

Another persuasive feature found in newspapers are opinion columns. In the week of his retirement, columnist William Safire wrote a farewell article for the *New York Times* and gave readers some tips on digesting the columns of pundits: (1) be careful of writers who start off quoting people on the other side of the political fence (e.g., a conservative quoting Bill Clinton, or a liberal quoting Ronald Reagan)—they may just be building credibility for what is to come; (2) be careful of writers who start off by admitting errors in a previous column—this too can be a lead-in to material that is difficult to prove but now seems justified in light of the previous honesty; (3) be careful of the term *respected analyst* when used to describe a source, especially if the person goes unnamed and their credentials unmentioned; (4) be careful of "insiderisms," or fancy jargon that makes the pundit seem like an expert who is in the know; (5) be careful of "snappers": a political harangue that is introduced by a historical allusion or anecdote that serves as justification for the outburst; (6) be careful of unexpected aberrations, given the pundit's known politics—this may just be a repayment to someone on the other side of the political fence for a past favor; (7) be careful not to send angry e-mails—the columnist may love to hear these things and might think, "Really got to them, ha!"[2]

Some students of persuasion refer to **frames** created by senders to focus receivers' orientation on some topic in favorable ways. Herbert Simons advises speakers to select helpful labels, definitions, descriptions, comparisons, contrasts, and contextualizations as "weapons in your arsenal of persuasion." He especially advises speakers to create frames in advance of debating the issue before an audience. A debater might say, "The victim here is not the person who was shot, it is the entire neighborhood that has to put up with these gang conflicts." The other side in the debate might then respond by accusing the first side of being unable to distinguish between literal and metaphorical statements because not the neighborhood, but the person shot went to the hospital. Both debaters are trying to frame the issue in ways that help their respective sides.[3] Those who use frames may actually be using one of Burke's pentad items to work as a frame for another item, because the scene in the above example, the neighborhood, is being used here to work as a frame for one or more of the other four pentad items (agent, action, purpose, and agency).

Receiver Skills for Motivation-Driven Messages

Here I would like to identify skills useful for consuming advertisements and for evaluating the propaganda we may encounter in the media or in public. In some ways, the skills for responding to motivation-driven messages concern what I describe in chapter 3 as compliance resisting, or the ability to control when we say yes or no to inducements created by professional compliance gainers. The actual compliance-resisting behaviors described in chapter 3 are mostly used in social conversations when a friend, family member, coworker, boss, or stranger asks us to do or not do one thing or another. But here, I will look at compliance resisting as more of an attitude than a conversational skill. Advertisers seek to get us to say yes when asked to purchase a product or service. Propagandists seek to get us to say yes to accepting the doctrines peddled. And those who would mentally coerce us to do as they want often seek blind compliance.

Responding to Advertisements

James Twitchell suggests some intriguing ideas about the roles played by ads in our lives.[4] He begins by reminding us that people have historically been driven to acquire objects for both the utilitarian value and the symbolic meanings ascribed to these objects. For example, you might own a DVD recorder because you want (1) to create a personal library of home-recorded movies (utilitarian), and (2) to gain control of the home entertainment at your disposal day and night (symbolic). According to Twitchell, ads help us assess the utilitarian and symbolic values of objects and services before we buy them.

Readers might try a self-analysis here and draw a box on a piece of paper, labeling the box "The Essential Me as Told by Some of the Objects I Have Chosen to Acquire." Now begin listing these objects in order of importance. You can choose objects from the general categories of clothing, jewelry, furniture, tools, entertainment devices, vehicles, real estate and buildings, tools, kitchen appliances, investments, insurance policies, art, novelties, supplies, and so on. How long your list is will depend on how tireless you are. Now ask what your motives were for buying or acquiring each item on the list. Were those motives more utilitarian or more symbolic? What does each item help you do? What symbolic things does the item help you accomplish? How debilitating would it be not to have the item? And can you remember when you decided this item was worth obtaining and why? Can you identify how the world of advertising participated in your decision, either directly or indirectly?

For more self-analysis, think about how a team of advertisers would categorize you as a type of consumer. The Stanford Research Institute has identified categories for consumers based on how motivated the consumers are to "acquire products, services, and experiences that provide satisfaction and give shape, substance, and character to their identities."[5] These eight categories of consumers are actualizers, the fulfilled, believers, achievers, strivers, experiencers, makers, and strugglers.

Actualizers are independent, and they take charge of their lives; they know what they want and are ready to do their own research to evaluate what they will acquire. They are also more impressed with the intrinsic value of things than with the extrinsic, or advertisement-added, values of things. Advertisers do not like these people and do not try to sell them things.

The fulfilled may drive something called a "town car." They are often retired and well-off, and they are mature, satisfied people who support the status quo. Advertisers like these people and do try to sell them things.

Believers are often religious, favor their own country's products, and like recognizable brands. Advertisers find these people's desired products and services easy to understand.

Achievers like to work hard, make money, and spend it. They often demonstrate their success by buying prestigious products. Advertisers smile at the thought of achievers at work.

Strivers look for upward mobility in a number of ways, including associating themselves with "uplifting" products. Younger strivers may become achievers someday; older strivers may simply become grumpy after years of hard work. Advertisers look forward to the continued success of people in these groups.

Experiencers "go for the gusto" and can be impulsive or even reckless. If they want something, they will find a way to buy it. Consumption is one way to fulfillment for experiencers. Advertisers fall soundly asleep at night with pleasant dreams about this group.

Makers are homebodies who like to do things for themselves, make things for themselves, redo the house, and so on. They are conservative, respectful, and suspicious. Advertisers may be uneasy with these people.

Strugglers are of little interest to advertisers because they have so little disposable income, although advertisers hope these people will become a more desirable consumer type one day.

Individuals can be members of more than one group over time. Complicated people may switch groups from week to week, to the extent they can do this financially. If you can place yourself in one of the above groups (other than the actualizers), you may occasionally watch an ad that seems to "tug at your sleeve" about its product, saying, "Psst, this one's just for you." If so, the advertising people have done their work for the product.

While advertisements do not really change our desires (which are built around terminal values), they do help channel and activate them. For example, it took an advertising agency, a long time ago, to get the companies that sold what was called "death insurance" to begin selling what they now called "life insurance." Similarly, "health insurance" is probably a better term than "sickness insurance." Would people today still own life insurance if there had never been ad campaigns for it? Yes, but perhaps the industry would be slightly smaller. You might try the following to build your skills at assessing the effects of product labeling and packaging. Select two household-supplies products that compete with each other, empty the contents of both packages into separate, plain containers, place the two containers side-by-side wherever they belong (kitchen, bathroom, bedroom), and use them interchangeably.

After some time goes by, try to assess the differences between the two as utilities. But also assess them from the perspective of the extrinsic values created for them by their names, advertising, and packaging.

Our skills as consumers of advertisements should go beyond the simple debate over whether or not to buy an advertised product or service: we must also decide if we are willing to buy into the ideals suggested by the product's or service's advertising. An ad for the Ford Mustang seems to say that the important things in life are shiny, new, strong, high tech, stylish, nimble, and on the move. The ad says this with a photo of a spanking new Ford Mustang parked in an open field on wet pavement. Parodying the famous words on the Statue of Liberty (see chapter 2), the ad boldly proclaims, "Give us your untamed, your assertive, your leadfoots yearning to be free." The ad suggests that consumers will find themselves by buying a Mustang. In another ad, an attractive young woman seems to have met the tall, well-dressed, handsome, apparently affluent man of her dreams. This ad for Calvin Klein's Eternity Moment perfume says, "Just one moment can change everything." The moment depicted in this ad is a romantic embrace: the man is lost in the dream as he looks down at her while she is looking off to the side, triumphantly, at the rest of the world. The ad suggests that the important things in life are being young, beautiful, well-off, and in love. From the perspective of this wish-fulfillment ad, who could quibble over the cost of the product when so much is at stake? But the values touted by the ad will be sadly, disappointingly short-lived if we take them too seriously.

However, it is children who are most in need of advertisement-consumption skills because the advertising world may be more powerful than the schools. As a consequence of the ad world's "education" process, some children may know more today about the way things work at McDonalds than at the local library. One of the things we learn early on is to suspend disbelief when we see people in ads going gaga over a product. Perhaps a good skill to master when giving your time to commercials is to reactivate the normal impulses to disbelieve that which seems at odds with personal experience. The ad world is not solely to blame for our unrealistic perceptions of ads, however. Many consumers *want* to believe in the ideals touted in ads. Thus, the skills needed for consuming ads overlap the skills needed for intelligent living in general.

The skills we need to be effective consumers require having a clear notion of what advertisements do for us and mean to us. We want to become connoisseurs of advertising so that we can consciously get the best deal we can in the entertainment-exchanged-for-attention bargain we enter into with advertisers. They grab our attention, focus it, communicate something. They then peddle our attention to sellers. We get entertainment, clarity about what values to ascribe to objects in the ads, and culture of a type in return. The more this becomes a conscious, intelligent exercise for us, the better off we are. But the more we are passive observers, using just our peripheral skills, the less likely we are to optimize our time exposed to promotions in the media. At a more practical level, it is also a good idea to learn to reject the hokum in ads (weasel words, glittering generalities, and so on; see chapter 14).

Propaganda Consumption Skills

Simons offers useful suggestions for skillfully consuming white propaganda in advertised messages.[6] He refers to "misdirection" tactics in ads where tricky wordings can mislead consumers, wording like "Nothing is better," which often refers to parity products that are all about the same in quality—hence none of them is much worse either. The same would be true of the claim "Nothing is proven to work better or last longer." "We are better" is also a problematic phrase because it does not say what the company ("We") is better than or better at. Some claims are true, but of no real importance, such as when a company brags that its product contains only natural ingredients, because both natural and manufactured ingredients can be good or bad, harmful or harmless, effective or ineffective. The claim "More hospitals use brand X than any other pain reliever" may be meaningless to the home consumer if, for example, most hospitals find brand X convenient to use only because it does not encourage small amounts of bleeding in patients who have just had surgery. Why pay twice the price for this pain reliever at home if you have not had surgery? Or perhaps brand X has been marketed more aggressively to hospitals. The claim "Thirty-three percent more cleaning power than another popular brand," could mean the company found only one competing product that fared poorly in just one performance category.

Simons also notes that ads sometimes say with pictures or visual rhetoric what they cannot say in writing because in writing they may be held accountable for any specific false claims made. Political stories that run in newspapers often use flattering or unflattering photographs of politicians or office seekers, depending on which party the paper supports. Ads for cleaning products may show, pictorially, unnamed competitor products doing poorer jobs. A dramatized television ad might show a person hopelessly incapable of keeping a closet looking neat, but who then uses an Easy-Organizer for their crowded closet, and the result is admirable order and lack of clutter. What is the Easy-Organizer Company claiming in its ad? Perhaps this: It will be just as easy for you with our product to make your own closets look this neat. You could never do this on your own without our product. Your closets will look neat forever and ever if you buy!

Anthony Pratkanis and Elliot Aronson offer useful suggestions for countering incoming political propaganda.[7] When you are consuming a propaganda message that may influence you in some way, they suggest, ask yourself the following questions: (1) "What particular things in the message are making me feel the emotions I am feeling about the overall message?" (2) "If I accept the sender's point of view, how might the sender (or groups aligned with the sender) benefit?" (3) "What are the basic issues identified in this message? How does the sender seem to resolve them? Are there alternate ways to resolve them?" (4) "Is the sender's past behavior consistent with what is being promised or promoted today?" (5) "Does the message contain statements that are rumors, innuendoes, or half-truths? Am I being asked to get on the bandwagon or to join the crowd? Does this message sound too good to be true? What might the people being criticized or disagreed with say in their own defense if they were here? Can I find alternate points of view, from separate sources, on this matter? What facts about this situation should I go learn about?"

You can apply these questions to editorials, opinion articles in newspapers, handbills hawked on the street, or political speeches. You could even apply them to newspaper reports that might influence your opinions, beliefs, attitudes, or behaviors (remembering that reporters and publishers sometimes pursue their own political agendas). Even college professors and textbook writers who take stands on social or political issues should get the same scrutiny everyone else does from you. This does not mean that you should be cynical about professional communicators. You can always temporarily give them the benefit of the doubt until you check into matters. Sometimes your job as a skeptical receiver can be difficult, so keep an ever-tentative mind until you are forced to make a decision by time constraints.

For example, I could tell you that a legislator opposes a law to make it harder for advertisers to exaggerate their products' qualities (e.g., "Smiley-Burgers will put a lift in your walk and a smile on your face every time"). It is true, you cannot imagine a fast-food burger always doing this, and such a law might seem a good idea. But before you think badly of this legislator, find out what the reason was for opposing the proposed law. Perhaps the legislator's answer would be, "Although I don't approve of advertisers making exaggerated claims about products, I still worry about infringements on freedoms of speech or the press. Sometimes well-intended policies have unanticipated negative consequences." Now you can decide tentatively which of the two points of view you believe more important in this situation and at this time. And next year you may want to vote for or against the legislator. Then you will have to reach a final decision. One other reminder is to wait before making a final decision to buy or not buy a product, vote for a candidate, believe a rumor true or false, or believe in or reject an idea. It is amazing how many things I have not bought that I would have bought had I acted at the earliest possible opportunity.[8]

Survival Skills for Indoctrination and Coercive Mind-Changing

We need to keep distinct the terms *propaganda*, *indoctrination*, and **coercive mind-changing**. Indoctrination requires that you as the indoctrinator have a unified or organized doctrine about the world. To get people to internalize the particulars of your doctrine, you have to first motivate them to listen and then to appreciate what you are saying. Over the centuries, preachers have commonly converted people to particular religions by first talking about eternal damnation in a fiery hell. Then the preacher instructs the listener on how to avoid damnation. In the early years of the twentieth century, political activists were able to motivate people to listen by first inciting fears about unemployment, poverty, and maybe even starving to death amid the negative consequences of the Industrial Revolution. Then they were often able to convert their listeners to one of the various "isms" that promised to bring a better day (if the masses would only join along with them the movement represented by the "ism" and abandon the discredited tenets of the existing culture).

Coercive mind-changing requires that the mind-changer have power over the listener physically or psychologically. The pure version of this relies heavily on **incommunicado incarceration**, which denies prisoners any information about what is going on outside the prison. This form of mind-changing is often built around obtaining confessions. These confessions, along with hostile statements made by prisoners about a home country, may also be useful during staged news conferences with world news correspondents. A lesser version of mind-changing occurs when the victims act as if they are being held in incommunicado incarceration when they are really not. Both *prison camps* (the conditions under which captured soldiers are held) and *interrogation-centers* (the conditions experienced by arrested civilians in a similar situation) are paradigm examples of situations where coercive mind-changing takes place. Domestic cult and religious conversion of whole communities are also paradigm examples of mind-changing, but without the use of physical force. Propaganda is much tamer when compared to these communication activities—although it can often be used as an important component of them.

Voluntary Exposure: In a Cult

Steven Hassan attended Queens College, New York, and while there was recruited by representatives of the Unification Church ("the Moonies") one day while sitting in the student union cafeteria.[9] As he tells it, he was invited to attend several meetings as a guest and he eventually joined for a period of several years, after which he became disillusioned with the cult and left to become a consultant providing "exit counseling" for people who wanted to leave cults or had already left one. He claims the recruitment process includes tactics that involve deception (e.g., telling potential recruits, "You can leave the weekend retreat for visitors anytime you want"—but not mentioning there may be no transportation back for a day or two after the recruits arrive); flattery, as in "You're so intelligent, and a great person"; and indoctrination that uses very carefully worked-out steps that take the recruits deeper and deeper into a commitment until they may eventually give all their possessions to the group, abandon their families, and stand out on sidewalks themselves recruiting and begging for money all day long. Hassan says the process relies on (1) a doctrine that is difficult to argue against and disprove in a short amount of time because it is convoluted and in some ways unverifiable, (2) a good-versus-bad sense of reality about everything, (3) an elitist outlook in which only the group's leaders know what is best, (4) a belief that "group will" is more important than "individual will," (5) a strict obedience to the group mission in words and deeds, (6) an attitude that happiness comes through good performance in pursuing the group's agendas, (7) a healthy dose of fear and guilt to keep members in line, (8) an ongoing string of emotional highs and lows, and (9) time distortion, which suggests that "past time is bad time," "present time is everything," and "future time is when rewards for being a group member will someday come to pass." The longer you stay in the group, the stronger the feeling that there is no way out (because of all the bridges you have burned).

Hassan claims to have developed practical guidelines for counseling the person who has spent time in a cult that uses indoctrination methods. He also suggests that should you undertake to help someone trying to leave a cult, you should prepare yourself emotionally because you may be in for a long battle that may wear you down. Then get a physical, and get yourself in good condition, or if you're ill, wait until you recover. Get help from as many people as you can. (Also, consult the campaign model I describe in chapter 13.) Next make a plan, start a set of files, collect phone numbers, consult professionals, and keep your helpers involved and informed. And contact a cult awareness center (leads can be found through a Web search with the search phrase {"cult awareness"}). But comparison shop, because any group can call itself a "cult help group," even a cult. When communicating with the cult member, try to build rapport and trust and try to understand their perspectives rather than being critical or hostile; let the person feel you are at least trying to walk in their shoes. Learn as much as you can about what thoughts and feelings are going on inside the person who needs your help. Become a human resource for the person and perhaps reacquaint the person with earlier social resources that were in place before he or she joined the cult.

Involuntary Exposure: Captive Status

Unfortunately, there is not much help to offer here should you become prisoner in a coercive mind-changing camp. But this is an extreme situation that few of us will ever encounter. The odds seem best for those in this situation to pretend to go along with the mind-changing but to resist it privately. Perhaps covertly seeing yourself as a professional who will study your jailer-controllers' techniques will give you a mission in these circumstances. Trying to stay balanced may help. And believing little of what you hear should help also. Remember that these people will be trying to break you down with stress and with their doctrine. Do not argue with them, but perhaps act as if you are trying to see their ways. Keep a low profile, and if possible, bond with other prisoners if you are given the opportunity. But people you meet in this situation may misrepresent who or what they are. Remember the material in this book on fact-inference confusion (see chapter 2). Perhaps the thought "Who wants to live forever?" will give you solace and peace. Meanwhile, conserve your energy when possible and keep your mind occupied with things other than what your captors want you to think about. And though it may sound cryptic, "Thinking out of the box" about the apparent realities you are confronted with may help.

Being Interrogated Psychologist William Sargant points to numerous studies showing that when individuals undergo severe trauma and stress, they become very open to suggestion.[10] They may even confess to things they did not do, but now temporarily believe they did do. Later when they recover, they may want to recant, but their confessions are now on paper and signed. Ruthless interrogators may stress such an individual with accusations, damning formal charges, sleep deprivation, or incommunicado status to "knock" them into a guilt-ridden, frightened, childish state of mind. If you are roused out of your sleep at three in the morning and then spend two weeks in solitary confinement without any idea of why you have been arrested, you will probably experience severe stress. And finally, there is the **interrogation**. When you are interrogated, the words *conspiracy, murder, theft, treason,* or *espionage* may be flung at you by people who seem disgusted by your very presence. In cases where you have actually done something wrong, they may try to finesse a confession by seeming to justify your motivation for committing the crime (your interrogator might say, for example, "I would have been tempted to do the same thing myself if what happened to you happened to me"). One common interrogator's tactic is to keep track of what you say in successive interrogations and then confront you with inconsistencies in order to jar new information out of you.

Author Charles Swencionis explains that Sargant's original work was based on a lesser-known theory developed by Ivan Pavlov (sometimes called trauma theory). When some of Pavlov's famous dogs were almost drowned one night by water leaking into their laboratory cages, they suffered severe stress.[11] This stress caused many of them to unlearn the things Pavlov had previously taught them with his classical-conditioning methods. Pavlov was greatly interested in the fact that some of the dogs now suddenly liked keepers they had previously disliked. Other dogs reversed the actions they had learned to perform on signal.

These insights provided by Pavlov may help explain battle fatigue and what today is known as *post-traumatic stress disorder*, which may in turn help explain how individuals can have their worldview changed by traumatic stress, breakdown, and adaptive recovery. These abrupt changes in the brain can be understood at several levels: (1) as neurochemical events, or brain-kindling electrical events; (2) as changes in conditioning and memories; and (3) as cognitive changes where the individual's basic premises about the world are challenged, become untenable, and are then replaced—unless the process is later reversed by a return to the individual's former living conditions and environment. In Swencionis's words:

> Pavlov believed the overall process [worldview changes due to traumatic stress] was the brain's attempt to avoid complete destruction: that it had to attempt to process trauma so great it called into question all it had ever learned. This is a theory quite different from the classical conditioning for which Pavlov is usually remembered.

Pavlov did his work under the watchful eyes of the Soviet secret police, who quickly saw the usefulness of such a theory for eliciting confessions from political prisoners. Their interrogation skills were apparently based on a combination of resources including what they had learned directly from the czar's secret police, and their historical knowledge of the Spanish Inquisition and the various purges of witches that had taken place in Europe in earlier times.[12]

Interestingly, Sargant in turn points out that interrogators even on law-abiding police forces sometimes think they have obtained a legitimate confession, without appreciating how much they themselves have caused the confession by breaking down the prisoner with stress and inadvertently planting subtle suggestions. In political tyrannies, the situation can be worse. You may fear a long prison term just for telling friends and relatives you are under investigation. Guilt might overwhelm you after you've had an innocent conversation with a foreigner, and this guilt may require that you prove yourself innocent of being an enemy of your own country.

What can you do when held captive by people who try to break you down in these types of situations? According to Sargant, it is important to avoid losing weight, worry less, learn to snatch sleep whenever and wherever possible, pay as little attention to indoctrination as possible, and think about things other than the indoctrination (but do not be obvious or rude in doing this). It is also very important that you keep the adult part of your personality in charge at all times by assessing your odds, planning little "successes," analyzing the interrogators, cataloging the number of specks on the ceiling, and shrugging off your fears with "brave talk" that works for you. At all costs, avoid "worry talk." Interrogators might encourage the more vulnerable, child part of your personality to come to the surface. But do not try to be brilliantly successful in your resistance. In Sargant's words, "The stake, the gallows, the firing squad, the prison or the madhouse are usually available for interrogation failures."[13] Perhaps you can try to seem as if your complete indoctrination is ever "just around the corner." Not surprisingly, insanity may make you totally immune to indoctrination because you may not correctly assess what is going on.

In the Bible we read, "Forgive them, Father, for they know not what they do." Beyond being a message of compassion, this message also has psychological power as a polemic. It marginalizes and redefines the power of oppressors to that of a mob using a sledgehammer to kill an ant. This image may not always reflect the reality at hand, but if your oppressors can distort reality to justify their actions, why not do it yourself, if it helps? The parental part of your personality can be used to see the aberrant "children" controlling you as ambitious "bad seed." For it is when you slide permanently into the frightened, pleading, guilt-ridden, child part of your personality that the end is near. Then you are most susceptible to accepting your jailers' indoctrination that you are guilty.

Anne Frank and Her Famous Diary Creating fear and trauma was a trademark of the Nazis, from their blitzkrieg war tactics and the terror campaigns they waged against populations that came under their control to their persecution of their own citizens who were believed not to support them. People who knew they would be persecuted by the Nazis often hid wherever they could, trying to disappear into the landscape. But the Gestapo, the German secret police, were efficient and ruthless in ferreting out those who tried to hide. Prisoners were tortured until they gave up the names of other people for whom the Nazis were looking. Some prisoners were traumatized by destructive medical experiments. Millions were sent to concentration camps. And as stories of the atrocities got out, anyone not on the good side of the Nazis lived in constant fear of the late-night knock on the door, or a demand in the street for their identification papers by the feared, plain-clothes Gestapo agents, who often held the power of life and death.

Anne Frank was a German-Jewish teenager who lived in hiding from the Nazis for twenty-five months above an office in Amsterdam. She was fifteen when she and her family were found in their hiding place and sent to a concentration camp at Bergen-Belsen, were she became ill and died. But Anne Frank's famous diary has long survived the Nazis. How did she hold up to the incredible trauma for nearly two years? She assumed correctly that the Jews being taken away were being murdered. Understandably, some of those around her were accommodating to the trauma, perhaps by signing official statements that they sympathized with the Nazis and approved of the New Order. But Anne seemed to survive by keeping the adult part of her personality in charge of things and by dedicating her energy to the diary. She writes:

> Eighty percent have decided to obey the dictates of their conscience, but the penalty will be severe. Any student refusing to sign will be sent to a Nazi labor camp.—May 18, 1943.
>
> I've reached the point where I hardly care whether I live or die. The world will keep on turning without me, and I can't do anything to change events anyway. I'll just let matters take their course and concentrate on studying and hope that everything will be all right in the end.—February 3, 1944.
>
> Mr. Bolkestein, the Cabinet Minister, speaking on the Dutch broadcast from London, said that after the war a collection would be made of diaries and letters dealing with the war. Of course, everyone pounced on my diary.—March 29, 1944.
>
> When I write, I can shake off all my cares.—April 5, 1944.[14]

On other occasions, the fifteen-year-old seemed to succumb to the ongoing trauma, with the child part of her personality coming to the forefront but then just as quickly giving way to the surviving adult:

But the minute I was alone I knew I was going to cry my eyes out. I slid to the floor in my nightgown and began by saying my prayers, very fervently. Then I drew my knees to my chest, lay my head on my arms and cried, all huddled up on the bare floor. A loud sob brought me back down to earth.

Alexander Weissberg and Zbigniew Stypulkowski Alexander Weissberg writes about having been interrogated by the Soviet secret police for hundreds of hours, having made two confessions, and having recanted both.[15] He was placed on what was called a "conveyor system," an endless moving procession in which the accused were kept under continuous interrogation day and night until breaking down. Since his examiners were working rotating shifts, Weissberg's interrogation could go on indefinitely. But he kept reminding himself that he could hold on "just one more night." A less-successful survivor, Zbigniew Stypulkowski, reported that when his examiner realized he was weakening, the examiner abandoned the hard-boiled approach and took a softer tone:

> I am sorry for you. I see how tired you are. I am happy to inform you, on behalf of the authorities, that the Soviet Government has no wish you should lose your life or spend thirty years rotting in some labor camp in Siberia. On the contrary the Soviet Government wants you to live and work as a free man.

A little later in the interrogation, Stypulkowski collapsed emotionally and began his confession, which was a convoluted mix of true statements and the false suggestions that had been put in his head by his interrogators over the last several weeks. They now had him, and any promises of leniency made by the interrogators over the last several weeks were inoperable. If he had been sent away to a forced-labor camp in Siberia, Stypulkowski might have been fortunate *not* to survive the dark, shoulder-to-shoulder, three-week boxcar ride to Siberia with its single relief-pot in the middle of the car and once-daily "soup" meals and stopovers to allow newly stiffened dead bodies to be tossed outside into the icy snow. The survivors of these rail trips sometimes found themselves standing half-naked in the Siberian snow and wind, only to have to build their own prison camps from which they could be worked to death. The Soviets killed millions with planned famines, executions, and forced labor with carefully calculated death-diets.[16]

Chapter in Retrospect

When responding to rational persuasive messages, you simply want to practice good critical listening and reading skills. This may mean overcoming the habitual barriers to effective comprehension you make for yourself. It may also mean constructing an outline of the persuasive message to see how its arguments are built. When responding to motivation-driven messages such as the ones used for advertisements or in favor requests from friends, you need to be more aware of exactly what appeals are being used. Responding critically to propaganda is more difficult, especially if it has been cleverly constructed to mislead you, or if you already accept its assumptions. It is understandably quite challenging to survive attempts by others to indoctrinate you or to use coercive mind-changing techniques to alter your attitudes. Being interrogated can become an endurance battle. But in these extreme situations, the more you can distinguish what you know for certain from what you are just guessing at or assuming, the better off you are. And making the implicit things communicated by your interrogators explicit in your mind also helps. Keeping the adult part of your mentality in charge when confronted with aggressive mind-changers is very important.

KEY TERMS

achievers	frames	listening barriers
actualizers	the fulfilled	makers
believers	incommunicado	skeptical versus
coercive influence	incarceration	cynical receivers
coercive mind-changing	indoctrination	strivers
experiencers	interrogation	strugglers

REVIEW QUESTIONS

1. What are specific differences between listening barriers and listening techniques?
2. What techniques do reading experts Mortimer Adler and Charles Van Doren suggest for reading critically?
3. What are the seven suggestions William Safire makes for critiquing newspaper columnists?
4. What is the difference between the symbolic and utilitarian values of consumer items?
5. Which Stanford Research Institute categories are liked by advertisers?
6. How can you protect yourself from propaganda?
7. How do the techniques of coercive mind-changing vary between cults and prison camps?
8. What is a lesser-known theory of Pavlov, described in this chapter?
9. How did Anne Frank cope with the intense trauma she experienced?
10. What do interrogations carried out in criminal or legal ways have in common?

SUGGESTED PROJECTS AND ACTIVITIES

1. Record and watch fifteen minutes of a news broadcast. Now write down what you remember about each of the stories in the broadcast. Then replay the broadcast, checking how accurate your notes are. Do you notice any patterns in whatever inaccuracies you find?
2. Critique a television commercial or magazine ad by identifying how it seeks to persuade or motivate. Can you spot any tricks of the trade in the ad's persuasion?
3. Find a political website that takes extreme positions, and analyze its propaganda. Write the website owners a critique of what you do not agree with about the site, especially that which seems dishonest or manipulative.
4. Find a biography or autobiography about someone who has been mistreated at the hands of captors. Analyze the experiences described in that book in terms of what we discuss in this chapter.
5. Research a well-known cult and write a report analyzing its methods and goals.

QUESTIONS FOR DISCUSSION

1. How would you rate yourself as a critical listener or reader? Why exactly?
2. Do you think the human race uses verbal communication more for the purpose of *socializing* with each other, *informing* each other, or *persuading* each other?
3. Do you think that you could survive a hostile prison camp that is run to coercively change its inmates' minds? Why? Why not?

Notes

1. Mortimer Adler and Charles Van Doren, *How to Read a Book* (New York: Simon and Schuster, 1972), 137–67.

2. William Safire, "How to Read a Column," *New York Times*, 24 January 2005, A17. I have included seven of Safire's twelve suggestions.

3. Herbert Simons, with Joanne Morreale and Bruce Gronbeck, *Persuasion in Society* (Thousand Oaks, CA: Sage, 2001), 382–83.

4. James Twitchell, *Adcult USA: The Triumph of Advertising in American Culture* (New York: Columbia University Press, 1996), 1–52.

5. Cf. the VALS 2 system as described by Russell Brayley and Daniel McLean, "Bookworms and Cyberheads: Does On-Line Instruction Reach All Students?" http://kolea.kcc.hawaii.edu/tcc/tcc_conf97/pres/brayley.html (27 June 2006); or search the Web using the search phrase {"Stanford Research Institute" VALS 2}.

6. Simons, *Persuasion in Society*, 275–98.

7. Anthony Pratkanis and Elliot Aronson, *Age of Propaganda: The Everyday Use and Abuse of Persuasion* (New York: Henry Holt, 2001), 341–48.

8. Purchase decisions should be organized into three separate phases: (1) deciding whether you really want or need to buy something in general; (2) deciding exactly what version, brand, size, model, and so forth you want to buy of that something; and (3) deciding where to buy that something after comparison shopping regarding price components, warranties, delivery promptness, convenience, return policies, and the like.

9. Steven Hassan, *Combating Cult Mind Control* (Rochester, VT: Park Street Press, 1990), 12–33.

10. William Sargant, *Battle for the Mind* (Cambridge, MA: ISHK, 1997), 155–65.

11. Charles Swencionis, preface, in Sargant, *Battle for the Mind*, vi–xvi.

12. Apparently, witches were sometimes "stooled," which meant they were tied up in a contorted way on a stool for four to twenty-four hours and tortured in various ways. Eventually, they admitted they were witches just to end the torture. Once someone was identified as a witch, the ensuing procedures would guarantee that a confession would be given, sometimes including naming other witches.

13. Sargant, *Battle for the Mind*, 267–68.

14. Anne Frank, "Diary Excerpts," Anne Frank Center, USA, www.annefrank.com/2_life_excerpts.htm (1 March 2005).

15. Robert Conquest, *The Great Terror* (Oxford: Oxford University Press, 1990), 121–31, 311–14.

16. Robert Conquest lists 14.5 million dead in just the "terror famine" of 1932–1933, which was used by the Soviets against peasants in the Ukraine. (This figure does not include the great purges conducted in later years against a wider selection of "enemies of the people"; and as even Nikita Khrushchev admitted after his retirement, the number of those killed was enormous, but who was counting?) Robert Conquest, *Harvest of Sorrow* (New York: Oxford University Press, 1986), 299–307. Apparently, stealing prisoners' clothing was common among the guards and other nonprisoners.

Selected Bibliography

Adler, Ronald, and Jeanne Elmhorst. *Communicating at Work: Principles and Practices for Business and the Professions*. New York: McGraw-Hill, 1996.

Ajzen, Icek. "The Theory of Planned Behavior." *Organizational Behavior and Human Decision Processes* 50 (1991): 179–211.

Albarracin, Dolores, Blair Johnson, Martin Fishbein, and Paige Muellerleile. "Theories of Reasoned Action and Planned Behavior as Models for Condom Use: A Meta-Analysis." *Psychological Bulletin* 127, no. 1 (2001): 142–61.

Algar, Selim. "Cruel Lotto Scam: Victim Loses 20G." *New York Post*, 2 August 2005, 29.

American Association of Advertising Agencies. "Standards of Practice." www.aaaa.org/eweb/DynamicPage.aspx?Site=4A_new&WebKey=d94ac5ca-e68d-4587-be89–5a8e7ea82e39 (23 April 2006).

Asen, Robert. "Seeking the 'Counter' in Counterpublics." *Communication Theory* 10, no. 4 (November 2000): 424–46.

Bahlmann, Bruce. "Broadband, HDTV, and Video Art: An Artistic Window with a View towards Next Generation Broadband Services." Broadband Properties, 8 April 2005. www.birds-eye.net/article_archive/broadband_hdtv_video_art.htm (27 November 2005).

Baker, Frederick. *Shadowing the Third Man*. Media Europa / BBC Arena, 2004.

Ball-Rokeach, Sandra, Milton Rokeach, and Joel Grube. *The Great American Values Test*. New York: The Free Press, 1984.

Bandura, Albert. *Social Learning Theory*. Englewood Cliffs, NJ: Prentice Hall, 1977.

Berger, Charles. "Slippery Slopes to Apprehension: Rationality and Graphical Depictions of Increasingly Threatening Trends." *Communication Research* 32, no. 1 (February 2005): 3–28.

Bergman, Teresa. "Personal Narrative, Dialogism, and the Performance of Truth in 'Complaints of a Dutiful Daughter.'" *Test and Performance Quarterly* 24 (January 2004): 20–37.

Berne, Eric. *Games People Play: The Psychology of Human Relationships*. New York: Ballantine, 2004.

Black, Edwin. "Gettysburg and Silence." *Quarterly Journal of Speech* 80 (February 1994): 21–36.

Borchers, Timothy. *Persuasion in the Media Age*. Boston: McGraw-Hill, 2002.

Bowers, John, Donovan Ochs, and Richard Jensen. *The Rhetoric of Agitation and Control*. Prospect Heights, IL: Waveland, 1993.

Brouwer, Daniel. "ACT-ing UP in Congressional Hearings: Counterpublic Oppositional Discursive Space." In *Counterpublics and the State*. Edited by Robert Asen and Daniel Brouwer. Albany: State University of New York Press, 2001, 87–110.

Brown, J. A. C. *Techniques of Persuasion: From Propaganda to Brainwashing*. Baltimore: Penguin, 1963.

Buller, David, and Aune Kelly. "Effects of Vocalics and Nonverbal Sensitivity on Compliance: A Speech Accommodation Theory Explanation." *Human Communication Research* 14, no. 3 (Spring 1988): 301–32.

Burgoon, Judee, David Buller, and W. Gill Woodall. *Nonverbal Communication*. New York: McGraw-Hill, 1996.

Burke, Kenneth. *A Grammar of Motives*. Berkeley: University of California Press, 1969.

Cairns, Helen, and Charles Cairns. *Psycholinguistics: A Cognitive View of Language*. New York: Holt, Rinehart, and Winston, 1976.

Chandler, Daniel. "Semiotics for Beginners." www.aber.ac.uk/media/Documents/S4B/sem02.html (1 Sept. 2005).

Chang, Laurence, and Peter Kornbluh, eds. *The Cuban Missile Crisis: A National Security Archive Documents Reader*. Washington, D.C.: National Security Archive, 1998.

ChangingMinds.org. "Psychology Theories." http://changingminds.org (7 November 2005).

Cialdini, Robert. *Influence: Science and Practice*. Boston: Allyn and Bacon, 2001.

Clevenger, Theodore. *Audience Analysis*. Indianapolis, IL: Bobbs-Merrill, 1973.

Cody, Michael, Mary Lou Woelfel, and William Jordan. "Dimensions of Compliance-Gaining Situations." *Human Communication Research* 9 (1983): 99–113.

Conquest, Robert. *Harvest of Sorrow*. New York: Oxford University Press, 1985.

———. *The Great Terror*. Oxford: Oxford University Press, 1990.

Cull, Nicholas J., David Culbert, and David Welch. *Propaganda and Mass Persuasion: A Historical Encyclopedia, 1500 to the Present*. Santa Barbara, CA: ABC-CLIO, 2003.

DeLuca, Kevin. *Image Politics*. New York: Guilford, 1999.

DeVito, Joseph. *The Elements of Public Speaking*. Boston: Addison, Wesley, Longman, 2003.

de Vreese, Claes, and Holli Semetko. "Cynical and Engaged: Strategic Campaign Coverage, Public Opinion, and Mobilization in a Referendum." *Communication Research* 29, no. 6 (December 2002): 615–41.

Dillard, James, and Eugenia Peck. "Persuasion and the Structure of Affect Dual Systems and Discrete Emotions as Complementary Models." *Human Communication Research* 27, no. 1 (January 2001): 38–68.

Doob, Leonard. *Propaganda: Its Psychology and Technique*. New York: Henry Holt, 1935.

Elwes, Catherine. *Video Art: A Guided Tour*. London: I. B. Tauris, 2005.

Festinger, Leon. *A Theory of Cognitive Dissonance*. Stanford, CA: Stanford University Press, 1957.

Finocchiaro, Maurice. "Dialectics, Evaluation, and Argument." *Informal Logic* 23, no. 1 (Winter 2003): 19–49.

Fishbein, Martin, and Icek Ajzen. *Belief, Attitude, Intention, and Behavior*. Reading, MA: Addison-Wesley, 1975.

Fortheringham, Wallace. *Perspectives on Persuasion*. Boston: Allyn and Bacon, 1966.

Foss, Sonja, and Karen Foss. *Inviting Transformation: Presentational Speaking for a Changing World*. Prospect Heights, IL: Waveland, 2003.

Freedman, Jonathan. "Research on the Effects of Media Violence." Media Awareness Network, 2005. www.mediaawareness.ca/english/issues/violence/effects_media_violence.cfm (13 February 2005).

Freedman, Eric, and Frederick Fico. "Whither the Experts? Newspaper Use of Horse Race and Issue Experts in Coverage of Open Governors' Races in 2002." *Journalism and Mass Communication Quarterly* 81, no. 3 (Autumn 2004): 498–510.

Gannett Newspaper Division. "Principles of Ethical Conduct for Newsrooms (US)." www.aceproject.org/main/english/ei/eix_o060.htm (24 April 2006).

Geis, Michael. *The Language of Television Advertising*. New York: Academic Press, 1982.

German, Kathleen, Bruce Gronbeck, Douglas Ehninger, and Alan Monroe. *Principles of Public Speaking*. Boston: Pearson, 2004.

Goffman, Erving. *The Presentation of Self in Everyday Life*. Garden City, NY: Doubleday Anchor, 1959.

Gordon, Ann, and Jerry Miller. "Values and Persuasion during the First Bush-Gore Presidential Debate." *Political Communication* 21, no. 1 (January-March 2004): 71–92.

Gottdiener, Mark, Karin Boklund-Lagopoulou, and Alexandros Lagopoulos, eds. *Semiotics*. London: Sage, 2003.

Grice, George, and John Skinner. *Mastering Public Speaking*. Boston: Pearson, 2004.

Hahn, Dan. *Political Communication: Rhetoric, Government, and Citizens*. State College, PA: Strata, 2003.

Hargart, James. "Semi-Subliminal World." www.subliminalworld.org/fulls.htm (29 January 2005).

Harrigan, Jinni A., Robert Rosenthal, and Klaus R. Scherer, eds. *New Handbook of Methods in Nonverbal Behavior Research*. New York: Oxford University Press, 2005.

Hassan, Steven. *Combating Cult Mind Control*. Rochester, VT: Park Street, 1990.

Hill, Charles, and Marguerite Helmers, eds. *Defining Visual Rhetoric*. Mahwah, NJ: Lawrence Erlbaum, 2003.

Honeycutt, Lee. "Aristotle's Rhetoric." www.public.iastate.edu/~honeyl/Rhetoric/cite.html (23 November 2005).

Hovland, Carl, Irving Janis, and Harold Kelly. *Communication and Persuasion*. New Haven, CT: Yale University Press, 1953.

Huckfeldt, Robert, Paul Johnson, and John Sprague. *Political Disagreement: The Survival of Diverse Opinions within Communication Networks*. New York: Cambridge University Press, 2004.

Jackall, Robert, ed. *Propaganda*. New York: New York University Press, 1995.

Jamieson, Kathleen Hall. *Everything You Think You Know about Politics: And Why You're Wrong*. New York: Basic Books, 2000.

Janson, H. W. *History of Art*. Englewood Cliffs, NJ: Prentice Hall, 1967.

Johannesen, Richard. *Ethics in Human Communication*. 5th ed. Prospect Heights, IL: Waveland, 2002.

Johnson, Danette, Maichael Roloff, and Melissa Riffee. "Responses to Refusals of Requests: Face Threat and Persistence, Persuasion and Forgiving Statements." *Communication Quarterly* 52, no. 4 (2004): 347–57.

Johnson, Thomas, and Barbara Kaye. "Wag the Blog: How Reliance on Traditional Media and the Internet Influence Credibility Perceptions of Weblogs among Blog Users." *Journal of Mass Communication Quarterly* 81, no. 3 (Autumn 2004): 622–42.

Johnson-Cartee, Karen, and Gary Copeland. *Strategic Political Communication: Rethinking Social Influence, Persuasion, and Propaganda*. Lanham, MD: Rowman and Littlefield, 2004.

Jowett, Garth, and Victoria O'Donnell. *Propaganda and Persuasion*. Thousand Oaks, CA: Sage, 2006.

Kellermann, Kathy, and Tim Cole. "Classifying Compliance Gaining Messages: Taxonomic Disorder and Strategic Confusion." *Communication Theory* 4 (1994): 3–60.

Kennedy, John F. "Cuban Missile Crisis Address to the Nation." www.americanrhetoric.com/speeches/jfkcubanmissilecrisis.html (20 October 2005).

Key, Wilson. *Subliminal Seduction*. New York: New American Library, 1980.

Kim, Min-Sun, and John Hunter. "Relationships among Attitudes, Behavioral Intentions, and Behavior." *Communication Research* 20, no. 1 (February 1993): 331–64.

Kirmani, Amna, and Margaret Campbell. "Goal Seeker and Persuasion Sentry: How Consumer Targets Respond to Interpersonal Marketing Persuasion." *Journal of Consumer Research* 31 (2004): 573–82.

Knapp, Mark. *Nonverbal Communication in Human Interaction*. New York: Holt, Rinehart, and Winston, 1978.

Kultgen, John. "Evaluating Professional Codes of Ethics." In *Profits and Professions: Essays on Business and Professional Ethics*. Edited by Wade Robison et al. Clifton, NJ: Humana, 1983, 225–64.

Kwak, Nojin, Ann Williams, Xiaoru Wang, and Hoon Lee. "Talking Politics and Engaging in Politics: An Examination of the Interactive Relationships between Structural Features of Political Talk and Discussion Engagement." *Communication Research* 32, no. 1 (February 2005): 87–111.

Labossiere, Michael. "Fallacy: Begging the Question." The Nizkor Project, 1999–2005. www.nizkor.org/features/fallacies/begging-the-question.html (9 February 2005).

Lariscy, Ruthann Weaver, Spencer F. Tinkham, Heidi Hatfield Edwards, and Karyn Ogata Jones. "The 'Ground War' of Political Campaigns: Nonpaid Activities in the U.S. State Legislative Races." *Journalism and Mass Communication Quarterly* 81, no. 3 (Autumn 2004): 477–99.

Larson, Charles. *Persuasion: Reception and Responsibility.* 10th ed. Belmont, CA: Wadsworth, 2003.

Leathers, Dale. *Successful Nonverbal Communication.* New York: Macmillan, 1992.

Lee, Eun-Ju. "Effects of the Influence Agent's Sex and Self-Confidence on Informational Social Influence in Computer-Mediated Communication: Quantitative versus Verbal Presentation." *Communication Research* 32, no. 1 (February 2005): 29–58.

Levinson, Martin. *The Drug Problem: A New View Using the General Semantics Approach.* Westport, CT: Praeger, 2002.

Liska, Jo Ruth, and Gary Cronkhite. *An Ecological Perspective on Human Communication Theory.* Fort Worth, TX: Harcourt Brace College, 1995.

Livaditi, Julia, Konstantina Vassilopoulou, Christos Lougos, and Konstantinos Chorianopoulos. "Needs and Gratifications for Interactive TV Applications: Implications for Designers." Athens University of Economics and Business. http://csdl.computer.org/comp/proceedings/hicss/2003/1874/04/187440100b.pdf (11 February 2005).

Luvera, Paul N. "The Art of Storytelling." Washington State Bar Association, March 2004. www.wsba.org/media/publications/barnews/2004/mar-04-luvera.htm (8 November 2005).

Maslow, Abraham. *Motivation and Personality.* New York: Harper and Row, 1970.

Matei, Sorin, and Sandra Ball-Rokeach. "The Internet in the Communication Infrastructure of Urban Residential Communities: Macro- or Mesolinkage." *Journal of Communication* 53, no. 4 (Autumn 2003): 642–57.

Matz, David, and Wendy Wood. "Cognitive Dissonance in Groups: The Consequences of Disagreement." *Journal of Personality and Social Psychology* 88, no. 1 (January 2005): 22–37.

Mazur, Michelle, and Pamela Kalbfleish. "Lying and Deception Detection in Television Families." *Communication Research Reports* 20, no. 3 (2003): 200–207.

McKerrow, Raymie, Alan Monroe, Douglas Ehninger, and Bruce Gronbeck. *Principles and Types of Speech Communication.* Boston: Allyn and Bacon, 2003.

McQuail, Denis. *Audience Analysis.* Thousand Oaks, CA: Sage, 1997.

McQuail, Denis, and Sven Windahl. *Communication Models: For the Study of Mass Communication.* London: Longman, 1993.

McQuarrie, Edward, and David Mick. "Figures of Rhetoric in Advertising Language." *Journal of Consumer Research* 22, no. 4 (March 1996): 424–38.

Mendelson, Andrew, and Esther Thorson. "How Verbalizers and Visualizers Process the Newspaper Environment." *Journal of Communication* 54 (September 2004): 474–92.

Meyerowitz, Joshua. *No Sense of Place: The Impact of Electronic Media on Social Behavior.* New York: Oxford University Press, 1985.

Mirzoeff, Nicholas. *An Introduction to Visual Culture.* London: Routledge, 1999.

Mongeau, Paul. "Another Look at Fear-Arousing Persuasive Appeals." In *Persuasion: Advances through Meta-Analysis.* Edited by Mike Allen and Raymond Preiss. Cresskill, NH: Hampton Press, 1998, 53–68.

Moy, Patricia, Marcos Torres, Keiko Tanaka, and Michael McCluskey. "Knowledge or Trust: Investigating Linkages between Media Reliance and Participation." *Communication Research* 32, no. 1 (February 2005): 59–86.

Murphy, James, and Richard Katula, with Forbes Hill and Donovan Ochs. *Synoptic History of Classical Rhetoric.* Mahwah, NJ: Hermagoras, 2003.

Muslim American Society. "Al-Qaeda Taunts Bush, Attacks France." Citing a report by Agence France-Presse, 24 February 2004. www.masnet.org/news.asp?id=989 (22 April 2006).

Nabi, Robin, and Alexandra Hendriks. "The Persuasive Effect of Host and Audience Reaction Shots in Television Talk Shows." *Journal of Communication* 53, no. 3 (September 2003): 527–43.

National Security Archive. "The Cuban Missile Crisis, 1962: The 40th Anniversary." George Washington University. www2.gwu.edu/~nsarchiv/nsa/cuba_mis_cri/ (10 November 2004).

Nichols, Bill. *Introduction to the Documentary.* Bloomington: Indiana University Press, 2001.

O'Hair, Dan, Rob Stewart, and Hannah Rubinstein. *A Speaker's Guidebook.* Boston: Bedford/St. Martin's, 2004.

O'Keefe, Daniel. *Persuasion: Theory and Research.* 2d ed. Thousand Oaks, CA: Sage, 2002.

Packard, Vance. *The Hidden Persuaders.* New York: Pocket Books, 1969.

Perelman, Chaim. *The Realm of Rhetoric.* Translated by William Kluback. Notre Dame, IN: University of Notre Dame Press, 1982.

Petty, Richard, and John Cacioppo. *Communication and Persuasion: Central and Peripheral Routes to Attitude Change.* New York: Springer-Verlag, 1986.

Pfau, Michael, Erin Szabo, Jason Anderson, Joshua Morrill, Jessica Zubric, and Hua-Hsin Wan. "The Role and Impact of Affect in the Process of Resistance to Persuasion." *Human Communication Research* 27, no. 2 (April 2001): 216–52.

Pratkanis, Anthony, and Elliot Aronson. *Age of Propaganda: The Everyday Use and Abuse of Persuasion.* New York: Henry Holt, 2001.

Puchta, Claudia, and Jonathan Potter. "Manufacturing Individual Opinions: Market Research Focus Groups and the Discursive Psychology of Evaluation." *British Journal of Psychology* 41, no. 3 (September 2002): 345–63.

Raghunathan, Rajagopal, and Yaacov Trope. "Walking the Tightrope between Feeling Good and Being Accurate: Mood as a Resource in Processing Persuasive Messages." *Journal of Personality and Social Psychology* 83, no. 3 (September 2002): 510–25.

Rank, Hugh. *The Pep Talk: How to Analyze Political Language.* Park Forest, IL: Counter-Propaganda Press, 1984.

Rauch, Jonathan. *Government's End: Why Washington Stopped Working.* New York: Public Affairs, 1999.

Reid, Ronald. "Newspaper Response to the Gettysburg Addresses." *Quarterly Journal of Speech* 59 (1973): 50–61.

Reinard, John. "The Empirical Study of Evidence: The Status after Fifty Years of Research." *Human Communication Research* 15 (Fall 1988): 3–59.

Rice, Jonah. "A Critical Review of Visual Rhetoric in a Postmodern Age: Complementing, Extending, and Presenting New Ideas." *Review of Communication* 4, nos. 1/2 (January/April 2004): 63–74.

Rideout, Victoria, and Elizabeth Vandewater. "Zero to Six: Electronic Media in the Lives of Infants, Toddlers, and Preschoolers." Henry Kaiser Foundation, Fall 2003. www.kff.org/entmedia/7239.cfm (13 February 2005).

Rogers, Everett. *Diffusion of Innovations.* New York: The Free Press, 2003.

Rogers, William. *Communication in Action.* New York: Holt, Rinehart, and Winston, 1984.

Romer, Daniel, Kathleen Hall Jamieson, and Sean Aday. "Television News and the Cultivation of Fear of Crime." *Journal of Communication* 53, no. 1 (March 2003): 88–104.

Roskos-Ewoldsen, David, Jessy Yu, and Nancy Rhodes. "Fear Appeal Messages Affect Accessibility of Attitudes toward the Threat and Adaptive Behaviors." *Communication Monographs* 71, no. 1 (March 2004): 49–69.

Rottenberg, Annette. *Elements of Argument: A Text and Reader.* 7th ed. Boston: Bedford/St. Martin's, 2003.

Rountree, J. Clarke, III. "Coming to Terms with Kenneth Burke's Pentad." University of Alabama, Huntsville. www.acjournal.org/holdings/vol1/iss3/burke/rountree.html (25 January 2005).

Rush, Michael. *Video Art*. New York: Thames and Hudson, 2003.

Safire, William. "How to Read a Column." *New York Times*, 24 January 2005, 17A.

Sargant, William. *Battle for the Mind*. Cambridge, MA: ISHK, 1997.

Schaffner, Brian, and Matthew Streb. "The Partisan Heuristic in Low-Information Elections." *Public Opinion Quarterly* 66 (Winter 2002): 559–81.

Schmitt, Kathleen, Albert Gunthert, and Janice Liebhart. "Why Partisans See Mass Media as Biased." *Communication Research* 31, no. 6 (December 2004): 623–41.

Schudson, Michael. *Advertising: The Uneasy Persuasion*. New York: Basic Books, 1984.

Signorielli, Nancy. "Prime-Time Violence 1993–2001: Has the Picture Really Changed?" *Journal of Broadcasting and Electronic Media* 47, no. 1 (March 2003): 36–57.

Simons, Herbert, with Joanne Morreale and Bruce Gronbeck. *Persuasion in Society*. Thousand Oaks, CA: Sage, 2001.

Skinner, B. F. *The Behavior of Organisms: An Experimental Analysis*. New York: Appleton-Century-Crofts, 1966.

Slater, Michael, and Kathleen Kelly. "Testing Alternative Explanations for Exposure Effects in Media Campaigns." *Communication Research* 29, no. 4 (August 2002): 367–89.

Society of Professional Journalists. "SPJ Missions." www.spj.org/spj_missions.asp (24 April 2006).

Stewart, Charles, Craig Allen, and Robert Denton. *Persuasion and Social Movements*. Long Grove, IL: Waveland, 2001.

Tannen, Deborah. *The Argument Culture: Moving from Debate to Dialogue*. New York: Random House, 1998.

Taylor, Philip. *Munitions of the Mind*. Manchester, UK: Manchester University Press, 1995.

Toulmin, Stephen. *The Uses of Argument*. Cambridge: Cambridge University Press, 2003.

Trafimow, David, and Krystina Finlay. "The Prediction of Attitudes from Beliefs and Evaluations: The Logic of the Double Negative." *British Journal of Social Psychology* 41 (March 2002): 77–86.

Trent, Judith, and Robert Friedenberg. *Political Campaign Communication: Principles and Practices*. 5th ed. Lanham, MD: Rowman and Littlefield, 2004.

Twitchell, James. *Adcult USA: The Triumph of Advertising in American Culture*. New York: Columbia University Press, 1996.

van Mulken, Margot. "Analyzing Rhetorical Devices in Print Advertisements." *Document Design* 4, no. 2 (June 2003): 114–28.

Wan, Hua-Hsin, and Michael Pfau. "The Relative Effectiveness of Inoculation, Bolstering, and Combined Approaches in Crisis Communication." *Journal of Public Relations Research* 16, no. 3 (2004): 301–28.

Warner, Michael. "Publics and Counterpublics." *Quarterly Journal of Speech* 88, no. 4 (November 2002): 413–26.

Warnick, Barbara, and Edward Inch. *Critical Thinking and Communication: The Use of Reason in Argument*. 4th ed. Boston: Allyn and Bacon, 2002.

Wenzel, Joseph. "Three Perspectives on Argument: Rhetoric, Dialectic, and Logic." In *Perspectives on Argumentation: Essays in Honor of Wayne Brockriede*. Edited by Robert Trapp and Janice Schuetz. Prospect Heights, IL: Waveland, 1990, 9–26.

Whaley, Bryan, and Lisa Smith. "Rebuttal Analogy in Persuasive Messages: Communicator Likeability and Cognitive Responses." *Journal of Language and Social Psychology* 19, no. 1 (March 2000): 66–84.

Whiteman, David. "Out of the Theatres and into the Streets: A Coalition Model of the Political Impact of Documentary Film and Video." *Political Communication* 21, no. 1 (January–March 2004): 51–69.

Index

AARP (American Association of Retired People), 283–85, 294n15

Abbot, Bernice, *185*

abductive reasoning. *See* visual rhetoric

Abelson, Donald, 359, 368n13

accept or reject persuasive message, *12*

accomplishment. *See* behavior: drivers and persuasion

achievers, consumer category. *See* Stanford Research Institute, consumer categories

act. *See* Burke's dramaturgic theory

activity. *See* models and diagrams for: advertising

Acton, Lord, 163, 294n18

actualizers, consumer category. *See* Stanford Research Institute, consumer categories

adaptors. *See* deception (and ethics): cues to, as identified in research

Aday, Sean, 336, 344n21

Adbusters, 334

ad hominem, 111

ad populum, 111

Adler, Mortimer, 371–72, 385n1

Adler, Ronald, 149–50, 166n8

advertisements: Bose campaign for noise reduction headphones,

306; ethics of, *127*, 128–29; features of, 327; and influence, 325–34; political, 326; responding to, 374–76; study of one-sidedness versus two-sidedness of, 234; utilitarian versus symbolic values of, 374; as visual rhetoric, 262. *See also* pathos in: advertising; public-service print ads: creating your own; subliminal persuasion; vices, appeals to for persuasion

advocacy ad. *See* advertisements, political

Advocacy Institute Training, 284

affection need. *See* human needs: Schutz

Agence France-Presse, 117n21

agency. *See* Burke's dramaturgic theory

agent. *See* Burke's dramaturgic theory

aggression (super-assertion). *See* behavioral avoidance tactics for compliance resisting

aggressive gamesmanship. *See* paths to influence model

agonism, 84

Ajzen, Icek, 20n12, 202, 220n11

Albarracin, Dolores, 239, 245n33

Albert, Ethel, 120, 140n2

Alberts, Jess, 65n15

Alexander the Great, 67, 159, 167n20

Algar, Selim, 270n30

allegory. *See* visual rhetoric

alliteration. *See* figures of speech

Allen, Bem, 244n16

American Association of Advertising Agencies, 127–28, 140n10

American Association of Retired People. *See* AARP

American Revolution, propaganda used, 67

American Temperance Society, 313

amphibole, 112

analogy warrant. *See* argumentation: Toulmin model of

analytical studies, *225*, 226–27, *255*

Anatol, Karl, 244n4

anchor. *See* social judgment theory

Anderson, Rolph, 362–63, 368n14

anecdotes or stories. *See* openers for speeches

anger. *See* Aristotle: paired emotions; behavioral avoidance tactics for compliance resisting

"animated wall pictures," 188

anonymous feature of advertising. *See* advertisements: features of

393